VIBRATIONS

THE ADVENTURES
AND MUSICAL TIMES
OF

David Amram

221 Method of teaching Composing

222 Teacher Theory

230 talking to Brownin

Thunder's Mouth Press
New York

278 COMMID

For Dimitri Mitropoulos

whose spirit lives in the minds and hearts
of so many people all over the world

281 About - time Disipline

Published by
Thunder's Mouth Press
841 Broadway, Fourth Floor
New York NY 10003

Copyright © 1968, 2001 by David Amram
Introduction Copyright © 2001 by Douglas Brinkley

Previously published by The Macmillan Company, New York

Library of Congress Cataloging-in-Publication Data
Amram, David.
    Vibrations : a memoir / by David Amram.
        p.   cm.
    Originally published: Vibrations : the adventures and musical times of David Amram. New York : Macmillan Co., 1968.
    ISBN 1-56025-308-8
    1. Amram, David. 2. Composers—United States—Biography.   I. Title.

ML410.A534 A3 2001
780'.92—dc21
[B]

00-046697

Manufactured in the United States of America.

People who are identified throughout the book by first names only have been given fictitious names.

Foreword

by Douglas Brinkley

THE thermometer read 105 degrees for five straight days. It was so scorching hot in Tempe during the summer of 1982, in fact, that I wore white tube socks over my hands just to start the ignition and grasp the steering wheel of my Chevy pickup with bad brakes. I had just graduated from Ohio State University and my life drifted in front of me like a dream cloud unencumbered by storm fronts. My grueling day job as a just-hired *Time-Mirror* employee was wiring Phoenix-area ranch houses for cable TV, then a new fad sweeping the country. At night I lounged in air-conditioned comfort at an Arizona State University dormitory/apartment reading various books about the fabled Beat Generation. These Eisenhower-era bohemians were now offering confused Reagan-era progressives like myself new nonconformist ways of looking at what critic Kenneth Rexroth once longingly called, in summarizing Carl Sandburg's populist oeuvre, "Old Time America."

On the Road, in particular, had captured my twenty-one-year-old imagination and its irrepressible author, Jack Kerouac, had become my literary lightning house, a charismatic prophet of rootlessness for the budding nomadic soul. It had been twenty-five years since *On the Road* was published and that July at Naropa Institute in Boulder, Colorado, there was a nine-day symposium paying homage to the classic Beat Generation novel. Naropa's promotional literature advertised that Allen Ginsberg, Ken Kesey, Gregory Corso, William S. Burroughs, and Lawrence Ferlinghetti would be participating, along with a composer named David Amram. His name was unfamiliar to me so I did some investigation. The card catalogue at the Hayden Library showed that he had written an autobiography titled *Vibrations.* I immediately checked it out and devoured the uplifting prose in a few long night sessions. I had stumbled upon a new American hero, someone whose Whitmanesque enthusiasm for democratic ideals reflected my own. *Vibrations* was a revelation to me. I identified totally with Amram's *joie de vivre* style that illuminated the pages of *Vibrations,* only unlike myself he was a musical prodigy, a *wunderkind* who had composed for Leonard Bernstein, performed with Jack Kerouac, jammed with Thelonius Monk, collaborated with Arthur Miller, recorded with Lionel Hampton, drank with Jackson Pollack, and acted with Allen Ginsberg. With *carpe diem* as his motif Amram had become one of the world's most accomplished composers, conductors, and instrumentalists on French horn, pennywhistles, piano, shanai, dumbeg, and other ethnic instruments from around the world. The indelible impression I got from reading this virtuoso's autobiography was that he was a one-man global jukebox who was also a gifted storyteller. There was something of the indomitable Pecos Bill in the unflappable Amram I encountered in *Vibrations,* it was as if this happy-go-lucky Renaissance musician could swirl a rope and catch a comet by the tail. By stark contrast, I was explaining to bored housewives in Mesa and Scottsdale the virtues of HBO. Somehow, getting Amram to sign my copy of *Vibrations,* which I had acquired in a used record store on Mill Avenue, had become an overweening objective of mine, a rite of passage so to speak, an initiation into the rarefied world of the Beats and classical music.

When *Vibrations* was first published in 1968 America was coming apart at the seams. The war in Vietnam had triggered a generational crisis. Hippies were burning draft cards and placing daisies in the rifles of National Guardsmen surrounding the Pentagon. The Kennedy brothers and Martin Luther King Jr. had just been assassinated. The Democratic National Convention in Chicago had turned into a riot when Mayor Richard Daley unleashed his police force on peaceful protestors. Doom and uncertainty hung in the air. Given this tumultuous environment it was quite a surprise when Amram published his charismatic memoir filled with upbeat nostalgia and compassionate reflection. Music was to Amram—even during the crucible of the Sixties—the great healer.

The significant thing about Amram as a composer, which he makes clear in this book, is that he belongs with those enlightened few who though well trained and proficient in traditional European classical music, have their roots in jazz. In his book review of *Vibrations* for

Saturday Review in 1968, Victor Chapin wrote, "His vision, which is that of all being part of a great whole, seems simple and obvious, but it is not, for composers have always been categorized and confined to schools or tendencies. The dividing line between one kind of music and another has been strictly drawn for centuries. However, as David Amram knows very well, it's all different now. He is the sort of composer we must look to save formal music from its own destruction."

As a coming-of-age memoir, *Vibrations* is richly anecdotal, comically inspiring, and notable for its uncompromising honesty. A bedrock optimist, cynicism is always frowned upon by Amram, negativity tossed aside as the tormented tool of the spiritually oppressed. Having composed more than 100 orchestral and chamber music pieces as well as numerous scores for Broadway theater and feature films, Amram has dazzled four generations of audiences with his versatility, raw talent, and timeless performances. But the fun of Amram's music—and *Vibrations*—lies in its surprises: his unlikely yet persuasive juxtapositions of seemingly disparate styles. Born David Wener Amram III on November 17, 1930, the cousin of conductor Otto Kelmpereer, this fast-paced autobiography begins with his cheerful childhood antics in Passagrille, Florida and his family farm in Feasterville, Pennsylvania. Almost from the cradle, music was Amram's lifeblood, and it's impossible not to marvel at the wholesome spectacle of this nine-year-old boy performing "Santa Lucia" on his trumpet with the intensity of the young Louis Armstrong on the levee. What makes the early chapters of *Vibrations,* however, much more than a nostalgic journey down memory lane, is his frank remembrance of growing up Jewish in an America ripe with anti-Semitism. "I found out what it means to be a Jew in rural Pennsylvania, 1939," Amram writes. "I was the only one in the school (my sister Marianna didn't seem to count) so naturally I was the logical choice to be beaten up and abused every day by my classmates. This was because many of the kids had parents who were part of the German-American Bund, a neo-Nazi organization." But thanks to his no-nonsense father, Phillip, David was steeped in traditions of Judaism and learned to stoically endure social ostracism, to work hard and prosper no matter what obstacles were thrown in his path. We learn in *Vibrations* that it was this adopted attitude of undaunted perseverance that would propel him all the way to playing jazz with Oscar Pettiford, Dizzy Gillespie, and Charles Mingus. In 1966, Leonard Bernstein chose Amram as the first-ever Composer-in-Residence of the New York Philharmonic.

What makes *Vibrations* such an enchanting memoir is the way the multi-instrumentalist Amram brings the reader along with him on his Horatio Alger-like journey to success. Void of pretense, Amram is just as proud of working at People's Drug Store in Washington, D.C. as penning the score for Archibald MacLeish's Pulitzer Prize-winning play *J.B.*, and scores for the award-winning films *Splendor in the Grass* and *The Manchurian Candidate*. There are stories of being a soda jerk, dairy farmer, bus boy, janitor, moving man, gym teacher, Army grunt, and amateur boxer. And along the way we encounter him in numerous locales such as Vermont, Paris, Athens, Sicily, San Francisco, Oberlin, Munich, and Washington, D.C., always with his trusty French Horn at his side. For aficionados of bohemian New York in the 1950s, *Vibrations* offers a special treat with tales of such Amram haunts as the Bleecker Street Tavern, Arts Foods Delicatessen, Johnny Romero's, and Washington Square Park. But Amram is no ordinary journeyman musician, for he is constantly composing, whether it's an opera based on Shakespeare's *Twelfth Night* with a libretto by Joe Papp, collaborating on the cantata "Let Us Remember" with Langston Hughes, or penning the chilling opera in remembrance of Holocaust victims, *The Final Ingredient* for ABC television. Always the wide-eyed student, Amram explains in *Vibrations* that it was alto saxophonist Charlie Parker who became his guru for all seasons. "His music made me aware that every sound is related to every other sound," Amram writes of his time jamming with Parker in 1952. "He was like an architect and a painter and a poet all at the same time. His attitude of an open mind and an open heart, of playing with anybody, listening to everything, trying to appreciate everything and then being able to distill all these experiences in his own way—all this affected me and a whole generation of people who were aware enough to get the *message.*"

Like his jazz and symphonic mentors, Amram's whole life has been dedicated to perfecting his art, to becoming a world-class composer, conductor, and multi-instrumentalist. There is an uplifting originality in both his music and persona. Reading *Vibrations,* one better understands what critic Nat Hentoff meant when he deemed Amram "a ubiquitous deliverer of good cheer." In his elegant memoir *New York in the Fifties,* Dan Wakefield wrote with great affection of the pivotal role Amram played in the New York art scene of that era when there was a cross-pollination of music, painting, and writing. There are references to him playing his French horn at clubs like Café Bohemia, Birdland, and the Five Spot, hanging out with legendary Abstract Expressionist

painters Larry Rivers, Franz Kline, and Willhelm de Kooning at the
Cedar Tavern, and participating in New York City's first jazz-poetry
reading, held at the Brata Art Gallery, in 1957 with Jack Kerouac.
Amram accompanied Kerouac with French horn, bongos, and occasional scat singing. Whether he was conducting a symphony or scatting
spontaneous lyrics based on a hillbilly lullaby, Amram never sneered or
cackled or over-delineated what constituted high versus low art. As a
musician he believed fervently in maintaining an open-door policy. In
other words, Amram was/is the world's great musical avatar of inclu-
sion, frowning on exclusion as a disease of conceit. Echoing Duke
Ellington, Amram's philosophy, simply put, is "No More Walls." This
is also the title of his influential 1971 double-album that combined his
symphonic work as a composer/conductor and his Jazz, Latin, and
World music compositions as a multi-instrumentalist.

Which brings us to the central importance of *Vibrations* as a cultural
and literary document. Long before Tower Records Stores had "World
Beat" sections for CDs or universities began teaching concepts of ethnic diversity, Amram was intuitively mixing folkloric and classical music
from all over the world in his repertoire. As the *New York Times* noted
in 1993, when reviewing the New York premiere of his violin concerto,
"Amram was multicultural before multiculturalism existed." What
other classical composer has dared to write a chamber music work like
Native American Portraits, incorporating Cheyenne, Seneca and Zuni
chants, that was premiered to critical acclaim at the Lincoln Center?
Or moves with ease from the Delta Blues to a Viennese Waltz to a
Cuban Guaguanco to Sephardic hymns? Or has put the prose of John
Steinbeck, Thomas Wolfe, and Jack Kerouac to music?

It was this effervescent, multitalented musician imbued with a zest
for life that I hoped to meet at Naropa Institute—and I did. After driving over eight hundred miles across the Painted Desert to the Four
Corners region through the spine of the Rockies I arrived in sleepy
Boulder at dawn. I had missed the first day of the symposium because
my truck broke down in Canon City. Anxious to make up for lost time,
I hurriedly set up my pup tent along a raging stream in Roosevelt
National Forest and headed to the University of Colorado auditorium
for an afternoon discussion on Kerouac's *Mexico City Blues.* The regis-
tration table looked like a concession stand at a Grateful Dead conference. A local bookstore was doing a brisk business selling such titles
as *Howl and Other Poems* and *One Flew Over the Cuckoo's Nest* to fans
eager for an autograph. I had brought my own dog-eared copy of

Vibrations with me and went looking for Amram. It didn't take me long
to discover him huddled near a dim stairwell, chatting amiably with a
few college students. His curly hair was unruly, matted locks sprouting
out wildly like the photograph on the cover of Dylan's *Highway 61
Revisited.* Around his neck were exotic chains and pennywhistles from
around the world. Even from across the foyer I could see he was exud-
ing a breezy charm. Somewhat shyly, I entered the small circle of listeners surrounding him. Immediately he made me feel at home, as if
we were long lost friends. "Hey Pops," he said, borrowing from Louis
Armstrong. "Where are you coming from?" This inaugural conversation lasted for nearly an hour, initiating a lifelong friendship. He signed
my copy of *Vibrations* "Keep on Truckin" which at the time was a reference to my road trip from Tempe to Boulder. Now, as I read the
inscription again eighteen years later, it stands as the perfect motto for
Amram on the occasion of his seventieth birthday and this elegant reissue of *Vibrations.* For one thing is certain: Amram remains the most
indefatigable musician of our time.

Douglas Brinkley
New Orleans
August 15, 2000

428 14 Hrs work on opera

451 TAN DAY 616?
     offer to teach

452 offer Bernstein Composer in Residence

Preface to the New Edition

IN 1968, when *Vibrations* was first published, most of my years had been spent participating in all the musics that my life had led me to. There was no easily definable category for what I was doing. *Vibrations* was written as a thank-you note to honor some of the great people from around the world I was fortunate enough to meet during my first thirty-eight years. In the year 2000, thirty-two years after the book's publication, many of the people I wrote about are no longer with us, but the enduring value of their work, and the shining light of their spirit and character, illuminates all of our lives in the new millennium. Dimitri Mitropolous, to whom the book was dedicated, Charlie Parker, Dizzy Gillespie, Thelonious Monk, Charles Mingus, Jack Kerouac, Rudolph Serkin, Edgard Varese, Franz Kline, Terry Southern, Leonard Bernstein, Joe Papp, Paddy Chayefsky, Archibald MacLeish, Mary Lou Williams, and many other men and women in the arts I was blessed to know and work with enriched the lives of everyone they touched.

When *Vibrations* was first published in 1968, anyone like myself (there were others) who was involved in many aspects of music, was considered hard to define. In 1968, record stores had no section for World Music, World Beat, or jazz using instruments and styles from around the world. There were scarcely any symphonic works being composed that used traditional Native-American, Middle Eastern, Afro-Cuban, or jazz roots, especially with the composer also conducting and soloing on several instruments. *Vibrations* helps to explain how I gravitated towards these different forms of musical expression. Most of my activities were a result of the extraordinary people I met, all of

whom shared something with me, with the unspoken understanding
that I would do the same with others. What I did and still do today
came naturally. Every note of my formal composed works reflect the
myriad experiences I was lucky enough to have shared with others. I
was simply following my heart and where my fate led me.

In the 1990s, when the term multicultural became an official watchword for the Arts, what I had been doing all my life suddenly had a category. Rather than being considered a gifted schizophrenic nut-case, I
was suddenly considered a pioneer, ironic since I was following the
Global concept of the arts, where the author could also be a performer
and improviser, in the footsteps of Bach, Shakespeare, Mozart, George
Gershwin, Dylan Thomas, Charlie Parker, Dizzy Gillespie, Thelonious
Monk, and Jack Kerouac, all of whom were multi-faceted, rooted in
tradition, adventuresome and had a World view.

Jack Kerouac, my collaborator in the first-ever jazz-poetry readings
in New York City at Brata Art Gallery in 1957, and in the film *Pull My
Daisy,* is now acclaimed as the towering figure of the era he immortal-
ized in "On The Road". Now his novels, poetry, and letters are being
studied and appreciated around the world, for their intrinsic literary
and spiritual value. And so are the works of many of the other artists
mentioned in *Vibrations.*

Jack and I both shared an interest and love of the music of Haydn,
Berlioz, Bach, Duke Ellington, Parker, Gershwin, Monk, and Gillespie.
Jack also encouraged me to share his admiration of Dostoyevsky,
Beaudelaire, Thomas Wolfe, Hart Crane, Dylan Thomas, Lawrence
Ferlinghetti, Langston Hughes, and Carson McCullers. Both of us
spent endless hours swapping talk about our adventures with other
artists in all fields of expression who combined the spontaneous with
the formal. We marveled at the extraordinary on-the-spot poetry of
Lord Buckley and listened together to the glorious compositions of
Bela Bartok which were inspired by folk music from the fields, the
streets, and the coffee houses of Europe. Jack encouraged me to write
my book the way I spoke and to dare to make it honest and natural.

Now as we enter a new century, many of the people I wrote about in
Vibrations are included in text books in our schools with their work representing the finest achievements of our generation. How we wish they
could be here to see the respect they are held in for their positive energy, purity of intent, and uncompromising idealism-in-action by a
whole new generation, *who discovered all this themselves!*

I am now able to give concerts as a performer of the musics I have learned in my life, where I often play, conduct, narrate, and combine the treasures of Europe's classic composers with music and musicians who until recently have been excluded from being on the same program with the masters of the past. Every time I conduct a symphony I think of Dimitri Mitropolous and all that he stood for. Every time I play I think of Charlie Parker, Dizzy Gillespie, and Rudolf Serkin, all of whom gave a struggling young composer-musician hope, inspiration, and encouragement. When I am at home on the farm, or on a plane, in a motel room, or any place it is quiet, I am constantly writing new music. I now know that every day my symphonic, chamber, choral, operatic, and ballet scores are being played somewhere and are being recorded by musicians I never met. This was my life-long dream and I never thought I would be alive to see it become a reality. I was grateful when I wrote *Vibrations* thirty-two years ago to honor those people who guided me on the path to pursuing my dreams. I am even more grateful today to continue on that path, living a life of music.

My hope is that readers of this book will be inspired to pursue their dreams and never give up trying. All the people I wrote about in *Vibrations* helped me to become stronger and more compassionate towards others. Those who were destructive and negative showed me how *not* to be. My life has changed over the last thirty-two years since *Vibrations* was written. I have a family and a farm to be responsible for. My sixteen-hour days are devoted to my family, and to composing, and when on the road, conducting, playing, disseminating, and sharing all I have learned with as many people as possible all over the World. My wild days and nights described in the book are long gone, but the spirit that led me through my early years, my thirst for knowledge, and my love of making music with and for others are still there.

True music from the heart is built to last, and in an ever-changing World remains a healing force. And the song and story in every person's heart is worth hearing. *Vibrations* is the song of the first half of my life.

1

WHEN we were living at my grandmother's house in 1936 I remember a sound that used to float upstairs while I was supposed to be asleep. It was like boxcars bumping together as a great steam locomotive pulled them slowly from the rail yard. This clanking and banging was my father, playing in the quiet of the night when all of us were supposed to be asleep. There was a wonderful old rosewood Steinway in my grandmother's living room, and as he would practice I would listen, fascinated as he attempted to play through the first movement of a Mozart sonata or Brahms symphony arranged for four hands. He couldn't play more than one chord without getting stuck. Sometimes after finishing a measure, he would go back again and start over. But somehow that sound of going back and forth and gradually getting to the end like a mountain climber who keeps slipping and sliding but still makes it eventually to the top—that was to me the first sound of music.

I remember going down to the creek near Shoemaker Road and dropping my blue bonnet in the water. When it floated away, I hung on to the branch of a tree and yelled "Help"—a word my sister had read aloud from a comic book. Sure enough, help came even though I wasn't sure what it meant. I also have vague recollections of being spanked for hitting my sister over the head with a toy truck when she wouldn't let me climb on top of her snowman, great Passover dinners with hot steaming mountains of food and me trying to learn the speech of the youngest son. Of all of these recollections, though, none is as strong as the impression of my father's playing.

On my sixth birthday my father bought me a bugle. My grandmother and grandfather, my aunt and uncle who lived across the way and all their children were there. It was the first and last happy scene I can remember. Within the next three years my grandfather, his son and my aunt's son were all to die. But at this time our whole family was together and the great feeling of tribal unity was terrific. When dinner was over, I was allowed to open my three presents. The first was some kind of terrible colored necktie like the ones worn in Our Gang comedies. The second was a sweater, with a note beautifully written by my grandmother in her painstaking, clear handwriting, telling me how glad she was for me to be having a sixth birthday. The third present was wrapped up in something a little larger than a shoe box, tied with a slick, wide red multi-bowed Woolworth-style ribbon. I ripped it open, went through all the shredded-paper filling and saw to my amazement and delight a regulation Boy Scout bugle. Its wonderful brass shine thrilled me before I even heard a note. As I reached out to touch it my father picked it up and proceeded to play it for half an hour. Possibly because of his mustache, which got tangled in the mouthpiece, or more likely because he had not played a bugle since World War I, the sound he produced was not one of overwhelming beauty. When at last he handed me the bugle I tried it for about thirty seconds and was able to make a sound with relative ease. This first experience was the beginning of a lifelong addiction.

Because my eight-year-old sister was sick and needed to be in a better climate, my mother took both of us to Pass-a-Grille, Florida, for the winter of 1936 and the spring of 1937. It was not what you would call a tropical paradise, but we loved it. We lived in a little ramshackle bungalow with a screened-in porch, thorny shrubbery outside and several nests of scorpions under the latticework. Across the street lived a man named Lester Jefferson, who—between bouts of gin and deep despair over the ruin the Depression had brought to his life—put together wonderful collections of seashells, which he'd meticulously mount on white pasteboard. My sister and I would watch him for hours. He would paste them together and notate them carefully with the Latin as well as the English names. Then he would get dressed up and, in spite of a case of the shakes, go out and try to sell them. But no one would buy, so he'd give some of them to his friends, go back to drinking and eventually smash the rest to pieces. There was also someone in the neighborhood who had a powerful singing voice. As my sister and I would lie awake at night listening to the ocean and hoping that no scorpions would sting us when we fell asleep, we could hear his whiskey baritone filling the air.

In those days Florida had a great atmosphere of nonchalance about everything. When my mother asked my teacher how I was doing, she said, "He's right smaht, but he cain't read yet."

I wanted to take music lessons at school but there was no music department and no musical instrument except an old beat-up piano that was never played. I thought it was probably just a prop with no insides. For some reason, however, I had a vision of playing the piano and being a composer, even though I wasn't sure what a composer did. My sister would read me the names of composers from piano music we had. They were beautiful editions with yellow covers, green borders and green letters. She told me that they were Bach and Beethoven and Brahms and other composers whose names I recognized because my father had plowed through their music.

I didn't learn much in school, but I had a wonderful time. Before lunch hour every day we used to go swimming and once we went to St. Petersburg and watched the old people play shuffleboard. We were taken out on a boat by an incredible sea dog with one arm who kept showing us his stump. He proudly told us that a shark had leaped out of the water and bitten off his arm before he knew it.

The only artistic event I can recall from my school years in Florida was when I appeared in a school play. Pop came all the way from Philadelphia to see me in the role of a yellow flower, and my sister as some kind of post-Crustacean sea creature. We also put on our own little show for him, which included a wild dance through our homemade orange grove. Because we had no real orange trees, my mother bought a tremendous bag of oranges for fifty cents and we tied them with green string to a scrofulous old tree. As my father arrived, exhausted from his trip down to our seaside slum, my sister and I went into this welcoming pageant. He wasn't too impressed with this, but my role as a flower in the school play interested him enough for him to take a picture of it, which I still have.

In the late summer of 1937 we moved from Florida to the large farm in Feasterville, Pennsylvania, my father, uncle, aunt and my grandfather had bought in the beginning of the 1920s. My father had a degree in agriculture from Penn State University and had been a farmer for four years before going back to school to study law and become a teacher. His brother had also been a farmer but then left

Feasterville to be a radio operator on a Grace Line ship and later take every other kind of job mentionable. But our land was still in good shape, even though it was impossible to make a living with that size farm anymore.

As soon as my sister and I moved in, we never wanted to leave. There was a whole pine forest, which my father and mother had planted when they were first married. There was a cemetery off in the distance and some fields of corn and alfalfa which my father farmed and a meadow where our few cows grazed.

From the time I was seven I began milking the cows and taking piano lessons. After a few months of milking, my hands got a great deal stronger, which impressed my piano teacher very much. She once asked me what I wanted to be when I grew up. "A farmer," I told her. I was fascinated with music, but even though I was only seven I could already milk cows and even began growing my own vegetable patch. I also knew about planting crops, chopping wood and clearing land. I used to ride on the back of the tractor with my father and knew how all of that worked too.

But my piano teacher seemed disturbed by this.

"You can't be a farmer," she said.

"Who says I can't?" I replied.

"Because no Jewish boy can ever be a farmer, they're not meant to be."

"Well, my father was a farmer for four years, and he still farms part-time."

"Well, he doesn't count," she told me.

Her teaching was more logical than her nonmusical moments. She taught my sister and me the Diller–Quail Beginners' Piano Book, but because we had heard our father struggle through much more complicated music we found these children's pieces amusing but boring. After playing through them for a while we would collapse into laughter, then begin improvising our own music.

Shortly after I began piano lessons there was a musical demonstration for my second grade. We were told that if we wanted to study any of the instruments shown, the school would provide them and give us lessons. I had no idea who the two demonstrators were, but they were fabulous showmen. They looked like Laurel and Hardy and in addition to playing the instruments they had a fantastic vaudeville-inspired floor show, complete with comic routines such as playing the instruments backward or upside down, swapping them back and forth and even using two at a time. This was irresistible for any second-grader, especially in the days before television. Such novelty acts could only be imagined while listening to Major Bowes' "Amateur Hour," a radio show that wasn't too often of too high musical caliber. When the two gentlemen began playing the trumpet, I knew this was the instrument for me. I began studying and took lessons at the Music Settlement School in Philadelphia whenever we made one of our occasional trips into the city. My teacher had large lips, thick glasses and a huge beaked nose. He gave me all kinds of ominous warnings of how I would lose my lip if I didn't practice properly and how I must always warm up at least half an hour a day and forty-five minutes before symphony concerts. Since I was only eight years old I didn't feel that any of these dire predictions of my demise in the music world particularly applied. But I was eager to learn, so I listened not only to his warnings and worries but also to his trumpet playing, which was excellent. I used to play with the mouthpiece a little to the side of my mouth with one shoulder hunched up, which upset my father. I remember him shouting at me to play sitting up straight without arching my body.

Shortly after I began my trumpet lessons, I went with my family and relatives to hear a children's concert at the Academy of Music with Leopold Stokowski conducting. "Peter and the Wolf" was one of the pieces performed and I remember a large police dog on the stage which represented the wolf. When William Kincaid played the celebrated flute solo, the dog began to bark. More important, when the three French horns played the menacing warning of the approaching wolf, I almost fell out of my chair. I remember a sensation going through my entire body at the sound of these three magnificent French hornists playing together. From my seat up in the peanut gallery I watched them stand up to bow, the spotlights reflecting kaleidoscopic colors off their shiny instruments, and I knew that someday I wanted to play at least a note on one of those exotic, wonderful-looking horns.

I got my chance about three weeks later in the school music room. While everyone was out to lunch I crept in and took out a French horn sitting in the closet. I noticed that instead of fingering with the right hand you fingered with the left; and rather than having trumpet-like valves, the horn had rotary valves with stemlike steel plates that were depressed to make the valve move. After I played two or three notes, I was surprised to discover how easy it was to make a sound but how hard it was to produce a really clear note. As I was experimenting I felt a sharp whack on my behind. The teacher had come back early from lunch and caught me playing an instrument that was not assigned to me.

"Don't you do that again or you'll be in trouble!" she shouted.

Because I liked her, I didn't offer any resistance. Guilt-ridden at being caught in this lascivious act of passion, I put the horn back in its case and crept out of the room to eat my fried-egg sandwich in shame. It was not for years that I got to play the French horn again.

It was during this time that I discovered jazz by listening to big band broadcasts on the radio. This was about 1938, when swing bands were in their full flower. Anyone who watches old movies on television knows that band leaders of the thirties were like minor movie stars. Harry James, Gene Krupa and Cab Calloway were as familiar to kids then as the rock stars are today.

I was always interested in different kinds of rhythm. I would sit around playing on toy drums for hours. One sound I'll never forget was the fantastic syncopated rhythms that our heating system used to make. It sounded like one long drum solo. I remember playing along with it, lying on the floor, wailing away with my ear pressed to the heater, and my knuckles on the grating. This began my informal rhythmic studies and I think somehow gave me a foundation for a rhythmic sense that I never lost.

When I was nine, there was a man who worked on our farm occasionally who also had his own gospel group. He had two sets of postcards that he would always show me. One was a set of carefully lettered pictures of him announcing services where he and his gospel group were performing. The other set was a fantastic collection of pornographic studies. Although the latter group made a far greater impression on me, seeing I was only nine years old and my imagination was somewhat limited in these areas, I do remember being interested in some of the songs that he and his gospel group played. Sometimes he brought his guitar to work and I used to play along with my trumpet. We mostly played old-timey blues, though I didn't know then they were called that. I was familiar with the melody for "Frankie and Johnny," which is based on the blues pattern, so he showed me, rather informally, that I could use the same chords to play a lot of blues songs. This is hardly revolutionary news, but in 1939 there weren't many opportunities for nine-year-olds to have such educational jam sessions, especially in rural areas. We worked up quite a repertoire and I might still be playing with him today except that shortly after that he was arrested for armed robbery. I remember how terrible I felt, because he had always encouraged me and he had a great musicality that I'll never forget.

In 1939 I gave my first concert performance with another budding trumpeter, Bobby Sye. He was a good, quiet boy who wore the kind of cap that professional golfers used. Whenever we visited his house to practice our trumpet duets, his mother would wash his face, clean his nose and invariably tell me, "I don't like that Roosevelt one bit, we can't have a man for President who cannot stand up on his own feet." Bobby would look embarrassed, but once she had finished her tirade against the Democratic Administration she would go back to her housework and let us play away. After we rehearsed a two-trumpet version of "Santa Lucia" and some march arrangements for two trumpets we would sneak out to the back of an old building that had once been a toolhouse, wind up a beat-up Victrola and listen to Harry James and Ziggy Elman records. This was the kind of music that the two demonstrators had played part of the time and this was how we really wanted to play. But we didn't know either where to get the music or how to play it.

There was one trumpet player in our school band who tried to play this way, but the music teacher always slapped him whenever he began to improvise during the hack music we were supposed to grind out during basketball or football games. Our raggedy band of students from the first to twelfth grades was supposed to cheer our team on, but sometimes we didn't have as many as eleven boys really able to play football and often their uniforms were homemade. We were always excited, though, because there was a chance our friend might do a little improvising before he was knocked down by our music teacher, who was also the band director.

When Bobby and I found out that the recital was coming up soon, we were scared to death since we would have to play in the auditorium in front of all the other students. So we began practicing like mad. On the day of our concert we were nervous all through classes. We even avoided getting in fights during recess, and when the classes were finally over, Bobby confessed to me, "I don't feel too good."

"I don't either," I said.

"Well," he said, "that's O.K., it won't sound any more lousy than the other kids."

Night came and we waited nervously for our big chance. Finally it was time for us to go on. We walked onstage with our trumpets and our music stands and both of us almost fainted before we even got to the center of the stage. Spotlights nearly blinded us. Petrified, I peered out into the auditorium, hoping no one would see me trying to recognize people in the audience. I couldn't see anything except a huge black hole like the ocean at night, but the rumble from the people out there was terrifying, like some gigantic sea monster. I had the feeling that as soon as I missed a note, some primordial jaws would come and snap us both in half.

Finally, after shuffling the music and fumbling with the mouthpieces of our trumpets and getting the water out of the instruments and trying to get in tune, we were ready to begin. The rumbling, which by this time sounded like the North Atlantic during a full-scale hurricane, suddenly stopped and that was even more frightening. Bobby was shaking so hard he could hardly put the trumpet to his lips. I was sure if I didn't begin right away I was going to pass out, so without waiting for Bobby, I signaled with my trumpet and started right up. The noise that came out was amazing. It sounded as if it were coming from beneath a pile of mattresses about a mile away, a tiny, pinched, warbling, quavering, nervous, frightened squeak. Every note sounded as if it were being shredded. Bobby joined me and he sounded even worse.

But when we finished "Santa Lucia" at long last, there was thunderous applause. We looked at each other in absolute astonishment. It was all we could do to control ourselves and not break down in hysterical laughter. Despite how terribly we had played, the audience seemed to love it. So we broke right into our final number, a march that sounded a little better. This really brought down the house, which we ultimately realized consisted of about thirty-five people, most of them parents, brothers and sisters of the performers, all dressed in coveralls, all beaming with happiness. When we had finished and the lights were about to go out, I saw my mother's ecstatic face smiling with pride. My father, however, had a kind of half-smile with his eyes up to the ceiling as if to say, "God, what that sounded like." Still, Bobby and I managed to make our public debut as trumpet players and we now felt that anything was possible.

Shor[...]
rural Pe[...]
Mariann[...]
to be be[...]
because [...]
American[...]
the same[...]
been brou[...]
Christian [...]
norant par[...]
stand that [...]
kind of sca[...]
whose famil[...]
Jew. My fat[...]
were not ign[...]

My grandf[...]
Sunday schoo[...]
Jewish and s[...]
but who were[...]
of the traditio[...]
In a certain se[...]
the idea of lea[...]

God from my father, who, when he read to us fro[...]
like the thundering voice of Jehovah himself[...]
My mother had also come from a religi[...]
never finished high school, entering the[...]
in order to send his brothers and s[...]
developed his latent scholarship[...]
and American writers. His da[...]
ish soul, fantastic warmth[...]
love of home, children[...]
cial and beautiful [...]
as close to Juda[...]
that we must [...]
day and g[...]
The [...]
day[...]

[...]son or Christ— the idea of lea[...] ...other cheek. But only as a stopgap. At the same time he taught me something very deeply rooted in the old Jewish tradition: an eye for an eye and a tooth for a tooth. He told me how when he was eleven some boys called him a kike and how by the use of his fists he had converted his persecutors into instant liberals. So I was given boxing lessons by my father and sent to a gym. By the time I was in the fifth grade no one called me a kike anymore.

We were brought up to believe as my father said that "by the sweat of thy brow, thou shalt earn thy bread." He was what is called in Hebrew the true "Al Kiddush Hashem." He taught us that there is no way to do anything except through hard work. He summed up the book of Job and the whole Diaspora by telling my sister and me, from the time that we could first understand, that life is no bed of roses. In a country where so much of the Jewish culture has become matriarchal, I had a patriarch for a father. In fact it wasn't until I was thirty years old and became interested in exploring my subconscious and unconscious Jewish roots that I was able to separate my idea of

ous family. Her father had
world of business at fourteen
sters through school. But he had
by pursuing the studies of English
ughter, my mother, had that great Jew-
, sensitivity, the feeling of empathy and
and family which is traditionally such a spe-
art of Jewish life. But she was not intellectually
sm as my father was. She was the one who told us
not bother our father when he would fast for the entire
to work in the fields from sunup to sunset.

little bit of singing my father did when he conducted the Fri-
night services was to affect me very strongly when I wrote a
riday Night Service of my own years later. And during Passover
services at the farm, all of us would play music. My sister and first
cousin had become wonderful pianists by this time, but my playing
was so terrible that I used the trumpet only. We would play some
jazz tunes, pieces from popular sheet music and some classical pieces
as well. Once as we were about to start our traditional Passover dinner, the doorbell rang and one of my Philadelphia cousins walked
in wearing an old fur coat like a college student of the twenties and
playing the bassoon! As we opened the door he finished playing "For
He's a Jolly Good Fellow," not exactly a traditional Pesach melody.
It was the first time I'd ever seen a bassoon up close since they were
too expensive for our school to have. After dinner he demonstrated
a little for me. I was fascinated by the sound, by the range and the
flexibility of what seemed to be such a clumsy instrument. For years
afterward I always associated the bassoon with a fur coat.

In 1940 I had my greatest agricultural year, planting a whole acre
of corn. I had learned how to drive a tractor, plow the land, plant
corn and keep it weeded during the summer. I used to have my
friends from across the way, Artie McCrae and Eddie Filemyr, help
me out. We would go weed for a while and then lie underneath the
cornstalks, staring up at the blue sky, telling jokes, talking about
girls, smoking corn silk and reading comic books by the hour. I
promised my father I would take all the money I made to buy stamps
for war bonds in exchange for letting me use the tractor to plow and

cultivate. Fall finally came, I got up early in the morning with Artie and Eddie, picked all the corn and put it in huge burlap bags. The grocery stores would buy a hundred ears for a dollar, and for the rest, my sister and I set up a roadside stand right off Bustleton Pike. We sold corn and lemonade right from the roadside. The Depression was beginning to ease off a bit and more and more people were coming to the Somerton swimming pool, which was only half a mile from our farm, so we used to get quite a few customers during the day.

It was during this time that I fell in love with a girl in school named Peggy Klink. She had beautiful black ringlets that came all the way down to her shoulders. She also had dark brown, nearly black eyes like a gypsy, beautiful dimples, and arms and legs just like those terrific dolls they used to have at big stores like Strawbridge and Clothier's in Philadelphia. She used to wear little checked gingham dresses that were always starched and clean, and while many of the other girls were very rough and tough because they had to be, she was very quiet, sweet and ladylike, with her little tinkling voice that sounded like an angel.

One morning just before I had to get up to work at the cornfield, I had a dream about her. I dreamed I was going to run away from school one afternoon with my trumpet, join one of the great bands that I had heard on the radio and travel around the world with her. She would be able to continue her schooling by bringing her books along. She could keep house for me. We would see the world together as I traveled with her and my trumpet case. Then when I became rich and famous at the age of sixteen or so we would retire and get married like a lot of other kids out in the country did at that time. With all the money I had saved, I would buy my father and mother a thousand-acre farm and they would go farming full-time with me someplace out west. We would all live together like one gigantic family and Peggy and I would send our children to the same school where we had gone. The dream stayed in my mind all day while I was working in the cornfield.

Artie McCrae finally said to me, "What's the matter with you, Dave? You look sick."

"I'm in love," I told him. "I've fallen in love with Peggy."

"What's so great about her?" he said.

Not wishing to tell him my dream, I went back to work with renewed vigor. When school started again I was ready to tell Peggy about my plan. But the first few days I saw her, I was so shy that I couldn't speak.

That weekend I went with Artie and Eddie to the movies in Frankford with some of the savings we had kept from our corn. We were loaded, with three dollars apiece, so we didn't have to sneak in through the back door the way we usually did. The movie was *Tom Sawyer*. We were scared to death, especially during the part where Injun Joe was waiting for Tom Sawyer in the cave. But it was then and there that I decided to run away from home. I went to Peggy the next day at recess to tell her of my outline for eternal happiness. She looked at me in that sweet way and burst into a gale of giggles and ran off by herself. I was really wasted by this rebuff so I went to Albert, one of the wildest kids in the school. I told him I wanted to run away to Philadelphia to make my fame and fortune as a musician and wanted to know if he wanted to go with me. He said "yes" right away because he hated school more than I did and being from a family of fourteen children, didn't like home much either. Right then and there we decided to run away as soon as possible. I had two dollars and eighty cents and Albert got a sack of food. The next day during recess we walked out of the playground and into the world. It was a cloudy day, not very good for running away, but we figured that this was a good time because the teachers were all inside.

After about three and a half miles or so there were police sirens behind us. We ran up and hid in the fields until they passed by, then continued walking and walking. Four or five hours later it began to get dark. At this point it occurred to us that we had picked the wrong day to run away. I walked down to Wally Freed's gas station where I had worked mowing grass, called up my father and told him that I was sorry that I had decided to run away and had changed my mind.

He drove Albert home.

That night when I ate supper, I noticed a look in his eyes of hurt and bewilderment. This made me feel worse than anything I had ever done in my life. It was impossible for me to explain to him why I had done it. I lay in bed that night listening to the great sounds of the country, the crickets and the distant birdcalls, the lonely wail of the last steam locomotive on the Reading line, and I knew that someday I would be gone for good; even though it wasn't with Peggy Klink I had to go and try something with music. I wanted to fly out there. I had seen that giant roaring silver streak just like the speeding silver bullet I always heard about on "The Lone Ranger." This silver streak was the Crusader, a luxury train that flashed from Philadelphia to New York at tremendous speed. Artie and Eddie and I would go to Somerton to watch it. We would throw pennies down the tracks and they would be squashed like gigantic pieces of chewing gum by the time the Crusader had sped over them. I could imagine myself on one of these big trains traveling with a band going to some fantastic place like Chicago or St. Louis. I didn't even know where they were, but I had heard them mentioned on the radio by different musicians and I knew what a thrill it would be to go. Peggy Klink rapidly vanished from my mind. The idea of being a musician someday and traveling never did.

One of the great sounds during those years in the country was the amplified parties at Polozkisky's neighboring farm. These took place starting in 1941, nearly thirty years ahead of their time. Once a year he would gather with the Polish–American clan from everywhere in the East and string loudspeakers from the trees, telephone wires, silo, barn, every high point. Then, turning up everything full blast, they would play Polish kazatskies at such an incredible volume you could hear the music for miles around. This, of course, would be accompanied by dogs barking and baying, cows mooing, horses neighing—a mélange of sounds which was unforgettable. After half an hour or so of roaring, Mr. Polozkisky would get to the microphone and start shouting drunkenly in Polish and end with a rapid-fire finale of swearing in English. This would be followed by someone trying to pull away the microphone while he shouted more obscenities into it and finally was drowned out by a half-hour of more kazatsky music. He and his family were tremendously hard-working people. This was their big blast of the year and the first electrically amplified music I had ever heard.

Finally it was time for us to leave the farm for good. Even though my father told us we would come back when the war was over, my sister and I knew we never would. We loved the farm more than anything else in the world. The last time up in my room with the great broad boards over a hundred years old, I listened to that sound of the crickets and birdcalls and cows mooing and trains in the distance. Then I walked down and saw the lights from the airport miles away shining for a second every minute or so as they swung around through the sky. I would come back to visit and see my friends, but I knew it was all over. We hadn't sold the farm yet, but we would. It didn't take much to figure out that since we were moving to Washington and my father was working for the government for almost nothing, we would have to sell it, and fast.

When we drove down the driveway next day and got out to Bustleton Pike toward Philadelphia, right around the corner where I sold the corn, there was Wally Freed's gas station across the street where I first heard cowboy music while I mowed the lawn. Crunched in the back seat surrounded by our baggage, I kept my eyes closed so that all those memories of the farm would stay with me forever.

2

OUR house in Washington was half of one of those two-family buildings divided down the middle. The first thing I noticed was how
narrow it was. Although it was four stories high it measured only
thirteen feet wide. There were all sorts of tiny rooms and little levels.
Actually no room itself was really all of thirteen feet wide at any
point, but it was our new home and we went into it cheerfully. Directly
next door to us was the Sheridan Square garage. That first night the
light from the garage streamed in my bedroom windows. I listened
for crickets but heard instead the clanging of tire irons, the laughter
and shouting of the men who worked the night shift at the garage,
the low voices and occasional singing that came from a Negro family
across the street and the occasional sound of guitar strumming and
radios blaring in the back.

Next morning, when I got up and looked around, all kinds of things
were going on: card games, crap games, numbers running and lots of
other urban activities. I could see that these black people were poor,
but they didn't have that slum look of stony despair that I had seen
in South Philadelphia. My father explained that a lot of these people
had lived in Washington for generations. I could tell they knew they
belonged, that Washington was *their* town.

There was one boy I noticed in particular that first day. He was
big and stocky and doing some shadow boxing. The next morning I
went out again. Most of the men were at work and those that weren't
were sleeping. I saw this big boy standing there. His voice was just in
the process of changing, so I knew he couldn't be much older than I

was. But he was much heavier, with broad, thick shoulders, and looked strong.

"Did you all just move here?" he asked in his southern drawl.

"Sure," I said, "I'm from Pennsylvania."

We began to talk a little. He told me he was fourteen, his name was Walter, he was one of eight children and he had two brothers in the army. He wanted to join the marines, but because he was only fourteen he couldn't get in. He showed me the socks and combat boots that another brother in the marines had sent him plus a Good Conduct medal, which he had pinned on the inside of his shirt. We played catch for a while. Then he asked me if I wanted to box with him.

"No," I said, looking him over. "You're too big."

At that time I had only been in fights during school—every day in fact—but I didn't know how to box that well yet and in a street fight situation I knew that he was too big for me.

"You want to wrestle?"

"Sure," I said, knowing that I couldn't get hurt that way, especially if we were to wrestle on the grass. We went up to the front of our house where there was a patch of green grass and started up. He was bigger than I was, but I knew a few tricks and occasionally got the best of it. Walter used only his weight and strength.

We were having fun digging up most of our eight-foot-square lawn when suddenly I heard a high-pitched nasal voice yelling out, "You gonna marry that nigger?" We both looked up and saw a truck that had stopped on Q Street. The man who asked me had on a cap and his teeth were brown from chewing tobacco. He had that really mean cracker look. The only time I had heard anyone called nigger was at the country school I went to in Pennsylvania. There was one Negro farming family and one of their three kids went to school with us. He was called nigger. At the time it didn't seem unusual to me, since I had always been called Jew or kike. It didn't occur to me that children would act any other way to people they thought were different. The way I'd been brought up, I figured it was other people's problem.

"Don't pay him no mind. Let's just go on to the back," said Walter.

"Look," the truck driver said viciously, "don't you be playing with no niggers. You're liable to turn black yourself."

I started laughing because the idea sounded so insane.

"Let's get out of here," said Walter. Walter and I still remained buddies, but this was my formal introduction to segregation in our nation's capital A.D. 1942.

A few days later I entered Gordon Junior High School. Because I had just come from a small rural school, Gordon Junior High seemed enormous. The playground alone was larger than the entire school area in the country. The atmosphere was also completely different because of the large number of students, the fact that it was a southern school, and the air of seething violence that seemed to be everywhere. This atmosphere of violence was constant and when it erupted, the teachers as well as the students seemed to take the idea of fighting for granted.

The moment I arrived I saw three or four serious fights in the school playground. Six or seven boys were holding someone's arms behind him while he was being smashed and stomped by two or three others. I was used to being in fights myself, but at least we used to go at it one at a time and when I got to be a good fighter myself, the fights finally stopped. But I noticed that here the parents of some of the smaller kids led them right into the school or they came in with older kids who served as protection. It took me a little while to realize there were several organized gangs in the school, including one called the Foggybottom Gang. My sister was going to boarding school in Florida because of her health. I was sure glad she didn't have to go through this with me. When we had gone to school in the country she used to lie down on the floor of the car on the way home so the kids wouldn't see her. She was terrified then because of the abuse I used to take being called a Jew. I had gotten used to it, but she never could.

But there at least she was safe on the floor of the car. In 1942 at Gordon Junior High no one was safe. Even teachers—those who couldn't fight back—were in danger of being punched, pummeled, kicked or even knifed. It was a madhouse and I enjoyed every minute of it. I had never liked school anyway except for music and sports, so the chaotic conditions in the classroom, with kids yelling and insulting the teachers, setting their desks on fire, throwing snowballs with razors and rocks inside, fighting and even one student being pushed out of the window—it all seemed wonderful and exciting to me. By the third day I felt at home. The classes were so backward that in about thirty minutes I could do all my homework and spend the rest of the afternoon practicing the piano or playing in the back with Walter and some other kids I met.

The fifth day in school I was coming from the science class when a boy named Joe pushed me on the shoulder and almost knocked me down.

"Watch that, Joe," I said.

He seemed surprised that I knew his name. "How do you know my name?" he said.

Suddenly the casual group behind him seemed to become an organized gang standing stiff and hostile. All the kids behind me also stopped and in a few seconds the immediate rumble was inevitable.

"Never mind how I knew your name, just watch who you're pushing," I said. With that he threw a right at me. Because I was expecting something like this, I slipped his punch. Next he hit me on the left shoulder, spinning me half around. Then he lunged for me and I caught him with my right elbow in the stomach, hit him three or four times in the face, put my leg behind him, hit him on the Adams apple and knocked him backward into a locker. He didn't feel like fighting anymore.

Then all of a sudden, one of the larger teachers materialized out of nowhere, hit me in the face and knocked me down. He then proceeded to knock four or five other students down as well while everyone else scattered. I was stunned. Kids who hadn't even had anything to do with the fight were lying on the floor, wondering what had happened. He pulled us all up and marched us to the principal's office. While we were waiting for the principal to come out, another teacher came rushing down the hall, yelling for the teacher to get to another class where a serious fight was going on. He left and by the time the principal came back, Joe and some of the other students had slipped out of the office, leaving just one other boy and myself. The principal was a kindly old man in his seventies and obviously was ready to retire. His name was Mr. Winston, a sweet old man with white hair, a white mustache, stooped and worn out by all the years in Washington's public school system and very upset by the chaos that had developed since the war began and the younger teachers were all away.

"Boys," he said in a genteel southern moan, "the good Lord didn't put you on earth to act like animals. Fighting is for animals, not for gentlemen. I want you two boys to shake hands and promise never to fight no more."

"But I wasn't even fighting," said the other poor boy, about to burst into tears.

"Don't sass me, son, I don't even want your name. Just don't let me see you in here again with fights. I don't know what's happened to this school and to young people today. In my day people would fight each other fair and square, out behind the schoolhouse. It's just with the families away, there doesn't seem to be any discipline." He looked through his thick glasses at both of us, almost expecting us to sympathize with him. "All right, boys," he said wearily, "you all go back to your classes and don't let me see you in here again."

We got up and left and went back to our classes. After a hysterical Latin class, during which the teacher, a kindly woman in her fifties with an incredible case of dandruff, was shouted down and almost knocked to the floor by one of the students, I left in disgust. I knew I wasn't going to learn anything this way. Outside, I saw Joe and the members of the Foggybottom Gang waiting. I noticed that two of them had knives, which I could see glinting in the sun. They were not switchblades but the kind of knife that is used for shucking oysters on Chesapeake Bay, easy to hide inside your pants and very sharp. I had heard of several stabbings the year before and I didn't want to be the first victim of the new academic year, so I went out the back way through the boiler room and walked home.

The next few weeks I figured ways of getting in and out of the school without being seen by this gang, who were obviously looking for anybody to pick a fight with. I wasn't afraid of fighting Joe again. I knew I could whip him, but I didn't want to get cut up by one of them or to be held and beaten. I figured eventually they would forget about me and find another victim, which they did.

Because I got plenty of exercise playing after school and playing hooky, I decided that rather than playing on the cement playground during recess, I would join the school band just for something to do. They already had about twenty trumpet players, but they needed a tuba player. So I went down to the band room, picked up a gigantic tuba and went into rehearsal. I didn't have any idea of how to play it, but no one there knew the difference anyway, so I used to fool around with the instruction book, learning the fingering and practicing reading the bass clef for the bass notes. After a few weeks I got pretty good at it.

I enjoyed the mellow tone of the tuba, but after my fellow students began throwing ice cream cones, popsicle sticks, Hershey-bar wrappers, quarters and even one gym sneaker wrapped in a jockstrap down inside the bell of the instrument so that I couldn't make any sounds during one of the march concerts, I went back to the trumpet.

Playing in the school band, I found some other kids who were interested in jazz. They told me a dance band was forming. I joined it and for the first time in my life was playing with a dance or "swing" band, as it was then called. I was only twelve years old and most of the kids were older, but they let me play because I had a good feeling for the idiom. We played old Glenn Miller and Duke Ellington arrangements. But I felt restricted just playing written parts. I wanted to wail. What made it worse was that the other kids played solos copied from records rather than making up their own. So after a while I quit.

Our front hallway was so narrow that the upright piano we had put near the door made it almost impossible to squeeze through. My mother let me paint a P-48 pursuit plane chasing a Japanese Zero down the stairs, possibly to indulge some latent patriotism she felt might be lurking somewhere in my soul. I used to come home from school every day, sit at the piano underneath my mural and play boogie-woogie for hours. Of course the harmonic pattern of most boogie-woogie tunes was the twelve-bar blues progressions. With Albert Ammons, Pinetop Smith and many others becoming very popular during this period, I was able to extend my playing of the blues. Meanwhile, I also developed a feeling for the music of the twenties by listening to old Louis Armstrong and Bix Beiderbecke records. To me it seemed related to other, more modern jazz. More important, because of Dixieland's ebullient use of contrapuntal improvising, I got in the habit of listening to the different lines together. In effect I was giving myself a very valuable course in ear training, though I didn't think of that at the time.

The Georgetown neighborhood we lived in was what Washington called a checkerboard neighborhood, *i.e.*, blacks and whites lived in the same block. I always heard a lot of music all around me and on hot nights people would come out with their guitars and sing and have parties. The music was fantastic.

The real turning point in my life as far as jazz went was just before I was thirteen and went to a party with some kids where a band had been hired to play. The band leader's name was Louis Brown. He had been a schoolmate of Duke Ellington's. Brown was an excellent pianist and had a soprano saxophone and drummer in his group. I had been told to bring my trumpet along and I did. Hearing these musicians play, I realized what it was really like to see a live jazz group. I had seen Duke Ellington perform when my father took all of us down to South Philadelphia once, but we were sitting up in the balcony and there wasn't that intimacy of a room when you're right there with the music. The effect now was overwhelming. While all the kids were partying, I just sat there transfixed by the music.

After about two hours Louis Brown came over and asked, "What's that you're holding there boy?"

"That's my trumpet," I said.

"You better come and sit in a little."

Without even thinking, I whipped out my trumpet and sat down next to the soprano-sax player. Without telling me what they were going to play, they went into some blues in B flat, the easiest key on the trumpet. When it was my turn for my solo and I began the first chorus, I got that sensation that has remained with me ever since whenever I play under good conditions and things are right. Everyone who has played jazz experiences this in some way or another and I'm sure they would find it equally hard to describe because it's so personal. It's as if you were suddenly floating miles above the earth but with your feet completely on the ground and your ideas almost coming out of the earth. It's as if the music were coming from somewhere else through you and out the end of your horn. You don't even think about music, what notes you're playing, what fingers you're putting down or anything. Part of this comes from the fact that you are listening so intently to the people who are playing with you and *they* are listening as intently to you. Suddenly everyone playing and ultimately even the audience becomes a part of the whole thing.

After I had done my five choruses and stopped, I saw that the members of the band were smiling at me and at one another. This made me feel terrific. They were really fine musicians and they dug me. After the tune was over, Louis Brown said, "I figured you'd go for that." The kids at the party were surprised. I guess I was surprised myself, but I enjoyed it so much I didn't even think about what I was doing. After I played a few more tunes, Louis came over to me and said, "Look, we're playing at the Elks Club next week down in South East, you know, the big one down there. I'll give you my number. Why don't you come on down and blow." I was so shocked, I probably looked puzzled, so he said, "Don't worry. It's all right if you are white. You'll get a dollar a night."

This was during the period of segregation in Washington when our nation's capital was as much the Deep South as Mississippi. Musicians are most aware of these conditions because in many ways they are the most telepathic and sensitive to their environment. But musicians have always somehow been able to be above it. I realized much later that the sense of brotherhood Louis had wasn't self-conscious or political; he simply thought I was a kid who might want to play and maybe I reminded him of himself when he was a kid. I feel the same way about kids today.

But I was really excited about this offer. I went home and told my mother, who said it was all right but I had to promise not to take a drink or go home with any women or smoke any cigarettes of any kind.

I called up Louis the next day. "Hi," he said. "We're goin' to hit ten o'clock next Friday. Why don't you come on down to my house Thursday and we'll run over some tunes."

When Thursday came, I went to his house. After he introduced me to his wife, he took me down to his basement studio, where he had his piano. I remember a sign on the wall almost like a monogrammed sampler: "Practice makes perfect." There were pictures all over one wall of famous musicians I'd read about, people who had been friends of his since the earliest days of jazz. We went over some different tunes together. Then he began to talk.

"The reason I like you is you got a nice sense of rhythm. You got real good time and you don't *rush*. Most musicians when they get excited start to rush, but you keep that time *steady*. That's the most important thing and you got that already. Now what you have to do is learn some more about *music*. You know, someday you could be like Vaughn Monroe or Carmen Cavallero or Kay Kyser and be a big band leader with your ability. You don't really know nothin' yet, but you can *play* and that's the main thing. Keep on with it." Then he began to play the piano and we played a little more. Finally he looked at me and said, "You sure you're goin' make it? We're saving a dollar to pay you, you know," with a twinkle in his eye.

I said, "Sure Mr. Brown, I can hardly wait. I'd like to play with you all the time."

"Well," he said, "I don't think that would be possible, but you can make it down to the Elks Club. They're pretty cool down there and they'd dig it." I told him that my mother had instructed me not to drink and he said, "Don't worry. We got plenty of ice cream there for you." Then we drank some iced tea and I went home.

The day of the job I was so excited that I fidgeted through the entire school day and could hardly eat supper. I rushed off with my trumpet, wearing a blazer jacket and what I thought were the sharpest clothes I had. I still looked pretty much like a hayseed though and I got there a half an hour too soon. I went to the room where the musicians were supposed to assemble and sat there with my trumpet case between my legs, staring at the floor and tapping my feet. The room was full of black men and they eyed me suspiciously.

Suddenly one man looked at my trumpet case and said, "You a photographer?"

"No," I said, "I'm Dave. I play the trumpet and I'm going to play with Mr. Brown tonight."

"Ooooooooo," he said. "You're a musician. Well that's crazy," and the whole room laughed and I could feel people warm up a little bit. For the first time I realized that when you are given the freeze, it also affects those who are freezing you so that they can't be as free with one another. Now they all began talking about their families and different events and I felt pretty good.

Then the drummer came in and saw me sitting there. "Hey, my man," he said. "You're right on time. That's good to be eager. Be sure you stay that way." He sat down and I continued tapping my foot and drumming on my trumpet case. He suddenly turned to me and said confidentially, "You do all right. You got real good time, but if you want to hit them high notes, you got to develop an embouchure. Look," and he took away my trumpet case. "Look," he said, opening his jacket. "Hit me there," he said. I demurred. "Go on, man, hit me. Don't be a sissy now. Hit me." I hit him lightly in his huge stomach, which felt like iron. "Come on, boy, can't you hit me no harder than that? I said *hit* me," and he crashed his fist into his stomach to demonstrate. I hit him as hard as I could and my fist bounced off. "Now you see that," he said, "that's my diaphragm. I used to play trumpet too until my teeth went bad, and I developed diaphragmatic breathing. That way you can play all night without getting tired." Then he took out my trumpet mouthpiece and said, "You know Louis Armstrong can pick his trumpet out of the case and warm up by hitting a high C just to start with?" He took my mouthpiece and showed me. "Breath from down here. I used to study real hard. I got the foundation for concert drumming and for brass playing. Get a good foundation if you want to go anyplace in music. You've got to get a teacher and develop that talent that you have or you'll just be nothing. And another thing, don't drink when you're playing, don't smoke and don't use drugs. Women are another thing, they make you feel good. They're good for you and relaxing. They're the ones that make you stronger. Them other things just make you weaker. If you're going to be a good musician, get a good foundation, be a lover and you'll be straight."

We began playing for the dance. After I played the first few choruses the place went into an uproar. People were really amused that a little white kid could play. Some of the remarks that I heard were: "He swings his ass off!" "That's Louie's son, that's Louie's son, that's his stone boy." People really seemed delighted that I was playing and I didn't get any more of those hate rays. In addition to the music, which was terrific, I saw the most incredible dancing I was to see for many years. Although this was old Washington with its segregation, terrible living conditions and unemployment, these people really knew how to party. The white zoot-suiters and jitterbuggers seemed dead in comparison. I noticed that each of the dancers had his own style and was really relating to his partner. The dancing became a personal thing between each of the partners and yet everyone seemed to be a part of the whole room, drawing from everyone else. Even the musicians were watching them and following them as much as they were following the music. It was a great experience. A lot of the words and language I heard that night back in 1943 are now considered to be hip. This was the old school of jazz, as I was to find out shortly. It gave me a foundation, an appreciation for many attitudes that helped me enormously as a musician.

Later there was delicious food and great thunderous declamatory speeches with phrases like "United We Stand . . . Divided [with a great dramatic pause] . . . We Fall," plus answering shouts of "Yeah man, amen, brother."

We played till about two in the morning. Gifts were given at the very end of the night to the different musicians with great ceremony and polish and laughter. My gift was a big container of ice cream, as I'd been promised. Everybody gave me a big hand and made me feel at home, so I ate my ice cream right up on the bandstand. The musicians all said good-bye and I took a bus back, one that left me within a half a mile from my house, and walked the rest of the way. This was my first professional engagement. Even though it was only for a dollar, I knew that I wanted to spend the rest of my life in music.

That winter I began delivering newspapers for the Washington

Star. My next-door neighbor had let me inherit his route, which was a big thrill for me. I was able to make some money on my own and also see some real adult life in Washington.

It was fantastic. During 1942 and 1943, wartime excitement had an entirely different form among adults than it did among us kids. As I was delivering newspapers from day to day I noticed that in the various apartment houses, men and women seemed to be constantly changing partners. Voluptuous women in their nightgowns would come to get their papers and I could hear laughing and drinking going on inside. Sometimes a man would come to give me a tip and I would hear or see a different girl in his bed each time.

I had never seen anything like this living in the country. I didn't even know any adults except my immediate family, Wally Freed and some people who would work on our farm from time to time. But being a newspaper boy, I found I was practically a part of some two hundred little households. Even though I was only twelve years old, women would flirt and proposition me occasionally, but I was too embarrassed to know what to do. During my route I was offered drinks, all kinds of drugs, sex and from the more conventional customers, sandwiches, hotdogs and sodas.

It was a fabulous job for a twelve-year-old hayseed and I loved it. On Sundays I would get up at five in the morning to deliver the Sunday *Star,* walking through all of the apartment houses while everyone was asleep. I would stop in front of each door and wonder who was sleeping with whom that particular night. Occasionally people I knew would be coming in late and they would greet me by name. That made me feel great. They would introduce me to their dates for the night and sometimes we would stand around and talk about baseball, the weather and even where to buy a drink. I had already found out one of the many alleyways close to Seventh and T streets when one of my customers drove me there one night on a bootleg whiskey drive. So I became a sort of adviser to the lost-soul transient government workers, soldiers, prostitutes and other people who were wandering through Washington.

I also had a large streak of patriotism. There was constant conversation among my relatives about the Jews in Europe and the gas chambers. I felt very involved with World War II and was heartsick that I couldn't go over and fight against the Germans. I collected salvage with my news wagon every day when I was done delivering newspapers. Because I was skipping school more and more frequently, there was plenty of time. Soon I became one of the school's salvage champs.

During one of my forays I ran into the janitor in one of the apartment houses where I was delivering newspapers. "I got some salvage," he told me. "Come on back here." He led me down into the boiler room. I looked around and didn't see anything but an old cot and some old blankets.

"Come on, where is it?" I said.

"You want some salvage?" he asked me.

"I have to hurry up, I have more papers to deliver."

"Here's the salvage," he told me and exposed himself. I started laughing and he got angry. "Don't laugh at me, you white mother-fucker," he shouted at me.

I got scared. "Listen," I said, "all I want is some salvage, old newspapers, tin cans, you know."

"Yeah, yeah, I know," he said, looking at me menacingly. "You come back tonight and I'll really give you some salvage, you hear?" He moved toward the doorway. "You want to lie down for a while?" he said, pointing to the cot at the end of the room.

There was a poker lying under the boiler. I picked it up and said, "You let me out or I'll bop you." He stared at me with a look of amazement, probably surprised to see a little boy acting so mean. I threw the poker at him and darted out of the door.

"Hey, come back," he yelled, running after me. I looked over my shoulder as I ran out of the doorway and I saw him still struggling to pull his pants up. I ran to my wagon, dumped the newspapers and ran home. I went in the backyard, where Walter was boxing with some friends, and told him what had happened.

"You wait right here," Walter said, "I'll get something to fix him up."

Walter came back about twenty minutes later with a brown package. I unwrapped it. Inside was the largest shaving razor I had ever seen in my life. It must have been for shaving an animal. It was six inches long.

Walter snapped it open. "You go back tonight and when he comes at you, get him fast. That's how you got to treat them fairies," he told me. "When they mess with you, just wait and when they get up close, whomp 'em. After you touch them up a little, they ain't gonna bother nobody no more. I did that once and the cat was in the hos-

pital for three months. If that don't work, I'll come over with some
of my friends tomorrow and we'll get him good."

"I don't want to hurt the guy," I said. "I just don't want him to
bother me."

But Walter insisted that I take the razor. "Listen, boy, if you
don't get that dude by tonight, we'll get him by tomorrow. If he digs
men he's supposed to mess around with men. He ain't supposed to
hit on no boys."

I put the razor in my pocket and went home. When it was time
to eat, I couldn't. Crazy thoughts were buzzing around in my head:
I didn't feel bad about hitting the janitor with the poker, but I didn't
want to mutilate him or see him hurt by any gang. My mother kept
asking me what was wrong. I finally told her what had happened,
only mentioning that he had propositioned me and leaving out the
razor. I figured the best thing to do would be to go and scare him.
Perhaps then he would leave me alone. I told my mother not to
worry—I wouldn't go back that night.

Next day I cut out of school at recess and spent two hours practicing with my razor until I could get it out as fast as Walter did. It
was all a matter of pulling it out from the left side, snapping it open
and standing almost in a crouch, all in one motion. When it was
executed right, the psychological effect was terrifying. I figured I
would scare the janitor so he would never bother me again. I didn't
want to hurt him.

When I went back on my newspaper route, I kept waiting for him.
Every time I heard a rustle in the hallway I stopped and went for my
razor, but there was no one there. When I went home I told my
mother again not to worry.

About three days later I found out from one of my customers that
the guy had been arrested for propositioning a young boy in the park.
In spite of that, I kept the razor with me until I graduated from
Gordon Junior High. Although I got into several fights, I never had
to use it, thank God. The only time I ever drew it out of my pocket
was when another colored kid I knew, a friend of Walter's, tried to
steal my newspaper wagon when I was down behind our house. He
was bigger than I was, finally knocked me down and started running
off with my wagon. I ran after him and when he stopped and started
to go for his knife or razor or whatever he had hidden, I whipped
out my razor. He was so astonished that he shook hands, gave me
the wagon back and never bothered me again.

I had been a Cub Scout when I lived in the country, so I joined the Boy Scouts the winter after I played with Louis Brown. We had a wild troop. It was there that I learned more about the superiority of the Marquis of Queensberry school of boxing over street fighting. I loved boxing, although it took me a long time to learn how to use the more graceful, sporting kinds of moves that really scientific boxing utilized.

When winter came that year, instead of dropping large hunks of snow off the Q Street bridge on the cars passing below, I went out on camping trips in Virginia. One time a boy I knew who was kind of a child prodigy in everything went with me. His name was Paul Gardescu. When we got to the campsite, it started pouring. While all the other boys were crying, Paul and I took off all our clothes to keep them dry, put on our ponchos, dug a hole in the ground, which we covered with boughs of a tree, then put up our tent, threw our clothes inside, built a fire, put our clothes back on and within twenty-five minutes we were sitting inside dry and comfortable while everyone else was freezing. Paul was a real outdoorsman. He was also the first friend I had besides my fellow newsboy Henry Scruggs who had many intellectual interests. All my other friends were only interested in fighting, trying to sneak wine and stealing. Two of my best friends were already in reform school for three years apiece. My father had gone overseas to New Caledonia as an agricultural adviser for the Board of Economic Warfare, so my mother took a job with the OSS. There was no one at home to tell me what not to do.

When my sister came back from Florida in June of 1943, my mother decided to have a little party for her so that she could meet some kids from Washington. We asked some of the children around the block and children of my mother's friends that she had met with her work at the OSS. I got all dressed up in my good suit, bow tie and suede shoes and spent quite a bit of the night putting calamine lotion on my pimples so that I wouldn't look too young in case any older girls showed up.

I played the piano for about two hours as the guests were walking in. They were rather surprised to open the door and find someone thundering away. They could just about get by me in the narrow hallway, but I thought this would be a wonderful way to greet them and also show that my sister lived in a home full of talented and cultivated people. I hadn't studied the piano formally since I left the farm, but I had been practicing and improvising every day. Finally when I got tired of playing, I walked upstairs and saw everybody sitting around looking nervous and embarrassed. So I brought out the Victrola and began playing my Dixieland records. Then I played the Bach Second Brandenburg Concerto. I noticed that the effect it had on the people was not so different from the effect it had on me. No one seemed to have noticed that it was different music. They were now talking and partying and having a good time. Then I put on the Dixieland music again and played along with the records. Because of all the noise I'd been making plus my frenetic personality, I managed to drive all the people to the other side or out of the room entirely. In fact, without knowing it I was a perfect host for my sister because I managed to get everybody away from where I was to wherever she was, although that was not always my intention. By the end of the night she had twenty admirers for the entire summer.

Shortly after this I went away to a wonderful work camp in Vermont. It was organized for city kids so that they could work on a farm and learn about outdoor life. Most of them were able to pay their camp tuition by working and I was thrilled to be able to go. By this time I felt as if I had lived in the city all my life, as if I was on my way toward becoming a very bad kid. It was the environment: violence and petty thievery, the supercharged, hysterical, sexually frantic atmosphere of Washington during this time. It was impossible not to be affected by it. When I got to Vermont and took one deep breath of that fabulous air, I knew that I was at home again with my soul. I remembered what my life had been like before we had moved to Washington. When I got out of the train and into the back of the bus on the way up to the work camp, I began crying, though I made sure no one could see me.

I brought my trumpet with me. During that summer of 1943 I used to play all over the buildings where we lived. A lot of the kids would sit around listening and I felt in myself for the first time that I maybe had something to say. It was as if I could only talk to them through my trumpet since most of the time I felt out of place. These kids were from New England. Without even discussing any of the experiences I had been through I could feel that they had led very organized, calm and conventional lives. They gossiped about the wonderful schools they attended, about fraternities, about athletic events like lacrosse and tennis. They also discussed World War II in great, sweeping generalities.

I found for the first time since I'd been in the first grade that I didn't have to fight. No one seemed to care if I was Jewish or not. There were no gangs, no violence and the countryside was beautiful. Even though I was almost the youngest kid in the camp, I was made a work leader because I knew so much about farming. Also, I used to sit in with the square-dance band and for the first time had a chance to play in odd keys like G-flat. The pianist of the band could only play the black keys. As a result the band played in keys that were unusual for ordinary trumpet improvising. Consequently, I made a great deal of progress on the trumpet that summer and began to practice very hard.

I decided to write my first symphony as soon as I got back to Washington. Although I destroyed it long also, I do recall elements in it which were similar to George Gershwin's work. But it wasn't because of Gershwin that I wrote it but because of what I heard from my introduction to and participation in jazz. It was also influenced by my continued interest in Bix Beiderbecke's jazz records—his great harmonic sense, his use of time and space, his fantastic artistry as a brass player. When I first heard the Brandenburg concertos, I noticed that by listening to each line I could also hear these pieces as a kind of baroque Dixieland. The polyphonic writing, the spirit and buoyant quality of Bach's Brandenberg concertos, were similar in many ways to some of these superlative Beiderbecke recordings.

The following spring I went to hear the National Symphony conducted by Hans Kindler, a great, towering, dramatic and tyrannic figure from the old school of conductors. The orchestra wasn't the best then, but no one in Washington cared. Especially those of us who canoed down the Potomac and brought our boats up to the edge of the barge to listen to the music.

I went with Sarah Mae, my beautiful neighbor, who was a pink Rubenesque beauty of staggering proportions. She was enough to blow any twelve-year-old would-be Casanova's mind. During the first half of the concert most of the music was of the pops variety. Already I could sense the difference between music that was written from the heart and music that was just trash, so at first I didn't pay much attention to it. I spent most of the time wrestling with Sarah Mae in the canoe, trying to take her clothes off. She tittered in that demure southern way. Even though we were good friends, she was embarrassed with all the people close by in the other canoes. So I gave up and concentrated on the music. After a lot of trashy potboilers, the program closed with, of all things, Beethoven's Fifth Symphony. Because the opening bars, which were rhythmically equivalent to the morse code for "V for Victory"—which must have been played on the radio on the average of once a minute during the entire course of World War II—the piece was as much a pop hit then as anything on the Hit Parade. Of course I had heard recordings of this piece before, but lying out there on the canoe, I heard for the first time how Beethoven used the opening four notes as the basis for the entire symphony. In some kind of primitive way I slowly became aware of the existence of form and development in composition, something altogether different from the freedom of improvising. I decided that I had better get a composition teacher and begin to find out more about this.

That night after I finally took Sarah Mae home, I gave my symphony one farewell glance, ripped it up and threw it away. I realized that if I was going to be a composer I would have to learn something about composing.

The work camp I had been going to had a winter school and the following fall I found out that they were going to let me into it as one of their experimental problem children.

I was overjoyed. I had graduated from Gordon Junior High School, but I loved being in the country and I knew that this school was very strong for music and that I could be in an environment where I wouldn't have to fight. It was a turning point in my life. For the first time I could look forward to school where I would be able to concentrate on studying. I knew I was smart enough to learn anything and to keep up with the other students. I was much more experienced with the outside world than many of them and even some of their parents I had met. I knew I would be all right now. I was back in the country.

So I felt right at home. Coming up on the train, I noticed two or three other far-out-looking kids who also must have been school experiments. As I got out of the train that beautiful fall day and rode up on the bus toward the school, I realized how lucky I was. My friend Walter was serving four years in reform school for robbing a liquor store and stabbing the owner. One of his friends had been shot and killed by the police. At least half of my class at Gordon Junior High had dropped out of school entirely. Some had joined the army or merchant marines, underage, and some were old enough to join even though they were still in junior high school. Three or four who were seventeen or over were serving jail sentences. Several of them were in the hospital. There had been stabbings and general panic. A new principal had been installed after I left. He was six feet six, had been a great athlete and was trying to establish discipline by unlimited use of physical violence. I was happy to be away from the whole scene. I thought about my Boy Scout friends like Paul Gardescu and as I looked at those beautiful green mountains I realized how much all of them would enjoy being out here. It was different from our farm, but it was beautiful countryside and I loved it.

3

I WAS walking by the record room one day after I had been in school a few weeks when I heard some beautiful trumpet playing. I ran inside and saw three or four kids lying on their backs listening to the Haydn Trumpet Concerto. I looked on the label of one of the 78-rpm records and saw that the trumpeter was George Eskdale. I was overwhelmed by the beauty of the piece and how terrifically he played.

"Who does this record belong to?" I asked. One of the students gave me a cutting glance and said, "They are the property of this school."

The other students looked away from me with a mixture of embarrassment, pity and amusement, but I was used to this treatment by now. I could tell that they thought I was a combination coarse yokel and city tough boy. I was smart enough to know that if I got in any fights or caused any trouble I would be the first one to be thrown out. So I cooled it. After the other kids had left, I looked through the rest of the record collection instead of going back to studying. I couldn't believe my eyes! There were thousands of records. They were by composers whose work I knew and loved plus other composers whose music I had only read about or whose names I had seen occasionally in music stores.

I noticed that there was no jazz and very little music of the twentieth century except for a few works by Gustav Holst, Delius, Stravinsky, Bloch and Debussy. But to compensate for this, there was an enormous collection of Renaissance and other pre-Bach music and hundreds of chamber works by the masters I had never heard. I stayed up until after midnight listening and every chance I got during

33

the year, I would run into the record room to lie there listening for hours. I realized that this old music touched something very vital in me. A whole different part of me identified with it and each piece that I heard pulled me back in time. After listening for a few minutes, I actually could feel that I was in Haydn's court, or in the chorus singing while Gesualdo conducted, or that I was playing the trumpet in an outdoor English celebration during a performance of the Trumpet Voluntary.

At the same time I was discovering this music, I played trumpet in the school orchestra. Because we did so much Bach I had a chance to really shine. The music director sometimes had the two or three of us who played trumpets sit in the balcony to play the various trumpet parts during the cantatas we performed. Because they were such extremely difficult trumpet parts, at least one of us was always bombing out and because I was the best, I always got the blame. The music teacher was a perfect gentleman, but he was also an insane music fanatic and when I or one of the other trumpet players would miss a note, he would say "God damn, Amram," under his breath, twitching with fury and pulling his neck muscles up and down in spastic motions until it looked as if his collar and tie would rip off. Soon my nick name became God Damn Amram.

Because most of these students were from tremendously success-oriented homes, when they saw that I was already a promising musician as well as a good farm worker, they treated me with a little more respect, though I can't say that I reciprocated. The work camp had been a wonderful natural atmosphere, but the school had a kind of a pre-Ivy League snobby atmosphere in spite of its radical political outlook and its crazy headmistress. The teachers probably represented the greatest assortment of crackpots of their era, a potpourri of the best and worst minds of their generation. They were overworked and underpaid.

The headmistress believed that the primary evils in the world were money, alcohol, businessmen, city people and towering above everything else—sex. She was smart enough to know that if she ran the students ragged from morning to night they would be too tired by the end of the day to do anything but collapse into bed by themselves. She also believed that every person was a Renaissance man or woman. She herself played four or five instruments badly, painted, wrote, skied and did everything with a kind of indomitable, clumsy good will that won over the motley group of teachers and students.

Still, I knew that most of these kids didn't really need this and I wished that the children I had been to school with in Florida or Feasterville and especially in Washington could have the chance to be in such a beautiful physical environment.

Towering above everything else in the school was the music director. Although he used to shout at me when he would hear me playing jazz on the sly (saying "God damn, Amram, can't you get that smell of smoke and the beer-sodden atmosphere of the dance hall out of your soul?"), still he encouraged me. I identified with him because I could see what a fanatic he was. When he would play Bach, he would get that far-out, rhapsodic look, staring at the ceiling the way I had seen some of the old jazz players do when they got carried away. He really made Bach swing even though he would have been furious if I had told him that. While I was not officially supposed to take any courses in composition or theory, he told me which books I could get to study on my own and that when we were singing or performing Bach to be sure to listen to the lines. I told him about my love for the Second Brandenberg concerto and he said that perhaps the next year the orchestra would play it to give me a chance to perform.

I was a fairly good student. My grades were about average except in music, where I did very well. I gradually found out that the stiff uptight snobbishness of the other kids came mostly from total inexperience in the world. They were simple nineteenth-century souls, carbon copies of their parents with no idea where anything was. I found out that many of them were really wonderful people underneath, despite their insular ways.

Nevertheless, I couldn't help feeling a sense of terrible injustice when I thought of all the bright kids I had known who could never make it to a great place like this. The peace and beauty of the country could straighten out any kid. In the short time I had been in Washington, my whole way of life had changed. If I hadn't been fortunate enough to come to this school, I might have ended up in real trouble. I began to think of the city as a place of evil and the country as a place of virtue (this was fortified when I began reading Walt Whitman's descriptions of New York). When I went out to the fields to practice the trumpet or walked through the woods by myself I felt as beautiful as the countryside.

I used to hang out in the barn a lot. I felt at home with the workers because they reminded me of country folks I grew up with in Feaster-ville. I loved the gruff, saturnine New Englanders. Since none of the other kids went to the barn unless they had to, the hands would talk to me. I would help them out, cleaning the stalls and the milking machines, feeding the cows and so forth. Generally I learned a lot about the real New Englanders, their families, how they had suffered unbelievably during the Depression. I discovered that great Yankee stubborn pride and the elegance with which these people could express themselves. Their speech was like Bach. Just as every note in his music was crucial, every word that they spoke in a conversation was crucial. Some of them sensed that while I didn't belong in this school, I was trying to make it. Early that spring one of them named Elmer, who played the trombone and piano, told me of a job that he had with the local square-dance band. I played with him once at the work camp so he told me that this job was a few miles away and I could come along if I wanted to sneak out with him. I was thrilled. About ten o'clock that night I jumped in the back of his dump truck with his guitar player and went about twenty miles to the barn where the dance was being held. This was a real farmers' square dance; it was quite an affair. The musicians all had flasks of whiskey with them and when they offered me a drink I couldn't refuse.

By the second set, everything was really swinging and the farmers were coming up roaring with drunken laughter and slapping me on the back so hard they almost knocked me off the bandstand. Everyone thought it was great to see a kid playing with the old-timers. At the end of the second set a perspiring, red-faced woman with a red fireman's bandana around her neck came over and offered me a small apple pie, only with her Vermont accent she said "poi."

During the third set, I noticed with astonishment that part of the music the violinist and pianist were playing was taken from a Bach cantata. I couldn't believe my ears, but sure enough the same refrain came up again. I asked the square-dance caller, who had studied some music. He told me that a lot of this music dated as far back as the seventeenth century and that while it was possible that this was taken from Bach, it was also possible that Bach had taken the same folk refrain and used it in his music.

The dance continued. Even though the music was stiff, ricky-ticky and angular just like the dancing, I realized that in many ways the whole buoyancy and excitement of the dancing and music was a lot like the dance I had played for at the Elks Club with Louis Brown

a few years before. There was that same naturalness and enthusiasm
and joy. I got the same great feeling being in there with my trumpet
and a part of it. Of course by the end of the night I was bombed out
of my head.

"Are you all right?" said Elmer as he was putting his trombone
away.

"Sure" I said, trying not to vomit. "I've been drunk before. It's
O.K."

"Don't say anything at school," he warned me.

"Don't worry. This is the greatest time I've had here all year." I
got underneath the tarpaulin in back of the truck. Every time he
would slow down, I would lean out the back and throw up. But with
that clear, crisp Vermont air, I felt O.K. by the time we got back to
school and snuck through the window into bed.

When I went back to Washington the following summer I got a
job in a People's Drug Store. It was the summer of 1945 and the
feverish excitement of wartime Washington had reached its peak.
That old successful American combination of money, violence and
sex had reached its apex with all the hysteria in the headlines.
Everyone was caught up with the scent of victory. There was an acute
manpower shortage, so that when I applied for a job as a soda jerk,
I only had to go to soda school for one day. A tired old hillbilly was
droning out the instructions on how to mix sodas and sundaes. He
would then ask a question about how to make one of the succulent
secret concoctions, picking someone at random. The response was
usually an imbecilic mutter followed by a blank stare. Obviously, with
so many able-bodied men and women in the armed forces, working
for the government and taking all the other jobs that were left over,
the cream of Washington's intellectual crop was not working for the
People's Drug Store that summer. He asked about five people in a
row how to make a black and white soda (vanilla ice cream and
chocolate syrup). Finally he asked me. When I actually told him he
immediately informed me that I had a job and to report to the Du
Pont Circle branch.

I showed up and began working. I had gotten used to working
hard all year at the school. I was in the northern Yankee work syn-
drome and my fellow workers began to stare at me with suspicion.

"Wha's yo' hurry, sonny?" I was asked by a whining, faded, plump
southern belle. She had fat feet that poured out over her shoes and

dyed curly hair and was called Shirley Temple by the other employees and some of the customers.

"I'm just tryin' to make me a little money, sugar," I said, jiving her with one of the white-trash, corn-ponisms I had picked up in Gordon Junior High.

"Don't be so fas' about it," she said.

I saw that in order to readjust I would have to get back into that southern groove. But a whole summer of slow motion would drive me crazy. I wanted to make some money fast, do some hitchhiking and maybe go up and visit the work camp. I knew I could stay up with some of the square-dance musicians or sneak into the barn or other hiding places I knew of.

The second day I was there a young pinch-faced fellow named Floyd talked with me. I told him I wanted to get another job so I could make some money and get out of Washington for the summer.

"Watch me," he said, peering surreptitiously from underneath his white soda-jerk's hat. As he rang up a sale for a bacon, lettuce and tomato sandwich, a malted milk and a cup of coffee, he only registered thirty-five cents.

"Hey, it was more than that," I told him.

"Says who?" Floyd responded, looking slyly over the open cash register. He put in the two dollars that was given to him, changed it, returned thirty-five cents to the cash drawer, closed the register, returned the change to the customer and put the rest of the money in a pocket underneath his apron.

"Don't you think you'll get caught?" I said, suddenly remembering several of my unlucky friends who were incarcerated at the moment.

"I've been here two years and they ain't caught me yet," said Floyd. "I make maybe a hundred and thirty a week extra this way."

"I wouldn't even need that much for the summer," I said.

"Well, it's real easy. Just pick your spots," he told me.

For the next three weeks I picked my spots. By the end of that time I had eighty dollars clear plus my salary, which gave me a hundred and fifty dollars. I was set for the summer.

The manager was heartbroken that I had to leave. "I'm sorry," I told him, "but I have to get back up to Vermont. I can't make it in this city anymore."

"You're the best worker we ever had," he told me.

"I appreciate that," I said, but I wanted to go back up to Vermont. I knew I could get a chance to play a little music there and anyway I wanted to get out of Washington. It was already becoming a bad influence on me.

"Listen," he said confidentially. "I'll give you a raise if you stay. We never had nobody work as good as you and I know you steal much less than any of the other boys." I looked surprised and started to panic. "I know, I know," he said, smiling in the same way that Floyd had. "I take quite a bit out of the register myself."

"I'm not a thief," I told him, getting angry. "I just took enough money to cover my needs. I'm afraid if I stayed in Washington, I might get into trouble."

"Lookie here," he said. "Don't you know the government, and the big businessman and everyone's a robber and a thief? All America knows that everybody's stealing from everybody. Don't you know that?"

"I'm sorry," I told him. "If I could work as hard as I wanted and everybody else was doing the same, I'd stay here for the summer, but having to work where everyone is loafing drives me crazy. It makes me feel like a bum and I'm not a bum and don't consider myself a thief."

"Well, it's wonderful to meet a boy with such ambitions," he told me as a last sales-pitch resort. "If you ever want to come back, you've always got a job."

"Thank you," I said. I'd only been back in Washington a few weeks and I was already getting that terrible feeling that I had before I left. I went home that night, got my overalls, my trumpet and a clean shirt, said good-bye and hitchhiked back to Vermont.

I made it to Vermont in six rides and two days. I went back to the work camp and really had a ball. At fourteen I was a lot taller than the year before and there were a lot of kids there that I knew. After one night of sleeping in the barn and two of hiding in someone's closet every time they made bed check, I modulated into the camp and ate meals with everyone even though I wasn't a member. I was even put in charge of the barn detail for a while.

One night there was a tremendous ringing of the fire bell and all the kids came running into the main hall. "The war is over!" someone shouted. It was VJ Day. The war was over. People were crying and laughing and shouting and I knew there must be something fantastic going on in one of the nearby towns. I ran over to the barn and saw Elmer, who was jumping into his dump truck. "Come on along," he said, and we roared off toward Brattleboro at about seventy miles an hour over the hills and around mountains. I heard those quiet Vermont hills suddenly being filled with car honks and yells and gigantic wah-whoos of joy.

After a trip that nearly took us off the sides of several mountains, we arrived at Brattleboro. This normally quiet town was like Times Square. In the few gas stations the attendants were running around doing a kind of war dance, waving signs saying "Free Gas" and yelling and embracing everyone. The farmers from southern Vermont and New Hampshire had convened there with whistles and horns tied on the backs of the exhaust pipes of their pickup trucks, beat-up old cars and tractors they had ridden in for the celebration. The din was unbelievable. It was probably the most exciting moment in this neck of the woods since the winning of the Revolutionary War. People were shouting, laughing, running around and hugging one another.

Suddenly a band began playing, a cross between what looked like a fire department band and anybody else joining in with a noisemaker or horn. Elmer got out his trombone, I took my trumpet and we just began blasting. It was too noisy to try to play any music, so we lifted up our horns into the air and just roared out shouts of joy. People swarmed around our pickup truck, cheering us on and yelling with excitement. It was not only that the war was over, it seemed to be the first thing these people had to really shout and whoop it up about for centuries. After a few hours, Elmer and I were tired. We were worn out from our blasting. More and more jalopies, pickup trucks and farm equipment kept coming in, almost all of them with some kind of noisemaker attached to their exhaust pipes.

As we were driving back toward the work camp Elmer turned to me. "How about that bomb they dropped on 'em?"

"I don't know," I said. "I heard something about it on the radio, but I don't know anything except of a place in New Mexico where they tested it. One of the kids from school is from out there."

"They deserved it, those bastards, they started the war."

"I guess so."

"Well, it's lucky we dropped it," he said. "It means a kid like you and all the kids won't ever have to go in the army again. You'll remember this day as long as you live. I remembered the end of World War I. They said there weren't going to be no more wars. Now

I know it. This was the last time. This will be one of the most wonderful days in your life," he went on as we bounced along the road
back to camp. "It's something you'll tell your children about, that
you'll never forget. The last war that ever was. Thank God it's over."
I was amazed to see tears come from his eyes as we drove along
through the cold, starry night. As the sounds of the party horns grew
fainter and fainter drifting over the great black Vermont hills, I
could hear Elmer snuffling and blowing his nose into his red farmer's
handkerchief.

By my second year in high school I found two friends who were
also interested in jazz: a quiet boy named Ken who plays clarinet,
and a terrific boogie-woogie pianist named John Phillips. Although
jazz was forbidden, we used to get together anyway and have sessions
for hours.
A wonderful English teacher who arrived and departed mysteriously during the year also played the saxophone. When he heard me
practicing one day he came over, invited me to his room, rummaged in his closet and pulled out a C-melody saxophone. He was
tall and lumbering and quiet and professorial. He also seemed very
shy and remote, a very somber kind of man who had obviously suffered a great deal. When he took out his saxophone, he produced all
kinds of sounds like slap tonguing, subtones, squeals, groans and
hollers, sounds I had rarely heard even on records much less live.
His whole face and huge body became animated. His gigantic foot
would begin tapping until his long carpeted slipper fell off, revealing
an enormous set of toes like the pictures I had seen of old Roman
ruins showing an archeologist standing next to some giant white foot.
I began playing with him. After about a week he produced a
wind-up Victrola with some battered old recordings of Bix Beiderbecke, some of the same records I had in Washington. Then Ken
came to play his clarinet. When we could we would sneak off to
where there was a piano and John would join us for jam sessions.
One day the teacher disappeared and no one seemed to know why.
He left me a note, however, in tiny organized handwriting, telling
me that I should keep on playing because even if they didn't like
jazz at school they did everywhere else in the world. He also listed
a bunch of records that I should buy and some arrangements that I
should get, including a large number of Duke Ellington's tunes arranged for clarinet, trumpet and saxophone. I sent away for them,

but because of the lack of a saxophonist, I rewrote them for viola. Needless to say, there weren't any violists at the school that could swing. Our plans for an underground band collapsed and Ken and John and I resorted to private jam sessions.

John got thrown out of school that year for drinking, smoking and raising hell in general. I knew where he was at because in many ways he was just like me. But he only wanted to play jazz and thought everything else was a waste of time. I tried to convince him that the classics were great too, but to him they were from the past and dead.

By the end of the year our group consisted of just Ken and myself playing duets out in the woods or away from the music room, where we were now banned because we played this kind of music. When I played with the square-dance bands now, they let me improvise more and even play one or two blues numbers late in the night. So I was able to keep up and get my kicks, at least a little bit.

I must have grown nearly an inch every few months during this period. I was always tired and always hungry. The school only had white bread, which I couldn't stand. We had never eaten white bread at home. I longed for some pumpernickel, rye bread, black bread, matzoth or anything but those terrible spongy, angel-food-cake, accordion-like flour pillows that were served to us every day.

I used to go to the cook when I did my turns working in the kitchen, but he told me if he fed me anything extra, he would have to let the other children eat more as well.

"I will even eat the slops," I told him. "Let me have the leftovers."

"I can't do it," he informed me, glowering from under his chef's hat. I could see he was a real organization man. But because I was really hungry I started to do something about it. After the brief spell of working for the People's Drug Stores I had sworn to myself that I would never steal unless it was necessary for my survival. Getting more food was necessary for my survival. There was no place to buy any food anywhere for miles and I would have had to get special permission to leave anyway. So with two friends I went back into the freezer about one o'clock in the morning when everyone was asleep. This was child's play in comparison to my junior high school experiences in Washington. With one friend serving as a lookout, I climbed on my other friend's shoulders, crawled over the top of the freezer, went between the pipes over the room to where the supply cabinet was, jumped down and entered the freezer, which didn't even have a lock on it. With no burglar alarms, no policemen and no pedestrians passing by, this was an extremely simple operation. I didn't want to take too much because I was only interested in getting enough to assuage my roaring appetite. Once a week I would go to the freezer and take meat, butter and cheese. And although I hated to do it, I also took a few loaves of that horrible white bread. That was all I needed. We had all the milk and vegetables we needed. The three of us would go out in the woods at night, have little barbecues and cook up our meat for the week. Then with our cheese and meat hidden in the windowboxes along with some fermented cider we had made, we would have midnight feasts while all the other kids were asleep. I found that with my supplemented diet, I had more energy and was able to function much better.

It was during this time that my life as a trumpet player reached a crisis. I had to have braces on my teeth. I had already played some jobs and begun composing and had seriously considered making a living as a trumpet player. With the braces, however, it became impossible to play the trumpet. The mouthpiece no longer fit. I couldn't see giving it up for three years. But because I only used the piano to help me in composing, to play jazz and to improvise, I seriously wondered what musical outlet was left as a possible means of support.

Then the school musical director decided that I should try the French horn, which had a smaller mouthpiece and could fit within the confines of my braces without hurting my mouth. Suddenly it seemed that the horn might be a new outlet for me, as well as fulfilling an old childhood dream. I figured that at least I could play this fascinating instrument a little bit. When the braces were off my teeth I could always go back to the trumpet.

Playing the French horn opened up another world for me. As I began rehearsing Mozart's Jupiter Symphony and other works, I found that I now had much more interesting parts to play. The horn was used orchestrally in many more ways than the trumpet. I also found that as a composer there were many more things I could hear. The French horn made me listen. There were so many colors that the instrument itself was capable of. Playing made me notice the other inner voices like the violas and how effective they could be in a well-orchestrated piece.

I began to play with a Renaissance music group that was composed of players who liked to sight-read pre-Bach music with each person taking any part on any instrument he could handle. During the next year we met frequently and played through hundreds of fascinating, beautifully written pieces of pre-Bach composers.

In 1945 there were still not that many kids playing French horn. I sat in the orchestra feeling like a star because I knew there was no one to replace me. In addition to falling in love with the French horn, I also fell in love with Holly, the first horn player, a beautiful doll-like girl a year older than I was. She had a page-boy blonde haircut, lovely guileless blue eyes and a fantastic figure. She was like a woman that was carved on the front of an old sailing ship. She had a lovely, completely feminine personality, quiet and unassuming, and she was very gifted in music. She also played the viola and the piano beautifully.

After a while we had the first happy romance of my life. On the clear days in the spring, we would walk for miles to find an isolated spot in the hills. We would lie on our backs holding hands, staring up at the clouds and the blue skies without saying anything for as long as an hour. We had that telepathic communication musicians have when they're playing. When we did talk it was mostly about music and the French horn.

I decided that I was not going back to the trumpet. Although I missed playing jazz, the horn was very rewarding and I felt I could do my jazz playing on the piano. I thought that someday I could possibly play jazz on the French horn, although this was something unheard of in those days.

Even though I was only in the tenth grade and Holly was in the eleventh, we discussed the idea of getting married. When I finally told her that she must marry me after I finished high school, she said, "I would, but the only trouble is I think you would stay out late all the time." Actually her prophecy was amazingly accurate for a girl of sixteen, although neither of us knew it then. But although we decided to give up our marriage plans we remained very much in love and never had psychological strains. Even though she played the horn much better than I did, she was still completely feminine and easily took the female role. She looked after me in every way she could even though I had no idea what the masculine role was at that time.

She played the Brahms Horn Trio. This piece took on a new meaning for me even though I had heard recordings of it by the great

horn player Aubrey Brain years before. I rehearsed the Mozart Horn
Quintet and performed it along with countless other arrangements of
Mozart horn concertos, Haydn's horn concertos, cello and vocal
music, some of which I transcribed for horn and piano.

Late that June I met Dimitri Mitropoulos. He came to visit our
place at the seashore with a friend of his who was working with the
Philadelphia Dell Concert series, where Mitropoulos was conducting
for the summer of 1946. He had two days off and wanted to go
someplace where he could relax and not be part of the music scene.
His friend and my mother had known each other ever since they were
children in Philadelphia.

We had a small, cheerful, simple house by the ocean and Henry
(my mother's childhood friend) thought that it would be nice for
Mitropoulos to get away there. Mitropoulos agreed to come because
he loved the ocean, as he did the mountains and just about everything else that had to do with nature. I was excited because even
though I was only fifteen I was already writing a trio for horn, violin
and piano based on the instrumentation of the Brahms Horn Trio.
I had heard radio broadcasts of Mitropoulos conducting but had
never seen him in person. Neither had my family.

My mother bought a lot of Greek food because she thought that
would make him happy and we waited eagerly for the Maestro to
arrive. It was a rainy afternoon when Henry finally drove up with
Mitropoulos. I noticed immediately that there was a constant electric
energy that seemed to emanate from him. As I saw him entering our
house I remembered what it was like to see Toscanini conduct when
I was eight years old and visiting New York. I remember turning to
a friend and saying, "His head looks like an electric light bulb."
This made all the people around me laugh, but it really was the impression I had as a child. Mitropoulos had this quality as well. When
I met him his eyes seemed to go right through me, through my sister,
my family and the entire little house that we lived in. He seemed to
be able to see everything in a glance. At the same time there was a
hint of a smile that constantly played on the corners of his mouth.
He seemed to have life completely figured out with a kind of Olympian chuckle about it all. He seemed totally aware of everything that
was happening, and able to cope with any situation. Still, he was full
of love and compassion for others.

For the next two days I sat quietly, listening to him talk. Whenever he said anything it was pointed, direct and eloquent. He had been brought up by priests and spoke almost like a priest or a saint. Rabbis I had heard, friends of my father's with their wild Talmudic logic—none of them had this man's burning angelic spirit. He wasn't concerned only with music, but with the whole mystery of life, the majesty of nature and man's relationship to it, and the inhumanity of man to man.

He was in the midst of such a discussion when a friend of mine named Sammy came in. Sammy lived about a half-mile down the beach and although he was only thirteen and a half, he had already been in jail three times for stealing and for two car smashups that he had been in as an unlicensed driver. He was six feet tall, over two hundred pounds and rather crude, to put it mildly.

When he came in I said, "Hi, Sammy," but my family and everyone else in the room gave him the freeze. It was such a bad freeze that he felt it immediately. After a few minutes, he got up and fumbled his way out of the house. My parents and the other people in the room looked relieved.

"Why did you treat the boy that way?" Mitropoulos asked suddenly. He then launched a whole discourse on how people forget that every man is their brother and that the teachings of Christ had taught him this if nothing else.

I found out later that Mitropoulos not only preached this but practiced it as well with every musician and every person that he knew. He slept on a hard bed, gave his money to needy musicians or composers and spent most of his time studying music, especially new music. He truly believed that men were brothers and that music was an aesthetic, spiritual, dramatic experience that brought people close together and made the multitudes one.

It was two days later, June 26, when I went to his concert, that I understood how much the personality of the conductor has to do with the kind of music produced. The program included Debussy's "Iberia," No. 2 of "Images" and Brahms's First. My mother drove my sister and me into Philadelphia to hear the concert. We arrived at the Dell and when Mitropoulos walked out on stage to conduct, you could tell that the musicians were glad to see him there. There was no looking at the floor, no zombie-like stares as if they were being humiliated by someone who was presumably going to lead them. They were *glad he was there*. And from the first downbeat to the last there was a kind of excitement I had never seen before at a concert. He seemed totally involved in the music and in the musicians, completely unaware of the audience. Some of his gestures were unfathomable and bizarre, but the music that came out was really inspired. I never realized the fire and passion that lay in Debussy's music until I heard this performance. The orchestra seemed as immersed in the music as Mitropoulos was. Because he used no score he was able to communicate with them directly, as if he were actually playing the orchestra. But at the same time he let everyone else play too. Sometimes he would lead and sometimes he would follow, but he was always with it and in it. He never seemed outside the music and he did none of the simpering and posturing and facial mugging that I had seen in so many older conductors who apparently felt it was necessary to interpret the music for the audience by accompanying each phrase with a facial gesture more grotesque than the last.

His nonshowmanship was the best showmanship I had ever seen. The sounds from the orchestra seemed to sweep the whole audience away. It was possible to visualize great mountains and forests at night, to hear the wind whistling through the trees, to feel the branches rubbing against one another. Mitropoulos' own roots in God and nature were so deep they seemed to project these true, natural feelings into the music and made it sound different from any performance of Debussy I had ever heard.

The audience went wild. Before Mitropoulos turned to them, he motioned to the musicians to stand up. But he did it as if he were thanking them, telling them how beautiful it was, asking them to stand with dignity and joy for the great experience that everyone had shared together. With this gesture of his arms the whole audience stood up even though he had his back to them. He then turned around and I saw those amazing eyes that seemed to grasp us all in one flicker, then go beyond us and become lost in thought, even as he was bowing. The tiny flicker played on the corners of his mouth as if he were saying that all the applause was unnecessary because the music had already said everything.

During the second half of the concert the orchestra performed Brahms's First. This was a piece I thought I knew backward and forward, being a horn player who loved Brahms. I had heard my father try to hack through it on the piano even though it took approximately two hours a movement. I had worn out several recordings of this work, had heard it performed many times and had even studied the score. But when I heard Brahms's First performed that night it was as if I had never heard it before. The great torrents of energy, the contrasting pastoral and reflective moments sounded completely different. I actually had a vision of Greece, which I had never visited, at least in my then-present incarnation, and it wasn't too much different from what Greece looked like when I did visit it eight years later. It was this mystical quality that Mitropoulos seemed to bring to the music and yet it was appropriate. He made it sound as if he had written the piece himself and yet I had the uncanny feeling that Brahms would have liked this performance more than any by the so-called Brahms experts, who made him drip with a lugubrious, Germanic, pedantic, heavy-handed sentimentality. Mitropoulos interpreted this as a free piece. I could see that he was trying to show the excitement that Brahms must have felt when he finished his First Symphony in his early forties.

Of course Brahms was always influenced by nature, writing most of his music in pastoral surroundings. Mitropoulos brought all of this out. The last movement had so much power and majesty that when it was over the audience came to its feet again. The orchestra also burst into applause even before Mitropoulos had a chance to ask them to rise. The musicians refused to stand when he motioned toward them. Finally he gestured as if to say, "I did nothing. Stand and do your duty." They stood, but they were all smiling and grinning and talking to one another, looking as if they had just won the World's Series. They didn't have that grim, gray look I had seen so many times when musicians go away disappointed because of circumstances they have to play under.

My mother said that we should go back and say hello because Mitropoulos and Henry were expecting us. I was so overwhelmed by the performance I didn't know what to say. I certainly didn't want to make small talk. When we got backstage Mitropoulos was standing by a wire fence, seemingly lost in thought while people stood and stared at him. My mother told him how much she liked the performance while I stood back. I heard him say to her, "What's the matter, didn't the boy like it?" Of course I went over immediately and told him how wonderful I thought it was. He then began talking about the Brahms Symphony and suddenly, in the midst of all those crowds of people, said he had looked at my trio while he was at our house and that I should learn how to modulate better. He actually told me the bar in which I should improve the modulation and how I should keep up my work in music. Then he went back into a trance and stared out at the people again from behind the fence.

What Mitropoulos told me that summer about modulating made me restudy my entire horn trio. I realized that although the melodic ideas were sufficient, the use of harmony in my piece was extremely pallid and primitive. I realized that if I could use more harmonically interesting lines in addition to the lines I had, it would add so much of a dimension that there would really be something to listen to over and over again. This was the kind of music I dreamed of writing. This was the test of good music: that each time you heard it, something new was there to hear and to feel.

I plunged into the study of harmony all over again. I sat at the piano for hours slaving over one or two measures, bashing away, hunting and searching, looking for the right notes. One day in the middle of the process I realized that the way I was playing the piano—backward and forward, slowly searching, finding, rejecting—was the way my father had played the piano in my earliest memories of music. I saw that his approach was almost a compositional one. I realized that the reason he was so laborious was that he wanted every note to be correct. If he missed a note, rather than going ahead, he would go back until he could make every sound the composer had intended even if it was completely out of meter and tempo. It was this painstaking and honest way of knowing exactly what I was doing that became the basis for my earliest compositional techniques. If I couldn't hear it in my head and write it down, I would just sit there pounding away at the piano until I could.

After completing some choral pieces, I got together with some friends at school who were pretty good singers. The thrill of hearing what I had written really got to me. The only instrumental piece of mine I had a chance to hear was an arrangement for our orchestra of a slow movement of a Handel organ work. The orchestra really ground through it. Every time there was a wrong note or a wrong entrance, which was most of the time, I felt as if someone were stabbing me.

One day the music director said to me, "If you're going to be a composer, you'll have to get used to this. It always takes a long time to hear music the way you would like to hear it and sometimes it doesn't happen until after you're dead. But if you're going to be a real composer, you'll go ahead and write anyway."

Truer words were never spoken.

The more I played Renaissance music, the more I found that while it was difficult to separate independent musical lines the way they moved melodically, or horizontally, from the way they sounded harmonically, or vertically, nevertheless that harmony was something that fascinated me. I felt I had a good natural lyric feeling but needed to develop a good harmonic vertical feeling, so that what I wrote wouldn't sound ordinary or primitive. The music of Debussy and Ravel and Stravinsky—especially the Symphonies of Wind Instruments, which was dedicated to Debussy—really caught my ear. These sounds were rooted in much older music but were still very new. I didn't have access to the scores or any formal way of studying them, so I simply bathed myself in the sounds and listened to the individual lines. Because I began composing more and more, I decided that I would try to stretch out and write what I heard and felt, even if it did go beyond what I had studied in harmony class.

I never actually saw a professional theatrical production until I was fifteen years old. My high school class went to see *Hamlet* in Boston. I was supposed to have read it, but I never finished it. I was caught in the excitement of the story of Hamlet and because I did not know the ending, was completely carried away by the climax of the play. I also recall that there was some use of music in this production, mostly recorded fanfares which sounded as if they were being played in a phone booth. Still, this left some impression on me. Later that year, there was a production at school of *The Man with the Flower in His Mouth* by Pirandello. I had acted in earlier productions that had been done that year. I had played Bushy in *Richard the Second*, but most of the classics didn't have roles that I could fill. My Feasterville accent eliminated me. I remembered the great sensation of shaking hands with Green and Bagot at the end of our big scene in *Richard the Second*. I really felt I was living it. But there was something that was very constricting about the conventional idea of theater for a performer, being stuck with lines and a director's dictatorial control.

Because *The Man with the Flower in His Mouth* required only a few actors and because Gordon Gould—who played one of the most brilliant Richard II's I've ever seen even though he was only a tenth-grader—had the lead in *The Man with the Flower in His Mouth* I was excused from my role as a thespian. It was decided rather that during one of the scenes in the railroad station, there should be music coming from a distant organ-grinder. Because it was very hard to find an organ-grinder recording, and because everyone at school knew that I was a budding composer, I was asked to write something that sounded like organ-grinder's music. Of course I said "yes" and wrote it in about ten minutes. It was for clarinet, oboe and French horn. It was not the totally conventional *um-pa-pa* grinder organ because at one point I had the accompaniment go into a different key to sound as if the mechanism in the organ broke down as the organs I'd heard in South Philadelphia often did. I did not really think that this ten minutes of work was the most distinguished that I would do in my life, but it threw my fellow actors into a state of ecstasy. "Superlative," "fabulous," "evocative," "magnificent" were the response from these young masters of hyperbole. It was my first experience with the kind but exaggerated reaction that people in the theater have for anyone who is disciplined and trained in a different art. While I thought that the organ-grinder music was quite effective and fun to do, it certainly wasn't that much musically. But apparently it had the kind of feeling that made the actors respond on stage. This was a gift that I have always seemed to maintain and while my interest was always in music, I think that my affinity for theatrical music is something that came naturally.

For the first time since I had planted my own cornfield with Artie McCrae and Eddie Filemyr back in the summer of 1940, I felt like my own man again. I was doing better in school. In addition to practicing the French horn, composing and working at my studies and listening to music, I read ferociously every chance I got. I remember being in the library once, putting my hand back over my shoulder without looking, pulling out a book and deciding that I would read it no matter what it was. It turned out to be *Cyrano de Bergerac,* which I had never even heard of. It was so exciting that I read it three times in a row. I read four of Thomas Wolfe's novels in the space of a month and also discovered Dreiser, Fitzgerald, Hemingway, Faulkner, Steinbeck and Dos Passos. I even tried writing poetry although what I wrote was pretty terrible. Once in a while I'd go out in the hills and try to sketch or paint landscapes, which were also pretty terrible, but these miserable efforts made me appreciate the great collection of art books in the library even more.

One day all these good things almost came to an end. A childhood friend of mine, Shorty, was in his room doing some sketching when another boy, Nick, came in and started an argument with him. He finally knocked over Shorty's water colors and although Shorty was small and slightly asthmatic, he became furious and he struck out at him. Then this bully, Nick, went out, came back with a sword and began threatening Shorty with it. He must have stolen it from one of the school's theatrical productions.

"Cut that out," I told him. I could feel myself beginning to get angry, something that had not happened since I had left Washington. It was a horrible feeling—like poison spreading slowly through my whole body. I became so angry at myself that I almost began crying in rage. "Stop it," I said, "God damn it, cut it out!" This only spurred Nick on. He hit Shorty broadside with the sword, not cutting him but knocking him over. Then he chopped the entire water color set, drawing board and table in half with the sword. I tried to control my temper, but I knew it would be too late.

He came at me with the sword, but instead of trying to defend myself, I said, "Please, please, stop it before you get hurt." I was watching him all the time as he swung the sword at me. I went to grab for a chair, but it was too late. I deflected the blow with my arm but it cut me high on the forehead right over my left eye. Blood ran down my face. I could hear Shorty whimpering in fear on the floor and saw him trying to crawl under the bed. Nick came at me with the sword again, but this time I had the chair ready and when he brought it down, I pushed up the chair and knocked it out of his hand. I dropped the chair and hit him a few times. When he fell down I started stomping him. When I felt my foot kick him in the jaw, I almost threw up, I was so horrified at what I was doing. Yet it seemed that all the rage I had ever known in my life was coming out all at once. I couldn't control myself. Some other boys came in and pulled me away. I didn't offer any resistance. I was glad because otherwise I might have killed him. Even though my head was hurt and I still have the scar today, I was furious at myself for losing my temper. I was afraid now that it would be all over, that I would have to leave and go back to Washington again. Several of the boys got together and decided they would say that we were wrestling and had an accident. I'm sure that the doctor at the infirmary knew that we were lying, but he let us go.

As I went back to my room with my head patched, I realized how sickening this kind of violence was. I decided right then and there that unless I was boxing someone with gloves on, I would never get in a fight again unless it was a question of life or death. And that's the last time in my life I ever touched anybody with my bare hands except in friendship.

When I went back to Washington that summer, I really began to miss jazz. I still played piano, but there was no one to play jazz with, so I played at home with records or whenever I would hear a good band on the radio. It never occurred to me that anyone would want to hear jazz played on the French horn.

One night I went to North Beach, about an hour's drive from Washington, to see two friends of mine, Spencer Sinatra, a great tenor saxophonist and classical flutist, and Dick Leith, a trombone player who played both jazz and classical music. Like myself, they were interested in all kinds of music and we had played together before in amateur orchestras around Washington.

I drove out to where they were working with a beautiful girl named Nöel and some other friends of my sister's from George Washington University. I hadn't played much jazz on the horn. Although Claude Thornhill and some other bands were beginning to use the French horn (Glenn Miller once had Junior Collins with him), the instrument was just about unknown in the jazz world except for large orchestras, which used it in a truly symphonic sense, not as an improvising instrument. But I brought my horn along and when I got out there, a Dixieland band was playing. Apparently it was Spencer's night off because he was a modernist. They were really wailing. I looked for Dick Leith but I couldn't see him anywhere.

As I was about to sit down I heard his unique rough-and-ready trombone style coming from far away. I jumped up from my chair to see where he was. He was standing in a phone booth about fifty feet from the stage, playing his chorus. He played two terrific choruses. The crowd cheered. Then as the clarinetist began his break, Dick went back to the phone conversation he'd been having before his chorus came up. When he was through with his call he gave me that knowing apocalyptic hipster wink and that sardonic smile, using only the very top sixteenth of an inch of the left side of his mouth. It meant come on out and blow.

So I came lumbering up with my French horn and played. Because they were playing Dixieland I knew a few of the tunes. I'd been experimenting with more modern kinds of playing because of the one or two Charlie Parker records I had heard. I found that playing horn with the band was completely different from playing the trumpet. I had all sorts of new ideas because the nature of the horn made you play differently. We really got into a few things.

After I'd been playing for a bit, a young trumpet player with that wide-eyed, vacant, outer-space stare and a slightly crouched posture came up. His head hung forward, bobbing somewhat. That bob became the mark of the bebopper from then through to the late fifties.

"My man . . . hey, baby," he said in a soft, somewhat affected voice, trying to imitate the Negro hipsters and not succeeding too well. He sounded like an after-hours whiskey salesman in the alleys around Seventh and T streets, speaking softly so that he wouldn't be heard. "Bruz, that's the coolest sound I've ever dug. You're a gas, Prez, you blow some gone French. Solid, you're a wiggie stud." Because I was familiar with only a little bit of this parlance and because he was trying so hard to be a hipster, I was really taken aback by this accolade.

"What do you mean?" I mumbled defensively.

"I mean you sound *goooooood*," he said with his eyes glistening. "Why don't you come in and blow with our band?"

"O.K.," I said, "after I've done playing with Dick." After I played the second set I joined my sister's friends and Noël, and we went to the bebop room. It was quite different. The scene where we'd been playing, people were dancing, talking and drinking beer, having a good time and joking with the musicians. Also the room was full. This other room was nearly empty and the people who were sitting there had the same vacant, stoned-out look that the trumpet player had. Later I found out they were high, but at the time I didn't know or care. It was my introduction to the world of the white hipsters, country style.

The band was playing lines from one of Charlie Parker's recordings, but I had no idea what they were doing. I thought the melody was based on the chord progression of "How High the Moon" but without playing the tune at first. Because the pianist and bass player were playing extensions of the chords which I could feel but could not identify, I was lost. The drummer was playing somewhat off the beat rather than laying it down. It was completely mystifying. The trumpet player played about thirty-five choruses with the sound no bigger than the sound of his voice but into the microphone so that we could hear it.

I turned to him and said, "What should I do?"

"Just blow, baby," he said. When my turn came I reeled back, put my horn into the microphone and just played anything that came into my head. I played as many notes as possible, all of them sounding wrong to me. When I paused to gasp for breath everybody would say, "Dig it, crazy." I didn't even know if I had finished the right number of bars or choruses when I finally stopped and I had no idea what was going on. As the first set stopped, I thanked the musicians for letting me play with them. "Look, I don't want to mess you up," I said, "let me just listen and see what's happening."

I stayed and listened about an hour and while I had the feeling that they were not sure what they were doing either, I saw that the kind of music they were playing extended the whole idea of jazz and took it away from its old groove of being good-time music. They were going somewhere else. These were people in the vanguard trying to find something of their own. I went back to the Dixieland band, played with Dick and told him about this new kind of music.

"Yeah, yeah," Dick said. "Those guys play some beautiful things, but if you want to hear what's really happening, listen to Bird records. Charlie Parker's the man. One of these days we'll get together and play some modern things, but remember, never lose the groove you have now. If you don't have the funk and swing in your music, it doesn't make any difference whether it's Dixieland or bebop or Beethoven. It still won't make it." And with one final wink I knew that my music lesson for the evening was concluded. We drove back to Washington mellowed by some Southern Comfort and some of that relaxed good cheer that southern girls seem to be born with.

My father had gotten a good job with a fine law firm after he left the government and had sold our little house on Q Street at a profit. Real estate prices had soared in Georgetown. So we used this as a down payment and got a nicer place in a different neighborhood in June, 1947.

I got a part-time job that summer and had the rest of the time free to practice, play music, work on my lessons and work on our new place with my father when he got home. It was the happiest I had seen him since he worked on the farm. I understood now that in a certain way his real art and love in life was farming, agriculture and doing work with his hands. As he used to say, "By the sweat of thy brow, thou shalt earn thy bread."

I decided that with my savings I would find a composition teacher. Van Lier Lanning, my horn teacher, told me of a wonderful man named Wendell Margrave, who taught at a small music school in Washington and had some summer students in composition. I felt I needed to study with someone, so I went to Margrave's house.

Doctor Margrave greeted me, sticking out his great paw of a hand, and with a booming voice welcomed me to sit down as if he had known me for years. He was so friendly that I couldn't believe it. He talked for about fifteen or twenty minutes, telling me what he had done that day, what he was going to be doing the next day, generally treating me as if we were old colleagues in music. He then asked me what I wanted to study. After we had talked for a bit he gave me some Bach inventions to practice and some exercises to work on.

"Bach's my man," he told me. "He's still the greatest of them all. You can spend your life learning from him." He then sat down and started to play the piano. I had never heard anyone play like this in my life. Although he occasionally missed notes, he played with such passion and enthusiasm and joy as his enormous frame rocked back and forth, I was afraid that he might crush the piano in half. The whole piano and finally the whole room was shaking. Yet it seemed appropriate to Bach's music. I also noticed that Margrave brought out each individual line. When he played fugues, he brought out the subject and the countersubject, looking at me knowingly each time a subject entered, as if we had written it together.

Just listening and watching him play the piano was a lesson in composition in itself. During the summer he showed me how to analyze music, ways of writing canons, fugues. Most of all, he encouraged me to follow my own instincts rather than copying anyone else. He told me over and over again that what I felt, I must do. The way my mind and my spirit led my instincts was what would make me a good composer. He gave me enormous encouragement for the work I brought him. Even though I felt like a musical illiterate in his presence, he really made me believe that he had faith in me and this fact alone meant as much at that point as all the music that he taught me.

Margrave was an amazingly accomplished man. In addition to being a first-rate composer, teacher and pianist, he also had a working knowledge of every instrument in the orchestra. He worked for the Navy Department full-time as a scientist, was a reviewer, music critic, writer, gourmet, family man and teacher living on an eighteen-hour-a-day schedule seven days a week with enormous energy and gusto and good cheer. He had none of the inhibitions that I found in many members of the classical-music fraternity. His gigantic, booming voice would roar a greeting to me every time I saw him. Beneath his great presence lay a very kind and gentle soul. He was one of those people that remained eternally young. I felt as if he understood me and identified with me better than most of the kids that I knew. By the end of the summer he had given me enough tools to work with so that I could educate myself in composition during my last year in high school.

That last year in school was a terrific one. I knew I would be able to graduate at seventeen, something that very few people would have believed when I entered four years before. I had come as a confused, upset kid but was leaving as a man. My horn playing was improving all the time. I played in concerts and did solos almost every week. I even enjoyed some of my academic courses for the first time in my life. English literature and history suddenly became fascinating because I saw how the cultures of different periods related to the music of the same periods. I was no longer afraid about going back to Washington after high school. With all the chances I had to play jazz or play with amateur orchestras, and with my new composition teacher, I felt that any of the bad life I had known was completely behind me.

To everyone's surprise Oberlin accepted me for the following fall. Overjoyed, I decided to catch a ride out to Chicago after graduation with a kid who was driving back and hitchhike the rest of the way to San Francisco, where I would visit Holly. I had been writing her all year even though we had decided not to get married. She told me I could come out and visit her. It would be easy to get a job in the booming post-World War II construction business.

During the speeches at our graduation ceremony a lot of the students felt sad and apprehensive. Many of them had never been

in the outside world in their lives and confessed they were frightened
of it.

But I could hardly wait. Even though the school had helped me so
much to find myself in music and to stay out of trouble, I knew there
was a whole other world out there of all kinds of music and people
and places to go and see and I wanted to be there with it. I said my
good-byes in a hurry, jumped in my friend's car and roared off toward the Golden West. All I could see as we were driving was Holly's
beautiful face in my mind.

During that summer with Holly I had my first conscious religious
experience in music. Although my background as a Jew conditioned
me for a whole other kind of expression much later on, at this point
in my life I was not aware consciously of my Jewishness in any musical sense. With the exception of hearing the shofar on Rosh Hashanah, and an occasional record of Near Eastern or Jewish music,
I cannot remember being aware of music in any way evoking a
specific religious feeling until the summer of 1948 when I was performing in the Bach B Minor Mass at the Carmel Bach Festival.

I was allowed to take ten days off from my job as a carpenter's
helper to go with Holly to this exciting festival. I played horn for
some of the concerts and sang in the chorus the rest of the time. Although I had sung the choral music of Bach all through high school
and had performed the trumpet parts in many of his cantatas, I only
thought of the music as music and had never had any apocalyptic
visions. In fact the only apocalyptic vision I had ever had was at the
age of seven on the beach in Florida with my mother at sunset when
I told her I saw God in the sky and went racing up and down the
beach until she calmed me down.

During the final rehearsal of the B Minor Mass, I noticed the
pause following the unearthly harmonic progressions of Bach's musical invention during "Crucifixus," the part of the text where Christ is
finally nailed to the cross and dies. These harmonies had always moved
me in a peculiar way since the first time I had heard them, but I never
gave it much thought except as part of the wealth and genius of Bach's
mind and music.

During the following section, the "Et Resurrexit," the trumpet
players had taken it easy during rehearsals because of the extremely
difficult entrance for the three trumpets in D. The first trumpet player
that summer was so temperamental that he would not play the part

most of the time. At the final rehearsal, however, the trumpet players decided that they would really do it and after we sang the final chorus of the "Crucifixus," there was an unearthly silence. Then the trumpets came soaring in with the great golden sound that seemed to come from heaven.

Suddenly it was as if I had seen a vision. The moment that the trumpets came in, I was overwhelmed by the feeling that someone who had died had been resurrected by a God in heaven. I realized it was a combination of the impact of the harmony at the end of the "Crucifixus," the very crucial silence during which time I was able to feel Christ being taken from the cross, the sadness of all those believers who watched him and then the great glorious moment that all the believers must have felt when they knew he had been resurrected.

I went back with Holly to the broken-down rooming house we shared with other young hopeful musicians and singers. We talked about this amazing moment in the Mass for most of the rest of the night. Holly was Christian, but her religion was nothing more than a kind of normal relaxed area of social life. Church was a place for her to go for weddings, funerals and get-togethers. But because of that unconscious near-madness that so many Jews possess and because of the necessity to discover everything in and out of music for myself as a personal experience, I actually had a vision of what the first Christians must have felt when they discovered that Christ had been resurrected. It was the closest I ever came to being converted to Christianity.

During the performance of the B Minor Mass I waited for this moment to see if it would happen again. It occurred even more strongly this time, but after the first few measures, the first trumpet player in his excitement and egomania played so loudly and ferociously that he missed about five notes in a row. He turned to his right to the other two trumpet players as if to indicate that it was their fault and they began missing too, and his face, which had begun to turn purple from overblowing, now began to blacken with rage. Still, the moment was there and has remained in my mind ever since.

Most of the rest of the Mass I felt was much more eloquent than any speech or sermon that could be preached. I began then, at seventeen, to think seriously of how I could write a piece someday that might lend itself to my religious convictions, even though I was not sure what they were. I knew that they were Jewish, but I was not sure what the Jewish experience was and more important what *my* Jewish experience was or how it could be expressed through music.

It was during this time that I became familiar with Stan Kenton's music. One of the members of the chorus—a superhipster, West Coast style, who was finally thrown out of the chorus for saying, "Yeah, dig it. Solid," and shouting with laughter during particularly moving parts of the Mass—took me over to his house one time between his finger poppings and shouts of ecstasy and played me all of Stan Kenton's music. This was also a whole new world to me because it incorporated a lot of classical devices. It had a feeling and a kind of frenzy that was almost like Khatchaturian's music.

I also heard more about Charlie Parker who had been out there and about Dizzy Gillespie. He had recorded with Bird. I bought as many of their records as I could and really started paying attention.

The rest of the summer I spent working like a dog. I carried shingles up on roofs, nailed down floorboards, hauled dirt, dug postholes, drove trucks and stayed busy every minute so I wouldn't be fired. I was three thousand miles from home and I had to make it for college. At the end of each week I would lay all my money, sixty dollars, on the carpet, where Holly and I would stare at it.

On nights when I wasn't exhausted, Holly and I would play music together, take walks and talk. I still thought she was an angel, but I felt as the summer ended that we would never see each other again. I had to find myself somehow in music and I knew it wasn't going to happen overnight. When it was time for me to leave California, we went to San Francisco to the Top of the Mark and watched the seals leap in the distance. As we held hands and stared off as we had done in school, we realized that our romance was over. There was too much difference in geography and temperament—she having grown more demure, placid, quiet and angel-like; I having grown more intense, wild, erratic, wrapped up in myself and not only staying up late at nights but sometimes staying out for three or four days in a row.

I made it back to Washington in exactly four days, driving day and night without stopping, sleeping in the crowded car I was a part-time driver for. I had to drive twelve-hour shifts and share the gas expenses. I got back to Washington, slept eighteen hours straight, packed my horn, my college suit, hid the three hundred and fifty dollars I had saved during the summer in the lining of my horn case so I couldn't get rolled, hitchhiked to Cleveland, Ohio, took a bus to Oberlin and got there one hour before the registrar's office closed.

The first few days, kids tried to get me to wear a freshman's beanie. "I only wear those in temple," I told them, and when I made it clear I was there to learn about music instead of college rah-rah life, they left me alone. The whole atmosphere seemed so cloistered and unreal to me that I concentrated on classes, composing and practicing.

At Oberlin I found my first full-time professional horn teacher, Martin Morris. He was a brilliant hornist who played with the Cleveland Symphony Orchestra and had a completely analytic approach toward horn playing. He was small in size, with a crisp, clean, scientific approach toward horn playing and teaching.

"I want you to approach each passage with a supersmoothness, with a supersuavity of tone and elocution, supersmooooooothness," he intoned, beseeching me and the other students who were cracking and burbling through the Kopprasch exercise book, the nemesis of all horn players. These exercises started off fairly difficult, soon became impossible, and ended up being so unplayable that if you could get through them there was something wrong with you. Still, they were the guideline of the old German school of horn playing, and as all the horn students would fumble their way through them, Martin Morris would gently remind us that conductors like the suave, liquid, supersmooooooth way of playing and that they got very upset when the horn players cracked.

When he mentioned missing notes, the common bane of all horn players, the back of his eyes would suddenly light up like phosphorescent beacons, glowing with fear and anxiety. A cold chill would pass through my body even though at the same time he tried to assure me and the rest of the students that it meant nothing and that all horn players have to be accustomed to failing as part of their job. The more he tried to tell us that it was all right, the more we felt like failures just listening to him. He would play the exercises himself with marvelous virtuosity, but when he missed a note, which was almost never, he would stop and say, "You see, did you hear that? That was because I wasn't concentrating." Then he would repeat the passage.

Martin Morris had a command of the instrument that was extraordinary and he was also very musical. All the students could tell that in spite of the fact that he tried to be so scientific, he was, like us, really a fanatic in his soul. He had that old-time horn-player romantic instinct of wanting to stand on top of a mountain and blast away for endless hours until every Rhine maiden within a hundred miles dropped whatever she was doing and came running to his side. He also was the first big-time musician that I'd observed for any length of time and I noticed his wild color sense. He would wear green-checked jackets, brown felt hats, strange knitted neckties, bizarre tweedy vests and huge custom-designed shoes that made his feet more comfortable. Although he was very small he had a pleasant, resonant, sometimes booming voice that sounded very much like a French horn. (Many symphony musicians have voices that match the instruments they play.) He also had the kind of studied, affected, somewhat mannered speech that I noticed in a lot of symphony musicians. I realized later that, being the first generation of American-born musicians who were working with fine orchestras, they were influenced not only by their European teachers' playing but by their accents as well. Because they were the first wave on the symphonic beachheads of America, they themselves had to come on like Europeans in order to get along. In Martin's case, as with many other members of the Cleveland Orchestra, the accent was a mixture of Ohio and Bavaria.

But the important thing I learned from Martin was that there was a serious and scientific side to music and that the horn required a lifetime of work. He also gave me that certain feeling of fraternity that all horn players have among themeslves so that, even though I was only seventeen, when I spoke with other horn players in the orchestra who visited us I was treated with a certain kindness and brotherly understanding that was very encouraging.

One afternoon while I was doing my harmony lessons outdoors, I saw a young man doing a frenetic series of calisthenics. Because of my interest in sports I asked him how he was doing a certain kind of headstand.

"Nothing to it, my man."

Taken aback by this hip response, I offered my palm, which he quickly put some skin to. He informed me that he was also a musician interested in the healthy life and his name was Paul Horn.

He was also studying classical music and was one of a whole generation that considered both traditions part of the total world of music. He told me a lot about the reed player's point of view and taught me to listen not only to Charlie Parker but the other great saxophonists that Bird descended from. Paul showed me Bird's relationship to Coleman Hawkins through Don Byas, Lucky Thompson, Wardell Gray and, most of all, Lester Young. He mentioned some young kids, Gerry Mulligan, Al Cohn, Stan Getz, Brew Moore and Zoot Sims. He introduced me to the composition "The Creation of the World" by Darius Milhaud, which was an attempt to fuse jazz and classical music. While we both agreed it was a marvelous composition, it was really more of an attempt to graft one kind of music to another, rather than something really organic. We both felt that you can't use jazz in a composition unless it's really a natural part of you.

I found after the second or third week that there were several other people studying composition who also played jazz and were interested in the new music of that time. Among them was another French-horn player named Ed London, and a pianist, Salvatore Martirano, who at that time had just finished playing with Johnny Bothwell and was coming to Oberlin to study composition. There was a brilliant pianist who was nicknamed Count Williams. He was from a town near Oberlin. Among other things, he could start playing something at a certain speed with a metronome, then as the musicians would play something else at other tempos he would follow, then jump back to the original tempo twenty minutes later and come out precisely on time with the metronome. His sense of simultaneous time was staggering. In the jam session we used to have with him, we got a whole new kind of poly-rhythmic idea which is never taught in composition, though it's present in most great compositions.

I was in terrific physical condition from having worked as a carpenter's helper all summer. Another friend of mine, Ken McIntyre, a pianist from Altoona, Pennsylvania, who was studying composition and was kind of an amateur strong man on the side, got me interested in lifting weights and in physical conditioning, something that has proved very valuable to me since then, what with the hectic life I've led. I found that doing road work, exercises and playing sports increased my whole orientation toward rhythm and coordination.

As the year progressed, I found many devoted students and by playing in the orchestra, learned a lot of new music. I had pretty good grades except in geology, when I failed to identify calcareous Tufa in the final exam and barely got by with a D-plus. But the atmosphere got me down. I felt the precious cloistered aura of the institution was more important than the students, and the blandness of the Midwest was driving me crazy. No amount of 3.2 beer could calm me down. Most of the girls were valedictorians and militant virgins and I felt that four years there would be like a stretch in a refined reform school. It was killing my soul, so in June of 1949 I decided I couldn't make it there anymore.

I KNEW I would never go back to Oberlin. I wasn't sure exactly what I was going to do in music or how I was going to do it, but I knew that there was something inside me that would never get a chance to get out there. I would miss Ed London and Salvatore Martirano and my roommates, Jerry Bidlack and George Lucktenberg. They were wonderful musicians and wonderful people, but my desire for freedom was too strong. The only time I ever felt free there was when we would all go to Elyria or Sandusky or Cleveland to have jam sessions or just to hang out with the hipsters, many of whom were steel workers.

At the end of the school year one of the kids was driving to Springfield, Massachusetts, so I threw my French horn and my belongings in the back of his car and we took off. I hitchhiked from Springfield to Vermont to visit my high school again. It was nice to see all the people, but as wonderful as it had been, I got the feeling after a day or so it too was an institution and when I left three days later I knew I could never go back there again either.

I hitchhiked back to Washington and decided to continue my musical studies on my own. My first instinct was to visit my first horn teacher, Van Lier Lanning, who had since become a conductor. He had been an excellent hornist himself, although he had not practiced in years. I remember when he picked up my horn, he would play until he turned purple. I could see that he had been so carried away with the love of the horn that he decided to become a conductor before he blew his mind. He had always spoken of the more romantic side of horn playing and how hornists, like boxers, had to keep in training each day, drink the finest of beers and liquors, only make love to the most sympathetic women so that their central nervous system would never be on edge, and many other bits of advice that thrilled my teen-age spirit. Most of our lessons had been of this philosophical nature plus listening to him perform until his lips gave out. At that point I wasn't able to play too well and he was unable to stand listening to me for too long a time.

I thought I would go back to play for him now to show him the progress I was making and see if he could recommend a teacher in Washington. He gave me a big hug and was delighted that I was continuing my horn playing as well as my composing. His wife came out to meet me with a few new children since I had seen him last. I heard a chorus of chickens cackling in the background. When he had been conductor of the Arlington Symphony Orchestra—which I had played for whenever I was in town—he would sell eggs after each performance. This impressed my mother, who had come to rehearsal once to see how I was doing. When she asked Mr. Lanning how my playing was coming along he told her what a fabulous artist I was going to be and then whipped out the eggs to sell her. She wasn't too impressed with his judgment of my horn playing, since she and my father had to listen to me blasting away at home every day, but she had been so happy to see the fresh eggs she bought a dozen to take home for my father.

After we had traded stories for a while I took out my horn and went through the warm-up floor show which I had picked up from all the other horn students at Oberlin and from Martin Morris. This was something that horn players spent more time practicing than anything else: a carefully worked-out maelstrom of notes, based on arpeggios that lie naturally in the horn's technique, interspersed with famous horn calls, scales, usually ending up with a few screaming high notes and then roaring down with a few more arpeggios plus a honking low note at the end. Then the horn player usually takes his horn out of his mouth, empties the water, tries to look nonchalant as if this were merely an exercise before getting down to the *serious* business of warming up. After I had gone through my minute-and-a-half preliminary cascade of warm-ups, he threw back his head and roared with laughter as I emptied the water out of my horn.

"Well," he said, "I see you have been seeing some other horn players since you've studied with me."

"Yes," I said, trying to sound like a blasé professional. "I would like to continue my studying though. Who do you know that I could study with?"

"I would suggest the first horn player in the National Symphony," he said.

I went to the National Symphony and heard the artistry of an excellent player named William Klang. Then I went backstage and asked him if I could study with him. "Sure," he said in a friendly, offhand way. He had a great lumbering way of speech that matched his huge, strong frame and his huge, strong way of playing. He had a unique way of sounding almost like a trumpet: very clear, strong, and bright. He played the horn more like a brass instrument rather than adhering to the German school of producing a deep, dark sound. When I studied with him, he showed me a whole new way of producing a tone on the instrument that was very practical for music that requires a lighter style. He was also the first teacher I had who would play duets with me by the hour. He was so physically powerful that he could play for hours on end without getting tired.

He also gave me a great many French études to study and for the first time I began to get some kind of insight into the French way of musical thinking from the viewpoint of a player. Even though these études were not representative of any particular school of French composition, they had a certain flavor, a point of view that was different from the German idea. This helped me understand the soul and spirit of much French music as a composer since it gave me something to cling to from my own experience.

When I used to go out to his summer place to visit him by a lake about fifty miles from Washington, I would hear him practicing as much as a mile away. Once he tried to take a dent out of my horn with his finger and almost ripped the bell off. Then to my amazement he took a broomstick and with a series of twists and whacks proceeded to knead the dent out entirely. His wife was English, a real music lover, who described for me in great detail the rich, full musical life in England.

Because of his kindness and even though I was not really ready for it he suggested I audition for the National Symphony. I was only eighteen years old and while I had some ability, I was still too inexperienced and too unsure of myself to be much help to any professional orchestra. This was my first audition for a major symphony orchestra, so I was terrified before I even got there. Like many good fighters, I lost the fight in the gym. I practiced until I thought my teeth would fall out. By the time I went to the audition I was not only a nervous wreck but had just about blown myself out in addition. Also my rather bizarre costume of mismatched socks, ill-fitting clothes, long hair and nervous, rapid-fire speech did not instil confidence. Howard Mitchell was very kind. He even gave me some excellent pointers on how to connect phrases and keep a line going all the time during many solo passages that I would be required to play as a hornist. He told me about his own student days and how he had hitchhiked and ridden freight cars to get from Nebraska to where he could study music. He told me how he had washed dishes and studied for years and about his slow climb through the ranks of being an orchestral musician to becoming the conductor of the National Symphony.

He also encouraged me with my composition. He told me that if I continued my studies, probably in a year or so I would be good enough to perform with the orchestra and even though I was not ready then, I left knowing that I would be soon. Rather than feeling that I had failed, I felt that I was on my way and that I was really becoming a horn player.

During the summer of 1949 a friend of mine and I got jobs rolling up sod. This was exhausting work, but it paid a dollar twenty-five an hour. I played centerfield on a sandlot baseball team in Maryland composed mostly of my fellow sod workers. We lost all thirteen games that we played. In fact, in the eleventh game our pitcher was hit with a line drive in the Adam's apple and because we only had nine men and he was no longer able to play, we had to forfeit.

When the fall came, I entered George Washington University. My grades were good at Oberlin, so most of my credits were transferable. I just signed up at random for any courses that sounded interesting. I knew I was going to study music now for the rest of my life anyway but thought I would be happier studying it privately rather than in an institutional situation. I found that because I was not emotionally involved in any way in my academic studies, I really began to enjoy college for the first time.

I was just about to turn nineteen, but the median age at George Washington University was around thirty. Something like fifteen thousand students attended this school. Almost all of them were veterans from World War II finishing school on the GI Bill. My sister was friendly with many of them. We used to go down to a little drugstore to drink coffee after school and I would listen to them talk for hours about the different theaters of combat that they'd been in and the places they had traveled to all over the world. College was not a game to them. They were there to learn. Without the GI Bill, many of them would never have had a chance to go to college full-time, so they were really taking advantage of it.

The whole academic-game world crumbled during this time. The teachers couldn't toy with these students, because many of them who had spent five years in a near life-or-death situation were so prepared for living that they could sense instinctively whether something was true or not. If a professor in any subject went into any kind of academic floor show, one of the veterans would raise his hand and challenge him. This good old down-home logic, mother wit, knowledge acquired through experience or even instinct for a particular subject would be enough to make the teachers backtrack. As a result, the teaching was on a higher level and the teachers were on edge because they knew that they were being paid attention to and questioned. It made it much more stimulating to be there as a student.

One of the oldest sophomores, called Pops, used to sit next to me in a gray cashmere sweater and nudge me in the ribs with his elbow, chuckling through his white pencil-line mustache every time he could see the teacher about to put himself out on the end of a limb.

"Watch him now," he would say, poking me and chuckling. "He's going to get it. You watch."

Sure enough, one of the students would slap him down with a pointed question that would leave the poor professor fumbling and stumbling. Pops had been a thirty-year man, retired as a master sergeant, and had decided to attend college. He planned on getting a bachelor's degree in ancient history. I asked him why he chose this of all subjects.

"Well, Dave," he chuckled, "I'm a study in ancient history myself, you know. All the places I've been in the army and on furloughs made me aware of history and the inescapable relationship between man and what's come before him. Just like the rise and fall of the tide. Nobody can escape being part of that sea of history. You're just a drop of water, boy. Never forget that."

He went on to tell me of his travels through Greece, Egypt, Italy, Sicily, Sardinia and how he even went over the hill, AWOL, when he was fighting in Italy, to go look at an art museum. "The flesh is weak," he used to say, bashing himself in his stomach, which was like iron. "But the mind . . ." and then he would point with his fore-finger with a drilling motion at the side of his head. "The mind, kid, keeps on until you hit the coffin. Even if you're going to be a musi-cian," he said, "you got to develop your mind. You take your sister now, she's a lovely lady and a fine scholar. You know when she brings up her family, those kids are going to be *smart*. They're going to be ready. You better believe that."

My sister was a terrific student. She used to pal around with the most serious students, all of whom were English majors. I used to listen to them discuss all the books that they were reading. They would get into violent arguments over the literary merits of Hazlitt and the influence of Kyd and Marlowe on later generations of play-wrights and poets.

Because the school was in a mild state of chaos and because the institution had been suddenly forced to adapt itself to the needs of the huge student body, it was more intellectually challenging than any other place I'd ever been in my life. The fraternity members only numbered about two hundred in a student body of fifteen thousand; they were completely swamped. When they drove around in their convertibles waving banners for school elections, thousands of ex-GIs would stand on the street corners booing them. I really felt at home.

I was practicing and composing harder than ever. It drove my poor parents and sister crazy so I bought a 1932 Plymouth for ninety dollars and used to rattle off into Rock Creek Park or even to the edge of the Potomac in Virginia to practice.

The largest class I ever attended was in *European History I* and *II*. The teacher was Dean Louis Kaiser. There must have been nearly two thousand people in the class. He spoke over a microphone and after hearing him for five minutes, I decided that I would have to become a history major. Starting with the cave man, he made all of man's history so fascinating that all two thousand of us would groan when the class was over because we wanted it to go on. In addition to the astonishing command of his material and his ability to relate political, social and artistic events that coincided with the historic ones, he was a spellbinding speaker and a great wit and could have made a fortune as a stand-up comic, priest, psychiatrist or a politi-cian. Even though he spoke to so many people, you felt as if you were alone in the class with him. Soon the back of my car was filled up with books about history, archeology, art and the literature of the Greeks and the Romans. At nineteen I felt for the first time in my life that I had really entered school. Dean Kaiser made me realize that learning could be a joy.

I ended the year with good grades, with great strides made on the horn and with my composing. I began looking at scores more and more, often taking them after school to the Phillips Art Collection, where it was quiet and I could study in peace. In the process, I became a painting fan.

I also began playing with several chamber-music groups and joined three amateur orchestras. Many of these orchestras would give concerts in different cities close to Washington.

One earth-shaking experience was the first time I performed the horn solo of *Oberon*. It was in the Mosque Theatre in Richmond, Virginia. The overture to *Oberon* begins with a simple three-note do-re-mi for D horn, followed by the orchestra. Although this is the complete antithesis of the barrage of notes all horn players use for warming up and impressing one another, I had been warned for many years that it is one of the most difficult solos to play in the literature because of its complete simplicity.

In order to be ready I got on the stage before any of the musicians and began practicing the three notes. Actually I had been practicing this excerpt for a week before and by the time the conductor came out on the stage I was certain I could do very well. I began to feel myself shake. To control this I leaned on the chair at an angle so that the shaking would not affect the mouthpiece coming into my lips but rather would just allow my stomach and back to tremble however they liked. As the audience applauded the conductor as he came onstage, I gave one fast practice entrance. I saw no possible way I could miss this solo, barring a sneak atomic attack. The conductor looked at me with that nervous imploring glance that conductors give when they know that a relatively inexperienced horn player can sabotage the whole evening.

I hit the first note perfectly, but it sounded as if I were playing in the Grand Canyon. I was so nervous, concentrating so hard, that my hearing had been accentuated as if I had been on some kind of LSD trip for a year. I couldn't believe I was playing so loudly. The first three notes sounded as if they were louder than the entire orchestra playing at its highest peak. Later I learned that in a certain stage of superconcentration and fright you can sound much louder to yourself than you actually do.

Somehow I managed to get through the entire solo without fainting from fright then asked the second hornist if I was playing too loudly.

He was a furrier who played for fun. "It sounded right fine to me," he responded pleasantly.

When I told my horn teacher about this he told me that this had happened to him when he had played Mendelssohn's nocturne from *A Midsummer Night's Dream* for the first time and also when he played the solo from the second movement of Tchaikovsky's Fifth. He told me about a hornist who had a special kind of health milkshake with raw eggs, wheat-germ oil, malt and Japanese tea, which was supposed to give you strength and to calm you down before playing big solos. He would always drink this religiously before playing the solo of Tchaikovsky's Fifth.

My eventual graduation from college was more important to my parents than anything else in the world. My mother's father had left school at fourteen in order to send his younger brothers and sisters through school. He had worked hard all his life but spent most of his spare time reading voraciously. He was a self-educated man and instilled in my mother an almost fanatic devotion to the importance of developing the intellect of her children. Of course that meant a college diploma. My mother's mother was also forced to look after her family and grew up with the same kind of attitude.

On my father's side of the family, the old Jewish intellectual tradition was even stronger. My great-great-grandfather, the first to come over in 1849, had been a kosher meat slaughterer in Echte, Germany. He was also a teacher at the village Hebrew school. Nearly all his ancestors had been rabbis. He landed at the port of Savannah, Georgia, and worked until the Civil War broke out. He had been a victim of religious persecution, which is why he came to America, but ironically he died of starvation during Sherman's siege of Savannah before he could see the end of slavery in the South. His son, my great-grandfather, was conscripted into the army and fought with the Georgia Rifles. He had received an orthodox Jewish education and was opposed to the bondage of any people. When the war was over, he decided to leave the South forever. He walked on foot all the way to Philadelphia, working his way up North. When he worked in a turpentine plant in North Carolina, the whole town came to see if he had horns on his head. He also had a touch of theater in his soul for he was a professional strong man as well, bending horseshoes and rifle barrels with his bare hands. This helped pay his journey, as well as keep any virulent anti-Semites at a safe distance.

After he arrived in Philadelphia, my great-grandfather worked as a ship's chandler on the Delaware River. His son, my grandfather, was chosen to be the scholar of the family. He spent his entire life studying and finally taught at the University of Pennsylvania Law School. His wife, my father's mother, won a scholarship to Bryn Mawr College but left after a year to get married. Her family had been mostly Jews from Poland and she had that great fire and ambition for learning. She herself was a very talented poet and writer who died very young. My father was brought up in this fierce intellectual tradition but wanted to be a farmer. He graduated from Penn State at twenty after studying agriculture but couldn't make a living farming. He entered law school at the University of Pennsylvania at twenty-four, an unheard-of age to matriculate in those days, worked his way through and graduated at the top of his class. He then taught at the law school there until we moved to Washington.

One consolation I had was my great-uncle, Harry Brylawski, who couldn't stand school and became a migrant worker, following the wheat harvest all around the country until he died. Another was my father's brother, who hated school and traveled around the world as a teletyper on ships, a mahogany cutter in the South American jungles, a used-book salesman and in dozens of other jobs, just to be able to make a living. I had been crazy about him since I could remember. He would tell my sister and me about all the wild places he had been and the people he had met all over the world. In addition, I looked more like him than I looked like my father and I had been named after him as well. My parents were afraid I would leave school as he had done, so my getting a degree was the most crucial thing in my life as far as they were concerned.

They both loved music but knew what a hard profession it was. I understood their confusion over the amount of time I was spending on my musical studies on my own. My practicing the horn and the piano, composing and keeping crazy hours the way I did were really wrecking their nervous systems. Since I had gone away to high school, I had spent very little time at home anyway. Now I realized the best thing that I could do for myself and for them was to leave for good.

That summer of 1950 I found a room on the fourth floor of a building where a friend of mine, Rudy, had a basement apartment. He had been a gym teacher at The Maret School but was leaving to get a job as an English instructor. He told me I could move into his apartment since he was getting another place. I knew it would actually be a relief for my family not to have me at home, but at the same time I didn't want them to think that I was putting them down so I told them that I had found a part-time job and would not be any drain on them and although I always would love them, I had to go. I had been living for the last six months with my girl friend most of the time as it was. But I had the feeling that if I began depending on women to support me, I would become like many of the musicians I knew who started out thinking they were very slick but as they grew older and lost their youthful appeal, ended up looking tired and castrated. I felt I had to be on my own to be a man and that if Annie, my girl friend, wanted to live with me she would have to stay at my place.

So I moved to 1815 Sixteenth Street, N.W., between S and Swan streets in what was a checkerboard neighborhood similar to the one on Q Street where we had first lived in Washington. I also got a job as a gym teacher at The Maret School and took most of my college courses at night. As a result, I had the daytime free to compose and the late nighttimes afterward to play.

As I ran across musicians in Washington, we began to have jam sessions in my basement. At first, it was just anyone who came by— a hillbilly guitar player, a bassoonist or a cellist from the symphony, a jazz saxophonist, anybody. If they were classical musicians then we would play chamber music or whatever music was around. If they were jazz musicians then we would play jazz, and if they were all there at once we would either have free improvisations or what we called "making a symphony," which was just someone starting out to play something and everyone else following.

Eventually the classical musicians who were interested in jazz would come down to play chamber music and then listen while we jammed. The jazz musicians became interested because they wanted to get together with classical musicians, an opportunity which at that time was very rare. Unfortunately in Washington, segregation was not only between the races but also between different kinds of musicians.

After about a year, my basement apartment became the focal point for visiting jazz men and jam sessions. Literally hundreds of musicians passed through Washington, wanted a place to blow or relax and would come down to my place. Because of its informality— reproductions of paintings all over the walls, a gas jet that was lit most of the time, orange-crate furniture and the ice-box full of yogurt, sour cream, borscht and other culinary exotica—musicians felt at home right away. There would also be a generous supply of girls, curious neighbors, in fact anybody that just felt like dropping in. Everyone knew that music was the food of love and we all played on, usually until the morning hours. Then I would compose, take a nap, and go to work.

My gym-teaching job at Maret, a French school for overprivileged children, was the greatest nonmusical job I ever had in Washington. Because I was an anti-institution man, I tried to make each class fit what the kids could do. I just considered myself the biggest kid in the class and we used to just go out and play as hard as possible until everyone was exhausted. I showed them all I knew about baseball, touch football, soccer, boxing, field hockey and also different calisthenics. I taught the boys from the first grade through the eighth grade and the girls from the first grade through the twelfth grade.

Some of the senior girls were only two years younger than I was and looked fabulous bouncing about in their gym outfits. But through a heroic demonstration of self-discipline I was able to cool it. I followed the old southern maxim, "Don't get your honey where you get your money." It was harder with the mothers of some of the six-year-olds, especially the divorcées who would come to school in their elegant furs and seductive diplomatic-corps perfume, inquiring of their children's health, meanwhile sidling up to me and coming on like gangbusters. They would tell me how marvelous it was that such a young man was working so hard, going to college and working at music, and what a pity it was that I wasn't able to find someone who could just send me to Paris for a few years to study with Nadia Boulanger instead of having to stay in Washington and be so busy. I agreed wholeheartedly but I knew that it was not the way I was going to make my mark in music. So I was polite but acted as though I didn't know what they were talking about and thus got them off the hook as well as myself.

Some of the older French teachers didn't like my rather casual approach to my job, even though I always showed up on time and worked like mad. They were of the old school and would have rather had a harsh disciplinarian. But because of the rotten schooling I had had through the first eight grades, I wasn't going to inflict any kind of poison on these beautiful kids. They loved their gym classes because they were able to have a good time as well as get the amount of exercise they needed. I felt that this was more important than making them into Olympic athletes.

My next-door neighbor was the theatrical director of Howard University, Owen Dodson. I used to see him occasionally when I was running off to school, rehearsals, a jazz job or my gym teaching. We would talk briefly. He was very intelligent, warm and fun to talk to. I wasn't sure exactly what he did at Howard University although I knew he was a teacher there. One day as I was coming back from teaching gym, he told me how much he enjoyed hearing me practice the horn, which I did every day in the late afternoon. The sound of the horn carried over the network of the fences in the back alleys, which were so much a part of Washington's lower-middle-class architecture. Apparently this sound had given him the idea of something he thought would be useful for his work.

"I would like to have something that sounds like that horn of yours for our production of *Pelléas et Mélisande,*" he told me. "Would you be interested in doing it?"

"Of course," I said. I knew Maeterlinck's great work although I had not read it since the eleventh grade. He told me there was also a chorus available.

I reread *Pelléas et Mélisande* that night and even though I had a class the next morning and a jazz rehearsal that afternoon before teaching gym, I was so excited about the play and the thought of writing music for it that I stayed up all night. Every place I thought there should be music, I would underline and write a little for it. Most of the musical sections were for solo French horn, which of course was easy to write since I could play it myself. The rest was for a small chorus and timpani, which I also decided I would play, knowing that when I was not playing the horn I could conduct and play the timpani at the same time.

The next morning I knocked on Owen's door. "It's finished," I said.

"That's wonderful," he said. "I had a feeling you could do it. But we have to show it to someone in the speech department who's a vocal coach and very well trained in music. Perhaps we can get together tonight."

I agreed and that evening, although I was rather exhausted from missing a night's sleep, I met with Fredrick Wilkerson, who was a speech teacher at Howard plus an excellent singing coach and well-trained musician in his own right. I played him the music on the horn and tried to croak through the vocal music. Wilkie, as we called him, also liked it and told Owen he felt it would be perfect for the play and not too difficult for the chorus to sing. We then had a delicious chicken dinner. Like so many people I'd met in the music world, Wilkie was a gourmet cook and I considered that chicken dinner to be my first commission as a composer.

We began rehearsals for *Pelléas et Mélisande*. This was the first time I had worked with actors of near-professional standards. Howard already had a drama department that was superb. There were some actors who had had professional experience and some who hadn't, but all were very serious about their work. There was a certain kind of tingle and excitement in the atmosphere that didn't seem to have the artificiality that we often associate with the theater. Everyone really seemed to care about what they were doing. Owen, who had been so kind and gentle in all the meetings I had had with him, was really a severe task master. But like a great conductor, every time he made a suggestion or said anything, it was for a specific reason. He always had something that he was trying to achieve. Otherwise he would keep silent and watch. He also had a phenomenal sense of the use of lighting. I believe of all the people in the theater that I've worked with since, I've never seen anyone with more of an innate feeling and a mastery of the use of constant lighting changes as a part of the rhythmic flow of the theater. There must have been two or three hundred light cues in the play, all of which flowed into one another. Owen was also able to adjust the lighting to the music even though this was way before there was any kind of modern mixed-media use of music and lights.

When the chorus had finally learned its music, we were all put backstage together. I conducted the chorus, played the French horn and bashed away at the timpani, while watching the script, listening to the actors, taking cues from the stage manager and observing the light changes. It was all very exciting and the entire production came off very well. It showed me how much my experiences as a jazz musician, a sideman in symphony orchestras, ballet orchestras and chamber groups had all added to my sense of timing and feeling for drama. It was something that seemed to come naturally. Owen told me that a sense of theater was something that could never be taught. He felt that good theater was an extension of music and, ultimately, of life.

I began playing jazz again on the French horn at this point, but I continued advancing my classical playing by further studies. My next teacher was Abe Kniaz, the new first horn of the National Symphony. He was an extremely complex, exceptionally intelligent person. In addition to being a masterful horn player, he was a superlative all-round musician, linguist, cook, and real old-fashioned Jewish intellectual. He constantly questioned, analyzed and searched the meaning of everything in and out of music and had an immense knowledge of the theater, literature, politics, painting and art.

Abe was adamant that I should complete my degree in European history at George Washington. Rather than being surprised or annoyed by the fact that I was also a gym teacher part-time, he thought it was excellent because it would make me a better-rounded person and probably a better horn player. He tried to have me analyze in myself why I wanted to play the horn so much. He felt that if I had some kind of intellectual detachment as well as my extreme emotional involvement, it would probably make me a better player and better able to function in the symphonic world. He also told me that I should never give up my composition even if I could never make a living at it because the satisfaction that I would gain from it would be more than I could imagine.

He thought I would be ready for the symphony within a year but that in order to prepare myself mentally and psychologically I should play with as many of the amateur orchestras around as possible. I was already playing with the Arlington Symphony once a week, but I joined the Department of Agriculture's Symphony Orchestra, the Washington Civic Symphony and two chamber groups so that I never had much time to sleep.

Abe suggested that I join the musicians' union. It wasn't really necessary. For the jazz jobs that I occasionally played, no one bothered to check whether you were in the union or not. But I thought it might be a good idea and went down and joined.

A week later I was called by the union for a job and was told that members of the National Symphony were also going to play. Of course I accepted and to my surprise, I recognized many of the faces of my heroes. But the job was playing for the funeral of the Mayor of Chinatown. Washington's Chinatown was not a very large area, but apparently the "Mayor," who was the number-one figure among the Chinese–American population, was also the leading numbers runner, drug dealer and white slaver in his two-block domain. He was being given a funeral with union musicians dressed in green bandsmen uniforms especially rented for the occasion. We drove out on the bus toward the cemetery. I was bursting with pride. Here I was playing a professional engagement with members of the symphony orchestra and getting paid union scale for it.

We got out of the bus and I was given my part, which I put in a band lyre. Rather than being any kind of Chinese music, it was Chopin's Funeral March. We then played some other, equally morbid Western selections and after the "Mayor" was laid to rest, drove back on the bus to Chinatown. Quite a few bottles of whiskey were emptied on the way.

"You see, kid," said an elderly musician who was about to retire from the symphony, "this is what you got to look forward to as a professional musician . . . real classy work." His cynicism didn't bother me because I knew that I was really on my way up that ladder and those Valhalla Rhine maidens were getting closer all the time. Also, drinking this much whiskey in the afternoon didn't hurt either. By the time we got back from Chinatown to be let off the bus, most of the members of the entire orchestra were roaring drunk. We got out on the street in Chinatown and began a Dixieland jam session. All the quasi-underworld figures came out on the street and clapped their hands to spur us on. Obviously there was not too much emotional bereavement on the part of the "Mayor's" friends. Possibly it was also the old southern attitude of the good times after the funeral, New Orleans style.

At any rate, we had a jam session for about fifteen minutes on the sidewalk. Then we were invited into a large Chinese restaurant, where we sat down to dinner. I really felt that I had hit the big time now. I had just joined the union and I was already invited for a dinner with these great concert artists. My head was spinning with excitement and whiskey. Then I suddenly heard chairs rustling to my side and looking over to the right, saw one of the outstanding members of the symphony brass section vomiting on the trousers of the waiter who was just bringing in the wonton soup. Dinner was postponed as most of our appetites vanished. I went home to my basement apartment and passed out.

In spite of this rather inauspicious professional debut I began getting quite a few more playing jobs. José Greco came to town and I was asked to play first horn for the two weeks he was there. His company was excellent and the music was marvelous. In one of the pieces, "The Three-Cornered Hat," I had a big solo. We also played Ravel's "Bolero" and several other works that had exciting horn parts. By the second night I was asked by the conductor if I would like to come on the road with him. I told him that I couldn't because I wanted to finish college and continue studying so that I could become at least a part-time member of the National Symphony the following year. The conductor was English and we got into a long conversation during one of the extra rehearsal periods that we had. He was extremely charming. Most of the musicians in the theater orchestra were in their late sixties or seventies, so I think he was happy to speak to someone young and enthusiastic.

I suddenly noticed a hate ray coming from the violinist who sat in the back of the section who was also the house contractor for the Gaiety Theatre. I remembered him when the Gaiety was a burlesque house and he played violin in its orchestra. Now the policy of the theater had changed, but he was still there. During rehearsals he would sit with his hat on and smoke while he nonchalantly sawed through whatever sections of the violin parts he chose to play in, knowing that his job was secure regardless of how he performed.

He came up to me and said with a deep southern accent, "Whah were you talkin' to the leadeh?"

I found out before that musical contractors and other house musicians always referred to the conductor as the leader regardless of whether he conducted a marching band or the Boston Symphony.

"He was asking me about another job," I said.

"You weh talkin' quite a long tahm," he said sardonically, blowing a thin wisp of cigar smoke toward my face and grabbing his suspenders in a defiant air like an old sharecropper or someone auditioning for the cast of *Tobacco Road*.

"We were talking about some other things as well," I said defensively.

"Look, son, lemme give you some advice. Don't nevvuh git frien'ly with leaduhs . . . they all pricks."

With this bit of fatherly advice, he went back to his chair. He was the first person who articulated to me the hostility that most musicians have toward leaders or conductors. I refused to feel this way because I considered myself to be part of music and an artist; besides, the conductor was very nice to me. When we had a wild party in my basement apartment for the cast, I invited him. We all had a good time. Some jazz musicians came over for a jam session, the Spanish dancers danced and I played a movement of the Brahms Horn Trio with the violinist and pianist, who always came to my parties.

I used to arrive at the theater early to practice the horn repertoire, also hoping that perhaps I would be discovered by someone who would whisk me off into some kind of magic world that I was certain lay out there for any musician who cared as much about playing as I did. I never found anybody during my preconcert warm-ups, but after the concerts I always met plenty of girls who were generally of a more stable variety than the ones I met in the bebop circles. One of them who came to the concert had been someone I had my eye on at George Washington University for four or five months. She was Jewish and looked like a Portuguese painting. She had a gigantic black braid, her hair coming below her waist when she undid it, and she was extremely knowledgeable about music. Even after we began living together, she would sit for hours listening to me practice and gave me a lot of encouragement. On many occasions she would discuss with me the fact that just playing the French horn might limit me too much and that I should consider my composing just as seriously.

At that time I felt that composing was something that I would do only for a hobby. As an orchestral musician I saw composers coming around occasionally to listen to performances of their work and I knew that they made no money writing this kind of music. They were lucky to even get their pieces played. I also couldn't stand the obsequious, apple-polishing manner that they assumed around conductors and performers even though I understood it was because they were so desperate to get their music performed. As a horn player during this time, I felt I had a certain kind of dignity and identity. I was only twenty years old, I was living with a beautiful girl, and while I supported myself mainly with my salary as a gym teacher, my money as a horn player was increasing every month. I was beginning to be quite a bit in demand in Washington. Also I was assured that I would become extra horn with the symphony the following season.

Because I used to go to so many of the symphony concerts and because of my association with Abe, I began to make friends with many of the horn players and other musicians in the orchestra who would come to my apartment to visit. I think they were interested in me mostly as some kind of crazy kid, but because nearly all musicians are generous to someone who is young and trying as hard as I was, they would also give me lessons and advice. I learned from string players how to approach the unaccompanied Bach sonatas, not so much as a horn player but as an all-around musician. They would show me for hours the tiny inflections in bowing. They brought over records of Fritz Kreisler to show me how this unorthodox master of playing could adapt all music to his own personality and make his personality seem the composer's personality. They also showed me how the art of rubato—playing out of tempo and yet making it relate to some kind of over-all tempo—was something that should be constantly in the back of your mind as a player, even at the same time that you were developing a fixed sense of rhythm.

I had cellists show me how they could produce different sounds and colors and how a string player attacks a note as compared to how a horn player would attack a note. I had clarinetists show me how they would diminuendo so low that it was almost impossible to hear them even in the same room and they tried to help me to do this on the horn. Oboeists and bassoonists showed me the problems they had with double-reed instruments, and Kenny Pasmanick, the great bassoonist with whom I played jazz, showed me many tricks about vibrato and phrasing and shading and colors which increased my knowledge not only in horn playing but about music and orchestration as well.

I also began to listen to all the old recordings of the Philadelphia Orchestra just to hear Marcel Tabuteau, the great oboeist who was the hero then of every orchestral player. He was so strong a musical personality that any conductor with any kind of intelligence would follow him and try to get the orchestra to phrase the way Tabuteau phrased.

Abe Kniaz, as well as my other friends in the orchestra, showed me how to take a huge breath to compensate for a place that was difficult and by breathing at a certain point, make the music itself breath. There were many tricks that I learned from the horn players:

how to have another horn player help you with your part so that you could sneak in a breath; certain ways of fingering and muting notes to attack what was almost impossible, like a fiendishly difficult entrance in the slow movement of Beethoven's Second Symphony; ways of fingering tricky passages like the one in *La Gazza Ladra*.

I was also introduced to the old New York Philharmonic recordings, on which I heard Bruno Jaenicke, the solo French hornist. His exceptional imagination, taste, sensitivity and sense of poetry made him a legend among all horn players. On the recordings he used a vibrato, which was very uncommon then. He played horn so superbly that from the minute he began until he stopped it was impossible not to concentrate and be absorbed by his playing. His playing became a model for me for years and influenced my instincts in music not only as a horn player but also as a composer. I found similarity between his playing and certain lyric players in jazz even though the discipline was entirely different.

My whole study of the horn during this time, because it was so broad and devoted, also turned out to be a study of orchestration, musical interpretation and music as a complete entity. I began the lifetime process of training my ear and my sensibilities to the inner meaning of music. I also began to listen to the horn players from Philadelphia, some of whom were in the orchestra that had shown me so much when I first heard it at the age of seven. They played mostly silver horns, which produced a different kind of tone than the brass horns we used in Washington. They were of an older German or Viennese school. Abe was more out of the Jaenicke school, although he had studied the horn in Philadelphia and really had a style of his own. But the Philadelphia players had something that was really more European. It was fascinating to hear, especially when they performed Beethoven or Schumann or Brahms symphonies. I began to listen more carefully at every concert the Philadelphia or other orchestra would play in Washington. I went with the other horn players in the National Symphony. We would listen and compare notes about how the horn players had interpreted the music as compared to the way other players did. Often, we would meet with the musicians afterward.

One night after the Philadelphia Orchestra had played I went with my hero, Marcel Tabuteau, to eat clams and talk about music. He told me something I have never forgotten. "Don't ever give up your composing. Try to write all you can every day. It's the best job in music, believe me. Even if you get to be first chair in a great orchestra, you sit in your chair and you rot. That's all that you have. Fortunately I teach and conduct too or I would die. It's just too frustrating playing with conductors and musicians that are too insensitive and have lost their love for music. Even if you can never make a dime in music you must continue your composition because you'll get more satisfaction from that than you ever will just from being a fine player." I looked at him disbelievingly. "I've heard that you're going to be a good horn player, but believe me if you give up your composing it would be a terrible mistake."

I saw Mitropoulos again when he conducted Mahler's First Symphony. By this time he had left Minneapolis and was the conductor of the New York Philharmonic. He had changed his conducting style so that it was not as flamboyant. He also seemed to have a certain new kind of calm when he conducted. Certain portions of the pieces he would not conduct at all.

His performance of Mahler's First that night was extraordinary. Although the orchestra in Washington, which he was guest conducting, was not of as high a caliber as the New York Philharmonic, Mitropoulos somehow seemed to capture the spirit of the work even with the mistakes that were being made. Rather than making faces or gestures at the mistakes, he seemed determined to keep a certain high kind of spiritual level in his work, perhaps with the hopes that the orchestra could match it. Most of the time it did. Of course one way to judge a conductor's ability is to hear an orchestra play a great deal of the time and see how it plays when different conductors are there. For Mitropoulos everyone gave everything that he could and in spite of the technical mishaps, the concert was a great success aesthetically.

Afterward I went to see Mitropoulos. He remembered me immediately and wanted to know how my composing and horn playing were coming along. His uncanny memory not only enabled him to conduct all scores from memory and speak five languages fluently (Greek, Italian, German, French and English) but also to remember names, faces, dates and events. I had been studying some of the rudiments of conducting which I felt were important for me as a composer and also to broaden my scope as a musician.

I told Mitropoulos, "Maestro, having studied a little bit, now I'm able to see and appreciate what you are doing."

"There is nothing to see, my boy," he said. "There is nothing to appreciate. There is really nothing to conducting." I looked shocked because I knew he would not put anyone on or humiliate anyone. "Nothing to learn," he said. "It's all in the music. You have to learn the music. Naturally there are many facets to conducting, to learning about different kinds of beats and different kinds of motions to produce a different kind of sound, many tricks to make players pay attention to you and infinite ways of achieving different results and making clear what you have in mind. You have to learn how to be able to say it through the baton and your hands and physical gestures without ever saying anything. But far more important and way beyond that is the music and the understanding and knowledge of the music. If this is really there, that quality will communicate to the musicians faster than anything."

One Saturday night I came home after playing a job. The usual mob of thirty or forty people was outside the door, waiting for me to come back so that the party could begin. I only knew three or four of them, the others being people who had heard about these sessions from friends. Opening up the iron gate of the door downstairs, I welcomed everybody in. As usual I got out my collection of saucepans, mason jars, paper cups, plates and empty bottles and handed them to everyone so that they could mix their own drinks. I only had Bring Your Own Bottle parties.

The party progressed normally, ending up with about a hundred and fifty people crushed into one and a half rooms, the police coming and yelling that this was a raid, half of the guests crashing out through the back door and hiding in the alley, the police leaving, the guests all coming back in and more guests arriving and finally the police coming back in plain clothes to join the party after they were off duty. I then played the Brahms Horn Trio, which was interrupted by gales of laughter when someone kept saying it sounded like "Yes We Have No Bananas."

I noticed a stunning girl with long black hair and dark, soulful eyes sitting quietly in the corner like a Buddha. We had a jam session a little later with seven or eight musicians and about five thirty in the morning there were only fifty or sixty guests left so I had a chance to do a little socializing. I noticed that the girl was still sitting in the same part of the apartment and I went over and began talking

to her. Her name was Maggie. She was from Dorchester, Massachusetts, and had come to study art in Washington.

We sat talking. I felt as though I were being lifted up off the floor
and flying right through the top of the building. We decided right
then and there that we would live together. A few weeks later I got a
letter from Rudy, who had had the basement before me. He was in
Nantucket. I had been the best man at his first wedding, but his wife
had been pregnant before he had met her, which he didn't know at
the time. After she had had the baby he left her, met a girl in New
York, fell in love and took her to Nantucket with him. His letter said,
"Boy, you have to come up here. We'll catch fish and live off the
fat of the land. It's beautiful and we can live right from the munifi-
cence of God's handiwork. Everything is here, a beautiful place,
beautiful people and a good job waiting for you when you get up
here. Hurry and come on up. Your father confessor, priest and
West Virginia hillbilly rabbi, Rudy." I told Maggie as soon as I was
finished writing the music for Howard University's production of
Hamlet, we would go.

The production of *Hamlet* at Howard University was the most
exciting theatrical project I had yet undertaken. Earle Hyman was
chosen to play Hamlet. Of course I remembered the excitement of
it from my high school days. A composer from the university had
been chosen originally but was unavailable, so Owen suggested that
I do it and I was happy to work with him again. I was allowed a few
instruments, so in addition to myself on horn, I had an oboeist, a
flutist and a percussionist. The oboeist and flutist both were first-rate
musicians, but the percussionist was really a pianist, Edward Schick,
with whom I had played chamber music for many years. He was a
theater fan and played the snare drum with his fingertips. The other
instruments he would figure out as we went along, just so that he
could work with us on the production.

Our little quartet couldn't fit backstage at the Howard University
theater, so we had to sit behind the audience. This made it very difficult to coordinate the music: the actors could not hear it as well as
they could have if we had been behind the stage, and because the
sound was emanating from the rear of the theater instead of from
the front, a great part of the magic that stage music can add to the
theater was lost. This taught me a lesson I never forgot. The sound
must be part of the play. In order to illuminate the play and inspire

the actors the music must come from the stage or under the stage or behind the stage as it was done in Shakespeare's time. When the sound comes from any place else it must be for a special reason, to evoke a special kind of effect.

After *Hamlet* was over, Maggie and I drove up toward Nantucket, stopping in Dorchester along the way to meet her parents. Her father had come over from Russia and was a steel worker. He had planned a career as an opera singer but had lost his voice as a young man. He still had a great love of music, was a real soul king and I dug him immediately. Maggie's mother was a sweet woman and treated me like her son right away.

Everything was great except suddenly I felt trapped. I began having a series of nightmares that when I went into the army and was sent to Korea I would immediately jump into enemy fire so that it would end my marriage plans once and for all. Every time I told Maggie that I really didn't want to get married she would get hysterical for hours until I finally assured her that I really loved her and wanted to get married after all.

We arrived in Nantucket and went to see Rudy and his new girl friend. He looked suntanned, healthy, but very worried.

"Listen, boy," he said, "things are sort of bad up here. I can't get off this island until I pay eleven hundred dollars on this house and my job fell through and I have to rent out my place. You can stay here on the sofa tonight and tomorrow night but then you'll have to leave."

My heart sank. This was to be my last summer idyll. I knew next year I would be in the army. And I had brought only fourteen dollars with me.

"O.K.," I said. "I'll look for a job tonight." I parked Maggie at Rudy's place and after going to all the restaurants and bars, found a job as a short-order cook.

I went back and told everybody that I had found a job. Maggie insisted that she wanted to work with me too because she didn't want me out of her sight for a second. Rudy told me that it would be easier to get a job working together and imperative if we were to get a place to live together to pretend that we were married, so I bought a four-dollar silver band and we became a common-law man and wife for the summer, with Rudy performing the ceremony.

I began working the next day, and because I was able to get out the orders fast, told the owner that I wanted Maggie, my wife, to work with me. That night Rudy's two male tenants arrived. One was a psychiatrist in Philadelphia and the other was an architecture student. They went into their bedroom immediately after giving the four of us hostile looks. Maggie and I were kept awake most of the night by their groans and shouts as they alternately beat each other up, made love and had long discussions about all their other romances, which we tried not to overhear.

Maggie and I were glad to leave Rudy and his girl friend to his new tenants and began looking for our own place. The rents were impossibly high, so we finally ended up in a room down by the gasworks with a Mrs. Mahoney (nobody ever knew her real name). She was a kindly old Irish woman with thick glasses, false teeth that hissed and clattered as she spoke and a gingham apron. The rent was thirty-five dollars a week and while she was explaining why it was the best bargain in Nantucket the three of us almost fainted when a gigantic blast of noxious air filled the room.

"That's the gasworks," she said, coughing through her apron, which she had pulled over her head. "It comes two times a day." (Cough, cough.) "It's not bad when you get used to it." She took off her glasses and wiped the tears from her eyes as we realized why we had found such a bargain.

She had a son named Frank, who had won a silver star as a medic during World War II and who informed us proudly that he'd been drunk for three years straight during his service and that when he finally got hit by a shell, he hadn't known where he was so it didn't make any difference. He showed us his citation, which he carried around, and also asked us to tap his hair, which was above the steel plate that he had in his head. He seemed like a very sweet guy, but we found out to our horror that night that when he would get drunk, he would come storming into the house and beat up his mother. We knew we were in for an action-packed summer.

The next day we both began working at a seaside café. I was the short-order cook. Maggie washed dishes and worked as a counter girl. We soon realized that it was Nantucket's leading gay bar, although in the daytime, conventional people would come in to eat hotdogs and hamburgers. Just about the time we were done work, the customers would come in for their cocktail hour, give us cynical glances and chuckle behind their hands. I spoke to the owner because he wanted us to work more than ten hours a day.

"My wife and I . . ." I said.

"That's not your wife," he said snidely. "I know you're not married."

I was impressed by his perception, but I insisted on the ruse. He insisted that we work twelve hours a day or get fired and because I had no money, which he seemed to sense, I had no choice.

"Listen," I finally said, "I don't mind working the time, but my wife is tired. She's just a young girl, you know."

"*Oh God,*" he said, "you bourgeois, middle-class people. You're dis*gust*ing. Why don't you go back to your farm in Idaho or wherever you came from."

I was reminded of the feeling that I had when the janitor sounded me in Washington in the boiler room, but now I was older and smarter and had my temper under control. I just turned my back on him, went back to my cooking and knew I would have to look for another job.

I found one at a place called the Center Restaurant. A young boy was sitting at the back repairing a bicycle. When I told him my wife and I were looking for a job, he roared with laughter. "O.K.," he said, "you're number forty-seven and forty-eight this summer."

"What do you mean?" I asked.

"Forty-six people have already come here and left."

I met the owner, who was the most sour-faced person I had ever seen in my life and spoke in monosyllables. I found out through the grapevine of bartenders, busboys and cooks that he had inherited a fortune but apparently was ready for a mental institution and was so paranoic he felt that the whole world was conspiring against him. Everyone would either quit or get fired because of his suspicion, fanatical cheapness and disorganization. I told him I would begin work but that I had to give my other employer notice. Even though I didn't like the guy I was working for, I thought it was only professional.

As I was cooking some omelets on the grill that night, having a ball jiving the customers—something that they enjoyed but that infuriated the boss—I heard someone say, "Dave, my man." I looked around and it was Richard Gibson, one of my friends from Howard University.

"Richard, what's happening?" I yelled out. I saw he was with a cute, curly-haired Jewish chick.

"How do you like my bagel baby?" he whispered in my ear.

"That's some real fine Sears and Roebuck merchandise," I whispered back.

"Listen, Dave," he said, "if anybody gives you a hard time about me, tell 'em I'm Cuban."

"What do you mean?" I said. "This isn't the South, man, this is America."

"That's what you think, baby."

I met his girl friend, who was a real doll, and when I poured them both a cup of coffee, the owner came up to me fuming.

"What do you mean serving that nigger in here?" he said.

"Man, are you kidding?" I said. "This is the state of Massachusetts."

"What do you mean serving that nigger?" he said, looking as if he were ready to start rumbling.

I was dying for him to make the first move because there were quite a few witnesses there. I caught Richard's eye and he made a gesture to cool it. I realized for his sake that I better.

"Look," I said, "he's a friend of mine from Washington and he's South American. Do you understand?"

"He's not South American. He's a nigger," hissed the owner.

Richard was very light-skinned and I knew he spoke French fluently, so I began speaking to him in French. He answered airily and I poured him and his girl friend some more coffee. The owner was flipping out with hate.

"If you don't believe me, test him," I said. "Ask him if he's a nigger and see what he says."

Another man came swishing up and holding a cat box in his hand. I could hear the cat meowing inside. He acted as if he were going to hit me with the cat box. I finally lost some control of my gentlemanly instinct.

"If you hit me with that cat box," I told him, "the only thing left alive inside this room is the cat."

They both really looked frightened and moved back. I felt that feeling of disgust that I felt when I had stomped Nick in high school, and even though I was furious, I was ashamed of myself even to allow myself this kind of violent feeling after quite a few years.

The owner motioned to his friend with the cat box. "You take over the grill," he told him.

"That's fine," I said. "My South American friend and his girl friend and my wife and I are going for a drink. Would you care to step outside and join us?"

Maggie came up and grabbed me, "Come on," she said, "we'll get a job someplace else."

I turned to Richard and his girl friend. "O.K., amigo," I said, "mucho trabajo aqui. Let's go a la casa por un tasteroonie."

"Hasta pronto," I said to the owner and his friend with the cat box as we walked out.

Just as we got to the door Richard turned around and said, "Be sure to come down to South America and visit me soon. I have a lot of friends there who would love to meet you."

We walked toward a bar to get a drink. It was a quiet night and we could hear the sounds of the pounding surf. The stars looked gigantic.

"When are you going in the service, Dave?" Richard asked me.

"Just about a year from now, I guess, Richard. As soon as I finish college."

"I'm due at the same time," he said. "Can you imagine going in and getting shot at in Korea to defend guys like that?"

Our next job was a little more pleasant the first day or two. We only had to work for ten hours and the tips were pretty good. I had a chance to practice again and to compose a little bit. Quite a few musicians were working there. We used to listen to all the latest sides and have jam sessions when we finished work.

The first day the chef quit and was replaced with a gigantic bruiser named Clarence. We were told before he came that he was a fantastic cook but pretty much of a juice head, and that when he got drunk he was impossible. Still, because of the prestige that chefs have in the restaurant business, a certain amount of temperament is allowable.

When Clarence arrived we could see that he knew his own importance. He must have been nearly six feet six, close to three hundred pounds, and he looked like he had just completed a year's run in *The Emperor Jones*. He had a great regal air about him, a low, booming voice, and he was constantly putting people on, then wait-

ing for them to call his bluff. His conversations were mostly monologues.

While he was working, he would ask questions and answer them
himself: "Say, Dave, you and your old lady are nice Jewish kids
here for the summer, trying to save up some bread so you can have
some little squealers soon, right? Groovy. I approve of that a hundred per cent. I got eight kids, three different wives and two unofficial. I worked on the railroad for sixteen years and could have retired,
possibly with a pension. I didn't make it. Why? Whiskey. Don't *never*
drink. Jews don't drink much nohow. Not cause they are cheap.
That's propaganda. Cause they're *smart*. They know what's happenin'. Jews know how to take care of business. I dig 'em because
they're hip with the dollar. They know the almighty dollar is where
it's all at. You say you got music eyes? Crazy. That mess that they're
doing now, I don't dig at all. Why can't these cats just get down
with the melody and say yes to their roots. Soul, Jim. That's all you
got to be talkin' about to be beautiful. Play pretty for the people,
baby. That's the key to success. Play pretty for the people and when
you get that bread hang on to it for dear life. You know Coleman
Hawkins? I used to see Hawk before you were born when he was a
kid. The father of the tenor saxophone. He still blows all these other
cats under the table. He don't need to play no bebop to sound good.
You know that Coleman Hawkins never bought a cat a drink in his
life. Never bought nobody a taste in his life. He's got real estate and
property all over Europe and a lot of places in America. He knows
where it's at. They'll never have no benefit concert for him. I was
in show business too, you know. I did some dancing, I was a valet
for a lot of leading personalities in the thirties, was a band boy after
I quit the railroad. I've done just about everything and I can cook
my ass off too. You'll never see me in the poor folks home. Well,
listen here, Dave, you and your wife are real nice people. But we
can't sit down here all day B.S.-ing, can we? We got some work to
do and if we sit here discussing all day long, nothing will get done.
Let's get down with it."

Clarence then proceeded to cook up an aromatic collection of muffins, fried chicken, hominy grits and other fabulous southern dishes
even though they weren't on the menu.

He put on his big chef's hat and came out from the kitchen. "They
goin' have to change the menu to fit me, you dig?" he said, laughing.
He knew that Maggie and I were a terrific audience and he was play-

ing to us. At the end of the day, he came out and bellowed to the roomful of hungry customers, "O.K., folks, here's what we have to eat this evening ladies and gentlemen. Some absolutely scrumptious fried chicken, Some deeeelicious hominy grits cooked in a superb southern style, some corn muffins. You seen all these great gastronomical selections in *Gone with the Wind?* Right?"

"Right," Maggie and I answered.

"Solid," said Clarence, holding the confused but spellbound audience in his grasp. "We're going to grease tonight, ladies and gentlemen," he said. "You spend your hard-earned dollar coming out to this ocean paradise, you're really goin' have somethin' out of sight. If you want to quench the fires of your burning stomachs with a little *ap*petizer"—and then he pointed dramatically toward me—"Dave and his charming bride, Maggie, will fix you up some fried eggs, coffee, bagels and lox and even a little anti*pasto* while you wait for the main course to be served. Dinner will be served in one half-hour."

He then returned to the kitchen and looked over his shoulder from the grill, laughing with us about his wild floor show. "Dig those people out there. They're all messed up in the mind. They don't know what's happenin'." In half an hour, the smells were overwhelming and dinner was served.

After the dinner crowd had left, we cleaned up and Maggie and Clarence and I talked about music. Clarence gave us another monologue until it was time to close. When we went home that night it looked as if we had found a job that was really going to be fun.

The next morning when Maggie and I arrived, there was panic.

"What's the matter?" I asked one of the waitresses.

"Clarence has been out all night. I heard he's supposed to be somewhere roaring drunk."

"That's no problem," I said. "This man really knows his business. He's the best chef out here."

A few minutes later there was an enormous crashing and Clarence came thundering through the door. He had his bags with him. "All right," he yelled, "who wants a drink?" He pulled out a bottle of Four Roses from a small bag that looked like a bag for bowling balls. I heard some other bottles clanking around inside. The waitresses withdrew in horror. "Come on, Dave, you and your wife have a taste with me," he shouted.

"All right, man," I said, and took a tiny sip and gave some to Maggie.

"Come on and take a drink. Don't be a sissy," he said. "I know Jews don't drink this early in the day. But then it's nearly Friday night. Have a taste." I tried again but couldn't force any more down. He took the bottle and *glug-glugged* an enormous quantity. Sighing and replacing the cap to the bottle, he looked at me and said sadly, "God damn. Whiskey's goin' be my downfall. I hate this stuff." He then went into the kitchen and I could see he was working up into an evil mood.

I was cooking the short-order morning breakfasts on the grill while he was supposed to be preparing lunch.

One of the waitresses came back to ask him what the lunch was going to be.

"Mind your own damn business," he snapped back.

"You can't talk to me that way," she said, and taking her order of English muffins, threw it in his face. He shouted and she ran out of the kitchen screaming. He grabbed a huge kitchen knife and, trumpeting like an elephant, came charging out waving the knife.

"Aheeee," the waitress screamed, scampering out the door. The customers sat terror-stricken at their tables.

"Everybody out," shouted Clarence, waving his knife. "Everybody out of here by the time I count three; otherwise you better say your prayers. One . . . two . . ." With a rumbling and crashing of chairs, the restaurant emptied in record time. Clarence turned around and there was no one left but Maggie and me. "Whew!" he said, wiping his forehead. "That bitch just about made me blow my cool. Well . . ." he said, taking off his apron and hat, "I guess I better get on out of here. You take care of yourself and your wife there, Dave, and if you're playing anyplace and I come up and say hello to you, you'd better play pretty. Remember what I said about Coleman Hawkins: never buy nobody a drink." He offered Maggie and myself another drink.

"No thanks," I said.

"Well, shit," he said as he put his bottle away, "you both cool, you know what's happenin' anyway. You're never goin' have too much to worry about. Stay beautiful," and he strolled out and Maggie and I cleaned up the wreckage.

There was no way to replace Clarence. Chefs were very difficult to find. I didn't know how to prepare the more complicated dishes, and I couldn't take the job even though it was offered to me. Anybody can be a short-order cook with a little experience and practice, but the planning and skill of a chef is something that takes years to learn.

A succession of chefs followed, but business was falling off. Everyone we worked with either was fired or quit. Maggie and I knew we would be next to go, so I looked around and found a job as a second busboy in the Opera House, Nantucket's best restaurant and bar. It was a marvelous job because the waiters were tops in their field. One was from Spain, one from Italy, one from France and one from Colombia, South America, and they were all big-money waiters in New York. They averaged three hundred dollars apiece each week in tips, which they divided. They gave a percentage to the first busboy and a smaller percentage to me. All I had to do was serve butter, water, fill the bread dishes and bring the orders to the waiters. I had a ball talking with the customers and listening to the piano player, Ralph Strain, who knew hundreds of tunes. Hearing him play, I learned the chord changes to a lot of tunes that I never knew before.

I also got to watch hundreds of different kinds of people including a party of yachtsmen who hurled butter on the ceiling with their knives as they got stoned one evening. I had a chance while I was standing next to my butter tray to hear the conversations of lawyers, doctors, businessmen, schoolteachers and lovers and eavesdrop on the kinds of minds I'd never been exposed to on such a personal level before.

I lost fifteen pounds during the summer because my food money ran out and because Maggie couldn't get a job by herself. The chef used to give me food, turning his back while I'd go into the freezer for eggs, butter and a little meat for us to cook when I got home. I was ashamed to have to do this so I decided to take another job in the mornings, replacing the Opera House janitor, who had left the island. It only took about three hours each morning and required cleaning off the tables, ashtrays, then sweeping and mopping up the entire place.

The third morning I noticed a funny smell when I entered the kitchen. When I struck a match to light the gas heater there was a tremendous burst of light. I fell down on the floor. Apparently the gas had been leaking all night and now exploded. I smeared myself with butter and bacon grease and called up the cops. They sent an ambulance down. Some doctors wrapped me up and asked me where I lived. They gave me a shot to stop the pain and it made me so high that I felt better than I had all summer. They drove me to Mrs. Mahoney's so I could tell Maggie I was going to the Nantucket Hospital. "Don't let him go," she cried, "I'll take care of him, I'll take care of him."

"Look, baby," I said, "I really got burned. I'll be back. Don't worry."

She was still crying, but fortunately the doctors took me to the hospital anyway. I had to fill out all kinds of forms including one that asked whether or not I was married. I figured it was best to continue the ruse that I was and put Maggie's name down as my wife. After eight days I got out of the hospital and although the explosion had burned my eyebrows, my hair, all the hair off my right hand, arm and some of my left hand, the doctor told me I wouldn't even have a scar. I decided it was time to leave and get back to my basement apartment.

With the compensation for the accident, we had just enough money to pay the rent, take the ferry back, get gas to drive to Washington and three dollars to eat with on the way. I stopped in New York to visit a friend and that night everything in my car was stolen. I was really beginning to get the feeling that Maggie and I were being pursued by bad luck.

In the fall of '51, I got Maggie a job as an art teacher at The Maret School. We were supposed to get married soon. A week later, when I was substituting for another teacher in history class, I heard a tremendous crash outside. I went outside during recess and found that my parked car had been smashed into and completely demolished. A week later, Maggie and I had our bimonthly hysterics when I told her I didn't want to get married yet. I realized that my guilt about not marrying her was a self-indulgence and I'd better just be honest and tell her to forget about it. It was awful having her leave, but later she married a lawyer. I've heard from her over the years and I'm glad she has a family and a happy life.

One of my friends from the time that I moved into my basement apartment was Malcolm Raphael, who worked for the CIA. He was the only CIA man I knew that played jazz piano and got high. I didn't even know what the CIA was then, but I knew that it was a top-secret organization. By the fall of 1951, Malcolm had told me that he had had it.

He was one of the most brilliant guys that I had ever met in my life and soon became the boy friend of my old luscious neighbor from junior high school, Sarah Mae, whom I'd had eyes for myself since the age of twelve. Malcolm used to come to our jam sessions and even played with us if there was no piano player available, even though he didn't know the correct number of bars or chord changes to any of the tunes. Many of us didn't either, so it didn't make any difference. He had such a wonderful disposition and attitude toward music that nobody minded when he would make mistakes.

Malcolm introduced me to a group of people late in 1951 who were what we called in the jazz world "wigs." The term "wig" referred to people of exceptional intellectual ability. A real cool "wig" was someone who was adjusted to the fact that he had exceptional equipment and was able to adapt socially to any situation. Malcolm was the coolest "wig" I had ever met in my life. Whether he'd be drinking with the professors of George Washington University or sitting in my basement getting high with visiting musicans, or at Seventh and T streets, or occasionally playing chamber music in a music lover's house, Malcolm was always so well adjusted that he was able to make everyone else feel at ease. He used to enjoy my great gourmet dishes and also my unconscious style of dress. Most of all, he appreciated what I was trying to do in music and understood the struggle that I was having. For that reason more than any other we became best friends. He'd been a ski bum before working for the CIA and a great ladies' man, so his romance with Sarah Mae and his government job were really a period of calm for him. My hectic activities provided him with enough kicks so that he no longer needed to expend his own energies.

I became extra horn with the symphony and to my thrill saw the first program of the 1951–52 season with my name on it, even though it was in parentheses to show that I wasn't a full-time member. After this I began working almost all the jobs in Washington when the symphony was busy and the regular hornist couldn't make it. I also played with the symphony when works were done that required extra horns, such as "The Isle of the Dead" by Rachmaninoff, the Mahler symphonies or occasional jobs where one of the horn players was sick. I also played many concerts outside the symphony when Washington union members had to be used.

I remember playing at a performance of Beethoven's *Missa Solemnis* with the symphony at the National Cathedral. Paul Calloway was conducting. I had just left my gym teaching job, which I couldn't afford to give up, and made the rehearsal with ten minutes to spare. Unlike the jazz scene where people would wander in at the nick of time or a few minutes late, I walked in and my eyes focused upon one empty chair. The entire orchestra was all there warming up along with the chorus and the soloists. The only empty chair was mine, the fourth horn chair. All of the musicians thought I must be crazy coming in so late. Fortunately I had a good low register and the horn parts were easy for me to play without much warming up.

I found that many members of the orchestra were really passionate music lovers. Most had spent years and years studying before they could get a job. Even though many of them were paid much less than they could have made at other kinds of work that required this much time and effort they still maintained their commitment to music. It was a great inspiration to be in this kind of atmosphere and it gave my life the only stability that it had during that particular period.

I was very tired those last six months, finishing college, waiting for the army, increasing my jazz activities, composing for Howard University, teaching gym and playing more and more frequently. But I loved playing the horn so much that it didn't even seem like work and my lessons got better all the time. I began playing the Brahms Horn Trio about once a month at different concerts and appeared with different amateur orchestras as soloist playing a Mozart horn concerto. I also began taking any job that came along that paid because I was just about to make a living as a horn player and this made me feel like a full-fledged pro.

I was called back to the Gaiety Theatre to play in a production of *The Student Prince,* and having written music for several plays by this time, I was rather critical of the production. So were the papers and it closed a week ahead of schedule. During one part of the show where I had nothing to play I emptied out my horn and did not realize that it was a dramatic moment of the show when the audience was completely silent. As I was blowing the water out of my horn, it made an inadvertent sound.

When the show was over the conductor came over to me and said in his strong Irish brogue, "Never fart at the conductor, son." Heeding the first advice I got from the Gaiety Theatre contractor about leaders, I accepted this advice without any backtalk. I began to think as I sat there playing um-pah-pahs and listening to the orchestra grinding out this terrible music, that perhaps I did not want to have to spend my life like these seventy-year-old musicians playing this trash. I decided right there in that orchestra pit that if I could not play with a first-rate symphony or get my own jazz group, I would think of horn playing as I did composing and figure another way to make a living.

One early Sunday morning after an all-night session, Ed Dimond, a fine pianist and arranger, told me that I should try to form a group that used some of the classical and jazz musicians who would fall by my basement. Three weeks later we had a group and were ready to wail. Our best soloist was my friend Spencer Sinatra, the saxophonist and flutist. He was now also playing with the National Symphony. The rest of the front line was Kenny Pasmanick, the solo bassoonist with the National Symphony who was also an excellent jazz man and myself playing French horn. For our rhythm section, we had Larry DiGuillian, drums, Norman Williams, bass, and Lloyd Lilie, a terrific pianist and accordionist who had introduced my sister and me to George Shearing's music. Our group played arrangements that all of us wrote. Some were tunes from records of Charlie Parker's, and ones that Miles Davis had written for his big band. Miles's playing appealed to me particularly because of his kinship with the French horn and because of the unique way he used the trumpet. We also tried collective free improvising. Spencer, Kenny and I also played classical trios, while the rhythm section rested.

Our first job was at a place called the Cross Town Restaurant. The owner, a very congenial man, thought it would be a good idea to have us as something different on Monday nights. The only problem was that while he was generally in sympathy with our music, his own taste led him to performing an act of his own. It was an imitation of Al Jolson, which was not exactly the same groove we were in. This was my first exposure to audiences as the leader of my own band. While a few hipsters wanted to come to hear our music, they were considerably outnumbered by the Cross Town's regular clientele, who just wanted to get drunk or to hear the Al Jolson imitations. When our group was playing what was then extremely far-out music, the Jolson fans and the heavy drinkers would sit dejectedly with their heads slumped down, generally mumbling to one another, "What is that crap?" or "Why can't you guys play something pretty? Where's the melody?" or "I thought you guys could play jazz," while our hipster audience, usually fellow musicians plus a few other fans who had come to our parties would sit there bobbing their heads in appreciation. Then when the owner got up to give his Al Jolson imitations after apologizing for five or ten minutes for having our group there, all of the hipsters would walk out in a mass demonstration against the desecration of their new art form. As a result, we were not an overwhelming success although we made our mark among the people that we thought were important. We got fired after two months but had a few other little jobs.

During this time, I sat in a few times with The Orchestra, a great band headed by the late Joe Theimer, one of the best big bands I ever heard in my life. Every member was an excellent soloist, as well as a fine section man. At the same time, Ed Dimond and Buddy Rowell, a whaling drummer plus jazz man, formed a terrific Latin band composed mostly of jazz musicians like me who liked Latin music, plus three fiery Latin percussionists. One of the percussionists had a day job working in a place that manufactured custom-made pipes. He had developed a tiny pipe for smoking pot. It was easy to palm and could get you the maximum high with a minimum amount of pot. Consequently our band always had a fantastic groove from the first minute of the rehearsal to the last minute of our job, wherever it was. At that time smoking pot was so little known it was almost a special kind of religious rite among musicians to make them feel closer to one another and to the music. We didn't go around advertising that we smoked it or try to get other people to smoke it. It was just something we did in order to appreciate music and live a little more on certain occasions when we got together. Almost like communal wine. The Latin musicians also felt the same way. They came from a culture that was much more relaxed than ours and they really dug the fact that there were some Americanos who liked their music and could play it.

It was during this time that Buddy Rowell and his wife, Stella, Joe Theimer's wife, Jo, and I went down to the Howard Theatre to hear Charlie Parker. At this time I had been listening to his records for over five years, most of which I had worn out from hearing them so many times. He was a legendary hero to all of us. Jo knew him, being an excellent jazz singer herself, and said she would introduce us all after the concert.

There was a special air of excitement at the Howard, as if the President were going to arrive or something. You could feel it all during the movie before the stage show, just like that buzzing one hears before the closed-circuit telecast of the heavyweight-championship fight: people not really concentrating on the movie but waiting for the great event to come. After the movie was over, The Clovers appeared, a fine vocal group. But even they seemed to sense that the big thing was going to come after them, even though they were wonderful crowd pleasers. We also noticed there was quite a smattering of white people in the audience, quite unusual for the Howard at that time. Apparently Charlie Parker's music had already reached people all over the world, even though he was not as well known in America as he should have been.

Finally the lights went down. The announcer came out and said, "And now, ladies and gentlemen, we present to you the world's greatest alto saxophonist, Charlie . . ." and before he could get "Parker" out, the piercing sound of Charlie Parker's saxophone broke from behind the curtain. The band began playing "Cool Blues." The curtain opened and there was the unforgettable sight of Bird wearing striped green pants, baggy at the knees, with scuffed brown shoes, one toe occasionally tapping every few measures, holding his alto, which seemed almost like a toy saxophone, he had grown so heavy during these years. His jacket, double-breasted, purple, was covered by huge lapels and was unbuttoned. Some kind of crazy orange tie bobbed up and down. He was playing with such concentration that the entire band seemed to be focused at the tip of his horn. Next to him was Kenny Dorham, a brilliant trumpet player, Teddy Kotick, the bassist, Stan Levy, the drummer, and Walter Bishop, Jr., the pianist.

The hush of the audience was unbelievable. As Bird played, there was a tremendous tension that could be felt by everyone in the hall. The only relaxed person seemed Bird himself, who was smiling affably except when he played. He had an incredible kind of projection in person that even his records couldn't capture. His records are great documentations of his amazing musical mind, but that night he played completely different choruses on many tunes I had listened to time and time again. Even if I hadn't learned his recorded choruses as I had, I could have sensed the abandonment with which he played. He was one of the true master improvisers. To him playing his horn was just like whistling or even more like thinking out loud. If you could imagine someone like Nijinsky or more recently Nureyev doing his famous leaps on a tight wire a hundred feet off the ground, no net below, blindfolded at the same time, this was how Bird played. He had such grace and abandonment and daring that after a while you didn't even think of it that way but just soared along with him. I saw that he and his music were much greater than even his legend.

After the show was over, Joe's wife said, "Let's go back and say hello to Bird. He's really a beautiful cat." And we all went back. Bird recognized Jo right away, greeting her warmly. Bird was nice to all of us, but he looked a little surprised at my outfit. I had on the shoes I wore as a gym teacher, which were called canoe shoes, sort of like sandals with a zipper in the middle, and my frayed suede jacket, which made me look somewhat like a good-natured juvenile delinquent, I suppose. But when Jo told him that we were all musicians and that I was a gym teacher too, he seemed very interested.

"That's crazy," he said. "We gotta talk some about my kids. They're going to school."

He had the kind of eyes that made you feel he had known you all of his life and could tell your whole story immediately.

"You wait for me, man," he said. "I want to drop off two people somewhere and then we'll hang out."

"Great," I said.

Buddy and Stella and Jo told Bird that we would have some of his friends and fans come to meet him over at my basement. So they left and I waited for Bird. He came down in a few minutes with two gorgeous girls all dressed to kill. I took them to my car, a battered 1932 Plymouth which featured a little rug in the back seat with two Tintoretto reproductions from the National Gallery of Art on either side just to make it seem more homey. Bird and the two girls got in the back seat. I was their chauffeur.

Suddenly his voice lowered to a basso profundo and he said, "O.K., take me to Seventh and R streets and hurry up." I realized that part of this was to impress the girls and I complied. "O.K., stop," he ordered like an emperor. I stopped the car and the two girls got out and he followed them. Just before he was leaving he whispered in my ear, "Don't go away, man. I'll get rid of these two chicks and then we'll have a ball. You dig?" His voice went softer, giving me that knowing twinkle.

"Solid," I said, and parked the car and waited. I saw them go into the house. After sitting about twenty-five minutes I thought perhaps he'd forgotten about hanging out, but out of respect I waited. About an hour later he came out and jumped into the car.

"Whew," he said, smiling. "Those two chicks sure make me appreciate my wife. Chicks like that are nothing," he said. "The only important thing is loving somebody. They make me realize how lucky I am to have a wife I love the way I do. And kids."

As we rode to my place we talked a little about music. When we walked down into my basement, it was already crowded with the cream of Washington's hipsters, who had somehow heard through the underground network during the hour and thirty minutes since he had left the theater that Bird was going to be there. These were people who had always looked at me rather askance before. They thought I was out of my mind because of the rustic way I dressed and because I played the French horn and was a gym teacher. They usually gave me the freeze. Most of them who were not musicians had never come to my jam sessions. It didn't seem like a hip enough scene because of the wild conglomeration of guests. Musicians themselves are very seldom snobs. The better they are, the more open-minded they are and the more they like all different kinds of people and experiences. But quite often fans of artists are exactly the opposite.

Still, here they all were in tribute to Bird in my cluttered-up down-home basement apartment. When Bird got to the doorway, the first thing he said was "Man, doesn't Modigliani have a lot of soul?" He recognized the Modigliani, one of many reproductions hanging on the walls, and was able to identify all the others as well. He looked around with his all-seeing eye and I got the message that he thought that a lot of people there were phoneys. "Man, what you got to scarf?" he said in a rather loud voice, thus showing everybody that he would join them after he had something to eat, getting them off the hook and at the same time being able to fortify himself before plunging into the den of vipers. I took him into my tiny kitchen and we opened up the icebox. When he saw all the wild collection of food, he roared with laughter. "My man," he said, "I see I'm in the presence of a stone gourmet!" We proceeded to make borscht and sour cream with all kinds of vegetables in it and some broccoli with sour cream and a crazy omelet I cooked up with fried onions, marmalade, maple syrup, bacon, tomatoes, covered with hot mayonnaise with some garlic fried in it and a little cheese sauce.

Bird was fascinated by my cooking and we both wolfed down portions of it, chased with some borscht and orange soda. I could see that Bird really enjoyed life and loved to eat. We talked a lot about the school where I was teaching because he was very interested in kids himself. I remember him saying that someday he hoped his kids could go to school with my kids and be able to get along. I never talked about racial problems to any black musician. It is as offensive as people coming up to me and telling me how great it must be to be Jewish before I've even said three words. Bird didn't mention it much either, but I could see that he was really conscious of the stupidity of our whole way of life and felt that the denial of people of each other on an individual human basis was even more upsetting to him than America's denial of him as an artist.

After we had finished our gourmet dinner we went into the other room, where his fans were patiently waiting, and he proceeded to sit back in an armchair like the king that he was and entertain everyone. I put on some of his records and he listened intently. During most of the others' solos he was laughing and giving encouragement to the musicians as if they were recording it at the time. At the same time, he was eyeing everyone in the room, answering questions, but still seeming to be somewhere else all the time. He reminded me of Count Williams from Oberlin. He not only had simultaneous time in his playing and got other people to play that way, but seemed to be able to operate on five or six levels at the same time plus another that was all his own. Because of his great warmth and kindness—he seemed more like a country boy than a great jazz musician—everyone in the room felt beautiful.

Many of us there that night are still friends today. I found that everyone that knew Bird well at all had a certain common bond just in the memory of him and his music. After the evening was finally over, he invited me to come back and see him, to talk to him about music and sit in with him. He also said perhaps he would come down to my basement and play. He was interested in the French horn and told me about the group of strings he had and that Joe Singer, the French hornist, was on the recording they had made.

As I drove him to his hotel, we talked about classical music. In addition to being so fond of Stravinsky and Bartók, he also loved the music of Delius. It was Charlie Parker that made me aware of Delius for the first time as a real orchestral innovator. Listening to Delius' music in a certain way made me understand Charlie Parker better and vice versa. Just before we got to his hotel we passed an outdoor hotdog stand and Bird's eyes lit up.

"Got eyes?" and I said, "Sure," so we stopped and had about four or five hotdogs and two sodas apiece. We said good night and he assured me again that he wanted me to come back and see him. I came back three days later after my gym classes. The afternoon show was still on. As I went backstage the aroma of pot was overwhelming. It seemed to be coming from the other side of the theater. One of the musicians in the house band was sitting there and I asked him, "Where is Bird?" He pointed his finger to the other side of the theater. I walked along backstage, where the sweet smell was getting stronger. When I got about thirty-five feet from Bird's dressing room, a chair and an arm with a joint of pot poked out. The chair rocked back, but there was no head visible. Just the back of a body. Then Bird's deep voice: "Come on in."

There were no secret mirrors or periscopes present, but I realized Bird could tell it was a friend by his telepathic sense, for which he was famous. He introduced me to Leo Parker, a great baritone player from Washington who, he explained, was not a blood relative although they had the same last names, but a soul brother nonetheless. I had my horn and Bird said, "Good, you brought it with you." He told Leo about me.

Then it was time for him to go on. No one backstage seemed to mind that he was smoking pot. It is a testimonial to Bird's telepathic powers that he was never arrested once during his lifetime for this or any other drug offense. As I went back to the other side of the stage with Leo to listen to Bird, we saw that the entire house band, which had just finished playing, was huddled around the side of the stage, listening to Bird. Then with the same announcement I had heard that first night, Bird started out again with the first of six shows he was to do that day. Every time I went to hear him, he played completely different choruses and got the whole band to play completely differently. It was really remarkable how he could set up a whole atmosphere. When the set was over he came out and one of the tenor players, a kid of no more than seventeen or eighteen, began to play so that Bird would hear him as he went by. Bird stopped and gave him a stern professorial stare, cocked his ear, looked at him and listened intently. He then gave a few words of encouragement. We went backstage and talked. I played for him a little bit. He played for me. We played together for a while. It's an experience I'll never forget in my life.

"I gotta go now," he said. "Go down and play with Kenny." He took me to Kenny Dorham, who was playing the saxophone with another bass player in an impromptu jam session down in the basement.

While Kenny was already known all over the jazz world as one of the great new trumpet players, he also liked to play saxophone. Bird introduced him to me and told him I was a fine French hornist. I played with Kenny and the bass player until Bird's next set. They showed me a lot of the new things that were being done in New York and told me about Miles's band with the French hornists Junior Collins and Gunther Schuller, and also about Julius Watkins, another great French hornist whom I worked with years later.

Bird came over to my place the final time to hear our little group with flute, bassoon and myself the night before he closed in Washington. We played his riffs and then did some free improvising. Bird was fascinated by the bassoon. Whispering in my ear, he said, "That cat's a bitch," referring to Kenny Pasmanick's bassoon virtuosity. He asked Kenny to play the famous bassoon solos from *The Rite of Spring,* Tchaikovsky's Fourth Symphony and many of the other bassoon solos with which Bird was apparently quite familiar.

"Why don't you play the saxophone?" I said to Spencer.

Spencer said, "If you were a saxophone player, you'd know why I don't play."

"Listen," said Bird to Spencer, "I know how you feel, but man," he said, "you have to love your horn and live with it and spend your whole life with it and after a while if you love it enough, it will become a part of you and you'll feel a part of it and it will love you and become your best friend." This was advice that later took me through some of the hardest periods of my life.

Bird had to catch a train. He said to me we'd have to play together when I came to New York and what a ball he'd had. I felt the same way. This was in the spring of 1952, the last time I saw Bird.

Charlie Parker's whole concept of music, his dedication to it and the spirit he created, influenced me as a composer as much as any other musician that I can think of. His music made me aware that every sound is related to every other sound. He was like an architect and a painter and a poet all at the same time. His attitude of an open mind and an open heart, of playing with anybody, listening to everything, trying to appreciate everything and then being able to distill all these experiences in his own way—all this affected me and a whole generation of people who were aware enough to get the message. Bird's whole life was dedicated to perfecting his art. While the whole era of bebop, the mystique and the social mores and patterns

have changed totally since his death, his music and the influence of
his music are stronger than ever.

Later in the spring of 1952 I met most of the other jazz men that
came through Washington, including Dizzy Gillespie who, with some
of the members of his band, camped out at my place overnight. I
wish they could have stayed forever.

In April I wrote the music for *The Family Reunion* at Howard
and Malcolm Raphael came to see it. We hung out all night afterward and went to Seventh and T streets to a session, then back to
my basement and talked until dawn.

"What do you think you're going to do when you quit the government?" I asked Malcolm.

"I'm going to the University of Michigan to study law. It may
sound like a cop-out, but I actually enjoy studying and my job with
the CIA is sickening."

"When I get out of the army I'll look you up or if I'm playing out
there in Michigan, I'll come by and see you."

"You'll have a ball in the army, David," said Malcolm, reassuring
me. "It will be the most fantastic sociologic experience of your life.
After your B.A. in history, it'll provide you with part of your credits
for a doctorate in lifesmanship with a minor in survivalhood plus a
diploma from the School of Hardknocksville."

"Solid, Malcolm," I said, "you've prepared me for Uncle Sam."

At my college graduation I played in the union orchestra, as I had
for other graduations that week. Before the names were called the
musicians came up and congratulated me. They were mostly symphony members. A few were from the old country and knew how
much it meant for musicians to have a college degree in a subject
other than music. They were as proud of me as if they were my own
parents and kept looking at me with admiring glances as the ceremony went on. When my name came up on the alphabetical list of
graduates it was passed by. The musicians threw their hands up in
the air in defiant gestures, but the ceremony went on. I saw my parents afterward, who were dismayed because they had never believed
that I would graduate from college anyway. I ran down in my bandsman uniform to the registrar's office and found out that I had forgotten
to pay my tuition and to register for the last term even though I had

taken all my courses and passed everything. She had my diploma anyway and gave it to me. It was just that some of the members of the university were so angry, especially since I was also playing in the graduation band, that the college wanted to give me a lecture before they gave me a diploma. I sent in the money for my tuition and shortly after went into the army.

5

MUSIC has been part of military culture since the beginning of time. The martial drums, the trumpets and the ram's horns go back way before the time of Joshua. Although many of us who play horns feel that those walls of Jericho were about to tumble down anyway or those shofar players must have had the strongest set of "chops" in antiquity; nevertheless, history is resplendent with descriptions of music that stirred men's blood to warlike passion. The bagpipe is still a stirring sound, the fife and drum and the image of the Spirit of '76 are still part of our popular culture. In America, much of this martial music has been transferred to stimulating the aggressive instincts of youngsters on the football field. The fatalities are considerably fewer, but the music isn't much more sophisticated.

I believe that the atomic era has changed the whole psychological relationship of man to his role as a fighter in an army situation. Those of us who were drafted during the Korean conflict knew that certain myths our brothers told us when they came back from World War II were simply lies, however deeply they were engrained in our culture, so it was impossible for us to enter the army with the customary savage and exorbitant sense of joy. Still, the number of war movies I'd seen as a child, complete with the symphony orchestra honking in the background to excite warlike passion, had brainwashed me to the extent that I still had secret visions of walking around without a shirt on like John Wayne, or smoking a cigarette with a carbine in one hand and a beautiful peasant girl in the other. She, of course, appreciated my liberating her country and was willing to return the ultimate sacrifice of herself as a reward to her savior.

I still believed in what World War II had accomplished and truly had an emotional involvement against Fascism. The entire European branch of my father's family had been killed except for one, who had hidden in a windmill in Holland all during World War II. I remember walking through Washington with friends of mine from junior high school in the middle forties with money we had collected from our jobs. Flushed with the success of having won an award for bringing in the most scrap iron and really feeling patriotic, we went to see a double-feature war movie, almost four hours of slaughter, pillage and rape, courage and bestiality, with good and bad guys clearly delineated and always with promises of sexual fulfillment for the victor. I noticed all the soldiers and sailors with their girls had a tremendous sense of excitement as they sat there watching some 4–F grade-B-movie star kill twenty thousand Nazis. I saw how the uniforms seemed to make the men who were wearing them more attractive and dynamic. I felt the irony of it all, as well as my teen-age frustrated passions, hearing those high, dry, hillbilly voices with the faces of farmers and grain salesmen who had suddenly at this cataclysmic moment in history become military Romeos.

Then there were the professional army musicians and bandsmen who had gone in during the Depression because it was impossible to make it on the outside. They didn't really consider themselves to be military men. They were all sergeants who referred to their work as a gig under the pretext that they were still civilian musicians and that their music job was how many times they showed up a week to play at the army or navy or marine corps band where they were stationed. Many were excellent musicians who used to play in the amateur orchestras I performed with. Some were doing their military duty in this way and a few preferred to remain for the full twenty or thirty years. I had a chance to join one of these organizations, but it would have required four years enlistment, which was too much for me to conceive of.

Still I felt I owed it to my country to make the military scene, so about a week after I had graduated from George Washington University I went down to my draft board to ask them when I would be inducted. The people at the draft board were very pleasant. I was referred to a middle-aged woman with that white hair with blue in it, a style still very popular in small southern towns, which Washington definitely was at the time. She also wore steel spectacles, right out of Grant Wood. I really felt that this draft board was an all-

American scene just like the Andy Hardy movies. In fact I identified with Mickey Rooney, even though I was much taller, since I was about to leave my innocent life as a red-blooded all-American pot smoker to serve Uncle Sam. I could already see that girl waiting in the fields with her hot peasant eyes focused upon me as I roared across the landscape with my carbine and French horn held high in victory.

The draft-board lady told me all about the military history of her family, leading way back to the Civil War, which she seemed to think was still in progress. After about two hours of this she declared that there was no record of me being registered. She saw the concern upon my face and said not to worry, as this happened quite often. Then she took me downstairs, where the other people in the draft board roared with laughter and told me how messed up the whole system was and not to worry about it. They finally located my papers and told me that in August I could report, assuming that I passed my physical. Some of my friends had figured ways of getting out of the army by saying that they were homosexuals, dope fiends or getting an elaborately forged doctor's report of illnesses that were difficult to detect, such as back ailments, brain damage or psychological problems including bed-wetting. I still felt that I had to go. I also figured that if the army was crazy enough to accept me, I could probably make a few improvements while I was there, so in a certain sense I entered with a crusading spirit.

I'd been a gym teacher for two years and was in terrific condition, so I went down to take my physical in a great mood. Everyone else was sitting there in a profound state of gloom and torture. I took the tests with no problems at all. The only thing I noticed out of the ordinary was one very nice boy from South America who obviously had polio with one leg so withered that it was like a branch of a small tree. He needed braces to walk on it. A master sergeant with a whiskey-reddened, blue-veined, glinting, pig-eyed, sneering face was shouting at this poor guy, telling him that all Puerto Ricans and spics were draft dodgers. Actually the person in question was the son of a Chilean diplomat and couldn't understand English. But the thing that amazed me was that they kept this poor young kid, who would not have been of too much value except possibly for target practice, waiting for nearly an hour while he was examined. They finally decided he was a cripple. This was my first glimpse of the "New Army."

We all drove back on the bus and I was told that I should report on August sixth for duty. I packed up all of my things and moved out of the basement apartment where I'd been living for two and a half happy years. I took one fond glance at the old pictures on the walls and the great collection of bottles that I had studiously put together in a huge collage. I showed up at the induction center with one civilian suit, my French-horn mouthpiece—since I was told that my horn would have to be delivered to me later at basic training—a copy of Walter Piston's book *Harmony* and a shaving bag, which I was told we were permitted to bring with us. I packed a razor, but the other usual toilet equipment I left out in order to put in one ounce of Chicago green pot, some of the finest that had come to Washington in years. I also brought a tiny pipe, which was about one and a half inches long and had been made by my friend, the pipe maker, who played in our Latin band. He spent days figuring how to construct a special pipe for me which would use up the least amount of pot and would be the most difficult for military authorities to discover, thus enabling me to get high whenever I felt that the pressures of the military life were too much for my delicate psyche.

I showed up early in the morning and was given an interview to determine what my military occupation would be. I brought along a copy of the National Symphony program, some reviews of music I had written for the theater and my mouthpiece in case there were any horns available. I was informed by the person in charge of giving out military occupation status that because I had a degree in European history, I must be categorized as a historical research assistant. I didn't qualify as a musician since my college degree was for another subject. With a little inquiry I was told that the entire Eastern Seaboard used perhaps four historical research assistants. The others were generally put into the infantry, where they could do their postgraduate work.

That evening I was approached by three young men who looked like junior versions of all the cops and Treasury Department men that I'd seen so many times when working as a jazz player. Once you had seen one, they were easy to spot because of the particular vibrations that they exuded.

"I understand that you're a musician," one of them said, starting off the conversation in a typically subtle fuzz fashion.

"That's right," I answered.

He then launched into a forty-five-minute discourse on narcotics and musicians whose careers had involved using drugs. He showed an extraordinary knowledge of pharmacology for a career infantryman. His two friends also joined in and made some halfhearted attempts at sounding "hip," but it was obvious to me that they were probably informers—part of the army undercover I had been warned about which was notoriously successful in whisking gullible hipsters out of the barracks and into the stockade. I disappointed them by feigning ignorance and indifference to the whole topic. Then I went outside with my shaving kit and smoked enough pot to turn on an entire battalion. And as I stood there with my shaved head, staring disbelievingly at the entire prison scene, I felt more as if I were in a movie with Edward Arnold as the warden and me as a lifetime convict waiting for my pardon, rather than the swashbuckling lead in a John Wayne picture. Suddenly a great rainstorm began. I was so fascinated with the whole predicament of being there that as the rain was pouring down in giant sheets I just stood there motionless. Then I put my pipe back in my shaving bag and wandered very slowly around the middle of the area, digging the rainstorm and thinking about what all of my friends in the real world were doing. Suddenly I looked around and saw other freshly shaved heads peering out of the dimly lit barracks windows surrounding the quadrangle, eyeing in amazement my solitary figure wandering around in the middle of a downpour. I returned to the barracks and in my sodden, saddened state realized that at last I'd become part of the United States Army.

I was sent from the Maryland induction center to Camp Breckenridge in Kentucky, where I was told that the basic training, especially during August, was really tough. I was looking forward to it because I enjoyed physical conditioning. To me the whole scene was wild with all these young boys who had never left home before suddenly frantic at being uprooted. It made me feel much older because of the amount of traveling and independence that I had had. As we passed Altoona, Pennsylvania, I remembered thinking of my friend from the Oberlin Conservatory, Ken McIntyre, the weight lifter and pianist-composer who was born there. I looked out and imagined that I could see his great form doing some body presses in back of one of the old quarries where the health fiends used to go. I hadn't seen him since 1949 when I left Oberlin and he had just gotten out of the army. As the troop train rattled and groaned toward Kentucky, I passed through many places where I had traveled, little towns that we had gone through at four o'clock in the morning on a bus ride to some job.

When we arrived at Kentucky we received the usual speech about how we weren't soldiers yet but were still civilians and had to be shipped into shape, etc., etc., and then we were taken to our barracks. After we settled down, a corporal grunted through another speech, announcing that he wanted to know if there was an experienced drummer in the group. No one jumped up so I went to him and said I could play well enough and that I would be happy to be battery drummer during basic training. He told me to go down to the band room, get a drum and try out tomorrow. I went down to the band room, where the regular Kentucky army band was stationed. To my great surprise I found out that there were more hipster musicians in the army than any one place that I had seen in my life. They were in their teens or early twenties like I was and almost all of them came on—whether or not they knew how to play well—as if they were deeply involved with the world of jazz. They all had their uniforms tailored a little differently to give themselves a particularly hip appearance and also had strange haircuts which could pass military inspection when tucked under their hats but were still long and un-military the rest of the time.

I asked for the drum and was told I could borrow it to practice for the night. Then one of the musicians asked me what I did. I told him I played French horn and some jazz. He suggested I come to a session later that night, so I brought the drum back with me to the barracks, practiced for a few minutes, put it into my footlocker, then went back to the band for my first session in the U.S. Army. The word got around that someone new had arrived who played jazz French horn. When I returned most of the band was there. This was because the four French hornists in the regular band weren't French horn players at all. One had been a radio station operator, one a gas station attendant, one a tree surgeon and the other a laundry truck operator. All of them had played a little trumpet at one time and managed to fake their way through a horn audition because the army standards were so low. So I was really a novelty if only because I knew how to play the instrument, not to mention jazz.

They gave me a horn and I started cooking away, playing all the latest things I had picked up from my final sessions with Washington's great jazz players—Earl Swope, the trombonist, guitarist Charlie Byrd, trumpeter Charlie Walpe, pianist John Malachai, tenor-sax players Ben Lary, Charlie Rouse and Angelo Tompros. I also knew some of the harmonically advanced tunes that Ed Dimond had taught me the changes to, when I played with Buddy Rowell's Latin band. After about five minutes the whole permanent band was there. They all told me after my sixteen weeks of basic training I was sure to get into their band. But if I went to band school, by virtue of some weird army logic, I was not permitted to stay at Camp Breckenridge but would automatically be sent elsewhere. I told them that since I was in the army I wanted to go overseas and see the world. I also knew that if I took eight weeks of basic training, then I could spend the other eight weeks in band school. After that, they were forced to transfer me elsewhere.

"What do you want to go into band school for?" one of the sergeants said, "Man, you know more about music than any of us here."

I explained that I found out that unless I went to band school for eight weeks I would not qualify as an army bandsman and I would have to be a historical research assistant, which meant the infantry. I wanted to be a bandsman so that I could continue to compose and play jazz too.

"Aren't you afraid of being sent to Korea or someplace overseas?"

"Not really. I'd much rather do that than be stuck in Kentucky for two years."

As I was walking home I heard some fine jazz coming out of another barracks window and wandering in, saw that it was a reactivated National Guard outfit, an all-Negro unit. I was surprised because the "New Army" was supposed to be integrated, but still the base band was all white and this band was all black.

There were many excellent musicians in this band and I spent the night playing with them and talking about music and musicians. This is where I met Maceo Hampton, a cousin of Lionel Hampton's, who was the first person to teach me what was then a new way of voicing simple chords, a system where the third and seventh are doubled so that a nonpianist could play many complicated chord progressions and substitutions with a minimum of finger movements. With this extremely simple device, I was able to spend hours figuring out my own ways of voicing chords. Maceo's lesson gave me a whole new way of using tonal harmony as a point of departure for my composing as well as playing.

When I got back the next morning and fell into formation with my drum, I noticed that the first lieutenant, named Stein, was looking at me fondly. Apparently he had checked my records and found out that I had played with the National Symphony, had gone to college and was really a cultivated Jewish gentleman in comparison with some of the other raw material that had yet to be whipped into shape for the firing lines in Korea. I thought that as long as he seemed to favor me, I would really try some of my superhip Latin counter-rhythms while we were marching just to see if I could turn on the atmosphere a little bit and take away some of that gray monotony that I already felt after one day. So I played the conventional military street beat the first thirty seconds. Then I started cooking. Some of the men ahead of me began to do a little mambo step as we were marching and after about three minutes everyone was doing little dances. As we passed the kitchen one of the cooks burst his head out the window and shouted, "You're wailing, baby, you're doing beautiful."

After a while Lieutenant Stein halted the troops and admonished the men. He told them that I was a very fine musician and they should take my music more seriously. In other words, he felt that the soldiers were laughing at me, so I really began stretching out, playing all the wild rhythms I could think of: seven against four, five against eight, all kinds of offbeats and skips and triplets. But Lieutenant Stein was so convinced that I was a good drummer he kept the pace and we completed our march painlessly.

Over the next two weeks I managed to keep myself sane by working out all kinds of drum patterns to see what I could come up with next and also by going to sessions every night with different musicians.

One of the most remarkable musicians I ever met in my life was stationed permanently at Breckenridge. The first time I heard him play, I thought it must be Bix Beiderbecke reincarnated. The sound, ideas and free-floating trumpet style were as fresh and beautiful as any jazz playing I had heard. As soon as I began to play with this guy, I got that feeling of slowly floating over the countryside, as if I had stepped out of a plane playing the horn and were lying back on one of the pillowy white clouds I had been watching from the window. His presence and listening powers had made me instantly high (on music).

After I finished my choruses, I looked up and saw him grinning. "Jerry," he said, and handed me a half-pint of muscatel.

We spent most of the night talking. Jerry was from Cleveland and lived for music. At the base, he had some kind of clerical job, but he was an outcast among the other bandsmen, most of whom were dance-band musicians in civilian life, more commercially oriented and more adjusted to the life of the sober, businesslike working musicians. Jerry and I became close because we had that bond of outsiders. Like many of the finest jazz musicians that I knew, he was free, idealistic and happy-go-lucky. But he was also unable to adjust to the army or to any kind of regimented life. He also had the distinction of being sloppier than I was.

One night we went to a jam session for the colored troops. The Negro captain looked at me in disbelief as I entered with my horn and said in a very soft, fatherly tone, "Soldier, you gotta shape up if you're ever going to make it in this man's army." Then Jerry came shortly behind me. With his long curls, baggy pants and scuffed shoes, he looked as if he'd just ridden a freight across the country. The captain said, again in a soft, kind tone, "I think you boys had better leave here. You both don't want to set a bad example for the troops."

We left and hitchhiked into Evansville, Indiana, the nearest place where the action was. The camptown of Breckenridge featured nothing but jukeboxes with hillbilly music. The one night spot had a memorable men's room consisting of nothing but a door leading to an open field. Jerry and I got high on the way into Evansville so that we would be oblivious to any small-town freeze. We went to the YMCA, which Jerry told me was the best place to pick up girls. You could be almost sure that you wouldn't get the clap at any church social function, a cliché but a true one.

At the Y, I met the other members of the band that he was playing with, mostly society and big band musicians who weren't really improvisers but were very good players. When they saw that Jerry and I were hanging out together, they immediately sensed a conspiracy. Some of the older musicians of the swing and Dixieland period had a certain hostility toward the beboppers just as the beboppers later had a hostility toward players who were doing the "new thing," and the "new thing" players had a hostility toward the rock and rollers, etc. Still they let us sit in and I found that Jerry adjusted to the sound of the French horn and made it comfortable for me to play. Until then, I was always trying to make the horn fit in with the inflection of the trumpet, saxophone or whatever other instrument I was playing with. But because he was such a good musician he made me like myself when I played. When an accordion player came to play with us later that night, we had such a good time that we began to work small dance jobs the remainder of the time I was in camp.

The worst thing about playing at Breckenridge was finding a horn, especially when I wanted to sneak off post. I could always squeeze in the trunk of a car till we got past the gate, or lie on the floor underneath a blanket or even inside a bass violin cover, but it was hard to get a horn, and each time I did, I would have to adjust to playing a different instrument. Finally the big moment came: my own horn arrived in the mail. All the people in my barracks were fascinated because most of them had never seen a French horn or even a French hornist up close before. I took it out and gave an impromptu concert. About twenty minutes after I'd started playing, the first sergeant came roaring out of his room and told me in no uncertain terms to put my horn away or he would shove it, which I told him would be a physical impossibility, but nevertheless I complied with his wishes. This particular sergeant and some of the corporals were furious at the way I'd been playing drums, but they were afraid to tell the lieutenant that I was not a real military drummer because they thought it was some Jewish plot. As ridiculous as this sounds, I was told this by one of the corporals who liked my unorthodox military drumming techniques. But I was also told there was a counterplot. During the time I went away for the Jewish holidays another man was going to take over the drums.

I really didn't care, so when it came time for the holidays, I got a room at the YMCA in Evansville close to the jam sessions and brought my horn along, as well as my civilian clothes, which we weren't supposed to wear. On the first night of Rosh Hashanah I went to a small bar and was sitting in with the band in my civilian clothes when whom should I see but Lieutenant Stein in the audience, popping his fingers and enjoying himself. Every time I looked over at him he would look away because he didn't want to acknowledge that he was in a goyish bar on the holiday evenings. I saw that apparently in spite of his fiercely outthrust lower jaw and his high military bearing he was really a hipster at heart.

Early the next morning I went to a rehearsal of the Evansville Symphony. It sounded pretty good. One of the French hornists told me I should come and play with them whenever I was in town. So one day I went to the school where the orchestra was rehearsing.

I was asked to play first horn, and during a break, a lady trombonist suddenly screamed, "Milstein's comin'! He's comin' hyar any minute now!" We all scurried back to our seats and began rehearsing the orchestral part of the Tchaikovsky Violin Concerto.

Sure enough, Nathan Milstein appeared. He stepped up on the stage still wearing his overcoat and stared in disbelief at this rather strange-looking community orchestra of plumbers, salesmen, retired music teachers, a few ringers in the service like myself, and high school students—all producing a rather un-Russian sound.

The conductor stopped us, turned to Milstein and said, "Are you ready?" '

Mr. Milstein said in a laconic tone with a rather sad look in his eyes, "No, but I don't think it makes any difference." He then took out his violin, tuned it rather rapidly and with his coat still on, ran through the first movement of the concerto, trying not to grimace with horror when some of the unbelievably out-of-tune sections clashed with what he was playing. At the end of the rehearsal I went over and told him that it was really a pleasure to meet him at last, how much I had enjoyed his playing and how I had heard him in Washington quite often. He was very gracious and told me that the Evansville Orchestra sounded much better at concerts than at rehearsals. He also said he was happy to see that there was some kind of growing musical activity in America because ultimately the entire musical culture depended on community participation all over the country, not just in the big cities. I saw that he was a certain kind of missionary too. It was a strange place to meet him. I never dreamed that the first time I played in an orchestra accompanying him would be in the army.

I went to a session that night, then returned to the barracks, when I found out that Louis, a great Puerto Rican pal of mine, had been elected to take over as drummer during my absence, thus completing the counterplot. He was a terrific guy so I didn't care. Also, he had some very good pot with him which we had been sharing, so we were very tight. In fact when we were both on guard duty we bought what we thought was the bargain of the century—enough pot to get us high for the remaining two years in the army, a whole shopping bag full for only thirty dollars. Two mysterious friends of his said they had grown it in a private field about a hundred miles away. I didn't understand Spanish well, but he told me the word his friends kept repeating was dynamite, dynamite, dynamite. So while we were on guard duty we took turns curing our fabulous bargain-discovery over the oven. As we walked around we would occasionally check the oven to make sure that it didn't get singed. After about three or four days we smoked the first bit of it, but it failed to do much except give us headaches. It was what they called in the trade, lemonade. We finally checked with another draftee hipster who was more familiar with plant life and he told us that what we had bought was alfalfa.

As the result of our experience in being burned, Louis and I were buddies. When he said, "Man, I'm sorry they asked me to be drummer," I said, "Don't be," and told him not to worry about it. He had great collections of Latin records, which he used to play in the barracks. After we got high he would read letters from different girl friends describing with great relish how they missed him and what a great lover he was.

The day after I got back, Louis looked rather nervous and when we started to march he broke into a mambo beat. Everyone was used to this by now, but in his excitement he accelerated the tempo into such a frenzy that it sounded like a tape machine speeded up into a series of hysterical rattles. The corporals and sergeants looked dismayed. They stopped us. He tried again. We started marching four or five times, but he got so hysterical it was impossible to march unless everyone broke into a run.

"All right," said a sergeant, "you'd better take over the drums again, Amram." So I was the drummer for the rest of basic training.

In the morning, we would run out of the barracks shouting, "Kill, kill, kill," at first in jest but later on with more and more intensity. With the constant indoctrination toward killing we became more violent as the weeks passed. There was one particular soldier who was beating everyone up in gym classes. Because I had told somebody that I had been a gym teacher, people kept trying to get me to fight with him. I didn't really feel like it, but when he finally challenged me I figured I might as well. He had what we call in boxing a "cute" style, keeping his hands up high most of the time and backing away and throwing right-hand leads, blocking most of the body punches with his elbows and doing a lot of fancy footwork. Because I knew he thought I couldn't box, I planned to get to him first and throw off his routine and timing.

When we started I feinted a left hand to the body and then hooked over his right to his jaw. He had moved his arm down to protect his side, assuming that was where I was going to throw the punch. A great roar went up from all the soldiers and a rather astonished look came over his face, followed by a slight laugh that he had been tricked by such an elementary move. We went at it for the next few rounds. I beat him and went on to become the battery champion. But none of the people at that time knew how to fight very well and when I was offered the chance to be on the boxing team I turned it down. I knew that eventually I'd be hit in the mouth enough times so that I probably could never play the horn again.

I didn't box much afterward, but before the eight weeks were up I was in the frame of mind where I really wanted to punish or hurt somebody in order to relieve tension, which all of us felt, being taken away from women and everything else important in life. By the end of the eight weeks I really felt like an animal, like one of those dogs I used to see as a kid that was kept out in the country tied to a stake at the end of a rope. I still seriously question the beneficial effects of this training for people who are planning to come back to civilian life.

My next eight weeks were in band school, which was actually at the other end of Camp Breckenridge. When I arrived I found that there was quite a bit of hostility directed toward me. Some of the bandsmen hoped I would stay in camp with the Kentucky band rather than being so anxious to leave. I had also dropped a few remarks to the bandleader to the effect that since I was drafted into an army that was fighting for freedom and equality for all people, I would feel funny playing in a segregated camp band, especially since a lot of my friends were in another band across the street. I told them that I would be happy to stay and play with the National Guard band across the street, but that didn't make too favorable an impression either.

At any rate, when I arrived at band school, aside from the feeling that I was overqualified, I saw the hate rays coming in my direction. I was already working weekends with Jerry and some musicians who were in special services, jobs regular bandsmen would have liked to have, so they were really out to get me. They knew that I could box, but they were not interested in engaging in any physical violence. In the army, fighting is not necessarily the best way to get at someone. I was put on permanent duty, stoking the barracks' fires, with the hope that by being punished a little bit, I might have a change of heart and join the regular band.

I wanted to leave Kentucky at all costs, so for the first three weeks I was a model student, tended the fires, managed to have sessions anyway and didn't have too much trouble passing my courses as a bandsman.

Around the fourth week, however, one particular sergeant started bugging me unbelievably. One day on parade I put a copy of *Jet* magazine in my band lyre. I had memorized the horn part for what we were playing, which was nothing but the *pah* parts of *um-pahs* anyway, and while I was playing my part I read through the latest *Jet* news.

The sergeant came over to me and said, "What's that you're reading?"

I said, "*Jet* magazine, sarge."

"How come you ain't got the music up there in that lyre?"

"Well, sarge, I've memorized it already."

"What do you think of all this training? Tell me the truth."

I said laughingly, "It's hopeless," and went back to reading my magazine and playing again.

That night I was called up and told that I had to go on stockade duty guarding prisoners. This was a job that was not too popular, since a great many prisoners had been escaping and often took the guards' weapons away and shot them. The stockade guards were mostly older men who had been in the army ten or fifteen years and had no compunctions about shooting anybody. Very few draftees were given this dangerous job. If you let a prisoner escape, you had to serve his sentence until he was recaptured.

I went on duty guarding the prisoners and I found all of them to be pretty much like me. They all hated the army and yet in some way were idealists, especially the ones who had joined up with the hopes of making a career out of serving their country. There were also a lot of hipsters, pot smokers, etc. During some of my tours of duty they would turn me on. The fact that I wasn't afraid was probably the only reason that I didn't get wasted. This turned out to be one of the most enjoyable jobs in the army. We would have long discussions about everything imaginable and when an officer would come around I would put a grim look on my face and the prisoner would appear to be doing some kind of work.

By then it was November and getting quite cold. The person who had taken over my job as fireman unfortunately was not too responsible. He was a trombone player from Minnesota who was addicted to strong drugs. He had a mason jar next to his bed filled with every type of pill and narcotic that I'd ever seen in my life plus some new ones. He took all kinds of pick-me-up pills in the morning, and cocaine, heroin, cough syrup and other opium-derived drugs to calm him down during the day, then something else to pick him up at night and finally a few bombers to make him sleep. As a result he was so high most of the time that when he tried to play the trombone his lips would usually pop out of the mouthpiece before he could make a sound, his face muscles were so frozen from drugs. Nevertheless, he was quiet and unhappy-looking, which made him seem like a good enough soldier.

He took over my job as fireman while I was gone and one night while he was nodding, the grates burned out. In order to punish us and humiliate him we were not allowed to have any heat in the barracks for four days. As a result some of the members of the band school began climbing in bed with each other at night, ostensibly to keep warm but actually forming romances that continued for the rest of the eight-week course. The few full-time homosexuals in the band were overjoyed and thought it was hilarious. Still clinging to my belief that women are man's only salvation, however, I took some bottles of terpin hydrate that a friend of mine had stolen from the dispensary and by drinking two bottles kept warm enough to go to sleep.

Toward the last week of band training we all got our orders. Some of us were to stay in the States, some were sent to Japan, which meant Korea, and a few were sent to Europe to replace bandsmen or infantrymen or whatever soldiers were coming home from their European tour of duty. I was lucky enough to be chosen for the European tour.

When the news came out, the sergeants in charge of the band were furious. One shouted at me, "God damn it, you fixed it all up in Washington beforehand, you son of a bitch." Of course this would have been impossible to do because the choices were made by some civilians from Kentucky who worked in an office and merely filed people's names. Some of my friends were not so lucky. Three of them later died in Korea. But I was one of the lucky ones being sent to Europe. I was also informed when I got the news that I had to go on KP duty. But I was so overjoyed to hear about going to Europe I didn't mind. My friend with the mason jar of drugs and I decided that the best way to get through KP this final time—since we had received our orders we would not have any more KP at Breckenridge after this—was to bring along some Dexedrine and Benzedrine in order to cheer on our efforts and while away the dull hours. After about an hour we were flying high, grinding our teeth, perspiring profusely, our eyes bulging from our heads and laughing up a storm as we threw dishes and trays and silverware at each other. We were really straining ourselves to do a super job for our final KP in good old Kentucky. The only trouble was that there was no hot water and because of an exceptionally greasy meal, there was a huge film of white slime that could not have been taken off the trays without dropping them into the ocean for a month. At any rate, we did our best and by nightfall we left the kitchen and went out to celebrate getting our orders.

The next morning about six o'clock the sergeant came storming in, almost crying. "Look at my hands," he said, "they're raw to the bone. The son of a bitches who were on KP yesterday left those plates greasy and the captain came to inspect and made all us guys come off post and leave our families and come back and wash the dishes all night. I wonder who those bastards were." My friend with the mason jar and I looked at each other and went back to sleep. Later we decided that we better skip breakfast until the hate clouds blew over.

When I went to lunch they were waiting for me and one infuriated noncommissioned officer said, "That's that bastard, that's him right there, give it to him, give it to him." I was all ready to start swinging, because if a higher-ranking enlisted man hits you first, it was understood that you could fight it out. In my frame of mind I was delighted to have the chance to flatten any of them. What they had given me was not a punch but a specially designed plateful of garbage with a kind of floral arrangement with mashed potatoes on top, sprinkled with cigarette and cigar butts in an original display.

"No thanks," I said, "too many carbohydrates."

"That dirty Communist Jew bastard," said one of the more liberal band members, "he had it fixed up in Washington and I wish the hell we could bring him back on KP but we can't. He's got his orders, that rotten son of a bitch."

With this great send-off I went to the PX and had some Coca-Cola with some aspirin in it and a goof ball to countereffect the depression following all the Benzedrine I had taken and the rather unpleasant reception I had received.

In a week I graduated from band school with a few days off before being sent to Camp Kilmer for my shipment overseas. As I went through the gates of Camp Breckenridge for the last time, I thought how the sixteen weeks had really made some kind of a change in my life. It made me aware that the revolution that was taking place in jazz and in America was something that I was really a part of. It was not something that was written about at the time or articulated by any leader but it was really happening. It still is today. All this was clearly brought into focus by the other young musicians I met when I was in the army who came from different parts of the country. All of them were touched by this new spirit. I found this wherever I went during my entire two years in the army.

After going home for a few days I was sent to Camp Kilmer, the clearing center for the troops that were leaving to go overseas or were coming back. I remember riding out on the train past Princeton, taking a peek at this little community and thinking of the life of all the people who were living there in a genteel Ivy-League fashion, then looking at myself and the assortment of characters I was with. Many of them hadn't finished grade school. I wondered which world was for real: the institution of the university or the institution of the army. Both made me feel like a victim.

Camp Kilmer was a great madhouse, swarming with troops coming back from Europe and Asia. The food was unbelievably bad. Epidemics of food poisoning were quite frequent at this particular time. So I skipped out for a day or two and went to New York to see some musician friends of mine. I also visited my sister. When I came back no one ever knew I had gone.

The next day I had my sailing orders. Fortunately I didn't eat that morning, for everyone who did got food poisoning. A group of us who weren't sick were taken to get the ship ready since it was supposed to leave for Germany the next day. For three days we stayed on the ship, wondering when it was going to leave. The soldiers were so sick they were unable to be transported from Kilmer. There was a great state of panic because of the amount of money it was costing to have the ship sit in port with just us few soldiers on it.

Another musician and myself played every night when we had done our work in the kitchen. One of the merchant seamen who worked on the boat was a great jazz fan. He told me that if I ate a lot of olives I wouldn't get seasick. He also mentioned all the musicians he knew and to show his appreciation of my dilemma, gave me a tiny bit of hashish, which I smoked up in a lifeboat the following night. I also met a sergeant on the boat who was only nineteen and had a record player with him. After our sessions we would sit around and listen to Beethoven's string quartets while he told me how he had been in Korea in combat for a year and a half and was now going to Europe. He already had ulcers and looked like a man in his thirties. He also had read everything by Conrad and Melville and was a great enthusiast of the art of whaling in the nineteenth century.

Finally the army decided it was not economical to wait and the other troops came aboard. The poor soldiers were still suffering from food poisoning. They all had the runs, hadn't eaten for about two days and looked like men who had just come from the battlefield and should be sent home, not overseas. As the boat started to pull out of the harbor, that famous swaying motion began and as they were about halfway through their first meal in two days, half of them got violently sick and, being too weak to get up on deck, threw up on their lunch trays. When that didn't bother me I realized that I had been so hardened that nothing could make me sick, so I stopped eating the olives, had a full meal and settled down to a pleasant cruise.

There was a pianist on board who played all the latest chord changes. He couldn't take solos, but he had a great knowledge of keyboard harmony and was interested in arranging and composing. We got together and decided that we were going to put on a concert. Right about then (it was January in 1953) we hit an enormous storm. When it was time for us to perform we went down to the recreation room. After about five minutes I looked over at the piano player as the ship took a particularly violent lurch. His face was contorted with terror.

"Look out, man!" he shouted, and jumped up into the air.

I did likewise just in time to avoid being hit by a great barrage of sliding chairs which had roared over from the other side of the room and would have smashed us against the wall. The ship really started rocking like crazy and we had to stop our little impromptu session.

I spent the rest of the trip sneaking out to the bow of the ship to watch the ocean, which was incredible. Enormous amounts of green-black water roared by us as the ship lurched its way over the hills of the sea. Gigantic waves smashed down below the troughs. It made the entire experience of being in the army worthwhile. I would have been happy to spend the entire two years right there on the boat, feeling the hypnotic effect of the sea.

We finally arrived at Bremerhaven harbor. I was really thrilled to see Europe for the first time. As we pulled into port I realized that my fantasies about intellectual Europe were accurate after all. I noticed that all the working men carried briefcases with them. I thought it was wonderful that even dock workers were so literate that they would bring their books and study materials with them. Later I found out that was the way they carried their sandwiches, but at the time I didn't know this and the sight of thousands of working men with briefcases really made me feel that at last I had arrived at the great center of Western culture.

As the boat floated into dock there was a band sitting outside to greet us. They were playing "I Wonder Who's Kissing Her Now" and the soldiers responded by throwing Dixie cups, candy wrappers and containers of coffee on the bandsmen's heads. The French-horn player had a gigantic mustache and looked sort of like a Russian bear playing the horn. To my amazement I noticed that he was playing without a mouthpiece. He had the end of the horn in his mouth, and was huffing and puffing and fingering and going through the motions of playing without actually making a sound. The other members of the band looked very cold and miserable. I sympathized with them, thinking it was a terrible thing for a brass player to have to put a metal mouthpiece to his lips sitting on the dock in near-zero weather. I didn't realize that through the magic of army planning, after being sent back and forth many hundred miles I would end up being in this band myself only ten days later.

I was sent with my fellow soldiers to Zweibrücken, where we were to be categorized. Although I informed the commanding officer that I was a bandsman, he told me that under the army regulations, all the troops in this shipment still had to go to Zweibrücken, while we waited to be processed, where there was nothing to do but drink beer. We were not allowed to leave the post, there were no facilities for playing music and only one Ping-Pong table for about a thousand people. I studied Walter Piston's book *Harmony* again and drank quite a bit of German beer.

Finally, I was brought up before an officer, who said, "I see you're a bandsman."

"That's correct," I replied.

"All right," he said, "you'll be sent to the Munich band school in Dachau."

"Dachau!" I said, getting a wild feeling inside myself. "Man, I don't want to go there, that's where all the concentration camps were."

Needless to say, this did not change the decision of the officer, and so I was sent way across to the other side of Germany with several other musicians, some of whom appeared quite nervous. They told me there was supposed to be a very tough audition and if you didn't make it you either had to stay in Dachau and study at the Munich band school, which was supposed to be the worst chicken-shit outfit in Germany, or you were forced to go in the artillery or infantry. While this presented no physical danger in Europe, it meant spending a lot of time on maneuvers and it was quite chilly at this time of year. I was looking forward to the audition. I knew I could certainly play well enough to be put in a band right away. The French-horn shortage in Germany was even more acute than in the States.

I arrived at the barracks at the band school, which ironically enough were right where the Dachau concentration camp had been. We stayed in the billets that used to house the Gestapo troops. Some of the prison buildings were still there as a kind of a museum. There was an old German who guarded the museum and since I spoke a little German he confided to me after a while that they hadn't done a good enough job on the Jews. This was a statement I heard reiterated quite often in German, usually in the privacy of someone's home, when, not realizing that I was Jewish, my hosts would bare their more intimate thoughts. I had had a music teacher as a kid who had survived Dachau. He had been a very fine violist before they hanged him by his arms for two days. He never was able to play well again, although he was a great musician. While he didn't dwell on his concentration-camp experiences I never had forgotten this, and the whole time I was at Dachau it haunted me. I wondered if some of the Nazis who had been responsible for this had lived in the same room I did.

Again we were not allowed to leave the billets, so I didn't get a chance to go to Munich, or any place else, but I noticed that there were also a great many hipster-style musicians in Germany, at least at the band school. Just before my audition, I met a grizzled old sergeant who told me about the crying need for French-horn players and how most of the bands were easy to be in. The only really bad ones were in France because the town was located so far from Paris, and Bremerhaven, because of the supermilitary nature of the first sergeant there. He also told me of the Seventh Army Symphony, an organization that was not together at the moment but which would be re-formed next year. He then launched into a tirade about how the beboppers were ruining the army and how these young whippersnappers would not carry their instruments in the regulation instrument cases but always carried their horns in corduroy or leather bags. I knew the reason for this was simply that if you carried your horn in a corduroy bag or a leather case or even in a paper bag as some musicians did, it was that much quicker to whip it out and begin playing. But the sergeant didn't see it this way and figured this was all part of a conspiracy against America. In a way he may have been right.

Although auditions are often difficult and nerve-wracking, the Munich band school audition was not one to inspire fear in anyone.

"O.K., soldier, let's hear your C-major scale," barked the warrant officer. I whipped off a three-octave special followed by a group of cadenzas, part of the *Siegfried* horn call and an excerpt from *Till Eulenspiegel's Merry Pranks*, all in rapid fire. Of course these are the things that I'd been warming up with since the age of fifteen. Most other horn players always did the same, so it wasn't much of an achievement, but the officer's eyes bulged.

"My God," he said, "you don't need to go to school. They're looking for guys like you. Get ready to leave by tomorrow."

"Don't you want to hear any more?" I said.

"No." It was probably the shortest audition I ever had in my life, a minute and a half at the most.

I was called that evening and arrived with an elderly Negro sergeant to report for shipment back to Bremerhaven. His name was Williams and he had just returned from Korea, where he had been shot in both legs. He was a career soldier, determined to make his twenty years and get his retirement. He had been in since 1940 and had spent nearly three and a half years of constant fighting during World War II—one of the rare people who fought in both the European and Pacific theaters of operation and survived. Now he had lived through combat in Korea and was still pretty much of a nervous wreck.

We were both informed that we were being sent to the Bremerhaven band at the port of embarkation. We got a map and realized that the route we'd been sent over made almost a complete triangle. We laughed at what enormous expense it must have been to send two men all the way around the country only to end up at the exact same place we had gotten off the boat just ten days before.

As we sat on the train, Sergeant Williams reminisced about old jazz days when he had worked as a tenor-saxophone player with territory bands all through the West and Southwest. He had run across Charlie Parker and the other greats on his travels through Kansas City before Bird had left. They used to play at what were known as "spook breakfasts" when many of the local musicians would come and jam while most people were just getting up. He was also a great boxing enthusiast and told me that I should not even think about boxing the rest of the time I was in the army or I would probably get banged up so much I wouldn't be able to play the horn. There was a sort of underground of boxers in the army just as there was with French hornists and people with other specialties. He knew most of the boxers that were stationed in Germany, including one who was in the Bremerhaven band. He also knew that the first sergeant of this band was notorious as the toughest in Germany and that the Bremerhaven band was also the best marching band, had the best physical-fitness record and did the best in the military aptitude tests of any band in Germany. They were what was called "R.A. all the way"—R.A. meaning Regular Army as opposed to U.S., which was made up of people like myself who had been drafted.

We arrived at Bremerhaven and were told that in a half-hour there would be a rehearsal. The band was preparing for one of its classical concerts—mostly Von Suppé overtures and other famous chestnuts from the world of pop-concert literature. They heard I was a good horn player, so I was asked to play first horn. We also did the overture to *Semiramide* though in a different key than Rossini had written it in. When I finished playing, all of the bandsmen looked at me in amazement. They had never had a French-horn player who was even halfway good before.

The first sergeant looked over from where he was playing piccolo and for the first time I saw his furious, hate-filled, animalistic face. When he was angry, which was most of the time, his face would turn almost black with rage, his eyes would light up with fury and he would bare his teeth like some enraged animal. He also had a low voice, speaking in grunts and monosyllables that were terrifying to hear. He had been made a master sergeant by the general of the post and because it was an American enclave, there was no place to go to complain about his treatment. He was literally the king and had every single person in the band under his control through a series of spies and finks. I could see he had it in for Williams. Often career noncommissioned officers had a grudge against other noncommissioned officers who have had combat experience. Our first sergeant had none, even though he had been in the army through World War II.

The warrant officer was the bandleader and technically outranked the sergeant. However, he was a sputtering, weak-mouthed, myopic, doughy, little guy who knew absolutely nothing about music and had not even learned how to beat four-quarter time after twenty-five years as a warrant officer leading a band. His attempts at conducting concert music were hopeless, and even though he conducted with a piano score, he kept getting lost.

"I can do my job as good as Toscanini," he used to remark, "but Toscanini couldn't do what I do and make these pieces sound good."

His knowledge of the rudiments of musical notation were also rather sketchy and he used to tell people to play louder during parts of the pieces where they had a rest, to play softly when the music indicated fortissimo, and when he tried to sing a part to make it clearer, he usually sang the wrong part. But although he was weak and incompetent, he was a kind person at heart. The first sergeant provided his muscle.

Most of the guys in the band were professional soldiers first and bandsmen second. They were almost all Regular Army men except for the French-horn player I had seen with the big mustache when I landed at Bremerhaven. One of the sergeants had escaped from the Bataan death march and, being a native of the Philippines, lived in the woods for four years before rejoining the army. He was never given any credit or money for his time while he was hiding in the jungle because he was not technically a prisoner of war. He was very bitter about this. He played bassoon and was so upset by the pressures from the first sergeant that he got his wife in the Philippines to write a letter saying that she was dying so that he could be transferred out. Other soldiers who were veterans of Korea also felt the same way. I thought I would go insane if I had to spend eighteen months under the auspices of such a sadist.

We played the concert the second day I arrived. It was the first time they had ever had a good French-horn player, so I was told by one of the sergeants that if I kept my nose clean I would make PFC and corporal right on schedule. If I wanted to reenlist, in fact, I could probably be a sergeant. I told him in no uncertain terms that I had not planned on a career in the army.

He looked disappointed. "Well, maybe you'll change your mind," he said, repeating a speech that various officers had given all during basic training. It ran approximately: "I know a lot of guys that try to work in music and they end up dope fiends and in jail or on welfare. But with the good old army you could play your music and have security too." I don't know many musicians who were converted by this sermon.

The morning after our concert we were told that it was time for a few boat jobs. There were two types of boat jobs: incoming and outgoing. The first boat job was in the morning, a farewell engagement. On board stood the sergeants and their wives with long leis around their necks. Many of the wives were crying. It was really sad to see how miserable they were. Most of them were leaving great apartments that had been given to them by the government. Now they would have to return to the various American Dogpatches, where they would have no more German servants and no more of the fantastic overseas benefits, which were finally eliminated a few years later following a congressional investigation. Also the prostitutes from town on their bicycles—all dressed up like American girls with sweaters, loafers and white socks—were out in full force, just like the chorus line from *The Threepenny Opera,* to say good-bye to their schatzies, who were mostly merchant seamen. The merchant seamen made so much more money than the enlisted men that most of the prostitutes belonged to them. The soldiers had to find romance elsewhere. Some of the girls were quite lovely and I eyed them carefully as we played through "Aufwiedersehen" and "Aloha," which brought more tears to the weeping wives' eyes. Then we went into some military marches as the ship let out a final gigantic honk.

As the ship sailed off I noticed something different about the third horn player's face. He looked over at me, surreptitiously laughing, and I saw that he had no teeth. He then took his false teeth out of his shirt pocket, slapped them in his mouth and grinned once more, toothily this time. His real kick was to see how many times he could sit with a horn in his mouth with no teeth in, pretending to play without anyone noticing. So far he had done this for two and a half months and no one had said a word. This was because of the staggering volume we played at. While the band's performance during our concert of the preceding night was not of breathtaking beauty, it was nothing compared to the raucous performance on the dock. Here the professional military men could really let loose their hostilities and aggressions. The out-of-tune blasting really made these old marches and sentimental songs sound quite avant-garde. The trombone player informed us on the way back on the bus that he was now the loudest trombone player in Europe since his chief competitor for this title had just returned to the States. He had been in the airborne and described with pride how on his third jump he had played the trombone all the way down even though this was against regulations and quite dangerous. He had also been in the Korean War and although he was thinking of getting out of the army, he didn't feel he could make it on the outside as a musician.

There was another trumpet player who had been in the service almost his full twenty years. He too had tried going back to playing with bands after World War II and just couldn't make the life or the music either. It was like prisoners who could never adjust to being out of jail. He and some of the other bandsmen generally liked army life. Music to them was just their way of getting through the army. They knew how hard it was to try to make a living playing and as military men they were doing a job that had a certain value. But I never could feel the psychic rapport with them that I had with most other musicians.

This band was in a powerful position with the general of the post and excelled in almost every area of military activities plus music for marching, concerts and boat jobs. The bandsmen were also protected from outside punishment for almost any crime. Those who made girls pregnant, got caught selling black-market cigarettes, were arrested for being drunk, disorderly or fighting, always managed to have it covered up. The most flagrant example was a really terrific draftee trombone player who was up in a room once with two prostitutes. He made love to them both and then tried to get paid for the cartons of black-market cigarettes he had unloaded. They refused to pay him and he got in a fight and cut the tendon in the back of his foot on a piece of broken crockery. He was staggering down the street when he was picked up by the German police, sped to the army hospital and stitched up. The report finally came out that he had cut his foot on a rock while marching. He even got a partial disability pension when he was discharged.

Because we were in the army of occupation we were not supposed to wear civilian clothes, but I bought a funky German suit. I used to sneak off post and go visit members of the Bremerhaven opera company, particularly the horn section. The horn players were fascinated to see someone so young who had already played in an American symphony orchestra and were also very interested in jazz. I became quite friendly with all of them. They used to attend our band concerts and laugh. I also saw my first productions of *Tannhauser, La Bohème* and many other operas I knew but had never actually seen staged. They left a lasting impression on me. When I couldn't risk wearing my one suit, I wore my uniform to concerts. People would generally step aside, look stonily ahead or look the other way, assuming that I must be of the comic-book, gum-chewing, Yo-Yo-spinning hillbilly music set, which was the predominant type of American soldier in Europe. Because I was so interested in music, and knew a little German, I managed to meet many German people, but because Bremerhaven had been so badly destroyed during the war and because it was an American enclave, a very chilly distance was generally kept.

On one of my excursions in civilian clothes I went to a bar that merchant seamen went to and was off limits to GIs. Their jazz pianist was also a fine classical pianist, as most of the jazz musicians in Germany were at that time. I couldn't stand it anymore. I had to play. After the jazz group I sat in with took their break, I began to play the Beethoven Sonata for Piano and Horn with the pianist. As I got to the end of the exposition and was about to go into the development section, I looked down from my music and saw a pair of white-laced brown boots. I looked up in surprise and saw an MP squinting at me.

"All right buddy, what you doin' here?" he said in a high, nasal voice.

"Ich möchte meine Musik spielen," I said in my best newly acquired German.

"Never mind that Deutsch shit with me, buddy," he snapped back. "I know you're an American with that God damn raunchy-looking suit. Even a Kraut wouldn't wear something that looked as shitty as that. Get the fuck over here."

Some of the prostitutes looked up, eagerly anticipating a possible rumble, and a merchant seaman, an extremely superhip Latin, shifted slightly to watch the happenings.

I tried to continue in German, but it didn't fool that MP too much, so I finally blurted out, "Look, man, I'm really going insane. I'm with the band and I just can't stand it and I'm a musician and I don't want to be in the army and if I didn't come down here to play some music I would have wigged out. I'm sorry."

The MP was so astounded by the series of non sequiturs I continued laying on him that he was struck dumb. By this time everyone was watching our confrontation. "All right, buddy," he whispered in my ear. "Just get out of here pretty soon and get back to the base," and with that he left the bar.

I stayed the rest of the night. We finished the Beethoven sonata and played the Schumann Romanze for Horn and Piano. I had found someone to play chamber music with for the rest of the time I was in Bremerhaven.

Three of the draftees in the Bremerhaven band were really fine jazz players. They were Jimmy Azarello, an alto player; Al Crossman, a trumpeter and arranger from Wallace, Massachusetts; and Oscar Dennard, a drummer. They were really the only free-playing jazz men located on this tiny base. We played together whenever we could, but we found that we could get many more chances to play with German musicians. I used to go to bars like the Ozeana in Bremerhaven, which stayed open twenty-four hours and had women that looked like they were right out of Little Abner: prostitutes on their last legs who spoke GI English and were interested in jazz. I used to sit in with the accordion player, who would do the best he could with boogie-woogie, which was for him the epitome of modernity. Because I had a scraggly mustache, the prostitutes would scream, "Dere's Harry Chames. Play dot horn!" Toward the end of the night they would usually end the music session by saying, "You better get you ass back before nineteen hundred, soldier, or you gonna be up shit's creek." I found more intellectual stimulation in other areas of the city.

In addition to the composing I was trying to do at the time, playing at these bars kept me alive inside somehow, and allowed me to forget the depersonalized feeling that the army gives everyone. In the spring of 1953 our little band was invited to Hamburg by the North West Radio Rundfunk to play in a jazz concert. Compared to Bremerhaven, Hamburg was like Mecca. It was a beautiful, sophisticated city with a real cosmopolitan atmosphere. The opera house was gorgeous and the radio station had the best acoustics of any place I had ever played in my life.

The real outlet for most classical and jazz musicians in Europe was not of course the army but musical activities that took place among the German musicians, who were all very kind to us. Even though I was in the army, there was a certain feeling of at-homeness as a musician that I never had known in America. Most musicians and composers I know who had been in Europe felt this way. It's because music is an organic part of life in Europe, not a distraction or something "good." It's something natural.

The whole feeling of our radio concert that night was one of naturalness. The audience seemed more relaxed and at home than any American audience I could remember, even though jazz is American music. They seemed to feel they were not coming to hear jazz but rather to hear music. Wolfgang Sauer, a blind German who sang like the old blues singers, was first. Then came a group with Jutta Hipp, a beautiful red-haired pianist who was called the Billie Holiday of Germany and one of the few great natural talents I ever met. After she played, our band played one of my arrangements based on *Till Eulenspiegel's Merry Pranks,* pretty corny now in retrospect but funny at the time. It was a big hit and we were asked to play on several other German stations.

While we were recording programs for these stations I had the chance to meet many German musicians, actors, radio announcers and directors. They all knew so much of what was happening in American art, music, theater and literature that it was embarrassing for me to realize how little I knew about what was happening in contemporary German culture, outside of the low life I had seen as a soldier.

I began buying German newspapers and magazines and in the process of reading about the new Germany improved my German.

In addition to playing concerts and boat jobs, our big band also played for special military occasions—whenever visiting dignitaries would come to inspect our base or for funerals or presentations of decorations. The last were the most moving. I remember one in particular, a forty-five-year-old private first class who had been recently busted down from master sergeant while he'd been stationed in Bremerhaven for talking back to an officer when he was critized for not having some of his equipment shined properly. Ironically, he was now being awarded the silver star for gallantry in action two years earlier in Korea. Seeing this leathery man standing at attention while his incredible acts of heroism were described was heart breaking. I could see how, in spite of his personal valor, the system had beaten him down. While he was brave enough to carry several people across a field being raked with machine-gun fire, he was not able to contain the anger at the hazing he received by his superiors, who had not been involved in combat and were determined to bust him. He had a kind of dignity standing there and I'll never forget his figure—the middle-aged PFC. We used to call him "Pop" and I was shortly to achieve the same rank that he had.

I made PFC almost to the day I was eligible and I was told again by the first sergeant that if I kept quiet and didn't bother anybody, I might even be able to be a sergeant before I got discharged, with broad hints that I should think about reenlisting. I made the mistake of informing him that I had heard about the Seventh Army Symphony and that I wanted to know how to apply for it because I felt I was qualified.

This set him into one of his famous snarls of rage. "You ain't goin' with no symphony or nuttin', motherfucker," he informed me. "No man ever get outta this band and you not goin' be first." The warrant officer came up to me that night, his soft, red face sputtering with fury, and he told me that if I thought I was going to leave the band to get into the Seventh Army Symphony, I was crazy. The general on the post had already been informed that I was indispensable and I was not eligible to apply for auditions.

This really made me sore. That night I went to the service club and began a series of phone calls to Seventh Army special services outside of Stuttgart. After a month or so of this I was told by the conductor of the symphony that I could not get out to take an audition. But because he knew I played with the National Symphony and because some of the musicians who were already there knew about me—an order was going to be sent down by a general who outranked the general of the Bremerhaven post, transferring me to the Seventh Army Symphony. He instructed me not to say anything about it so as not to upset anything—just wait until the order came.

One day in the middle of June, the magic news of my deliverance arrived. I received orders to be transferred from the Bremerhaven Band to Seventh Army special service headquarters. I was then to be reassigned to a phantom company, an artillery outfit I never saw until a few days before I was discharged fourteen months later.

The members of the band were stunned when they heard the news. I was the first person who had ever been able to transfer out from under the evil aegis of the first sergeant. Some of the guys in the band gave me a party, which was only marred when Harris, the saxophone player and a hopeless alcoholic, began rolling down from the top of the hill where we were wining and broke a rib. Otherwise it was a typical army party, with everyone getting deliriously drunk to escape the horrible imprisoned lives away from women and all the good things we were forced to leave.

I went down to say good-bye to the musicians in the Bremerhaven opera. They gave a performance of *Tannhäuser* again. Afterwards I went backstage and sat with the musicians, talking about music and different styles of orchestral playing. The German horn players had a whole different way of playing, using a very muted style. We were in a discussion about the techniques of playing with a clear, bright sound for French Impressionist music and modern music as opposed to the dark sound for Brahms and the robust sound for Wagner, when suddenly one of the clarinet players in the Bremerhaven Opera came lurching over to me and began a tirade of old hip expressions from the late 1920s and early 30s. "You American, I know you like to play it hot, kiddo. You'll have a hotsy-totsy time here, brother," etc. This was the first of many Germans I was to meet who had worked in America in the twenties and thirties and then had come back and still spoke the kind of slang that was completely outdated except on The Late Late Show.

It was during this final night in Bremerhaven that I realized how much the military experience was accepted and even admired by ordinary German people. Many of the musicians I met and spoke to were generally sensitive, kind, intelligent, gracious and extremely friendly. Nevertheless, they invariably would show me pictures of when they were in the army. They meant this as a fraternal gesture and would show me these photos with a smile. Some of them had been in during the end of the war, when they were only thirteen or fourteen years old, yet all of them had pictures of themselves, shy children looking bashful in their Nazi uniforms. As my friends from the opera were teasing me, I saw how insane the whole idea of army was. Seeing these people who were in the German Army that had killed six million Jews, I still could not help but feel some sense of identification with them: they were also musicians and loved the same life that I wanted to return to.

I told all the musicians that I would be sure to visit when I came back. The Seventh Army Symphony was scheduled to give a concert in Bremerhaven a few months later. Then I went to the Ozeana to say good-bye to the musicians I had sat in with and to some of the prostitutes I had gotten to know on a nonprofessional level. One of the prostitutes, Helga, a tall blonde, gave me her address and made me promise to call her when I came back. Although she made her living from merchant seamen, most of her boy friends and lovers were people in the army. She was fascinated by the politics of status in army life and especially how it existed in the world of enlisted men.

"That's good, Dave," she said, shaking her head with admiration. "You're really going to make it. I understand that symphony has the men out on TDY [temporary duty], but they'll never have to return to their outfits until they get discharged. I think you have yourself a great deal. Be sure and call me when you get back and we'll go out and celebrate. You could probably even make sergeant before you get discharged. There is much more room for advancement up there at Seventh Army headquarters than there is here."

I remember thinking how far-out it was that she was a more persuasive salesman for military life than anybody I met the entire time I was in the army. I took her address and phone number and promised I would call her. I caught the bus back to the barracks and went to see Sergeant Williams to say good-bye before I left. He had grown more and more retiring since we came to the band, a complete loner. It was obvious that they were waiting for him to crack so that he could be busted. But he refused to be antagonized or led into any trap. He was a real Zen master and had his ego so under control that he was always able to differentiate between his inner self and the system that the army imposed on his outer being.

I knocked on his door and he told me to come in. "Well, Sergeant Williams, I guess I'm leaving the band before you," I said.

"That's good, Dave," he said, motioning for me to sit down and offering me a glass of brandy from his footlocker. "You deserve it," he said. And the way he said it made me feel that I didn't. He read this look on my face and said, "I understand how you feel, but you have to understand that I made my choice and I live and die by that. For a black man of my era the army is the best place to be. A lot of my friends are dead or institutionalized or strung out on drugs or still in that MF bag."

"MF bag" is an old musician's term meaning "motherfucker bag," referring to black people who become victims of their grinding poverty and of the ghetto. Without knowing it, they are forced to believe the myths about themselves and constantly act out their own racial stereotypes.

"The only way that the sergeant is going to get my stripes is to kill me," said Williams matter-of-factly while he sipped his brandy. "There is no way they can bust me and if the North Koreans couldn't shoot me out of my stripes, no peacetime master sergeant is gonna bust me out. I think every man gets what he deserves and with all the times I was shot at before I even went into the army and from the background that I came from, I'm doin' fine. You see, I'm a soldier, buddy," he said with a pride that I heard from very few military men but that always filled me with a certain kind of respect. "Naturally, I'm a musician in my soul, but I had to put that part of my soul aside to keep the rest of me together. You see, in seven more years, I'll be able to retire and I'll still be a young man and I have one hundred and fifty acres that will be paid off by then. It's a place a little over seventy-five miles from Phoenix and when I'm not there, daddy, nobody even gets to say my name unless they're especially invited guests. My friends have an open door to come and groove and you know that includes you. And with my retirement pay and with the disability I'll be able to claim by showing them how bad my legs *really* are when I get discharged, I'll have enough money just to work the land myself and grow cattle and a few crops and do some gigging on the weekends. I still have some connections out there for playing music too and I'll be straight. By that time I will have found myself some delicious, young European mama that wants to settle down with an old agriculturally inclined tenor player and we'll groove, so really all this other jive is incidental. My only advice to you for the rest of your short visit as a guest of the army is to cool it, Dave. Don't try to fight it because that's like trying to knock out the ocean by punching at the waves. The only way you can make it in the army or in life is to let a lot of the nonsense wash right by you. It's going to be there anyway, so it's necessary to even pay a lot of things any mind. The time to make your stand is when it's something that really concerns *you*. *All* of you if it is something that is life and death, *period*. You see, if I'd gotten upset every time somebody called me nigger or if some of the crackpots in Korea said I was a soldier of the imperialists or whatever abuses people try to lay at each other, I wouldn't even be here today. You dig? But seven years from now I'll have my scene cooled out until I die and then we'll see where it's at. That's why a cat like this sergeant and this warrant officer or all the stooges they have in the band can't even touch me. They are speaking to a land baron and they don't even know it."

By this time we had drunk most of the brandy and it was almost time for me to get up and start packing. Then, as a piece of final advice, he said, "Remember the other day when you were sparring with Crawford?"

Crawford was one of the musicians that Williams had told me was a boxer.

"He wasn't beating up on you because he knew that you were a French-horn player with good chops. In the future if you entertain any thoughts about fisticuffs, don't drop your right hand when you throw your left jab because if you do, someone's going to left-hook you in the choppers so hard you'll never be able to hit any more high notes. In fact, my advice to you, Dave, is to quit boxing and just continue working out and doing the exercises. You have a nice face and can bag young, groovy chicks till you're fifty if you keep in shape, so why get it all smashed up trying to prove you're a man? If you want to be a fighting Jew, serve in the Israeli Army after you're done with this army and be a hero that way, you dig?"

I suddenly saw what he meant. Since that day in 1953, while I continued working out, exercising, doing road work, calisthenics and all the exercises boxers do while in training, I've never been in a fight. It always seemed ironic to me that I learned this kind of pacifism from a professional soldier.

I thought about my first sergeant as I left. I couldn't hate him. He was doing his job and doing it well. He was a professional soldier, just like Williams. I was an amateur.

It was the army I hated, and the fear of him I felt deep inside. The shame I felt at being afraid filled me with hatred and violence. I thought I had lost all of that long ago, but I hadn't.

The train rocketed off. When we finally arrived at Stuttgart I was amazed by how beautiful and modern the city was. Bremerhaven was still in ruins from the war, but apparently Stuttgart had been so badly bombarded that an entire new city was built. The gleaming white buildings with their modern designs were stunning. I took an army bus from the train station to the Seventh Army headquarters. There I was told to report to Sergeant Berry. As I was climbing the last flight of stairs to the top of the barracks, I heard a confusing mixture of sounds. A cellist, a violist and a bassoonist and several violinists were all practicing at the same time, a brass quintet rehearsing Hindemith's "Trauermusik," a jazz band somewhere and two or three hillbilly guitars with amplifiers twanging aimlessly away. As I got to the entrance I could also hear some actors shouting out Shakespeare, and a lot of other voices yelling, laughing and carrying on.

I got to the top floor and witnessed a panorama of total confusion. The wall lockers were covered with pictures and reproductions of paintings. Even though it was in the afternoon, the barracks were in a complete mess. All the musicians, whom I assumed were members of the Seventh Army Symphony, had long hair and were wearing sloppy, half-army, half-civilian clothes. I noticed one fellow playing the cello who was wearing an air force uniform and another cellist with a French uniform. Also, I saw an old Filipino sergeant cooking a great-smelling rice dish on a hot plate and a young private who was reading *Steppenwolf*. He looked at me and said, "God, what a great book this is," and then went back to reading it before I could say anything. Next to him was a giant stuffed bear on wheels which was tied to his ankle with a rope.

"Excuse me," I said, "I'm supposed to report to Sergeant Berry."

"O.K.," he said, putting down his book. He led me to a door, then giving it a kick, said, "Sergeant Berry, get your fat, white-trash, cotton-picking, ex-paratroop, cracked-vertebrae, derelict, ice-cream–scooping, tired, old Kentucky homebody ass up off of your government-issued bed and give this poor boy genius some advice."

I was astounded. I'd never heard a private speaking to his first sergeant in this fashion.

"Ah, come on," croaked the sergeant, sounding like Andy Devine. "I'm trying to get some sleep, Wolfram. Quit bugging me."

"Get your ass up," said Wolfram. "I say, get that ass from thy battered bed or I will flush thee down the head."

"All right," said Sergeant Berry in his croaky, persecuted voice. "What's your name, son?" he said to me.

"Private David Amram US52192619 transferred from . . ."

"Never mind all that shit," said Sergeant Berry wearily. "Just try to find an empty bed and take it. This place is a mess," he said in a confidential tone, although it was rather obvious anyway. "I've been in the army seventeen and a half years and because I stopped in the third grade they're trying to throw me out, but I'm going to make it and get my pension. You know, I never saw anything like this sympathy. That's what we call it, 'The Seventh Army Sympathy,' har, har, har," and he burst into a hilarious cackle.

"Ah, shut the fuck up, you old fat fart," shouted the young, sensitive-looking violinist with black horn-rimmed glasses who was practicing the Kreutzer Sonata.

"That's no way to talk to me, son," said Sergeant Berry. "I thought you guys that played that sympathy music were suppose to be cultured. You see, I'm in charge of all these special-service barracks. This room is the Seventh Army Sympathy. The next room there are the hillbilly entertainers. These here shows have traveled around Germany. We got stand-up comics, magicians, a tap-dancing team, there are three gospel groups, some rhythm and blues bands and God knows what else. We had some great stars here. Eddie Fisher was here," and then Sergeant Berry proceeded to read off the names of the show biz greats who had passed through the portals of these sloppy barracks. "I don't know what would ever happen if there had been an inspection here," he said nervously. "We have an agreement with the commanding officer, Captain Gonsalves, not to have any inspections and in turn for that the guys always tuck their hair into their hats when they go to play at other bases."

I found an empty bed, got out my horn and started practicing. There was so much noise and activity in the barracks that I didn't think anyone had noticed me. Then a short, pugnacious-looking fellow came over. Eyeing me with fierce blue eyes, he said, "I'm Bill Gaffney. They call me 'Spike.' I hear you used to box too."

"Yeah," I said. "How'd you know that?"

"Some of the guys told me about you when you flattened that guy in basic training. I was in the artillery band with somebody who'd been in basic with you. I was going to continue boxing myself," he said, "but one day I got the instructor mad at me for not doing what he said and he knocked me out. After that I decided to quit boxing."

"You're right," I said. "I quit myself."

"I play the oboe," he said. "If you want to play some duets later or play some chamber music, let me know. We don't start rehearsing for three more days. I was in last year and, man, it's the greatest. We get to travel all over Germany and do whatever we want to. This is the best job in the army and the orchestra is really terrific sometimes."

Just then Sergeant Berry came out and shouted in his croaky voice, "Chow time. Get them egg. Get them egg!" A booming chorus of "Get them egg. Get them egg" rolled out from everyone in the barracks, but I noticed that only about five people started for the mess hall. The others dropped their instruments, their books, their music or got out of bed and started rummaging in their footlockers. Suddenly I saw that almost everyone had his own hot plate like the Filipino sergeant I had seen and everyone started cooking in the barracks. It was a wild cross section of gourmet delights and in about forty-five minutes the whole barracks was filled with the delicious aroma of home cooking.

Spike invited me to eat with a viola player named Midhat Serbagi and his brother Richard, who was the man I had seen wearing the air force uniform. He had somehow transferred into the Seventh Army Symphony as a cellist. No one was quite sure how he or the air force ever got away with that one. Midhat had prepared some Umjedra, an excellent Lebanese dish. We talked about all the news of the group of young musicians that we knew who were around our age. It turned out that almost everyone I met in the Seventh Army Symphony knew almost all the other young symphonic players, composers and conductors of my age group. I also ran across Sergeant Lou Blackburn, whom I had not seen since I was at a jam session with him at Camp Kilmer, and many other musicians who were now in special services whom I had jammed with briefly somewhere or other before or during the time I was in the army. For the first night since I had been in the army—and it had been almost a full year—I went to sleep feeling pretty good.

Two days passed and finally it was time for us to rehearse. An hour before rehearsal, about twenty more soldiers came in. They had gone to different countries on furloughs. Some had forged passes and came back under the fence. Some had gone on pot-buying expeditions to places as far as Holland. Three or four just came into the barracks to get their instruments and find out the schedule. One of the soldiers had been living off base with his German girl friend for the last six months and had also taken an unofficial five-month vacation with her in Greece because he played the violin so badly that the conductor thought it would be better not to have him around.

We went to rehearsal. Actually the orchestra was amazingly good. Three of us, James Cook, James Tankersley and I, alternated playing first horn. The first-trumpet player was Kenneth Schermerhorn. He played as well as any trumpet player I could ever recall hearing in my life outside of the great Marchand and I found out later that Kenny had studied with him. The strings of course were a problem, as they are in most orchestras, but the players we had were excellent for the most part. There just were not enough of them.

In typical army fashion there were also a few men who had never played in any kind of an orchestra in their lives but somehow were put there. One trombone player who was fortunately about to be discharged couldn't even read music. His specialty seemed to be getting outrageously drunk and after several hours of going "hee hee hee hee hee" through some kind of delirium, dripping his 240-pound hulk onto the floor from the top of his bunk. He would then pick himself off the floor, take his trombone into the men's room and urinate into it, after which he would fall asleep in the shower. I don't know what the Marquis de Sade would say of this exhibition, but unfortunately his showmanship was a lot better than his musicianship. The whole time he sat there he never made a sound; he just moved his slide back and forth. We all covered for him because we didn't want such an eccentric soul sent back to his outfit to be crushed by military life.

During the rehearsal the conductor told us, "Now, gentlemen, we have our favorite tenor, one of the great tenors of the century, our own Captain Gonsalves." All the soldiers applauded and to my surprise, a short, rather good-looking, intense young man came up and sang some arias from *La Bohème*. He was a remarkably good singer. By having a first-class orchestra to accompany him, he was really getting his kicks in the army. Possibly for that reason he was letting us get away with murder when we weren't playing. I also found out that another major motivation for his concert performing was to pick up women, which he was quite good at, even when he wasn't singing, but apparently, as he confided to us later, he found a higher type at concerts than he did at the officers' club.

We rehearsed for almost eight hours. I was pretty exhausted by the end and had a headache as well. I had never rehearsed that much in my life. And while the other musicians were exhausted too, it was really fun because we were young men all doing what we loved to do. I certainly didn't feel like I was in the army anymore.

During the next two weeks we rehearsed as much as eight or ten hours a day getting our repertoire organized. We were to tour many concert bases and some civilian places as well. We were told that if we did as well as we hoped to, we would be invited to the Passau Music Festival and possibly be continued on a permanent basis. It really got to be like one big family. Many writers, comedians, comics, jazz musicians, gospel singers, actors, acrobats and sword swallowers and even a great trio of harmonica players who lived with us in the barracks are still friends of mine today. All of us hated the army for the same reasons. While we were regimented in music we were devoted to something with real standards that required real ability and was involved with a real idea.

We piled onto the bus and began a five-week tour. We played many small army bases, some civilian concert halls, and once were driven to a completely empty field with no stage, no chairs, no lights, no music stands, just a field with a few cow pies in the middle of a farming area that the United States Army was using for its spring maneuvers. A troop of soldiers in full field uniform marched over the hill and sat down. We had to play from memory with everyone standing up, which was quite difficult for the cellos. At some outdoor concerts the violinists would stop playing because they were afraid the glue in their fiddles would melt from the sun. We played one concert for a group of mentally disturbed patients, two or three of whom became violent during the fast movement of Schumann's Spring Symphony. In almost every case the concert would be preceded by a speech by some officer in that mechanical, nasal, honking, dry, rasping military voice, spouting out doltish clichés.

During our first tour one or two musicians were discharged and one or two replacements would show up. The conductor of the orchestra, Andrew Heath, would inform us in a very genteel fashion as each soldier was being replaced.

"Now, gentlemen," he said one time in his beautiful, Harvard tone, "today we are very fortunate in having a fine artist to play the clarinet, Dino Lavelli. Dino is a marvelous clarinetist and I think you'll be thrilled with his approach to orchestral playing." Dino stood up and took a bow, looking like Chico Marx with long black curls. He had wide brown eyes that were popped open most of the time, a look that comes from sniffing cocaine. He also had a certain kind of nervous dart to the eye that you see with many young guys who spent a lot of time in reform school. Dino sat down, the first clarinetist graciously offering him a chair. But as we played, the shouting, squeaking, squealing sounds that came out of the clarinet made it clear that the army had made a mistake again.

"Jesus Christ," Dino said after rehearsal, "I never played that kind of shit before. I only used to play in the square-dance bands and Festa jobs up in Massachusetts. There is a lot of good work up there. How are you supposed to play this kind of crap?" he asked, looking around for some advice. "Am I supposed to follow dat guy when he's waving his arms?"

Realizing we had to cover for him the same way we did for the Marquis de Sade trombonist, we gave him a fast lesson in faking. He played third clarinet and spent the rest of his time helping out Ed Murray, a saxophonist who had gotten with the symphony because at one time they thought they were going to do a piece of Gershwin's that used a saxophone. Since the piece was no longer in the repertoire he stayed on as a sort of road manager. Ed was studying to be a pharmacist, so he was our liaison with German doctors in our constant endeavor to keep the venereal-disease rate as low as possible. Dino was very helpful as the assistant road manager except that because of his hoodlum background, he would usually miss the bus when we left town, being with a girl someplace or in a fight or passed out somewhere. He would manage to hitchhike, beg, borrow and once even steal a motor bike to arrive at our next destination in time for the concert.

It was during this first tour that we were joined by Ezra Katzman, a huge pianist who was quite talented except that during concerts he would always get lost and improvise. We found out a few months later that his practice of getting high on pot before every concert didn't seem to help his classical technique too much. He would be so stoned that his mind would start wandering and he would forget which piece he was playing. Once during the C Minor Piano Concerto No. 21 by Mozart, he began playing the opening measures of the last movement of Beethoven's Emperor Concerto. The effect was quite startling and unfortunately we were playing before a German audience and they were rather surprised by this unorthodox interpretation. Realizing the mistake, he began improvising and continued to improvise through the concerto and actually ended up playing the right music with the orchestra for the last twelve bars. After a stunned silence, the audience burst into thunderous applause. Some of the members of the orchestra got together after the concert and thought the next time we played the Mozart Concerto, we would begin the last movement by playing the orchestra part of the Emperor Concerto. But we were afraid that Ezra's mind might not slip into that. Thus whenever we played with him we always gritted our teeth, waiting for when he would begin to start sliding into the other reaches of his subconscious.

He was really the original Mr. Camp of the army, with an incredible air of mock pomposity. He had convinced all the brass in the army that he was one of America's greatest concert artists. The fact was he had worked as a demonstrator in a piano store before he went in the army and really only knew about five pieces, none of which he could remember too well especially when under the influence of marijuana. Yet the esteem with which he was held by the military establishment was unbelievable. When the officers would give speeches before our concert, they would include phrases like the "very famous and fine," "real well-known piano player" and "first-rate, top-drawer musician" Ezra Katzman will play his interpretation of that wonderful number, "The Twenty-first Mozart Symphony Concerto for the C-Minor Piano." During these long introductions, Ezra would be preparing himself, puffing away on his last poke of grass before coming out to slaughter whatever piece he was going to play.

We completed our tour and the reports were so good from the military bases that it was decided to extend the orchestra for at least six months. This met with a great round of bravos from all of us because it meant that we could stay together and play music and not have to go back to our old outfits. We were told that we had been invited to play at the Passau festival. As resident orchestra we were to play two Menotti operas, several concerts, Carl Orff's opera *Die Kluge*, some chamber concerts and accompaniment for one of the ballet companies. We spent three terrific weeks in Passau working on all this interesting music. When there was time off from rehearsals, we would jump in the Donau with the native kids and let the swift current sweep us down about a half a mile. Of course we had to be careful not to land on the other side because that was East Germany. Apparently this had happened and not too many people had come back.

I also had the chance to play first horn in *The Barber of Seville*. It was a complete production with a great deal of time spent rehearsing, so I had a chance to really study the opera and realize for the first time the brilliance of Rossini's work. I saw that in addition to his impeccable clarity of musical expression, he also had a true dramatic instinct. The way the opera was staged, I saw the possibilities of writing modern opera in a way where the music was of paramount importance. The atmosphere of great music and true dramatic situations eliminated the necessity of gigantic sets, opulent costumes and all the things that I felt instinctively were such an encumbrance to most American operatic productions.

We had some late-night jam sessions with the Black Watch bagpipers who were performing at the festival and also had a chance to meet the beautiful dancers from the Spanish ballet company. Some of the musicians later took furloughs to visit these girls in Spain.

Because the orchestra was so well disciplined by this time and because we played with such a spirit, the impression we left was strong enough to get us offers to play all over Germany. We began a schedule that was unbelievable. Because almost all of us were in our early twenties we could take it and, in fact, we enjoyed it. My friends Spike and Midhat bought an old Mercedes-Benz and we used to follow the orchestra bus in our car. Sometimes when we would have a day off between concerts, we would forge some passes, syphon a tank of gas out of an obliging army vehicle and roll off to visit an interesting country. There was always a concert to be heard, an opera to see, a ballet production or an art museum. We would stay up all night, drive to see whatever we could and somehow get back. The amazing thing is that no one ever missed a concert, came in late or played badly. There were so many fine musicians in the orchestra that we made sure that the music was the important thing and not the army.

It was at this point that Captain Gonsalves decided that we should be militarized a bit. By this time my nickname was Long Hair, because I had managed not to have it cut for the six months I had been with the orchestra. I had devised a system for piling it under my cap so that when I lifted my cap off my head, it would all fall out like a mushroom. It was so long by this time that even German men, who had long hair themselves, were shocked. We were also quite boisterous and not too discreet sometimes in our behavior when we were visiting other army installations. Often when we would show up at an army installation we would be greeted by derisive shouts of "There comes them symphony faggots." But by nightfall we made sure the best-looking girls ended up with us. I remember one tortured, perplexed-looking thirty-year Regular Army man who obviously fancied himself as a great Casanova staring in disbelief as some of us returned with some of the young German lovelies after a concert. Up to this point I think he was convinced that everyone that played the violin must be a homosexual. He was almost in a state of shock.

Suddenly with a revelatory spark in his eye he said, "I know how you guys do it. I heard about you musicians. You all eat pussy!"

Because we had created a good reputation in a musical but not military way, Captain Rodriguez was forced to assign a lieutenant to travel with us and whip us back into shape. His name was McCauliffe. He was a business student who had been in the ROTC, a typical ninety-day wonder, fresh-faced, pompous, innocent, about our age but with one-hundredth of our experience. When he first arrived he immediately demanded an inspection. We all stood at attention, trying not to make him appear foolish. Most of us looked like survivors of Valley Forge by this time, with holes in our clothes, long hair, small beards, goatees, mustaches, frayed shirts, unshined shoes and corroded buttons.

As he began to interrogate David Moore, a great Negro bass player, listing off all the violations of military dress, David, a master put-on artist, kept saying, "Yes sir, yes sir," in a crisp, military way. After about the two-dozenth violation, he suddenly boomed out in a low voice, "Yes suh! I do dat fo' you, massuh. You is my white Saviour!" This completely blew McCauliffe's ROTC mind. Convinced that here was a simple Negro soldier trying to make a career in the army but led astray, Dave's Amos and Andy completely destroyed him. He jumped back in disbelief and fright. We didn't want to be cruel, but a roar of laughter went up that was deafening. Poor McCauliffe turned completely red and ran off the inspection field.

That was the only inspection that we had. Two nights later he was out with us drinking after the concerts. We clued him into the way of charming the girls. Being semi-brainwashed by the military way of life, he would usually start up his conversation with local women with "I understand that you are proud people. It's an awful thing when a proud country like Germany must lose, but in defeat you can still maintain your dignity and pride. We of the United States Army are here to help you find the freedom you all desire. We are here to help you maintain those ideals that millions died for. The sacrifices shall not go in vain. By the way, would you like something to drink?" Then he would stare at the floor, turning red and shuffling his feet, trying to think of something interesting to say. Usually after the first five minutes of his openers, the girls would walk away.

After spending some time with us he gave up his military routines entirely and in about three weeks was a changed man. His uniform was sloppy, he was laughing all the time and was living the romantic life that his Calvinistic forebears would never have dreamed possible. Instead of the missionary converting the heathen, McCauliffe went native himself and the Seventh Army Symphony continued to play and live in its inimitable style.

After almost seven months of continuous work and extremely successful concerts, Seventh Army headquarters suddenly decided that the symphony was a waste of time. We had played for German audiences with great success, to the amazement of the critics and a public who only had seen Americans getting drunk, fighting, listening to hillbilly music on their transistor radios and generally being more obnoxious than even the Germans themselves were when they were tourists. In spite of the fact that we were setting a better image of America than any other organization in the army, the military people felt that while it was good to continue the hillbilly bands and the juggling shows, the symphony was not really necessary.

Fortunately our conductor at that time, James Dixon, was the protégé of Dimitri Mitropoulos. When he wrote Mitropoulos about the situation, the Maestro, who had a concert scheduled in Germany, made a special trip to Seventh Army headquarters and spoke to the generals. He was so persuasive that the symphony was continued for several more years.

After this Mitropoulos threw a party for all the members of the orchestra. Incredibly enough, he remembered me immediately. We had a marvelous dinner in a German restaurant and afterwards Mitropoulos had a question and answer period in the great tradition of Greek philosophic gatherings. We would ask him questions and he would ask us questions, often answering them himself. It was a kind of Socratic metaphysical discussion. He told us that as in mountain climbing, where each man depends on the other, so had our spirit kept the orchestra together. By utilizing our positive energies even in a military situation, we could serve our country and also continue to develop ourselves for civilian life. In a few hours he renewed our whole sense of dignity and our faith in music.

He also spoke at great length of how music was a mountain and that every one of us, every musician, every composer, every man-made sound was a pebble in that mountain. He spoke of his own boyhood in Greece, where he was raised by monks, how he studied in Berlin. Much of his success in music was, as he said, being in the right place at a given moment. His chances had come, like so many other conductors', when someone was sick. But, he said, "You not only have to be there, you must be able *to do* it when you are lucky enough to be called upon." He spoke at great length about the symphony as a drama, visually as well as in terms of sound and how important it was to be involved in the music even during the rests.

From that night on whenever Mitropoulos conducted in Germany almost the entire symphony would go if we were anywhere even remotely nearby. He was always delighted to see us backstage. He remembered most of our names and he also asked me to show him anything that I was writing. All of us were deeply impressed by his great spirituality and his realness. He made us all decide that if *he* were a general, we would follow him into battle to death if necessary.

Shortly after Mitropoulos visited us we began a tour of cities in northern Germany and I noticed that Bremerhaven was on our schedule. I was really excited because in a sense I felt like a local boy making good, coming back home to my old haunts. Many of the people from the band had left, but I wanted to see those that I liked, including Sergeant Williams and George Napuda, the horn player with the huge mustache. I wrote Helga a letter and told her I would call her when we arrived. None of the other members of the symphony had been in Bremerhaven before except when landing there originally.

As soon as we got there I went back to the barracks to visit and get some belongings I left there. Unfortunately there had been a flood in the basement and all my letters, music and reproductions of pictures were destroyed, including some compositions that, I must say in retrospect, I am not too sorry to have lost. I asked about Williams. Unhappily, I was told that he had been busted to a private, transferred out and was in an infantry unit somewhere around Orleans in France.

Going back to the barracks and seeing people I had known was like returning to a prison. I saw how grim and horrible the atmosphere was and couldn't believe that I had spent nearly five months there. Most of these men, when they were not cowering under the tyranny of the miserable first sergeant, spent their time in their rooms drinking, talking or masturbating. It was a depressing atmosphere. I had to leave. I invited all of the guys to the concert. I had also invited the people from the opera house, and with three hours or so until the concert, I went down to the Ozeana and saw the afternoon shift of prostitutes, some of whom remembered me. In the seven or eight months since I had left, they all seemed to have aged incredibly.

One in particular remembered me. "Hey look," she shouted out, "dere's Harry Chames, but he don't got his mustache no more and he got long hair now. Shit, look at dot soldier's fuckin' hair," she bellowed with glee. "Buddy, if you don't shape up, get a crease in you pants, shine dem shoes, get dat greese ofen your tie, shine dat brass and get back to der barracks by oh-seven-hundred, your ass goin' be in a whole lot of trouble, buddy."

She was interrupted by one of the other lovelies at the bar, "Slim ain't mit de band no more. He mit der symphony now. He mit de big time," she said seriously. "God damn," said the first one, "you some hot shit now. Come here and let me kiss you," she said. Remembering her baroque sense of humor, just as she was about to place a smacker on my cheek, I turned to the side in time to avoid her high-heeled shoe kicking up into my groin, a specialty I recalled watching her perform on some of the poor love-starved enlisted men while I sat in with the band. "Hee hee hee hee" she said, "you remember me real good, don't you?"

I called up Helga. She really sounded glad to hear from me and was happy that I had written her. "My boy friend is leaving tonight," she said. "I'll come to the concert and we'll go afterwards and have a good time and I'll pay for everything."

"That's O.K." I said. "I've saved some money and I was going to do the same for you."

"Listen," she said, "you done real good. I was afraid you might be doing stockade time because you always had that wild look in your eye like you might fuck up real bad, but it sounds like you're doing O.K." Even though I had not really known her except seeing her by the boats with her bicycle as the different customers would leave for their ships, her voice sounded very warm, as if she was genuinely glad to speak to me. I really felt as if the concert we were playing in Bremerhaven were a command performance before the European heads of state. We played in the same hall where I had played my first concert with the Bremerhaven band and it was beautiful. I wasn't even nervous when I played the famous horn solo in the slow movement of Tchaikovsky's Fifth. Horn players had good days and bad days. There's really not much you can do to control your feelings. I was so happy to be back and hear myself play in that hall. I could see how much I had improved as a horn player since I had arrived in Germany more than a year before and it gave me that extra confidence. The conductor, James Dixon, had me stand and take a bow at the end.

Afterward we all went out and made the rounds. I sat in with every band in town. Then Helga said, "Come on. I'll take you home with me and have the cabdriver wait outside my house until morning and he will drive you back to your bus."

"Wow," I said, "don't do that. That would cost you all kinds of money."

"Come on," she said, "old friends are best and you're a good one." On the way back in the cab she started to talk about music. It turned out that she was familiar with the work of almost every composer from Monteverdi up through Anton Webern and Schönberg. She knew a lot about contemporary music and many procedures used by contemporary composers. Like so many of the people I met in Germany, she had a very fertile, well-disciplined mind and even though she was a professional prostitute, she was more stimulating to talk to than many women who are involved in more legitimate occupations. After spending the night with her, I hated to leave, but by this time, after thirteen months in the army, I was used to saying good-byes.

I found out that the following summer I could be discharged from the army in Europe. If so, I would have a chance to play the horn for the America Houses and tour Germany as a civilian. The America Houses were an excellent group of small cultural centers sponsored by the USIA throughout Germany. Of course I leaped at the opportunity and when I was asked for one reference, I gave Mitropoulos' name. While I was in Berlin I was assured that I would have a job touring and playing the Mozart Piano Concerto and the Brahms Horn Trio after discharge from the army. My experience in the army was turning out to be more helpful to my work in music than I could have imagined.

When we went to Austria we played Tchaikovsky's Fifth again for the last time. Sitting in the same hall where I had seen the Vienna Philharmonic perform a few weeks earlier, I was terrified at having to play. Fortunately, I managed to calm myself by staring at a gorgeous girl in the third row. When she looked at me with gigantic green eyes out of the Middle Ages, I got so Zenned-out that I almost forgot to start playing.

By this time the symphony was at such a high level that it was better than many of the professional orchestras in Europe. Because it was now made semi-permanent, auditions were held and excellent musicians were being accepted. The standards were higher, but it lacked some of that campfire spirit and insanity that had made it so attractive to me when I first arrived.

When we came back from Austria and had a few days off, I was asked by someone in the special services to write some incidental music for a play they were doing based on a James Thurber story. The adapter was Buck Henry, and Paul Lief was the director. Paul told me what was needed for the play, which included a small ballet with two swisher-dancers who had managed to pass all the army entrance exams and were having a ball making it with each other and everybody else they could lay their hands on. They were very knowledgeable about music, however, with a very good understanding of rhythmic problems. There was so little time that we all agreed it would be best if I wrote the music to the choreography. So we went over the entire dance, counting the steps together. Then I composed music that fit what they were already doing. I completed the whole score in four and a half days, staying up day and night, with some friends helping to copy the parts for xylophone, timpani, clarinet, bassoon and French horn. It was to be a special performance to show all the Seventh Army big wigs the high caliber work that was going on. Since the symphony had already performed so much, this time they wanted to show all the dramatic talents that were part of our Patch Barracks madhouse.

We rehearsed for a day and a half and everything seemed very well synchronized. But just before the performance was to begin I looked around frantically for Rick, the clarinet player. It was time for the overture, but Rick was nowhere to be seen. He was apparently down in a trailer with some gypsies and had forgotten about his performance.

"Get Kenny," I said frantically. I knew Kenny Schermerhorn could sight-read the clarinet part on the muted trumpet, transposing it down an octave when necessary. While someone went to find him, a colonel came backstage in a cold rage.

"Why don't you begin, soldier?" he questioned me, his voice filling the whole backstage with the cold, dry depth of his withered, sexless soul.

"I'm waiting for the clarinet player, sir." Surveying the scene like General Sherman about to burn Georgia to the ground, he turned his eyes toward me and said, "It looks like you got the musical personnel here to do the job, soldier. Let's get on with it."

"Listen, Colonel," I said, "I'm the composer and I wrote this music for certain instruments. If the clarinet player doesn't show up, someone is coming to play his part."

"I don't care what you wrote it for, soldier," said the colonel, zeroing in for the kill. "If you don't start playing by the time I'm in my seat, you're going to be doing some stockade time, and if you don't get a haircut by the next time I see you, you might do life." With this he stalked off. Just then Kenny came bursting in with his trumpet. We played and although the muted trumpet didn't exactly sound like a clarinet, the music went quite well. It was the only composition of mine I had performed in the army except for a few jazz tunes.

Rick came back the next day to apologize and tell me about the wild scene he had had with the gypsies. To pacify me, he invited me down to the gypsy trailer and gave me an enormous reefer, made of a German newspaper rolled up like a huge cigar full of pot. He then introduced me to a lovely gypsy girl in the adjacent trailer. We smoked up all the pot, not wishing to leave any incriminating evidence lying about. The trailer camp was rocking that night.

Whenever the symphony had a few days off, we would go to the Jazz Keller in Frankfort. This was Europe's number-one jazz hangout. No one ever worked there for pay except the waiters, but musicians from all over the world would drop in to play when they came through town. Midhat and Spike would gas up their old Mercedes and we would take off, zooming down the Autobahn. Usually, Fred Dutton, our first bassoonist, squeezed in with his bassoon case and bass. He had recorded with Dave Brubeck and was my unofficial instructor in chord changes. We also played jazz duets with horn and bassoon, which really knocked out everyone at the Keller. Midhat and Spike would sit around, meeting the local lovelies, while Fred and I were wailing away.

One morning as the dawn rose over the shabby streets of Frankfort, all of us were walking back from a session when suddenly Jules Greenberg, a percussionist in the orchestra, turned to me.

"Hey, Dave. Today's Yom Kippur. Let's go to temple, just like the old-time Jews used to. Up at dawn, and spend the day in prayer."

"Solid, Jules," I said. "I need some soul." We left everyone else and walked to the broken-down old temple in Frankfort, Germany. The building was scarred by bullet holes and attended by perhaps fifteen or twenty poor, ragged Jewish elders, the pitiful handful left of what had been a thriving Jewish community before Hitler. As we went through the service and I saw these old men sitting there, I began to see my father's face and my grandfather's and my great-grandfather's and my great-great-grandfather's, of whom I had a daguerreotype at home. He had come from Echte in Germany. These people really were my brothers. Perhaps if my great-great-grandfather David Moses Amram had not come to America I might have been in that synagogue or more likely dead by the hand of the Nazis. Still, this was not an experience that created blind hate toward the Germans or any kind of nationalistic sensation. It was rather one of a deep identification with people I knew were my own.

The man in front of me had a beak nose, sallow face and burning eyes. He was a Jewish working man, with enormous yellowed hands, probably a butcher or a laborer. His croaking voice reminded me of my father. My father never sang this way when I was around, but I heard him sometimes when he was alone in his room. There was something in this rough singing that really got to me.

I began to listen more closely. This singing and moaning and wailing really moved through my entire body. And I knew what they were singing. It was about the whole experience of myself and my ancestors. In these shabby surroundings with a group of survivors who would die and leave no offspring, I knew that I had heard for the first time the Jewish experience as expressed through music. It was simple, eloquent, wailing, the kind of feeling I had in my French-horn playing since I began the instrument. I always made such a melancholy sound that even my teacher Abe Kniaz, used to tell me not to play so Jewish. It was also something that had attracted me so much to jazz, a kind of a wail, an old, deep, beautiful feeling that came from way way back.

Jules and I stayed all day. I felt as if waves were rising and breaking over me each time a prayer was said or music was sung. The rabbi had a great, full white beard, ancient eyes and long white fingers that fluttered when he prayed. He reminded me of the Rembrandts I had seen at the National Museum in Washington.

After the services were over, Jules and I went to speak to the rabbi.

"New York? New York?" he asked, looking quizzically at us, deep into our eyes.

"Philadelphia. *Wir sind von Philadelphia.*"

"Good boys. Good boys," he said, and gave each of us a hug.

We went out on the street and walked for a while in silence. Then we spotted a second-floor restaurant where we knew that a post-Yom Kippur crowd would be eating up a storm. I was so hungry from fasting I got dizzy at the sight of all these people wolfing down their food.

"I'm starving," said Jules.

"Me too," I said, and we went upstairs and had a feast.

Because I had officially taken only two days off since I had been in Europe, I had almost a month's furlough time coming. Adley, a wild bass player, and I decided to go to Rome. We planned to meet there, so I took the train by myself and couldn't believe how beautiful Italy was compared to Germany. When I first got there I spent most of the time studying the antiquities, since my major had been history. I really pounded the streets like a seasoned tourist.

One day when I was alone in an art museum, I saw a beautiful young girl with a camera case. Feeling the irresistible urge to meet her, I went up and said, *"Come si chiama questo in italiano?"* She answered me in Italian, but I quickly discovered she was German, so we began speaking in German. Then in English. Then in French. She also could read and translate Ancient Greek, being an archaeology student. We decided right there in the art gallery to go to Greece together. She had to go somewhere first so we arranged to meet at the youth hostel in Catania, Sicily.

I arrived at this small fishing village before she did, so I struck up a conversation with some of the local boys. Most of them had never spoken to any Americans and somehow, with my broken Italian, they got the idea I was a fisherman. My hands were calloused from carrying so many bags around. So when they felt them, they thought they were seeing a genuine American man of the sea and got very excited. They all brought their brothers and sisters down to meet me and recited lines from their English books like "The horse and carriage wait outside for you, sir." Apparently the educational system was training people to be servants, nineteenth-century style. They also told me about the fathers' cutting up the faces of boys that went out with their daughters and warned me not to come on with any girl. I ate seaweed out of the water although I can't recall the name of it and we had a kind of jam session with the kids in the village who played different instruments. One thing I also found out to my delight is that while the Sicilians were very proud and terrific fighters, they all hated the army as much or more than I did. We really had a wonderful time.

Finally the German girl, whose name was Ilse, showed up. We took the train to Brindisi and from there a boat to Greece. Because she knew Greek fluently, we were able to visit all the antiquities and she could translate everything immediately. We visited Aegina, Suniom, Delphi, Marathon and many of the magic places that made Greece the most moving, spiritually, of any country that I've ever been in in my life. I felt at last that I had returned to something that was deep and ancestral in me.

One day I told her how awful I felt having to wear a uniform, which automatically branded me as being an overfed moron in a peacetime army, while there were friends of mine in Korea getting shot at and sometimes killed. I even thought the color of our uniforms was ugly. She suddenly said, *"Unsere waren schön."* (Ours were beautiful.) I estimated that she was five years old when World War II ended. Her father was a very successful lawyer, her mother a well-known scholar. But the strain of German militarism, stupid pride and chauvinism was apparently ground into her as well.

When we left Greece I told her I wanted to see her in Germany. "You have to wait until you get out of the army," she said, "I can't see you when you're wearing a uniform. I would be disgraced if I were ever seen with someone in an American uniform. You have to understand that."

Suddenly my sense of proportion returned. It was just like the first day with my head shaved standing out in the rain. I was still just a soldier, a digit. Of course this is a tremendously valuable experience to share with other people. Guys who have been in jail have a certain kind of jailhouse wisdom. People I had known who had been in reform school, smugglers, numbers runners, dope pushers and other people in outside groups—all had a certain kind of perception and vision that was more acute than those whose lives moved in ordinary circles. But I think that the army also kills something in most people which takes them years to recover. And the peacetime army is particularly degrading. Its atmosphere forces everyone to act in the most brutal and selfish terms, the philosophy being to find the easy way out or fake it. Rather than teaching discipline and making a man out of you, the army destroys one's manhood. I think it has wrecked more characters than it's helped.

I finally said good-bye to the army at a great big party, where I was presented with a jacket especially made up with master-sergeant stripes, hash marks for fifty-two years' service with every medal awarded plastered on one side plus a tremendous series of marksman's medals stretched all the way down the other. On the lapels were sewn "RA all the way," "God Bless Mother and the Home" and a big dollar sign. I wore the jacket around the base with the orchestra silently cheering me on, but when an MP threatened to lock me up, I had to take it off before I could get over to the Seventh Army headquarters.

I was sent to my phantom artillery unit with my French horn. They were dying to process me so I would be discharged on time. They had never had anyone receive a European discharge before and were frantic for fear they'd be one second late and get in trouble for costing the army extra paper work and money. I was told to go out and do extra work, cleaning up the lawn and so forth, but I decided that I had done my all for the army. For nearly two years I had been playing professional solo horn at $105 a month. Someone else would have to clean up the cigarette butts and wash out the toilet bowls. I told them that it was against my convictions to obey orders anymore and went into Frankfort to see some of my friends. I saw many musicians and found a place to live after I was discharged, a great apartment right next to the railroad station.

Finally my discharge papers were ready. Packing all my belongings in a big straw box and duffel bag, I walked out the afternoon of August 6, 1954, two years minus five hours, twenty-seven minutes and thirty-five seconds from the time I had gone into bondage. My heart was soaring. I was going to Frankfort to move into my great apartment, where I would write music, play jazz at the Jazz Keller around the corner, eat Jutta Hipp's goulash and visit the friends I had made in Germany. As a *civilian*. No more uniforms, no more restrictions. I felt as if I had been shot out of a cannon. I realized for the first time what it meant to be free and how lucky I was to be more involved than ever with my music.

I knew I would have much harder roads to hoe but I had made it through the army. I thought about three friends of mine who had been killed in Korea and another one who had been killed in Germany in a training accident. I also thought of my cousin, Dave Powell, a beautiful trombone player, who had been blown to pieces in World War II. Nothing was ever found of him but his dogtag. And I thought about all my relatives who had been fried or gassed to death in Germany. I loved America and would go home someday. I even would go out and fight if necessary, but I could never serve again in a peacetime army.

As most people who served in the military know, for some reason your mind blots out every memory except the enjoyable ones. To this day I still can't remember seeing a friend of mine wounded in basic training although it happened in front of me; or some of the brutal beatings that I saw given in the training camps in Kentucky; or the name of the guy next to me in basic training who had such a bad knee he could hardly walk but because he was Sicilian and couldn't express himself well was almost beaten to death because people thought he was shirking. When he was finally sent out on maneuvers in the middle of the winter, he almost died of pneumonia right in front of our eyes before he was finally taken to a hospital.

The army probably trains more people into becoming adult delinquents, arsonists, rapists, homosexuals and criminals of various types than any other force in the country. Anyone who's been in the army knows it's probably the most destructive and degenerate atmosphere a young man could possibly be put into. It's controlled by people with a death wish, people whose impotence leads them to acts of incredible sadism. Maybe the best solution for our country would be to take convicted murderers, rapists, muggers, arsonists, criminals, homocidal maniacs and homosexuals with a violent nature and have them as a professional full-time army. This is essentially what the Foreign Legion was like and they were certainly an effective group of hired assassins.

I'm afraid the image of John Wayne charging with his carbine over his head and his shirt off had vanished forever as a symbol in my mind. In fact, I knew it would never mean anything again to young people in this country.

I was lucky enough to continue with music. Many fine musicians I knew were not so fortunate. Excluding those who were killed and those who came back maimed or with ruined nervous systems, many never recovered from the years of forced layoffs from practicing and playing during crucial, formative years of their youth.

The only other solution I thought of on that memorable night was to draft all super-patriots over sixty-five into the army. Many such men seemed to have a war-like nature, judging from comments I had heard. What an idea: a senior citizens' army of sadistically inclined shuffleboard players!

Even though I had enjoyed boxing, and even though I like to fish and I own a gun, the army made me a confirmed pacifist. Of course because of my army training, I know many ways to cripple or maim. This is one achievement I take no pride in. Most musicians I know feel the same way. From living together in our music we learn brotherhood, harmony, compassion, love and the elevation of the spirit through the joys and sorrows expressed in so many different kinds of music from so many different kinds of people all over the world. If Western society can ever catch up with the message of its music we may still be saved. And if the world's generals and statesmen could all get together for a jam session or some chamber music, more good would be accomplished than wrecking young people by training them in the art of legal violence.

"Jutta . . . I'm out, I'm out!" I shouted as I ran into the tiny room where she was staying. I could smell some of that excruciating goulash that she was cooking while I was running around the room, hugging her, laughing and dancing. Jutta finally got me to sit down and eat some goulash. I went out to play with her on her job and after that we went to the Jazz Keller to have a big celebration with Albert Mangelsdorff, his brother and all the musicians I had met during my time in Germany. I felt like I wanted to stay in Europe for the rest of my life. I was so disgusted with the army that I didn't want to go back to America again for a long time. Every place I had been to in Europe, I felt at home. Whenever I walked down the street with my horn, people seemed to understand that I had a skill, something that was important, possibly something that might even give them some pleasure. All over Europe, music was so much more a natural part of every person's life. It was not "culture" or something you forced down people's throats like castor oil. Rather it was as much a part of their life as baseball is of ours. Everything was so much older and as I was becoming increasingly aware that I had an old soul, I felt I'd come home again. And now that I was a civilian in Europe for the first time, I felt this oldness even more strongly than ever.

My landlady was a staunch old German type who loved music and the horn, was interested in jazz and took a keen interest in my compositions. She was also very critical of the different girls I would bring around to visit. If she thought they were not up to her high standards, she would give me a tremendous lecture on the value of maintaining one's social position. She had a remarkable lack of judgment of character and would end each lecture with the statement *"Aber ich bin kein Engel"* (But I'm no angel). To pacify her, I used to play a few choruses of "Over the Rainbow" and if that didn't work I would try the overture to *Tannhäuser*.

After I had been in my apartment for a while I became very adept at hanging from a pair of rings that were attached to the ceiling. They were like the rings used in a gymnasium. I found it was a terrific way of clearing my head when I was practicing or composing. I got so that I could hang upside down for three or four minutes. At night I would watch the astonished faces of the people from the tramcars going by. They would look out from their window and see me staring at them upside down from the ceiling of my second-story room.

It was during one my upside-down athletic demonstrations that Jay Cameron arrived with some friends, dancers and musicians, from Paris. He told me that I should come work with him, at least for the Christmas holidays. I had met Jay at the Jazz Keller when I was in the army. He was tall, extremely thin and looked like a cross between a farmer and a scarecrow. Even though he was constantly living on the edge of disaster, he had a kind of Olympian calm, gentleness and maturity that I found in very few jazz musicians of my generation. He had played alto when I first met him, but since he had moved to Paris recently he began taking up the baritone seriously and had gotten into a deep study of harmony and harmonic substitutions. As I went through my athletic paces, Jay introduced me to a whole new world of chords and chord substitutions.

"You've got to come to Paris, Dave," he told me, "that's where it's really happening. It would groove you much more than Germany. It has comfortable living, a chance for you to work with your classical music, horn playing and compositions too. Deutschland is passable, but Paris is so soulful you'll never leave once you get there. The French are so hip in every way it's unbelievable. Not only intellectually but musically—the way they dance, every way. Next to New York this is *the* city, and you'll be there in time to catch just that last bit of post-World War II cosmic cheer."

I had felt all this during my two brief visits to Paris, but I had traveled so much in the last few years that I thought I'd like to settle down in Germany until Christmas, at least. I showed Jay my schedule. "Man," I said, "I've got to play Brahms's Horn Trio in twenty-three different cities in these America Houses all over Germany. And I want to go back to all the cities where I played when I was in the army and see them as a civilian, visit the musicians and go back to the art museums and be in these places just as a person, not as a soldier."

"Groovy," said Jay, "but don't forget Christmas Day, we've got a gig. Here's my address." Jay gave me his address and phone number. I talked to his friends in French and broke out a huge bottle of the nearest thing I had to French wine, a gigantic container of liebfraumilch.

They finally had to catch their train, so we weaved off to the bahnhof. I said good-bye to all of them, knowing that I was going to see them all soon. Before I went back home I sat down in the station to order a bite to eat. But after a while I noticed the waiters kept looking at me in a strange way, talking among themselves and not filling my order. Finally the head waiter came over and spoke to me in French. At that point I realized that I had given my order in French. Grinding my brain cells back into German, I ordered some herring and sour cream, wolfed it down, skipped my post-midnight visit to the Jazz Keller and collapsed into bed. In a few days my tour for the State Department would begin.

I had concerts in almost every part of the country, crossing and crisscrossing familiar trails that I had ridden in army buses, on trains, hitchhiking and in the old beat car that Spike and Midhat and I had traveled in. Because of Mitropoulos' recommendation, I was able to choose the musicians I wanted to play with. I got the violinist Lewis Kaplan and pianist Thomas Hutchings, both of whom had played with the Seventh Army Symphony, to be my companions for our concerts. I was also able to wangle the services of Midhat, who volunteered to come along as page turner. He was thinking of changing from violin to viola, and trumpeter Kenny Schermerhorn, now the Seventh Army Symphony's conductor, was nice enough to let him leave the symphony for a while to go on tour with us. We had a rigorous schedule, but being young, enthusiastic and ambitious, we liked it.

When we played in front of German audiences we would walk on the stage and already their bodies seemed to lean forward, so eager were they to listen. From the moment that the first sound was made, there was an almost deathly hush. No matter where we went in Germany, there was always this incredible hush and a tremendous kind of listening that was different from anything I'd ever experienced before. All the times I had performed the Brahms Trio in Washington, the musicians and myself always had to concentrate like mad, fighting the static of people laughing and shouting at my parties or staring out of the windows when we played it in a regular concert situation. There were certainly many people in America like myself who loved music so much that they would die for it, but they were always in the minority. Here in Europe it seemed so natural that it seemed inconceivable that people all over the world would not appreciate music this much. It made Lewis and Tom and myself play better than ever before.

Often after the concerts I would run across many of the German jazz lovers that I knew from the many hours I'd spent jamming in my trips through Germany. There was one terrific jazz club in Heidelberg called The Cave. It was really just like the students' caves must have been hundreds of years ago. And somehow it had the cultivated, buoyant atmosphere that I imagined the authentic old Heidelberg must have had in the days of the real Student Prince. I didn't expect to see the people inside singing and swaying and clicking their glasses to Sigmund Romberg's music, but I did notice that there was a much lighter and cheerier atmosphere here than most of the places that I had been to in Germany. The girls were exquisite and even the American soldiers that were there seemed good-natured. A tenor player from the Midwest who played a lot like Lester Young, an MP sergeant in the army, a wonderful German jazz bass player, a visiting Dutch pianist, an English drummer and myself began cooking. We played till only eight or nine people were left, then went out to an apartment and spent the whole night talking.

The entire atmosphere of The Cave and of the apartment we went to was different from that of most of the other big German cities I'd been in. The people were extremely open-minded, and didn't have the patronizing attitude I often felt Europeans had toward Americans. They were the most liberated Germans I had ever met and I was fascinated, listening to them describe what they felt would be the new Germany. The man who had the house was a professor at the University of Heidelberg. He and his young wife felt that a whole new generation of people were going to create a world in Germany that would be free from the terrible, stiff, inhibiting traditions that created the master-servant relationship among different classes and allowed someone like Hitler to take over.

As I listened to all this I kept thinking of the time I was going to a session at the Jazz Keller. About a block from the bahnhof I noticed a policeman and a huge crowd of people standing silently by. I went up with Carl, a native of Frankfort and a fellow musician, and we saw some cops beating a man. As the cops were pushing him into the back of a police wagon, they kept poking him with their clubs and kicking him and twisting his arm while he howled in pain. The police seemed to be enjoying their work. I'd seen police something like this before in America but never this rough. But the thing that really amazed me was that in a crowd of several hundred people, there wasn't one sound. They were standing, watching a perfectly harmless-looking man getting almost murdered and they seemed to be approving of the policemen's efficiency.

"Jesus Christ, stop it!" I yelled out.

"Why don't you quit that?" yelled Carl. Though I noticed that he was speaking in English.

"You Nazis!" I yelled out. I couldn't help it.

"Stop that, you Nazis!" yelled Carl, also in English.

People looked at us coldly but still silent. They then turned back and stared in silence as the policemen took the man away in the back of the police wagon. I could still hear him screaming in pain; they were obviously still beating him. This is what I was afraid was the attitude that was going to make it difficult for a new Germany to have much of a chance.

When I told this to the professor, he laughed.

"That's the whole point. It's the passivity and blind respect for authority that makes the Germans potentially dangerous. We're not violent. We're too easily led."

I stayed an extra two days in Heidelberg and every chance I had during the time I was in Germany, I would come back to The Cave and visit the professor and his wife, in addition to a lovely girl I had met there who was attending the university. The morning before I left, after the girl had made me a tasty *frühstück,* the great German cold breakfast, I lay back in bed, thinking how much like a king I felt, being taken care of this way. Just the little things that she and other European girls did, like pouring cream in my coffee, really knocked me out. They were such tiny things, things you would never ask a woman to do, and yet they seemed to want to do them just for the sake of pleasing a man.

Suddenly she turned to me and said, "Have you noticed how cold our generation is becoming?"

"What do you mean?" I said. "I don't feel cold toward you."

"You know what I mean," she said. "It's all so impersonal, everyone seems so cold and dead and even lost. You have so much life. That's because you play music and you can express something."

"That's not true," I said, "I just dig being alive, every heartbeat is a groove. Jesus Christ, I could still be back in the army. I'm just so happy to be free, I feel like I'm flying all the time."

"No, no, that's not what I mean," she said. "If you were a woman you would understand. There seems to be no poetry or romance in general in the world. Tell me honestly, Dave, have you ever been in love since you left the States?"

"Sure," I said. But I thought about it and I realized I hadn't really been. With all my traveling about, my romances were often short-lived and dependent upon where I happened to be and whom I happened to be with. It all seemed so natural in my circumstances that I had never thought about it before.

It was during one of our sessions at the Jazz Keller that I met Gunther Schuller. He had heard of me through John Lewis, whom I met in Rome when I was on a furlough and who knew about my playing. Gunther, who in addition to being such a fine composer, was an excellent French hornist and had always been interested in jazz. He liked my playing and told me to call him when I came back to New York or write him if I needed any advice. He said he would help get me into the Manhattan School of Music to study horn with him and composition with Vittorio Giannini. I think if it hadn't been for my association with jazz, I never would have met Gunther this way and perhaps would have delayed my return to America.

It was also during this time that Bird was supposed to come and record in Germany and I was supposed to be in the session. But he tried to commit suicide and never made it over.

Albert Mangelsdorff, a marvelous trombonist whom I had jammed with many times at the Jazz Keller and I formed a group. Between my engagements for the America Houses and my writing, we played quite a few concerts. One notable one was in Heidelberg for a gigantic audience, followed by another all-night session at The Cave, followed by a post-mortem philosophic seminar at the professor's house. Albert had a way of making the trombone sound as much like a horn as I could make the horn sound like him and we made several records for the Armed Forces network when we got back.

As we continued our tours with the America Houses, we noticed that there never seemed to be any American officials present. Everytime we went to play at a new America House, the German people would say, "We're terribly sorry, but Mr. and Mrs. So and So wanted to come to the concert tonight, but because they were ill or had a previous engagement . . ." or some other excuse. Finally when we came to the America House at Frankfort, one of the people who worked at the America House turned out to be an old Jazz Keller aficionado.

"Tell me what's happening, man," I said, "the Amerikaners don't seem to be hip to the big new sounds from Doucheland." This was the name that some GIs and hipster Germans who had a good sense of self-deprecating humor used when they referred to the Fatherland.

"Well," he said, "you can't expect to see those guys here. They might come out to hear Elvis Presley or Lawrence Welk. They don't want to hear no Brahms."

"Isn't this a drag. You're interested in jazz and here they are in your country and they don't even want to hear your music even when it's played by us."

"Well, Dave, like they say to the Israeli ambassador, you're a very young nation."

I was ready to visit Paris around Christmas. I had been there once while I was in the army and again for two days to see my sister and her husband when they had first arrived. But I really didn't know anything about it, except that it had seemed mysterious and beautiful and seemed to cross my mind more and more during these five months that I had been out of the army. I had been in Germany for almost two years now. I had been to more than a hundred cities and knew people in every part of the country. I knew some of the landscapes and city streets better than I knew many parts of America. I learned different accents and different dialects of the different parts of Germany, so that I could tell where someone was from by hearing them speak and how they were dressed. I admired the incredible industry that seemed to fill everyone. Still there was something that I knew was wrong and I could feel it in most of the German people I had known outside of the musicians. I sensed the new spirit, and the professor from Heidelberg and his wife were talking about it in many of the young people. But I also saw an enormous blind spot. In any kind of discussions that even tended to remotely relate to their possible responsibility for the horrors their country had wreaked upon the world, the ultimate answer seemed to be "Well, we are Germans." This was always preceded by the fact that they had been fighting the Russians, that they liked America and how terrible it was to have Hitler but that really he wasn't much different from Churchill or Roosevelt and that all world leaders were responsible for many of the atrocities.

Also, many older women after asking me if my mother did not miss me and if I did not want to go home to her, would say, "Why did you people bombard us?" I must have been asked this fifty times in restaurants, railroad stations, railroad cars, run-down restaurants, everywhere. The greatest line I had heard was two days before I left for Paris. A girl came up to me and said, "I hear you're leaving us for a while, Dave. Well, I certainly shall miss you, you're one of the greatest musicians we've had come down here. I loved the way you play jazz."

"Thank you," I said.

"It's amazing that you can play jazz so well."

"Why do you say that?" I asked.

"I never realized that you were American," she said. "I didn't think that Americans could play jazz that well."

In the last analysis, the places, the few people I'd grown close to and the musical experiences I had in Germany were priceless. I said good-bye to everyone as fast as possible because I hated sentimental farewells. My last time at the Jazz Keller we had a celebration drink. Everyone said, "We know you'll be back, Dave," and I knew they were right. The next morning I walked over to the bahnhof with all my belongings stuffed into my straw box and went to Paris for the weekend. I brought my box along just in case I wanted to stay. I stayed for almost a year.

6

I ARRIVED in Paris December 24, jumped into a taxi and asked the driver to take me to the Left Bank or wherever else he thought I could find a cheap place to stay. After stopping at two or three run-down hotels, we went to a tiny hotel on rue Monsieur le Prince. I got out and when the concierge showed me what she assumed was a charming room, a little larger than a phone booth with a wall-to-wall pistachio-colored moldy rug covered with wine stains, I eagerly accepted, paid the driver, took in my gigantic straw box and called up Jay. I was ready to wail.

It turned out that the owner of the bistro where we were engaged to play that night had decided he wasn't sure if he was going to pay us or not until he saw how many customers were coming for Christmas Eve. This was hardly the Yuletide spirit, but I found it common procedure among the French low-life type of businessmen, especially when they knew they had a bunch of desperate expatriates working for them. But in spite of this initial setback Paris was so fantastic I decided it would be my second home for the rest of my life. The lights, the international army of lovely girls and the food surpassed any dreams I had ever had of paradise.

I made the rounds with Jay, sitting in at all the jazz clubs which were then going strong: the Ringside, the Club St. Germain, the Mars Club and the Hôtel des États Unis, which became our personal after-hours spot.

New Year's Eve I worked with Jay, the French pianist Réné Utreger, and Kansas Fields, the drummer, who had left America years ago. We played at an American air force installation and as I spoke during intermission with the Frenchman who worked in the cafeteria, I realized that in some ways I felt closer to him and to the American musicians like Jay and Kansas, who had had European experiences like mine, than I did to the men who were stationed there. But even though I was still bitter about the army, when I heard those accents it made me homesick inside in a way. Hearing those dusty voices from Kentucky and West Virginia, the crisp, cold New England accents from Boston, Maine and New Hampshire, the honeyed croon from the Deep South, the old cow-puncher drugstore-cowboy twang and drawl of the westerners—all the voices and sounds of these guys and the innocence most of them had in their eyes made me realize on that New Year's Eve that America was my home and that somehow I loved it, even though I didn't understand it and felt lost and out of place there most of the time. I had the first inkling that evening that I would have to go back some day.

After the job was over I talked about this to Jay, who smiled his philosophic smile. "I'm not ready quite yet," he said, "and I know America is not ready. If neither of us is ready there's no point in my being there. I think I'll probably be ready way before America is, and when I am, I'll go back. As far as I'm concerned any place I play my horn is home." As we drove back from the air force base and approached Paris, I saw those shining, winking lights almost like a huge flying saucer ready to take off. Although I missed America for the first time, I certainly wasn't about to leave.

At my first place in rue Monsieur le Prince the concierge used to wake me every morning with *"Monsieur Amram, vous êtes en retard, vous savez?"*

"Ja, ich weiss," I would answer and mumble something else in German. I was used to waking up and speaking in German and I would automatically do this before switching into French. Then I would drag myself out of bed, usually past noon. Often the door would open a few inches and I would see the darting brown eyes of the concierge's daughter peeking in while she dusted the door or used some other pretext to see who had spent the night. The daughter was very pale with black hair and dark brown eyes. Although she was only twenty, she already had that wise, slightly worn-out, sophisticated look that so many French girls had. She had a high, clear, virginal voice and we used to have many discussions about the most mundane events while she was presumably dusting something. We surreptitiously eyed each other, talking about French Indo-China, the beauty of the

Italian landscape as seen from the train, how cold it was that winter in Paris and other assorted excuses for flirtation. I knew that if I made one false move, I could be shot, jailed or deported. Still I found her lovely and enjoyed knowing a girl I could talk to in this way, if only for a change.

After about a week the girl introduced me to her father, who looked like a stereotype Frenchman from an old Marx Brothers movie. He actually wore a beret, had a huge cigarette holder with which he constantly was smoking Gitanes or Gauloises, and rivulets of leathery wrinkles on his face like an animated French prune. He would squint from behind the clouds of smoke, punctuating every four words with *"n'est-ce-pas?"*, making it impossible to disagree with him. Sometimes he glanced at me and then at his daughter and zoomed back again just to check out the action. There wasn't any, of course, except for the muted vibrations that passed between us. His monologues reminded me of Clarence, the Nantucket cook, except that they were not as interesting. Both his daughter and his wife would sit quietly without yawning, shuffling or looking bored, never saying a word. If nothing else, he was really the man of the house, even though his wife apparently handled the business details and everything else.

After about ten days the conversations became so long that I thought I had better move. I hadn't come to Paris to listen to this man talk. I began to have visions of being locked in my pistachio-carpeted room, handed food once a day by the daughter as she did her dusting, then being put into a strait jacket and confronted with her father for four hours of monologue a day until I finally went totally mad.

I found a beautiful place at 50 rue Mazarine called the Hôtel de L'Université. The room was even smaller than the one I had at rue Monsieur le Prince, but it was less expensive and had not only a toilet in the hallway but a small bathtub! This was really living. When I told the manager that I was a composer and musician she was thrilled and engaged me in a long discussion about the musicians and composers she had known. She also told me of a piano store where I could rent a piano for four dollars a month complete with candle holders on either side. When the piano was moved into my room there was hardly room for anything else. But it didn't matter. I ran out, bought some candles and sat there in the warm, flickering light. It was really too much. I felt all I needed now was a quill pen and a white wig and I could really join the masters. I also figured it would create a great atmosphere for girls, especially when they asked me to play my latest composition. Of course, because of my limitations as a pianist, I would improvise about forty-five choruses of the blues. But they would invariably say, "How marvelous to be able to write down your thoughts in music." At first I would try to explain that it was possible to compose music without being able to perform it on the piano, especially if it was for thirty or forty instruments that didn't include the piano. But this thought seemed to elude too many people, so finally I gave up and whenever I was requested to play something I'd light the candles, sit down and start wailing.

The neighbors in my building were a kind of United Nations of cheerful ex-patriots and lost souls. There were actors, dancers and singers who were traveling through Europe from all parts of the world; a wild young Swedish girl who was an amateur occultist and had a great collection of African carvings, shrunken heads, witch doctors' potions, American–Indian magic wands and pictures of swamis. Above all, she loved to cook succulent, steaming Swedish feasts. There were also strange old French pensioners who would salute me and sing like a French horn whenever they saw me; students from all over the globe—a great assortment of sympathetic souls.

Across the street was some kind of decorating firm, and I noticed the fourth or fifth night I was there how beautifully the apartment above was decorated. As I was admiring the home, someone whom I presumed was the owner of the shop came in with her lover or husband or whoever it was. I didn't consider myself to be a Peeping Tom, but I was hypnotized for an hour by a theatrical production that was really an education. After that I kept my curtains down at night so I could get some work done. But if I would open them to let some air in about ten thirty any night, they would inevitably be there, cooking away in a great display of bon vivantism.

Around the corner was a wonderful French market. With the little money that I had, I would buy huge chunks of cheese, *vin ordinaire,* vegetables and a little fish. Ravenous with hunger, I'd often eat most of it before I even got back, to the dismay of my more gourmet-minded French neighbors. I would also watch the wine trucks while they were making their deliveries. The working men occasionally sampled their wares by slugging down an entire bottle of wine in one series of ecstatic gurgles. After being conditioned by countless books and movies to respect the highly refined European palate, it really did my heart good to see these working men socking down bottles of wine as they stood in the back of the truck. It definitely helped me overcome my American-oaf complex.

There was a marvelous restaurant right around the corner from me called Sous L'Arche. The French working men would come in there in their undershirts. It looked just like Renoir's Luncheon of the Boating Party, which I'd seen so many times at the Phillips Art Collection in Washington. Perhaps because of this casual atmosphere, the few French musicians I took there recoiled in horror. But in spite of occasional cockroaches on the floor and the somewhat gamy atmosphere, I thought I had hit the top gourmet spot in Europe. For ninety-five cents you could get a complete dinner with wine. And right around the corner was a *frites* place where you could get a pile of French-fried potatoes and a small steak for even less. I was in heaven. The only other restaurant I had been to was an Indochinese restaurant and in spite of my sturdy stomach, I got so sick that I was immobilized for two days.

I continued making the jazz scenes with Jay, who introduced me to almost every musician who was working in Paris. Some of them, like Henri Crolla, remembered me from the few brief days I had spent there on furlough. There was a group of us who were playing what was then the new thing in jazz. Since Charlie Parker had come to Paris for his concert in 1949, there was a legion of confirmed Bird lovers all over France who felt they could no longer play in the style of the twenties and thirties. They included Raymond Fol and Martial Solal and Maurice Vandair, three brilliant pianists, and Henri Renaud, who, while he didn't have the technical facility of the other three, knew all the tunes and created a great groove while he played. There was also Pierre Michelot, a bassist who was as good as I've heard anywhere, and one drummer, Jean Louis Viale, who was familiar with the technical advances in jazz that Max Roach and Kenny Clark had introduced. There was also an extraordinary saxophone player, Barney Wilen, who was sixteen at the time. and a tenor player named Bib. Because none of us was working very much we used to have sessions almost every day. We would go to various musicians' apartments, hotel rooms or basements similar to mine in Washington and work out the new musical ideas that were just becoming familiar in Europe. I would often play piano if one of the regular pianists couldn't make it, and began to apply the different voicings and harmonic ideas that Maceo Hampton had clued me into back at Camp Breckenridge in 1952. I found that the more I worked, the more versatile I became and the more variations I could find on the few simple chords that were the basis for all the music we were playing. From the simple basis of a few major, minor and diminished chords, a whole vocabulary could be created that went beyond what Ravel and Debussy had achieved harmonically. By using—or at least hearing—the counterpoint, I saw it would be possible to employ these elements consciously in composition much as Milhaud and Stravinsky had done at one point in their development.

The more I played at these sessions, the more I could hear in my head at night a kind of music that I realized one day I would have to write. The pieces I was writing were still much more traditional. I was afraid to use in my compositions the feeling that was becoming so much a part of my life. I wrote a great many jazz tunes and sketches where I used these ideas freely, but I was still not ready to commit myself to using this part of my vocabulary in my pieces. I knew they were there and that someday, in order to create an honest expression of my experiences, I would have to state them musically.

I also found my jazz horn playing was improving since I was playing with musicians who were more musically advanced than my friends in Germany. But my wisdom teeth were killing me so much at this point that I realized that if I didn't have them taken out pretty soon I might not be able to play anymore. Reluctantly I decided that I would have to give up my good times and see a doctor for the first time since I'd been in the army.

Somewhat hesitantly, I decided to tell my sister about this. I knew that one of the beautiful things about her husband moving to the Paris branch of his bank was that they could get away from his family and my family. They could start their own life here. And because he was much more conventional and came from a calmer family background than we did, I didn't want him to think that he had married into a family of lunatics. So I figured it would be best if I didn't see them too often until I got more settled down.

In the state of confusion that I had lived in, I had lost their address. But I remembered the bank he worked for, so I thought I would go and see him. I hadn't shaved for a week or had a haircut since I had gotten out of the army. My one suit didn't look too sharp either. Also, I must have been a little bleary-eyed, because I hadn't slept in two and a half days and was also zonked-out from an eight-hour session I had just completed.

When I walked into the bank I didn't get a very warm reception from the guards. They looked at me as if I were going to pull a robbery or ask for a handout. I asked for my brother-in-law and after some trepidation was led back to the cage where he was selling travelers' checks. I could see he was really paying his dues in the banking business and felt sorry to see him there, a lean, handsome young man from the beautiful hills of Lancaster County, stuck behind these bars cashing travelers' checks when I knew he would rather be out in the fresh air doing anything else. I felt as if I were visiting an in-law in jail.

I stood in line without saying anything. When my turn came he looked up, glanced a little and said, "Yes?" I realized he didn't recognize me. I was going to put him on with a few hilarious routines that I had planned, but I realized as he looked at me in horror that there was not too much possibility for rollicking humor in the situation.

"I just want to find out the name and address of a good dentist from Mari and also to send you both my best. I forgot your number. Excuse me, man."

When he saw it was me he really blanched in spite of himself. He was a true gentleman and would never snub anybody, but it was obvious I was not representing the best interests of his career by my appearance at that moment.

"David, it's wonderful to see you," he said softly, looking nervously about, hoping no one would realize who I was.

"That's O.K., man, we don't have to go through all that," I said. "But just let me have the number at your house and I'll call you sometime."

"I'll tell Mari I saw you. She'll be delighted to know that everything is going so well," he said.

I took the name and address of the dentist that he gave me and called him up right away. I told him I was Mari's brother and he asked me on the phone what was wrong. I told him that I was a French hornist, that my teeth were bothering me and I was afraid that I might have to have them removed.

"Ah ha," he said on the phone and went into a philosophic discussion of the French horn and its use since the time of Bach and how he loved the sound of *le cor,* as it was called in French. I kept

putting money into the phone box as he kept on expounding the
beauties of the French horn. After about fifteen minutes I asked him
if it would be possible if I could see him about my teeth.

"Better now than later, my son. Come tomorrow and we shall
take out those teeth with no pain or discomfort whatsoever." Then
he talked about my sister, what a lovely person she was, what an
exquisite neck she had and all kinds of pleasant sundries. He spoke
like an ambassador from the court of Louis XIV. It really grooved
me to speak to such a civilized and cultivated dentist, especially after
the myriads of hard-working, studious and unpoetic dentists I had
known in America. But I was really more worried about my teeth
than anything else at this point and I double-checked with him to
make sure I had the correct appointment time. I called up Jay and
the other musicians and told them that the few jobs that we had
booked for the next month would have to wait because I had to
have my wisdom teeth taken out.

The next afternoon, I got as cleaned up as possible and brought
along all the remaining money I had saved from the army except
what I had left over to pay my rent for the following month and a
little bit to eat on. The dentist came out to meet me. He was as tall
as Charles de Gaulle and cordial and charming. He looked astonished
when he saw me. I think he had expected to see an imposing figure
from the classical music world. I was obviously not his dream of
the embodiment of one who had played the glorious sound he had
described in such detail the day before. Still he invited me into his
office, looked at my mouth, gave a few pokes and said, "Very
simple, it will be of no consequence whatsoever." He then gave me
about eight shots in the gums and another shot in my arm which was
enough to send me into a state of Nirvana for the rest of the day.
As he chiseled and chipped and wrenched inside my mouth, he continued his conversations about the wonders of music and how attractive he thought American girls were. While they were accused
of being cold and distant, he felt that they were fascinating, charming
and very quaint. I could see he was really a dedicated old lecher and
had big eyes for my sister even though he knew she had just been
married. But because of all the cotton and clamps and hammers I
had in my mouth, all I could do was grunt and groan approval to
whatever he said.

Finally, with a great flourish and display, he finished yanking out
both wisdom teeth and showed them to me proudly. He then instructed

his nurse to put them into a little box so that I could keep them as souvenirs of my pleasant afternoon in his office. Sewing up my gums, he then said, "Come my son, we will celebrate your successful operation of these formerly troublesome teeth." His nurse then brought in two glasses of champagne and he insisted that I drink one. I was still so high that I couldn't feel anything, but I sloggled it down.

"My son," he said, "if you have any pain, take these pills. They will alleviate any discomforts whatsoever."

I thanked him, put the pills in my pocket and staggered out of the office. As I left, a woman dressed in furs approached the doctor. It was obvious he had warm relations with all his patients as he gently slipped his hands underneath her coat, fondling her tenderly while he kissed her on the earlobe. Well, I thought to myself as I lurched out, I guess the French people really do have the right idea about life after all.

The dentist had suggested that I spend a night or two with my sister in case I had any bad aftereffects from the operation. I was feeling dizzy and could hear the pounding of the chisels in my mouth, so I called up Mari and asked her if it would be possible to spend the night at her house. "Sure," she said, "you know we'd love to see you." So I went up to her apartment, walked up the five flights and found out that the heat in the building had just broken down. She was standing there with her husband, shivering. "Come in," she said, "it's wonderful to see you again. You're looking sort of green though."

"That's O.K.," I said, "the doctor told me I'd be all right by tomorrow and in case I have any pain he gave me these pills."

"Have something nice and hot to eat," my sister said to me.

"No thanks," I said, "I'm not hungry. I think I'll just lie down for a while." I lay down on the couch and while she put a blanket over me, I conked out. I woke up in about two hours with the sound of pavement breakers crashing all around me. Whatever magic potion he had given me to kill the pain had worn off. I really felt like I was going mad. My sister was standing over me, as apparently I had been groaning in my sleep. I tried to talk to her, but my whole face had swollen up so much I couldn't say anything. By groaning and grunting she figured that I wanted some of those magic pills the doctor had recommended for me. She gave me the box. There were about eight pills inside and the instructions were to take one pill every four hours. The pain was so severe that I took two and swallowed them. After about twenty minutes of excruciating pain nothing happened. I indicated to my sister that I wanted another one. She looked at me sternly. I shook my head to show her that I wasn't trying to get high but was really in pain. I took a third pill and still nothing happened. She took the pills out and looked at them carefully underneath the lamp.

"Surprise," she said, "they're just aspirin." For the next four days I lay on my sister's couch, groaning and trying to sleep. Her husband tried to be a good sport about it, but after the second day he got a little tired of seeing his brother-in-law day and night whenever he came into his living room, moaning on the couch.

Even though the pain was killing me and I wasn't able to eat or scarcely move, I really felt sorry for him, so as soon as the swelling subsided enough, my sister gave me cab fare so that I could get back to my hotel room. I went into hiding because I looked like I had just gone fifteen rounds for the World's Heavyweight Championship with my guard down the entire time. When I pointed to my mouth and tried to indicate through a series of gestures that the dentist had taken out my teeth, the hotel manager thought that it was splendid. "You'll play more beautifully than ever," she said graciously.

I stayed shut up for about another week. Only Jay and a few other friends came to visit me. I was able to play a little piano although the bouncing around jarred me. I did some composing, but a lot of the time I just spent sleeping. It was the first rest I had had since I had gone into the army over two years before. I pulled some of the books out of my battered straw box and read Ernest Hemingway's short stories and *From Here to Eternity*. I felt that the main character, Pruitt, reminded me of Williams and many other guys I'd known in the army who were idealists and got crossed by the system. I also went through some paperbacks: *New World Writing* and the *Paris Review,* where I read an interview with William Styron. Styron said that a writer's main job was to write and not be too pompous or waste time giving too many interviews. I liked his candor throughout the interview and because he sounded so for real, I bought *Lie Down in Darkness* and *The Long March*.

His style really knocked me out. He wrote almost the way the symphonic composers of the twentieth century whom I admired the most at that time—Mahler, Ravel, Prokofiev, Shostakovich, Stravinsky, Bartók—composed. He had a great mastery, clarity and sweep that I hadn't seen in many American composers' work and I wondered if any of us would ever be able to achieve anything near the power of what our novelists had achieved. I was sure that the jazz musicians already had. The trouble was that jazz musicians were forced to compete in the area of popular music, even though with what most of us earned playing jazz we might have questioned the extent of our popularity.

As I continued reading, I began to think that perhaps someday I would be able to write music that might have some of the quality that I felt in some of these writers I was beginning to admire more and more. I also thought from what I kept hearing in my head that my music could never take the route that composers were supposed to follow in 1955; I could never join others in chasing the ghosts of Schönberg, Webern and Berg. I loved their music, but I was from Pennsylvania, not Vienna. I felt that if I was going to accomplish my dream, I would somehow have to write down what I felt and what I heard and hope that it would have enough impact to mean something to musicians who played it and eventually to people who would hear it.

I became so possessed with this idea that I forgot about my teeth. Between reading and composing, I made plans to set the works of some of our authors to music. I was not sure exactly how, when and where I would do it, but I filed it in that part of my mind that had been earmarked for many, many years for future compositions and I never forgot it. When the chance came years later to write this work, that compartment opened up immediately.

A few days later I got a phone call from Sandra Calder, whom I had taken around to some of our jam sessions. She wanted to know how I was and told me that she was going to meet her father and would I like to come along. She also told me Edgard Varèse would be there. I had known Varèse's music for a long time and had always admired his great sense of color and texture and form. He seemed to me one of the true genuine avant-garde musicians of his time and a man who had a real vision in his music rather than being a phony or a sensation seeker. From his music, he seemed like an artist with a real visionary point of view.

"I'd like to but I don't think I would be very good company," I said. "I look as if I've just been run over and I can hardly even drink."

"That's all right," she said. "Everybody will understand and we'll be among friends."

So we went down to the Deux Magots. It was the first time I had been out since my operation and the first time I had planned to spend an evening in Paris without my horn in my hand. Sandra's father, Alexander Calder, was as expansive and jolly and delightful as his mobiles. His wife was very quiet and obviously completely devoted to him. They were a great couple and made me feel comfortable immediately. After about five minutes of listening to him talk I laughed so hard that I could feel one of the stitches break in the back of my mouth. I had a few Pernods and really felt terrific. He described to all of us the first job he had and how he had complained to the foreman when he was working that the light about forty feet above his head was too dim and was going to hurt his eyes. Because the company refused to change the light bulb, he left the job and began to pursue his dreams.

Suddenly another man, bigger and more bearlike than Calder, came up. He almost knocked over the table, embracing Calder in a big hug. This was Edgard Varèse. He had bushy eyebrows, incredibly alive piercing eyes and a wonderful, expansive quality.

"What do you do?" he said to me gruffly. I didn't want to tell him I was a composer because I felt that I was still too much of an amateur, so I just sat there.

"He's a wonderful French hornist," said Sandra Calder.

"All musicians are idiots," Varèse said, staring at me. I started to laugh. He gave a great roar of appreciation at my response and proceeded to talk for about half an hour about various musicians that he knew all over the world, the different playing styles of the different sections of every one of the major orchestras in the Western Hemisphere. All with great knowledge and affection. I confirmed that night something I had always instinctively felt: a man had to be a master musician in order for the music to sound masterful. Although Varèse was considered in those days far out and obscure, he knew as much about instrumental playing as any musician or conductor I had ever spoken to. He knew and cared as much about the classical works as anyone and had an enormously broad mind for all kinds of music including jazz, which he also talked about with great relish and enthusiasm. His openness reminded me of Mitropoulos and while he did not articulate any great religious or philosophic ideas, he obviously lived them. I felt just meeting him made it worthwhile coming to Paris.

Other people came by to say hello to Calder—writers, painters, artists, musicians I had heard of since my childhood—and I noticed that they all had the same thing in common—a kind of natural openness, frankness and lack of pretense, and particularly great kindness to the young people at the table. Neither their hard-earned reputations, their notoriety nor their years seemed to present any barrier between us. They wanted us to communicate directly with them.

Throughout the night Calder managed to keep everyone laughing. It really made me proud of being an American again. I was happy to see such a group of wonderful people, especially after having been cooped up in my room. I forgot about my teeth and even though the stitches kept popping, I laughed at all the terrific conversation.

About two days later I ran into Jean Davidson, the son of the sculptor Jo Davidson, who was a friend of the Calders. He invited me to a party, where I met another group of people from all over the world who were as educated, intelligent, alive and interesting as any people I had met in my life. Again there was no pomposity or pretentiousness or uptightness. We were all having a ball.

Jean was also a great talker. His range of knowledge about everything was so astonishing that even though there were some beautiful girls at the party that I'd wanted to meet, I listened to him for nearly two hours straight as he displayed the recesses of his exceptional mind. As I listened to him I realized that I would have to read some of the French authors and philosophers he was describing. He traced back the social, economic and political influences that had been brought over to America at the time of the French Revolution. Beginning with Hawthorne, he talked about writers, painters, poets, musicians and how they fought the same battle throughout America's history. It was enough to bend any French-horn player's mind.

While he talked, a beautiful girl with coal-black hair and intelligent, burning eyes came up and sat down next to me to listen. Jean said, "Giovanna, dear," and went right back to where he had left off. She was so wonderful it really made it hard for me to listen to Jean's conversation, as fascinated as I was. She sat completely quiet. I could feel those heavenly, tinkling vibrations emanating from her like electrical charges. Even in my wildest fantasies as a soda jerk in the People's Drug Store, I never dreamed that I would be sitting somewhere surrounded with people like this. My mind was really soaring with all the conversation, the wine and mostly with Giovanna's presence.

After about fifteen minutes Jean paused briefly to light a cigarette, which had been dangling in his mouth for the last half-hour. He had been talking so much that he hadn't had time to light it and both Giovanna and I had been so spellbound by his conversation that we hadn't thought of interrupting by lighting it for him. As he leaned over to strike a match, I introduced myself to Giovanna. Jean, being extremely aware and sensitive, gave one fast dart with his eyes and went over to talk with some other friends.

I found out that Giovanna had just been divorced from a poet, had come from Milan and not only seemed to know more about everything in the way of music, art, poetry, dance, ballet, and politics but also was extremely soulful and down-home, warm and feminine. We arranged to meet the next day and she became my girl friend. She was a few years older than I was and much more sophisticated in every way, but she never lorded that over me. She knew how broke I was and even though she didn't have much money herself she would occasionally get me a meal. When we would make love and hadn't gone out to dinner she would say, "This is Parisian dinner." She would also tell me in moments of passion that I looked like Jesus, which made me a little nervous at first but it clued me to the whole relationship of church and life among so many Italians.

Giovanna also gave me a lot of books to read and told me if I was going to be a composer it was just as important for me to develop my mind as well as my sensibilities in order to make the long haul. "If you're to be a real artist, it's your whole life that's involved," she said. "It's so easy to be a genius in your twenties. In your thirties it's a little harder and in your forties, there's almost nothing left. You have your whole life and you must constantly prepare and discipline your mind and your spirit as well as gratifying and stimulating your senses." She had a great knowledge of classical music and was one of the few people I tried to play one of my compositions for, even though I could not hack them out any better than my father used to hack out the pieces he tried to play.

Just about the time my final savings were running out, I got a job with a great new band that was going to play at the Rose Rouge. This was the club that had started Juliet Greco and other stars. The owner, Nico, had sold it to an enterprising young Egyptian named Paulo. He had long hair that came almost down to his shoulders— quite unusual for French businessmen during that period—and was about six feet four. If anyone kidded him about his hair, he gave them one menacing glance and they generally stopped. He had been a student in Paris but wasn't able to get any of his father's fortune into France, so he had existed doing various kinds of hustling for two years until finally he smuggled in a giant share of the loot. Because of his hustling activities he became hopelessly enamored with the nightclub life and decided that he wanted to form his own club. So he bought the Rose Rouge and decided to install a modern jazz band.

We had seen him many times at sessions, bobbing his head up and down with long locks flopping about, but none of us realized he wanted to start a club of his own. All the musicians liked him because he was a straight person and enjoyed music. To be accepted, you didn't ever have to act hip with musicians. You just had to be for real in whatever way was real for you. Paulo was his own man and we all dug him.

One night he and Sadi came over to a place we were all jamming. Sadi was a Belgian vibraphonist who had run away with a circus when he was a little boy. During all the years he traveled with the circus he practiced jazz on the side, finally bought a vibraphone, came to Paris and began working as a jazz player. He was a great showman, in addition to being a great musician, and when he would hit different notes on the vibraphone, he would sometimes pause, physically accompanying the held note with incredible facial expressions, interpreting the dramatic and poetic influences of each sound that often seemed to give him so much pain to play. The show-business training hadn't gone to waste. Just watching him play the vibraphone was as good as three rings in any circus.

With a good front man who was also such a good musician, Paulo figured we could form the most sensational band of the season. "How wonderful it would be to have something new and vibrant to enrich the jazz scene in Paris."

"Yeah, oui, that's right, man," we all agreed. Most of us were half-starving to death anyway and any job anywhere, especially for money, was a great improvement as far as we were concerned.

"We'll open up in the Rose Rouge in a month," he announced. "Christian Chevalier will write the arrangements. All of you can write some arrangements. We'll have great acts that you can play for, a group of African fire-eaters and dancers I know of and we'll really make the Rose Rouge into a swinging place."

"Oh solid, crazy, groovy, magnifique," came the response from all of us.

"Sadi will call all of you for the first rehearsal," said Paulo. Two hours later the band had been formed. It included Bobby Jaspar, a Belgian tenor player, Jay Cameron playing baritone, Roger Guerin, a Frenchman playing trumpet, myself playing French horn, and several other excellent musicians from different countries. Because rules were still lax we didn't have to worry about work permits. Paulo seemed to be pretty well versed in the kinds of payoff that were necessary. It was hard for us to believe that suddenly we had found a patron of the arts, especially for the art of jazz.

A week later quite a few arrangements were written and we all got together for the first time. The band was composed of enthusiasts who all wanted to play anyway, so the rehearsals would always end up in jam sessions. Paulo was thrilled to see how all of us enjoyed our work. I took Giovanna to some of the rehearsals. She really enjoyed the music we were playing, especially the more stomping numbers. I found the music fun to play but also thought that something of this nature could be done in chamber or symphonic compositions that could really be good music, not necessarily restricted by the four-quarter or twelve-eighths time, which was used in all our pieces. Still, for what it was, it was excellent music to groove by and of course when the soloists were allowed to improvise, especially Bobby Jaspar and Jay, it became real art.

We finally had our big opening and all of Paris' supreme hipsters came: Nico, who had owned the club before, Juliet Greco, actors, musicians, the cream of the nightclub and gangster worlds. We were told we could get about seventy dollars a week, which made us plutocrats in the jazz world. I was down to my last three dollars, so I was thrilled and so was Jay, who had been living like a miser for the last few weeks. Giovanna came and we ate the delectable food that was served for everyone there. The band swung all night and everyone seemed to love it. The acts went over very well and everybody said what a swinging modern orchestra it was. It looked like we would have a lifetime job.

The only thing Paulo hadn't counted on was that the regular audience after the opening night was not Paris' supreme hipsters but usually businessmen from different parts of Europe who came to see cabaret entertainment. A big stomping band with unfamiliar chords, rhythms and melodies, composed of egomaniacs who took as many

choruses and did as much improvising as they wished, was a complete groove to those who loved music. But the ordinary clientele
were looking for something else. They probably would have preferred
an accordion or a violin or a string trio. By the second week attend-
ance had fallen off. Usually when the band started playing we managed to drive everyone out by the second number, except for the
music lovers, who usually sneaked in free to catch our music. The
waiters thought we were terrific. But even though they admired the
freedom and creativity of our new forms they became rather upset
when they had no customers to wait on, since they depended on tips.

We were in heaven, however, and after each night's work, would
run off to a jam session at the Hôtel des États Unis in Montparnasse.
We were accompanied by Paulo, who kept remarking how wonderful it was that musicians would play for no pay and yet enjoy it
as much or even more than the regular salaried jobs they had.

The Hôtel des États Unis was the focal point of all the jam sessions
during 1955. Don Gias worked there, a marvelous ex-patriot pianist.
He loved jazz, was studying composition and by one or two in the
morning was delighted to have people come sit in with him. After a
few weeks it became the Mecca for all the modern jazz players who
came through Paris. We had sessions lasting until dawn. In addition,
the proprietor, Walter Bryant, would stand up and recite some Shakespeare if he was so inclined, inviting any other people who were visiting to get up and perform spontaneously. The atmosphere was so
friendly that as you were playing you could walk out and make a
date with any girl in the audience. There was no wall between the
performer and the audience whatsoever. It was like one big party
all the time.

It was there that I first met George Plimpton, Terry Southern and
what was known as *The Paris Review* group. At the time I didn't
even know that they were writers or remember that *The Paris Review*
was where I had read the Styron interview. They were all there because they loved spontaneous jazz and were having a good time. We
all used to hang out together, having a ball almost every night of the
week.

Somehow I still managed to get up each afternoon, write music all
day, go to my job at the Rose Rouge, then back to the Hôtel des
États Unis at night. These crazy hours were hard on Giovanna, but

she saw how much I was enjoying myself, so for a while she went along with me.

Paulo decided that there was only one way to save the Rose Rouge from going under financially. One night he bounded in before we were due to start work and cried, "I've figured out how to do it. We have a great new vocalist coming in who will make this town alive again."

"Who's that?" we all said.

"Look," he said, showing us a picture of a luscious young blonde that looked as if she had just been selected the beauty queen of some pageant for the most beautiful Swedish girl of the century. We all stood there gaping at her picture.

"*Merde alors*," said one of the musicians, "she doesn't have to sing looking that good, all she has to do is to show up."

"Now remember," said Paulo, "this is going to save us. She is a very good musician, so I don't want any of you to come on with her —you know what I mean—until the job is over. We can't offend her or we'll be sunk. We need a drawing card, and I think Mona can do it for us." He looked at the picture fondly. "Mona McKay, what a beautiful name," said Paulo, shaking his head in wonderment as he stared at her stunning photo. He decided that we would all go out to the airport to meet her and her accompanist. They were just leaving from what we were told was a highly successful engagement in Morocco. Mona had agreed to work in Paris for a percentage of the gate just in order to be back in the city of lights for a while. Apparently she had a rigorous schedule. Jay had heard of her because she had played in some of the theaters in New York years ago. We figured she must have done that when she was in junior high school.

Some cameramen came out with us to take a picture of the band meeting Mona. Jay and I decided that we would change instruments, so I held his baritone sax and pretended to play it while he held the French horn straight up in the air like a unicorn's horn. We all stood around posing as the airplane landed and taxied down the field. We could all see our jobs at the Rose Rouge stretching out for another year and maybe one of us, if he was lucky enough, could spend one night of incredible ecstasy with Mona. Looking at her picture with those large, clear eyes and that lovely skin, you could not only feel her soft, smooth youthfulness, you could even smell her.

A hush fell over the band. We saw a few people get out and way in the background we saw a figure dressed in white accompanied by a man with a beard and an attaché case. Even though it was dark we could see her white suit coming through the night and we were sure it must be Mona. No one else would wear a white suit that tight-fitting unless she was in show business. We waited and waited and finally after Mona came through customs, Paulo went dashing through to meet her. He came back a moment later, his face ashen white.

"Hiya, honey, it was good of you to bring the boys out to meet me," honked a brazen voice like an old Ethel Merman record broadcast over a public address system in a ball park somewhere. Mona came striding out, took one look at the photographer and threw her hands over her face. "Get that fucking camera out of my face," she said. "I'm not made up, Jesus Christ honey. I just come from entertaining five hundred fucking lousy soldiers, holy shit."

We were all shocked to hear the quality of our dream girl's voice, not to mention the language she was using. When she took her hands away from her face we were really shocked. We figured that Mona's grandmother must have come in as a substitute. She must have been at least fifty-five years old and she looked like every year had been a hard one. We looked at one another in bewilderment.

"Hiya, fellows," she said, eyeing all of us lasciviously and giving a little bump and grind. Paulo looked as if all the blood had been drained from his body. "Well," she said, "let's get that God damn picture taken." She jumped in, pulled her arms around Jay and me, and the photographer snapped away as she beamed contentedly.

"Boy, they're rough riding," she honked into Jay's ear. "Those God damn airplanes are horrible. You play French horn hhhhnnnnh-h?"

"Well," said Jay, "not really."

"Well, baby, I hope we can make some money in this joint. I've been on the road since World War II and I'm tired."

We all rode back in the bus in silence. The musicians were taking sympathetic peers at Paulo, who had his head in his hands.

"Let this teach you a lesson, Dave," said Jay. "Remember that you can always retouch a photograph, but you can't retouch the truth."

As we rehearsed that week, however, we could see that Mona really knew her stuff. Her voice was frequently horrible, but she had the real old-time vaudeville show-biz kind of style that could conceivably attract an audience. Paulo was such a groovy guy that anytime he would make a suggestion we would listen to him. But

Mona was not quite so open-minded. "I know what the fuck I'm doing, baby," she would tell him every time he said something. Finally he gave up.

A few people showed up for her opening, but the problem was that the audience was European rather than from the Bronx and they couldn't seem to identify with her style. The French newspaper described her *"La Blonde à la voix de noire"* (the white singer with the black voice), but she sounded pretty Irish to me.

Her accompanist was a real hustler, however, and because he knew some high society, managed to wangle us a job playing in a huge party in a chateau outside of Paris.

"Well, fellows," Mona rasped as we all got in the bus, "we've got it made. We're going all the way to the top." We all liked her by now. She was absolutely straight to the musicians. "Fellows," she rasped, "we're gonna knock 'em dead tonight. We'll be playing for royalty, crowned heads of states maybe, princes, big New York international society people. We'll go in there and do our stuff and who knows? We might even get to play some high-class work. *Class work,* that's what I want fellows." Because most of the musicians were not familiar with these phrases they just nodded contentedly. Our band was really swinging by now and all we wanted was to blow, whether it was in a chateau for the international set or in a poorhouse. As long as we got paid enough to live on.

Sadi took out his bongos and played on the bus. This job had really boosted his spirits because the Rose Rouge was in trouble financially, what with our super hipster band frightening away most of the customers. Sadi felt bad. He couldn't play any kind of music except what he felt. All of us were the same way, but Sadi wanted desperately to please people. He couldn't understand why his band wasn't popular. It was full of wonderful musicians. All the real music people liked it, but it just didn't seem to go over with the public.

"It's too far ahead of its time," he used to say, and shake his head sadly.

The chateau was really gorgeous. A stream flowed through the beautifully manicured lawns. There was a great main house, small houses on the side, old servants' quarters, beautiful beds of flowers and a whole area next to a lake especially constructed for the party. A massive green hedge circled around the back of us and the bandstand was over in the corner. We started to play and people slowly ambled toward us.

It was the most freaked-out collection of faces I'd ever seen in my life. Most of the men looked like cadavers. Before the first set was over, five or six of them had propositioned us in between numbers. Most of the women had that vacuous, bored, sexless-dull degenerate look I had seen in the Rotogravure sections of Sunday Hearst papers in America. They were the society page come to life. They had mastered the art of looking bored and were stuck with it. Their faces seemed frozen in a mask that never changed except when their eyes would slowly move from one direction to the other, always retaining that thick veil so as not to register any emotion. They were beautifully dressed, all seemed to have very white skin and stood in that affected way as if they were dropouts from a ballet school. No one was dancing.

After the first set Paulo came over, glowing with pride.

"You sound terrific. They're not dancing yet, but they'll catch on, don't worry."

Mona decided to sing the second set. During the first set she had met a friend of hers, an industrialist from New York. But when it looked like the band wasn't going to make it, he had left her standing there alone. Being a pretty hearty soul, she went over to the bar and had about seven Scotches. When she came back on again she delivered a great brazen monologue with her Bronx-French accent. In no time at all our entire audience ran behind the other side of the chateau. Dauntless, she brayed through three more songs. We figured by this time everyone had gone back to Paris, but when she stopped, people gradually drifted back again.

They still looked bored, so Sadi decided that we should play something more lively to get the people into the groove. He sat down at the bongos and began playing one of the pieces that featured him as a soloist. He was a great bongo virtuoso as well as being such a fine vibes player and we had a kind of African number that was really a cooker. In the middle of the solo that used to really gas everybody in Paris, one of the strange-looking men came up, picked up Sadi's vibraphone sticks and began hitting his vibraphone gently.

"*Salut! Cochon! Fils de pute! Emmerdeur! Con!*" The man looked up, shocked. These are not complimentary phrases in French and generally musicians playing at society parties of this type were not on very personal terms with the audience. At society parties they were generally treated like servants at best, so the man couldn't believe it. "If you touch those vibraphone sticks I'll knock your face in," said

Sadi in English. He grabbed the sticks and was about to hit him, but the man scuttled off, astonished.

Sadi was really bugged. "All right," he said, "fuck these people, let's play some music." We then went into our most avant-garde repertoire, featuring advanced, abstract jazz tunes with maximum improvising, changing of tempos, cadenzas and long solos.

During one tune in which I didn't have a solo I was delegated to steal some liquor for the band. I jumped behind the hedge, ran around the back where the liquor table was and told the bartender that Monsieur La Touche had requested to see him immediately because there was some problem about getting some kind of liquor and that he must go to the chateau right away. I finally convinced him of this outrageous lie even though there was no Monsieur La Touche While he ran off I grabbed a few bottles, sneaked past the hedge, nodded pleasantly to the parking-lot attendant and went back to the bandstand. We began bombing down the bottles like mad plus a few joints of pot mixed with hashish. By the end of this set we decided to keep on playing.

By this time the guests were losing their blasé expressions. Now they were looking horrified. The more astounded and angry they looked the better we played. We were going to bombard them with good music until it killed them. Roger, our star trumpet player, requested a piece featuring him. He started off his usual solo, but when the band came in he suddenly stopped, took off his coat, tie, shirt and pants, and went up to the microphone in his undershorts, pointed his trumpet toward the audience, leaned back and started wailing chorus after chorus, getting more abstract sounds like barnyard chuckles, beeps, bloops, howls of pain, shouts of rage. It was a real avant-garde performance mixed up with some swinging and wailing. It was so powerful that the people were just hypnotized. Then he stepped off the bandstand and began walking around through the audience, blasting into people's ears while they stood frozen.

We continued playing in this vein till a few people finally began dancing. About twelve people really dug us. Apparently they were swingers but didn't want anyone else to know that they might be enthusiastic about life. Suddenly George Plimpton popped up.

"Well, David," he said, "your band is making quite an impression this evening."

"I know these people don't dig it, man, but you know we've got to spread that message."

"David, I'd like you to meet Mr. Maclair," he said, introducing me to a tall gentleman.

"Hi, Mr. Maclair," I said, "it's great to meet you."

Mr. Maclair then told me that he owned several steel empires and would like me to play all of his parties in New York.

"I presume you're a friend of Meyer Davis and Lester Lannin." I told him that while I knew of these two society-band leaders, I was in a different groove.

"Don't you usually play society music?"

At first I thought he was putting me on.

"No, Mr. Maclair," I said. "Usually I don't play this type of commercial music like we're performing this evening. I play—you might say, more jazz-oriented music."

"Oh," he said very pleasantly, "if you ever do want to play for one of my parties in New York, be sure to let me know."

"That's very kind of you," I said, and I staggered off. I really never could believe that people couldn't hear. I figured that Mr. Maclair must have made so much money that perhaps the sound of all those dollars rubbing together had deafened him totally. We went back and continued playing. Pretty soon only about twelve people remained. They all started dancing like mad. The frozen expressions disappeared from the women's faces and they looked like they were having fun. Paulo had met some girl who had sent her husband home and was grooving like mad.

"Beautiful, beautiful," he kept telling us, shaking his long hair and almost ripping off her clothes with his enthusiastic dancing. *"Bravo, les musiceans!"*

We continued playing and drinking and smoking until dawn. The twelve people who were still there came back on the bus with us. Back in Paris, we all had a party at some enormous house in which we passed out, getting up just to have a fast meal before going right back to work that night.

Musicians from every school of jazz would come to play at the Hôtel des États Unis. Don Byas, the great tenor man who was a link between Coleman Hawkins and the most modern players of that time, played with us a few times. He had migrated to Europe quite a while before, had stopped drinking, became a real health fiend, married a European girl and was also an enthusiastic underwater diver. He had done some music for a film about different species of fish using different kinds of music for each school of fish. It was beautiful. We talked about composition whenever we played together.

Albert Nicholas, who must have been in his seventies, played with us. He was interested in all the modern tunes and if he didn't know the one we were playing, he would ask the piano player for the chord changes and then would invariably say, "I'm gonna go home and practice that one. Tomorrow night I'll be back and you'd better look out boys cuz I'll *tear it up!*" Sure enough, Albert would come back and know the tune inside out.

American servicemen who were visiting Paris, as well as musicians from different bands, would also come in. I remember once a bassoon player I had known in the army came by.

"Hey, Dave, how ya been?" he said, his eyes glowing with enthusiasm.

"Great," I said. "Paris is paradise."

"I've only been in Paris one day on a furlough and I've gotten me a gig," he told me excitedly.

"Hey, that's terrific," I said. "Where are you playing?"

"Well," he said, "it's not exactly a music job. It's more—show biz.

"What do you mean?" I asked him.

"Well," he said, "I was in a music store looking for some cane to make reeds for my axe and this cat came up and sounded me and after a whole lot of weirdness he's got me working in an exhibition."

"No kidding," I said.

"Yeah, that's right. I'm working in an exhibition, man. It pays me eight thousand francs a shot. I go in, get juiced out of my head, turn on and make it with this chick. People watch. The first gig, they just had this real old nice English couple sitting there holding hands. They must have been in their seventies. I got two more dates tonight and a matinee tomorrow afternoon. It's going to pay my whole furlough."

"That's wild," I said.

"Well," he told me, "I'm still interested in playing music. I don't plan on doing this for my life's work." He had time before his next show started and took out his bassoon. Apparently his theatrical work hadn't hurt his playing because he fried through a few choruses of "I Can't Get Started," using the new substitute changes that Clifford Brown had introduced.

Waiters from the Rose Rouge as well as performers from different traveling groups would come to hear us play. Terry Southern was

always there, a thin, quiet, cool, mysterious cat who constantly
seemed to be somewhere else except when he'd break everybody up
with his ability to sum up a whole situation in a few wry words. Baird
Bryant and his beautiful wife at that time, Dinny, were also regulars.
Baird was making a film called *The Vipers*, based entirely on a piece
of music by Stan Kenton, showing him and his friends riding on
motorcycles through Paris with dissolves of people dropping out of
airplanes, parachuting into Japanese bathhouses, bombs exploding,
great scenes of love. It was truly a mind-bending abstract movie that
made you high just by watching it. It was the best experimental film
I had ever seen. Baird had also written a book in ten days to make
some fast money. It was a takeoff on pornographic books and was
so funny that I wrote a tune named after it, called "Play This Love
with Me."

One of the finest jazz singers I had heard in Paris was Lobo Nocho.
He was also an excellent drummer and dancer, all of which he did
to support his main interest in life, which was painting. He was from
Philadelphia and after World War II had decided to settle down in
Paris and study and live. He knew nearly every fine jazz musician
I had ever met in my life plus hundreds that I had read about. He
had a wonderful occult quality of the supreme hipster in the best
sense of the word. He was someone who was truly aware, spiritually
turned on and always inspired. He had an innate understanding of
almost any person he met. Knowing several languages, he could
make anyone, from a nervous American tourist to a weary, cynical
proprietor of a French tobacco store, feel at home and relaxed just by
his presence. He was even able to talk to the trees and if an animal
came by on the street, one look from him and it would come over
and sit obediently at his feet. Most of all, he had a great sense of
humor about himself. Whenever he would call someone on the phone,
he would invariably say, "Hello, this is God speaking."

He was working across the street from the Hôtel des États Unis
at another little club and he used to hang out with us between sets.
One night he invited me over to sit in with him. He sang a few
tunes and I played in the background. Then he played drums as I
played.

"Dave," he said, "I have to tell you something. You can really
play that horn. I heard you play when you first came to Paris and
you didn't even know I was listening. I also knew you had your

teeth taken out and the rest must have done you good because you're playing better now than you did before."

"I'm glad to hear that," I said. "I can't really tell what I'm doing, man, I just want to blow."

"That's beautiful," said Lobo, "but if you're going to be a musician and you've been given a gift by God, you have a responsibility. You could do for that horn what Charlie Parker has done for his instrument. There are not too many cats out there playing the French horn."

"I know, Lobo," I said. "I work hard at music, man. I play a lot for nothing and most of my composing I do for nothing, but it's serious to me even though I have so much fun doing it."

"I know all that," said Lobo, "I'm thinking about something else. I'm talking about *you*. If you're really going to do anything substantial in music, you've got to straighten yourself out."

"What do you mean?" I said. "I think I'm pretty cool."

"You are, you are," said Lobo. "But let me ask you a question, Dave. How old are you?"

"I'm twenty-four," I said. "I'll be twenty-five this fall."

"Well," said Lobo, "you must be old enough to look in the mirror."

"I don't even have a mirror in my room. I'm not interested in that narcissistic crap."

"It's not narcissistic, Dave. It's self-respect," said Lobo. "The first time I saw you I said, 'My God, that cat can play the horn that way. He's got all that music inside him and he's gone to the doojie, you know.' [Doojie was one of the terms for heroin.] Now I know you never use no stuff even though you may smoke a little pot now and then, but you looked so sloppy that I figured you must be strung out on drugs. If you're going to want people to know how beautiful you sound, you have to look beautiful. You've got to be beautiful all the way. I don't mean that you have to go to a hairdresser, but you have to respect yourself and stand up straight and love yourself if you want people to love your music. I bet you haven't combed your hair, pressed your suit or really gotten straightened up since you've been in Paris."

"Well, man, I guess you're right," I said. "I don't really think about how I look. Since I got out of the army I've forgotten about all that. I don't put it down. It just doesn't seem important to me. At this point I don't really care about anything except music and having each heartbeat be an ecstatic experience."

"Well, that's very fine and poetic," said Lobo, "but if you're going to be a musician, baby, you've got to think about something else. Look at me. I'm not the greatest singer or the greatest drummer, but I've got to support my painting habit. How do I do it? Baby, when I show up on the gig, I look like a million dollars, and I feel better too and people treat me with more respect and dignity. This is baby stuff, man. I know you know all this anyway. It's just that you're all up there on cloud nine and you don't give it any thought and you've got to, at least when you're working."

Lobo was right. Although I was functioning on several levels at quite a frenetic tempo, I was really so disorganized that I probably was not working as efficiently in any area as I should. I wasn't really too worried about it, but the fact was I would be able to accomplish more in music if I tried to become even remotely organized in some way. I always showed up for work ahead of time and played well, but I began to wonder if I would be able to play better and write better if I were organized.

I thought about it after I left Lobo that night. I realized that perhaps in music there was something besides satisfying myself and my fellow musicians. The way Lobo described it, it was more than art and self-expression. It was as Mitropoulos and so many other people had indicated but had never articulated to me: music was a divine mission.

I continued my classical playing whenever I had a chance. Robert Kornman, an excellent composer, conductor and pianist, had chamber-music sessions.

One night I was told that I was to appear with some French musicians at a soirée. "Get dressed up," I was told. "This is a big occasion. All the musical élite of Paris will be present. They're performing the works of a new young composer and you must be there to play."

"That's terrific."

I sent my suit to the dry cleaners although it didn't do too much good, and I showed up that night at an enormous old house on the Right Bank. The composer, a very young and handsome boy, had been living under the patronage of a mysterious woman who apparently took in young men as her showpieces. If they were homosexuals, that made it easier for her, since they would spend more time around the house rather than running out looking for chicks. He was obviously earning his board. I could see from the constrained look he had on his face that he really was more of a chauffeur than an artist-in-residence. But as we used to say, *"Chacun à son groove."*

The other musicians arrived and we sat down in a huge glittering ballroom with a grand piano. The young composer came out and we were presented parts for woodwind quintet and piano. We went through the piece before the guests arrived and it was very nicely written: good sounds, well orchestrated for the instruments with a good flow and a nice sense of form. He played his part beautifully and we were looking forward to a fine concert.

The atmosphere of the place really made me feel as if I were in a book by Marcel Proust. The Old World elegance, the slightly faded, luxuriant satins and silks and twinkling lights and dusty chandeliers. It was the embodiment of the American's dream of European splendor.

The guests started arriving. Most of them were in their sixties or seventies. The ones who spoke French with a thick Russian accent reminded me of the waiters at Ratner's, the great Jewish restaurant in New York. The only difference was that these fellows didn't have a towel over one arm. These distinguished emigrés who were being introduced by their titles might or might not have once been White Russians, but they definitely sent out vibrations of being either waiters or cabdrivers now. When they smiled, their gold teeth showed profusely. Their rusted medals clanked decorously from their shiny, slightly moth-eaten tuxedos. I felt a real twinge of sadness as I saw the ratty entourage arriving. I knew that the Czar of Russia was never going to leap out of the balcony tonight.

The next group that arrived were mostly Frenchwomen in their sixties, seventies and eighties, generally overweight, in evening gowns and escorted by effeminate young men who fawned over them with an inordinate amount of attention.

Finally a great hush came over the room as a marvelous-looking woman arrived surrounded by an escort of grim-looking bespectacled types. I was told by the French bassoonist, "There she is, the grande dame."

He didn't have to tell me who it was. I realized it must have been Nadia Boulanger, the great composition teacher I had heard so much about since I was a child and with whom every composer in America wanted to go and study. She had beautiful eyes and I felt good just seeing her, even though the people with her looked nervously about as if they were with the heavyweight champ and didn't want anybody getting too close to touch.

Finally we sat down and began to play. The pieces went quite well except that the composer kept getting lost. One time when we couldn't cover for him, we had to go back and start again from the beginning.

I felt as if I were in a wax museum. I really wanted to cry for all the people that were here, reliving a bad imitation of what once must have been so glorious and exciting and meaningful. I knew I wanted to spend my life in music, but I certainly could never live with the idea of trying to please a gathering of this sort. Any contemporary artist would have to find his audience from the present and the future, rather than trying to appeal to people who obviously associated music and art with something that was out of the past. As I saw the dreary expressions of the waiters and cabdrivers and widows and escorts, I realized that this was more like a costume party than a concert. The music was just an excuse for a social gathering. This was a perfectly good excuse, but it did not seem to me a reason for anybody to write music or perform it. At best it was simply the tail end of bygone times.

As soon as we were done playing, people rushed over to the hors d'oeuvres and began eating with more fury than I had ever seen at chow time in the army. I suddenly realized why most of these people were there. They were hungry! Not for culture but for something to eat. I stared in amazement as tray after tray of hors d'oeuvres down to the last piece of watercress were gobbled up furiously by the bemedaled men. These cats were really starving. The elderly women and their escorts munched daintily and drank a little, but the White Russian contingent was really scuffling. It seemed as if they needed the benefits of the Bolshevik Revolution as much as anyone who was in Russia at the moment.

The other musicians and I all went up to the composer-pianist and congratulated him. I wanted to get a better look at Madame Boulanger, if not to say hello, but the people that were with her were so sinister looking, I decided to skip it.

It was my night off from the Rose Rouge, so I called up Giovanna, who had wisely decided not to come to the soirée. We went over to the Hôtel des États Unis, where some of the African fire-eaters and drummers who also worked at the Rose Rouge were sitting in along with a terrific trumpet player from a traveling Italian commedia dell'arte group. As I was playing, I saw how lucky I was to be able to play jazz, to be doing something that was alive and unpretentious. Here the whole atmosphere was so warm and real and electric. The music was the important thing. I was sure that when Beethoven, Bach, Mozart and Brahms were writing music, they felt the same joy of life and vitality. I just hoped that jazz music would never become mummified or put in the kind of museum atmosphere that I had been in earlier that night.

When I told Giovanna what the experience had been like, she said, "That's because Paris is not a great musical city. If you ever came to Milan or Rome or any of the Scandinavian countries or England, you would find a freshness and spontaneity and creative atmosphere that would make you happy as a musician and a composer."

'Well, people don't feel stiff about jazz over here," I said.

"That's only because of you young musicians that bring your joy with you. The French romanticize the jazz musician. But when this passes it will be hard for them as well. The important thing that you learned tonight is that you must be in the environment that makes you feel alive. You can't control what your music will become and how it will affect people someday, but you can control your life and who you are with."

In a way I saw that she was on the same track as Lobo. I decided that I would only spend time in scenes that made me feel good and made me want to continue with music.

The session was so great that night that by the end I had completely forgotten about the enervating, uptight atmosphere of the soirée earlier. We all went out and got hot rolls and coffee. Then Jay, Giovanna and I walked down to the Île St. Louis to watch the sun rise.

Things were pretty hard for Paulo and the Rose Rouge. Although every jazz man in Paris would come there at least once a week— sneaking in with the musicians or sitting at the bar and buying one drink for four hours—the place was really dying. The big spenders who could keep it alive were staying away en masse. If they did come they would leave in horror as soon as our band began stomping. Paulo could have gotten rid of us and changed the format, but he was determined to go down swinging.

One day he came in beaming. "I've got it," he said, shaking his long hair triumphantly. "We're going to appear in the Palais with a stage show and create the sensation of the decade." We were still on the job at the Rose Rouge at night, but we decided we could rehearse the theater show in the daytime and fit the schedule around the acts we had to play for. Everyone in the band thought this was a marvelous idea. It would give us an extra income from the theater and real exposure for our great sounds.

About a week later we began rehearsals. We all arrived promptly at ten o'clock in the morning at the Palais, eager to play, even though Jay and I had only had a few winks, having been up at the États Unis the night before. Generally when an orchestra rehearses in a theatrical situation, the dramatic part is worked out in advance and then the orchestra is called in. It's carefully broken down so that the orchestra spends most of the rehearsal time playing in order to save money for the management. This had been my experience playing in ballets, operas and theater music in the past. However, the director of the show apparently had another system. He gave a moving oration to the band before we played a note, describing with sweeping gestures of his arms and tossings of his head how this would be epic theater, a variety show utilizing the creative force and electric talent of everyone of us. Mixing the vim and vitality and energy of jazz into the popular theater for the first time would eventually whip up such a frenzy of excitement on the stage that it would become a tidal wave of emotion charging down over the audience, inundating them in a cataclysmic torrent of ecstasy. He was quite a talker and even though my French was pretty good at the time, I needed some help with translation of his Racine-inspired purple prose. Even Jay couldn't understand part of what he said, but Bobby Jaspar translated it for us, and the musicians, while they listened respectfully, laughed for days afterward and imitated his great oratorical style.

After he had completed a speech that would have made Demosthenes proud, followed by a stunned silence on our part, Sadi, the bandleader, said to him, "When do we begin playing and what order do we play the music in?"

The director looked slightly hurt but then brushed the mundane implications of this question aside. "This is not the point—this is not the route we are undertaking," he said. "We are one great force. We are the center of the wheel whose energy will radiate through the spokes to the entire city of Paris! I must ask you gentlemen to sit here until you are cued to play. Every artist in the entire program is going to be here so that we can all get a sense of one another. In this way we shall be like one great family, one organism breathing and moving and creating together. Each of us will take something from the next. I am depending upon your vitality and creativity to make this a great success."

He then snapped fingers dramatically and a scrim was lowered, hitting some of us on the head because we were sitting too far forward. About forty-five minutes passed. Every time we tried to warm up we were requested not to play so as not to destroy the atmosphere. As we sat there we saw that the director was in a heated conversation with a thin man who was doing some kind of solo act, surrounded with a battery of old beat-up instruments.

"He's discussing with him the effectiveness of using the guitar in one of his routines," Sadi said, hopelessly throwing up his hands.

"Why do we have to sit here?" asked one of the members of the band. "Can't we go away?"

"Look," said Sadi, "I'm sorry, but we have to stay here. This guy is crazy, but he feels we all must be here."

Time went by and more members of the newly formed troupe arrived. Some of the strippers showed up looking really beautiful. One in particular was fabulous. She was a gypsy and knew some of my friends with whom I had stayed in the gypsy trailer camp in Germany.

I was about to get her phone number when the director called her and the other dancers over. He then proceeded to give them a speech similar to the one he had given us but in terms of dancers' orientation, speaking of movement, the use of the body in space, the timeless rhythm of the dance and how they could make the stage rise to new heights and lift the audience to new planes of spiritual awareness. I don't imagine many strippers had received an indoctrination of this sort. The girls seemed to be quite impressed with his elocution. The dancers took off their coats, put on their costumes and were ready to go. After twenty minutes one of the dancers went over to the director, who was still talking to the man with his great barrage of battered-up old instruments, and asked him if we could rehearse the number.

"No, no, no, my dears," said the director. "Not yet, we must not break the rhythm. We are one organism, you know. One stress or strain can spoil the inner energies."

After about another twenty minutes, the director finally summoned the soloist to come on stage. "Now," he told him, "before you begin the show, the band will play five minutes. A marvelous piece of work, I must add," he said, looking at us fondly. "Then you begin your routine as we have discussed it. Are you ready in the lights?" By this time we had been there three hours and the lighting man had gone off to get a drink. Another twenty-five or thirty minutes went by and finally he came back.

"O.K.," said Sadi. "Vas-y." He stomped his foot and we began to play our first number, the opener. We wailed away and everyone looked happy to see us finally begin to do something.

We completed our five-minute number and the solo man came out on stage. His first routine was in English. He had a surprisingly good imitation of a hillbilly accent. "Hi, ya all," he said. "How ya all doin'? I'm a big cotton-pickin' Georgia farmer. Bon jewer. I'd like to sing a song for yew." He then picked up his guitar and began singing "I've Been Workin' on the Ra-yel-road."

After about seven bars the director said, "No, no." The boy looked up. "You must turn," the director said, "not so far to the right. If you lift up your knee, that is really too much of a Central European gesture and attitude." The novelty singer looked mystified. "No, no, no, you must do it thusly." The director then did something that looked like any Frenchman about to sing a popular chanson. This began a tremendous argument, which finally involved Sadi and the strippers and members of the orchestra. The director remained adamant, but after another twenty minutes of arguing it was decided that the boy could leave the gesture as it was but that he must face farther downstage.

"O.K., ça va," said the singer, and he began to continue where he had left off.

"No, no, no, no," said the director, "we must not stop the rhythm. How can I tell? How can the lighting man tell what we have accomplished? From the beginning, please."

The singer obediently started into his number.

"No, no, no," said the director. "From the *very* beginning." So we started from the very beginning with the blackout, played our five-minute piece again and the singer came on for his number.

This continued for the rest of the day. After about six hours we finally got through the first number and began with the strippers, but with every single gesture the director would leap up with some subtle suggestion. By seven o'clock they were hurling off their clothes so hard they sounded like black jacks when they hit the floor.

We were all so tired and so depressed by the director's great creative-family approach that we all hated one another and could hardly wait to get out. I never wanted to see a woman take off her clothes again in my life, unless we were good friends. That afternoon killed whatever remote voyeurism I might have ever had lurking in my soul.

The next week we continued rehearsing in this insane fashion. Ten days after we began, the show opened up and was an incredible fiasco. There was no pacing, no timing, no applause and even our swinging band could not do much to change the sullen and hostile expressions of the faces in the audience as they sat through what was probably the most boring and disorganized variety show of all times.

Paulo lost none of his enthusiasm. "When this band catches on," he said, "it's going to be something. We're just playing for the petite bourgeoisie. But when the word gets around among the people *in the know,* we'll be a sensation."

Another two weeks went by. Finally Paulo called all of the musicians together after work one night.

"Gentlemen," he said, "I love you and I am heartbroken to tell you, but this is our last night. You've been so wonderful, I'm paying all of you a few extra days' salary and I know that being such fine musicians, you'll be able to get other jobs. The stage show is closing tomorrow and the whole Rose Rouge is closing. I don't have a dime and I'm too much in debt to continue and I don't want to ask you to work for nothing."

None of us knew what to say. We all knew that barring a miracle, Paulo would have to fold, but we hated to see it happen because he was such a wonderful person to work for. It seemed such a pity that he hadn't had more experience before he had undertaken such an ambitious adventure. I had never seen such affection of musicians for their employer as we all felt for him that evening. We all took our pay and invited him out to dinner and went off to the Hôtel des États Unis for a mammoth jam session.

I had saved up some money, so I wasn't really desperate for work. Also, because I was available, I was beginning to play on some jazz recordings where different musicians had decided to use a French horn. I took one day off, went to Giovanna's house and slept for twenty-four hours in a row. I woke up feeling great and the next day made a record with Lionel Hampton, later released in the United States and the first commercial recording of me playing jazz on the horn. The band included Nat Adderley and Sascha Distel. I also began work on writing some little pieces for a jazz record of my own, which I was going to make with Bobby Jaspar playing saxophone and flute, Maurice Vandair playing piano and harpsichord, myself playing French horn, Eddy D'Haas, a fine bassist from Holland, and an excellent French drummer.

I always sat around on a bench outside the Rose Rouge with Terry and my other American pals. After the sessions we would go out with Lobo and Jay and others and walk around Montparnasse and Saint-Germaine-des-Près, listening to those fabulous birds serenading us each morning. This gave me the idea of writing a piece. I played it on the piano for Terry.

"A groovin' gas, mon vieux pot!" he exclaimed. It was just a sketch called "The Birds of Montparnasse," for flute, harpsichord, French horn, bass and drums.

During the time I had off I wrote and arranged enough music for a whole record for our little group and we recorded it. We later found out that Bobby was signed with another record company, so no one could legally release our album. I got hold of some copies though and gave one to Terry and Baird Bryant and Lobo and kept one for myself.

Giovanna found it more and more difficult to keep up with my impulsive way of living. I could hardly blame her. I knew that we would have to part, even though I cared for her so much and admired her. I gave her my only copy of the record as a gift.

She had pictures of New York, mostly postcards, all over her apartment. They were conventional shots of the skyline and the city. She spoke in glowing, romantic terms about New York.

"Wouldn't you like to go there?" she said to me. "Wouldn't your chances for music be better there?"

"I don't know," I said. "I was going to go there before I went into the army, but I really love Europe and feel more at home here. I've never had so much fun or felt so free. I've met more interesting people and got more ideas for my music and more inspiration for living than I ever did in the States."

"Yes," she said, "you'll feel that way for a while, but you can't stay here forever. Eventually you'll have to make your stand at home, you know."

"Maybe so," I said, "but I consider myself to be a citizen of the world. My music's got nothing to do with that nationalistic crap. I love America and when I see what beautiful people from America are like over here, it gives me a whole new insight into America, but I'm in no hurry to go back."

"Well," she said, "I think New York must be the most marvelous place in the world. I would love to be there with all that excitement and energy and newness. We're so old here, you know. I prefer Paris to Milan, but I am sure New York must be what Paris was like hundreds of years ago."

I had been thinking about going back but not enough to do anything about it. I figured that if the jazz records I made in Paris created some demand for me as a player that I might go back. But if I could continue to make a living playing here, I would stay. Possibly I could study composition again with a French teacher on the GI Bill. The problem was it seemed almost impossible to get the GI Bill at any music school in Paris. I knew I could study at the Manhattan School because of the conversation I had had with Gunther Schuller about a year before, but I didn't want to give up the joy of being in Paris. I had really found my spiritual home.

I was at a session one night at the Caméléon on Rue St. André des Arts where Henri Renaud was playing with his quartet. He was not a brilliant technician, but he more than made up for it with his wonderful "comping," the ability to accompany by playing chords at just the right moment, thereby inspiring you to think of things that you would not otherwise have played.

That night when I was sitting in he said to me during intermission, "Dave, our saxophone player is leaving to take a job in Belgium for a few months. How about joining my quartet? You can be featured and it will pay fairly decently."

"Just let me know when," I said.

"You can start next Monday," he told me. "We've been playing together so much anyway since you've come to Paris, you may as well get paid for it."

I played with him for the rest of the night and went home feeling wonderful. When I got there I had a call at the hotel telling me that Lars Gullin, the outstanding Swedish baritone saxophonist, Bobby

Jaspar and I were to play in a group with Raymond Fol as part of a big jazz concert. It looked like I could stay in Paris forever. I went to the Hôtel des États Unis the next night because I wanted to play and also so that I could be in good practice for the concert that was coming up later that week.

"Dave," Jay said to me when I came in, "there's a girl that I want you to meet. She's just a friend of mine and you might dig her." I came over to the table and there sat a beautiful blonde. I didn't think she was Swedish or Scandinavian or German or English. I couldn't figure out what she was. There was something very exciting about her that was really different. "Dave, meet Laura," Jay said.

"*Enchanté,*" I said.

"I'm sorry," she said sweetly, "I can't speak French." I was startled. She was American. For the next twenty minutes we talked. This was the first time I had spoken to an American girl that I had had any eyes for since I'd come to Europe nearly two and a half years earlier. The only American girls I had seen were usually the wives of officers or sergeants when I'd been in the army or tourists. I would always help them out if they needed directions or wanted to translate something, but with all the fantastic girls from Europe I had met, it never would have occurred to me to waste one minute with any uptight American females.

As I talked to her, however, I realized that although she was very American, she wasn't uptight at all. Maybe I had changed enough so that it was no longer necessary for American girls to have that tense quality with me. As she talked, I realized that what I had been reading about in jazz and music magazines was something that she not only knew about but was deeply involved in. She knew almost every musician I had heard of, was familiar with their music, their records, their compositions, their work and was really part of the scene that I dreamed about while I was in Paris.

"You've got to come back," she told me. "It's tough, but things are wailing back home."

"Well," I said, "maybe so." That sort of turned me off a little bit because I didn't want to think about returning, any more than I did when Giovanna had mentioned it. I went up and played a set with the band, then sat down and talked to her some more.

"Whew!" she said. "I don't know anybody that's doing that in the States. The only other kitty that plays French horn is Julius Watkins. He's a fantastic player, but he has a whole different direction that he's taken in his playing. You'd dig him back though. He's a beauty. You could do a lot of work. Of course you have to get yourself together."

"What do you mean?" I said.

"Well," she said, eyeing me up and down laughingly, "you're not exactly one of *Esquire*'s ten best-dressed men. That sloppy style is out as far as musicians go. They're wearing Italian-cut suits now."

"I saw Bird play and he didn't look like any fop," I said.

"Yes, baby, but there's only one Bird," she told me, "and he'd be working more if he did."

Lobo came over and joined the discussion. I saw that she and Lobo knew something about life that I was not tuned in to, and for the next three days we hung out together constantly. I gradually felt myself being pulled into a new kind of attitude that I always seemed to reject before. It was something that seemed purely home-grown, purely American without any pretensions or self-consciousness at all. Their awareness of situations and analyses of things I had taken for granted or paid no attention to most of my life seemed almost to strike a mystical chord. They both loved music, but they considered it to be part of the whole world rather than the whole world itself.

The afternoon of the third day, we went up to Lobo's room and sat around a gigantic water pipe puffing up some pot which Laura had brought with her from the States.

"This is pure soul dynamite," she said, running her fingers through her blonde hair, then gesturing them in fluttering motions up toward the skylight. "It will take you away out there," she pointed. I looked up and saw the trees, those curly white clouds and the beautiful blue Paris sky above. They began talking about the Bible and religion. We got higher and higher while they got deeper and deeper. Suddenly a sensation started down in the heels of my feet. I could feel it in the back of my spine, spreading out on either side all around me like a belt. It was as if I were being unzipped from some cellophane container I had been in all my life, almost like a fetus being born and coming out of the sack for the first time. I felt as if I were being bathed in light. I looked up through the skylight and the incredible blue that came down there seemed to be God coming down and enveloping me in his presence.

I looked over at Lobo, who simply gave me one nod. I looked over at Laura and she was smiling faintly. I was speechless. I sat there for two hours with this sensation and decided to change my life. I decided at that moment to go back to America, study composition, play music, get my life completely together and become a new man.

I finally stood up and said, "Lobo and Laura, I'm leaving. I have to go get cleaned up."

I went home and bought a black suit at the corner with most of my remaining money. Then I went up to my room and stood in the shower for about an hour, scrubbing every bit of dirt that had collected there over quite a period of time. I scrubbed my hands and my fingernails for nearly half an hour. I took out my horn and shined it, cleaned up my whole room, mopped it, straightened out all my papers, put on a clean shirt, tie and my new suit, shined my shoes and went out and walked around Paris with my horn.

Every time I would look up in the sky, I would get this feeling of being high again. Either I had been touched by God or I was about to lose my mind forever. I finally went to the Hôtel des États Unis and sat in and played. I didn't say a word to anybody.

Jay came over to me afterward. "You sound great tonight, Dave," he said. "But you look sort of fucked up. What's the matter?"

"I've been touched by the hand of God," I told him.

He looked at me for a minute. "Uh oh," he said, "don't forget about your concert tomorrow night."

"Don't worry, Jay," I said, "I'll be there."

"I will too," he said. "I'm playing with another group." He chuckled and went back to finish eating his chili.

The next day I met with Lars Gullin, Bobby Jaspar and Jay's group. I hardly said a word to anyone. As we were rehearsing, I felt all my thoughts going through the music and it was as if I could think and have the sound come right out of the end of the horn without even knowing that I was playing.

I heard Lars talking to Bobby after rehearsal. He said, "I heard a lot about that cat when he was in Germany. He sure plays good, but he's really out of his mind, isn't he?"

"No," Bobby said, "he's just very impressionable."

Backstage that night was pandemonium. Because it was one of the big jazz concerts of the year, all the musicians from Paris were hanging out backstage and because heroin was becoming more and more popular, people were shooting up, sniffing from the ends of screwdrivers and mirrors, plus smoking pot, hashish and snorting cocaine. I said no to everything. I just wanted to play. The tunes we

were playing were "Autumn in New York," "Now's the Time," and
"The Way You Look Tonight." Raymond Fol had written an ar-
rangement for which I held a note at the end of "Autumn in New
York" for almost a minute.

"Are you sure you can do that, Dave?" he said. "If you get nervous, we can change it."

"It's fine," I said to him. I felt I could do anything. The concert
started and I sat on the side of the audience where my sister was
sitting. I hadn't told her about my experience, but she and her husband seemed to be enjoying the music, which made me glad.

As I looked at her, I realized how much I had loved her all my
life, without ever being able to tell her. I thought about the time
back in Florida when I was six years old. I had had a similar religious
experience with my mother on the beach and told my sister about it.
I remember how she had laughed and poked fun at me. I also remembered another time when we nearly had been trapped by a fire
on our farm. As we ran out to the brook to escape, she turned to me
seriously and said, "Do you think that was God's will?" I had never
discussed anything of any spiritual nature with her, but at that moment it was beautiful to have someone of my flesh and blood that I
was so close to. I was happy to see her sitting there with her husband,
listening to the music.

I went backstage and as the other band was finishing their number, someone came running up and said to Raymond, "Man, did you
hear the news?"

"What's that?" Raymond said.

"Charlie Parker is dead."

We all suddenly seemed to shrink. Everyone backstage quieted
down. All the heroin and other drugs were quietly put away. People
just stood there in silence while the band onstage, oblivious of this
terrible news, kept on wailing.

Finally Bobby spoke up, "Well, he was our number one man,"
he said. "The best thing we can do in his memory is to keep on wailing better and more beautiful than ever."

All the musicians were nearly crying. We didn't say anything to
one another. It was announced that we were to go onstage.

As I played my chorus for "Autumn in New York," I kept thinking about Bird and how many times I had thought about him and
how strange it was that something like this should happen just now.
It all seemed related in some way.

The next tune we were playing was "Now's the Time." Raymond made a speech saying that this tune was written by Charlie Parker and would be played in his memory. He said it so straight it wasn't morbid or maudlin or phony. We could feel the reaction and spirit of Bird hovering over the whole hall. It might just have been the state that I was in, but I could feel his presence as much as if I had just seen him a minute before. Then we played "The Way You Look Tonight" and in the series of choruses I played, something seemed to break loose inside of me. I played for about fifteen minutes without stopping. Raymond and the other members of the band kept encouraging me. For some reason that I never fully understood, something died inside me that night and something new was either born or released for the first time. I felt a real determination and force inside myself that had to get the music out at any cost and at any price.

Lobo and Laura came back after the concert. "Well, Dave, I guess I won't be seeing you for a while," said Lobo. I didn't say anything. "I know you're going to go back home. I could hear that by what you were saying when you played."

"You were really cooking, Dave," said Laura, looking at me. "What's the matter, baby? You look like you're losing your mind."

"I don't know," I said. "I just know that I've got to get back. I have to get into music all the way no matter what."

"You don't have to worry," said Laura. "You'll do fine."

We went out that night and talked about Bird for several hours. Lobo said not to feel bad because the thing that would make Bird the happiest would be to know that all the musicians that he had turned on with his music were playing more than ever. He didn't want his playing to stop anything; he wanted it to start something and get something going in the world. His music was the quintessence of the life force and it was up to those of us who lived it to keep that spirit alive.

Lobo finally left us alone and said, "You two youngsters better hang out together for a while. I'm going to feed my number one baby, Sha-ba-da." This was the name of Lobo's beautiful dog.

"Do you want to come home with me?" Laura said.

"Sure, I was just going to ask you to my place to see my piano with the candles."

"Jay told me about it," said Laura. "You're a pretty corny cat but I dig you anyway." We went to her house and when we woke up the next morning I never felt better in my life. This was the first American girl I had been with for so long and the first hip girl I had ever had any romantic feelings toward. All of the other hipster girls I had known had really just been friends. Most of my romances had been with more docile types.

But I noticed that Laura didn't feel well. "What's the matter, baby?" I said. "Can I go and get you something to eat?"

She looked at me and her eyes narrowed. "Jesus Christ," she said angrily, "you don't know about anything, do you."

"What do you mean?"

She got up and went into the bathroom. When she came back out, I could tell from her eyes as much as the cotton swabs on her arm that she had taken her morning shot.

"You didn't know I was just a fucking junkie, did you?"

"No, I guess not," I said.

"Well, life is one big series of surprises."

"Listen," I said, "let me help you. You don't need to take that poison. You're too good for that."

"Forget it, baby," she said, "you save yourself, that's enough. Don't bother to save me."

For the next few weeks I did everything I could to try and stop her from using drugs. I had stopped taking anything since my vision and I found my senses growing more and more acute. I began working at the Caméléon. Laura would come down to listen all the time and I saw a whole network of junkies that she was involved with. There was really nothing that I could do short of becoming a junkie myself. I had never touched heroin, having known so many people of my time who were either dead, institutionalized or walking zombies as a result.

I told Lobo about this. "I knew that, man," he said. "I figured you must know just by looking at her. I guess you love her so much that she made you blind."

"I don't know what to do," I said. "I really dig her. Do you think maybe she would go for a cure?"

"No," said Lobo. "She's a grooving chick, but that's her scene. She's not a physical addict as much as she is a mental addict. She has a beautiful mind, but she doesn't want to be hurt by things and she hasn't learned that the only way you don't get hurt by life is to face it straight ahead and after a while those things that seem like they'll hurt, just bounce off. Remember, you heard it from God first," said Lobo, laughing.

A night or two later I saw Laura leave with another musician who I knew used drugs. I didn't see her after that. She just disappeared.

When Henri Renaud left Paris during the summer, I took his place as the leader of his quartet while he was gone. With a lot of Americans visiting, the audiences picked up and we started having packed houses.

A young American came in one night and asked if he could sit in at the piano. His name was Hal Kaufman and he wanted to be a lawyer or a doctor. He sat down and played some thunderous piano but mostly in the 1920s style.

"Look," I said, "our piano player is leaving tomorrow. You can work with us, but let me show you some of the chord changes and what's happening now." I wrote out a few chords and showed him a few voicings. He was so fast that by the end of the evening he had memorized everything and started his own way of playing. He told me all the things that were happening in America. I mentioned that I was going back and with his organized approach to things, he asked me when, how, where and so forth.

"I'm not sure," I said. "Gunther Schuller told me he could help me to get into the Manhattan School of Music."

"Well, you'd better write him a letter," said Hal. "Write him a letter and book your passage now or you'll miss the boat. If you want to get the GI Bill, you've also got to get working on that."

That night I went home and wrote Gunther a letter telling him I wanted to come back to study that fall. I had been in touch with him periodically but had never been certain as to when I was going to get back, if ever. I wasn't certain exactly what date I would leave. I remembered that the Manhattan School of Music opened at the end of September and as a result I decided to go back about that time. But because of the crazy way I was living I still made no definite plans.

One night at the Caméléon a bunch of young American students asked if they could sit in. Because so much of my playing came as a result of playing with other people, I said, "Sure." They were not that comfortable playing our kind of music, but for the next week they played with me each night. Finally they asked me if I would like to go back to New York with them on the *Groote Beer*, a Dutch student ship that was leaving toward the end of September. That fit in perfectly with my unplanned plan, so I again said, "Sure," and arranged to be taken aboard as a student with the band, even though most of the kids were still in college and looked a little younger than I did after nearly three years of rampaging around Europe.

This meant that I had to say good-bye to all the friends I had known in Paris. It was really sad. I knew I wouldn't be back for a while.

When I went to say good-bye to Raymond Fol he said to me, "Dave, when you come back again you will have no more youth."

I thought about this and about musicians like Stephan Grappelly, who was probably then in his fifties and still had the spirit of a kid. I went back to where Stephan was playing and sat in with his band on my night off.

"Do you think I'll lose anything by going back?" I asked him.

"My boy," he told me with his great charm, "once you've been to Paris you never lose it as long as you live." I heard in his violin playing that night not only the gypsy elements and the old honky-tonk jazz, but the French sophistication that he brought into his playing, that gaiety and joy that The Hot Club of France jazz musicians had.

I also went to hear Albert Nicholas and Sidney Bechet. Sidney was in his late fifties and Albert was in his seventies.

What a unique art form jazz was. Imagine if one could go and speak with Monteverdi and Josquin Des Prez and Bach, run down the street and hang out with Schubert and Brahms, have a drink with Mussorgsky, then go to supper with Bartók and end up talking to Arnold Schönberg and a fifteen-year-old electronic composer, all in the same day. In jazz this was still possible. Some of the oldest masters were still alive. I never saw it more clearly than that last night in Paris.

I also said my good-bye to Sascha Distel, whom I recorded and jammed with many times, to Jay, Bobby, Giovanna and Rene Utreger. Rene's friend Jerry Gray, an American who had been married to the late Wardell Gray, was over in Paris visiting. She asked me to call her at the Alvin Hotel when I came to New York so that she could tell me where to hear and play music.

I also went around to discothèques, where I first heard the recordings of the then emerging Sonny Rollins. From his recordings and the ones of Thelonius Monk I could tell something new was happening. It was almost as if Charlie Parker's death had made it possible for others to be heard. Although it broke every musician's heart when he died, it seemed that his life had been a sacrifice for all of us, that it opened up the doors for the kind of music he had been playing for the last fifteen years. This was one of the forces that was pulling me back to America, in addition to my own desire to continue composing.

I felt that there would be better training and more opportunity for my music in New York than there ever would be in Paris. Being in Paris made me feel the soul of America more strongly than ever.

I packed everything I had into my old straw box and shipped it to Holland. On the way to Rotterdam, I stopped to see Albert Mangelsdorff and his brother Emile and Jutta Hipp and Carlo Bohlender and many other friends in Frankfort.

"Be sure to come back, Dave," they all told me, even though they seemed to sense that it would be quite a while before I returned. We had some great jazz sessions the last two nights and I finally left for Holland.

I got to Rotterdam and jumped into the boat. Suddenly I was surrounded with American students again after all these years. It was wild. I met with the musicians and found out that all I had to do was play with the Dixieland band in the early part of the evening.

"This is a fantastic gig," I said to the trombone player. This turned out to be the understatement of the century, since I only had to work about an hour a night. I had no place to compose, so I wandered to the piano room the first morning and met a piano teacher from New York. We played the Beethoven Horn Sonata, a Mozart horn concerto and much of the music that I had for horn and piano. After lunch we would drink beer, which was only a nickel a bottle on Dutch ships, play some more music, then after supper I would work for an hour with the Dixieland band, then have a jam session up on top of the boat just beneath the lifeboats. The kids who were interested in more modern jazz would come and listen while we played through the night. I spent the eleven days doing this. It made my reorientation to America very easy.

7

WE STEAMED into New York Harbor on a beautiful sunny day. The Statue of Liberty looked like a lovely lady toasting our return. It had been nearly three years since I had seen America. I felt like an immigrant arriving in a new country.

An older girl was sobbing at the rail. "Isn't it beautiful?" I said. She cried even harder.

I listened to her sobbing and figured each tear was like a flower she was giving in her bouquet to the States. "It's wonderful coming home again. You know, it's been nearly three years since . . ."

"Quit bugging me, you dumb schmuck!" she cried. "I can't stand coming back. I hate New York. Rome was so beautiful. And Paris. And now, to come back to *this!* Ech-h-h! Boo-hoo-hoo-hoo. Go *a-way,* you creep!"

I figured she wanted to share her homecoming with herself, so I ran down below, said good-bye to the musicians and got my belongings together.

When I got off the gangplank, the vibrations coming through the soles of my shoes felt different. This was *American* cement, Hoboken, New Jersey, cement. It was beautiful. I was really back. The acrid, smog-filled air smelt lovely and the rough, snarling voices of the cab drivers and dock workers shouting over the rumble of trucks, the screeching of brakes and horn honks—it all sounded terrific.

Hugging my French horn, big suitcase and knapsack (my big straw box came about a week later), I took the tube to Manhattan. I called Rodney Dennis, violist and musicologist whom I knew in high school, to see if I could find a place to stay till I found an apartment of my own. He said, "Sure thing, come on over," and I went to East Twenty-eighth Street, where he and his wife were living. On the way I noticed that some people were staring at me. Not being very badly dressed, I realized it must be that strange look in my eye. I was still recovering from my pre-psychedelic religious visions. I felt I was on a mission.

I got to Rodney's house and met his wife. As I was unpacking, there was a knock on the door. It was Ken Karpe from the upstairs apartment, coming down to visit Rodney. I knew as I looked at him that he was a nouvelle vogue hipster, but knowing that Rodney was rather conservative, I didn't say anything that might sound too weird. Besides, I still looked like such a hick I figured Ken and Rodney would have no idea where I was at. I just wanted to find a place to settle. No scenes. However, when Ken saw my waterpipe he asked me to come upstairs. His apartment was beautiful, and he had an enormous record collection. I found that Ken and his fiancée, Sylvia, were very interested in jazz and they asked me to come by some time if I felt like playing. He had a Steinway baby grand. I wanted to talk to both of them more, but I had to go hear some music and play if possible. That's why I was back. I went downstairs. I'd been in New York two hours and already had a place for jam sessions.

After Rodney's wife had cooked us a delicious American-style dinner, we decided to walk down to some of the jazz places in the Village. I had heard about the Open Door and it was still open. With my French horn in my hand, I walked in and spoke to the manager in my most cheerful European way.

"Hey, I've just come back from Europe. Do you need a French-horn player to work here?" The manager bared his fangs. It was my first experience with the old New York snarl.

I got the idea that the answer was no since the manager pushed us out on the street with his stomach. I went over with Rodney to the Café Bohemia.

While we were walking there I said, "Gee, Rodney, that guy wouldn't even let me in to play. I feel like blowing. If you can't sit in, how are you suppose to ever get a job in New York?"

Rodney gave me the classic answer that I still remember. "Amram," he said, "I don't know that much about the jazz world, but I'm sure that's not the way to go about it."

When we got to the Bohemia I decided to cool it and just listen. I walked in and saw a very well-dressed young man playing the alto saxophone more or less in the style of Bird. He kept playing and playing. I was surprised because usually in Paris we would never play more than five or six choruses to give everyone a chance. About the eighth chorus I noticed that the saxophonist began to repeat a one-note figure throughout his chorus and develop it almost the way Henry Purcell did in his variations based on one note. After the alto saxophonist had played about thirty choruses, which were spellbinding, he sat down on the side of the stage at a desk and began to write music while the pianist began to play his choruses. This surprised me to put it mildly. I noticed the pianist was playing with his eyes closed, looking as if he were in pain. He was really wailing in a certain kind of a way that sounded familiar. I was sure that it must be George Wallington, the composer of "Lemon Drop," whom I had seen playing ten years before. Also playing bass was an old friend I had met with Bird four years ago, Teddy Kotick. I asked a guy at the bar and found out that the alto saxophonist was Jackie McLean. It was almost like it was when I saw Bird for the first time. His playing was completely different from anything I had heard since I left America.

I was really hypnotized. As the night went on, I heard a terrific trumpet player, Donald Byrd, and other musicians that came by to sit in. They all were playing something new to my ears. I spoke with Teddy Kotick and he reminded me of my basement days in Washington. He told me to come down to the union floor and said if I had any jobs to let him know.

"Man, are you kidding? I just got here," I said.

"That's O.K., there are not many French-horn players. You never know," he said. "You might not work for years, you might work tomorrow. This is New York." He said, "Come back after you've been in town a while and sit in with us. George is pretty nice about that."

The drummer in the group, Will Bradley, Jr., saw my horn case and came over to tell me some places where there were sessions. Rodney and I hung out there until early in the morning and then went back to his house.

"I don't know what you see in that music," he said. "It all sounds the same to me."

"It's hard to explain, Rodney," I said, while trying hard to explain. "I know that from your point of view it doesn't seem to have much variety and contrast, but you have to listen to it in a different way and get inside of it to see what the musician himself is saying. You have to feel the way he treats the notes and the way he creates a line and a sense of space. It's almost like composing on the spot. It's such a personal kind of music that you have to listen to it in a personal way, especially when you hear people that are improvising in their own way like these guys were, not just copying somebody else from a record."

"Well, I'll have to try harder," said Rodney, who eventually did become a jazz fan.

In the next two days, I enrolled in the Manhattan School and found an apartment on the Lower East Side. The third day I was in New York I called up Jerry Gray and went to see her at the Alvin Hotel. There was a young musician visiting her when I got there named Freddie Redd. He told me that he played piano and after talking to him a while I said, "Man, how come there aren't places to play all over the place? In Paris we could play anywhere. What's happening here?"

"There are places," said Freddie, smiling.

"But people seem sick and depressed here," I said.

"Well," said Freddie, laughing, "that's New York."

Five days later I walked into Birdland and ran smack into Leonard Feather, whom I'd seen last in Europe. He remembered me and asked me what I was doing. Bud Powell was playing and Charlie Mingus was his bassist. Mingus came up to Leonard Feather and told him he was forming a group of his own called the Jazz Workshop. Leonard introduced me to Mingus, who gave me a deep look.

"Hey, how are you, Mingus?" I said. "I'm Dave," and put out my hand.

He still gave me that deep look and then suddenly changed into a smile and said, "Hey, Dave," and shook my hand. Then he said a few more words to Leonard Feather and went back and played.

After the set was over he came back to the table where we were sitting and suddenly said to me, "How would you like to go on the road for $125 a week?"

I was rather taken aback by this because while Leonard had told him I was a good player, he had never heard me play and any young musician in New York would have been happy to play with Mingus.

I said to him, "Man, one of the reasons I came back to America was to get a chance to play music, but I'm going to try to go the

Manhattan School of Music so I don't know if I can go on the road or not. I want to study composition again."

"That's cool," he said. "Be at my house this Thursday at three o'clock in the afternoon. You see a friend of mine, George Barrow. He's the tenor player of the group. He'll show you how to get out there." He gave me George Barrow's address and phone number.

After I said good-bye to Leonard, I went down to my Lower East Side apartment feeling terrific. I'd only been in New York for five days and I was already going to work with Mingus. I called up George Barrow and we drove out to Mingus' place to rehearse. I played the written parts and then improvised. After playing two or three choruses I stopped and the other musicians looked pleasantly surprised.

"Hey," said Mingus, "you can play the parts and swing a little too. I think you'd be fine."

"There's only one trouble. I'm not a member of the union yet."

"That's O.K.," said Mingus. "Those union cats always try to hold someone good back. We'll go down there and make a case."

Mingus and I went down to the union a few days later and the union officials, even though they were not what you call jazz fans, obviously held Mingus in awe. There was no one else at that time that could play bass with his virtuosity or who had his astounding ideas in composition and improvising. He was ten or fifteen years ahead of anyone else in jazz. But the union rule was that you had to live six months in the city before you could work a steady job. I had only been in town a week.

"Can you find me a French-horn player that can play my music?" said Mingus.

The officials looked at each other. After a few minutes they told me I could open with Mingus in November at the Bohemia, but that was the only steady work I could have for the first six months.

"Those cats aren't really so bad," said Mingus as we left. "They just don't know what's happening when it comes to music."

"Thanks for helping me," I said.

"I'll see you at rehearsal," said Mingus. "How's music school?"

"I'll start next week," I said.

"By the time we go on the road you'll make it. You can learn more playing with me than they'll ever teach you there."

"I'll see you at rehearsal," I said.

I began to restudy theory, harmony, counterpoint, orchestration, and play in the Manhattan School woodwind quintet. Because I already had a B.A. in European history, I didn't have to take many academic subjects. It was a long trip from the Lower East Side up to One Hundred and Fifth Street, but I enjoyed it and I found that I could even do some of my work on the subway each way. The student body was very enthusiastic about music, very sincere and dedicated on the whole. The atmosphere of the school was warm and friendly. The teachers would often eat lunch with the students and meet with them informally.

There were also many excellent musicians at the school. Donald Byrd, the trumpeter I had heard my first night in New York, Buzz Garner, another man I had played with in Paris, and a whole army of bass players, pianists and drummers, including Phil Brown, whom I had known from the time he had played with Stan Getz in Washington—all were studying there. I saw many familiar faces from bands I had played with and orchestras I had played in and musicians I had seen in Europe, even guys as far back as junior high school.

My composition teachers were Ludmila Ulehla and Vittorio Giannini. They had their own system of teaching. They were not only excellent theorists but excellent composers. They thought that rather than teach the students any particular school of composition it was best to ground us in the traditional way. Giannini felt that after giving the composers the tools of the trade, it was then up to them to make music. There were six of us in Giannini's class. Some were interested in being songwriters and arrangers. A few wanted to be composers. Giannini was not too interested in jazz, although he played piano in dance bands in the twenties and could play ragtime when he was in a cheerful mood. His passion was orchestral, symphonic and operatic music. His mastery of music was so complete that he was able to read any score like a newspaper. He could sit down at a piano and sight-read the most complex orchestral work and could also hear it in his mind at sight. He never used the piano when he composed and wrote so quickly that the ink couldn't dry fast enough for the speed of his hand.

All the students would bother him with silly questions to challenge his knowledge. He took it all good-naturedly with a regal air. His answers always made profound musical points, which he assumed the students would really get or not get at all. He wasn't interested in showing off. He was only interested in teaching music.

Once, after a series of silly questions about why certain chords were more effective when they were voiced a certain way, Giannini went from behind his desk, lifted up the lid of the piano and crashed out a low C octave with his left hand and held it.

The class looked astonished.

"Listen," he blurted out. There was a great silence in the room and the octave chord rang out.

"Listen," he whispered, and we all listened. He put his head inside the piano to demonstrate the point. All of us heard the octave gradually die. The point he was making was that music is ultimately something to be *heard*. If the composer did not listen and hear, in his mind and with his ears, he certainly was not going to write any music that would mean anything emotionally. Without feeling very strongly how music should sound, he could never write anything that could communicate to people.

My other teacher, Miss Ulehla, was a born theorist and probably one of the most knowledgable teachers of harmonic procedures for twentieth-century music. She also wrote excellent music and was enthusiastic about teaching. She encouraged any original ideas that any of the students had no matter what style they wrote in. She was very quiet and serene and extremely gracious to all of us. She tried to fill in the gap that Giannini might have left for the students who were more unsure of themselves.

She also had a wonderful approach toward teaching orchestration. We would learn the rudiments of each instrument, take it home, then write pieces for it to play for the class. It was the first time that I had seen orchestration taught the way I believed it should be: the composer or student composer actually took the instrument in his hands and made a sound on it. While some of the pieces and the performances by the student composers were pretty far-out sounding, it was great fun and also an excellent way to learn.

I also enjoyed playing in the woodwind quintet. Gunther Schuller was our faculty coach as well as my horn teacher. His knowledge of modern music showed in the pieces he had us play, such as Irving Fine's Partita, works by Nielsen, Hindemith, and compositions by student composers as well. When the woodwind quintet was broadcast on WNYC, we would call up Gunther to see if he had heard the broadcast. He was a great teacher as well as an accomplished hornist, composer and conductor and because he also had such a genuine interest and affection for jazz and for young people, all the students loved him. Occasionally he would come to our concerts and that would make us play a little better. When I told him I was going to play with Mingus in November, he promised to come down to the Bohemia and listen.

Mingus had final rehearsals at the Bohemia the afternoon we opened. Even in the afternoon the atmosphere was full of excitement. On the walls were huge photographs of Miles Davis, Charlie Parker, Dizzy Gillespie, Max Roach, Bud Powell and many other greats who had changed jazz forever. Just looking at their pictures made you want to play.

The Bohemia was packed with all kinds of people, including some gorgeous girls. In addition to that were many fine musicians in the audience. I played through the sets with Mingus and everyone in the band seemed happy. The arrangements were often completely different from the way we rehearsed them. Some of the things we did on the spot, but I was able to get into the groove right away. You just opened up and let the telepathy flow. I didn't even feel tired when I went to school the next day because I was so elated from playing.

The weeks went by like minutes. When Mingus wasn't rehearsing or working, we would go down to hear Miles play at the Bohemia. He was making his big comeback and it was during one of these nights that I met Monk. At this time Monk had been forgotten by much of the jazz world and was nearly unknown to the general public. I was thrilled when I saw him and told him about how great I thought his recording of "Little Rootie Tootie" was. We talked a while and I told him about Paris and about having seen Bird a few years ago. Then he said, "Give me your number." He pulled out an ancient address book that had numbers and names written all over at every crazy angle and seemed to be falling apart in all directions at once.

"Maybe I'd better write it down on a card," I said.

"No, no. That's cool. Just let me write it here."

After about four minutes of thumbing through pages, he found one tiny blank space and very meticulously wrote down my number.

"Now you write down my number," he said. I wrote it down and the next day after school I called him up. "Hey, Dave," he said. "Come on over."

I went over and began the first of a series of after-school sessions with him. We would sit around for hours, talking and listening. I watched Monk listen to the radio, or to whatever people were saying or whatever was happening. Part of his fantastic power was to be able to absorb anything, use it himself and make it his own. He would listen to the radio for hours without even bothering to change the station. Somehow listening with him, you could feel that there was something in the music, no matter what it was. His remarks and comments on music were unbelievably perceptive. I played him a composition of mine and he seemed to understand what it was all about. He also told me that he liked my horn playing and that he would come by and visit me.

A few days later he trudged up the six flights of stairs in my building and we spent the whole day jamming, talking, eating and generally hanging out. Musicians that hang out simply stay together, talk, share ideas and listen to records. Instead of having a jam session, they have a kind of verbal, psychic, spiritual, telepathic session. I played Monk some more of my music and records I had made in Paris and told him about music school. He again invited me to come by after school anytime, which I did. He also taught me some of his compositions.

Just before Christmas, Mingus came back to the Bohemia. The second night there I met Max Roach, who asked me if I would write some arrangements for his group. Apparently the word had gotten around that I was a composer as well as a horn player. I wrote a tune and called it "In Monk's Garden." Max and his co-leader Clifford Brown liked it and decided that they would put it in their repertoire. The group Max and Clifford had with pianist Richie Powell, tenor saxophonist Harold Land, and bassist George Morrow was extraordinary.

The day after I met Max, I met Sonny Rollins who had just come back from Chicago. I had just been called by Betty Rollins (no relation), a student at Sarah Lawrence, and asked to bring a band to play at school. She was on the ship that I came back on and now wanted to have a jazz group come to Sarah Lawrence. I asked Sonny if he could make it.

"Can't you make it a little more than that?" he said.

"I'm sorry. That's all she's giving us."

"O.K.," he said. "I'll be there. Who else is going to be in the band?"

"I don't know," I said. "I'll go down and try to get Teddy Kotick and some other guys I know."

"Well, we'll have a good time," he said.

I went down to the union floor for the first time to look for Teddy and try to find a drummer and pianist. The floor was the most insane scene I'd ever witnessed. It looked like those pictures of Wall Street during the stock market crash only with about ten thousand musicians. You could see when you walked in that the group was divided into different sections. First there was what was called the Toupee Clique—guys mostly in their forties, all of whom wore toupees and had dyed waxed mustaches. They were the commercial-killer types who had most of the club dates and Bar Mitzvahs sewed up. They were surrounded by guys who were not quite in that scene but were looking for that type of work. They didn't talk to anybody else.

Then there were the regular society musicians who were a little better dressed, not quite so mean-looking but had shifty eyes. Some of them were angling for those great jobs on the big passenger boats, which were well paying. Others were trying to break into the Meyer Davis office. They also had no time to talk to anybody else. Then there were the Latin musicians. They were easy to spot because they were much more friendly, many seemed stoned and they laughed a lot. Often, the Latin drummers had their congas with them. The symphonic section was also easy to spot. These musicians looked like most symphony musicians do everyplace, rather conservative but always wearing strange color patterns—greenish tweed coats with baggy pants, hand-knit ties and often space shoes. They were quiet and serious-looking. There were also some marvelous retired symphonic musicians from the old country in their seventies or eighties still trying to make a come back with long, flowing hair in the Franz Liszt style, often speaking Italian, German and French. Listening to their conversations about the great conductors and soloists they played with was worth the trip to the union floor. Then there were the swing men who dressed more or less in the 1940s style and who had a different kind of language.

Finally there was the bebopper's section. These were all guys who knew there would be no work. I could tell from their slouched positions and the leather bags they held their cases in that they were beboppers and post–beboppers. They would get together to find out whether there were going to be any sessions that weekend, who had some good pot or just to talk endlessly about music, chord substitutions and what was happening.

In addition to thousands of voices, names were constantly barked over a loudspeaker. Later I found out the musicians would pay fifty cents to have their names called out with the hope that the repetition would inspire other people to hire them or make it look like they were busy, even though everybody was hip to this hype. I began to realize that most of these musicians were out of work for the moment or they wouldn't have been there.

I finally spotted Teddy. "My man, I have a great gig with Sonny Rollins coming up this Saturday night. How can I get a rhythm section?"

"Well," he said "I don't think I can make it, but . . ." At that point I was almost bowled over by an army of bassists and drummers. Within three seconds I had a bass player and a drummer. I'd already asked an outstanding young pianist, Cedar Walton, and there was Sonny on saxophone and myself on French horn. So we had our quintet.

I had not heard Sonny play in person, but his records had really knocked me out. His whole extension of what Bird had done, the West Indian feeling that he got in some of his music, plus his humor and his whole way of using a tenor saxophone, were unique. I could hardly wait to start work.

When we began playing at Sarah Lawrence that night, I was completely overwhelmed by Sonny. I'd never heard anything like this in my life. His records had captured nothing of the real Sonny Rollins. He was able to take one theme and develop it almost symphonically, making the saxophone an entire orchestra playing and answering itself. Eventually he extended this style of playing into some recordings, where he would play unaccompanied saxophone.

As we were playing a familiar tune he suddenly stopped, turned to Cedar and asked, "What was that you were playing?" Cedar was so surprised that he stopped playing himself. "What was it?" said Sonny. Cedar told him. "I just wanted to see," said Sonny. Then he went back and played about ten more choruses and each time he got to the part with that chord, he used Cedar's alteration as the basis of alterations for all the other chords. I realized without his explaining it that a large part of his phenomenal mastery of playing came from the fact that he knew every single note of each chord and all their substitutions. I saw how much the brain as well as the feeling played a part in this kind of music and what a refined art jazz had become. The fact was, jazz men were exploring harmony in a way that had not been done since the time of Debussy and Ravel. While most classical composers had abandoned harmony altogether, it was being rediscovered, reexplored and reexpressed by the jazz men, who had a profound influence on my composing.

As the evening progressed, the music got so exciting that the president of the college got his clarinet and sat in with us. We were asked to come back and play another concert a month later. The girls there were lovely and we hated to leave.

Late that night we went to my house and I cooked an avant-garde vegetarian meal. Then we went down to the Café Bohemia and although I wasn't working there that week, all the musicians from Mingus' band had come to sit in and we played again.

I continued to see Sonny many times after that. Although we never worked together again, we played together many, many times. He kept up an interest in my composition and also encouraged me as a horn player. He knew how much I was scuffling with the French horn. Whenever he introduced me to a girl he would say, "This is David Amram, a very excellent French *horn*ist," with a dramatic pause before the "hornist," and a significant look to make me feel good.

On Christmas Eve of 1955, I played the Bohemia again with Mingus and ran into Lionel Hampton, whom I had not seen since I'd been in Paris.

"You're doing great, kid," he said to me. "You're working in New York City." He and many other fine musicians of his era had to wait ten or fifteen years to be able to come to New York and then many years before they could work there. In years afterward when I was out of work and broke and pretty desperate, I always remembered what he said.

As 1956 arrived I found that I was beginning to compose more than ever. School seemed to stimulate me into writing music. When I wasn't working at night I would jam with other musicians. Then I would go home, do my studies, then my own composing. By that time, it was usually time to go to school. After two or three days of this in a row, I would be so tired that it was hard for me to concentrate on everything.

I had a terrible problem collecting my GI payments. It required taking a whole day off from school to go and usually after waiting for hours I would get the same answer: "I don't know what it is, but the check seemed to be delayed. I'm sure this will all be straightened out, if you come back in a week or so. Don't worry, you'll get your money." It was very discouraging because my budget was tight, to say the least, and I was just about penniless at this point.

By February I was flat broke. I began working at odd jobs, doing manual labor or going to shapeups in the Village or elsewhere. In the early morning you could show up and do any kind of carpentry or moving work. I felt the strain, but as long as I was making music, nothing else mattered. My rent was only forty-eight dollars a month, so I didn't have trouble meeting that. I also kept going down to the union hall every Monday, Wednesday and Friday afternoon, hoping for a job.

The jam sessions at Ken Karpe's apartment on East Twenty-eighth Street served as a catalyst for some of the best jazz of the middle fifties. Because of Bird's death, many musicians felt that a leader had disappeared. Miles Davis said that New York would never be the same without Charlie Parker. Bird was missed by thousands of people who knew him, people from every walk of life. During the last years of his life he was employed less and less, so he spent an enormous amount of time with young musicians who were coming along, painters, poets, in fact just about anyone who had any human quality. In a way the jazz world was tied together because of this loss.

The sessions at Ken's started during the time I was working at the Bohemia with Mingus. One night after a job I invited Mingus, Oscar Pettiford, the renowned bassist and trumpeter Art Farmer, for a session. When we all arrived there were other musicians already playing. They were amateurs and when they saw Oscar, Art and Mingus, they stopped. Everyone sat around looking uncomfortable. Ken's wife at the time, Sylvia, was a fantastic hostess, one of those women who was able to make everyone feel at home just by those qualities of sweetness and awareness and consideration that she had. But even she was having a hard time cheering everyone up. Sometimes when Oscar had a few drinks he would start shouting at people, but it was always in mock anger and with that wild sense of fun, hoping that they would respond and call his bluff. He began to grumble as everyone sat around staring. Finally someone took out his horn and Mingus sat down at the piano. Art Farmer and I joined them.

We all had such a good time that we played until about seven in the morning. We decided that those of us who weren't working would meet Saturday at midnight and those who were would come over after three. The next week more musicians came and within a month we had the most exciting sessions imaginable: Monk, Jim Hall, Zoot Sims, Joe Gordon, Chico Hamilton, Gil Coggins, Lefty Sims, Freddie Redd, Nobby Totah, Chuck Israels, Willie Jones, Cedar Walton, Art Taylor and the whole new group of musicians who had just come from Detroit; fabulous baritone saxophonist Pepper Adams, trumpeter Thad Jones, Doug Watkins, Paul Chambers, Tommy Flanagan, and Elvin Jones. All were there plus many more musicians no one had heard of who were really something. Max Roach's whole group with Clifford Brown, Richie Powell and Sonny came frequently.

The younger musicians like myself referred to these sessions as "school." I was not working too much, so when Saturday rolled around I would have a complete rest so that I could play twenty-four hours straight. I was on the first of one of my post-Army health kicks. Thad Jones used to kid me because at nine o'clock one morning before we ate some waffles at Bickford's, I ran around the block three times.

At these sessions musicians would wait and wait just to play. One time the drummer Philly Joe Jones complained because we played one tune which he timed with his watch for an hour and twenty minutes. He swore he would never play again unless people limited the number of their choruses, but fortunately he changed his mind and came back the next week. When the audience comprises mostly people that really listen, the standard of playing changes. There's always a relationship between the musicians and the audience. But most of us in jazz were used to the fact that especially during the late forties and fifties not many people were atuned to what we were doing, so we played more or less for one another, hoping, of course, that people would eventually react. And when there was an audience reaction, you could feel that the music was almost pulled from you by this psychic rapport.

I felt like this a few times when I played at the after-hours place at the St. Theresa Hotel in Harlem. It was nicknamed The Hole, and Joe Knight, a wonderful pianist from Brooklyn, used to play there with his trio from three until nine in the morning. With that audience you could really feel the interest in the music. It was like having a conversation, talking with a few hundred people. But usually this was not the case in clubs, so most of us got used to playing for one another. At Ken's the audience comprised the greatest musicians, and the greater the musician, the better he can listen.

At Ken's house the whole atmosphere was so beautiful that we would stay until we were exhausted. Some of the sessions would last as long as twenty-four hours, with different shifts coming and going. Some of the superenthusiasts like myself, Freddie Redd, Gil Coggins and Willie Jones would stay around the full day and then go "hang out." Some of us would go to my apartment on the Lower East Side and play for a day or two afterward. I would skip school on Monday, play a little more, fall asleep, get up, eat, talk about music all day, listen to records or analyze the solos of Sonny Rollins, Miles or Monk on their most recent recordings.

At that time John Coltrane had begun playing with Miles, but he had not developed his style to the extent that he did during the last few years of his life. He was an outstanding player and all the musicians liked him.

Through the sessions I became very good friends with Richie Powell. He used to talk to me a lot about symphonic compositions he was interested in and also about the French horn. He suggested trying to find a style that would suit the instrument. Clifford Brown also used to speak to me about this and mentioned that my playing would sound better for jazz purposes if each note was articulated rather than trying to imitate the saxophone. It was almost impossible for anyone to hear specific rapid notes when played, except for possibly another French-horn player or a well-trained musician. It was from Clifford Brown and Richie Powell that I got a new approach toward playing the horn in jazz.

The one thing I learned from Ken's sessions was the tremendous harmonic knowledge all the musicians had at this point. Every saxophone player or trombone player or trumpet player was a master at keyboard harmony. Although there were many pianists eager to play, they had to jump in fast because every horn player there could play excellent piano. If they didn't play solos on the piano, they all had a thorough knowledge of harmony and voice movement and could accompany beautifully. Horn players also had a way of not playing too much behind a soloist but rather feeding just the right chords that would fit the style of the soloist. It was sort of a super-informal workshop and something that I've never seen before and doubt will happen again for quite a while.

One Monday night I decided to go up to Birdland and hear some music. Monday nights were jam sessions and I knew that toward the end of the evening I could sit in. I got past Pee Wee, the tiny doorman with the high voice who recognized me from the times I had been there before, and went over to the bullpen, the crowded section on the left where the most devoted listeners and musicians sat. Others stood at the bar, digging and talking about music. I heard a cooking set, but the smoke was getting in my eyes. When I stepped out into the street during intermission I heard a familiar voice.

"David, the sour cream king. You're back."

I turned around and there was Malcolm Raphael. I hadn't seen him since the night we had spent together before I went into the army.

"Malcolm . . . steineroony . . . burger . . . voutissimo!" I said, shouting with happiness and almost breaking his wrist as I gave him some skin in a mighty fashion.

"Dr. Amramstein . . . horn-spielovitz!" he replied bursting into a warm, modulated baritone cackle and taking off his glasses, rubbing the bridge of his nose and putting them on again. This was a gesture that he often would use when he was suddenly struck by something unexpected. We went into the bar next door, where he told me he had gone to the University of Michigan, gotten his law degree and passed his bar exam. Then he had decided he didn't want to practice law in Michigan so he was in New York.

"That's great," I said. "Where're you living?"

"Well, at the moment I'm sic transit mundi. I still have my convertible M.G. Everything I own is in the trunk, including a law degree. I've got to pass the New York Bar exam so that I can afford to become America's leading stride pianist. My erudition didn't make me a sellout. I'm still broke. But *brilliant*."

"That's a gas," I told him. "I have a big four-room apartment right down in the heart of Old Ukrania on the Lower East Side. You can come and stay there. As long as you're not bitten by rats you'll find it's great atmosphere for studying."

We went back to Birdland and I told Pee Wee about the sessions we used to have in my basement in Washington when Malcolm had played with some of the musicians who were now working at Birdland. He let Malcolm in free. We listened to the session and I sat in on the last set. Then we went back to spend the night talking, as usual.

"I don't want to put you out, David" said Malcolm, a little concerned, as we trudged up the six flights.

"Don't worry, my man," I said, "You can stay here in peaceful surroundings. It will probably really be just what you need to pass your bar exam."

When Malcolm entered the room he blanched a bit, took off his glasses and rubbed his nose. There were four or five people in my apartment, which I honestly forgot to tell him about. Because of my casual style of living, I had become adjusted to being able to work whether I was completely alone or with ten or fifteen other people around, sleeping, eating, practicing music or whatever. My powers of concentration had grown stronger, even if my powers of organization hadn't.

Malcolm looked around. "Maybe if I come back later it would be a little less crowded," he suggested tactfully.

"That's cool, Malcolm," I told him, "I have another sleeping bag here."

"That's no go," said Bill, an old friend of mine from Washington. He had been a drummer and was now working in the daytime to get himself straightened out so he could play again.

"Look," I said, "while you're away during the daytime Malcolm can use your sleeping bag and while you're sleeping at night he can study."

"Well," said Bill, grumbling, "why can't he use Bashir's bed when he's out working in the daytime?"

"That's when Edith is sleeping in it," I told him.

We had worked out a system of sleeping in shifts that would have made the Hilton management jealous. In the midst of all these people coming and going, smoking pot, shooting up drugs or saying their prayers (as Bashir would, five times a day), practicing, having endless discussions about Buddhism, the True Islam, Hinduism and whether or not Adlai Stevenson would make a Yin or Yang president—I would practice the horn or the piano and do my latest studies for school. I just didn't have the heart to kick these people out in the streets. As I was the only one who could guarantee the forty-eight-a-month rent, I didn't mind. Malcolm offered to chip in a little on the rent.

"Man, that's the best news I've heard from you since you quit the CIA. If you've got it, that would be a real treat. Most of my other tenants at the moment aren't doing so well financially." Malcolm pulled out his wallet and laid a crisp twenty-dollar bill on me. As I snapped it a few times admiring it, everyone in the apartment woke up and came around as if they had heard the opening chords of the Eroica Symphony. We all stood in silence, admiring the green and white beauty of Andrew Jackson.

"O.K.," I said, "the delicatessen is still open, let's go down and get some soul food." We all scampered down the stairs.

"Zikel," I said to the old owner, a Polish Jew. He and his wife had survived a concentration camp and they still had their tattoos on their arms. He looked nonchalantly at all of us. "I'd like you to meet my friend Malcolm."

"A wonderful boy," said Zikel. Then he whispered, *"Iz er a Yid?"* (Is he Jewish?) I pointed to my heart, to my head, to Malcolm and gave him a wink. That meant even if he wasn't, he was the greatest.

I still hadn't learned the art of ordering food in a scientific way. Malcolm watched in amazement while I spent the whole twenty-dollars getting creamed herring, olives, artichoke hearts, frozen blintzes, three dozen bagels, a pound of sweet butter, four jars of Mother's gefilte fish, six pounds of beets, half a dozen eggs, two half-pints of heavy cream, six bottles of Dr. Brown's black cherry soda, two jars of marmalade, some maple syrup, two pounds of macaroni salad, a quart of sour cream, three pounds of potato salad, and six eight-inch smoked white fish that were lying sadly on their sides, covered with flies.

I looked at Malcolm. "Don't worry, pops," I said to him, "we're going to have a real old-time feast just like we did when Charlie Parker came to visit us that night in my basement."

We went upstairs and took out my old straw box and the card table, which I wrote music on. We placed an old towel over it and spread out a great banquet with candles. I then got my own home-made borscht from the icebox and made a white fish, marmalade, spaghetti and sour cream omelet with maple syrup, brown sugar, chopped onions, oregano and garlic, with bagels and artichoke hearts on the side, topped by a dessert of blintzes and Dr. Brown's black cherry soda. It was a little too flavorful for my other tenants. While I scarfed up a storm, Malcolm surreptitiously ate up the three pounds of potato salad while he told me all about his experiences in law school, his romances and his plans after he passed his bar exam.

The following weekend at Ken's jam session, Oscar Pettiford announced he was going to form a band. We had a nucleus that came every week to play and Oscar decided this group of superenthusiasts could make a great new sound in jazz. He hired Julius Watkins, the brilliant French hornist, and myself; a harpist, Betty Glamann; a flute and saxophone player, Jerome Richardson; Gigi Gryce, who did most of the arrangements as well as played a superlative saxophone; Sahib Shahab, who was a mainstay at Ken Karpe's sessions and had a quintet of his own for a while that featured Tommy Flanagan, a pianist who also was in Oscar's band. J. R. Montrose also played saxophone and the trumpets were Art Farmer and Ernie Royal. Jimmy Cleveland played trombone and Osie Johnson was the drummer. Needless to say, it was some band!

Ken Karpe told us that if Oscar was going to form this band there ought to be a concert for it and he decided to have an Easter Jazz Festival at Town Hall. Although Ken had never produced a concert, we were sure he could do anything. With his sharp suits and attaché case, he looked like he could never lose. In addition to Oscar's band, Ken told us Thelonius Monk was going to play at the concert with his quintet and trio. He had Ray Copeland and Sahib Shahab in his quintet and they also played in our band with Oscar. So we all rehearsed a few times and felt ready for the White House.

I had spent the whole night before the concert completing a piece featuring Julius Watkins and myself with the band. We only rehearsed it twice, but when we performed it that night, it sounded as if the band had been playing together for over a year. That's how great the musicians were. It was really an all-star band. Every member had his own band on the side.

After we finished our set, Monk sat down at the piano. Our band remained onstage to listen. The communal feeling was overwhelming. As Monk played, all the musicians looked at him with so much love it just about heated up the stage. The audience could feel it too, seeing all these musicians listening and looking intently and they began to pay even more attention.

Monk played fantastically. He had been really struggling the last few years and at that point had more or less retired to his apartment. I had never seen him perform except at his house and at my place once. This was the first time I saw what a really natural showman he was. He brought down the house. In spite of the fact he was neglected by much of the music world, he always had a following. He was unique and he couldn't be anybody but Monk. He had his own style of playing and his own technique, just as he had his own style of harmonic usage, of time relationships, of dress, speech, walk and mannerism. He was a total individualist and as a friend of mine remarked to us after the concert, "It sounds as if that music is coming right out of his head into the piano."

The concert was a great success artistically, even though Kenny lost his shirt financially. He didn't care. The concert was so beautiful that he felt he had made a great contribution to music and to all his friends who had come and played at his house so many times.

The sessions at Ken's came to an end because of an awful event. It was shortly after our concert at Town Hall that Clifford Brown and Richie Powell died in a tragic car accident. Kenny and I had been with Richie just a few weeks before when he was getting his marriage license. His wife had also been killed. Clifford Brown's funeral was in Delaware, but the service for Richie was right outside Willow Grove, Pennsylvania, where I used to go as a kid to the amusement park. Ken and I made this sad trip up on a beautiful day. People showed up from all over. His father and mother were comforting all his young friends, who were trying not to cry but couldn't help it. When I saw Richie in his coffin I couldn't believe he was gone. He was someone who had so much music in him. Even though he had been overshadowed by his brother Bud, Richie had something unique of his own to offer as a player and as a composer. Listening to the few records that he and Clifford Brown made is an experience that never fails to move people even after so much time has passed.

We drove Richie's father back to New York. He told us proudly how Richie and Bud had studied and practiced so much all their lives. It's a shame that so few people know how much time and effort jazz musicians put into their music. Jazz is a whole area of music that has yet to be appreciated. Its ultimate importance has not yet been realized. Its influence is felt, but the music itself fails to support but a handful of its practitioners. Even though it has lost a great deal of its popularity at this writing, it's still being performed all over the world today. As fine as the players were then, there are thousands of brilliant players today.

The standards keep getting better as the horizons broaden. The teen-age jazz player today has the vocabulary of Charlie Parker, Sonny Rollins, John Coltrane and Ornette Coleman. He also has a knowledge of classical music and quite often composes, arranges and plays several instruments. The future of jazz should be as important and unpredictable as its past. Whether or not it becomes an all-engulfing force of popular music is beside the point. Beethoven's last string quartets aren't as popular as some of his symphonies, but they still hold a unique place in the music world.

Often when I sat up at night on the roof copying music, I could hear the singing coming from the synagogue next door. It was an old, broken-down temple like the one I'd been to in Frankfort. Most of the congregation were elderly Polish Jews who had escaped from the old ghetto only to come over to this new American ghetto instead. It seemed ironic; yet when I watched them in the park and occasionally talked in Yiddish to them, they seemed completely resigned and unaffected by it all. I would see them sitting on their roofs on fair spring days or watching solemnly as the Ukrainians played their guitar music and accordions quietly at night in Tompkins Square Park.

There were mostly older people living on my block and while there was a large mixture of Puerto Ricans and Negroes, everyone got along amazingly well. It was really a true melting pot. Most of us were in the same boat. We all lived there because that was the rent we could afford. Although there were a few bad gangs, they would leave you alone if they knew you weren't going to bother them. There was a certain kind of honor present in the neighborhood then. It wasn't called the East Village but simply and definitely the Lower East Side. The artists that lived there fitted in very well with the community because they had respect for their neighbors and their neighbors' conditions.

At the synagogue next door I would see a lot of people entering the temple on Saturday and on the holy holidays. I could see them from my roof as if I were watching a religious procession from a mountaintop. When I heard the singing, it seemed to tell me that there I was again, that I was being followed around by something very old inside me. It seemed to be beckoning me back to the fold. Sometimes I'd sit in the hallway with my ear against the wall. I didn't want to go to temple while my life was still so wild and disorganized. I used to have long discussions with Bashir and had even considered becoming a Muslim because intellectually a lot of its tenets appealed to me as much as Judaism. Still I felt that even though they were both close as brother religions, I couldn't convert.

I spoke to Malcolm about this, since I found him to be a philosophical sage in addition to such great company.

"You just continue in your travels, David," he said. "You have to realize that part of your tradition is to doubt everything and then to rediscover it inside yourself."

"It's nothing intellectual, Malcolm. It's something I feel." I took him next to the wall in the hallway to listen to the singing. "Isn't that something?"

"Man, that's real soul music," said Malcolm. "Those cats are wailing in there."

"I know, Malcolm, it really gets me."

"Well," said Malcolm, "we don't even have to go into your collective unconscious to find that this is part of your vocabulary as a composer. If you know who and what you are and never forget it, it'll be a lot easier for you to try to sound like David Amram. You have a natural lyrical gift, so the best thing is to develop that in yourself."

"Well," I told him, "I'm not trying to copy the tunes they're singing here, but I sure would be happy if my music could get some of that impact and power." We went up to the roof. Bashir joined us and we sat there listening to the old men singing. Then we looked across the black tar and gravel roof, up to the Con Edison towers where the East River was dimly sparkling. An occasional tug would go by, softly mooing. We could hear all those old souls from Poland. Their voices made me feel the ghetto walls in the old streets and past that back to Medieval Europe.

As the first school year came to an end, I dropped out. I hated to leave, but I was stone broke. My GI payments were still three months late and I wasn't getting any work playing the horn. The only way I could get by was going to shape-ups for a day's work, painting, moving furniture, cleaning—anything at all to get enough to make ends meet.

I was writing more and more music on my own. My piles of sketches and parts of various pieces got larger than my composition assignments. I wanted to study for four years, but I knew I really didn't need school to make me compose. I loved the Manhattan School and my teachers. I was so ashamed to drop out that I couldn't even tell them in person. I didn't want to look like I was begging. I simply stopped showing up.

Things hit an all-time low. New York was becoming a dragon I had to fight every day. I used to sit on the tar and gravel roof of mine and look out through the smog at the poisonous clouds blowing from the chimneys and think of how hard it was to survive, much less become a composer and all-round musician. Malcolm had moved off with his girl friend. Bill, my old acquaintance from Washington, had stolen a week's earnings I had left out on the piano and cut out. I was stuck with other people who had come for a night but somehow never left. Shoplifters, drug users, connections—it didn't seem to matter to me somehow. But after my apartment was robbed for the second time, I threw everyone out except Bashir, who was staying there because he was a real friend. He was also an excellent singer and musician and had taught me a lot about the Muslim religion and its moral tenets. He never said a harsh word to anyone. No matter whom he was with, he would try to help them straighten themselves out even though he was in desperate financial straits himself.

One night Bashir and I went to the Club Harlem. I played with the band and he sat in the corner looking on disapprovingly, as everyone was swinging with the music, drinking and generally having a merry time.

When we left he said to me, "Those people are fools, how do they think they're ever going to get out of these conditions? If they don't stop those stupidities they'll be slaves forever. Drinking and smoking and taking drugs helps to keep them down and they don't even know it. You can never understand this, Dave, unless you are in it. You can't imagine what it's like, seeing your own people remaining so backward and acting so foolish. It's heartbreaking, but we're trying to change and enlighten these people so they'll straighten up and act like men. As long as they continue with this foolishness the system's always going to beat them. You've got to have skills and you've got to have tools."

Two weeks later, my apartment was robbed for the third time. I realized I was down to nothing. I had all my instruments and valuables in the pawn shop except my good horn. I wasn't getting any jobs playing and although I appeared at some of the shape-ups, there wasn't much work there either. I was rummaging through my straw box to see if I had left any money in my collection of music and letters that hadn't been stolen. Suddenly I came across two war bonds I had bought with the stamps from the money I had made planting the acre of corn I had harvested with Artie McCrae and Eddie Filemyr in Feasterville. As I looked at the war bonds my mind went back to when I was ten years old, in love with Peggy Klink and driving my tractor, milking cows and dreaming of being a musician.

Here I was, twenty-five years old with nothing. I really felt blue. For a minute I thought I wouldn't cash those war bonds. I felt by turning them in, I was cashing in the last of my innocence and dreams. I just sat there on my dirty linoleum floor and thought about what I was doing and where I was going.

After about half an hour I decided things couldn't be any different and this was the way it had to be. Everyone else I knew had paid dues and I was still paying mine. I went down to a place on the corner and cashed them in.

Terry Southern had returned from Paris a little after I did and had brought the copy I had given him of the jazz record I had made with Bobby Jaspar. On it were some of my compositions, one of which was a favorite of his, "The Birds of Montparnasse." I had used flute, harpsichord, French horn, bass and drums. He liked it so much that he played it for Al Avakian, a film editor and an old Parisian expatriate like us.

Terry called me. "What's happening, mon vieux?"

"Rien, Terry. Je suis wasted."

I went over to see Terry at Al's house. Al liked the record and had already taped it himself. We spent the night reminiscing about Paris and old friends there. Terry told me not to feel blue. He was wasted himself.

A few weeks later I received a call from Hal Freeman. He was a friend of Al Avakian's and when Al played him my piece "The Birds of Montparnasse" he liked it so much that he decided he wanted me to do the music for his documentary film *Echo of an Era*. He knew nothing about me except what he had heard from Terry and Al but most important from my music. I told him in all fairness that while I had written music for some plays, and while of course I had been composing a good part of my life, that I had never written music for a film.

"No problem," he said. "I can show you everything you need to know in an hour."

The next afternoon, he did. The mechanics of writing music for a film is probably one of the simplest problems that any composer has to face. Although there have been many articles from Hollywood's leading hacks describing the immense complications of fitting music to a film, anyone with a third-grade education and any kind of visual sense can write a film score. The basic ingredients are: (1) a stopwatch, (2) a metronome and (3) the ability to divide feet and frames into seconds. And for those who have trouble with division and multiplication, there are plastic wheels that convert the number of feet into seconds.

Quite simply, when you have decided where the music will begin and where it will end, you measure that particular length of film on a Movieola, which has a footage counter quite like an old-fashioned car speedometer. If it is to be music for ninety feet (60 seconds) followed by a different kind of music for twenty feet (13.5 seconds) then the only problem is how to make sure before you get to the recording session—where it is very expensive to keep musicians waiting—that the music will be the exact length. This is figured very simply by the number of feet you can have. If there is to be one minute of music and the tempo is appropriate to the visual image of a metronome marking a quarter-note equaling 60, then there have to be exactly sixty beats. This would mean that if the piece is written in three-quarter time, you would have twenty measures of music. By setting the metronome at this speed, and checking it with a stopwatch, you can be certain that a piece of music of a circumscribed length will work out to 60 seconds. If you conduct a little too fast, of course, you can slow up at the end, or if you fall behind, you can speed up at a certain place. Sometimes this is done deliberately, to emphasize a dramatic moment, but the mechanical part is extremely simple.

The most difficult part in writing film music is deciding where the music should start, where it should stop and the nature of the music as it relates to the entire fabric and structure of the picture. The composer must decide how the music, as it appears throughout the film, can best serve to aid the entire picture, to give the picture an additional form and possibly to accentuate certain parts of the movie which might not come across as well without music.

The idea of the orgiastic, roaring orchestra, 110 men all honking as loudly as possible, playing the same melody over and over, is quite familiar to American filmgoers. Often movie music of this kind steals quite liberally from other composers at will. This whole idea of film music is quite fortunately just about dead. It originated, I believe, during the days of the silent actors when those great thespians of the silver screen were put in the mood by a borscht-belt type of violinist who would sit on the side of the sound stage sawing away some old Bessarabian melodies to make the actors feel something.

I told Hal Freeman that this kind of music was not the genre I could do successfully. I told him most movie music made me sick and assumed that if he liked my piece "The Birds of Montparnasse" he was looking for something other than reheated Wagner with a side order of Montavanni. He assured me that he was interested in having some kind of music that related to the film and was also good music on its own. He said that the better the music was, the better chance it had to relate to a visual idea of a high caliber. The intangible factor was how the music and film related to each other. He discussed this at great length. He was a professional film editor, a graduate of St. John's College and very dedicated to film making as an art.

He spent the day telling me about the real artists of American cinema who worked in documentary films: giants like Flaherty, Francis Thompson, Alexander Hammid and younger men like Leacock, Pennebaker, David Young and others. This was the only kind of cinema that continued to grow as an art form. Nothing else interested Hal. He felt that cinema was more than something to pass the time of day, more than a diversion to enable an audience to get off the street and forget their troubles.

Hal explained to me that he would help me as much as he could with the mechanics, although he assured me that there would be little trouble. He told me he would lend me his Movieola and wanted me to decide where I thought the music should be and what character I thought it should have. He had spent nearly two years working on the film with writer Arnold Bloom. He wanted me to take my time so I could do my best.

Not only that, but he offered me some money! The most I had received for composing until then was five dollars for writing music for *Hamlet* at Howard University. When he gave me a hundred dollars in advance, I almost passed out. I couldn't believe that someone would pay me for doing something I had been doing all my life for nothing. Needless to say, I didn't turn the money down. It might have sounded like a token payment, but to me it meant food.

The next day Hal brought the Movieola up to my house and we began to watch the movie. It was all about the history of the Third Avenue El, filmed in color. It began with shots of the El rocking toward the viewer, followed by a flashback showing its history. The entire flashback was constructed by the ingenious use of stills from the eighteen nineties. People then thought the El represented the coming of Armageddon as well as the end of the horse and buggy era. It was a great group of pictures, painstakingly selected from the Museum of the City of New York.

The old drawings and cartoons were all edited so brilliantly, even in the rough cut, that I liked the film immediately and knew that somehow I would be able to write music for it successfully. The end of the picture returned to a real shot of the El again, showing New York in the fifties, just before its demolition. Hal told me that there would be music, some narration, but no dialogue or sound effects. The music would have to play an important part and he kept stressing that I should feel free in composing it. He explained to me that even if some of the music didn't fit exactly, he could adjust the film. On the other hand, I could adjust the music as the film changed if he decided to make changes later.

With this kind of wonderful working relationship, I sat down as soon as Hal left my place and watched the film for about twelve hours. Every few days I would have a friend look at the Movieola with me. Watching it with someone gave me more of a feeling of theatrical involvement by picking up their reactions to the film. This was the same kind of orientation that I had always gotten from the theater where the actors pick up things from one another, from what the audience is feeling and from the whole telepathic feeling of the theater. Because this does not exist in films until after they are completed, I found it very helpful to watch it with people who were seeing it for the first time, not to discuss the music but just to be aware of their feelings as they saw the same thing I was watching.

Hal came back in about three weeks and asked me if I had any ideas. I sang him the theme that I used for the El in the beginning— one that I developed through most of the picture—and played him other parts of the music. I decided to use tenor saxophone. My friend George Barrow and I wanted to form a group anyway. We were no longer with Mingus. I asked George if he would also play flute, which he was studying and doing very well on. I knew bassoon player Dave Kurtzer, who played baritone saxophone as well, so I decided that the wind instruments would be flute, French horn and bassoon for one part and then tenor saxophone, French horn and baritone saxophone for the other, so that three of us had two different combinations of instruments to play. In addition I used bass violinist Arthur Phipps, pianist Cecil Taylor and percussionist Al Harewood. I used this group not only in the traditional jazz rhythm section way but also like a small chamber ensemble.

What I was doing was what I've always tried to do—simply write good music and to let it be called whatever it was. Some parts were out-and-out jazz, although this was all written out except for eight bars that Cecil improvised. The "classical sections" had the urgency of jazz because of George's beautiful playing and because of the kind of music I wrote. During some of the film that showed elegant old horses and carriages, I wrote some of the wildest jazz, and somehow it worked in relationship to the picture. Throughout the picture, I wrote sections of music wherever I felt they would fit. Somehow in my mind I knew that the film would come to life in a different way with the addition of this music. What I tried to do was not to write background music but to treat the whole situation as if it were ballet in which the music and the visual image become one thing.

Hal came back in another two weeks to go over the whole film and was rather surprised to find a small army of people sleeping at two in the afternoon. I explained to him that some of them had come over to watch the film and we sat up all night looking at it over and over again. The cinematic soirée was followed by a jam session and some additional merriment, which had resulted in our sleeping late. A friend of mine from the army, Ali, a devout muslim of the Ameer sect (not the group of white-haters but the true Islam), got up to perform his ablutions and a few other friends stirred about. Hal looked a little distressed, but being a true gentleman, said nothing to make anyone feel uncomfortable. I told him how much I thought the film held together after repeated viewings and how I thought the music would fit and make the film a different thing. I was just discussing with him the possibility of lengthening the ending because of the musical idea I had and because of the beauty of the final shots of the subway when I was interrupted by Joe, a saxophone player who had been at the session.

"Man," he said enthusiastically to Hal, "that flick is a stone freak natural gas! It blew my mind bruz! Out of sight, baby. You cooked your ass off terrible, *terri*ble, real *bad!*"

While all of these were the highest accolades that could be given to any film maker in the world, Hal's St. John's classical-oriented background had not prepared him for these colloquial expressions. He looked rather flabbergasted. I explained to him that this meant his film was already being well received. He said that he would come back tomorrow so we could go over the ending to see if we could possibly stretch it out or if there was a way I could do something musically that would achieve the same result.

The next day he came back. Everyone had left my apartment except for Charles Mills, who was sleeping off one of his monumental hangovers. Because he had been carousing for over a week without going to sleep, he was lying in the same place twenty-four hours later, on the floor on my sleeping bag. He looked like a middle-aged Boy Scout on a camping trip, snoring peacefully with his white curls sprawled out on the sleeping bag just as if he were in a state of Nirvana at Yellowstone National Park. Even an occasional cockroach crawling out from beneath the many layers of linoleum lined with chewing gum, bobby pins and old Dick Tracy comic books did not disturb his peaceful slumber.

After about thirty seconds of puzzled silence Hal whispered "*Who is that?*"

"Don't worry, my man," I answered him airily, "that's my composition teacher."

We decided that I could record the music at the end the way I wanted to and that he would make the film longer or we could cut the music in another place, if necessary. I also decided to make a shorter version in case that would work best for the film as well. I had no feelings about that. The Bartok Violin Concerto has two endings and no composer minds making something longer or shorter as long as it is his own work and can be controlled by him so that it comes out in good taste, expressive and part of the whole.

Hal left and I got to work. A few weeks later, I called up the musicians and we went to Bell Sound Studios to record the music for the film. Because we didn't have the equipment to see the film and record the music simultaneously, I simply used a stopwatch, a metronome and played the French horn while conducting by nodding my head and signaling with my left elbow.

We recorded all the music in one day and it came out splendidly. Then Hal laid in all the music. All of it fitted perfectly except for the ending. Hal decided to use the long ending and fitted this part of the film to the music. About two months later, I saw the film with the music and the narration and it was really a treat. There was going to be a showing at the Brooklyn Museum and Arnold Bloom, one of the writers who worked on the film, lent me a dollar so I could get to Brooklyn and back to see it. Watching the film with a real audience was a fascinating experience. Unlike the theater, the work was completed by the time the audience came and I didn't have to go back and change anything. Although the film was only sixteen millimeters and was designed to be shown in museums and for civic groups, it was blown up to thirty-five millimeters and shown in regular movie theaters a few years later. It was a wonderful introduction for me to learning how to write for films and served as a great apprenticeship for my later work.

A few days after I had finished recording the music for the film, George Syran gave me a call. He had gone to the Manhattan School of Music with me the previous year and was one of the many excellent young all-round musicans who was getting a degree in music, working on his classical playing, and also a fine jazz player. He had a job playing with a trio in New Hope, Pennsylvania, for the summer. But he had another engagement for the weekend and wanted a substitute. He called me up and asked me if I would go.

"Sure," I said, "I never really worked on piano, you know, except in Paris when I used to show up early at the Rose Rouge to play with Jay Cameron, but I sure would like to do it."

"I know you've played the piano at a lot of sessions when piano players weren't there and you'll have a ball," said George. "It's a real relaxed job and they're beautiful guys to work with." The guitar player in the trio was Al Schackman, a fabulous musician, whom I had heard play at several sessions.

I got a ride to New Hope and the three of us sat right down and started working. It was my first job playing trio piano and we all had so much fun that even the people that owned the place came out to listen to us. I found out that Chan Parker, Charlie Parker's wife, had a little shop nearby, so I went over during a break to tell her about the time I spent with Bird, how much he had meant to me and what an inspiration he still was. She was just as sweet as he'd described her, and their son looked exactly like Bird. I talked to Al about her. He also felt that the whole atmosphere was different just with the thought of Bird that seemed to vibrate around New Hope every time musicians would get together. He still seemed to be that force in people's minds that he was when he was alive.

As we played that night, the smells of the countryside were beautiful. We were playing outdoors and I noticed the aroma of the grass, the wild hay, the flowers and summer leaves. It reminded me of our old farm.

I went to the bar to get a drink during intermission and noticed the familiar accent the barmaid had. I was sure it sounded like the way people used to talk in Feasterville.

"Do you know where Feasterville, Pennsylvania, is?" I asked.

"Sure," said the girl. "It's not far from here."

"What!" I said incredulously. "That's where I'm from."

"You don't know too much about geography. This is Bucks County. You're only a few miles from there, you know."

She said know like ne-*ow,* and that nasal country sound threw me right back to my childhood. I had a real urge to drive over and try to find where the farm was, but I knew I couldn't. I didn't have a car and somehow I didn't want to look back. The present gave me enough to think about.

Playing with Al Schackman was like having a jam session and by the second night it wasn't even like a job anymore. During intermission of the second night a man came over to me and asked me to sit down at his table. He was dressed in a very flashy style, like the Basque gangster, Henri le Gitan, I had known in Paris. His clothes were cut a little tight and extremely loud, but were of a very expensive material. He was with a friend of his, Doc. His name was Morris and he told me he would like to manage me and get me a contract as a piano player.

"Well thanks," I said to Morris, ready to get up and leave. I was already a little skeptical of people who were going to do something fantastic for me. You always met them in bars and they always ended up trying to get fixed up with a girl, buy some pot or bust you. After a while, I realized that Morris was serious. He wanted me to audition for a friend of his at Decca Records, who was an A&R man.

"I appreciate that," I said, "but if they decide they want me to make a record, I want to do it with my own group."

"What group?" said Morris, looking confused. "I thought this was your group?"

"No," I said, "these are wonderful musicians, but actually this is George Syran's group. You should get in touch with him. He's the real trio pianist," and I wrote George's number and address down and gave them to him. I could tell he was never going to look at them.

"We think you got something, kid," said Doc, flashing a Broadway smile at me, brighter than his glittering pinky ring. "Kind of a wonderful, primitive quality. Like Thelonius Monk must have had when he was young."

Great-great-grandfather David Moses Amram (1789–1864) and his son, my great-grandfather, Werner David Amram (1832–1913)

Werner and his son, my grandfather, David Amram (1866–1939)

Grandfather and my father,
Philip Werner Amram, in 1918

My father and I
in 1964

Early spring in Feasterville, 1936, five and a half years old

First grade, Pass-a-Grille,
Florida, 1937

My parents, Emilie and Philip, and my sister Marianna on
the farm in Feasterville, early summer 1937

My sister Marianna and I under a painting of us,
ages two and four, at the Jersey shore in 1945

On the farm
in 1938

California, 1946

With my horn in 1947 (*Photograph by David Lattimore*)

An outdoor jam session in Bremerhaven, February 1953

Dimitri Mitropoulos during a rehearsal as Music Director of the New York Philharmonic (*Photograph by Fred Fehl*)

Christopher Street, New York, 1958

Davis Park, Fire Island, 1962. Working on "Dirge and Variations."

Speaking to the members of the American Association of Psychotherapists at the Waldorf-Astoria, October 5, 1963, on "The Creative Use of the Unconscious by the Artist" (*Photograph by Esther Brown*)

Arthur Miller at my Sixth Avenue apartment, working on *After the Fall* in late October 1963 (*Photograph by Inge Morath of Magnum*)

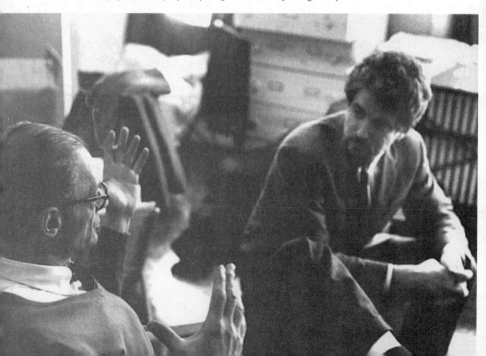

Working with Joe Papp on *King John*, 1967 (*Photograph by Henry Grossman*)

With Leonard Bernstein at Philharmonic Hall in 1967 (*Photograph by Henry Grossman*)

George Barrow and I at the Dave Lambert Memorial in Tompkins Square Park, New York, 1967 (*Photograph by Henry Grossman*)

With friends at Davis Park, Fire Island, 1967

Recording the music for *King John* at the Variety Arts Recording Studio, summer of 1967. Left to right: Lynn Berman, the author, Dave Moore and Midhat Serbagi. (*Photograph by Henry Grossman*)

My concert debut as a conductor, conducting the "Shakespearean Concerto" in Corpus Christi, Texas, 1967 (*Photograph by Fred Eberstadt*)

During a break in the filming of the 1959 historic beat film, *Pull My Daisy,* featuring an original music score by David Amram, who also appeared in the film, the composer (top right, hand to mouth) shares ideas with some of his collaborators, including (left to right): poet Gregory Corso (back to camera), artist Larry Rivers, author Jack Kerouac, and poet Allen Ginsberg. *Pull My Daisy* features Jack Kerouac's narration and a title song by David Amram, with lyrics by Jack Kerouac, Neal Cassady, and Allen Ginsberg. (Photograph by John Cohen)

Composing the "Autobiography of Strings," 1959. (Photograph by Baird Bryant)

"Are you kidding?" I said. "Did you ever hear any of Thelonius Monk's records when he was young? He was a piano virtuoso when he was young. I'm just a beginner, let's face it. I can play, but my real instrument is the French horn.

"The French horn?" said Morris incredulously.

"Yeah," I said, "I can really play the French horn. I played with Mingus and Oscar Pettiford and a lot of guys. That's my instrument and I've already recorded on a record with Lionel Hampton and a lot of other musicians in Paris."

"Well, I'd like to hear that," said Morris, "but I want you to audition as a pianist."

"I will," I said, "only under the conditions that you'll come and hear the group I have with George Barrow, Arthur Phipps and Al Harewood. George is the tenor player that I worked with with Mingus, and Arthur and Al are friends of ours. When we play together, we have a wonderful groove.

"All right," said Morris, "that's fair enough. Have another drink."

"No thanks," I said. "I'm not much of a drinker."

I went back and played. They sat there listening and told me they would be sure to call me in New York. I gave it no more thought. When the job was over I said good-bye to Chan and her son and went back to New York.

Sure enough two days later I heard a familiar Far Rockaway blast coming over my phone. "Hello, David, this is Morris from New Hope."

"Hello, Morris," I said.

"I want you to come today or tomorrow to Decca Records and audition."

"O.K.," I said. Arthur had a day job and couldn't take off, so I called Tommy Potter, whom I had known when I lived in Washington. I had jammed with him at the Club Bengasi in 1951 when he was passing through.

Then I called up Malcolm and said, "Malcolm, you might never have passed the bar exam in New York, but you've got yourself a job as my common-law lawyer to protect me against this guy Morris. I'm auditioning for Decca Records."

"Great," said Malcolm. "Who's in your band?"

"Me," I said, "I'm auditioning as a pianist."

"Are you kidding?" said Malcolm. "I could give a better audition on piano than you could."

"I'm hip," I said, "but maybe they'll give our group a chance to record if they like me. If they don't, I'm not going to do it."

I went with Malcolm to Decca Records and against Malcolm's advice forced the astonished A&R man to sign a piece of paper saying he would not release the recording of my audition without my consent. Looking at me like I was crazy, he signed the paper anyway. I then played three tunes. Because I had been playing piano for a few weeks, I really had my piano playing together.

Malcolm looked surprised. "Say, man, I didn't know you could do that," he said.

"Well, I didn't either, but I've been practicing a little bit."

"That was beautiful, kid," said Morris.

"Thank you," I said. "Let me know what happens because I want you to hear our group."

Morris called back the next day and said that Decca Records was interested in recording me as a jazz player. "I'll do it," I said, "but not recording with a piano trio. I'm not ready for that as a pianist and anyway I've got a terrific group."

Two days later, Morris came trudging up the six flights of stairs where George Barrow, Arthur Phipps, Al Harewood and I were ready to audition. Morris looked around and winced.

"Uh oh," said George, looking at me and winking.

We played through some tunes and really sounded good. The whole tenement was rocking. Morris flashed open his coat when we were done, revealing his ruffled shirt with purple studs partially covered by his white-on-white tie. He threw his arms up in the air, popping out his glittering gold cuff links. "Wonderful, fellows, wonderful! Yeah yeah, real soulful. I think you got a splendid group here. Come here for a minute," he said to me in a sinister voice and took me into the other room. "I don't like that bass player," he whispered to me, "and the drummer sounds a little, well you know, not too swinging. And that tenor player," he said, "I don't know if he's really the right man for your group."

I smelled a rat. "Look, Morris," I said, raising my voice, "what is it you got on your mind?"

"Well," he said, "you know mixed groups are harder to sell . . ."

"Come off that jive, Morris!" I said in a loud voice.

George came up to the door. "Everything O.K., fellows?"

I was really mad. Morris must be kidding, I thought. "Everybody's got mixed groups, man. This isn't 1935." I was about to really lose my temper.

"What is it exactly you don't like about our group?" said George.

"Oh, nothing," said Morris. "I think it sounds excellent. With a little shaping up you'll be ready to record for Decca."

"What kind of shaping up?" asked George, boring in.

"Well," said Morris, "you know, those little rough edges. Those— the little—nuances that make a difference between great and good."

"Like what?" said George.

"Well," said Morris, getting a little flustered, "I'm sure everything will work out all right."

"This is our quartet," I said. "If you want to record it, great."

"You'll hear from me," said Morris.

"Oh boy," said George after Morris had left. Arthur and Al laughed. "You just about blew our recording, Dave. You've got to learn how to talk with these people, man. They're businessmen and if they can make you lose your temper or lose your reasoning they'll take advantage of you. Logic, remember you've got to use *logic,* you've got to out-think them at their own game and it's not hard. It's mostly common sense. Just stick to the truth and logic and never lose your temper. You know about boxing. Well, when I studied with Cus D'Amato, that's the first thing he taught us. As fighters, we must always be thinking ahead of our opponent and never lose our temper."

We stayed and played some more.

The next day, Morris called back and started on the same old tack. He thought it would be easy to sell me as a trio pianist and that if I had a piano trio with two other white musicians I could make a fortune. This time I was prepared. "That's wonderful of you, Morris," I said, "and I appreciate it, but I really think that with our quartet we'd do a lot better." I kept trying to be logical, businesslike and nice, but toward the end I got disgusted in spite of myself. "It's our quartet or nothing," I shouted. "If you bring up any racial matters or try to interfere with my music again, you can find someone else's blood to suck."

"O.K., O.K., kid, don't get mad," he said. "Your group is going to be marvelous." He called us up a week later and told me that I was to sign a contract for a year with Decca, give him ten per cent of the advance and make my first album the following spring.

"*Our* album," I said. "There are four of us playing."

"Right, right, right," said Morris.

One night late in August after I had come back from a floor-cleaning job, Charles, my composition teacher, came by and told me that there was a session right across the street. I had only taken three lessons from Charles, but we hung out a lot and talked about music constantly. We went over and I played. Chet Baker was there. He had just returned from Europe. He played my French horn for a while and sounded great. We talked a lot about the use of the French horn and how it differed from the trumpet as a jazz instrument. He felt it would be difficult to find the right style for playing jazz on the French horn. He felt I was on the right track.

He had to catch a train, so Charles wanted me to come and visit Willis, a friend of his in the Village who had a lovely seventeen-year-old daughter.

"Isn't it late, man, it's two thirty in the morning?" I said.

"It's O.K., it's O.K.," he said, "he stays up late, man, he stays up late. He only sleeps three hours a night. He runs a big business during the day, but all night he stays up communicating with people from outer space."

"No kidding?" I said. "I've got to meet him."

We went over to Christopher Street, where Willis lived. He had a very nice apartment and a beautiful daughter, just as Charles had said. As we walked in he was sitting hunched over a Ouija board, pushing a shot glass around the board and taking notes.

"Oh hello, Charles," Willis said, "Nice to see you."

"This is one of my friends, Dave," said Charles, "one of my students."

"Dave," said Willis, "you're just in time. Hold this glass."

I touched the side of the Ouija board and I felt a motion. I noticed that he seemed to be pushing the shot glass.

"You see, you see, you see," he said, "she's out there." He then showed me a whole series of letters he had received from a girl in outer space. The letters described her measurements, how much she weighed, what she liked to eat and the fact that she liked mature men. This guy's out of his mind, I thought to myself. He then proceeded to show me all his books about flying saucers. He told me about the flying saucers he had seen and how he had been in touch via his Ouija board with people from outer space for the last six years.

"Charles," he said confidentially, "there's going to be a landing in your area next weekend. Why don't you go out there and make a report for me?"

"O.K.," said Charles, giving him a conspiratorial look. "Dave and I will go check it out." We sat there for another hour or so, but after his daughter went to bed I could see no reason staying with this maniac anymore. I finally got Charles to leave.

"Man," said Charles, "this guy seems like he's crazy, but his daughter is so beautiful I wouldn't mind taking an interplanetary voyage on one of his flying saucers just to get to her. She may be thirty years younger than me, but I love her and she's going to be my seventeenth wife." Every time Charles met a girl he liked, he asked her to marry him immediately. Often, they accepted on the spot. Marriage proposals were rare in our circles.

"How about those flying saucers that are landing?" I asked.

"That's fine," said Charles. "We'll see them. Five days from now come up to my roof and we'll say hello to the saucer people."

I came by five days later to see Charles and he was just finishing the second movement of his symphony. His impeccable handwriting and sense of order seemed incongruous to many people, but I understood it was all part of him and that was the way he was. He seemed like a nut, but in his music he was devoted to the point of near-madness.

"O.K., Dave," he said, "I'm finished. Let's go out and celebrate."

"How about the saucers?" I asked.

"Don't worry," he said. "they won't be here for another four and a half hours."

We walked over to the West Side to the Village and sat in Sheridan Square park. A friend of ours, Rocco, came by.

"Hi, Charlie, how's your symphony coming?" Everyone in the Village knew Charles and loved him.

"Great," said Charles, "I've just finished the second movement."

"Listen," said Rocco. "I've just got some bennies, if you'd like a free score."

"Well, an occasional stimulant never harmed anyone," said Charles.

I had seen Charles at Jim Atkins' before I had met him formally, sitting there with his railroad hat on and his bloodshot eyes looking as if they were going to burst out through the sockets. He would slump over his coffee, grinding his teeth and perspiring from bennies.

"Well, Dave," he said, "here's to the saucer folk." He started popping them down like candy.

"Wow," I said, "how many of those do you take?"

"Don't worry," he said, "we've got thirty here, we'll take ten apiece."

"O.K.," I said. I gobbled them down and after a few minutes I began feeling a little more highly strung than usual. After about twenty-five minutes my mind was spinning, my heart felt as if it were going to pop right out of my body and I was grinding my teeth till I thought my fillings were going to come out. Every word that Rocco and Charles said as they began talking about extraterrestrial objects and the dynamics of space sounded like gems of wisdom.

"What we better do now," said Charles, "is calm down a little."

We went over to the Bleecker Street Tavern and drank a bottle of wine. All the hobos from the Mills Hotel looked like medieval holy men. I thought perhaps I was in the fourteenth century.

"How do you feel?" said Rocco.

"Well," I said, hearing my teeth grating in my head, "pretty weird."

"I'll tell you what," he said. "In order to calm down a little bit, we'll go over to Fred's house and take a few goof balls."

Fred was a chef we knew who always used to take quite a bit home from work. We used to go to his place to eat the chickens and turkeys he'd bring home. He loved Charles and Charles's music and he seemed to like me.

We went over there and Fred greeted us with a "Oh no, here come the three Bobbsey twins. You cats look torn up. What will it be, chicken cacciatore or goof balls?"

"Both," said Charles. We sat down. Fred turned out some chicken cacciatore and looked inquisitively at me. "You look pretty wigged-out there," he said. "I think these will calm you down."

"What are they?" I asked. My eyes were so extended I could hardly see anything.

"They're sleeping pills," he said.

I swallowed them and began to feel a little better as the numbing influence counteracted the Benzedrine and wine and I began to feel myself coming back to earth a bit. I ate the chicken and felt a lot better. Rocco began telling us about the fifteen years when he had been in the army as a professional soldier. It had trained him for his life as a vagrant, sleeping on the street all these years and still keeping his health.

"I've been sellin' pot and smoking since I was fifteen years old and I am a tower of health," he said, "I can't understand what people have against it." He then surprised us by pulling off his shoe and taking several reefers out of his sock. After we smoked them all up they seemed to destroy any neurologically disturbing effects the Benzedrine tablets had given us.

We had another glass of wine and then Charles said, "Now I'm beginning to feel relaxed. Let's go over and look at those saucers." We trudged all the way to his house on the East Side and sat up on his roof. We waited and waited and waited without seeing any saucers. I was really disappointed because I really wanted to see a flying saucer more than anything else I could think of.

"Well," said Charles, "I am one-thirty-second American Indian and part of our culture is to have patience." He then let out three thunderous war whoops, began to do a little rain dance and passed out. We all lay down on the roof and while we were waiting for the flying saucers to appear, fell asleep.

I woke up the next afternoon, went back home and looked out of the window to the street six floors below. Jesus Christ, I thought. I thought of all the great health kicks I'd been on and really felt that I was becoming wasted slowly but surely.

I went back to work, writing some music, and the phone rang. It was a girl I had known from Paris named Irma. She had gone over as a model and had wound up with a truck driver who wanted to be a saxophone player. I had let him sit in with me at the Caméléon because he was a very sweet guy even though he was just a beginner at music. I dug her and knew she instilled confidence in him.

"How's Frank?" I asked. "Is his sax playing coming along?"

"Oh, he stayed over there. He's not into anything. He needs someone to push him," she said, "but you sure were groovy to him and I appreciated it and that is why I called you up. I've got this guy who is taking me out to Ocean Beach on Fire Island. He's sort of a klesmer, a schlemiel, a real klutz, but you might like to get away to the beach. It's really beautiful there, so why don't you come along?"

"Listen, baby, I'd love to, but I've only got five dollars to my name," I told her.

"That's O.K.," she said, "he has a lot of money and he's a big spender. You don't have to pay for a thing. I've already told him about you, that you're my friend, and he loves music."

"Well, that sounds great," I said. "Maybe I'll bring my horn and we can play some."

I packed up my French horn, my gym trunks, which I had used to do my roadwork in the army, a towel, and I was all set to go. Irma was looking more lovely than ever and I was sorry that I wasn't able to take her out myself. We went out and met her friend, Irving, who had a loud voice, was a flashy dresser, tall, good-looking. Within fifteen minutes he had told me all the things he excelled in and mastered. He had been a professional boxer, a symphony clarinetist, an airlines pilot, anything that you mentioned, he had done it better than anybody else. After a few minutes I found out that he was also a liar, which he had forgotten to mention in his list of credits. He had a lot of energy and I enjoyed hearing these great series of achievements pouring from his lips, especially when half an hour later he would contradict them, saying that he had been somewhere else at that time. He would repeat the same story but in a different context without remembering it.

When we got on the ferry there was hardly anyone on the boat, so I took out my horn and played a few tunes. I played some classical horn pieces and then played some jazz.

"What do you want to be, a bum all your life?" Irving suddenly snapped.

"What do you mean?" I asked.

"Look," he said, "I used to play that type of music up in the mountains, you know, the Catskills, and I could have been a great jazz musician. They said that I was going to be one of the best of all time. Benny Goodman was frightened when he heard me play, but I gave it up. It's like being a tennis bum or a ski bum, only you become a jazz bum."

"Well," I said, "I just love playing music."

"You'll be a bum," he said, and continued the lecture all the way across on the ferry.

When we got to Fire Island, I saw to my astonishment that the ocean and the bay were only a few hundred feet apart. There were no cars but acres of beautiful girls. Even though Ocean Beach had cement sidewalks and a few stores, it still had a wonderful smell and a joyous, free atmosphere I hadn't felt in years. Also, I had never seen so many beautiful girls, thousands of beautiful Jewish girls swaying and undulating up and down Main Walk, swinging their hips, shaking their breasts and staring with burning eyes at all the men as they walked back and forth, looking for action. I had never seen anything

like it. Underneath their green eye shadow was a combination of
hunger, coquettishness and scorn.

For all my insane living during the year I had been in New York,
I hadn't been having too many romances. All the getting high that I
had been doing probably was making me act so strange that I was
scaring women off. I realized that I would have to go back to my
healthy way of living soon. Apparently Irma's date hadn't been informed that I was impoverished. When he told me how much my
room cost, I told him that I was sorry that I had only five dollars. I
slipped him the five and he arranged for me to sleep on the back
porch for the two nights we were there.

The owner of the house was a schoolteacher who had been fired by
the Board of Education for being a member of the Communist party.
Consequently he was very glum. His wife kept shouting and screaming at him while his children cried, so I didn't spend too much time
at the house. I walked up and down the beach a lot, looking at that
beautiful ocean and smelling that great air. Feeling the wind and the
sand really brought me back to life again. I thought about what I had
been doing and realized that I had spent almost an entire year in
New York. Although I had dropped out of school, I really felt that
I had gotten started as a composer. I had completed a film score,
which was something at least, had several good lessons with Charles,
had a record contract and was working hard on quite a few pieces.
In addition, my horn playing and piano playing were really coming
along and at least I had been able to make it through one year in
New York.

Irma and her date had a fierce fight as soon as he found out he
couldn't sleep with her. And even though the people that owned the
house were fighting and shouting and their kids were yelling and most
of the people around seemed drunk most of the time and the place
was full of smiling girls looking for husbands, it was still a paradise
for me. Those two days were like a year's vacation. When I got back
to the city I felt as if I could start all over again.

One September afternoon, Ken Karpe called and told me about
the plans that the Stevenson headquarters had for jazz. They were
located in a first-floor showroom a few blocks above Birdland. Ken
was put in charge of jazz after he had suggested the idea to them.

"Think of it," Ken said, his promoter's eyes flashing. "All the

musicians who want to swing with Stevenson and hate Eisenhower
can get together and session in his honor."

"That's great," I said. "We all want a place to play anyway. This
will be a ball." Freddie Redd, Willie Jones, Al Cotton, Kenny Burell,
Pepper Adams and many others became regulars immediately. We
were cooking there day and night, to the astonishment of the volunteer workers, who had to go through endless series of phone calls
and manipulations in order to get the big-time theatrical names to
appear to say a few words. The Jazz for Stevenson was rocking the
whole place by the time the volunteers came to open things up. The
session would start in the afternoon and continue until they finally
threatened to lock us in by throwing the lights off a few times.

"It's extraordinary, these jazz boys' political loyalty and devotion
to the liberal cause," said one professional volunteer.

"That's right," said Ken, looking at us and grinning.

We didn't care if General Grant got reelected. We just wanted to
blow.

More and more musicians kept coming by. Stevenson could have
swept Local 802 in a landslide. If someone stepped out, someone else
would jump at the chance to play, picking up whatever instrument
was available until the owner returned.

During one memorable session, Mingus played bass, I played
drums and Steve Allen came and played piano. "I'm not really used
to playing music like you guys do," he said, but when he sat down
he really played very well. I was so impressed by seeing a big-time
TV personality this close that in the beginning of the second chorus,
the combination of my excitement and inexperience as a drummer
got me so nervous I kicked over the sock cymbals, which crashed
down, narrowly missing the piano. Allen leaped up, looked over at
me, made a joke, sat down and continued playing.

Tony Scott, Gigi Gryce, Gerry Mulligan, Bob Brookmeyer and
Zoot Sims came by. The place was always packed with musicians.
Finally at the end of the campaign, we all sat down and listened to
Stevenson's final speech on television. He was conducting his campaign differently from the 1952 one and was obviously trying to be
more of a politician. Everyone listened as he spoke on TV and finally when he mentioned how America should be, he said that he
wanted it to be a beautiful place for many different people. Suddenly
in the great list of names he mentioned Willie Mays. A groan went
up from the musicians.

"What's the matter?" asked one of the campaign managers, looking nervous.

"Lady," said one of the musicians, "he ain't going to get the black vote coming on with that jive."

"What do you mean?" she said indignantly. "He has an excellent record with the Negroes."

"An excellent *record*? How many did he sell?"

The woman looked confused.

"Look," said one of the musicians, "Willie Mays makes about ninety thousand a year. He makes more money than Stevenson does. What the hell does Willie Mays need his help for?"

"Well," she said, "you have to realize of course that he was being symbolic."

"Well," said the musician, "we don't need nobody to be symbolic, we need somebody who's going to *do* something for real, now, N-O-W, for everybody. All black people don't want to be athletic stars. Look at me. I'm a perfect example. I'm nearsighted and I got flat feet. I couldn't get a dime to walk a dog. Some of us want to be doctors and lawyers and some would like to be able to make their living as musicians, especially after studying for twenty years."

The woman slunk away and I heard her speak to Ken. "What's the matter with these musicians?" she asked indignantly. "I guess they just don't understand anything about politics. They just don't know who's with them and who's not, the poor things."

We were sad to see Stevenson lose because we figured if he won, the White House would be rocking with music for the next decade.

A day or two after the election, Ken called me up and told me that I could make some fast money. "I know from your moving-man stints and the health kick you've been on lately that you're in good condition, Dave. You're a real health bug still, right?"

"Well, I'm in a health slump at the moment, but I can still make it, Ken. What's up?"

"Show up in two hours at Studio C on West Forty-eighth Street," he told me. "We're going to be extras on a television program and make seventy-five bucks tax free in two days."

"Wow," I said, "I'll be right up. In fact, I'll be ahead of time."

I showed up and found out that Ken had somehow wangled his way into being one of four extras who carried Jackie Gleason on stage, dressed up as an Arab. Ken had known the assistant casting director, Honest Abe, who apparently took ten per cent of the actors' income in lieu of the fee that an agent would usually get. For his ten per cent he guaranteed not to report any of us to the television union. For this show they were looking for four guys over six feet tall who were strong and reliable. Of course both Ken and I were perfect types. Especially since we were stone broke. Honest Abe was very friendly and told me that if I gave him his ten per cent payoff (donation was his way of saying it), he could probably get another show for me.

Well, I thought to myself, I finally found myself a patron. I could envision myself with a show each week, being able to resume my composition lessons and quit any work outside of music forever. As I walked around and sounded out the other extras, I found out that only one of them had any acting experience. One was a city cop, one was a salesman in a department store, one was a medical student—all of them had somehow gotten in touch with Honest Abe, who actually helped them to support themselves by working in this desultory fashion. It was during the last days of live TV in New York and everything was so disorganized that nobody knew the difference. Also, from what I'd seen of some of the professional acting on TV shows, there wasn't much difference anyway.

We got dressed in our Arab costumes and I called up everyone I knew in New York to have them watch my TV debut. We carried Jackie Gleason out on his rickshaw and it was lucky all of us were strong because he was pretty heavy.

Just before he was about to go on stage he said, "I can't get out of this thing." Three or four flunkies came in. "Skip it," he said imperiously, and with one swipe, knocked the whole side of the platform off so he was able to leap out.

After the show was over, Honest Abe told me that I had given a first-class performance and I could have a job on Bob Hope's show. "Of course, there'll be a donation."

"How much does it pay," I asked.

"$175."

"You got yourself a new star," I said.

A few days later I showed up and this time I was to be an air force pilot officer who pulled Bob Hope offstage. I hung around for two days doing nothing, making more money than I ever had since I came to New York. I felt somehow that it was wrong, but Honest Abe told me I was a good boy and should go and start taking some pictures of myself around to casting agencies. I could probably make myself a career out of being a professional extra. Roy de Carava, the photographer who had come to all Ken's sessions, was a pal of mine and knew how I was scuffling. He told me he would take some pictures of me for this purpose. Although he never did this type of work even for big money because of his reputation as a great artistic photographer, he did me this favor.

I got my pictures taken and made a few rounds, seeing casting agents who were even younger than I was, and I figured that in a few weeks I woul never have to have a day job again. My icebox was jammed from the money I got from the Bob Hope show.

Still, I thought it was wrong of me to be taking work away from real actors, so a week later I went back to the shape-ups and day jobs.

I felt better. I didn't want to be a scab actor.

A neighbor of mine, Betty Lou Fitch, who was an accompanist with the Mary Anthony dance company, came by my house and told me that the New York Shakespeare Festival, then in its infancy, was looking for someone to write music for *Titus Andronicus*. Apparently some people in the cast had heard about some of the productions I had worked on at Howard University and had recommended me to Joe Papp. Because I lived on Eighth Street between avenues B and C, and the church where the festival was then performing was on Sixth Street between avenues C and D, I thought it was not too much out of my way to go and meet them.

I went over to the Emmanuel Presbyterian Church on East Sixth Street. As I passed the children playing on the street, I noticed a group of young men with extremely long hair. They were actors waiting to audition for the festival company. When we got inside I saw them staring nervously at me as I waited in line. Even though I was not coming to audition as an actor, I could feel their paranoid reactions and understood how difficult it must be for an actor in New York. Imagine someone who is going to play the part of a great nobleman who with a wave of his hand could send ten thousand men to their death, yet in real life hopes that he can get a part that pays him thirty-five dollars a week if he's lucky.

I met the directors, Joseph Papp and Fred Rolf. Fred Rolf had a dashing look, sort of like Basil Rathbone, and Joseph Papp had long hair, an extremely energetic manner and brown eyes that looked as if they knew you right away. Their touch of elegance made me forget my shabby neighborhood and its aura of extreme poverty, especially when I noticed both men were wearing Chesterfield topcoats with black velvet collars. This impressed me for some reason and I began laughing. I was wearing my old, gray, moth-eaten sweater that I had brought back from Paris with me, and needed a haircut and a shave. The more that they spoke to me in their measured, theatrical well-modulated tones, the more I shuffled and mumbled and came on with my hip talk.

For some reason Joe Papp said I would be able to do the job very well. I had not seen any rehearsals of this play, but I had been taken by a friend, Julie Eastman, to see *Julius Caesar*, the preceding summer when it was at a park on the Lower East Side and I had enjoyed it very much. My only criticism was of the music. They had taken the recorded sound track of the score for the movie *Quo Vadis*. It was not exactly in the Elizabethan spirit as far as I was concerned.

I went to several run-throughs of *Titus Andronicus* and was very much impressed with Colleen Dewhurst, then an unknown but brilliant actress, Leonard Stone, who played Titus, Rosco Lee Browne, who played Aaron the Moor, and the many other first-rate actors who appeared in this difficult play. In spite of its contrived plot the play had a certain kind of power. It was as if one were watching the birth of a new genius. To me the play had everything that Shakespeare did later so much better.

There was no budget for me, the actors, the director or the musicians, so I got in touch with some of my old friends at the Manhattan School of Music and I asked them if they would come and record the music as a favor. They all agreed. When I finished writing the music and copying all the parts myself, we went to an old studio where demonstration records were made, mostly for Puerto Rican bands. As we walked into the studio, our ears were bombarded by Pachangas, mambos and many of the fiery sounds of Spanish popular music. I rehearsed with my group and as we began to record, a large group of Spanish musicians came to the studio. I saw them gesticulating through the booth and I heard one shout, "Meng, that soun's groovy!" They asked the engineer where our band was going to be playing. I explained to them that this was not a demonstration record but rather music for a Shakespearean play. That seemed to dampen their enthusiasm somewhat, but I invited them all to the play.

I didn't know about the art of splicing tape, so a lot of our mistakes had to be kept, including a drum solo where the drummer goofed. He unintentionally hit a crashing rim shot on the side of his drum in the middle of a very serious march. The actors eventually did a kind of mambo step each time that *splatt* interrupted the drummer's rhythm. The music was later cued in by someone who ran the tape recorder, coming in just at the right times throughout the play.

I hoped the music would make some contribution to the whole general atmosphere by virtue of being good music as well as relating to the production itself. Although this is the one piece of theater music I've written that I would not publish or allow to be used in any other production, I still listen to it occasionally with enjoyment. It has a certain freshness that I like, but I don't feel that it measures up to other scores that I have written for the theater.

Joe Papp, however, wanted me to work for the festival the next summer.

"I like your music. You frightened us a little at first, but you have something. Keep it up. I'll see you next summer."

"Solid, mein liege," I said.

"You might get that sweater cleaned, Amram. The health inspector would have arrested us if he'd seen you wearing it during rehearsals. Here's two dollars."

I took the money, bought some beets and sour cream and had a theater party for Betty Lou, her boy friend, Carl Macbeth, Freddie Redd, Malcolm and Randy Weston.

After Ken Karpe's sessions at the Stevenson headquarters there weren't many places to play again. I began to go down to the Bowery to a place called the Five Spot, where merchant seaman Don Shoemaker was playing with a bass trumpet player named Dale Wales. Cecil Taylor went with me.

Friends of mine from Paris went there and it really became a great place. I saw Jay Cameron again and a lot of painters I had met at the Cedar Tavern, all of whom were interested in modern music of any kind.

Don and Dale were bighearted guys and would let us play whenever we wanted to. Everyone was dumbfounded by Cecil's playing. He was completely original. The painters felt instinctively that he was a great artist. Once when he was playing in a particularly vigorous vein, one of the hammers inside the piano flew out. The bartender came over and tried to throw him out. I told him that if Cecil left I was leaving too, and because a lot of painters had come to hear us play, the bartender relented and Cecil continued. His whole approach to improvising was completely different from anything that had ever been done in jazz and really knocked people out. We used to come back and play a lot and finally when Don's group left, the Five Spot decided to continue with their jazz policy. Cecil worked there for a month with Steve Lacey, soprano saxophone, Dennis Charles, drums, and Buell Neidlinger, a virtuoso bass violinist. They had an exceptional group and the Five Spot began getting more crowded every night. Then my group was asked to come in and we stayed for eleven weeks.

During this time, painters began coming in droves to hear the music and meet other artists. Bill de Kooning, Franz Kline, Joan Mitchell, Herman Cherry, Boris Lurie, Mike Goldberg, Roy Newell, Alfred Leslie, Norman Bluhm and many, many others who lived just a few blocks away would come every single night. This was the first time I really became interested in modern painting. I would talk to the painters during our break and they would invite me to their shows and their studios. The painters taught me to see again, and this taught me to hear. They introduced me to a whole new world, which I felt helped me as a composer.

Beer was only fifteen cents a glass or seventy-five cents for a whole pitcher. On Monday, my night off, I would come and sit in because it was so much fun. Jack Kerouac used to come, many old friends of mine who I knew in Europe, people from the army and old friends from Washington. Whenever any band came into town and wanted a place to blow, it would come down and sit in with us.

Once the union delegate came to check up on us. We were supposed to be working with a quartet, but there were eighteen men playing when he walked in and he shouted that if that ever happened again I would be fined and thrown out of the union. He came down once again and there was Woody Herman's band—about fifteen people— but the music was so great that he just sat, listened and walked out without saying a word.

Most of the time, though, our quartet worked only with a few people sitting in during the last hour. Valdo Williams, the pianist, was a Canadian-born musician who had his own style and was also a very accomplished composer in his own right. The bass player was Allie Richardson, who was able to play six or seven hours a night without even drawing a deep breath, and the drummer was Dennis Charles, who also was a very individualistic kind of player. Sometimes John Orr would play bass. George Barrow had another job so he couldn't play with us. Still, it gave me eleven weeks to really work out my new approach to the horn and in the course of all this the Five Spot made its name.

I was making $85 a week, so I didn't have to work during the day. I was in heaven.

About the sixth week I was at the Five Spot, a fellow came up who introduced himself as Dan Cowan. He was one of the best French hornists in New York. He told me he was interested in the way I played. He told me that if I played the horn differently with a different way of placing my mouthpiece, I might be able to do more of the things I was trying to do and get a better sound. Junior Collins had been in a few days before and some other French-horn players like Jim Buffington, who had tried to help me out as much as they could when I first came to New York. They all came in to listen and to encourage me. Ed London, my friend at Oberlin, had come to New York. He was completing his Ph.D. in composition and he sat in a few times. We would often play; two French horns with the rhythm section, and it sounded great. He had really become a master jazz player and it was wild playing with him again after nearly eight years.

I invited Dan to sit in, but he didn't want to. He had a fine ear and played some jazz, but he was content to dig us. Like some of the greatest musicians I knew, Dan seemed to always analyze any situation, musical or otherwise, almost immediately. He told me where he lived and said we should get together sometime so he could give me some French-horn lessons. Because of my hectic schedule I told him that it might not be for a while, but that we would definitely get together. He also knew how to play the violin and was interested in writing, painting and literature.

Sometimes we would go out with the painters after the Five Spot closed. If the girl I was with didn't mind listening to other painters talk about their work, we would stay up till dawn. During those winter nights, the conversations kept us warm. We would sit listening when Ray Parker, Alfred Leslie, Stanley Twardowicz, Paul Yakovenko, Mario Yrissary or Jimmy Cuchiara would let us visit their houses or studios. Otherwise we'd go drink coffee at the Sagamore and talk about their work.

The painters not only made the Five Spot grow from a Bowery bar into a jazz center, but they also created its atmosphere. They were genuinely interested in the music and they felt that what we

were doing was serious music. They were not like most jazz fans,
who just wanted to come in to pick up chicks or make the scene.
They actually liked the music. They were open-minded to any kind
of music. It was like a party every night playing there.

By the end of our eleven weeks the Five Spot was really getting
famous. *Esquire* magazine came down and did a whole writeup on
Upper–Lower Bohemia with a two-page picture of our band playing.
The Tonight Show came down and I spoke about our group and jazz
and what it was like playing music. I didn't say anything spectacular,
just the truth.

Naturally the owners had to capitalize on their new-found success.
They had given our group a chance for eleven weeks, a long run in
New York, but then we were replaced. Groups with bigger names
came in and the prices went up. The Five Spot had really made it
and although it lost a little of our early pioneering spirit, it still was
a wonderful place to go to.

I found during my last three weeks of our job that I was composing
more than ever. Playing all night gave me more energy. I began to
feel really alive in New York for the first time. My playing was different than it had ever been. I wasn't as relaxed as I had been in
Europe or Washington, but I knew more. I was still fighting inside
myself to get something new out. Working at the Five Spot gave me
a terrific opportunity to try out different things. Because we were
the only band and everyone in it was young and strong, our sets
would last longer than an hour.

I didn't have one smoke or one drink during the eleven weeks that
I was there and I really got those healthy vibrations going inside me
again. I was living with one girl about two blocks away from there
and another girl was living in my apartment. Between the two of
them and a few dozen beauties who would always come around when
musicians were playing, I spent all my spare time romancing or composing instead of getting high or hanging out. By the time the Five
Spot job was over, it was time to make our record for Decca and I
felt in fabulous shape.

George Barrow and I made the record with our quartet in the
spring of 1957. We had all worked on the Third Avenue El film the
preceding summer and after our audition for Morris, we had played
an occasional job together. I wrote tunes and arrangements for the

whole record, except for Arthur's composition "Phipp's Quips." Ken
Karpe wrote words to one of my songs, "Someday Morning Will
Come." One tune I entitled "Lobo Nocho," named after Lobo. It
was my way of thanking him for steering me to better paths. I hadn't
always followed his advice, but I remembered it.

We rehearsed for two months so that the record would be the best
possible. By our last rehearsal we really sounded good. Most of the
music was improvised, but it was also classical-sounding and different
from most of the things that were being recorded then.

When we finally came to the studio we really felt we were ready.
We knew Morris wouldn't bug us too much. What we weren't prepared for was the incredible producer Decca Records had assigned
as our A&R man. Compared to him Morris was an Albert Schweitzer.

Our man was a classic of the old music-business type. Usually the
rejects that couldn't make it in the other areas of music were stuck
in jazz. They were generally escapees from the garment district who
smoked pot two or three times in high school and fancied themselves
as the penultimate of hipsterdom. Morris told me this particular A&R
man had his own publishing company. What Morris didn't tell me
was that it was a common procedure for original tunes to be illegally
taken by the publishing company of the A&R man, who then wouldn't
report record sales but kept the composer's, as well as the publisher's,
royalty.

This guy immediately antagonized all of us with a twenty-five-
minute lecture on race relations, how he'd had nothing against Negroes
(they were usually his best friends) and how he wanted us to play
when we recorded. He seemed to think that the members of our
group had just arrived from the cotton fields of Georgia, had been
on relief for the last fifteen years and had only played washboards
and primitive instruments before. In fact all three of them were very
sophisticated and accomplished musicians. The bassist, Arthur Phipps,
was a graduate of the New England Conservatory, played the flute
very well, was an excellent photographer and was employed full-time
by the U.S. Government. The drummer, Al Harewood, was one of the
best in New York. He had great finesse, originality, good taste and
was an ideal ensemble musician, always sacrificing his own brilliance
for the sake of the music. George Barrow was also another super-
gentleman. So we were really offended by this man's behavior, especially before he had even heard us play.

The idea was to split us up as a group. Then they could control us. George had worked with other integrated groups and had seen this happen before.

"I'm telling you," said George, "it's divide and conquer, divide and conquer. That's all these cats know. They see we're together. You watch. If he can't turn you against us, he'll try to turn us against you. As long as we know what's happening, everything's cool. Just keep your temper. Don't be gorilla-ing these cats. And don't look so bugged. Let's just play."

Our first session went well in spite of everything. The A&R man strutted about, shouting, popping his fingers and even doing a little dance to show us how to swing.

"Swing, swing, God damn it, swing! What the hell's the matter with you boys?" he whined. "You call that a swinging sound?" He screamed at Al Harewood after a take. *"Thud-de-thud, thud-de-thud?* What's that? Where's your rhythm? Didn't you ever hear Big Sid Catlett?"

"That was twenty years ago, baby," said Al.

"Don't give me that Crow Jim shit," shouted the A&R man, seeing a possible opening. "Your kind of drumming is killing jazz. *Thud-de-thud, thud-de-thud.* Can't you get zip-a-zip? Zip-a-zip?" He began dancing again. "Those big band days. Gone forever. Swinging drumming is a lost art. Why don't you play with some soul instead of that cool stuff?"

To demonstrate his point he threw his pencil against the drum and came within inches of dying. Al had worked too many years to have someone hurt his instrument.

Next he shouted, fumed and yelled at me, trying to rattle us. But we refused to have our music ruined by him. Perhaps he thought this was the best way to work in music, but it was not the way to get any kind of results. Good music is produced in an atmosphere of love and cooperation and joy, not hate and oppression and bullying, especially when the hater is incompetent and ignorant. The great thing about the new pop music is that it's done by young people with other young musicians. The old cigar-smoker types are now back where they belong—in the slot-machines racket or selling hot fur coats— not in the sacred art of music. But during this time, this is what most of us had to put up with. Otherwise, we went unrecorded.

As the A&R man got more evil, Morris got more frantic.

"I think your man is wigging out," said George.

"They both are," I said.

"You better tell your landsmen to cool it before they get heart attacks," said George.

As the A&R man was shouting and protesting, Morris would come up, throw his arms around him and say, "But Dave is only a nice boychickle, a nice boy! Good God, how can you speak to a nice bubbala like that?" Morris was really coming on with the old hamisha crap till it was sickening. All our quartet wanted to do was make good music. We were the artists. They were supposed to carry us. We had to carry them. It made it more and more difficult to record. Morris and the A&R man kept staring at us, shouting over the loudspeaker, and running from the control room, whining, "Swing, swing!" At the end we were laughing. We couldn't help it. They were both acting like summer-camp directors gone berserk.

In spite of everything, we managed to complete our record. Fortunately the tape editor at Decca was excellent and we had good takes of everything. We listened to the pressings and were really proud. At least we had something down. We figured it might help us get some work. But they should have put out a record of Morris and the A&R man. It would have sold a million.

About a week later we were asked to pose for a picture for the cover. When we got to the photographer's studio there were four white wigs, the kind that Mozart and Haydn wore. We refused to put them on. The photographer couldn't believe it. They weren't used to musicians talking back, especially unknown musicians. Finally they asked us to have one picture taken with the wigs on and one with the wigs off. We refused to do that, knowing they would use the picture with the wigs on. Then, hoping to sell George the idea, they whipped out a picture of Louis Armstrong wearing a long white gown with angel's wings pasted on his back.

"Look at this," they said. "This is the great Louis Armstrong and look how he's dressed on the record cover."

George then launched into a tirade that could have got him elected as president of the musicians' union. He said how musicians were not clowns and entertainers but artists and while he loved Louis Armstrong's music, we were from a different era and so were most of the musicians at Decca Records who had recorded in the last thirty years. We also questioned the wisdom of wearing white wigs as we were playing jazz, not baroque music. Finally they gave in.

A week after our record cover was done I did a session for a little company that hired teriffic musicians to just come to the studio without rehearsing and start wailing. Everything was recorded. Later I found myself appearing on three different records, all of which were taken from that one session. We were only paid, of course, for one recording.

This was the way most LP records were produced in the late fifties and was one of the things that hurt jazz. Thousands of records were put out with the hope that one of them would catch on. As a result the market was flooded with second-rate work that only confused the gullible public.

I'll continue playing jazz until I drop dead, whether I get paid or not, because it's an important part of my life. But the scene itself is often still as depressing and backward as it was in Al Capone's time. The dishonesty and lack of business ethics, the low-life, gangster-style people who are still involved in much of it, and the poor way the music is promoted and handled are inexcusable. While much good is being done today in the presentation of jazz by a few idealistic souls, the answer of course is that the musicians have to become more and more involved in every single detail if they want to end up with anything. Just as boxers are now much more business-oriented before they even get to the point of fighting, musicians are becoming the same way, not because they are harder or less soulful, but because they're tired of being cheated and exploited.

James Dixon came to visit me that spring. He had come to town a year before, but my life was such a mess, I didn't want him to see me then. We had been buddies in the army and I respected him and his teacher Mitropoulos so much that I felt I would rather see them both when I was doing a little better.

Late in April I answered the door and there he was, looking like a multimillionaire.

"Hello, old stick buddy. Mind if I come in?" he said cheerfully. We talked for hours. He gave me some money, I got my clothes pressed and we went to see Mitropoulos.

It was wonderful seeing him again.

"How is your music coming?" he asked. "I expect good things from you. You are an old friend. You must not let me down."

We went out to eat and I listened to the Maestro and Jim talk about music and conducting.

After we walked Mitropoulos back to the Great Northern Hotel, Jim insisted on treating me to a cab ride downtown. When I took off my suit, I found a ten-dollar bill in the side pocket. Jim had sneaked it in. I bought my groceries for the week. I hadn't gotten a dime since my record was made and was about to resume day work again. I decided to go to see Doc, the music publisher who had two of my tunes. On the contract, it said I should get a dollar for each one.

I walked all the way up to the Brill Building and showed him the contracts.

"Ha-ha-ha-ha!" he roared. "Hey, Yetta," he shouted to his secretary, "get a load of this. Two dollars. Ha-ha-ha-ha!"

He wouldn't give me the money. I went to the union floor. I didn't want to go to any sessions or get turned on. I wanted to work. There was nothing. I went by a musicians' bar to borrow carfare after the union closed. No go. I walked all the way down to the Lower East Side. It was a sunny day, with a cool spring breeze, but I didn't feel too cheerful. The next morning I was back at the shape-up. I might be down, but I definitely was not ever going to be counted out.

Around the middle of May I got a call from the Shakespeare Festival. Stuart Vaughan was going to be the artistic director for the summer. He had seen the production of *Titus Andronicus* and had liked my music so much he wanted me to write the music for all their plays for the summer season of 1957.

By this time I had been promised so many jobs that hadn't come through that I didn't put too much faith in anything, but I was very pleased to hear from him. I showed up for the rehearsals in June. A lot of the actors were as broke as I was. Some of them, like Ed Sherin and J. D. Cannon, would lend me carfare, and wouldn't even let me repay them. A lot of the others would sneak up to Joe Papp the way I did to ask for some sandwich money. They had dignity and pride and weren't scroungers. It was just that they spent so much time working on their parts that they had to quit their day jobs and didn't have any money. It dawned on me that I wasn't the only artist in New York who was struggling.

As I saw how magnificent some of these actors were, what a great feeling they had for the classics and how hard they worked on their roles, I began to enjoy the rehearsals for *Romeo and Juliet*. Briarly Lee, who played Juliet, was really magical, and Steven Joyce, who played Romeo, was sincere and young and passionate. J. D. Cannon's Mercutio was better than any I had ever seen. The whole cast was excellent and the feeling that they had was like a jazz band performing well together.

There was just enough in the budget for a token salary for about seven musicians. Stuart and I got together several times to discuss it. Finally I played the score for him on the piano as I heard it in my head. He had played trumpet himself, so he was sympathetic and trusted me, even though my stumbling through on the piano must have sounded like a nightmare. Because I didn't want to start orchestrating it until the final changes had been made, I ended up having exactly three days and seven hours to complete it in time for the recording. I sat down to work for eighteen hours straight, sketching out the score. After thirteen hours had passed I began to feel pretty funny. My body felt completely numb. I touched my stomach with my hand and realized that it was ice cold. Even though it was in the eighties, I was numb from sitting so long in one position. I stopped working, went up to the roof, did some exercises, came back and had all the parts copied on time.

We recorded the music for *Romeo and Juliet* in an office building. Joe always managed to find some way of doing the impossible and he got a friend of his from CBS who had been an engineer for dance bands to come and record all the music and also to help us splice it afterward on a home tape recorder. During some of the most tender and lyrical music for oboe, flute and bassoon, a great thunderstorm started outside. Because the place wasn't sound-proofed, it took us several takes to get a tape with no thunderous interruptions.

Joe listened to the rest of the music, beamed proudly and left us to finish it. He really loved and understood music and he knew that there was no point in interfering. Whenever he made a suggestion, it was for a reason. The musicians liked him and were happy to work even for the tiny amount that we got. (I was getting five dollars.) We also used some excellent musicians to sing some madrigals that I wrote, plus three trumpet players and two horns for some of the other music. Maurice Peress played the trumpet and it was here that our long association in music began. The other French-horn player was my old friend from Oberlin, Ed London, who had gotten his Ph.D. in composition since I saw him at the Five Spot. Like me, he played jazz, was writing music for a Shakespeare festival—his was in Antioch, Ohio—composing and playing the French horn.

The next week *Romeo and Juliet* opened. I sat there groaning with pain each time the tape recorder either broke down, broke the tape or ran too fast, coming in with a twan-n-ng. Still, the music made its point, and most important, the actors liked it and felt that it really helped them in their performance.

About the third night Steve Pace, a painter who used to come to the Five Spot every night, came up to me. He had his customary fiery look, a sort of a blustery scowl that hid the tremendous kindness and gentleness that you could see if you looked closely in his eyes.

"God damn it," he said to me, "when I saw you at the Five Spot I always thought you were full of shit playing that jazz on the French horn. How could anybody play in a barroom and not be full of shit? That's what I always thought and you know it." Actually, Steve had come almost every night and spent several hours quietly listening to the music while everyone else was talking, so I knew he must have enjoyed something about it. But I knew he was trying to make a point. "I have to tell you" said Steve, "I was really happy to see your name on this program and know that you wrote the music. It's beautiful," and with that he spun around and walked off. I never had realized that anyone would notice the music for the play outside of the actors and the musicians who had played it. It made me happy to know that someone who knew another side of me had heard something I wrote and liked it.

Just after *Romeo and Juliet* opened and I was about to begin work on *Two Gentlemen of Verona,* Midhat came to town. I hadn't seen him since I'd gotten out of the army, but I'd heard he had been study-ing viola at the New England Conservatory on the GI Bill. He came thundering up the six flights of stairs with his brother Richard and Dave Moore, the bass player from the Seventh Army Symphony.

"Man," he said to me, looking me right in the eye, "you look *horrible.*"

"Thanks, Midhat," I said. "It's great to see you."

"Come on," said Midhat. "I'm not putting you down. You look terrible, man, what the hell have you been doing with yourself? Shit, look at this place." He came over and began kicking the wall by the bathroom.

"Watch it," I said, "the whole place will fall down."

"Jesus Christ, man," he said, "what are you doing living in a shit hole like this?"

"Well," I said, "it's forty-eight dollars a month."

"Ugh," said Midhat. As he opened up the icebox a great horde of cockroaches scampered out from underneath. "This is ridiculous, man. You're supposed to be an artist. You can't live in a crap hole like this."

"Well, Midhat," I said, "I've been here now almost two years and I'm still alive."

"Wouldn't you like to live someplace else?"

"Of course. I'd move in a minute if I could find any place this cheap that was any better."

"Well, I know of a place," he said. "There's a lot of them."

"How d'you find them?" I said.

"Look," he told me. "Just look in the Sunday *Times* or *The Village Voice* when it first comes out. We'll go out tomorrow morning and look in the *Times.*"

Dave Moore had a job and had to run off.

Midhat and Richie sat down and we talked about old times, what they had done, their brother Roger, who was going to become an actor in New York, and all the guys that we had known in the army. Then Midhat cooked up some Umjedra, the delicious Lebanese dish he'd made in the army, and told me he was going to move to New York soon too.

As we were eating our steaming plates of Umjedra, he suddenly jumped up. "What's that?" he shouted. I looked over. "Oh," I said, "just a little animal life." A rat had peeped out from underneath the radiator. I was still scared of rats but was used to seeing them occasionally and hearing them scurrying in the walls. I'd killed one once with a monkey wrench. The Lower East Side was in such terrible shape that rats were just a small part of the danger in these tenements. The worst danger, as I explained to Midhat, was that the ceiling could fall down on you while you were asleep. And when you were out in the street or the hallways, you constantly had to look out to make sure you were a step ahead of anyone that might try to mug you.

"Jesus Christ," said Midhat, "I'm not sleeping here."

"Come on, man," I said, "that rat won't bother you."

"You're out of your mind," said Midhat. He and his brother stayed anyway, but they got me up early the next morning. We got a copy of *The New York Times* and I went looking for a place. Within a week I found one on Christopher Street. It was also a six-flight walkup but only cost fifty-four a month and was in a much nicer neighborhood than the Lower East Side. Ruth Astor, who was a friend of Dave Lambert's, brought over her Volkswagen. We jammed all my belongings inside of it and in two trips made it over to Christopher Street. The last trip I followed her on my bicycle.

So I moved into Greenwich Village. It was July, 1957, and I was about to complete the music for *Two Gentlemen of Verona*. I was still broke, but when I sat up in my new apartment, I felt pretty good. I had made a record for Decca, I was making occasional recordings with other jazz groups and getting my music played with the Shakespeare Festival. I also had quite a large pile of compositions, completed, uncompleted and nearly completed as well. I might not have looked so good to Midhat, but I was advancing artistically and I hadn't been beaten yet.

MY NEW apartment on Christopher Street was designed a little differently from my place on the Lower East Side. Instead of being a railroad flat, you walked through a hall, about three feet wide, then arrived in the kitchen-bathroom. On the right side was a small room that I decided to use for the bedroom, and on the left side was my one-room music room, living room, studio, study, dining room and closet.

The first day I was so tired after lugging everything up the six flights that I lay down on my sleeping bag and slept. As I lay on the floor that first night, I realized to my pleasure that I didn't hear the sound of one rat scratching. This was a relief. However I did hear a rustling about 2 A.M. I thought perhaps it was a group of mice. I listened, half-dozing, finally got up, went into the living room and turned on the light. There was a tremendous whooshing sound like a huge bed of leaves being blown away on a gusty fall day. I saw a black sea of cockroaches, a whole army, skidding across the linoleum to their hiding place. I had never seen so many cockroaches in my life. I was used to them from the Lower East Side, but I was astounded to see so many. And I was very impressed with these cockroaches for climbing up so high in the building. In cockroach distance, it must have been the equivalent of a three-mile climb for a person with very short legs.

I looked under the linoleum where they had hidden. Rather than the layers with the hairpins and old newspapers that I'd had in my East Side apartment, there was just an old moldy floor and no roaches to be seen. I heard the whooshing growing fainter and realized that they were in the walls. There was probably a tremendous cockroach community in the building and perhaps throughout the entire block. It might eventually overthrow the entire city. With these thoughts, I dozed off to sleep and the next morning got up and started finishing the music for *Two Gentlemen of Verona*.

Romeo and Juliet had gone beautifully, but *Two Gentlemen of Verona* seemed as if it would be the sleeper of the season. No one was really that familiar with the play. The cast had worked so hard on *Romeo and Juliet* that when we began to sandwich in rehearsals between the performances of *Romeo and Juliet*, everyone was exhausted. Jerry Stiller and Ann Meara were in *Gentlemen*. They were fabulous and kept the whole cast laughing as we rehearsed out in the steaming, sunny fields of whatever park we were working in that day. The actors all wore overalls and old straw hats. It looked like the cast of *Tobacco Road*. With all the beards, the Shakespeare Festival looked as if someone were filming the life story of Vincent Van Gogh. We were a pretty ratty-looking crew, but we all had that old campfire spirit and the actors were terrific. Jerry and Ann kept everyone's spirits up with all their clowning and improvisation and jokes.

I wrote the song "Who Is Sylvia?" before writing the rest of the music. Although there had been so many versions of this, I decided simply to do it the way I felt it in terms of the lyrics and our particular production. There was also a little ballet and quite a bit of incidental music between scenes, music for the transitions in the forest and a great many other places where I was free to write almost anything.

Spencer Sinatra, my old friend from Washington, had moved to New York and told me he would play flute. David Kurtzer and Al Epstein played bassoon and oboe respectively. Jules Greenberg, whom I had gone to the temple with in Frankfort, Germany, in the army, had moved to New York and he played percussion. The harpsichord-ist was my friend from Washington who'd played percussion for *Hamlet* in 1951, Edward Schick.

I really felt at home with these musicians and we all went down on the subway to WNYC in high spirits to record the score. Joe had apparently wangled some way of letting us use their facilities. After we completed taping the entire score in one hour, the station manager came running out as the engineer was about to give us the tape.

"Hey, you can't take that tape," he said. "That belongs to the station. This isn't a recording studio."

"But we're doing this for the Shakespeare Festival," I said. "It's nonprofit, you know." I had already found this out as the stock phrase that was used whenever people wanted to get me to play for nothing.

"We're nonprofit too," said the station manager. "Get out. Right now."

Well, I thought to myself, I guess I won't be hearing any of that music for a while. I told Joe.

"I haven't even heard it, Dave," he said, "but I know it's beautiful. We'll scrape up the money and pay the musicians and we'll do it again somehow." A day later the musicians came back and we went to Carroll Studios, run by Carroll Bratman. He was a former percussionist who had the greatest selection of percussion instruments in the world. He had helped the Shakespeare Festival out before by lending us instruments. He let us use the studio as a favor in order to tape the score again. We managed to record the music and it came out even better the second time.

Two Gentlemen of Verona opened and was the surprise theatrical hit of the summer. It wasn't until opening night that everything seemed to work. The spontaneity and naturalness of the actors, Stewart Vaughn's sympathetic and relaxed direction, complemented by the whole atmosphere that Joe had already set up around the Shakespeare Festival, made it irresistible. People stood in line for every performance. I went to see it almost every night, just to watch the brilliance of the actors, to meet friends and study all the reactions to the show and to the music and its use.

A lot of the painters that I had known from the Five Spot came to see it because it was free and because they were interested in Shakespeare. They liked the idea of the Shakespeare in the Park as a wonderful kind of venture in the theater. They were interested in the idea of music as one spatial element in the theater. They would often talk to me in terms of rhythm, lights, time and form, with the music being one element, part of a giant chiaroscuro, almost a visual element of the total theatrical experience.

As I was having a discussion with some painters after one of the shows, Dan Cowan, the French-horn player I'd met at the Five Spot, came up. "That was nice, Dave," he said, giving me a wink. Coming from a musician of this caliber, that was a higher compliment than a thirty-two-page report would be from anyone else. Dan went over all the music and commented on each section very briefly. He told me he had recognized my horn playing in one of the cues and how if I developed a different way of playing I would be able to get the kind of sound I was looking for. He'd been able to hear, even over the recording system, exactly what I was doing wrong as a horn player. Still he could sense what it was that I was trying to do.

"I wish I could pay enough to get someone like you to play horn in the recording," I said. "My chops aren't too good, but we've got a budget problem, as you know, so I usually play all the percussion instruments, horn, trumpet, harpsichord, organ, flute and recorder and anything else I can to try to save the money."

"I'll be glad to do it," said Dan. "I can even help you to get some other good musicians who would enjoy working on it too."

The painters were with us, so we got into a conversation again about Matisse. They all felt that his importance as one of the great giants of the twentieth century was just beginning to become recognized. The painters also felt that his paper cutouts done in his last years were going to usher in a whole new era in the visual arts. As they sat there speaking about hot and cold colors, form, shapes, design, ideas and involvements, I realized that they were similar in a way to musicians but that they had to articulate their feelings in a much more verbal way. When I spoke to Dan we could say the most cliché things or almost nothing and with a look and a gesture express ourselves. Simply by the sounds of our voices we could communicate. Words weren't as important as they seemed to be to the painters.

My life was beginning to come together a bit. I was still in desperate straits financially and didn't know what I was going to be doing next or how I was going to do it. Our group wasn't getting any work. I was still taking day jobs here and there, playing jazz whenever I could. My composition work was still in a disorganized kind of rudimentary stage, even though I was writing a great deal and had huge piles of sketches, notes and incomplete pieces scattered all over my apartment. Still that night, as Dan and the painters and I talked, I began to have the feeling that my association with the painters, with Dan, who had achieved something on the horn I had never been able to, with some of the young composers and conductors I knew—all these different worlds of jazz, classical music, theater and art were coming together. I felt that I was in some way part of something happening in my time and that I was able to learn and advance my thinking every day, as an artist and as a man.

Dan came over to my house and we talked a great deal that evening about music. He told me how he'd studied the French horn and violin since he'd been a kid in Brooklyn, how he'd worked with some of the greatest musicians in the world, such as Bruno Jaenicke, a horn player whose records all of us had listened to for decades. Dan explained to me how his violin playing had helped his horn playing and his horn playing had helped his violin playing. He also told me about his interest in painting, how he had studied acting with Morris Carnovsky, and of the writing that he had done. He had an incredibly active mind and was able to speak more eloquently than any musician I ever knew. Just when he had led you down some avenue of thought, he would suddenly cancel it out with some self-deprecatory remark in the tradition of the great old Jewish comics, then start on a new tangent. In spite of his quick mind, he really had the old down-home soul that made him a great companion and friend. He had been through a lot of hell and agony himself, but rather than being bitter, he seemed more alive than any other free-lance musician I had ever met who had managed to survive in New York. He played with symphony orchestras, with Broadway shows, with chamber music groups, and when he had free time, he would play for fun. He was a real old pro with an amateur spirit.

Just before I began to attend rehearsals for *Macbeth* I got a call from a man with a voice and style of speech that sounded like my old friend Morris. He told me he had a real hip jazz club in Wildwood, New Jersey. He had heard our group was the greatest. He told us we would all get a hundred and fifty dollars a week, could swim in the day and swing after dark. I called up George and we got our group all set to go. I was thrilled. I called him back and told him we were on our way.

I told Joe Papp that I had to go away to play but that I would get *Macbeth* finished in New Jersey. Because I was only getting five dollars a play, he understood.

George and I went with our quartet to Wildwood. The owner told us that we could only get half of what he told us on the phone. We stayed in the bar, watched the TV broadcast as Floyd Patterson knocked out Hurricane Jackson in the tenth round and drove back

to New York somewhat discouraged but all the wiser for my mistake
—one that I've never made the likes of since.

Even though I felt stupid for having been conned, I realized it was
my fault for being so dumb. I no longer could excuse myself if I was
exploited. Dan lent me fifty dollars and I paid off the bass player
and the drummer for the day they had wasted. George wouldn't take
anything.

"It's my contribution for your tuition for business school," he told
me. "You can make it up later. Next time you'll know better. Or else.
Use your head. *Think*." I started thinking and decided I'd better
write the music for *Macbeth*.

A few weeks later I got a call from Betty Rollins, the cute girl
from Sarah Lawrence who had hired me to play there when I'd first
come back from Europe. She was still in school, so I assumed she
wanted me to play again.

"No," she said, "of course you're welcome to, but that's not why
I called. I'm acting too, you know, and my representative, Barna
Ostertag, heard your music this summer in the park and wants to
know if she could help you in any way."

That sort of stopped me cold. "That's funny," I said. "Since I saw
you I had one or two—you know—slow periods in music." I was
trying to think, as George had suggested. "When I worked as a TV
extra a little bit, I got some pictures made up and when all those good
reviews came out mentioning my music, I got the copies on a piece
of paper and made some photostats and took them around to two or
three music people I know."

"What happened?" she said.

"Nothing," I said. "The receptionist usually gave me the old
Queens Boulevard hate rays and intimated that if I didn't leave right
away, I would be thrown out by somebody bigger."

"Well, I think you'll find that Barna is a little different," said Betty.
"She's really a terrific person, a real lady and not artificial in any
way. Most of all, she mentioned your music to me and then I told
her how I'd known you on the boat. Why don't you come up and
see her?"

"Great," I said. It was hard for me to imagine that after two years
in New York a reputable business person would actually be interested in me. Ten per cent of me wouldn't pay anyone's light bill. So
far the only things that I hadn't done for nothing, outside of working

at the Five Spot, were for the lowest-type, grade-Z con men. After my experience with Morris I didn't think much of managers. I thought I would call up George Barrow because he still had a much better business sense than I did. He was more mature, even though he was only a few years older.

"What do you think, George?" I said.

"Listen, Dave, just sit and *listen* and see what the woman says. Don't tell her your hard-luck stories, just *listen* and see if she makes *sense*. And get cleaned up when you go to see her. Don't go up there looking like a beatnik."

"Well . . . ," I said.

"Come on. You don't have to jive me. You still look sloppy most of the time. And remember, more important, don't get angry. You've got to learn to cool yourself and control yourself. This is *business*."

"O.K., George, you've inspired me again. I'll let you know what happens." I got all dressed up and went to meet Barna in her office on Fifth Avenue. I walked in and she was a cute little lady with a low voice, short, curly hair and a great collection of golden trinkets that looked like she'd been assembling them for years. They jangled on both of her wrists. She also had a lieutenant colonel's gold leaf on her lapel and when I looked in her eyes, it was like looking at somebody that was five thousand years old. Right away I could see that she was smart and deep, had been through everything, but still came out swinging. I was speechless. I just stood there looking at those eyes and she looked me up and down.

"I just want to say," she told me, "that I thought the music I've heard of yours is very fine."

"Well, thanks," I said, shuffling back and forth. I began a long monologue, telling her of all the troubles I had had for the last eight years.

"Do you think you would like to be a composer?" she asked me quietly.

"Well, sure," I said. "I've been composing now since I was thirteen or fourteen. That's quite a while, you know," and then I delivered another long monologue, shuffling about. She was the first business person I'd ever talked to that actually paid any attention to me and the fact that she was concentrating on what I said made me extremely nervous.

Finally she interrupted me rather sternly. "Don't fidget so," she said. I looked surprised and calmed down. "And stand up straight.

You must not slouch. You're a man, not a boy. If you want people to take your music and you seriously, you have to present yourself the way you really are inside."

That really floored me. I sat down. She then talked to me for about an hour and a half, giving me advice, asking me questions and filling me full of a kind of calm I had never experienced since I'd been in New York. I could see she was completely contemporary, even though she was in her fifties, and she had the spirit of a child. She told me about how she had been an actress, how she had gone overseas in World War II and worked with soldiers, how she had come from Piqua, Ohio, helped build the Goodman Theatre in Chicago and worked her way up as a performer, finally as a representative and now was opening her own office. She had mostly young actors who were beginning. To my astonishment I found out that she had been the representative of Earle Hyman, who had played Hamlet in the Howard University production for which I had written the music back in 1951. She had had one other composer briefly, but he wasn't a serious person about his work. He wanted to be commercial and had left her.

She said she felt something for my music. I told her I was getting only five dollars a play as a composer. As a jazz musician I got whatever I could for the kind of music I wanted to play. I felt I probably would never make much money. She then asked me what I really wanted to do ultimately.

"My dream," I told her, "has always been to be able to find the time to write pieces that can be performed in a concert hall, in opera houses and in people's homes. I want something to leave behind me when I'm dead. My story—my sounds—to show the way I felt about music and about life—music that can stand on its own forever."

She told me that if she was to work with me the most important thing would be for me to have to learn to budget my time so that my own work could be the number-one priority in my life. If we were fortunate enough to be able to make any money at all, I wouldn't have to do odd jobs and daytime work. Then I could set aside time to complete pieces every year regardless of what else I was doing. Eventually I would even be able to turn down work in order to pursue my own private dream. Again I didn't know what to say.

"It will be an adventure," she said. "We don't even need to sign a contract. Our faith in each other is more than sufficient for that. I don't really know that much about music, but in exchange for what

I can teach you about what I know in dealing with people and in acting like a responsible adult as well as a responsible artist, you can teach me about music and what musicians go through."

I was really moved by that. My mind flashed back to the famous story Joe Louis had told about his manager. As a highly talented but poorly managed young boxer, he'd been told by his manager that whether or not he would be able to be champion, they could sure have fun trying. I left Barna's office and for the first time since I'd been in New York, I felt I could trust someone who was on the other side, someone who was in the world of business who would not try to sell me down the river and force me to be something that I felt in every fiber and nerve ending in my body was wrong, cheap, vulgar or a sellout. I realized as I walked back to Christopher Street that while I'd been scuffling for these two years, I'd been doing things that I believed in and that now perhaps I could find someone who could help me, if not financially, at least by giving me advice and the wsidom of a lot of experience.

I got home and called up Betty Rollins. I told her how much it meant to me to have someone like this help me in any way.

"I knew you two would get along," said Betty.

The Shakespeare Festival decided to move to have a winter season. They moved into the Hecksher Theatre and their first show was to be *Richard the Third*. After looking around for an actor they found a young unknown who had worked out of town but had never had a good part in New York. His name was George C. Scott. I came to rehearsal the third day and sat there hypnotized like everyone else.

"This guy is too much," I told Tom Gruenewald, who was now the stage manager. "Yes," said Tom in his calm, controlled way. "I think he'll be first-rate." Even though George C. Scott was rehearsing in his T-shirt he was able to create a whole atmosphere around him. He looked and acted like a king. I noticed that whenever he was on-stage, all the other actors gave performances that were better than when he was not on stage. He could not only command attention, he was able to turn on the whole cast with his presence.

I watched the limp George created for Richard. It gave me the idea to write special music that Dan played on the viola da gamba which became music for Richard every time he had one of his gripping moments of silence. Knowing he had the audience in his pocket even before there was one, he would limp about the stage, filling the empty theater with the atmosphere that he seemed to be able to create with a movement of his hand or the twitch of an eyebrow.

There was almost sixty minutes of music in the play. Because my neighbors were already going crazy from my practicing and composing, I went up to Dan's eighteen-dollar-a-month apartment on Tenth Avenue and West Fifty-ninth Street, where other musicians and painters lived. While he slept, I would sit up nights plunking away at his old upright piano. Then he would get up in the morning and play some of the horn music, the violin parts, the viola da gamba parts and anything else that he could, just to encourage me.

A friend of Oscar Pettiford's named Janet Stewart, a lovely lady who lived on Park Avenue, had heard us play at Birdland with our band in the spring of fifty-seven and invited Dan and me to come up for some chamber music sessions. She had seen the Shakespeare in the Park that summer and was happy to know that some of my music was getting played. There were people she knew that she thought might enjoy meeting a young composer.

Dan looked suspicious. "It's cool, Danny," I told him. "She's not a soirée giver or a head hunter. She's a real lady."

We both went up to Janet's place. Dan agreed that she was a charming, gracious, warm, fun-loving woman, almost like you would imagine a queen to be back in the Middle Ages. We would play music and she would sit there beaming and then when we finally would say, "Hey, Janet, do you mind if we stop for a few minutes?" she would agree grudgingly. Dan and I would run back to the kitchen, make ourselves gigantic sandwiches from the huge piles of succulent meat and cheeses that packed her icebox. In ten minutes we could eat enough for a whole week. We didn't make anything fancy. We just took two pieces of bread, slopped on some mayonnaise and horseradish, jammed everything we could between the slices, and wolfed them down.

The third time we went, Dan scurried around the kitchen and found some terrific prewar Lapsang Souchong tea, which Janet didn't even know was there. He offered to make some. Because Dan was also a great gourmet cook, not an avant-garde one like me, he began making little feasts during our breaks. I'm sure that Janet's cook would have been very jealous if she could have seen the fabulous impromptu ten-minute dinners we would eat. As Janet would smell the great aromas floating from the kitchen, she would say, "Dan, what are you cooking now?" As he ran about the kitchen with the speed of light, mixing, throwing things in pots, burning, turning, boiling and stirring, he would go into tremendous comic routines in order to be able to keep up his unbroken flow of cooking.

Several other good musicians came. Israel Citkowitz, a fine composer and pianist, Michael Smith, who was then a student who played the recorder, and Frank Corsaro. Frank had just finished directing *Hatful of Rain* and was doing very well. It starred Ben Gazzara. Ben and Frank were real people. I met them at Birdland when I played there with Oscar Pettiford. I had talked to Frank briefly just to say hello and didn't realize he was so interested in music. When he arrived at Janet's, Frank turned out to have an amazing lyric tenor voice and really loved to sing. He would begin singing Shubert lieder and while Dan and I were out in the kitchen scarfing up a storm, we would hear his beautiful Neapolitan medieval choirboy voice floating through the kitchen doors.

"Hey," said Dan, "this guy's really got some hell of a talent."

"Em, em," I would say, chewing up my week's meal. We performed Benjamin Britten's Serenade for tenor, horn and strings, with the orchestra part being played on the piano by Israel. Dan and I would alternate on the horn. Dan would bring his violin and we'd play the Brahms Horn Trio. Then Frank would drive us down in a taxi to Twentieth Street and ask us if we wanted to take the taxi down to the Village.

"No, Frank, that's O.K.," I would always say. "Dan and I are going to walk, it's such a beautiful night." I guess he knew we were lying when it was snowing and raining, but he was too much of a gentleman to have the cab go farther. He realized that we were too broke to pay. So we would get out and say good night and walk down the remaining fifteen blocks or so.

I had completed the music for *Richard the Third* and at one of our chamber music sessions with Janet, I asked Frank if he would sing part of the music. We needed someone who sounded like a monk and Frank had exactly that unearthly, eerie, beautiful quality. He also was studying piano and was interested in directing opera. A week later, Frank came up to the studio and spent hours recording the music. Then, a chorus of actors arrived and hummed while Frank sang. I played the bells while Dan helped the singers out, playing the viola da gamba softly to give them their pitch.

After about six hours, the engineers were groaning.

"I feel great," said Frank.

"I wish I'd written more," I said. "You're the Renaissance champ."

Richard the Third opened and was a great success. George C. Scott began to get the recognition he deserved. I heard about the dues he had paid before he could even get a good acting job. This gave me a lot of encouragement and hope for myself. He had worked at every kind of day job imaginable. He had toured and acted in little companies all around the country, so that by the time he got his chance, he was ready. As Dan had remarked, George was so obviously a real trouper that when he got his opportunity there was no question of whether or not he would make it.

Frank introduced me to a lot of people who worked in the theater and told me he would try to help out my music in any way he could because he really felt that I had some contribution to make to theatrical music. I told him that while I enjoyed writing incidental music, to me it was like being an accompanist. It was fun, and master composers like Beethoven and Mendelssohn had written theater scores for *Coriolanus* and *A Midsummer Night's Dream* that stood on their own, without the plays. Still it was only a small part of their total work in music.

"You know," said Frank, "you should think about opera or maybe musical comedy."

"I'll be perfectly honest with you, Frank," I told him, "I can't stand musical comedies. To me that Bronx-housewife-style singing is worse than anything in borscht-belt history. They use all these great musicians, singers, actors, dancers, set designers and everybody to produce something that ends up being just a lot of garbage which would be better off at a summer-camp show. I know I'll write opera, but I'd go to the electric chair before I'd spend five minutes on a musical. I think it's the lowest form of music that there is. All those fine players having to blast out that junk. Musicals are sickening. Once you've played *The Student Prince*, you've had it forever."

"Well," said Frank, "on the whole, you may be right, but there are a few exceptions. Have you seen *West Side Story*?"

"No, I haven't," I told him. "I'm not trying to break your heart, but I don't go to shows or concerts unless I can get in free."

"If you get a chance," said Frank, "see it. It's worthwhile."

A week later my aunt Louise came to town. She was my mother's sister. She and her husband had always been great to me since I was a little boy. I used to play "Old Man River" with her husband, my Uncle Kirsch, whenever I would visit their house in Philadelphia.

Louise called me up and said, "This is your Aunt Louise, dear. I know you're busy, but I'm just in town for two days and would like to take you to the theater. What would you like to see?"

"How about *West Side Story*?"

"Fine," she said, "I'd like to see that myself."

I sat flabbergasted. Somehow Leonard Bernstein had managed to beat Broadway at its own game and sneak in nothing but real music, not once in a while but throughout the entire show. I was really impressed and while I still didn't want to write a musical comedy, I saw that at least it was possible to work in this area.

I decided that any incidental music I wrote from now on I would keep in a new pile, because the short overtures, dances, songs and musical transitions had merit of their own. I stored them behind the piano. By now my pile of new and old pieces was growing so gigantic that I hardly had any room left in my apartment. I decided that I was going to complete one piece, using what I had heard and thought about for the last few years.

I told Barna this and she was very happy. "When you have finished that piece, I'll be more happy than if you were a millionaire and so will you." The piece I had already partially written and had in my mind was a trio for saxophone, French horn and bassoon. It was one of nearly a hundred works I had in various stages of completion. It was the same instrumentation I had used for the Third Avenue El movie. Although that music stood on its own, I didn't feel it would be interesting as a suite. I wanted a real four-movement work. The thought of the timbres and the sounds of these three instruments suggested something in my mind that made me sit down and start grinding away with the idea of having George Barrow and some other friends play it. I began to work on this piece every chance I got.

Just as I was stone broke again and about to go looking for a day job, Oscar Pettiford called up. He said that the all-star band was going out on tour for a while. I was happy to go. Even though I knew there wouldn't be much money, I wanted to play with all the fellows again. It would give me a big boost, after all this time with Shakespeare, to get back into the twentieth century. I also felt it would help me in writing my trio.

It was a treat to see all the musicians. I missed playing with them, and we all got to rehearsal early, so we could hang out. Some of the guys had heard my music for the Shakespeare Festival.

"Yeah, I heard you. Ya-bah-dup-a-deee," said Jerome Richardson, the tenor-sax player, singing a fanfare I had written a year ago. That cheered up my whole week, because I had jammed with Jerome up at Minton's in 1955 when he worked there. He knew as much about classical music as he did about jazz, and was completely schooled in theory and played four instruments equally well. The whole band was well schooled, for that matter.

"The bread might be a little sad," Oscar warned us after our rehearsal. No one said anything. All of us loved Oscar. When he could not always pay us the full amount each night, those of us without families would take the smallest amount. Of course when he had the money we would always get it. Having a band like his was a constant struggle. Nevertheless, we always had a ball.

Our trip to Florida turned out to be the longest one-nighter I'd ever played. The regular trombonist disappeared and in his place came another player nicknamed Porkchops, who engaged me in a nonstop conversation that he began by saying, "My main man, every French-horn player that I ever knew was either out of his mind or a faggot!"

"I'm not either," I told him.

"That's splendid," he said, "I dig you back anyway." And he launched into this fantastic story of his life, of his five wives, his years as a pimp, his drug habits, the time that he served in jail, his army experiences, his days as a merchant seaman and many other of his experiences that go into making up the life of a supreme hipster.

When we got to the train station at Washington, he said, "I'll be right back, Jim, I'm just going to take me a little stroll." Another member of the band said, "I bet he gets busted before he walks around the other side of the block." And of course he did. But the police could find nothing wrong and had to release him. He continued strolling around the block and came back and informed us that there were no happenings in Washington. "This used to be a swinging town years ago, but man it sure is a drag now," he said. "I was checking the sounds and there ain't nothing shaking." We then got on the train and about two o'clock in the morning got off at some scraggly town. We were taken in a broken-down old bus to the airport. From the airport we flew to some place in Florida where another bus met us, even more broken down than the first. From there we rode through the Everglades without stopping because our white driver informed us, looking at Ed London and J. R. Montrose, the other white guys in the band, with his steely blue Cracker eyes, "You boys would be dead in a minute." He looked as if he wanted to complete his prophecy himself.

I noticed at the bus station that the black people of Florida—and this was before any of the freedom marches—were astounded to see a Negro band leader with three white musicians working for him. The musicians who were from New York were upset by the terrible living standards in Florida and by the terror you could see in most of the black people's faces. It was a sad sight.

Finally we got to the university. Oscar was in a very bad mood and refused to get out of the bus. "I'm going to sleep here," he growled. He proceeded to lie down in the bus and conk out. We were given a room to change in and some supper since by this time it was six o'clock at night and almost time for us to play. Some of the last-minute replacements like Porkchops had never seen the music before and we were supposed to have an extra rehearsal, but Oscar was sleeping so we had our supper and tried to rest for an hour. We woke up Oscar and began our job. Because some of the people hadn't played the music before, the band didn't sound nearly as good as we did at Birdland. The kids at the concert dance really enjoyed it though. They recognized the names of many of the musicians in the band who were known in the jazz world and cheered us on.

Afterward the college president had a reception for the band, a very formal affair. Oscar was sulking in the corner, angry at the way the music had been played.

Finally one of the musicians went over to Oscar with the college president and said, "Oscar, I would like you to meet the president of the college."

Suddenly Oscar's face broke into a demonic smile. He threw his arms around the startled president and said, "Hey, motherfucker, what's happening?" and began bear-hugging him and shouting with laughter as only he could do. The president and members of the

faculty were rather startled, but it broke the freeze and after that we
had a ball the rest of the evening. Oscar was the most honest and
kindhearted man I ever worked for. His craziness was part of his
great gift, which was why musicians would do anything for him. By
the end of the evening he had charmed everyone on the faculty. We
stayed up till four that morning. Then we got back into the bus and
headed for New York. We arrived in Manhattan about fifteen hours
later through another series of train rides, plane rides and bus rides
with short stops here and there to go to the bathroom or get something to eat.

When I got back to the city I realized that we had traveled for
almost three days straight in order to play for four hours. I really
began to admire musicians who can make one-nighters for years and
years.

A week later we had our last big job. It was a concert in Springfield, Massachusetts, where Dinah Washington also appeared. There
were only about eight signs in all of Springfield, no advertising in
the papers or anywhere else. Only twenty-five people showed up at
the armory because no one knew about it. Oscar had a good name
at that time, but Dinah Washington had a very big name, which could
have filled the house. She was upset too. She sat in and sang with our
band and we sat in with members of her band and we spent the whole
night having a session. Only the family men got paid whatever Oscar
could scrap together. The rest he paid out of his pocket.

We all knew as we drove back from Springfield that the band was
finished. We felt sad. As soon as Oscar sensed this, he started shouting, laughing and bellowing at us to liven things up. He wasn't about
to let anyone feel sorry for him.

"You going to do more Shakespearing?" he asked me, as I walked
with him to Twenty-eighth Street when everyone else had gone their
way.

"Sure," I said. "I hope we can still play. If I can help any way—
you know, copy parts or anything . . ."

"Help? *Help?*" shouted Oscar, as if he were being attacked by an
army of Venusians. "What the hell are you talking about? Do I need
your help? Listen, Dave, you help your*self*! Get it all together. Be
as good as you can be. Write as beautiful as possible. You can do it.
Don't worry about helping nobody, man. That's jive and you know
it. You keep writing and don't let nobody stand in the way of what
you got to say. We're all blessed by God to be in music. O.K., let's

have a little taste at my house. I love French horns. When we work again, I don't want you guys to miss any more notes and mess us up. I *listen*, you know. I hear *every*thing."

We went to Oscar's apartment and started drinking ale.

"Isn't life beautiful?" shouted Oscar. "We've got the most gorgeous band in the world. Yeah! And don't make no noise," he roared, pouring out more ale. "My son's sleeping and he's got school tomorrow. Cheers, Dave."

"Cheers, Oscar," I whispered.

"God put us here to blow. Man, if you talk any more trash I'll cut my French-horn section. I'll replace you with *mello*phones. Didn't we sound fine tonight? What a band!"

We stayed up all night and Oscar showed me an Indian dance he had learned as a child. When his son got up to go to school we were dancing in a circle. His wife cooked us breakfast and I finally went home. I could have stayed for days. Oscar was the best company in the world. He had the biggest heart of anyone I ever worked for. He was one of those people who showed me the power of the pure positive approach toward everything. By utilizing your own energies and your own life forces you can affect other musicians and other people and even change the whole atmosphere from being uptight or negative or depressing into being joyous.

After Oscar's tour, things got pretty slow. The weather was getting cold and I was broke again. Dan came over and helped me paint my apartment. We painted it mostly black and white in honor of Franz Kline, whom we used to hang out with all the time at the Cedar Tavern. We put one gigantic dot of yellow over the bathroom door in order to celebrate Franz's return to the use of primary colors again. I started going back to the shape-ups. I didn't like going out there and shivering on the streets. In a way I felt sort of ashamed that people who knew me would see me out there scuffling for manual-labor jobs, so I decided to work on the night shift at the post office.

It was down on Chambers Street and we had a wild collection of workers. They could have formed a Chambers Street Branch repertory company, a symphony orchestra, a jazz band, a novelists' workshop—all the fine arts were represented there in full. I saw people I had known from all over the place. I ran into one of the old-time workers who used to come to the Five Spot every night when I had played there. He pointed out to me who the two cops were who were spying on people who were stealing mail. It helped to pass the hours, watching the cops in action. I saw them busting several people so cleverly that no one knew who they were. I finally began warning people and suddenly the two cops disappeared.

At first I used to work rather lackadaisically, going with different friends I knew to the men's room. We would get high, but I found it made the hours seem longer, and I didn't seem to enjoy getting high much anymore anyway. We would also go back in the baggage room and drink wine, which was more sociable.

After a few weeks, I figured the only way to stand the post office was to work as hard as possible. I began working like a fiend. I would go to the face-up table and work like mad. The face-up table was where the letters went through an enormous machine that put a date on the letters and canceled the stamps. I would stuff gigantic quantities of mail through, then run around with my cart to the sorting tables, sort mail, heave mailbags around and do every kind of work I could in a frenzy.

"That guy's crazy," said some of the old-timers, looking at me. I figured it was the only way I could make it. After a while I found that it began to pick up my spirits again.

Whenever I got bugged, I could always watch my fellow workers. One old man, a Hasidic Jew with a beard down to his waist, long sideburns and a long-billed fisherman's cap, used to stand in front of the mailboxes where he was sorting mail, rocking slowly back and forth on his heels, dipping into his baggy coverall pockets occasionally to get some saltines to munch. After twenty minutes of rocking he would make one great lean forward and with the bill of his cap resting on the top of the sorting table, fall asleep, standing up for as much as an hour before he would wake up again and resume his rocking.

There was one Negro transvestite who used silver hair spray, wore floppy cashmere sweaters and did imitations of Brigitte Bardot. There were also some far-out postwomen too. One, Frankie, was so tough that when some guy made fun of her for being gay, she knocked him out with a left to the stomach and a right cross to the jaw. After that she was left alone. There were also opera singers on the way up who would entertain us with their vocal prowess, bellowing out arias at 3:30 A.M., and several dozen aspiring stand-up comics who would snap out their routines for hours. It reminded me of the atmosphere of Patch Barracks in the army.

It was nice to have an assured income again. Oscar's band had not paid much, so I was just about even. I borrowed a little more money from Dan and owed him about ninety-five dollars. One day when he was up in my place giving me a horn lesson, one out of the hundreds of armies of traveling musicians, drug users, wanderers, vagabonds, struggling artists, students, old friends and strangers who knew my address came by my place for a handout. Although my life had gotten more organized and I was more serious, I still felt an obligation whenever anybody wanted anything to give what I had if I had it. I still seemed to feel guilty if I didn't. I gave the guy five dollars that I had just borrowed from Dan. After staring sullenly at both of us, he left.

"What the hell did you do that for?" said Dan.

"Well, Danny," I said, "the guy needed some money and I had it."

"The hell you had it," said Dan. "You just borrowed it from me. Do you think I'm lending you my money so you can give it to a bunch of bums that hate you more after you give it to them? That's ridiculous."

"Well, Danny," I said, "I just think it's right."

"Bullshit," said Dan. "You're trying to compensate for some kind of guilty feelings and think you're being St. Francis. If you want to be a humanitarian and a human being, give your money and your kindness and your love to your friends and the people who really deserve it and need it and appreciate it. If you were independently wealthy, it would be different, but you're not. You're being a fool and you'll only be exploited and weaken yourself by being an easy mark. I don't mind giving you the money, because you're a nice person, but these people would leave you lying in the gutter. Most of them are philistines. Some of them probably come from well-to-do families anyway and are just playing beatnik."

I thought about what Dan said and I realized he was right. There were more and more people like this in the Village—drop-outs from society who instead of writing their families for money, seemed to prey off people who really were scuffling like I was. Also, I found they never would pay you back.

But I told Dan about another time when I had walked all the way from Eighty-fourth Street to the Lower East Side because I couldn't borrow any money for carfare. I had walked through some of the musicians' bars and no one would even give me subway fare. After that I always vowed that whenever any musician would ask me for money, I would give it to him, at least a quarter so that he could get to where he was going.

"That's different," said Dan. "We all do that. If someone's a pal, you share your last meal with him. But these people aren't musicians or friends. They're anti-lifers. That guy's face was the face of a real art hater." After that I tried to be a little more sensible.

We began rehearsals of *As You Like It*. George C. Scott played Jaques and was sensational. Jerry Stiller and Ann Meara also had wonderful parts. Tom Sankey sang "Blow, Blow, Thou Winter Wind" and some of the other songs I wrote. The play had a lot of songs and dances and even a harpsichord overture, which I recorded myself. (It took about forty takes.)

Christmas Eve I was off from the post office. I got together with some old friends of mine from Europe I had run across at the Corner Bistro. In the course of our celebration, we smoked up quite a bit of Panama Red TNT pot. I spent most of Christmas Day wandering around the streets in a near-catatonic state, thinking I was Santa Claus. I took a little nap and that night decided to finish the music for *As You Like It*.

I sat down and couldn't write. For the first time in my life I wasn't able to sit down and compose when I felt like it. I just couldn't get my mind together. I realized that because of all the pot I had smoked I had been slowed down to the point where I couldn't compose, so I decided right then and there that I would never again do anything that would interfere with my composition. If I ever did get high again it would have to be during a period when I wasn't forced to use my mind actively. I couldn't put down pot or start crusades to burn up all the pot fields in the world—far from it. It was something that I enjoyed and it gave me certain insights, pleasure and closeness with many people. But it was something that I felt I no longer needed except once in a great while, because it interfered with the thing that was the most important and crucial in my life, which was being able to write music. If I couldn't do that, there was really no point in my being alive.

It was during this time that Howard Hart, an old friend of Charles Mills, my composition teacher and a fine drummer himself, started to have some poetry readings with jazz.

"Are you going to play drums?" I asked.

"Hell no, man," he said. "I'm going to read my poems." I knew Howard had written some wonderful poems that Charles had set to music, but I didn't realize how much and how well he had written until he started showing me his work. He had a great many poems, some of which I found very beautiful, all of which were very well suited to music. He brought over his friend Philip Lamantia. When I played while Howard and Philip read, it was cooking. We could see that we really had something.

Jack Kerouac was in town, so he agreed to be MC and do some reading too. We went to the Brata Art Gallery on East Tenth Street and had the first jazz poetry reading in New York. The place was jammed even though it was pouring rain that night. There were no advertisements, just word of mouth. It really went over great, and when a drunk from the Bowery came in with a bottle of wine and offered it to everyone, Jack Micheline broke the silence by taking a sip and saying, "You see, the poets and the winos are coming together at last." Everybody laughed and we continued the reading with Jack and other poets in the audience coming up and reading their poems while I wailed away on the French horn.

We had a big party afterwards. I hadn't seen Kerouac since *On the Road* had come out. He told me he would come by with Philip to visit me and that we should get together and do some more readings. Howard decided to have some evenings at the Circle in the Square theater with him and Philip and Jack as MC.

Jack and Philip and Howard would drink enormous quantities of Thunderbird before the performance, but because I was playing I only drank a little bit. After intermission, as the audience sat patiently waiting, they would usually be out drinking more Thunderbird or seeing their fans on the street and I would be stuck all alone in the middle of the theater-in-the-round, having to entertain people by myself. I would usually start off with some kind of sociological description of how jazz poetry was born, and no one could tell that I was kidding for the first few minutes. Just about the time that they would start laughing, I would play the horn to be serious again and sometimes would play for ten or fifteen minutes all by myself right in the middle of the stage until the poets eased back in and began their reading. After a while they liked it so much that this became part of the act.

Jack was a fantastic improviser and when I was playing he would be able to make up words to go along with the music on the spot. He used his voice just like another horn, using words like notes. He had an extraordinary ear. Philip had a powerful dramatic-reading style and delivery. Howard had a wonderful, sincere quality that made him sound like an old French troubadour from the past. I found that my theatrical experience helped me to instinctively time when and where I should play the horn and when I shouldn't. Sometimes I played jazz, sometimes classical music, mostly just music to fit the nature of each poem. I would always go off to the post office after the shows.

One night when I was off, Jack invited me to go to Brooklyn College, where he was giving a lecture to a group of English students about his work. He told me Philip and Howard were coming along and said I should bring my horn.

They all came by my place and we took the subway to Brooklyn College. It was supposed to be Jack's reading and lecture. He was to talk about *On the Road* and the literary influences in his work. He decided to bring us along to give him moral support. The bottles of Thunderbird started appearing and by the time we got out to Brooklyn College an hour behind schedule, all of us were quite torn up. The place was packed. Jack was one of the shyest people I'd ever met in my life when he was sober. Because he had struggled so long before he'd been discovered as a writer, his overwhelming success and the sudden pressures were a lot to take. When he was around a lot of people that he didn't know, the only way he could face them was by drinking. Still he always maintained his sweetness and kindness.

As we lurched into Boylan Hall at Brooklyn College where Jack was going to give the lecture, the students looked rather astonished. The English professor was very cool however. He introduced Jack, who told a few stories and anecdotes and then said in the tradition of the Zen master, he would let the students ask questions. When someone asked a long, involved question about whether or not Stendhal or Proust was more of an influence on his work and whether or not Celine influenced him stylistically in any way, Jack would say something like "You've got the answer in your question, and it's a beautiful answer." He was putting everybody on in a way, but in another way he was trying to show them that the writer says it all in his writing and for him to answer the question as if it were an English class would be dishonest. Finally the students kept getting more and more hostile because they wanted to be told something definite.

One student got up and said, "How come I love your books and the characters in your books and I hate you?"

"You don't hate me," said Jack. "You love me and I love you." It went on like this and the rumbling and the confusion grew more intense till finally a cute little fellow with Harpo Marx curly hair, bright blue eyes and an insane leprechaun smile raised his hand and stood up. "Jack," he said, "when you take those trips out across the country hitchhiking, walking, bicycling, sleeping out in the fields at night, traveling on freighters to foreign countries and when you go to Mexico and out into the desert—doesn't your mother ever get worried?" Everybody in the place cracked up. He had brought the house down with his question and good vibrations were restored.

After that Philip began to read some poetry, Howard read some poetry, Jack read some poetry, I played the horn and what started out as chaos became very beautiful. The students loved it. The English professor was happy because although this was not what he had expected, he wanted to show his class most of all that writers or artists were real human beings. Some of the students, including the young guy who'd asked Jack about his mother, stayed afterward. He introduced himself as Lenny Gross. He wanted to be a writer too and he and some other students invited us all out. We stayed up most of the night having a party, ending up in Manhattan. It was the greatest group of students I'd ever met and it made me feel like I was back in school again, except the kids were much hipper than the kids were when I went to school.

Jazz poetry became a fad, which fortunately had a very short life as the music was not generally related to the poetry and the poetry not altogether related to the music. Often the poetry was of a very amateurish quality, but it was fun while it lasted. All of us who could improvise poems or limericks on the spot felt that jazz singers like King Pleasure or poet-comedians like Lord Buckley and Lenny Bruce were much closer to what jazz poetry really was. Still, with the great evocative powers that jazz has, it can be used with poetry. I did make one recording with Philip Lamantia and Howard Hart in which—as a result of our having worked together for a long time—the poetry and music were related.

Our final concert was sponsored by the Paper Book Gallery at the York Theatre and Richard Avon, the good-hearted impresario had only sold seven tickets the night before the concert. He asked me if I would give away a few free seats. I went to the Cedar Tavern, the Corner Bistro, the White Horse Tavern and many of the bars on MacDougal Street, so when the night of the concert came the York

Theatre was packed. Howard Hart and Steve Tropp were the poets. One of Steve's poems had the line ". . . and then I saw the light of her neon vagina," which was the most memorable literary moment I experienced in jazz poetry. We had a post-poetry party afterward, ending up at the Five Spot, with poet Arnold Weinstein joining us.

Our record for Decca finally came out nationally but nothing ever happened. For the final humiliation, *Downbeat* only gave it two and a half stars.

When I went into Jim Atkins' cafeteria one night, two guys who used to come to the Five Spot shouted out my name. "Hey, Dave Amram," yelled the taller of the two. "You only got two and a half stars there, champ. You better sharpen your shovel, pack your axe and git back on the farm."

But his friend stopped him. "That ain't right," he said. "I heard that record and it was a groove, man. You got your own lyric thing going. You just keep swingin' your own way with George and fuck the critics. They don't know nothin' about music. They *all* full of shit."

"I go for that," said the first guy, "but I still think you ought to go back to the farm. You play too pretty to stay in the city." I sat down at the counter and talked to them both and we looked through the other reviews. So many recordings were being released every month, it seemed impossible that this could continue much longer without completely destroying the market. We had worked on our record for months but a lot of recordings including ones I had played on were simply jam sessions where we would go out to New Jersey, sight-read some pieces, improvise and then the entire amount would be put out on records every few months under a different leader's name as a different record, all taken from one session. Eventually, we all had to suffer if the companies rushed to put out all these records without promoting any of them.

Still, the sound that I'd gotten with George on my jazz record encouraged me to work even harder on my saxophone trio, which was really taking a beautiful shape. I had completed two movements. I thought I would rehearse it with George when we could find a bassoon player who had the time and when I had a chance to finish the last two movements and then copy out the parts.

James Dixon came to town again for his annual visit and for the first time didn't have to lend me ten dollars. I took him out and told him the work I was doing and he was very happy to see that I seemed to be getting myself together. He took me up to the Great Northern Hotel to see Mitropoulos, who looked older and more troubled. He was under a great deal of strain, but he was very kind as always and happy to see us. We went out and he took us to a terrific dinner and then we went down to Forty-second Street and saw a double feature including a Tarzan movie.

"Isn't it curious?" he turned to us and said. "They have some really fine composers writing music for those movies. What a pity that these men must waste their talents and be ignored this way. It really is a shame that they don't utilize them in writing concert music as well. It's a tragedy to have a gift for composition and to throw it away." After the movie was over, he looked at me. "James tells me you're not wasting so much time anymore in trying to find yourself." He looked through me as if he knew everything I had done since I had last seen him a year ago. "I haven't heard from you. You might have been dead," he said.

"Well, Maestro," I said, "I hate to trouble you when you're so busy."

"I'm never too busy to see someone who is my friend," he said. "You and Jim are like my sons. The sad part in growing older is that you can become so busy with people that you have no time for your real friends. I hope to see some of your compositions again soon."

"I promise you I'll show them to you, Maestro," I said.

"How is your jazz work coming?" he asked.

"Fine," I said, "I'm still playing."

"Who is the latest thing now, Dizzy Gillespie?" he said, smiling.

"No," I said, "Sonny Rollins and John Coltrane, Bill Evans and Miles Davis."

"Oh," said Mitropoulos, "I've heard the music of Miles Davis, but I don't know much about the work of the other three. The only criticism I have of the jazz world is that every six months the heroes change."

Jim and I left the Maestro after a while and the next day went to watch him conduct at the Metropolitan Opera. He had gotten us both tickets. Afterwards we went out again and he and Jim spoke about opera.

Suddenly he turned to me. "You must write opera," he said. "It's the greatest art form. With your interest and fine work in dramatic music, you could write a good one." He looked at me as if to say that that ended the discussion.

"I will, Maestro," I told him.

Jim had to go away the next day because he was working at the New England Conservatory. We talked about our old friends in the Seventh Army Symphony and compared notes and found out how many of them were working hard in music, playing in the good orchestras, conducting and composing, and how lucky we had all been to be together in the army in such a happy situation. We both decided, however, that neither of us was about to reenlist.

The saxophone trio was finally finished and the parts copied. Just before one of our chamber music sessions with Dan, I ran into Spencer Sinatra. He had left Stan Kenton. He hadn't played the saxophone for a while and had been concentrating mostly on his flute playing, but he agreed to read through my piece at Janet Stewart's house. Dan, Spencer and a bassoonist played through the whole piece. It was wonderful to hear a piece played all the way through by professional musicians and I decided I would add a fourth movement, an epilogue, just to end the piece. The fourth movement was to be similar to the music I had written for Ettore Rella's play, *Sign of Winter,* and I completed it in a few days.

I began working on a string quartet immediately afterwards and sketched away on many ideas in addition to rummaging through what must have been three hours of incompleted string quartets I had already begun.

The next production in the Park was *Twelfth Night.* As I watched the rehearsals, I saw that the balance of comedy, bitter-sweet tragedy, romance and the musical character of Feste could all make a marvelous opera. Frank Corsaro, who recorded many of the songs that were used in the play, also thought it was a good idea. Joe Papp said he would like to adapt the libretto and we agreed that we would cut the play but use only Shakespeare's words. We thought we could use some of the music I had written for the Central Park production as a basis.

In the fall of 1958 Stuart Vaughan was offered the artistic directorship of the Phoenix Theatre and asked me to be the composer and musical director for him. This meant that for the first time in my life I would have a tiny but guaranteed salary for a whole theatrical season. This seemed incredible to me, after nearly nine straight years of financial panic, excluding the two years I spent in the army. I accepted the job as musical director with thanks and realized it would also give me a chance to work on my concert music because I would not have to work at day jobs.

The first play at the Phoenix was *The Family Reunion.* I had worked on it before in 1952. Looking over the old music that I had done then, I didn't feel any bit of it was appropriate except for the overture. Six and a half years later I still felt the old overture I had written captured the essence and spirit of the play. This was a piece I had played quite often on piano for Thelonius Monk when I used to visit him after music school. It was one of the compositions I could perform on the piano and I was quite fond of it. I also played it for Stuart, who liked it as well.

We decided that the rest of the play would be different musically from what I had done before. Because of his training in music Stuart was not afraid to be different and wanted me to write certain parts of the music in as free and as far-out a fashion as I wanted to, to fit the scenes where Harry sees the apparitions.

I was filled with more energy and happiness than I had ever had since I'd come to New York. I knew that I could squeak by now without having to take any day jobs for the rest of the year. I would have to live extremely cautiously and still might need a few jobs outside music once in a while to help. Barna wasn't making enough off me to pay for postage stamps, but she knew I had finished my saxophone trio and was working on my string quartet and some other pieces. When she spoke to me she felt that our plan was beginning to work.

"It's going to be a long, long road," she told me, "it's going to take your whole life and long after I'm gone you'll still have to struggle, but at least you're getting started in a sane and sensible direction and learning slowly how to use your time and act like an adult. If you don't learn this as an artist, you can be the most talented person in the world and still won't be able to achieve anything. It's *never* going to be easy."

One morning as I got up to go to the rehearsal of *The Family Reunion* I saw Joe Papp's picture on the front page of the paper. There was a story about him saying that he had been fired from CBS because of some congressional investigating committee. I read this story and I couldn't believe it. He was doing more to bring free theater to New York, help out actors and give unknown people a chance than anyone else in the city. Without him, God knows what I would have been doing at this point.

I called him up right away. "It's nice of you to call boychick," he said. "I've been wiped out twice before and I built myself back and I'll do it again. Even if they kill me they can't stop the idea of the Shakespeare Festival. It's too important for the city and for the theater. These guys just come in town for one day and try to wipe out everybody. McCarthy's era is supposed to be over. If they think they're going to get me to testify to squeal they'd better forget it. I'm not a fink. This is ridiculous for something that goes back years before and I'm going to sue through my union and try to get back my job at CBS. They're never going to get me to lie down."

I was sickened. It seemed incredible that someone who had been so useful to the New York community could be the target for such an outrage. I went to the Phoenix Theatre and everybody there felt glum. Stuart was crestfallen. Even so, he said, "Remember, Joe is a fighter. He's at his best when people are trying to put him down. He'll come out of this and come out better than he was before. Cheer up."

A week later Joe called me up. "David," he said, "you know how much I think of your music. I'm stage manager now for a play called *Comes a Day* with Judith Anderson. Cheryl Crawford's producing it. It's on Broadway and I told the director how much I think of you and he wants to hear your music."

"God," I said, "that's great!" I called up Barna and she told me to go and meet Miss Crawford and play her my music and worry about the money later. I went up and met her and she and the director liked my music, so I was hired.

I'd never even been to a Broadway theater in my life except for the time when I saw *West Side Story* with my aunt, and I was petrified. I walked backstage and met Judith Anderson. She had heard some of the music that I had done previously. She looked at me with her deep, burning eyes and said, "I like your music."

I didn't know what to say, so I put out my hand and shook her hand and said, "Really?" Then her eyes took on a different color and it showed me how stupid I was for not being able to take a compliment.

"Yes, really," she said, looking at me with such intensity that I thought she was going to burn a hole through me.

"Thank you," I mumbled, and walked off. Joe came over to me. "Don't be scared of these people, you're as much of an artist as anybody. Don't worry about people's reputations. As long as you have respect for them they can feel that and that's enough."

I met the director. "Well," said Robert Mulligan, "you must be the greatest composer of the century. Joe Papp has been talking about you incessantly ever since he got this job. I know his judgment must be good because he was the one who told me about George C. Scott, and George is great in the part."

I didn't even know that George was in the play. He gave me a hug when he saw me. This was his first Broadway play too. The cast also included Brandon deWilde and Michael Pollard. Barna told me that even though I would get very little money for doing it, I would get a chance to write some music for a good play that was going to be on Broadway.

A week and a half later there were two big ads in the Sunday *Times,* one for the Phoenix, announcing that I was writing the music for *The Family Reunion* and was the music director, and one for *Comes a Day* mentioning that I was writing the music. People started calling me up to congratulate me and two days later I went over to Ken Karpe's house with a big bottle of Courvoisier to celebrate. This was the first time I visited them without having to have Sylvia make me something to eat. I had gotten an answering service a while ago, hoping that someone would call me for a job, and Kenny asked me how my service was.

"Great," I said, "I'll call them up just to show you." It was the same service that Ken had. I called them up and there was a message saying that I should get in touch with Elia Kazan.

"Groovissimo," said Ken. "I'm not at all surprised, and you know something, Dave? He'll really dig you, just be yourself."

I was amazed and checked in the phone book to see if there was more than one Elia Kazan. He wasn't listed. I called the next day and it was the director. I was told by his secretary he wanted to interview me about the possibility of writing music for a new play by Archibald MacLeish called *J.B.* She suggested that I bring some of my music and recordings of any works that I had. I got some tapes and the Shakespearean music and the jazz record that I had made for Decca. None of my concert music had been recorded at that time.

I went to Kazan's office and when he walked out to meet me I had the feeling as soon as he looked at me that we would be working together. He seemed to size me up in about a hundredth of a second, register approval and then resume his normal inquisitive glance.

"I've heard a lot about you and I've heard some of your music and I like it. I'd like you to read this play and maybe you could write the music for it. It's not like anything that you ever worked on before, but I think we could do something terrific. Let me hear your records and I'll call you tomorrow."

I left his office in a daze, finding it hard to believe that I would be chosen from nowhere to work on a play of this magnitude. I went home and read the play. The way Archibald MacLeish had conceived the whole story of Job was extremely touching and original and the characters were all very American, in the older sense.

The next day at eight o'clock in the morning my phone rang and I heard a voice say, "Hello, this is Elia Kazan." I heard my jazz record playing in the background. I knew that he must have liked it. "Listen, I like your music and I'd like you to do this," he said. "I want you to come this afternoon and meet Alfred DeLiagre. He's the producer. Wear a tie and a suit if you have one."

I had one good suit, which my mother had bought me as a present when I got out of the army. When I finally came home from Europe I had picked up the suit when I passed through Washington on the way to New York but I hadn't worn it in three years. It was still hanging in the closet and the pants needed to have cuffs put on them. I ran down to the tailor on the corner and told him I had to have cuffs put on them in the next hour and a half or I might miss the greatest job of my life. He got so carried away by my excitement, although I don't think he understood what I was babbling about, that he told me he would finish them in an hour. I then went and borrowed some money from my downstairs neighbor, Marty Tobias, a commercial artist, and went out and bought a pair of brown desert boots, which I thought would be extremely dressy-looking with my sharp brown suit. Then I ran to the barbershop on the corner which I had passed for a year and a half without ever going in. The barber had gotten used to seeing me walking by with my long hair and waved greetings back to me.

"So," he said, "you've finally come in. You want a shoeshine?"

"No," I said, "I need a haircut real fast. I got a big job coming."

I got my hair trimmed, got my suit, and being more dressed up than I had been since I lived in New York, treated myself to a taxicab up to Kazan's office, already feeling like a millionaire.

His secretary tried to suppress a smile as I walked in. She examined my yokelish outfit and told me to sit down and wait in his office. As I was waiting I could hear him having an argument with someone. Finally he came out with a tall, distinguished, extremely polished-looking gentleman, whom he introduced as Alfred DeLiagre.

"Well," said Mr. DeLiagre in cultivated and highly theatrical tones. "You realize of course, we would like you to play some music for us for the play, but since you have written none for *J.B.* as yet, I would like to know a little of what you have done."

I rattled off my credits. He said, "You seem to be doing extremely well for such a young man. Still I'm not certain that you could do something of this nature. Do you think you could?"

"I'm positive," I said. "I think the play is great." This made Kazan smile and I found out through the years I've known him that he appreciates enthusiasm in others as much as he has enthusiasm himself for his work and like so many highly accomplished people, respects energy and honesty more than pretension.

He and Mr. DeLiagre went back into his office and I could hear more arguing. I thought to myself, well, it was wonderful to almost have a chance to work on this, but certainly they're not going to hire someone like me.

They came out about ten minutes later and Kazan said, "You're going to do the music for *J.B.*, kid." I shook hands with him and Mr. DeLiagre and left the office so that I wouldn't faint right there.

I called up Barna and told her that Kazan wanted to use me. She was quiet for a moment, then I heard her breathing a sigh of happiness. "Well, dear," she told me, "in one year we've been very, very lucky. I know you'll do a fine job. By the way, how's your string quartet coming?"

"It's wonderful, I'm really moving along."

"Good," she said, "Don't forget that we must continue having you develop as a composer. That's the most important thing, isn't it?"

"You know it," I said. She knew as well as I did that the pieces that I'd been writing all my life wouldn't bring a dime but that they would keep me alive as a composer and as an artist and as a man. As thrilled as I was at having a chance to work on something that seemed this great, I knew it was not the end in itself.

I was being paid more for working on *J.B.* than all the other composing I had done in my life put together, and was even going to get $25 royalty for each week that the play ran. I met with Kazan a day later and we went over the entire play, discussing it from a philosophic point of view and then getting down to the specifics of each scene. From the script, Kazan described to me how he envisioned each scene, how it would be staged, how the costumes would be, how the characters would react to one another, change during the play and what the music should be like. When the play finally opened it was remarkably close to these ideas, which he seemed to be improvising as he spoke. He told me that there should be certain sounds and certain feelings and that I must judge what to do and how to do it by watching the play, by being there at rehearsals and by seeing what happened.

He told me that even before I saw one particular scene, I should write the music for it and that the music would help him. I wrote some songs that the children sang and one or two other very simple sketches that I could play on the piano for the actors. I attended almost every rehearsal from the time they began. We added the music piece by piece. As rehearsals progressed, I cut out certain sections, added other sections and by the time the play went to Washington for tryouts I really felt as if I were a part of it. I spent my twenty-eighth birthday making last-minute changes.

It was strange being back in Washington again. I hadn't been there except to visit once or twice since I had left in August, 1952, to go in the army. Six and a half years later I was coming back with some music I had written for a play that had one of my old heroes, Raymond Massey, in it as well as Pat Hingle and Christopher Plummer. On the train I had been thinking of seeing Raymond Massey in those war movies back in 1942 when I used to sneak into the theater when I was living on the farm. Artie McCrae, Eddie Filemyr and I used to go through the back door, and save our money for popcorn. I remembered one movie I sat through four times. Raymond Massey was in it with Errol Flynn and played a German officer.

I told Massey how much I had enjoyed his performance. "Yes," he said, laughing, "I'll never forget that movie. We figure that Errol must have killed at least ten thousand Germans single-handed in that one film alone." Although he was such an established actor, he was really kind and gracious to everyone and when we got to Washington I noticed that he was always the first one on the stage practicing, trying out the spectacular set that Boris Aaronson had built. He practiced his moves and his lines and worked with the enthusiasm of someone a third of his age.

"Look at him," Kazan used to say, "look how Ray goes. Isn't that great, he's just like a kid. What a cast we've got." Kazan was like a super-electric-charged flying saucer, sending out sparks and radiation wherever he went. He was always burning with so much energy that as soon as we walked into the theater or a room where anyone was working with him, everyone could feel those vibrations and it made you try twice as hard.

The music had really come off beautifully. Although Archibald MacLeish didn't really want any at the beginning of rehearsals, he liked it so much that he decided that he wanted to add more. Christopher Plummer was a natural musician as well as an actor, so we used to have great jam sessions after the play each night in Washington. After the rehearsals we would go up to the place where the actors would congregate. Chris would play the piano, Pat Hingle would play the harmonica and I would play the French horn.

James Baldwin was along on a grant, working on the play as an observer. I had known Jimmy since I had moved to Christopher Street in 1957. We used to hang out together at the Riviera, down the street from where I lived. He had heard some of the earliest music that I had done. He was just beginning to be recognized nationally as a writer. We used to discuss *J.B.* and the theater and the whole idea of the use of poetry and drama. He didn't like the play as much as I did, but his criticisms of it were extremely incisive.

We went around Washington together and I showed him a few of the places where I had been as a kid. I told him about some of the wild experiences I had had and he told me a little about his boyhood in Harlem. I hadn't read much of what he had written at the time, but I could see he had it rougher than me. Much rougher. We both agreed we didn't know any artists in America who seemed to have a particularly easy time of it in the beginning.

Some of the actors in the cast began to bug me, telling me now that I was working on something that was going to be a hit, that I should get as much money as possible and get a very strong agent.

"We know your agent," they told me. "She can't do you any good. She's just one person, she doesn't even have a secretary. You've got to go to some big organization like MCA or William Morris if you're really going to make it, otherwise you're always going to be small potatoes."

"Listen," I said, "people in big organizations like that have slammed the door in my face all my life. I have never been able to get past the receptionist. This woman was interested in me when I wasn't even making a dime and she's interested in me becoming a better composer and an artist. As far as I'm concerned I'll stay with her until she tells me to leave. She's someone I can trust. That's something that money can't buy. And she's plenty smart too."

They seemed convinced that there was some easy way to do things, that everything depended on connections and power. This might be true in the acting profession, although I doubt it, but it certainly isn't true in music. Outside the commercial areas in music you can only achieve your desires through the quality of the music itself. All that anyone can do to help really is to make it possible for the composer to have his music heard.

There was one scene that never seemed to come off in *J.B.* During the simulation of an atomic bombing the play seemed to collapse. I suggested that I go back to New York and record something. Elia Kazan had liked my other ideas so much that he granted me permission. The play opened with a very simple trumpet call, played by Maurice Peress, which later was used in different ways throughout the play and even sung by the chorus of old women. I thought of it as being a sort of Old Testament wailing-wall horn, much like the music that had affected me so much since I had heard those old men singing in the Frankfort synagogue. I thought the music for the bombing scene should be completely different from this. Rather than suggesting something from the past, it should be the most horrible sound of the present or the future. I wrote it on the train going back to New York.

When the musicians came in to record this piece of music they thought that I was insane. "Jesus Christ," said Midhat, "stop making faces like that or I can't play."

Maurice and everyone else really got frightened as I ran around the room crashing on instruments and trying to make them play something that would make it sound like the end of the world. During the nineteenth take, I played so violently I threw my back out. But this was a good take. Perhaps the grimace of pain as I heard my sacroiliac popping inspired the musicians to play a little more horribly than seemed possible.

When I went back to Washington with this gruesome-sounding music, the whole cast came out to applaud, even though I had to hobble up onto the stage because my back was killing me.

When we got to New York we were really confident that *J.B.* was going to do very well. When the production finally opened in New York, the combination of the lighting and music, the acting and Mr. MacLeish's beautiful play was really one totality, thanks to Kazan's masterful direction. Even though we opened during the newspaper strike in 1958, the reviews were read on television and it was a great success. The actors were stunned. Many of them had been working for years and years and never had been in a Broadway hit.

I went with Kazan and some others to Howard Dietz's house. His wife, Lucinda Ballard, had designed the costumes and was one of the people who had recommended me to Kazan. I thanked her again and she said that she was happy not just for my sake but also because the music had helped out the play and that in the theater we all try to do our part as well as possible for the whole. Mr. Dietz was as kind and funny and warm a host as his lyrics would suggest and the room was full of all kinds of people that I never thought I would meet in my life. John Steinbeck was there with his wife, plus many other well-known authors. I had been reading a lot of Steinbeck's work in the past few years and I wanted to set something of his to music. But I was afraid to ask him, so I just sat and listened to him talk. As I sat there in that beautiful apartment drinking Scotch, I forgot all about my cockroach-filled apartment and realized how lucky I was.

The next morning I went down to the theater with my hangover and stood outside for an hour watching the lines of people waiting to purchase tickets. But I didn't have time to sit back. I was suddenly being bombarded with offers to write music for all sorts of different theatrical productions.

I told Maurice about my string quartet when I went over to visit him and his wife, Gloria, and cute baby girl, Lorca. He was still living in his basement apartment on Thompson Street.

"I've got an orchestra this summer, Dave," he told me. "If you don't have a performance for your string quartet why don't you think of using it as a basis for a short work for string orchestra? You can use some of your jazz experience and make a really valuable contribution to string orchestra literature. There are not too many pieces written for string orchestra and it might be a good idea."

"Well," I said, "let me think about it."

I went home and looked over my string quartet. Actually some parts of the quartet had a great deal of jazz, some of which was written from actual figures that I used to play on the horn and the piano. Of course, I had changed the writing so that these figures would fit the limitations of string instruments.

I began to think of this piece almost as an autobiography in music from the time when I had first gone on the road with different bands and orchestras, traveled through Europe, in fact everything up through now. I trusted Maurice implicitly because he was such a gorgeous trumpet player and such a good friend.

I called him up. "Maurice, I'll have it done by June twelfth."

"Great," he said. "We'll program it."

I was really excited. I was going to have a professional orchestra perform my music for the first time. I had mounds of music sitting around the apartment. The earliest orchestral pieces I had written in high school were too amateurish and crude to play now. A lot of the other pieces I had destroyed. I went through the gigantic pile of other music I had lying around and began working away like mad.

I decided to use the sonata-allegro form as a basis for the piece. I tried to use the spirit of jazz in a way that wouldn't sound cheap or out of context but rather in a way that would enable the strings to play comfortably. I hoped the members of the string orchestra wouldn't think of the work in terms of *jazz* but rather of *music*. After working in both for so long I no longer saw a distinction, except the distinction that existed in other people's minds. There may be differences in terms of idioms, in approach and performance techniques, but ultimately it's all part of a world that expresses itself through a beautiful series of sounds. There was no reason I could not combine these sounds in terms of my life experience to make my own kind of music. I also knew that Maurice would be able to conduct the parts that did require some knowledge of jazz rhythms and to help the string players to interpret them.

A friend of mine, Seymour Wakschal, a violinist for whom I was writing a sonata, came by my house and gave me some suggestions about how to write jazz-inspired figurations to make them playable for strings. He and Midhat were two string players I knew who both loved and understood jazz. He told me to write what I felt and heard and he and the other string players could help me to work out any technical problems or problems of interpretation.

Seymour and I were close in many ways, besides music. He had played all his life but he wasn't a child prodigy either. He had been a real tough guy as a kid, and in his youth in Brownsville used to leave his violin on the pool table and go to the movies. When he came to the pool hall, if anyone had moved the violin, they would have to fight with him for the privilege of having touched his instrument. He had been a brilliant violinist since the time when he was a little boy but had been a little crazy. He was such a tough kid he had even fought an exhibition with Beau Jack, the former lightweight champion. He told me that Beau Jack had almost killed him and after that he decided not to box anymore. He still had a bad temper. I used to try to tell him how he must learn to control it as I had done and that musicians had no business being fighters or boxers. He had large hands, which would never lead you to suspect that he could play the violin, but he was in fact an extraordinary player, very musical, sensitive and with a real appreciation for every style of music, from Bach through the most modern composers. He wanted to play string quartets and chamber music as well as being soloist.

When we first met, he was playing in a small orchestra in the back of the second violin section. It was just a job for him because he had given recitals and had his own string quartet previously, but like so many others, he was in a period like the kind of slump athletes occasionally go through. As we got together more and more, we managed to cheer each other up. He also introduced me to other musicians who worked as free-lance players around the city. They were all honest, unpretentious, regular people interested in a great many things besides music and anxious to help me with any of my music when they could.

CHRISTMAS DAY, 1958, I began working on the music for *Antony and Cleopatra*. George C. Scott and Colleen Dewhurst were to star. It was being done at the Heckscher Theatre, where George had first done *Richard the Third* a year and a half earlier. Joe Papp decided to do it as a reading. There was almost no set and very simple costumes. I noticed how much George had grown already as an actor. He seemed to have even more skill and grace and assurance than he had when he had played Richard and Jaques. Colleen also seemed even better than she had been as Lady Macbeth. The music was very simple. Since it was being done indoors, I wrote the entire score for trumpet, viola, bassoon and percussion. Occasionally there were some fanfares, but this seemingly limited combination of instruments was sufficient to carry the musical burden through the entire play, without being repetitive. It opened January 13, 1959.

The day after opening night, I was called by Alfred Leslie, the painter. I used to go by Alfred's house several nights a week after I was done working at the Five Spot and sit up all night talking to him, listening to his radio, eating minestrone soup and drinking wine. I would usually be so excited by the end of the night that I couldn't go to sleep and whatever poor girl was with me would have to listen to me ranting and raving until finally Alfred would wake up the next morning and politely ask us to leave. I hadn't seen him lately because I knew he was hard at work with his painting and I hadn't had much time to do anything but work either.

"Davy," he said, "I'm making a movie." I didn't say anything. Alfred was always interested in movies and had always told me he thought I should try to write popular music because he thought popular culture was just as important as so-called serious culture. I always would explain to him that "commercial" musicians were a different breed. They could be fine talents, but they were different because of their intent—money first.

I thought perhaps Alfred was joking about his film. "I'm really serious," he said. "Robert Frank is going to be the photographer and we're doing an idea that I discussed with Jack Kerouac. Jack told us this marvelous story one night. We taped it and we're using it as the outline for the scenario. Everything will be improvised and it should really be fun. Allen Ginsberg is in it. Gregory Corso, Larry Rivers and thousands of other popular figures from the Third Avenue film world."

"That sounds wild," I said. "How come you called me? Do you want me to write the music?" I was starting to get a little nervous about time, since I was working on a violin sonata for Seymour, my "Autobiography for Strings," *The Beaux' Stratagem* for the Phoenix Theatre, which had to be completed by February, plus *The Rivalry* by Norman Corwin, which was opening on Broadway February 7 with live musicians, which meant I had to spend a lot of time at the theater.

"Yes," said Alfred, "and we want the music recorded in March."

"Well," I said, "I know it would be fun, but let me think."

"Don't think," said Alfred. "Come over here tomorrow after midnight because we're going to all get together and talk about it and we'd like you to be in the movie too. You could be Mezz MacGillicuddy."

"Who the hell is that?" I asked him.

"He's a hip tape man."

"What's a hip tape man?"

"Come tomorrow night and you'll find out. He's sorta like—you know—like a disc jockey, hip musician, advertising man, wandering minstrel bohemian."

"Come on, Alfred," I said. "For God's sake, I'm not like that and nobody else we know is either."

"That's the idea," said Alfred. "It is supposed to be a wonderful and unique character that's not like anybody or anything in the world. Jack says you'd be perfect."

"How come he wants me to do something like that?"

"Actually he doesn't," said Alfred. "He wants you just to be yourself, but we have to think up a character. Everybody in the movie is just going to be themselves and improvise. You can play the French horn or do whatever you want to."

"Well, that might be fun."

The next night I went over to Alfred's. He and Kerouac, Gregory Corso, Robert Frank, Allen Ginsberg, Peter Orlofsky, Richard Bellamy, who ran the Green Gallery, and some others were sitting around Alfred's studio. We spent about two hours drinking wine and each of us was given a copy of the scenario, which was really just a few pages of sketches about a guy who worked for the railroad and brought his friends home for a party. After their goofing around, his wife got mad and threw them all out. Delphine Seyrig was supposed to be his wife. She was the only person in the film who was a professional actor. The other girl in the film was Ray Parker's wife and she only had to sit around and look beautiful, which wasn't hard because she was one of the most gorgeous girls in the history of Greenwich Village, the Lower East Side and all the rest of New York.

Delphine looked very nervous as she saw all these wild-looking people in the room sitting around and talking and laughing and having a good time. Because she'd studied acting professionally, she tried occasionally to make deep and profound remarks about characterization and the hidden meaning of the scenario. This was met with raucous laughter and a lot of clowning around because none of us were interested in psychoanalyzing the scenario. There was nothing there but a bunch of sketches and we all decided we would have a ball and do just whatever we wanted to.

A few days later, between rehearsals of *The Beaux' Stratagem* and *The Rivalry,* I started going over to the filming of *Pull My Daisy,* as it was eventually called. Alfred had rigged up all kinds of lights all over the ceiling of his studio and had put quarters and nickels in the electric fuse box so that we could rent extra-high-powered lights and not blow out the fuses the first day.

It was a madhouse. If things were getting dull, Allen and Gregory would start cutting up, take off their clothes and threaten to jump out of the window or pour water on anybody that looked like they weren't interested. There were also a few onlookers sitting around getting high. Most of us were drinking wine and trying to think up outrageous jokes that we could pull on Robert Frank so that he would laugh so hard that he wouldn't be able to film us in action. Robert was a great photographer. He was very serious. but it was often hard for him to know where to point the camera. When Alfred would try to direct us into doing something, we would all do something else in a different place to see if we could confuse everybody.

Poor Delphine would pace up and down on the side, having practiced something that she was going to do and when she would begin acting, Gregory would say, "Come on, come on. Stop that shit. This is supposed to be real and poetic, beautiful and soulful. Not that show-business bull shit. This is life and truth and God touching us all with his divine finger of reality. Later with all that acting. This is rea-al-ity, captured forever by the sacred box of the angel Robert Frank."

Alfred would say, "That's terrific, terrific, terrific. I've never seen anything like this. It's alive and spontaneous." Then he would take me aside and say, "Davy, this is going to be an epic. This is going to be an American classic. I've never seen anything this spontaneous or beautiful in my life. I'm going to start producing movies all the time. We have a production company. Do you know what its name is? G String Productions. That's right, G String Productions. We're going to make Hollywood come to its knees by really showing them how to make movies. All right, all right, quiet down, everybody. Let's stop all this nonsense. Now . . ."

Then he would give a series of detailed instructions. Everybody would laugh and start doing something else and Robert would silently walk around photographing it. This went on about eight or ten hours a day. Because I couldn't think of anything to do, I figured a whole way of throwing grapes, plums, nectarines, bottle corks, matchbooks and anything up in the air every time I was supposed to act. I would catch them in my mouth as a means of adding visual continuity to the film. I had practiced this in the army whenever I was on the verge of insanity, so I could catch anything like trained seals do, as long as I had time to see it. I was almost as good as Joe DiMaggio in the outfield. To top this, for the close-ups, I would hide the grapes and oranges in my mouth, impaled by a toothpick. When I was supposed to deliver my line, I would smile, open up my mouth and slowly take out the toothpick with some gigantic piece of food on the end. I even tried to light a book of matches on my tongue, but I was afraid I might burn my lips.

In one scene I was supposed to leave the bathroom as a cowboy who had gone there to get high. In the bathroom, I found a toothbrush that belonged to one of the kids in the cast. When I came out, I began a great shoot-out with Gregory Corso, who responded perfectly. At the moment we were to draw, I whipped the revolver-toothbrush from the holster and brushed my teeth furiously. Everytime I would think of anything to do, everyone else would think of something really insane and Robert would dash around the room trying to film it all while Alfred was shouting encouragement and directions at all of us.

My sister was visiting town and wanted to come to one of the rehearsals of something I was working on. I told her I couldn't bring her to any of the plays I was working on because theater people got very upset when visitors came to watch if they weren't associated with the production. But I told her she could come to see the filming of the movie.

"I would really enjoy that," she said. "I've admired Larry Rivers' painting and I like Allen's poetry very much. They must be extremely interesting people to work with."

"You're not kidding," I said.

She turned up at the studio and it was bedlam as usual. Allen refused to put his clothes back on during one of the scenes, while Larry Rivers was shouting that he was stealing the scene from him. Larry said while anybody could draw attention being nude in a movie, it took a really great actor to give that kind of performance that was breathtaking just from the psychological point of view.

When Allen refused to cooperate, Larry started walking all around the room, playing the saxophone, which brought shouts of dismay. Meanwhile poor Delphine was having a tantrum because no one would rehearse something she thought of doing. Alfred was shouting at everyone. Robert was walking around the room looking philosophical.

"Is this what the film's about?" my sister said.

"No," I said. "They're just having a—I guess you might say a kind of separate preparatory session or informal rehearsal period. Gregory," I said, "I'd like you to meet my sister Mari."

"Hi," said Gregory, "you're beautiful. Would you like to marry me?"

"That's very nice of you," said my sister, "but I'm already married."

"Oh," said Gregory, "how about being my girl friend?"

"No," she said, "thank you very much, but no."

"Well, it was nice to meet you," said Gregory, and he walked back and started dancing around the room with everyone else.

"All right," said Alfred, "let's go into that scene where you're having a jam session." We sat down and began to have a jam session with

Larry playing the saxophone and me playing the French horn. Just as we were filming it, two men came in and started to move an enormous painting out of the room.

"That's great," shouted Alfred. "Film that, Robert. For God's sakes, man, that's extraordinarily beautiful." Everyone got up and started dancing around in front of the painting while the poor baffled moving men, blinking in the bright lights, tried to wrestle the enormous painting out of the room and down the stairs.

My sister stayed all day and watched. "Is this what the movie is going to be about?" she asked.

"No," I said, "eventually it's to all be cut down to fit Jack's original idea."

When *Pull My Daisy* was finally finished, a few days later, Robert explained to me that they had thirty hours of film and it was going to be cut down to twenty minutes. After this, Jack was going to come in and narrate what had been cut down and I would write the music. "O.K.," I said, "just let me know when. I have to get back to work on my other pieces."

I went back and started working on my violin sonata, "Autobiography for Strings" and the music for *The Rivalry*. I had been postponing the last because of my rehearsals for *Pull My Daisy,* but now that my stint as an actor was over, I was glad to get back to composing. *The Rivalry* had a fine cast. Richard Boone played Lincoln and Martin Gabel played Douglas. Nancy Kelly played Mrs. Douglas and the play was all about the Lincoln–Douglas debates.

Word got back to Mr. Gabel at the first rehearsal I'd attended that the producers thought he looked too tall. The shoes he was wearing had slight lifts, making him perhaps three-quarters of an inch taller than he was anyway.

"Listen," he barked at the stage manager, "if you want to hire a midget, go out and tell the producer to get Ted Atkinson."

After that, nobody bothered him anymore. I admired his spirit because he was peppery and lively and a terrific actor with a lot of power, style and a great sense of humor. At lunchtime he shouted out, "I'm starving. Who will get me a sandwich?"

Everybody had left the theater. "I'll be glad to, Mr. Gabel," I said, and when I came back he said to me, "You're the type of maestro I appreciate." After that, just because I had gotten him a sandwich, he really went out of his way to be nice to me and to all the musicians who were in the show.

Richard Boone, who was known mostly as Palladin on TV, played Lincoln. He was a very fine stage actor, very humble and quiet with that kind of inner strength that made him believable and touching as Lincoln. Nancy Kelly was perfect as Mrs. Douglas. The director of the play was also the writer, Norman Corwin. He enjoyed having these great actors working for him so much that he would sit at the back of the theater roaring with laughter at the jokes and twinkling with joy when he wasn't laughing. He would come up and hug Miss Kelly and slap Richard Boone on the back, tell Martin Gabel how great he was and say, "Let's take the whole thing again. That was really a treat to watch." This was a rather free style of directing, but the cast was so fine and the material was so interesting that it really didn't need someone hovering about the theater trying to psycho-analyze everybody.

Norman Corwin would occasionally hum an old Civil War tune and say, "That's what I love. You got it? You got it?"

"Sure," I said, "but you know I'm going to write my own music."

"Definitely," he said to me. "I heard that music you did for *J.B.* and it was beautiful. Just watch the play and get the spirit and do whatever comes into your mind. I know it will be fine."

I wrote the music for *The Rivalry* in four days. It took about fifteen hours a day, but I got it done. I wrote three little marches, which I entitled "The Alf Landon Victory March," "Colonel Kreplach" and "Lincoln, Douglas and Stalin." The titles were only to cheer up the musicians, for the names of the marches did not appear in the program. They were scored for piccolo, trumpet, trombone, drums and cymbals. The cymbals player also played guitar and banjo in other parts of the play and the piccolo player, Spencer Sinatra, also played flute with the guitar and the banjo. The trumpet player and conductor was Maurice Peress and the drummer was Jules Greenberg.

After I'd finished the music and was about to copy the parts, Barna called me up. "I've got some wonderful news," she said. "They're going to pay for copying."

"Boy," I said, realizing I had really hit a new peak in my life as a composer. "I'm finally going to have someone copy the parts for me." Closing my eyes with bliss, I realized I would be able to save hours of eyestrain. I could even have a nap before the first rehearsal.

I called up Maurice and asked him whom I could get who was a good music copyist. I didn't want to ask Arnold Arnstein, the world champion copyist, because it was such short notice. I figured it would be such a simple job that it would be better to give someone a chance who really needed the money.

"I know just the person," said Maurice. "She's a beautiful girl and she always wanted to meet you anyway. Her name is Judy. She's an excellent copyist and she can do it very well."

"It has to be done in two days," I told him.

"That's all right. She's fast and efficient and really needs the money."

"Great," I said. I called up Judy and she really sounded very businesslike.

"Bring the music right over and I'll begin it immediately."

She was a very lovely but tense-looking girl with a brilliant mind, snowy skin, a winsome smile, and a great knowledge of music. "I really need the money," she said, "but I hate copying music." I was sort of taken aback by this. She then told me for about an hour she had worked for some music copyists and thought it was demeaning and degrading work, but that she would do it for me because she realized how tired I must be and she felt sorry for any composer that had to do this horrible job himself. I began to get a little worried, but she assured me that she would do a beautiful job. She showed me some of her work and it was terrific. "Call me up tonight and I'll probably have it finished," she said.

I went over to rehearsals at *The Beaux' Stratagem*, which was opening up two weeks after *The Rivalry* at the Phoenix. Then I went home, worked on the violin sonata for two hours and then decided I would call up Judy to see how far she'd come. Her answering service told me that she wasn't home but to call later. I kept calling every hour and at two o'clock I finally got her in.

"Hi, Judy," I said, "how are you coming with those parts?"

"Oh, my God," she said, "I haven't started them yet. It's such a pain copying music. I always put it off till the last minute, but don't worry. I'll get it done. I wouldn't let you down."

"O.K.," I said, and hung up. Most of that night I had nightmares of being at the first rehearsal with no parts. The next day I spent working on the violin sonata, "Autobiography for Strings" and going to another rehearsal of *The Beaux' Stratagem*. That night I called up Judy again.

"I haven't begun it yet," she said. "I'm not in the mood, but don't worry. I'll get it done. Call me up in two hours." I called her up about nine o'clock at night.

"I haven't started," she said. "I just can't stand doing it. But don't worry about a thing. When is your rehearsal?"

"Thirteen hours from now."

"That's O.K.," she said. "I'll do it."

"Listen, I'd better help you. If those parts aren't done I've had it."

"Well, I'll tell you what to do. Come over and buy me some supper and just keep me company."

I went over with two dinners from Bickford's. She talked for about an hour and a half and was fascinating to listen to. She was a brilliant conversationalist and was well versed on many subjects. The only thing that she didn't seem interested and enthusiastic about was copying music.

"Well," she said, "I guess I'll begin." She got out all her ink, paper, rulers and must have spent nearly an hour setting everything up, adjusting the lights, putting pillows in her chair, squinting at my score, checking the music and walking around the room. It was nearly one thirty in the morning.

"I'm about to start," she said. "We still have nine hours left. That's the only part I like about copying music—the excitement of trying to figure out whether or not you'll get done on time."

"Well," I said, "I guess that's exciting for you, but I'm really pretty worried. You know I only have a little bit of rehearsal time and I've never had live music in a show before."

She sat down and looked at the music for a half an hour. "This is really fascinating," she said to me, "the way you've made these few instruments sound. I like especially the way you've written the piccolo part. It's sort of a humorous takeoff of Civil War music and still, it's very fine counterpoint." She then began to discuss the uses of harmonically oriented polyphonic writing in twentieth-century music and how tonal music still could sound exciting if the voicings and the textures were used in a fresh and original way.

"Hey, I'm really glad you like my music," I said to her, "but it's two thirty. We've got to get this done." At three eighteen she began copying the first note.

"Listen, maybe I'd better go home," I said. "I don't want to bother you."

"No, no, no," she said. "I can't stand being alone when I'm copying music. I really hate it and I have to have your company right now or it won't get done. I won't get done."

"Yes you will, yes you will," I said, and we reversed roles. I kept talking to her and she kept telling me how tired she was. After about an hour she said, "Good, it's done."

"What's that—the piccolo part?"

"No, the first measure."

"Listen, I'd better start copying with you."

"Oh, no. That makes me nervous. I'll be fine."

Time passed. She clutched her forehead. "Oy, I've got a terrible headache. Can you go out and get me some aspirin?"

Things continued to grind on in this fashion. Finally at six o'clock in the morning, after apologizing for half an hour, I sat down and started copying furiously, faster than I ever had in my life. I didn't even look at the score most of the time because I had memorized most of it. She had just completed the piccolo part and part of the trombone part. The rest of the music I copied myself and arrived at the rehearsal hall two minutes before we were to start. The musicians sounded great, but we had to spend most of the time correcting the piccolo part into which she had copied mostly wrong notes, even though it was painstakingly done in beautiful handwriting.

After this experience, I either copied the parts myself or got Arnold Arnstein to do it for me. I decided that I was still too young to be a philanthropist.

The guitarist and banjoist, Jerry Silverman, was a well-known virtuoso and had written several books on folk music. He had played the guitar in *The Power and the Glory* for the Phoenix production, for which I had written the music. I had never written for the banjo, although I had fooled around with it. Jerry showed me the best key and positions to write for banjo, so I wrote additional music for solo banjo, and some pieces where the banjo played with the tiny orchestra.

At the beginning of the second act, Jerry came out dressed like a pre-Civil War sharecropper and played a stunning improvised solo leading into the music I had written, as Martin Gabel sat, quill pen in hand, writing one of Douglas' great speeches. Jerry was such a good player, he kept making his solo longer and longer. Finally, about the third preview, Jerry was still wailing away when the lights came up and Martin Gabel sat writing until the audience must have thought he was completing *War and Peace*. Finally he leaned over and said sotto voice to Jerry, "What is this—banjo time?" After that Jerry cut his solo down.

Most of the music went very well. The musicians came out in Civil War costumes and played a few times. It was really a delightful show. The only trouble was that because Mr. Corwin had not had any experience working on Broadway, he didn't know all the technical problems of lighting in a show. In addition, our particular lighting crew was a rather eccentric and temperamental one. Often the lights would start flashing or go off in the middle of a scene. Then Martin Gabel would begin improvising. In the middle of an impassioned speech he would say, "Don't mind those lights flashing off, ladies and gentlemen. Don't mind those flashing lights. Even in darkness, even in light, I continue to say," and then work back into the original passage until the next technical mishap occurred. Occasionally the sets would not move when they were supposed to. Often the lights would come on on the wrong part of the stage. But by opening night everything went very well. It had a respectable run of nine weeks.

Almost every few weeks I was writing for some new play. We had our own little informal gang, a kind of chamber orchestra that would get together for each job. Seymour, Midhat, Marvin Feinsmith, an outstanding bassoonist, Dan Cowan and all the other musicians felt free to criticize me if they felt I had written anything that was unplayable, and would shout at me if they thought I wasn't conducting well.

"For Christ's sakes, Dave," Seymour would yell after performing something with grace and feeling. "Why don't you learn how to conduct?"

"Jesus, Dave," Dan would say, "how in God's name are we supposed to come in when you don't have any beat?"

"I'm doing the best I can. You didn't get lost, did you, Dick?"

"Nah," Dick Berg, the French hornist, would say stoically, as he lit a large black cigar. "But I can't tell what the hell you're doing. Just beat the time out clearly—don't paint pictures."

I had the good fortune of having friends who were terrific players working with me. They also didn't care whether I ever hired them again or not. They knew that I wasn't a masochist but that I was trying to learn to conduct. Because they were all outspoken types like I was, conducting my pieces became a new part of my schooling. In most professional situations, musicians never say anything because they want to be hired again. They figure that it's not their job to tell the conductor whether or not he is being clear. Most conductors are lost a good deal of the time anyway, and musicians accept this. They just read their parts, try to follow one another and hope that they can get through the piece well enough to be employed again for the next one. If, when I was working as a horn player in orchestras, I had told every conductor when he was unclear, I wouldn't have had much chance to play music. I would have been talking all the time.

The more I conducted, especially with a small group full of critics like this, the clearer it became that the most important thing for a conductor is to know the music beforehand, to prepare entrances, and to be clear. A minimum of talking and maximum of preparation is essential. I also learned that hearing music, composing it, and conducting it are different skills.

At Seymour's suggestion, I began studying with Jonel Perlea, the masterful conductor who unfortunately had lost the use of one arm through a stroke. With the use of the other arm, he made more music than most conductors I had seen all my life. He was a hard taskmaster, but the lessons I had with him gave me a whole basis for studying on my own and watching other conductors.

I went to see Mitropoulos again in the spring of 1959 when he was conducting at the Met. Because of the studying I had done, I appreciated more than ever his mastery of the art of conducting. No one seemed to be able to conduct operas as well as Mitropoulos. He was always in control. He knew the music perfectly. He set up an atmosphere and indicated through his hands, eyes, body and his entire personality the way he thought the music should be. He knew how to lead and he knew how to follow. I watched his performance of *Tosca* with renewed appreciation.

"Maestro, I have to say now that I'm beginning to study, how much I have learned from watching you," I said to him afterward.

"And I have to say to you again as I did to you a few years ago," said Mitropoulos with his incredible memory, "that there's nothing to conducting. It's all in the music. Perhaps you understand that a little better now than you did when I told you the first time." And he gave his great smile.

During the spring I was asked to lecture to a group of people at the ANTA Theatre about composing dramatic music. Other people from *J.B.,* including Kazan, were there. When it was my turn to speak, I gave as direct and as honest a speech as I could about my method for composing music in theater. It was simply that I had no real system but tried to make each play a unique situation. I explained how I thought music should start and stop, the use of repetitive themes and their alterations, the dramatic fabric of the play and its relation to a musical scheme, and other basic ideas I had about music in the theater.

Just as I left the stage I was motioned aside by the stage manager. "A phone call for you, Dave," he said, "very important, someone screaming at the other end of the line." I picked up the phone and heard a tinny screaming sound before I even got the receiver to my ear. It was my Italian landlady. She was hysterical.

"Your water leaking all over the floor below. Everything a-leaking. *Ma si scostumato cornuto!* What'sa matter with you. You're notta good boy no more. Hurry up a-home!" She began crying.

I raced out the stage door of the ANTA Theatre. I knew that the plumbing, which had been leaking for months, had probably given out and was flooding the whole building. I had complained many times, but of course nothing had ever been done about it. Most of the winter I had used an electric blanket and had the oven going to augment the erratic heater. I began to think what a drag it was to be living in such a dump. Also my two rooms were completely filled with music and books and records by now.

Close to a full division of cockroaches had moved out of the music room and were laying siege to the kitchen. I had visions of an army of cockroaches being drowned in a sea of tepid water filled with garbage.

As I was hurrying out of the theater, a woman from the audience ran out on the street after me. "It must be marvelous being such a great success so young," she said, "so young. You've done so wonderfully." I wanted to invite her down to see my apartment, but I thought it might be rather inappropriate and anyway I didn't want to shatter her illusions.

"Thank you," I said. "I consider myself to be very lucky." I sped downtown, opened the door, called the plumber and decided that I'd better look for a new place before the whole building fell down.

The Beaux' Stratagem at the Phoenix was a completely different kind of play. June Havoc was the visiting star. It gave me a chance to use a small chamber orchestra. The play was delightful and I also had a chance to write several songs with a small orchestral accompaniment.

During the opening I sat on the stairs between the lobby and the men's room, eating a take-out Chinese dinner. I had been so busy I hadn't had a chance to eat much, sleep much or do anything except to write music and go to rehearsals. I had just finished chop-sticking my way through a delicious container of sweet and sour shrimp when I heard a familiar voice whispering to someone over my shoulder. I looked up and saw Malcolm with his girl friend tiptoeing in late for the first act. I knew that he couldn't see me because it was dark, so I crept around to the other side of the theater and lay down in back of the center aisle.

As Malcolm walked by, I extended my palm and whispered, "Mr. Steinaroony." Malcolm looked down aghast. I saw his girl friend trying to pull him away. "It's me, Malcolm. I'm wigging out. Don't leave me lying here."

"I'd like you to meet David," he said to his date. "Is that you?"

"Yes, Malcolm," I told him. He squinted down to make sure. "I just wanted to welcome you and your lovely friend to this production. This drama world's getting me. Everybody takes themselves too seriously. Got eyes for some shrimp?"

"Later," he said, and he and his girl friend tiptoed over me and entered the mausoleum silence of the audience, which treated this comedy like a state funeral.

After the production was over and the last of the grim-faced audience had departed, I went back to the Chinese restaurant with Malcolm and his girl. We talked over all the things that had happened in the last few years.

"You certainly are eating a lot," he told me.

"Man," I said, "it's great to be making some money." We went out that night and ate piles of food at Grant's on Forty-second Street around four o'clock in the morning.

I was called to do the music for *Kataki* the day after *The Beaux' Stratagem* opened. It was a play directed by Alan Schneider, with Sessue Hayakawa and Ben Piazza, written by Shimon Wincelberg. I read the script and it was fascinating. It was about an American airman who was shot down on an island with a Japanese who couldn't speak English. I thought it would be a chance to do something interesting musically. I began eating constantly at the rehearsals and when the rehearsals were uptown, I would go to the Turf restaurant. During my first three years in New York, I used to get one piece of cheese-cake whenever I was lucky enough to have thirty-five cents. Now, I would buy a whole cheesecake and eat it during rehearsal. Then I would go over to John Molfetas' Greek restaurant and eat two complete meals. All during the rehearsals I began eating a ridiculous amount of food. Rather than buying a car or splurging money, what I didn't spend on getting my music copied, I spent on eating. I began to gain weight for the first time in my life.

While *Kataki* was progressing, I got to know a great girl with Malcolm at the White Horse Tavern. Most of the girls there at that time were the hard-drinker, sour-puss, Vassar drop-out types, vaguely interested in literature and never interested me. But Emma was different. The night we met we were all sitting around and the Clancey Brothers were in the back singing as they had been for years. I had come in to get a half-and-half and at least one of their delicious knockwurst sandwiches. Because of my good cheer at fortune's change, and the enormous appetite that I seemed unable to to control, I ate four knockwurst sandwiches. As I stood chatting with the owner, Ernie, and was polishing off my fifth, I heard a girl's voice saying, "Good Lord, look at the way that cat eats!" I turned around and saw Emma sitting there with Malcolm and Doris Moreau.

I had first seen Emma when I came back from Paris. She had been with Boris Grgurevich and some other pals of mine whom I had seen outside the Café Bohemia when I first worked there with Mingus. Because of the distance that musicians seem to have from other mortals when they are thinking about music, I only noticed her obliquely. But I dug her even then. I saw that energetic brown twinkle coming from her deep, dark eyes. Her body was like the Modigliani nudes I used to have in my Washington apartment. The black ringlets of her hair, her girlish voice and fast, devilish wit really got to me that evening in 1955. Because she was with Boris, I didn't come on with her since that would have been a violation of any gentleman's principles.

Still, I can honestly say that I didn't forget her either and when I saw that she was sitting with Malcolm and Doris Moreau, another old friend of mine from Paris, I grabbed the remains of my knockwurst sandwich and as I jammed it down my mouth in a paroxysm of gluttonous joy, I sat down with Doris, Malcolm and Emma.

"*Ça va bien, coco?*" I said to Doris, peering to the right as I talked to Doris on my left, trying to catch Emma's twinkling eyes.

"God," said Emma softly, "the human garbage can is loose in the land."

"I can't stand watching this," said Malcolm. "David, this is Emma. See you later." He got up and left.

"Would any of you girls like a sandwich?" I said, offering the greasy remains of my knockwurst sandwich as a desperate come-on.

"Oh," said Emma, fluttering her eyelashes and rolling her eyes in the back of her head. "Why don't you just relax and drink your half-and-half and stop eating for a second. You're the most frantic person I've ever seen in my life. Relax." She began stroking my arm and holding my hand and suddenly I felt completely relaxed.

"I remember you," I said. "Remember when I was at the Bohemia . . ."

"Yes," she said in a world-weary fashion. "We don't have to go through all that."

I realized that I didn't have to even come on with her or go through the usual floor show that seemed to be necessary to break down people's barriers. So I sat there drinking my half-and-half and listening to Emma and Doris talk about Paris. As they spoke about old friends and familiar faces, clubs that I had played in and coffee houses, I could see the city of Paris coming back in my mind and I realized how much I missed it. I wanted to go back some day, but I had the feeling it was going to be a long time before I could. I still hadn't regained the cosmic cheer that I had there, but at least I was surviving, and to do that in New York was really quite an achievement.

As I was in the middle of my daydreaming, I saw Emma looking at me with a smile flickering over her face. "God," she said, "you're in another world."

"No, I'm not," I said. "I was just thinking about Paris when you two were talking."

"I remember seeing you when you just got back," she said. "You were slim."

"Yeah, well, ha ha," I said, looking down at my waistline. The pants of my old suit were about to explode, I'd gained so much weight.

"You were really attractive then—at least you could have been," she said. "Don't you have any idea of your appearance and what you look like?"

"Sure," I said, "but—well, you know, I guess I don't think about it as much as I ought to."

"Well, you ought to," she said. "That's all part of it, you know." She reminded me of Lobo. I suddenly wondered if I was about to have another religious experience. I realized she was just talking to me like a person and when I held her hand under the table, I could feel that wonderful warm feeling of communication go right up through my arm to my shoulder and through my entire body. It felt like some kind of wonderful drug—not the way drugs really feel, which is artificial, but the real thing—life.

It felt so great, I just sat there for a few minutes not even drinking my beer. She looked over at me, obviously pleased but chuckling. "My God," she said, "you're crazy. You're out of your mind. You're out of your blooming mind, governor."

"Let's go," I said.

"Doris," she said as a way of departure.

"Shpater, mamacita," I said, and we left the White Horse Tavern. We walked around the street for about an hour just digging each other and talking. Suddenly she stopped when we got to Thompson Street and stared down.

"What's happening?"

"Don't you see?"

"See what?" I said.

"You don't see? So few people do. There are diamonds in the sidewalk. See that glitter? I love to see those diamonds in the sidewalk." They looked like thousands of glittering jewels in that filthy old Thompson Street sidewalk underneath the lamp, shining and flashing like the lights at Orly airfield at night when you taxi in for a landing."

"That's great," I shouted. "Wow, what a sight!"

"Oh, my God," she said wearily, "what a shlugger you are. Can't you appreciate something in a quiet way?"

"You're right," I said, "I know I probably seem like a drag, but I'm pretty tired. I've been working like a dog."

"Well," she said, "if you're a musician you're supposed to, but you have to learn to relax once in a while too."

"Well," I said, "I've got plenty of time for that. Anyway, everyone else I know has been relaxing for years. I'm trying to make music."

I stayed at Emma's house for a week. She knew a lot about relaxation. She lived in a fifth-floor walk-up right outside a cab garage—

a little north of Hell's Kitchen. Hundreds of taxicabs were downstairs. I could hear the drivers shouting and yelling all night long. Her apartment was like my apartment on the Lower East Side but without rats. She'd somehow managed to give this tawdry railroad flat a kind of wonderful European atmosphere.

I found out that Emma worked for the Maritime Union and shipped out every few months when she needed money.

"That's really something," I said. "I finally have a lady merchant seaman for a girl friend."

"Well, not exactly," she said. "I work on the ship as a waitress; I don't steer the ship. Still, it's a groovy way of seeing the world." She told me stories of all the countries she'd been to and the places she had visited and the wild scenes on shipboard and the fascinating people she'd worked with, and finally, about her writing. She showed me part of novel she'd written and it was really funny and brilliant. She seemed hung up though and didn't believe in herself enough to commit herself to the idea that she was a writer.

"You can really write, Emma," I told her. "You should save some money and write."

"I know," she would say. "I know I can, compared to most of the crap that you see. I know how well I could do, but it's the scene. The scene gets me down."

"There is no scene. We have that scene in music too, you know, but you can just ignore it and make your own scene. You can blast through and do your own thing."

"No," she said, "I wish it were that way, but it's not. Without the people behind you, you could just be out there forever."

"That's not true, Emma," I said. "You've got it, baby. You have the words written down on the paper. No one can ever take that away from you. If they are good they'll be here ten years from now and way after we've died. If they're really nowhere, they can promote it like mad and it will be forgotten ten years from now. It's just like music. If you write it down and you have it there in a legible form and it doesn't get burned up, it's going to be there and someday it will come through."

"No," she said, "you're very sweet and you have a lot of energy and drive, but I don't think you understand how things work yet."

"I don't think that's important. The main thing is to do it. I never finished music school, you know. I wanted to, but I ran out of money and I was too disorganized then anyway. I've never even been to Tanglewood. I've never had a fellowship. I've never had a patron and I don't even know the people in the music establishment— whatever that is. Except for Dimitri Mitropoulos, I don't even know anybody in classical music that could be helpful, but I'm writing my music and now I'm starting to get some pieces played."

"Yes," she said, "but you have to do all that work in the theater. I've read about that."

"Sure, but that happened mostly through accident and chance and being ready. I've been ready to work in music all my life and now I'm finally getting the chance to squeak by so that I can spend a little more time on my own work. And if I can do it, Emma, anybody in the world can."

"No," she said, "you're still very naïve. You'll see."

I used to have arguments with Emma and try to encourage her to pursue her own dream and her work, but it was difficult. In a way she was so sophisticated, but in another way her constant concern about the politics of the New York world of fine arts, publishing, literature, social climbing and all the other refinements of urban living which I had been oblivious to and contemptuous of really worried her. Still, she was the first girl I'd been with since Laura in Paris that seemed to have that kind of hipness and compassion, and she didn't use drugs. She was great company and we used to sit for hours and hours as I worked like a fiend on my "Autobiography for Strings," orchestrating it and copying some of the parts. She was an excellent cook and kept shoving plates of food in front of me while I worked.

I was told to write any kind of music I wanted to for *Kataki*. I had some flute solos that I wrote in addition to percussion music played on a large group of Eastern instruments. When the score was done, everyone was pleased, including me. But at the first rehearsal, Sessue Hayakawa stopped at the end of a long musical interlude during his pantomime and refused to continue.

"What's the matter, Sessue?" said Alan Schneider. Sessue had a brilliant way of taking command when he wanted something changed, usually by pretending not to understand English, although he understood and spoke it fluently.

"That sound like Chinese music," he hissed furiously.

I spoke to him afterward and he gave me a little chuckle. "It's all right," he said. "Just the director keeps talking and bothering me. He should leave us alone and let us work it out ourself." Because

Alan Schneider only had two actors to shout at instead of an entire cast, and because he knew I was the youngest member of the production team, he began screaming at me. I knew he didn't really mean it, so I decided to pull a Sessue Hayakawa myself. I would just sit there and when he was done shouting, go ahead with whatever I was saying or doing as if I hadn't noticed it. Alan had a big heart. He just got so carried away, he couldn't help it.

During one of the final rehearsals of *Kataki*, I came with Midhat, who had played viola in the part of the score I had tried to make sound like koto music. Alan went into one of his tirades again. There was a small invited audience. I began to boil a little in spite of myself. I didn't like being insulted in front of other people, especially strangers, and I guess I must have begun to lose my temper.

Midhat grabbed my arm. "Come on, man," he said, "let's get out of here. You're really starting to get somewhere in music. You don't want to go to the electric chair now." I left with Midhat. "Whew," he said, "I haven't seen that look on your face since the army."

"Yes," I said, "I guess I have to study with Sessue Hayakawa and learn some more about that Zen mastery of self-control."

When I went to Emma's afterward, I told her about it. "Don't be silly," she said. "Don't let these people bug you. Don't even get involved or bother. Just be on a total level of satori. They're completely untalented anachronisms anyway. The whole Broadway scene is dying. I don't see even why you want to work in that area."

"I don't particularly," I said, "I love the theater, you know, but I'd just as soon work only for the Shakespeare in the Park, the Phoenix and no one else. Only for people that are really beautiful, where they want to use my music and my abilities creatively. Schneider's a brilliant director too. He likes me. He just goes crazy sometimes. But this play is really terrific. If the play and actors are good enough, I don't care if the director flips out once in a while. Actually he's done a good job. You'll have to come see it."

"O.K.," she said, "I'd like to see you in a tuxedo anyway."

When we went to Philadelphia for the previews, the play was very well received. The music sounded beautiful and some of my relatives showed up and congratulated me.

"Thank you," I said, "but you haven't heard any of my concert music yet. You've just heard what I've done in the theater. Tiny pieces."

"Well, when are we going to hear the Philadelphia Orchestra play something?" they asked.

"Just be patient," I said. "It takes a while."

After the show was over we had a meeting because, as we learned, there were some financial troubles with the play. I went upstairs and there was a group of backers and businessmen, mostly smoking cigars and looking nervous, pacing back and forth and speaking in guarded, hushed tones. Over in the corner was Sessue Hayakawa with a gorgeous girl who was trying to set up an interview with him for a local television program.

"He write the music. I am the star," he kept telling her. I noticed that his broken English was hypnotizing her. After a few minutes she was really bowled over by him.

God, I said to myself, if he can do that in his seventies, he's really something. He was one of the most ultra-supreme hipsters I'd ever met. Nothing seemed to faze him. After the backers' meeting was over, I saw him leave with the girl interviewer. I decided I'd have to speak to him and learn some of his Zen magic in its practical form. The only other kind of Zen magic I knew much about was what I had read from the works of uptight Western Zen experts. From their photographs, most of them looked like they were escapees from some kind of terrible rigid Episcopalian background. Hayakawa certainly didn't give this impression.

The next night on the way back from Philadelphia I spoke with him.

"Yes," he said, "this is really an extremely strict science and discipline and religion, you know. It's like studying music, but it's also a full-time devotion. I was in a monastery for years and I still go and meditate once a year. It's the study that enables you to unite your mind and your body and your spirit with everything. You can become one with the universe only when you realize that you already are. Then you have control of yourself. I was in Philadelphia once before, a few years ago. It must have been before the war. A man came up with a gun and tried to rob me. I simply looked at him and decided I would turn myself inside out."

"How did you do that?" I asked. I had never seen anyone that could act like Sessue Hayakawa could, but still I couldn't imagine him turning himself inside out.

"I simply put my hands in my pockets until he went away. I discouraged him so that he left without any violent feelings whatsoever."

"How did you do that?"

"Very simple," he said. He put his hands in his pockets and then he stared at me. I watched his eyes and suddenly I was sure that he *had* turned himself inside out. Of course he hadn't, but in some way he managed to make himself nearly invisible. I think he did it with his eyes. He almost hypnotized me on the spot by hunching his shoulders forward, pushing his hands down in his pockets and making himself almost nonexistent. Then he snapped back and so did I. "You see," he said, "I turned myself inside out. Just one of the many disciplines."

The rest of the way back he spoke to me about Japan, about the golden days in Hollywood when he'd been a film star and then about Japanese music. "I will give you a record," he said, "of a Japanese flute player. It's recorded on Japanese Victor and you can copy it and give it back to me. I like your music very much for *Kataki*, you know. It's not at all Japanese, but it's very personal and I think it relates well to the play and the production. In the theater one does not have to be literal anyway. The theatrical truth is a subjective thing."

When we got back to New York, Hayakawa gave me the Japanese record and I copied it. Most of the pieces were simple Japanese folk melodies, embellished by a flutist, but his playing was something I had never heard the likes of before in music. The only thing they sounded remotely like were some of the old Israeli melodies I had heard played on a wooden flute or some of the recordings of Arab singing that I had heard at Midhat's house from his great collection of Lebanese, Greek, Turkish and Arabic music. The music Hayakawa lent me had a quality that completely created a climate, a sense of time and world of its own.

As I listened to this recording it gave me the idea of trying to write a piece from my own experience for solo flute. Obviously it would be impossible to write anything like this Japanese piece, because the instrument, the scale and the temperament, the rhythmic conception and its improvisatory quality would be nearly impossible to reproduce in Western terms. I decided I would write my own piece for solo flute and began to plan it in my mind.

My time sense was getting so finely attuned that I was able to think of many things at the same time. Just before *Kataki* opened, I saw the final editing of *Pull My Daisy*. I went that night to Jerry Newman's studio with Jack Kerouac and while I played horn and piano as I had done for our jazz poetry readings, Jack improvised the narration, watching the film for the first time. He listened on earphones as I played.

"Perfect," said Alfred Leslie, when we were done. "We can use that for the music."

"No, we can't," I said. "We'll do a little better." I finished the music for *Pull My Daisy* three days later, staying up twenty-four hours straight.

Anita Ellis sang the song that Allen Ginsberg and Jack wrote entitled "Pull My Daisy." The orchestra we used included my jazz quartet with Sahib Shahab playing alto, dubbing in the sax parts where Larry and I played in the film. Midhat played viola, Ronnie Roseman played oboe and English horn and Jane Taylor played bassoon. We recorded at Reeves Sound Studios, and it was my first experience conducting and recording my music in a top-flight studio.

"Do you want to celebrate?" asked Robert Frank when we were done. "Alfred and I will go out tomorrow night."

"I can't," I said. *"Kataki* opens tomorrow."

"You're on a pretty tight schedule compared to the Five Spot days," said Alfred.

"I think you've got a point there," I told Alfred as I said good-bye to the musicians and rushed off to the dry cleaners, where my tuxedo had been since the opening of *The Beaux' Stratagem.*

I got all dressed up the following night, although it was quite a struggle getting into my tuxedo. I told Emma I was coming up in a cab, and the people in her building looked surprised, seeing me galumphing up the stairs, all dressed up and carrying a corsage. When Emma saw me in my tuxedo, she was really surprised. She was even more surprised when I opened my coat.

"Oh, for God's sake," she said, "I'm not going to the theater with you looking like that. Are you *crazy?"*

"No, it's O.K.," I said, "it's dark in there and I'll wear my coat the whole time."

I'd gained so much weight, I could no longer fit into my tuxedo. My fly couldn't zip, so I had bought five or six huge safety pins that they use on baby's diapers and had managed to close the pants enough so they wouldn't fall off entirely. I had planned to wear my overcoat through most of the performance, just showing the top of my tuxedo and the bottom of my pants.

"You're in*sane,"* she said. "I'm not going."

"No, no, it's O.K.," I said, "I'll keep my coat on."

I finally convinced her to come. Hayakawa was so brilliant that Emma and I were both crying by the time he finally died at the end of the play. Even though I'd seen his performance so many times in rehearsals and at previews, he was such a consummate actor that each night I really felt as if I were seeing it for the first time. Afterward we saw him backstage for a while and even though it was his opening night and people from all over the world had sent him telegrams and were there to see him, he took a few moments to talk to Emma. I could see that they dug each other right away. They were both superaware people and I saw that in his presence, she became very girlish.

When we went home she said to me, "I realize how happy you are with your relative financial stability, but you have to go on a diet. Have you ever been on a diet?"

"No," I said, "I've been on some starvation diets, but those were unintentional."

"I mean a real diet," she said. "It's crazy that you should weigh this much. How much do you weigh?"

"I don't have any idea," I said. "I haven't weighed myself since I went into the army. When I boxed as a light heavyweight, I was always under the weight limit of a hundred and seventy-five pounds, so I never bothered to check it." I got on her scale and to my amazement I weighed two hundred and thirteen pounds.

"The way you eat," she said, "it's not surprising. I don't even want to go out with you if you gain any more weight. We'll look like Laurel and Hardy."

For the first time in my life I went on a diet. Instead of eating a whole cheesecake at the Turf, going to Grant's and eating five or six hotdogs, pizza pies and my usual gourmet thrill dishes, I began eating three meals a day like other people did. I hadn't done this on a regular basis excluding the army since I'd left home at the age of nineteen and I found it was very relaxing. In three weeks I was back to my normal weight.

"You see," said Emma, "now you look almost subhuman again."

Although *Kataki* opened and closed rather quickly, everyone seemed to like the music and I began getting phone calls day and night from people to write music for every conceivable venture. I told Barna that I wasn't interested and because of the summer work that I was assured of having, I felt that I could take off from May until the following fall after I finished "Autobiography for Strings" to write another piece for oboe, two horns and strings.

"Wonderful," she said, "that's the most important thing." While I was completing "Autobiography for Strings," I stopped work on my violin sonata and began the "Shakespearean Concerto," for oboe, two horns and strings, and still planned my solo flute piece although I wasn't sure who would play it or what form it would take.

I won the Obie prize given by *The Village Voice* for my work with the Shakespeare Festival and the Phoenix Theatre as the best achievement for music off Broadway. This was the first award I'd ever gotten for any music I'd written.

In addition to writing music for the Shakespeare in the Park production of *Julius Caesar*, I also went to Stratford, Connecticut, and wrote music for a production of *Romeo and Juliet*. Then I came back to my apartment on Christopher Street—I still hadn't moved—and worked on "Autobiography for Strings." A week later I got a call from a music publisher who said that they would like to publish my music. They offered me enough of an advance so that I could put a down payment on a good piano and move to another apartment. Barna thought it would be a good idea, but I wasn't so sure. I knew that these people were not involved primarily in classical music and that's where I wanted my music to be.

"Look," said the enterprising young man at the publishing company, "you're working in the theater, stay there."

"Yes," I said, "but I've also been writing concert music for a long time."

"Listen," he said, "there's no money in that. It's hopeless. Less and less people are going to concerts and no one wants to hear symphonic music. Do that for a hobby, otherwise you'll end up as an old man teaching in a music school. Be realistic."

"I am being realistic," I said. "If I can get someone to publish my concert music, I'm not interested in whether the rest gets published or not."

"I'll tell you what we'll do," he said, "if you'll go with us, we'll get all of your concert music and publish that too."

I suddenly saw my music being played all over the world. "Really?" I said. I was so anxious to have my pieces published that I was stupid enough to believe him.

"Of course," he said, realizing that he had trapped a sucker.

I still didn't think I should do it. Something in my stomach told me these people were like jazz-business people but with a college education. Barna felt it couldn't do me any harm and it would give me a place to move some of my piles of music. After we signed with them I brought in piles and piles of music for the next three weeks. My arm got sore from signing statements saying that all these different pieces belonged to them. I don't know where they could have put them all and I can't even remember how many pieces I gave them or what they were. I was glad to have them out of my apartment so they wouldn't catch fire or be destroyed some other way. But the publishers were mostly interested in music for the plays and began giving me offers to orchestrate musical comedies and write music for all kinds of commercial ventures, which I refused to do.

"Never, never," I said, "forget it."

After a while they realized I meant it and stopped calling me. I began calling them up once a month to ask them when they were going to publish my concert music. The answer was always very mysterious.

With the money that they gave me, I decided that I would move. Stuart Vaughan told me of a great apartment on Sixth Avenue at the corner of Eleventh Street over a store. It was vacant and it was only eighty-five dollars a month.

I called a friend of mine, Dick Bessemer, who was also a friend of Emma's since his days as a merchant seaman. He was an artist, a writer and just about everything else. He had been a pal of mine since I first came to New York and I knew he was a great apartment saver. He and Dave Lambert were the best in the Village. Dick told me that he would help me fix up the place and put down some tiling so that I could make it into a tiny apartment and studio combined. He also told me that he would help me move. He had always dug my music and now told me he wanted to see me enter the adult world.

Dick fixed up the place on Sixth Avenue and it looked like heaven. With the last of the money that I got from the publisher, I made another payment on a good used Baldwin baby grand and fixed up the rest of the Sixth Avenue apartment myself. I got my belongings ready and Dick came to Christopher Street to help me.

"Listen, man," said Richard as I was piling stuff up. "You can't take all that junk with you."

"What do you mean?" I said. I had a lot of furniture that I had made out of orange crates and old boards, old chairs I had gotten out of the streets; magazines and papers and letters from Europe; old arrangements and compositions that I had written years ago wrapped up in string; pictures, papers, old ragged clothes—piles and piles and piles of junk.

"If you take all that stuff," said Richard, "you'll have to find another apartment to live in. Just take your music and leave all your other crap behind. The Goodwill Industries or Salvation Army won't even take all that junk. You must be out of your mind."

I didn't want to let these things go, but I saw Richard's point. I was looking back less. If I had a relatively ordered place to live in, my life might become more ordered. Since I was working so much and so hard, I would need all the concentration I could muster to continue as a composer now that I was finally getting the chance to function as one.

We spent the whole day moving my stuff. The only thing I kept from my past were some posters I had when I was playing Germany and Paris, some of the books that weren't stolen from me when I was on the Lower East Side, all the music I had kept from my publisher, my one brown *J.B.* suit, my tuxedo and my horn. The rest of the stuff I left in the apartment on Christopher Street.

It was June, 1959, and at twenty-eight I had finally found a pretty nice place to live. There was nothing inside but the piano, a sleeping bag and a card table. I figured that I could furnish it gradually and really get more organized than I'd ever been before in my life.

My first public performance in concert with professional musicians took place that month, during Maurice Peress' series for NYU. Up until then all my music that had been performed professionally was for the theater, the film about the El and my jazz work. All my other concert music was lying about in drawers, shelves, lost or scattered about in various parts of the world. It had been performed by friends of mine and in school, but that was the extent of it. I found great kinship with Charles Ives, who also wrote a great deal of music that was not performed but that he kept working at for his own pleasure. Now people were not only interested in what I wrote but were actually starting to play it.

The day before the rehearsal, the copyist Arnold Arnstein called up.

"It's done," he said.

"That's terrific, Arnold, how can I thank you enough?"

"You can thank me enough by not waiting till the last minute. How do you modern composers expect to get works performed when you finish so late? Are you trying to kill me? I'm only human. We had to stay up all night. As far as I'm concerned, you can thank me by never writing another note of music. All of you are the same. What's next?"

"A concerto for small orchestra, 'Shakespearean Concerto.' "

"Well bring it in *early* this time. Does it sound any different if it's copied a few weeks before the performance instead of five minutes?"

Arnold was the best copyist in New York, so I couldn't argue.

"You get my point?"

"Yes, Arnold, you're absolutely right."

"Good," said Arnold. "I know you'll be just as late the next time. Good luck with the performance. Who's conducting?"

"Maurice Peress."

"Never heard the name."

"You will. He's for real."

"He knows?"

"Yes. He's not the fake-issimo school."

"Good luck with the performance. And *please*—bring the next piece a little *earlier*—you guys are *murdering* us."

I got the parts and they were perfectly copied without a mistake. I took them to Maurice's place and we discussed the piece.

"I like it," said Maurice. "It's honest music. It sounds like you."

"That's good," I told him. "It's dedicated to your daughter."

I showed Maurice the final score with the dedication to Lorca Peress. He wanted to wake her up, but since she was only two years old, his wife decided to wait until morning.

"Autobiography for Strings" was an attempt to describe the first twenty-eight years of my life in music. Of course it was a very tangential description because the piece was only nine minutes long, but I tried to capture the joy of playing jazz and traveling around the world. It was a musical distillation of what I had done in jazz and also included many of the feelings that I had experienced as a French-horn player. For example, in the second measure of the piece, the cello played a bass line reminiscent of one of the phrases Miles Davis played at the end of one of his most famous choruses. It was a kind of trademark for jazz musicians. When I played part of it on the piano for him, Freddie Redd told me with a twinkle in his eyes that the bass lines were the best lines of my piece.

Ultimately, jazz was only an element of the whole, but it was jazz that inspired me and helped me write the piece. We had a three-hour rehearsal for the whole concert, but there was only twenty-five minutes to rehearse my piece. Because of the excellence of the New York musicians, the string players were able to read through it quite well the first time. Just before the concert began I saw a friend and fellow composer, John Huggler.

"Wait till you hear this performance. The first time a professional orchestra plays your piece is something that you'll never forget."

He was right. Even though there was so little rehearsal time, the performance was enough to convince me that I should continue writing for the concert hall for the rest of my life even if nothing else ever got played.

Dan, Malcolm, Emma, Larry Rivers, Al Leslie, Joe Papp and countless friends from the Lower East Side and the Village came. I had my first party in my Sixth Avenue apartment after the concert.

Seymour and Midhat, who played in the orchestra, cornered me. "That was pretty nice, Dave," said Midhat. "Write some more, *right now.*"

"It was all right," said Seymour. "Now you can finish my violin sonata. Greenwich Village is full of geniuses who don't do anything. You better produce—or *else!*"

"It was good, Dave," said Dan. "But I can't judge it objectively until I hear it backwards and sideways through plastic earphones, programmed by four computers. This is the age of mechanical art, doncha know?"

"Bravo, governor," said Emma. "When are you going to change those curtains? They look like leftover slave costumes from *Ali Baba and the Forty Thieves.*"

George Barrow, Arthur and I appeared on *Look Up and Live*, a TV program that devoted one half-hour to jazz. We played "The Birds of Montparnasse," some blues, and I spoke about jazz and concert music and the affinity I felt for both. Nat Hentoff was the commentator. Bill Evans and Sadik Hakim also played.

"Well, pardner," said George Phipps when we were done, "the Amram-Barrow quartet may get discovered yet."

"When we finally do, we'll have a lot of material," I said.

"What pieces are you doing now?" said George. "I thought 'Autobiography' was a big step forward musically."

"I'm finishing a piece for small orchestra, 'Shakespearean Concerto.' I put the violin sonata aside for a while."

"Well, let me know so I can hear it. But you'd better write something else for saxophone soon or I'll boycott your concerts."

"Shakespearean Concerto" was built around the theme of its second movement. The melody was one that I'd used in the production of *Twelfth Night* the year before. It was a song that Feste sang at the very end of the play, my own setting of "The Wind and the Rain." The melody stayed in my mind long after the play was done. I also planned on using it as a basic motif for the opera I hoped to write someday based on *Twelfth Night*.

Joe Eger had suggested I write "Shakespearean Concerto" for two horns, oboe and strings so it would fit into a program that he was doing where the Mozart Divertimento for oboe, two horns and strings was also being performed. I wrote the second movement first because it was something that had been in my mind and I had material for it. The rest of the piece was in no way Shakespearean but simply music, using the oboe and the two horns and occasionally a single violin and viola as solo instruments pitted against the rest of the string orchestra. It was very much like the way these instruments might be used in a concerto grosso except that I tried to use the oboe and the horns in an orchestral context. I used jazz elements, including a fiery figure for the horns in the last movement similar to a figure that I had played at the Five Spot as my sign-off.

Toward the end of the summer when I almost had the "Shakespearean Concerto" completed, Dan suggested that we go to Provincetown with his beautiful girl friend, Eva Textor. Emma had shipped out to make some money and see Egypt for the first time, so I went with Dan and Eva. They knew some people there, so for four days I had the chance to be at the seashore again. It was the first time I'd been in Provincetown since 1946 and it was the same wonderful, wild, hectic scene as always.

When I came back, I felt so good from having been out in that fresh salt air that I finished the "Shakespearean Concerto" by the end of September. When Joe Eger rehearsed it with his small orchestra, which included Walter Trampler and Karen Tuttle playing the violas and Lois Wann as the oboe soloist, he decided that he would perform it at Grinnell College on tour and then in New York. Because I had been taking some conducting lessons again with Jonel Perlea, I conducted the first reading of it myself.

As we went through the piece, I realized that I had had the chance to complete and hear three substantial concert pieces during the past year. These were pieces I would not throw away, revise or use as the basis for other pieces. These were actually the first three pieces that I felt were any kind of statement that I could be proud of. These were compositions I would put in a new kind of pile. They were my beginnings as a man. As I heard these wonderful musicians playing through my work and how involved they were in the music, I saw that whether or not I appeared to take myself seriously from now on and whether or not people thought that I was serious, nevertheless I was finally getting my chance to write music and hear it played. I was twenty-eight years old and really cooking. I felt that these pieces, while they were only the beginning of my dream, were definite statements of what I felt about music and would serve as points of departure for where I wanted to go.

When I wrote the music for *Lysistrata* and *The Great God Brown* the following November, John Perras told me that if I wrote him a solo flute piece, he would perform it in his upcoming recital in January. Because of the idea I had had for a solo piece since speaking with Sessue Hayakawa, I stopped the violin sonata after completing the second movement and began work on "Overture and Allegro" for unaccompanied flute. The first movement was simple, plaintive and sad. The second movement was the most extended use of jazz ideas that I had ever written. Because of the flexibility of most flute players, especially young American flutists, I was certain that if I was actually able to write down on paper some of the more idiomatic jazz ideas, they would be playable and come off spontaneously enough to give the spirit and the essence of jazz without sounding like a concert musician trying to copy a jazz player. John slaved over the piece and finally decided that it was effective, even though it was rather unprecedented in solo flute literature. He decided to program it for his recital.

A few days later I was called to write the music for *Turn of the Screw*, a television drama that was to star Ingrid Bergman. John Frankenheimer was the director. He and his wife were familiar with the music I had done for the Phoenix Theatre productions and the Shakespeare in the Park music, although they had not heard of my concert music.

I had never met John Frankenheimer and when I went to meet

him he said simply that he liked my music and would like to have me work on this play. He stressed the fact that he wanted real music, not television music or background music, but the best music that I could possibly write to fit the dramatic situation, using whatever instruments I wanted to.

I told Barna and she was overjoyed. "You'll be able to have a little of your music heard all over the country on this program," she said. "It's not like having your own work performed, but you'll be part of a whole and it should be a wonderful experience. Just as I told you when we met, they will have to come to you. Also this will give you a chance to write some more pieces when it is over. How is your violin sonata coming?"

"I almost have it finished," I said.

Working with John Frankenheimer was really wild. He had a great visual sense and a wonderful flair. And even though he would shout and scream at the crew and the cameramen until he would turn purple with rage, everyone liked him because no one took it personally. He just wanted the program to be good. He drove himself with such relentlessness that everyone clamored for the chance to work with him.

Throughout it all, Ingrid Bergman had a great detached calm. She saved her energy and emotions for her acting. She was so forceful and pure in her performance that it seemed each time, whether in a run-through or in the final taping, that it was really happening before your eyes.

The program was beautifully done. When I went out to Brooklyn for the final taping, John said, "You realize when this is over, you'll only have seventy-two hours before it goes on the air."

"It's O.K., John," I said. "I have all the music in my head and I'll be able to time it and write it down somehow." I'd decided to use violin, flute, French horn, bassoon, piano and percussion for the entire score. I felt that this would be enough and would capture the feeling.

While I was watching the final taping a man from the advertising agency who was sponsoring the program came in and began to tell me that I should plan on conducting a football march to be played with a superimposed Buick automobile over the final credits of the program.

"I have music I've already written for the final credits," I told him, "based on music that the children hear and sing in a little song I wrote for them. It's almost like chamber music and I think it would be much more appropriate for the program than a football march. I don't know if you've read the script or not, but the Henry James novel was not about the life of Jim Thorpe or any other famous football players."

"Ha ha ha," he said. "Very funny. You'd better prepare yourself for a football march."

"Listen," I said, "you could pay me a million dollars and I wouldn't do something like that. Who the hell are you?"

"I represent the people who are paying for this program," he said in a dry, relaxed tone. I realized that he was so impressed with his power that he couldn't even bother to be rude to a pip-squeak like me.

"Well, it's not going to happen," I told him. "Maybe you can brainwash the public with your poison on other shows, but not this one. We're artists, man." I went to John and told him. "Listen," I said, "they want to have some kind of weird football music at the end of the program."

"That will never happen," said John. "Don't worry. I wouldn't hire you to do some kind of garbage like that." John came in and gave the man one of his shouting specials. Then—as a fantastic tactical maneuver—during the time he was supposed to film one of the possible end credits with the football march, accompanied by an automobile superimposed over the top, he had cameramen suddenly appear during the final credits in their shirtsleeves, leering into the screen so that it was impossible to use it. They later decided to put the football music on after the program was over, while announcing the next week's attraction.

"I hate to shout like that," said John afterward, "but that's all these people understand. If you try to talk to them about art or be logical, they don't seem to get the message. They need to hear the entire hundred-and-ten-piece orchestra of rage."

As soon as the taping was done, John and I went over to the NBC building and he ordered two cots. "We're going to need these," he said. "In between mechanical work and dubbing, we can put these cots in the newsroom and catch a nap every once in a while." We walked in with our cots and put them in the newsroom. People looked rather askance at both of us. "Don't pay any attention to them," said John. "I don't work for this network on a permanent basis and I plan to keep it that way. Anytime you have a few minutes off, use that cot. We've got to get this show done on time."

"We will," I said. "Don't worry." While it was being filmed I had to time with a stopwatch every section of *The Turn of the Screw* that needed music. Because of the enormous expense of replaying video tape over a machine at that time, I had no chance to watch a final screening. Since it was impossible to dub the music in with the video tape, I had to get exact timings while the tape was being filmed and spliced, then write the music and time it, then mix the music in with the final tape without any second chance. If any of the musical sections were not exactly the right length, the whole tape would be ruined.

"Can you do it?" said John.

"Sure," I said. "What else can I do? It's too late now. Anyway, this one will be a challenge."

I sat inches from the man who was splicing the tape while John subtly tried to urge him on. The splicer was from Jamaica, Long Island. He had a gigantic pair of scissors with which he would cut the video tape and he seemed completely unconcerned about anything to do with TV. He was only interested in talking about blue fishing and the weather conditions off Montauk Point. "I caught me some stripers and blues the other day. About thirty-five miles out. It was blowing up pretty good." Snip, snap and he would cut the tape, crimp it together and Ingrid Bergman would go from one part of the nineteenth-century country home to the other as smoothly as if there were no camera change at all. "Then we went up and we thought maybe we seen some tuna. They was jumping, you know, flashing in that water. But we lost 'em when we tried to gaff 'em. He musta weighed fifty, fifty-five pounds. Big bastard. But we didn't have anybody who knew how to gaff." Snip, snip, snip and the two children were suddenly confronted by the ghost of Quint as another splice was made. The splicer's monologue would have been more appropriate for *The Old Man and the Sea*, but while he went on with his fishing tales for three and a half hours, I timed the music at the places that I saw it should start and stop, and getting out the notes that I had made, began composing on the spot.

For the next fifty hours, I composed, copied parts that I couldn't rush to Arnold Arnstein, and occasionally would go over to the cot and conk out. After an hour's sleep, one of the people in the production unit would wake me up. John and I would go down and get some delicious sandwiches at Reubens. Then I would go back to sleep for a half an hour and get up and write some more music. Most of the music had actually been sketched or was in my head. It was just a question of organizing it, rewriting it and making changes. Seymour Wakschal and Dan Cowan and the other members of our six-man chamber group were alerted and when it was nearing completion, they came zipping into NBC studios to record the music.

John was really understanding. "Just take your time," he said. "I don't care how long you take, let's get it perfect." We spent eight hours recording. Norman Ogg, the sound man, was calm and patient throughout it all and even though it was such hard work and I was so tired, it was really fun. There was a lot of music in the program and I had complete freedom to do whatever I wanted.

We got the music tapes done and while they were downstairs being edited, John and I slept for three hours, the longest nap of our working marathon. We were roused from our slumbers just in time for the six-o'clock news. We tip-toed past the newsmen, who by this time seemed to accept us as permanent fixtures, and went into the control room, where the mix was going to be made. Because no one was sure how to do music this way—video tape was relatively new—I suggested that I sit next to an engineer and when it was time for each musical section to come, I would cue him a split-second early so that he could start the music tape right on cue. If the music came out exactly the way I thought it should, it would synchronize with the picture. If it didn't, well, they still loved me in the post office.

We began. Each musical section fitted perfectly.

The crew members were astonished. "It's not so hard," I told them. "All you need is a stopwatch and some imagination." Apparently they were bowled over by the mystique of how hard it's supposed to be to write music for a dramatic situation and have it come out the right length of time.

"I just finished writing a twenty-two-minute piece," I told them. "You don't have to be a genius to write something thirty-eight seconds long." We had to make three complete versions of the program. One for the East Coast, one for the West Coast, which was sent out by airplane, and one for the Middle West. The three programs were to be shown more or less simultaneously, but there was no national hookup as yet.

We were done a few hours before air time. "Do you want to conk out again on the cots?" said John.

"No, I'd never wake up," I said. "I want to watch the show." John went home to the Dakota and I went over to Midhat's house. He had also played in our little chamber orchestra and had decided to have a big Cantonese dinner-TV party to watch the program. "I think you'll really enjoy it," I said to Seymour and Midhat. Dan of course had read the play and being a real intellectual, spent about an hour discussing Henry James's place in the literature of the nineteenth century, and whether or not the ghosts were actual, symbolic, an aberration on the part of the nurse or simply a belief that there were ghosts. Or perhaps was *Turn of the Screw* merely a realistic portrayal of an actual mysterious occurrence in Victorian England.

When the program finally came on and the music began playing, everyone put down their chopsticks and sat transfixed as we watched the beginning of the program. I was really happy that the musicians had already recorded the music, so that they would have a chance to see the program, watch the great artistry of the actors and see John's brilliant work. I thought to myself what a shame it was that John had to sit at home and couldn't be here with the musicians seeing his fellow collaborators' reaction to the stunning visual impact and dramatic power of his program.

As soon as the music stopped and the children appeared on the screen, Midhat got up with his brother and went over to serve himself more egg rolls.

About thirty seconds later Seymour said, "Hee, hee, hee, dig that kid. Man is he *weird-looking.*"

A minute later everyone was up, eating, drinking, talking, laughing and only Emma, Dan and I were watching the program.

"For Christ's sake, shut up," said Dan. "You bunch of peasants. Watch the program. It's beautiful."

"Ah," said Midhat, "I've seen these TV shows before. We'll wait till the next music cue."

The three of us watched the program, oblivious to their talking and laughing and drinking, but one second after the next music began, although it was so soft it was almost imperceptible, there was a deadly hush in the room. Everyone scampered back to the television set to listen to himself playing and watch the program. As soon as the music was over, back they went to the table, drinking, talking, laughing.

"Oy vey," said Dan, shaking his head, "what a bunch of morons."

"Oh well," said Emma, "this is the age of specialization."

By the last forty minutes of the program, however, all the musicians became interested in the entire program and by the end of the show everyone was really very moved. Miss Bergman's performance was so powerful that it was as if she had been right in the room. The phone kept ringing all night long as friends of Seymour's, Midhat's and

Marvin Feinsmith, the bassoon player, called up to congratulate them on their playing. Every one of the musicians had had real solos to play, and the music actually sounded like a chamber music performance, not like some kind of tinny canned music.

All of us had worked together now on quite a few projects. Seymour was working on my violin sonata, Midhat was working on an old viola piece of mine, Marvin had worked on my saxophone, horn and bassoon piece with Dan. Jules Greenberg and I had played together for years since the army. It was really a kind of workshop situation for all of us and because of this the performance of the music for *The Turn of the Screw* was really musical and free sounding, in addition to fitting the dramatic situation.

John told me he would have more work for me and I realized that because of all the offers I was getting, I would definitely not have to worry about working in the post office that Christmas. I had to write a score for *Peer Gynt* at the Phoenix. I wanted to work on completing my violin sonata, as well as "Overture and Allegro" for flute, which was to be performed soon. I decided that I had better get some sleep first. I slept for fourteen hours and when I got up I went right to work.

I realized that there was no more time in my life to waste. My days as a wild man were over. All my energy from now on would be devoted to my music. I was already turning down more work each day than I had ever been offered in any year of my life before. I realized that I could simply sit home from now on, answer the phone, write music for any project that I was asked to and have very few worries. But as I resumed work on my flute piece and the violin sonata, trying to be as polite as possible to people who were calling me and explaining to them in as little amount of time as I could that I had work of my own to do, I realized that I was just beginning on the long road that would occupy the rest of my life. It was a new kind of struggle. It was a struggle for time and a struggle to continue with my work and get that music down on paper. I wasn't able anymore to get it out just by playing.

By the end of 1959 there weren't even that many places to play. I still went to sessions once in a while, but most of my playing was done at home. Instead of playing for eight or ten hours, I would compose for eight or ten hours. I missed playing and the brotherly feeling with other musicians, but when I would see them, they understood. "You're just saying the same thing in a different way," they'd say. "You're still blowing, man, but you're doing it on paper instead of with your horn."

That's what I felt that I was doing. My best blowing still hadn't been heard by anybody, but it was being written down. I was about to complete my fifth piece in a year and a half's time.

10

ON THE FIFTH of January, 1960, John Perras gave a concert at Carnegie Recital Hall, which included my "Overture and Allegro" for unaccompanied flute. It went very well and even got a good review in *The New York Times*, which shocked most of my musician friends, since they had also thought it was a good piece. I went with a lovely seventeen-year-old girl whom I had met at a health food store. She giggled with pleasure when the piece was over. She was such a sunny soul, I dedicated the piece to her. When we went to the health food store owned by Mr. Damer on Eighth Street the next day he was bubbling over with enthusiasm.

"That's a real fine review you got there, keep up the good work," he said. "What will it be, watercress and mangoes on pumpernickel or Joyanna health drink with some wheat germ oil and some blackstrap molasses on the side with a little yogurt? It's excellent for the pancreas."

He wore a white doctor's smock. I used to love going there, not only to eat the excellent salad but to watch his incredible put-on with the customers. He was the hardest seller of all time. I used to watch his quasi-medical diagnosis of people's health when they'd walk in off the streets. Some stumbled in out of curiosity or because they thought it was the entrance to the shoe store next door.

That morning we settled for green artichoke spaghetti with meat substitute and Tiger's milk. Afterwards, I walked my tower of health back to her apartment. Since she wasn't going to be eighteen for another month I decided not to serve any prison time now that I was doing so well in music. She thought this was hilarious and began roaring and giggling, trying to get me to seduce her while making humorous references to how I would look in a prison uniform.

I went back home and right to work. *Peer Gynt* was opening the twelfth of January. I knew I would not have much time to relax afterwards, because I had to complete the music for *The Fifth Column,* a television play based on the Hemingway play, directed by John Frankenheimer. It was to be taped January 29.

The day after I completed the music for *Peer Gynt* I began going to rehearsals of *The Fifth Column.* The cast included Richard Burton, Maximillian Schell and Sally Ann Howes. Richard Burton and Maximillian Schell were not internationally known at that time although they certainly were well respected among actors. As rehearsals progressed, I played jazz during lunch time and Richard Burton came over and began reciting Shakespeare. I stopped to listen.

"No, no, continue. That's what I used to do in pubs when I was a young boy. I used to recite poetry and Shakespeare to jazz. I love to do it. Are you going to play again?"

I played and he recited Shakespeare. He was wild. He had several cans of beer with him and gave me one. We had a ball during most of the rehearsals. I noticed that he had the same thing in his work that Ingrid Bergman did, a tremendously natural way of acting. He never seemed to be pretending; he always made you feel that you were there.

The music for *The Fifth Column* was for full orchestra. It was the first time I had the opportunity to conduct and record music that I had written and orchestrated for a small symphony orchestra. In addition to the CBS musicians on staff, I brought in my own group of henchmen, a wild, young, happy-go-lucky lot. After the regular staff musicians at CBS overcame the shock of seeing all these sloppily dressed, wild-looking young musicians, they had a good time too.

At the same time, I worked on my violin sonata, starting to complete the third movement, a theme and variations. Seymour would come over every few days and shout, "Whatta ya got done now?" I would show it to him. He would look it over, play-stop-start-practice and then say, "Is that all?"

"Well," I would say to Seymour, "I've been pretty busy."

"Busy, shit," he would say. "When are you going to get this God damn sonata finished?"

"I'm sorry, Seymour. I'm doing the best I can."

"Well, hurry up. You told me you were going to have it done by New Year's."

Seymour sometimes spoke in a brusque manner, but he played with sensitivity and refinement. Each time I heard him play part of my sonata, it inspired me to work hard on it no matter how tired I was.

As I was coming into the home stretch on Seymour's sonata, Sidney Lumet asked me to write music for *Caligula,* the Albert Camus play. Sidney had thought he would do this at the Phoenix once before, but funds were not available. Now it was definitely being done on Broadway with Colleen Dewhurst and Kenneth Haigh in the cast. They were both as fine as any classical actors that I had worked with. I began on the music immediately. Because Chandler Cowles, the co-producer of *Caligula,* had produced Menotti's first operas, he was very sympathetic to the demands that I felt were necessary to write music for the play and we had quite a large orchestra for the theater. Strings, percussion and a brass choir.

The music went extremely well, but at first Kenneth Haigh was very angry. It was because of a long cello solo during his first entrance. This music was associated with him throughout the play. It was nearly two minutes long and it was Sidney's idea. After Kenneth got used to the music, he began to like the idea and we became good friends. I would go back to his dressing room and while he was every inch the tortured Roman emperor on stage, he was a mad Irish-English hipster-philosopher backstage. He had an improvisatory quality of freedom in his acting which reminded me of a jazz musician. If someone would change one tiny line or bit of action, he would change his performance to match it. No matter what happened he was there.

When *Caligula* opened February 15 all of us felt that no matter how long it ran, we had worked on something that we would remember all our lives. Camus had died in a car crash before the opening. All of us felt that much more strongly about his loss and the power of his play.

I invited Dimitri Mitropoulos to the performance. It was the last of my music that he ever heard. I saw him sitting in the audience and his great bald head reminded me of that first time at the seashore in the mid-forties. Although he was no longer the conductor of the

Philharmonic and his health was very poor, he had lost none of his dignity or nobility.

"Maestro, I'm really honored that you came," I said to him afterwards.

"I enjoyed your music, David," he said. "It was very interesting and appropriate and well written. You have made wonderful strides since that time nearly fifteen years ago when we first met. You even learned to modulate." He gave me a darting glance and I could see that familiar flicker of ironic laughter drift across his lips. "You must go now," he said. "There are many important people here for you to meet, I'm sure."

"Well, Maestro," I said, "you're the only important person for me here."

"You're a good boy, as you always were," he told me. "I'm happy that you feel that way about me. It's good you have such loyalty to your old friend. To tell you the truth, I'm not feeling very well. I'll go back to the hotel."

"Let me walk you back."

"No," he said, "you must stay here, this is your night. We'll see each other again."

I insisted that we walk together the few blocks back to his hotel. As we got close to his hotel he said, "Would you want to do anything else besides music?"

This sounded like a strange question, but knowing how he asked questions to give answers, I simply said, "No."

"Neither would I," he said. "I thought about it many times, but the more I work at music, the more I know how lucky I am to be a musician. Without it"—and he shrugged his shoulders expressively—"I do not know what I would do. Without music I can't imagine my life having meaning. I can't even climb mountains anymore since my health has been bad. I should not smoke and even my one big meal a day should be supervised more carefully. Still, music gives me that joy that it always did." He took another look at me with his wonderful piercing eyes. "Aren't we lucky?" he said. I couldn't think of anything to say. "Good night, my dear, work hard, I'm proud of you."

I walked away to go back to the theater. I was to hear from Mitropoulos once more in a letter, but that was the last time I ever saw him.

I turned down all other work and plunged into the violin sonata full speed ahead in order to finish the last movement. I was just about to complete the last page when I got a call from an old friend of mine whom I remembered vaguely from the Five Spot. It was Whitey Lutz.

"Hey, Dave," he said on the phone, "I remembered those great poetry things you used to do with Jack Kerouac two years back. How about having a concert at Town Hall and you swing it on the old French horn and we get some great poets and go!"

"Whitey," I told him, "I think my jazz-poetry days are over except at parties. What would be great would be having a concert of my music and Charles Mills's music. I learned a lot being with him and it would be great if his music could get more of the recognition it deserves."

"No," said Whitey, "I remembered your music from the Five Spot. I want it to be yours or I won't do it at all. If it goes well maybe we can do Mills's music on the second concert."

"O.K.," I said, "but if you want a concert, I don't want to play the French horn. I can do that anytime. How about putting on some of my concert music. I have a whole bunch of pieces that no one has ever heard."

"O.K.," he said, "we'll have a concert, you tell me what pieces you want and how many instruments and I'll pay for all of it."

I was stunned. Whitey and his wife were older people who used to come to the Five Spot regularly. I had no idea he knew I was a composer, but apparently he remembered me from the eleven weeks I had played there, three years before in the winter of 1957.

Again, I suggested to Whitey that I share the program with Charles Mills. I didn't want to have a whole evening of my own music.

"It's you or nothing, Dave," he told me. "That's what I want."

Charles Mills had always been an inspiration to me. When I had spoken about his music with Mitropoulos, Mitropoulos said he was one of the most important American composers. Mitropoulos had played Mills's "Theme and Variations for Orchestra" and he admired his work very much. Because of Charles's erratic nature and the difficulties all composers face, he did not have his rightful place in American music as far as many of his friends were concerned, including me. Whitey thought if the concert went well enough then perhaps he could do some of Charles's work as well.

I told Barna. She was bowled over to think that someone would want to sponsor my music with no strings attached. I decided that since it was a whole evening of my work, if I were to conduct it as well it would be too much of a one-man show. Besides, I felt that Maurice Peress understood my music as well as any conductor I knew. It also meant that he would have the chance to conduct in Town Hall and get paid for it.

I told this great news to Maurice. He thought the best idea would be to have the two small orchestral works and some chamber works. He felt that they would be possible to rehearse and we could hire a small orchestra within the budget. Also, the two orchestral works would balance the chamber works. He also suggested that I use some of my Shakespeare music in concert form. We decided that the program would start off with the incidental music for *Twelfth Night*, then the violin sonata and then "Autobiography for Strings." He felt that the second half would be a good place to program the "Overture and Allegro" for flute, the trio for saxophone, French horn and bassoon and finally my "Shakespearean Concerto" for the final work. When Whitey gave us the budget, I started working like mad, calling up musicians who would be interested and would have the time to perform the music. Seymour agreed to play the violin sonata even though I had not completed it and also to be concertmaster in both of the orchestral pieces.

Whitey wasn't sure exactly when, but he told me the concert would be sometime during the first ten days in May.

Seymour asked me, "When are you gonna finish the sonata? For Christ sakes, do you want me to sight-read the last few bars? Are you gonna write it during the night of the concert?"

Finally we were told that the date for the concert would be May 8. I called Seymour and told him that the violin sonata would be done any minute. I was really in seventh heaven. All my recent pieces would have first-rate performances and my friends would hear my music at last.

I was called by Cantor David Putterman of the Park Avenue Synagogue, who wanted me to write a sacred service for the following year. I told him absolutely yes and spent the rest of the day thinking about being a Jew and Jewish music.

I had thought about *J.B.* in terms of the story of Job. The music I had written for *J.B.* even made Moishe Halévy, the head of the Habima Theatre, think that I was Israeli before he met me. But I had only used my religious feelings in a natural kind of a way without giving it any conscious thought.

Cantor Putterman told me that the Park Avenue Synagogue had been commissioning composers each year to write a new setting for the Friday night liturgy. I had met Cantor Putterman in the summer of 1957 when his son Zev, a friend of mine from the Village, had brought him to Central Park to see the production of *Macbeth*. At that time he told me that someday he hoped I could work with him. Now the moment had come.

I went to visit him at his house in Westport. He showed me the parts of the service and told me to call him if I needed any advice or had any problems.

Only a few days later I received another call from Westport. It was my old friend Andrew Heath, who had conducted the Seventh Army Symphony before James Dixon. He was giving a piano recital the following fall at the Metropolitan's Grace Rainey Rogers Auditorium and wanted to know if I would write a piano sonata for his recital. He was a very fine pianist and an all-round musician. I told him that I would. I had an idea for a piano sonata and many sketches for piano music, most of which had landed in various wastebaskets. I told Andrew I couldn't start on it until the summer because of my other commitments. But if he could wait, I could send approximately one movement a month during July, August and September.

Cantor Putterman was only able to offer me one hundred dollars for the sacred service I was to write. Andrew, with a wife and four children, offered me no money at all. I didn't care. These were first-rate people who came to me because they were interested in my music. I was still living modestly and knew I could afford to take the time off to do it and pay for the copying as well. I would have loved to be remunerated, but this was the spring of 1960. I felt I was lucky even to be asked. No one was going to force me into being Mr. Background Music now.

As I was getting ready for my concert, I received two offers to write film scores within two weeks. It seemed as if this was my time of testing to see whether I was really a composer or not. So rather than make myself nervous I decided to write the music for both of them. The idea that I might not be able to complete all these projects never even occurred to me. I accepted both film commissions joyfully.

The first offer was to write the music for John Frankenheimer's *The Young Savages*. I was told I'd have to leave for Hollywood at the end of September and would have six weeks to write the music. I figured this would give me a chance to complete my piano sonata. When I came back I could work on the sacred service. The other film, Elia Kazan's production of *Splendor in the Grass*, was going to be done in New York City and I was told that I could record the music for that when I got back from Hollywood.

I thought that if I continued my new-found organization of each day and did not contract any kind of sleeping sickness, I would be able to complete all my own work during the year. I knew I would have enough of an income to turn everything else down. My theatrical commitments were *Henry V, Measure for Measure* and *The Taming of the Shrew* for the upcoming summer in Central Park. I enjoyed doing music for Shakespeare plays so much by this time that I didn't even consider it work. Instead of going to play tennis or to the movies, or bowling, sitting around coffeehouses or bars, I was able to spend the time writing music for Shakespeare.

I plunged into all my work. I started the piano sonata, beginning with the second movement, a lullaby which was based on blues, and began visiting Cantor Putterman to get help with the transliteration of the Hebrew for the sacred service.

The news got around that I was going to have my own concert and I got calls from all kinds of old friends. Because ticket sales weren't exactly booming, Whitey's management told me I could give out a few passes. Having mastered the art of papering the house at jazz-poetry concerts, I went about the task with calculated abandon. I covered the Cedar Tavern, the White Horse, the Corner Bistro, Johnny Romero's, the Bleecker Street Tavern, all my haunts on the Lower East Side, coffee shops, Washington Square Park, the Art Foods Delicatessen, Mr. Damer's Health Food Restaurant and all the other cultural centers where concert lovers meet to eat. I told Whitey that whether or not he actually made any money, he would certainly have a full house.

Seymour would come over to my house to work on the violin sonata and we would spend all night calling up musicians to tell them of changes of plans, schedules and so forth. We also got together with Maurice and checked over all the parts before rehearsal. The night before our first orchestra rehearsal, I slept on the floor and Seymour used my bed to lay out all the orchestral parts, which he was still working on furiously, checking all the bowings and phrasings, until I woke up and we went to rehearsal.

At the first rehearsal some of the musicians seemed angry. Like Seymour, they were all young free-lance players, ambitious, outspoken and great performers. Everyone wanted to be concertmaster. They grumbled and growled and refused to sit down.

They were really giving Maurice some bad vibrations, so after the first hour of rehearsal, I got up on the podium and gave an impassioned speech telling them how much it meant to me to have my music played. I knew every one of them was a concertmaster in his own right. I really meant it, but they were so astounded that a composer would even have any considerations for their feelings that they burst into applause.

After that, no one gave Maurice or Seymour a hard time. They all played like angels and by the time the last rehearsal was over, the music sounded terrific. Seymour looked like a ghost. In addition to practicing the violin sonata constantly, he was also concertmaster in "Autobiography for Strings," "The Shakespearean Concerto," and was constantly bowing the parts, arguing with Maurice about how he should conduct the piece, arguing with all the musicians about how they played their parts and telling me how I should have composed different sections better. Without his amazing drive, knowledge and Elizabethan cheer and energy, the concert probably would not have come off as well as it did.

When the night of the concert finally came, Town Hall was packed. The entire downstairs section was filled with people in dirty raincoats, overalls, long hair, berets, scarves, corduroy suits, dark glasses and—most important to me—smiles, happy receptive faces. They were all friends of mine from days in Paris, the Lower East Side, the Village and people I had known who had come from all over the country to attend this concert on May 8, 1960. There was not that uptight world that seems to be so much a part of the concert scene, especially where contemporary music is concerned. People were coming to hear the music and to enjoy themselves.

Russell Oberlin sang the counter-tenor parts for *Twelfth Night* with his matchless skill. Seymour played the difficult violin sonata so well that, sitting from the side of the auditorium, I could see the fiddle players standing backstage in the wings with their mouths open. Maurice conducted "Autobiography for Strings" and the orchestra played it perfectly. After intermission John Perras played the solo flute work and the saxophone trio was performed. People clapped between movements because they enjoyed it so much. I suspect it was the easiest piece on the program for them to hear the jazz influence that they expected in my work, not knowing anything else about me.

"Shakespearean Concerto" really set the place in an uproar with its bubbling ending. I was so carried away that when Maurice motioned for me to come up for a bow, I dashed down the center aisle in my tuxedo and since I was wearing sneakers, managed to vault up the stage with one flying leap to the pleasure of my old gym students who had come all the way from Washington to see their old teacher. It was as much fun as any jazz concert that I had participated in and everyone seemed to enjoy themselves.

Next day, some of the critics accused me of everything except advocating the violent overthrow of the government. The *Herald Tribune*, however, was very laudatory except for the last paragraph, which said I knew nothing about form.

"Don't worry," said Maurice, "those are beautiful pieces. Just keep on writing, that's the only important thing. Some day all these pieces are going to be performed all over the place and everyone will forget what the critics said." I'm happy to say that Maurice was right.

Even though some members of the critical fraternity had a rather dim view of my talents, I was approached by several music publishers, many musicians requested copies of my music, which they wished to perform, and I was asked to write more works. Most important, Andrew Norman wanted to sponsor recordings of most of the works for the concert. No strings attached. He liked the music and wanted to have it recorded. Otherwise, as he said, it would be performed, enjoyed, then lost forever.

The day after my concert, I went to the first production meeting for *Splendor in the Grass* and found out that the Dixieland training I had in Washington when I had played with Louis Brown at the age of twelve had not gone to waste. Some of the music for *Splendor* would be Dixieland music and the rest would be symphonic. I wrote a few tunes, which Kazan was going to use to help the actors get characterization. He was also happy that I was having the chance to work on *The Young Savages* and get experience on a feature film before I started *Splendor in the Grass*.

I was lucky to find a place on Fire Island that summer. This time it was not sleeping in the back of someone's porch. I had actually graduated into a full-fledged shareholder, sharing a house with Dan Cowan, Sy Mottel, a theatrical director, and a friend of Sy's who had some mysterious job in a talent agency which seemed to change each time we questioned him. He would gesture expressively with his thumbs and fingers when referring to the gigantic deals he was closing, but fortunately he had no trouble raising the rent money.

After the recording of my music, Dan went down to the Casals Bach Festival in Puerto Rico, to play in the orchestra. He wrote me a letter to say he was getting married toward the end of the summer. He had met a lovely girl who was also a musician and they were engaged. I was really happy for his sake although I shuddered at the thought of him bringing a sweet innocent young thing out to the depraved den of Ocean Beach. My memories of the battalions of sultry stenographers, swinging and swaying up and down the boardwalk, did not seem like an ideal place for a honeymoon, but I never questioned Dan's judgment or experience.

While Dan was away, I went with Spike Gaffney, the oboist in the Seventh Army Symphony, to a party for the *Provincetown Review*. I used to play piano and horn whenever they had parties. I would either go with a band or alone just for fun. Their parties were held at the Socialist Hall. There were always a lot of friends there, people who had been to my concert and people I had known from the Five Spot, the Cedar Tavern and from Paris. They were just folks.

As I was playing "Well, You Needn't," one of my favorite Monk tunes, I spied a lovely girl with doelike eyes, dancing with a huge oaf to my right. I noticed that she kept pushing him away and by the time I had finished playing I was happy to see that he had given up. I thought I should at least say a few words to her before someone else came over. She had a sweet, innocent look like a deer, trapped in a menacing horde of beatniks, including myself. I wanted to protect her from the outside world.

"Hi," she said. "You want to dance?"

"You know it," I said.

We began dancing and that old feeling came over me. I thought I was being electrocuted. After about two minutes I decided to abandon any of the usual formalities and asked her if she would like to come to Fire Island with me the following morning.

"We can catch the seven o'clock ferry," I said, "and I have some terrific lemon meringue pie in my icebox we can eat until then." I thought a come-on like this would be irresistible. I didn't even know what I was saying, but she was so lovely I would have said anything just to even get a chance to talk to her longer.

"Well," she said, "some people think I'm a witch. When I'm sixty years old, I'm going to turn all green, have warts and moles and go around putting hexes on people."

"How old are you now?"

"Twenty."

"Well, I think you're lovely," I said, "and I don't think that you'll ever be a witch."

"Well, you never know," she said, "life is far out for us druids."

She then told me about the history of the druids and we went over to my apartment with some other people and sat around all night eating my lemon meringue pie, drinking some Filipino beer which I had gotten from Igor's Art Foods Delicatessen, eating some macaroni salad, which I had in the icebox, and waiting for the sun to come up so we could drive out to the Fire Island ferry.

We roared off at dawn. Just as we hit the Midtown Tunnel she said, "No, no, no, I can't do this. Take me back. This is insane."

"Not really," I said. "That salt air and sunshine will knock you out. It's the greatest."

We went out and spent the summer together.

I had to come into the city to work on the Central Park Shakespearean productions. Spike would drive me in in his beat-up old convertible. As I was copying out the music in the back seat, I would stand up shouting at him while my poor druid companion would cringe in her seat, assaulted by the horns honking behind us and my screaming at Spike to try to help him zigzag through the traffic so that we could save time. In addition to watching the rehearsals and recording the music, which didn't take that much time, I also had to see the music publisher for *Splendor in the Grass* at least once a week. He was a very sweet guy, but he was not exactly an avant-gardist. For him, Sigmund Romberg was the king.

"That's nice, nice, nice, nice," he would say, patting me on the shoulder. "But it's too weird, it's far—*out!* It don't sound—mel*odious!*"

"I think it's pretty," I would say lamely.

"Change that bridge!" he would say, zeroing in for the kill. "It's too hard. No kids can sing that. It's too far out. Change that bridge or it will never sell a copy."

"Look," I told him. "I'm not trying to be the king of movie music. Kazan likes this melody and I think it's beautiful and it's the best music I can write. You'll have to take it like it is."

The rest of the time I would go to the Shakespeare in the Park or spend the day at the beach. It was my first time outdoors since I'd been fifteen years old. My friend was really more of a cherub than a druid. She was an ideal companion and I even thought of marrying her. She would pitter-patter in the house like a small Anglo-Saxon Japanese geisha girl, her doelike eyes batting, her soulful freckles and cute figure driving all the aging stenographers into fits of rage and jealousy as she really showed Ocean Beach what it meant to be a lady.

I knew that I should get a piano to complete my piano sonata, and Dr. Jules Eskie, a dentist who was staying in Ocean Beach with his family, told me that if I went to his house in the suburbs, I could borrow his. He and his wife, Jo, were really friendly down-home people.

"Just go in the house some morning," he said cheerfully. "The door's always open. Just go in the front room and take that piano and it's yours for the summer. My son never practices it. What good does it do there?"

I got together with my friend Dick Bessemer, another moving man, Seymour and Dan Cowan. We all jumped in the back of a small moving truck after having a quick gourmet breakfast at the Twin Brothers about five in the morning. We whisked out in the rattletrap old truck to Dr. Eskie's suburban house. As we walked in the door, all the dogs in the neighborhood began barking. Seeing all these bearded, raggedy Greenwich Villagers walking into a charming home and carrying out a piano was a little too much.

"We'd better get out of here," said Dick, "before they set up a police barricade."

Neighbors were peering suspiciously out of windows and doorways.

"It's O.K., it's O.K.," I yelled at them. "Dr. Eskie said we could take his piano. We're friends of his. Fire Island. *Mishpucha*. Patients. You know. Fire Islanders."

We piled in the truck, feeling as if we had just pulled a great bank robbery, and caromed off to the ferry, while I serenaded the neighbors, playing in the back of the truck. We put the piano on the ferry, then had it transported to the house at Ocean Beach.

The seaside was an ideal place to work. I really felt completely healthy for the first time since I'd been a kid. I decided no matter what else happened in my life, I would have to wangle some way of being close to the ocean every summer.

I began work on the Yigdal, the final section of the sacred service, and completed it in two weeks of steady work, putting aside my piano sonata. Somehow the Hebrew gave me a feeling that seemed to sound from within my bones. This language was a lost tongue. It gave me a feeling of going way back into something that I had been and that had been lost. I felt the music come out of me naturally.

The Yigdal almost wrote itself. I realized that there was something in this kind of way-back wail no matter how sophisticated a form it took that was in all my music. It was not the moaner-groaner, *oy vey ist mir* school, mostly music that came from Russian and Polish club-date orchestras. What I was doing went way back to some of the old Hebrew family trees of my father's that had roots in the fifteenth century. I felt the music I heard in my mind for the Yigdal even preceded Maimonides' thirteen Articles of Faith, written in the twelfth century, which the Yigdal was based on. Without using LSD, magic mushrooms or anything else, the Hebrew prayers turned me on to the whole pre-Christian era.

The Shakespeare Festival had a benefit in East Hampton and Joe Papp asked me to come and contribute some music. Midhat, Spike and Seymour were all visiting me at Ocean Beach.

"Let's go," said Midhat. "I'll play your piece for viola and piano, 'The Wind and the Rain.' Seymour can play the violin sonata and Spike can turn pages."

"I'll stay here and guard the door against ghosts, hobgoblins, and visiting stenographers," said my girl friend.

The four of us left and went to East Hampton. The benefit was well attended. Midhat and Seymour played beautifully and Joe Papp raised quite a bit of money. As I was about to drive back to Bay Shore and catch a ride back to Ocean Beach, I heard a familiar girlish voice.

"Ahoy, governor. Groovy sounds, I say."

It was Emma. I hadn't seen her since she had shipped out.

"Emma, I thought you were in Egypt."

"I was. Now I'm here. Come and stay with me."

"I can't. I have a little druid soul mate waiting for me in Ocean Beach."

"Ocean *Beach*? Fire *Island*? Uch-h-h! How can you stand those people?"

"They're O.K. They don't bug me. I almost have my piano sonata completed."

"Come on. I'm going back to sea in a few days."

I stayed for two days.

East Hampton is a beautiful place and Emma was staying in an enormous house. Everyone that dropped by was a high-pressured type, on the make. Not for a good time but for professional reasons.

"I don't dig it here, Emma." I said the second day.

"How do you ever expect to make it anywhere else?" she said, looking at me coolly. "Everything in New York is done through social contacts. All the important people in the arts, literature and communication pass through here."

"This is summer," I said. "You can meet every important person in the world and that won't get one page of your book written. It certainly won't make you write better."

"What does quality have to do with it?" said Emma bitterly. "They control the whole system. Look at the crap . . ."

"I know about all that. You've said that before. I'd better go."

"Wait, wait," she said. "There's a great party. You've *got* to go. We're all leaving in an hour."

"I'm not even dressed," I said. My good suit was in Spike's car, which he had driven back to Bayshore. All I had was a T-shirt, moccasins and Farmer Brown coveralls.

"You don't have to dress. You're an artist. A poor, struggling young composer, don't you see? All part of the game. Perfect."

"No," I said. "I don't want to look like a bum."

"It's informal," she said. "Come on, we're late."

We arrived and it looked from a distance like a plane crash on someone's lawn, with the spectators mobbed in a circle. Emma yanked me into the crowd.

It was too late. Everyone was exquisitely dressed, in ultra-chic informal attire. I felt like the maintenance man.

A woman in a khaki safari suit, complete with a white Frank Buck-style pith helmet and shades, sidled over. She introduced herself and when I looked through her shades, after checking my raunchy appearance in their rose-tinted reflection, I recognized her. She had been in quite a few jungle movies in the early 1930s. I'd seen her on The Late Late Show.

"I enjoyed you in *The Hidden Diamonds of Zanzibar,*" I said.

"Oh, that's all behind me now, dear," she said, clutching my arm and throwing some of that white-Jungle-goddess movie charm my way. She felt good. At least she was warm and had some life force emanating from her. But she must have been in her fifties and I was with Emma. I really missed my druid love and thought I'd better get back to Ocean Beach fast.

"I love contemporary music," said the Jungle goddess. "Since my husband passed away I've . . ."

I got her message. I saw the stocks, mutual funds, securities, capital gains, bank accounts, furs, diamonds, chauffeurs, pools, travel, buying concerts and conductors, bribery, girls on the side, months going by without composing: Destruction.

"It was great meeting you," I said.

"What's the matter?" said Emma. "She's *loaded*. You could conduct concerts of your music all over the world. You'd never have to write a note of music for a play or movie in your life. She really has the hots for you. Face it, David. You've *got* to have a patron. That's the way it's done."

"No it's not," I said. "Not my way or anybody I ever admired. That's *really* selling out."

I went back to Ocean Beach. It might have been plain, but it was great for me. Emma's view of being an insider made me decide maybe being an outsider wasn't so bad after all.

Toward the end of the summer, Dan asked me to be his best man. The wedding was going to take place at the Marlboro Music Festival at the end of its season. His wife was a lovely girl as well as being a great violinist. We both drove up in the black Volkswagen, which she had lent Dan, and jabbered away like madmen about the meaning of life, the significance of marriage, the future of music, whether or not abstract expressionism would continue in another form. Suddenly I noticed that we were sixty miles off course.

"Jesus Christ," said Dan, "I can't be late for my own wedding dinner. Still, it's such beautiful country, it's really worth it. What a view!" We must have driven ninety miles an hour and arrived at Marlboro just in time for the big dinner that was being thrown in Dan's honor the night before the wedding.

I went into a side room to change and a young fellow with curly hair came over and said, "Hi, I'm Michael Tree."

"It's a pleasure to meet you, Michael," I said. "I've heard a lot about your playing and I'm glad to meet you."

"That's wonderful," said Michael. "Would you mind trying out this fountain pen for me. I can't seem to get any ink out of it."

"Sure," I said. I thought it was funny even if I was a composer that he would think I knew more about a pen than he did. After all, he was an accomplished violinist and was more tactically oriented than I was and besides—*ba-Llah-mmm!!!* A huge explosion rocked the room and I thought perhaps I'd been caught in another gas conflagration as I'd been in Nantucket that horrible morning long ago. I was dizzy. Michael and three or four other musicians who popped in from the hallway roared with laughter.

"It's an exploding pen," they shouted gleefully. I was so frightened, I thought perhaps I would have to go to the Brattleboro hospital.

In spite of this cacophonous introduction, Marlboro was a very civilized place. The dining hall was packed with enthusiastic young musicians and their wives, families, dogs and children. Everyone seemed to love everybody. The atmosphere was friendly. I saw musicians I hadn't seen for years and the feeling was beautiful. I met Rudolf Serkin, whose playing I had admired since I was a child, and he was extraordinarily kind and gentle.

He gave me a quick, darting glance and reminded me of Mitropoulos. In one brief instant he could look at you and seem to size up everything. I felt too shy to say anything. I admired him so much I was speechless. I also met his son Peter, who was twelve years old then and brilliant. He and I sat up talking about flying saucers and astronomy most of the night after everyone else had gone to bed. He had a really way-out original mind, a great sense of humor, and was as bright as a forty-year-old man.

The next day I went out and played wiffle ball, sort of like baseball, with the musicians. I'd never seen a place where so many musicians had so much fun. They were at the end of their season and they were preparing the wedding for the new bride and groom. They decided to play the first movement of the C-Major String Quintet by Schubert as the wedding music. The dining hall was decorated with bundles of fern leaves, pine boughs and wild flowers. All kinds of wonderful food was set up, with a square dance to be held after-

wards. Dan really looked the happiest I'd ever seen him. His bride
was blushing and cheerful-looking.

A squirrelish-looking female violist came up and put her hand on
his arm. "Well, grandpa," she said, "you're finally getting married
again, eh? How do you like the idea of being *trapped?*"

"What are you doing around twelve o'clock after the wedding?"
said Dan. Giving a squeal of horror, she edged away. "You see,"
said Dan, "there are always people who try to bug you. Nothing is
sacred anymore except life itself. Wa-hoo!"

The wedding ceremony was beautiful. I was so interested in hearing the first movement of the Schubert quintet that I almost forgot
my cue as best man and Dan had to yank me forward at the end.
After the marriage, we all went to Mr. and Mrs. Serkin's for a reception and I had to make a speech. I just said how wonderful it
was for my friend Dan who was such a fine musician to be with his
brother musicians on this beautiful day. Then there was a big celebration and just before I left to go back to New York, Rudolf Serkin
came over.

"Have you written any music for us poor pianists?" he said, smiling.

"I'm finishing a piano sonata, Mr. Serkin," I told him.

"I would like to see it," he said.

I almost passed out. He was one of the greatest pianists in the
world and I was flattered that he'd even talk to me. "I'll be sure to
mail it to you," I told him.

I went down to watch Dan and his wife take off. Late in the afternoon Seymour called. He had borrowed a car, but it had blown up
on the way and he was hitchhiking to get to the wedding.

"Where's Danny?" he screamed.

"Well, Seymour, the wedding's over," I told him. "He drove away
on his honeymoon."

"God damn it. He can't do that. What the hell . . ."

"Look, Seymour, I know he wanted to see you, but he had to
leave. The thought's the important thing."

"To hell with the thought," said Seymour. "I wanted to see that
guy. God damn it. I bought a car for eighty dollars and it blew up!"

"Well," I said, "as long as you're O.K."

"Well, I am coming up anyway," said Seymour, I would have
waited for him, but I wanted to get back to Fire Island to my druid
angel, so I got a lift with a bass player and took the train out to
the Island.

In a week, I finished the last movement of the piano sonata. Much of this piece represented my feelings about the piano sounds I loved in jazz, especially the work of Thelonius Monk and Bud Powell. I also utilized a lot of my own improvising techniques on the piano. The final movement was a theme with variations based on a melody I had written in 1957 for a production of *Macbeth*. I wrote a whole set of variations in which I used the piano coloristically to exploit every possible sound and mood as if it were an orchestra.

I went to see Andrew Heath again. He told me that when I got back from California he would have the piano sonata memorized. I visited Kazan and went over the notes that he had made on *Splendor in the Grass*.

It was time to go to California. I'd never been to Hollywood in my life and I was really excited. I had all kinds of wild fantasies like everyone, of tap-dancing with Betty Grable, playing croquet with Fred Astaire, having lunch with Lana Turner and after I finished my brilliant film score, pressing my fingertips into Graumann's Magic Chinese sidewalk or whatever it was called.

I had to leave on Flight 817, United Air Lines, September 30, 1960. Dan and his wife and my druid angel and Spike waved me off.

"I'll be back with a suitcase full of money," I said. "Isn't that great, Hollywood, California. Too much. They're paying for my trip. Really something, isn't it?" I could hardly believe it. I was going to Never-Never Land, not as some yokel on a bus tour, but as an employee to write music for what appeared to be a marvelous and adventurous movie.

I got on the airplane full of hope. I could see the cigar-smoking executives badgering me with million-dollar offers while others decided to film my life story while I was conducting the Los Angeles Philharmonic and playing with my jazz group in the afternoons, saving the mornings for hanging out with the health cultists I had read about. Then I could return and compose forever.

When I got off the plane in Hollywood, the first thing I noticed were the terrible expressions on the faces of the policemen who were there. Even the worst MPs in the army and the German officials who looked the most ex-Nazi were nothing compared to these Los Angeles cops. They were really unbelievable. My first few seconds in

Los Angeles were already preparing me for the end of twenty-nine years of a moviegoer's brainwashing.

I went to the Montecito Hotel, where all good New Yorkers go when they first come to Hollywood. At the old hotel I saw a little bulletin board. It had many names of actors that I knew from off Broadway and the Shakespeare Festival and I even saw my own name there. The man at the desk asked me what I was doing. When I told him I was writing the music for *The Young Savages* his face lit up.

"I know John," he informed me confidentially. "I've been in two hundred and twenty-eight movies. If it weren't for my arthritis, I would still get some of those old fast-action roles. I've played enough gangsters to serve at least a thousand years in jail. I've played chauffeurs, con-men, hustlers, organ-grinders." He then reeled off an enormous list of his film credits, a kind of panorama *Who's Who* of all the grade-B movies made during the thirties and forties. He was the first of many people I met in Hollywood, all of whom seemed to be movie actors.

After I got a half-hour précis of his career, I excused myself and went up on the elevator to my room. An unattractive man with a crew cut rode up with me. Noticing my French horn, he asked, "Are you a musician?" I should have realized then that anyone with such a lame come-on was not worth talking to.

But because I wanted to seem like a true humanitarian I said, "Yes." Having broken the ice, he then asked me if he could come to my room for a drink. "I don't drink, my man," I said, trying not to hurt his feelings. When I got off the elevator he followed me to my door.

"Do you mind if I come in?" he said. I didn't say anything, just tried to give him the freeze. "I'm an actor," he informed me.

"No kidding," I said, "where have you acted?"

"I've never acted anyplace," he said, "but I'm going to be in the movies pretty soon. I can feel it."

"That's great," I said. "If you don't mind now, I have some things to do before I go to work tomorrow, so I'll see you. Good luck with your acting."

"Care for a blow job?" he said as he began to walk out the door.

"No thanks, that's not my scene," I responded. He then walked out casually. He provided my introduction to the second part of some of Hollywood's grotesquerie: the deadly attitude toward sex, not as anything to do with love or life force or as the great religious, physical and spiritual expression of salvation and rebirth, but as something that you offer someone like a cigarette or chewing gum.

I got up the next morning and saw John Frankenheimer, who told me I could watch the rough cut of the film. I was also supposed to meet Mr. Integrity, one of the executives connected with the film.

"Watch out for these bastards," John warned me. "These are Hollywood boys, Dave. This is different from New York. Nobody's an artist out here. Just watch out."

With these cheery words of advice, I prepared to meet Mr. Integrity. I had read a great deal about his crusading liberalism as a cinematic pioneer. I read of how as a fighting champion of first-rate art films he let nothing stand in the way of artistic merit. I had read his press releases for years and believed them. I even felt that I knew him.

We were finally introduced. Mr. Integrity was a short, nice-looking Jewish man with a Madison Avenue crew cut with that little part on the side that seems to be hollowed out by the barber. The thing I most noticed about him was his eyes. They were like so many people's eyes that I was to see in Hollywood. He would talk, looking at my ear, my shoulder, over my head and quite often turning his head around to look out the window. I was amazed to see him answering the phone and speaking to someone else while still thinking he was speaking to me. He would even speak to me but answer the person on the phone. About every five minutes his eyes would look at me with a sad look like two pieces of overripe Camembert cheese.

Each time the eyes would be directed toward me the question would always be "How do you like Hollywood? It stinks, don't it?" This would be followed by a frightened expression of pure terror waiting for the answer, followed by a look of hostility quickly modulating into a complete glassy stare as if he were dead; then the eyes would start roving around again.

I told him about my work in music and my views on music and film music and film making. Suddenly he pierced me with the strangest stare I had seen yet. His eyes remained unchanged, as if he were paralyzed. Finally I said, "Mr. Integrity, stop giving me that ray!" Suddenly his whole face contorted and twisted and he began staring up at the ceiling. It was like the expression I had seen on people who took forty or fifty pills a day, as if some new kind of spansule had exploded in his system and caused a neuro-muscular-vascular change.

After our conference ended I left with John to see the film. I noticed that he looked a little shaken.

"What's the matter man?" I questioned him. "Did I say something wrong?"

"Listen, Dave," he told me. "This isn't New York. You've got to remember that. This is a different scene. Don't tell these people everything you think."

I figured if I'd gotten through the army without groveling I was certainly not going to toady for people like this. I found out much later that outbursts of rage and anger were the only way you could make yourself clear in Hollywood.

I went to see the screening of *The Young Savages* and was really impressed. Although parts of it were Hollywood at its worst, there were flashes of brilliance that John had brought with him from his television days. I could see that the musical possibilities were enormous. I decided to use a jazz orchestra for the parts that were concerned with life in Spanish Harlem and to use an ensemble of fifty-five men for the parts that could be more symphonic, even though the orchestra music had elements of jazz in it as well. I was sent to see the studio music director to get oriented.

"O.K., kid," he said, "I want you and your helpers . . ."

"Excuse me," I said, interrupting him. "I don't use any helpers. I write my own music."

"Look, kid," he said "I've been in this business for twenty-six years. You don't have to bullshit me. Everyone out here has ghost writers and helpers."

"I'm sorry," I said, "I write my own music."

"Well, all right," he said. "A lot of kids do when they first come out. At least tell your orchestrators that . . ."

"I'm sorry," I said, interrupting again, "I don't use anyone to orchestrate my music either. I orchestrate, compose and conduct my own music."

"What?" he said, looking at me as though I were insane.

"What's so amazing about that?" I inquired. "It's not that hard."

"All right," he said, "I know plenty of wise guys who thought they knew it all. When you get to the studio you'll see. If you go over time, you'll never be asked back here again. The best way to succeed in this business is to be like everybody else."

"Look," I told him, "I'm not trying to succeed in this business. I was asked to do one film. I'm trying to succeed in music."

With that he changed the subject. "As far as the orchestra goes," he said, "I'm going to introduce you to the contractor and he'll get the men for you."

I met the contractor. He looked like a Coney Island, Surf Avenue, pool-hall hipster, police informer and numbers runner. He had on several pinky rings, a toupee, loud mismatching clothes, pointed shoes and that sleazy Damon Runyon look that you see in so many low-life people who have been able to survive hustling on a small scale and have achieved a certain stature in the lower echelons of the criminal world.

"I've got the greatest orchestra you've ever heard, sonny boy," he told me.

"Wait a minute," I said, "I haven't even told you what instruments I need yet."

"That doesn't matter," he said, hitting me with a sales pitch automatically. "We have the greatest fellows in the world out here. Our boys can do anything. You name it, we've got it."

"Actually," I said, "I have a few musicians in mind already."

"Look, kid," he interrupted me. "What the fuck do you know about Hollywood? You're from New York, ain't you?"

"Yes," I replied, "but I've been a musician since I was eleven years old and I also play French horn. I know a lot of great jazz and classical musicians who are living out here and I want to use them to play in the orchestra."

"We have our own men," he said, giving me a deadly glare.

"That may be so," I said, "but there are no more permanent studio orchestras. All of us all over the country know that. I'm a member of the Union and I know I can hire any man who's a member of this local."

"All right, who do you want to use?" he said.

"I'll get the musicians I want to use and I'll give you the list," I told him. He looked furious as I left.

I called up my friend from the Seventh Army Symphony, Stanley Plummer. Even though he played second violin in a string quartet with Jascha Heifetz, Gregor Piatigorsky, and William Primrose at Heifetz' home, he had never gotten a job playing in any kind of studio recording because he was not in the clique. Every violinist knew of him because he was teaching at the university and because he had appeared as a soloist with the Los Angeles Philharmonic. Still, no one would give him a movie job.

"Stanley," I said, "I want you to be concertmaster and select the orchestra. Just get the best musicians in Los Angeles. I don't care if they like contemporary music, if they're nice people, killers, men, women, black, white or whatever. Just get all the people who are the most beautiful free players so we can have a cooking orchestra." Whenever there is any problem in choosing musicians the best person to ask is a fine artist because they always place music before politics. Of course if you live in any particular city long enough you can find out for yourself.

For the jazz group I decided I would ask Harold Land, whom I had not seen since he left the Max Roach–Clifford Brown quintet in early 1956. I had written an arrangement for them in 1955, but I had not seen him since. I was driving around in a rented car trying to find Harold when I saw that *The Connection* was playing. I recognized a friend of mine's name on the marquee and stopped. Suddenly I saw George Morrow, the bass player who was also with Harold Land when they both played with Max and Clifford's group.

Leaning out of the window, I said, "George, what's happening?"

"Crazy, Dave," he said. "What are you doing out here?"

"Listen," I told him, "I'm doing this wild film about New York and there is a part where we need a jazz group. I'd like to get a band just with Harold, you, a good drummer and myself."

"Who's going to play piano?" he asked.

"I think I will," I said. "I brought my horn out, but my chops have been sort of bad anyway because I'm changing my embouchure, so I'll play piano."

"Groovy," he said. "I can get in touch with Harold and get a drummer that I know from San Diego and we'll come by the hotel and visit you tomorrow."

The next day Harold came by with George and Leon Petties, a wonderful drummer from San Diego. We had a session.

"We don't even need to rehearse," I said. "I'll just write out some simple things and we'll go in and play for the picture and it will come out great. We'll just go in and have some fun and play some real music. Maybe we can go in and show them what some for-real music sounds like in a film." They all agreed that this was the best way to do it.

Stanley gave me the names for the symphony orchestra, so I went back to see the music contractor. He looked quizzically at the names. "Who's Harold Land?" he inquired.

"If you know anything about jazz," I said, "Harold Land is one of the best tenor-saxophone players in the world. He played with Max Roach and Clifford Brown's quintet and he's a terrific player."

"I never heard of him," he said. "He can't be any good. Where is he from?"

"About eleven blocks from here," I replied.

"Who's these other two guys?"

"George Morrow and Leon Petties." I told him what great musicians they were and that we'd already had a jam session and they more than met my qualifications. He had listened so far with growing hostility.

"Are they schvartzes?" he said, leaning forward intimately.

"I don't think they would ask if we were kikes," I replied.

"All right," he said. "You do it your way. You'll be sorry. Them schvartzes never show up on time."

"Duke Ellington has been showing up on time for the last thirty-five years," I replied.

"All right kid," he said, "you'll learn. You have them beatniks, schvartzes, dope-fiend musicians on that record date and you'll never be asked back to Hollywood."

"I don't care," I told him. "I'm just trying to make my music sound good. Here's the list of the musicians I want for the orchestra." Most of the classical musicians he knew, but when I told him I wanted Stanley Plummer to be the concertmaster he grew furious.

"Who the fuck do you think you are?" he asked in his rather aggressive style. "We got all these great violinists here. Do you think they're going to sit behind some young punk and play good?"

"That's my worry," I replied. "I'm conducting the orchestra and I want my music to sound good. There are a lot of solos and I know Stanley can play them beautifully. He still loves music with his heart and soul. He's not a commercial killer."

"What do you mean?" he questioned, looking more like a killer than he did commercial.

"I mean when you play for real, that makes it sound for real. It'll make my music sound better," I answered.

"Impossible," he said.

"Look," I said, taking out some music I had written. I noticed suddenly a blank expression come over his face.

"I don't read music," he said.

"Well, you know. At least you play an instrument. There's certain kinds of music that . . ."

"I don't play no instrument either," he told me.

"How come you're a contractor then?" I said.

"Listen, kid," he said, "you're never going to be a success in Hollywood. You ask too many questions."

"Just get those musicians," I said. "You're going to be out here the rest of your life. I'm just here for one picture. Do what I want and don't bug me."

Seeing that we'd reached an impasse, he left and I went back to the Montecito to work on the music. A little later the phone rang and it was Mr. Integrity. "What are you doing choosing some unknown kid to be a concertmaster?" he barked over the phone. "The men won't play."

I couldn't believe my ears. Mr. Integrity, pioneering, liberal crusader of the artistic film world, the man whose press releases constantly mentioned how he broke away from the shackles of the old Hollywood to search for new artistic standards was telling me whom I should have for the concertmaster of my orchestra. "The men won't play for him," he kept repeating. "The music director's very disturbed." Finally I blew my cool and shouted at him the same way that I had heard him shout at other people.

"Get this straight," I shouted, "leave me alone and let me do what I want. Most of the music you hear out here is stolen from the cesspools of used-up hacks. I'll do something that will make your picture better than it would be otherwise. I don't care if I never come to Hollywood again, but I want to make this music good because it will have my name on it and I don't want to do something I'll be ashamed of the rest of my life."

"That's wonderful, kid," he said, his voice suddenly changing into a seductive purr. "I think you have great talent. Keep up the good work."

With this about-face he hung up the phone and I went back to writing the music. About two weeks later the score was complete and we went into record. I had all kinds of instructions that I had written into my score to tell the musicians how to produce certain nuances. After the first few seconds I realized it was unnecessary. Even reading it through the first time, the members of the orchestra played so beautifully that there was really nothing for me to do but hope someone would miss a note so I would have an excuse to go back and hear the music performed so well again.

The only unpleasant thing was the hate rays that the violinists were directing toward Stanley. But being a cosmologically cool cat himself, he just acted as if he didn't notice it. For the first hour and a half of our recording I noticed that the musicians had that dead look that I've seen on the faces of people who are wonderful artists and are forced to play recordings. Usually they have to perform the kind of trashy music they are ashamed to even think about. As a result, they have to turn themselves off, as if they are in another world. But after about two hours, when they saw that I was really trying to prove something with my music and what a good time I was having, the atmosphere began to change. By the third hour they were often roaring with laughter between takes, especially during one cue when in the middle of conducting I started playing the French horn and conducting with my foot.

"What's that laughing?" the musical director said, running out with a wrinkled look of anxiety spreading across his suntanned face.

"Listen, man," I told him, "we're just having a good time. Go away and quit bugging us." After that we had no more problems and we finished recording the entire score two hours ahead of schedule.

One night when I was off, I went to hear Ornette Coleman. He was playing in Hollywood, and I hadn't heard him since the Five Spot.

He and his group sounded beautiful. Don Cherry was the first trumpeter I had heard play the new way who could make so much music. He had his own sound just as Ornette had his. Scott La Faro was playing bass and I talked to him afterward.

"I love playing with Ornette," said Scott. "He's some composer too. He wrote five new things yesterday. He composes all the time. The more I get into his music, the more I dig it."

"It's funny seeing you guys out here," I said.

"It's funny seeing *you* here," said Scott. "You going to settle down here and make a million?"

"Are you going to join Lawrence Welk?" I countered.

"Crazy," said Scott. "You know Ornette's back trying to get our money. The owner doesn't want to come across with all the bread. So Ornette offered to shoot craps with him and settle it that way."

The group came out and played once more. I could hear Ornette's composer's brilliance in his playing. They were all cooking. They really made me miss New York. I felt as if I were serving a jail sentence, even though I was getting paid well for my crime. I knew I could never stay in Hollywood. Ornette's group reminded me of when I heard them at the Five Spot and when I played the Five Spot. Somehow that shabby Bowery bar seemed more beautiful to me than all of Hollywood.

The next day it was time to record with the jazz group. Harold and his group had a job in San Francisco and they agreed to come back and miss a night's sleep to make the date. But naturally they wanted their plane fare and Harold wanted double scale, seeing that his improvising was a large part of the contribution to the music. This was not only more than reasonable, it was the barest of necessities and only fair.

"Let me talk to these guys," said the music director. "I know how to talk to them schvartzes."

"Listen," I said, "if you speak to them, they won't even show up for the job."

"What do ya mean?" he said. "I got the greatest musicians," and he reeled off the names of hot-shot hipster musicians of the thirties, all of whom had settled down to the lucrative film-music recording work at the expense of giving up their individuality. While they were excellent players and deserved the money they made, they had lost that fire and spark that great improvisers have. The real jazz players have it because it means more to them than anything else in their lives and they spend hours a day perfecting it.

"Don't worry, man, I'll pay the plane fare and double scale myself," I said.

"Listen," he said, "them coons are going to take the money and not even show up. They'll never get on the plane that early. They're unreliable."

"The date went great yesterday, didn't it, and the concertmaster played great, right?" I said.

"Yeah," he said, "but that's different."

"I'll be responsible and if they don't show up I'll play everything on the piano. Don't worry." I realized that half of this man's obnoxious behavior came from his own insecurity and the fact that he knew he was completely unqualified for his job. Like many people in Hollywood, he was overcompensated for work he was not really equipped to do.

I showed up at the studio a half-hour ahead of time to practice the piano parts because I had spent so much time writing and studying the orchestral scores that I conducted the day before. I wasn't really that familiar with the tunes I had written for the jazz section and during the parts where I improvised I wanted to be able to look at the film while I was playing, so I wanted to know the chord changes by heart. Five minutes after I got there, Harold, Leon and George arrived, twenty-five minutes head of schedule, and we sat down and just started playing. By the time we were ready to record, we were way ahead of schedule.

The session went off fantastically well. It was more like a party than a recording date. (After the picture came out, Columbia Records released an album, one side the symphonic music and the other side us playing jazz. Although it wasn't around very long, we got great reviews and it's still something that's performed on some jazz shows. In terms of jazz life that's pretty good longevity.) As we were playing, people from other sound studios gathered and by the end of the three-hour session we actually had a large crowd.

"Where did you get those boys from?" I was asked.

"They live a few blocks from here," I answered. "Right in Los Angeles. They're natives."

One of the tunes I named "Harold's Way," and the other version "Harold's Way Out." That's because there was a street close to the studio named Harold's Way, and as we played Harold Land's great smoky, serpentine sound filled up the whole studio with a kind of soul and warmth and realness that was not part of the Hollywood movie scene at all. On one particular tune I got so involved in playing that I continued even after the filming was over and played about a two minute chorus, which later was one of the most frequently played sides on the sound-track record.

Harold said, "Yeah, Dave, you *played* on that one."

"I didn't even know what I was doing, Harold," I said.

"That's the way you play the best sometimes," he said.

The next day I saw Mr. Integrity again and he wanted to know if I would stay out till the following spring to see if there was any other work around.

"Man, I don't like it here at all," I said. "I want to go back. After I finish the music for *Splendor in the Grass* I have several chamber pieces to write, an orchestral work and a sacred service."

"A sacred service?" he bellowed. "How many people do you think are going to hear your chamber music and sacred service? A few hundred, if you're lucky a few thousand? If you do music for films you'll reach people all over the world."

"My name might reach people all over the world," I said, "but my music wouldn't because they're not going to be able to hear it. I don't want my music to be in the background all my life. I want it to be in the foreground."

"You're a talented boy. I'd think it over carefully. You could do very good here if you'd learn to play the game. Look at me. I used to be a dancer and an agent. I thought I'd burn up the world. I starved. I finally got wise. Now I live great. I have a beautiful painting collection. I'm a totally adjusted happy man." Then his eyes began to go through their modulating series of looks.

I left and went back to the Montecito. The next day the mix began. During the mix there were three men who worked for the master control board: the sound-effects man, the music man and the dialogue man. For two days I kept quiet and watched the three of them trying in every kind of ingenious way to make their part the loudest because Academy Awards are given to sound effects men and to music men. As a result there was a constant conflict. The dialogue man of course had to make sure that the speech was heard. In control of these three people was a master mixer who tried to balm everyone's feelings. Like most of the technicians, these people were extremely good at their jobs because in Hollywood the technicians were the only people that really had a definite skill. Their function was to constantly save all the genius' errors, chop up and doctor the yards of mediocrity to make it come out like a cohesive film. While most Hollywood movies are far from masterpieces, the dissolves, the sound effects, the mixing, the lighting, the editing of movies, are usually close to perfection.

I respected these men for their workmanship. Most of them were Southern California farmer types. I just kept quiet. During the whole day, the introductory music was mixed and while the credits were run, the two different gangs in the film, both represented by a different kind of music, were shown walking down the street. Because there was a theme for one of them which occurred later in the picture, I was rather shocked when a distant truck that was shown a few blocks away in the film began approaching and the sound-effects man turned up truck noises until they obliterated all the music.

"I'm not trying to interfere with your job," I said, "but would it be possible to turn down the sound effects at this point a little so that you can hear the music at least enough to know what the theme is. It occurs later on in the picture and the audience should be familiar with this in the beginning so that they can identify it every time they hear it."

The sound-effects man turned around and gave me an awful glare as if he had caught me robbing his orange grove. "It will take a bigger man than you to make me turn down this mixing pot, sonny," he said icily.

A little later Mr. Integrity walked in and in order to impress upon him what a good job he was doing, the sound-effects man boosted the lever controlling the mixing pot as far forward as it would go. When the image of the truck appeared on the screen, the howling squeal was deafening. Because of Mr. Integrity's highly nervous nature, he let out a squeal of his own and showed some of his old training as a dancer by leaping about a foot and a half in the air and spinning around the room in a paroxysm of pain.

"Stop that! Stop, stop!" he shouted. "It's *killing* me!"

The sound-effects man, like most other people in Hollywood, was extremely respectful of anyone who was in a higher position than he was. Without saying a word, he leaned over his mixing pot and turned the sound down until it was almost inaudible.

I found that during the mix and cutting of the picture, everytime anyone said *anything* about the picture—even one time when I suggested that an entire scene be cut—the suggestion was taken. No matter what it was, nearly anything that Mr. Integrity heard, he would take seriously and put into effect. It was unbelievable, especially after reading about his pioneering, crusading, liberal, tough-minded idealism as an independent film maker. I think his publicity agents would have had a more interesting story if they had written how he really was.

Finally the film was completed. As I was about to leave, Mr. Integrity said, "Listen, you did a good job. We're going to have a preview and I want you to come and see it."

"Great," I said, "I want to bring along a wonderful girl I met."

"No can do," he said.

"Why not? She's not a reporter. She would just like to see what I've been doing for the five weeks I've been here."

"No," he said, "no one can come. No one knows where the theater is and you can't bring her."

"Then I'm not coming," I told him. When I got back home, his secretary called me up and said, "Look, don't make waves. Do what he says."

"I'm very sorry. I'm not a slave. If there were tickets for sale I would buy one. I just want to bring someone with me. I found out that the people who are working on the film are bringing their wives. I want to bring a girl with me."

"You don't understand," she said. "These previews are as secret as the atomic-bomb tests were during World War II. They are so worried about actors and other people coming and filling out the cards."

"What cards?"

"You'll see," she said. "White cards are given out and then the people who have seen the film will fill them out and say whether or not they liked certain parts."

"Well, I'm not coming," I said. "I'm sorry." A few minutes later she called back and told me that Mr. Integrity had invited me and my girl friend to meet everyone at the Chinese restaurant. After dinner we went on the bus to the preview, which was way out in some farming community about eighty miles away. Everybody in the bus looked as if they were driving to witness an execution. During the film, I sat back with my girl and we enjoyed watching it. As we left afterward we saw Mr. Integrity. His face was ashen.

"How are the cards?" he said out of the side of his mouth. "How are the cards?" There was a grim conference afterward, during which all the cards were studied as if it were a jury voting on life or death. I noticed that most of the people watching the film seemed to be farmers and I had heard that when the weather got cold, people would leave during the middle of the film to make sure that their oranges were safe and that sometimes these films would not get released because the producers seeing the audience walk out on them would feel it had no appeal. With the addition of two or three key cities, these previews determined the film maker's decision on the reaction of the entire world audience, a procedure that explains the quality of most films that are released. It also explains the number of bombs at the box office. One of the questions on the card was how people liked the music. Apparently a lot of people did, because I was told the next day I would have to write some more.

"For what part of the picture?"

Mr. Integrity said, "The love scene on the roof."

I felt there was plenty of music under that scene. Any more would make it sentimental and sloppy. It was an embarrassing scene of a boy and a girl standing on a roof talking about their parents with two actors that looked like dropouts from Hollywood High with those young professional show-biz faces. The way they tried to register any kind of emotion would make you leave them no tip after they served you a banana sundae.

"Listen, kid, this part needs some music. You better think about it because if you leave now, we're going to fly you back."

"I'm sorry, I have work to do. I'm not going to write music for that part," I said, and left for New York.

The day after I got back home I received a phone call from Mr. Integrity. "If you don't come back and write music for that part, we'll take your music and play it backwards," he said.

"How about playing it sideways?"

"Listen, kid, I'm not kidding. If you don't come back, we'll use someone else's music."

This was a common practice. Because I didn't want my name on any of the garbage usually used, I had to agree to go back. Two days later I was flown back to record three minutes of music. We recorded it, the musicians went home. Just as I was leaving the studio, I saw Mr. Integrity skittle like a crab across the recording-studio floor.

"Hi," I said. "How did you like that? As long as I came all the way out here I hope you heard it."

"Don't worry, kid," he said. "I'm sure it will be fine," and he continued to wherever he was going.

Ultimately, no music was used in this scene anyway. But when I went to see the final version of the film I noticed that the piece I had recorded had been used someplace else, where it was completely inappropriate.

Right after I got back from Hollywood I began work on "Discussion for Flute, Cello, Piano and Percussion." Oscar Pettiford had died and I was writing the piece in his memory.

On the night of November 2 I went to the corner of Eighth Street and Sixth Avenue to buy a paper. There, in black, impersonal print was the news that Dimitri Mitropoulos had died while conducting a rehearsal of Mahler's Third Symphony at La Scala, Milan. I read the article twice, folded up the newspaper and started walking.

I walked all night until the sun came up the next day. Every time I tried to think about something else, I saw his face. I could see the wing collar he wore when he conducted. I could see him bowing to the orchestra, bowing to the audience and looking far off, the way he always did when the music was over.

He had always heard something no one else did, because he knew something no one else did. You could tell it just by being in his presence. Now, no one would ever know his secret. All we could do was remember that face and the eyes that looked as if they were from another time. The half-flickering smile, the great domed head, the compassion and sense of irony that he radiated in his gentle, loving way. I knew he had simply left his body behind. He didn't need or want it anymore. The report said that he jokingly told someone he was like an old car, slowly breaking down and that when he conducted he no longer found his body of much use to him.

It seemed so clear to me as I walked. Of all the people I had ever met in my life, Mitropoulos alone knew that the body was only a vehicle for the soul. It was almost an encumbrance to him. Everything else, except the life and language of the spirit, was almost silly to him.

As the sun rose that morning, the day had a calm, yellowish, dusty glow. I had not lost a hero, father, brother or friend. For the rest of my life I could think of him and try to fathom the secret that he had left his countless friends all over the world. At best, all the thousands of musicians I had met could leave the world their music. Mitropoulos had left the world his soul.

I resumed work the next day. As I worked on my music, I thought about what Mitropoulos had said when we went to the movies on Forty-second Street a few years before. I remembered how he felt doubly sorry for film composers who did nothing else. First, because most of their music could scarcely be heard. Secondly, because they became slaves of the easy way and did nothing else.

I saw in the year 1960—just a few days before my thirtieth birthday—that I could become Mr. Background Music if I wanted to, what with the work I had done in the theater, television and now two big films. Because I always knew that my job in life was to try to have my music add something to the world, the only way films could be useful would be to interest people in my other music. I decided I had better limit the amount of work I was going to do in this area. I could probably become a millionaire if I devoted myself to this work and nothing else. I was able to write music for these films very fast and very well. I could conduct, orchestrate and play some of the instruments during the recording. But even if I would improve the standard of film music, I would lose the meaning of my life in the process.

After *The Young Savages* I could hardly wait to finish the music for *Splendor in the Grass* and get back to my own work full-time.

Working with Kazan again was very stimulating. Somehow, being in New York made the film more real. It was like the atmosphere when *J.B.* was being done. Because of Kazan's theatrical mastery, he tried to make the actors feel as if they were a part of a situation that was real and alive, not merely puppets to be photographed. Kazan invited me to come and watch the filming so that I could feel I was a part of the film. I even appeared in one of the scenes as a member of a band, dressed in a tuxedo, playing my French horn, while Pat Hingle told Warren Beatty how to survive if the stock market crashed. Our quartet and Maurice Peress all ran around the set in our 1929-style tuxedos, feeling like the Barrymore family.

We had a terrific band for the film including Buster Bailey, a veteran clarinetist who was there when jazz actually first started. His contribution, George Barrow's sax solos, and Maurice's trumpet playing made the entire film more joyful and alive.

Unlike the Hollywood system of decisions through rampant paranoia, Elia Kazan would not allow anyone to tell him what to do. He welcomed suggestions from everyone, but he was the final boss about everything.

After I had completed the score, Jack Warner came to New York to see a preview. Apparently he fancied himself as a kind of stand-up comic. After he had completed a few jokes that I remember my grandfather telling me and I failed to laugh, he suddenly looked at me and said, "Who are you, the undertaker?"

His retinue automatically roared with laughter.

"No, I'm David Amram," I said. "I wrote the music."

"Well, here's another bright boy," he said. "Listen, there's a lot of young people nobody knows about, they got a big break working with this guy, Kazan. Leonard Bernstein did his first film score, *On the Waterfront*, for him. Who knows?" he said, looking around at his retinue and throwing up his hands, "this boy may be another Leonard Bernstein." Then, looking at me again, he said, "Who's greater than Leonard Bernstein?"

"Beethoven," I answered. Mr. Warner turned back to his retinue and didn't bother me anymore.

As we watched the screening of the picture I noticed him slumped on the seat and for the first hour heard him occasionally snoring. He woke up during the picture and would drop off again.

After it was over he said to Kazan, "Very nice, Gadge, I call that a real slice of life. I've only got one criticism—that part where the girl is yawning, cut it out."

"What?" asked Kazan, getting a little edge.

"I said, cut it out," said Jack Warner. "I don't have yawns in my movies, it makes people fall asleep."

Look who's talking, I thought.

Kazan said, "We'll do it my way, Jack."

"O.K., Gadge," said Jack Warner, and looked at his retinue to calm them down as they were getting nervous that someone seemed to have disagreed with the Pascha. "After all," he said expansively, turning to his retinue, "he's a genius, you know."

After the music for *Splendor in the Grass* was finished, Andrew Heath performed my piano sonata at the Grace Rainey Rogers Auditorium of the Metropolitan Museum. It went very well and I was proud of his performance. He played the entire work from memory. A lot of our old friends from the army came to hear him.

I worked on "Discussion for Flute, Cello, Piano and Percussion" at my usual keyed-up pace. Because of all the percussion I had used in *The Young Savages* I felt at home with these instruments. When we rehearsed it, all the musicians felt that I had written my best work yet, incorporating jazz and Latin American elements into a concert piece. Of course the use of the instruments, in addition to their bizarre coloristic effects, made it possible to make more definite the implied jazz elements that I had in so much of my music. In the opening flute solo, I tried to paint a musical portrait of Oscar's personality. "Discussion" was done on the same program as a brilliant piece, "Progressions," by Harold Farberman for flute and two percussion instruments and "Sequenza" by Luciano Berio. The whole concert was a great success for John and for all the composers involved. It really encouraged me to get back to work on my sacred service.

Many of my friends couldn't understand how I could work day and night on a piece for which I was being paid nothing. I stopped trying to explain why I was spending the next four months writing a work for one hundred dollars. I knew why.

11

I HAD promised Stuart Vaughan that I would do the music for *Hamlet*, which opened March 16. But every other second of my time day and night was devoted to my sacred service. I didn't answer one letter, go to any parties, movies, concerts or bars. By April it was completed and we were ready to begin rehearsals.

The opening three notes of the service provided the unifying motif for the entire work. I imagined them as being symbolic of some kind of giant ram's horn. I realized when the service was nearly completed that these three notes were similar to what I had heard the old man singing in the synagogue in Frankfort seven years before. Somehow his croaking voice in the middle of a prayer had stayed in my mind. His old, craggy face and the whole scene of that service returned to me again as I completed the final pages.

In spite of our many arguments, philosophic discussions and constant concern about how the prayers could be most effectively set to music, Cantor Putterman and I always agreed about one thing: Maurice Peress would be the ideal conductor for my sacred service. Maurice seemed to have an instinctive feeling for liturgical music. His father was an Arab-speaking Jew from Iraq who played and sang beautifully. His mother was from a very religious family in Poland. Maurice, like myself, was a runaway from home who had come up the hard way in music. He had worked in every area of music but never lost his direction. He had that old lyric feeling when he played the trumpet and when he conducted.

Maurice began to accompany me each week as I worked with Cantor Putterman. The cantor was a man who was a truly old soul. Even

385

if we never got together without arguing, I loved him like a second father and he treated me like his third son. His knowledge of Hebrew and the subtle inflection of the prayers, the accents and drama of the religious text was extraordinary. When he sang the traditional music to the prayers, and especially "the counting of the Omer," it sounded as if he were going back five thousand years in a time machine. I always felt I was listening to a voice out of the desert. Even though he was in his sixties, his tenor had a quality that could reduce you to tears within a second. It had a melancholy, wailing-wall sound.

It had been a long time since my grandfather had taught me Hebrew as a little boy. My father had taught us Sunday school on our farm. I remembered how we had talked about the men who wrote the Bible. My father felt they were probably Hebrew shepherds who lay in the fields with their sheep, staring up at the stars to think about God. Hearing Cantor Putterman talk and sing brought back that old mystical feeling. He made me aware of the poetry and soul of Jewish music and consequently made me look deeper into the eyes and souls of my fellow Jews and non-Jews alike. In a certain way I went through what so many other people in America go through when they find the greatness and poetry in their own heritage. I could just be more me than ever, and enjoy it.

The experience of writing the service was like a delayed Bar Mitzvah for me. I had never had one because my father was away during the war. When my mother and I wanted to join a synagogue in Washington, the admission fee was almost half my father's yearly salary as a government worker. As a result, I became a temple drop-out for the next seventeen years.

But during the time that I wrote the sacred service I gained a new part of my manhood, even though I was thirty instead of thirteen. It didn't make me suddenly feel like a professional Jew. I was a professional musician. It didn't make me want to go out and slaughter the goyim, although there was certainly enough precedent for that kind of violence in the Old Testament. Nor did it make me want to renounce my American citizenship and join the Israeli army. What it did do was to make me aware of the great brotherhood that I had with all men. It made me understand that the love of nature, the joy of the physical as well as the spiritual world, was a natural part of my tradition. I saw that the Calvinistic attitudes of so many assimilated Jews no longer had to bug me because they were values designed for someone else, not me. I saw that my feeling of always being an outsider was something that was natural and that by acknowledging my own ancestral vibrations I could enjoy life every second just by knowing more who I was.

As the months went by my whole life began to make more sense. I realized as I got into the core of my own feelings that Allen Ginsberg, while he looked like Karl Marx and came on like Bhudda, was like me. I had felt a kinship with him when we worked together on *Pull My Daisy* the year before. Even though we had different habits of living, there was a certain Talmudic rhythm and great yea-saying energy in his finer works that predated his debt to Walt Whitman. He had the old Jewish wail.

I really looked forward to the first performance of my sacred service. With Cantor Putterman's unique artistry, the rehearsals and the fine choir, we had prospects of an excellent performance. I was given unlimited free passes because the temple held almost two thousand people. So I went down to the Village with friends of mine a few days before the premier, spreading the news and the passes around.

The night of the performance there was a fantastic turn-out. People from the theater whom I had worked with, many concert musicians, like Felix Galimir, who was to help me so much at Marlboro, the great jazz pianist Randy Weston, Dan, Seymour, Emma, my druid maiden, Spike, Midhat, Malcolm, painters, writers, poets and pals. It was a beautiful event. Afterward we had an *Oneg Shabbat,* a kind of reception with cookies and tea in the basement of the temple. My father was called up on the platform with Maurice. He looked so pleased, some people thought he was me. Mel Brooks came up with Anne Bancroft and whispered in my ear, "Man, you're the Jewish Bach!" Friends from the Village and the Lower East Side who had never even been that far uptown in their lives were there. Jewish hipsters who hadn't been in a temple since they were children were there. It was a wild event and somehow very meaningful in a contemporary way. The non-Jews enjoyed it as much as the Jews and as Horty Lambert said to me afterward when we all went down to Dillon's tavern in the Village, "Old friends that pray together, stay together." It was really a treat and that's part of what religion should be.

I had sent Rudolph Serkin my piano sonata a month after Andrew had performed it, and to my amazement, he wrote a letter back, telling me that he would like me to be a guest composer at the Marlboro music festival for the summer of 1961. I was surprised that he had remembered me, much less would offer me this position. I was told that I could come during August. The way my schedule was arranged, I felt that this would be satisfactory if I planned everything right.

Jerry Tarack had asked me on behalf of the Beaux Arts Quartet to write a string quartet. I thought about it and couldn't resist the opportunity. I rummaged through all my string quartet sketches that night and with the exception of one that I was especially fond of, threw all of them in the wastebasket.

I went up to Marlboro as the guest composer in August. I had a Norwegian girl friend and we stayed in a kind of attic in one of the dormitory buildings there. The musicians rehearsed my "Discussion for Flute, Cello, Piano and Percussion." It was to be performed in two weeks and I had almost fourteen hours to rehearse it. I was able to attend other rehearsals and concerts and be with the performers all the time.

It was the nicest time I had ever spent with musicians. I brought my horn along to play a little jazz and some chamber music. The musicians all worked like demons. They all took turns waiting on the table and working in the kitchen. Every night, there was a concert. Often people who did not play during the regular weekend concerts for the public would play in the dining hall. Everyone else would show up informally in shirt sleeves to listen, applaud and encourage their sound brothers and sisters. The most accomplished instrumentalists, many of them famous concert artists, would play with beginners. It was really what Rudolph Serkin dreamed when he created Marlboro: a true republic of equals.

Serkin set the whole tone of the place. He had such love and fondness for everyone there. He cared so deeply for all that was good in music, it was impossible not to feel joy and happiness whenever he was around. He was like a father to all of us. Musicians would come hundreds of miles to visit and feel the wonderful atmosphere. At Marlboro the musicians and their music were what was important. There were no conductors, no patrons, no authoritarian figures to relegate the performers into the roles of cabdrivers or servants.

I heard marvelous music day and night. Everyone seemed interested in my music and encouraged me to continue composing. They read through a great many works of mine, making them sound better than I imagined was possible.

I heard Michael Tree and David Soyer perform Kodály's Duo for Violin and Cello. It really made an impression on me. Watching David Soyer, tall, dark and foreboding, playing the cello, and Michael Tree playing the violin part with all of his heart and soul reminded me of jazz men I knew. They were both wailing. The summer before when I had met Michael and he had handed me the exploding pen, I knew what a fine player he was, but his practical jokes made me forget how serious he was about music. Now I saw that he was completely carried away when he performed, sometimes almost jumping out of his chair with excitement.

A few days later he and David told me they were forming a trio and wanted to know if I could write a piece for them, to be performed in about a year.

"Sure," I said. I told them that I would have to finish my string quartet first but that with a year's notice I certainly could write something for their trio. It really made me feel good to be asked. I went with my horn and my girl friend down to a rehearsal room and began having a jam session with a cellist and pianist. After a while Myron Bloom played horn and I played piano. Chris Von Baeyer, the cellist, and Mike Bloom were improvising like mad. It sounded so good, I stopped to listen.

"What's the matter?" said Myron jokingly. "Run out of ideas, Amram?"

"No," I said, "I was just listening to how great you two sounded together. That's a terrific combination, just the horn and cello."

"Why don't you write a piece for horn and cello?" said Myron. "I have a concert next spring in Cleveland. If it's any good, I'll play it there."

"Solid!" I said, excited.

I decided that after I finished my string quartet, I would write my piece for horn and cello next and call it "Three Songs for Marlboro." I figured I could do that between the time my quartet was done and the time I would have to work on another project.

A few weeks later, Maurice Peress gave me a call. "Davy," he shouted over the phone, "you'll never believe it."

"What's that?" I said. Whatever it was, I was ready to believe it.

"I'm one of the three new assistant conductors with the New York Philharmonic this year." I almost didn't believe it. Maurice was finally getting some acknowledgment for his talent.

"Now when someone asks you why you get that unknown cat to conduct your music and says who the hell is Maurice Peress, you'll be able to tell them. Can you imagine that?" he said, laughing. "It's really wonderful. I'll be able to learn so much and it will be a real experience. I never even knew Leonard Bernstein and he picked me from the whole group of people. It's really exciting."

I was happy. I had had so much good luck since I met Maurice, I was glad to see that it was starting to be shared by my friends as well. Midhat had gotten into the Metropolitan Opera Orchestra, Ken Schermerhorn was now conducting all over the world, Ed London was teaching at Smith and composing better than ever, Dan was happily married, playing the French horn and painting away like mad, and Seymour was working a lot more too, though he wasn't getting as much of a chance to play solos as he would have liked. He performed the Mozart Violin Concerto in the park during one of our concerts that summer and did very well. Spike was starting to play a lot, and Jay Cameron, back from Paris, was tearing up the jazz world, along with Pepper Adams and most of the musicians who had played with Oscar.

It seemed as if all of us who had come together by chance had begun to have good luck. I hoped that it would continue that way. I moved back to Sixth Avenue and worked on my string quartet day and night.

The Beaux Arts Quartet decided that they wanted to play my piece at Town Hall the following February. They suggested I have another Town Hall concert. I decided to have my "Discussion," piano sonata, which Richard Goode from Marlboro was interested in performing, and my new string quartet done in the first half, and the sacred service for the second half. George Shirley agreed to sing the cantor's solos and Tom Pyle got a chorus of professional singers. I wasn't able to run the concert myself so we had a professional concert manager put on the concert. I thought I might break even.

Dave Lambert's ex-wife, Horty, told me about a great place outside Woodstock that she was sharing with some other people. She suggested I go there with my Norwegian girl friend because with the piano that was already there, it would be a wonderful place to compose and it only cost twenty dollars a month for a share.

We took the bus to Woodstock and I spent the next six weeks completing my string quartet and beginning work on "Three Songs for

Marlboro," my piece for French horn and cello. I spent New Year's Eve ushering in 1962 with my girl friend, and Bob Ray, a fellow Greenwich Villager, and his girl. When I thought about the madhouse of New York, I realized how great it was to be out in the country.

Shortly after New Year's Day I was well into "Three Songs for Marlboro." It was a weekday, I was all alone and my whole body felt like ice.

"My God," I thought, "I must be dying." I had spent the whole night dreaming of the piece I was writing. In my dream I found that because of being in the country, it seemed that I could think more simply about the music and get to the essence of the pure expressive sound I was after. The French horn and cello had a very bucolic kind of feeling as I imagined them playing together. I remember dreaming about the sounds coming from snowdrifts and frosty, ice-covered fields, surrounded by winter-white hills.

When I woke up, I found myself in an icelike state. I realized something was wrong. I touched my head and it was like ice. What a drag, I thought to myself. Next month I'm having a whole concert of my music at Town Hall and I'll never live to see it. Who the hell wants a memorial concert at my age? I lay in bed for another hour, trying to imagine what my funeral would be like and who would come to it, what kind of speeches would be made, and whether or not any of my music would be performed during the services. I also wondered how many of my old girl friends would come to the funeral. A lot of them came to my concerts and were all very friendly, but, I suddenly thought, suppose none of them show up at my funeral. That would serve me right for never having gotten married. No sobbing wives and ex-wives, no sobbing children, no mourning grandchildren. What a drag to die so young.

Finally, I thought, before I expired I would at least get as far as the window to see the snow-covered fields. I didn't want to die looking at that crummy brown wallpaper, with its grim floral design like an old calling card from the Depression.

I got up, and except for the fact that I felt so cold, I seemed to be all right. I noticed that I could see my breath quite clearly. I touched the side of the wall and it was like ice. Good Lord, I said to myself, there is no heat! I looked out the window at the thermometer. It was seven degrees below zero. I went over to the radiator. Nothing.

Apparently the heating system had completely broken down during the night. The inside of the house was subzero. I'd never been this cold, even in the army. I began rubbing myself, slapping myself, and putting on my clothes, trying to get warm. I lit the oven and the stove. I turned on the hot water in order to warm up my hands which felt frostbitten. Nothing happened. I ran outside and saw under the house that some of the pipes had already burst. I called up the heating man and he told me that this had happened in a lot of places because of the tremendous cold snap that had developed overnight. I called up Horty Lambert and told her that I would be glad to help pay for the damage, but I suspected that our winter hideout was over. It had been great while it lasted.

I came back from Woodstock and felt trapped in New York. Because I had spent nearly two months in the woods, the city began to make me feel closed in. I began thinking about the countryside again and how good it was to live there. I knew that if it hadn't been for New York, I might not even be working in music except as a hobby. I was grateful, but the most elegant parties, the greatest buildings, the most important musical events—anything and everything seemed pallid in comparison to the joy I felt in my spirit by the seashore or out in the country.

I knew that of any city in the world except Paris, New York was my home for the rest of my life. Still I felt trapped being back and this was augmented by the fact that everyone else seemed trapped too. Even people who lived in gigantic floor-through apartments with doormen, elevator operators and servants were trapped. We were all victims of the foul air and the soot that came creeping over everything, accompanied by the ingenious nemesis of man—the indestructible cockroach. The cockroaches had found me again. My Sixth Avenue apartment was crawling with them when I came back. I launched an all-out war, a blitzkrieg followed by a pincers movement. After emptying eight cans of insecticide, I killed the majority of them in one final skirmish in the kitchen, flushing out a hidden horde that had encamped inside my hot plate. I almost asphyxiated myself in the process.

I sent "Three Songs for Marlboro" to Arnold Arnstein to have copied. The performance was supposed to be March 6. I figured that Myron Bloom, the French hornist, and the cellist would have time to practice it. As I prepared for my concert, I got a call telling me that John Frankenheimer wanted me to come to California again to work on the movie *The Manchurian Candidate*. He sent me the script and

I thought it was very interesting. It was different from the book and I could see that there were possibilities of composing something exceptional for the film. I knew I could use the money, because it looked as though my concert might not break even.

As it turned out, it was very fortunate that I worked on *The Manchurian Candidate*, because otherwise there would have been no concert. Not realizing the cost, I did whatever my concert manager told me in the way of advertising and also paid all the expenses, including a professional thirty-two-voice chorus, musicians and soloists.

A few weeks before the concert, toward the end of January, I was commissioned by Lumadrama to write music for a text by Archibald MacLeish, to be performed July 4 at Independence Hall. It was called "The American Bell." It was written about the founding and meaning of the Liberty Bell. Mr. MacLeish had quoted speeches from the famous men of the time who created the Declaration of Independence. He also wrote poetic interludes of his own. It was a beautiful and moving text. I was told that I would be able to use members of the Philadelphia Orchestra to record music for it.

As February 20 approached, I realized that all the money from *The Manchurian Candidate* and "The American Bell" would be needed to cover the probable loss from the Town Hall concert. What had started out as a simple one-man show had become a financial nightmare. Because I had been burned so many times myself, I was not going to short-change any musician or pay them a penny under what they usually got. I was not about to become a whiner. I had worked for too many. I decided before the concert, however, that this was going to be the last one that I would ever sponsor myself. From now on, I would just write my music. That was my job. Someone else could have the pleasure of producing it.

The concert was a financial disaster except possibly if you were looking for a 100 per cent tax deduction. From an artistic point of view, however, it was beautiful and rewarding. All the musicians played superbly. The new string quartet sounded marvelous and was very well received. George Shirley sang the sacred service magnificently. Maurice conducted as he had done at the Park Avenue Synagogue and seemed to have more confidence and skill than ever.

At least I had heard all these pieces performed brilliantly. It was worth it even if I felt I would never use my own money to do it again. I still felt that it was better that I had paid for it than if I had to go out and grovel, spending weeks, months or even years searching out potential patrons with the hope that they might throw me a few crumbs. Some people in the arts spent a great part of their lives doing this. I had to be my own patron. I might be broke again, but I was my own man.

My spirits were soaring in spite of my sinking finances because of a girl I had met a few days before at a party at George Plimpton's, where I was playing the piano. I had gone to many of George's parties since I came back from Paris. A lot of people that I had known there still hung out with George. He had known me since I played at the Hôtel des États Unis and was always for real. I'd been talking to Terry Southern about how Ornette Coleman and John Coltrane were going one direction, while Miles Davis and Bill Evans were doing something else. Terry always loved jazz and knew a lot about it.

Suddenly Terry looked over and his face fell in surprise, bewilderment and admiration. Because he was always such a cool cat since I had met him eight years before in Paris, I was surprised to see him register so much emotion in one evening, not to mention in one second. I looked around and almost fell out of my chair. There was the most extraordinary-looking woman I had ever seen in my life. When she looked at you, you felt that her eyes were burning right through you like laser beams. She was nearly six feet tall and had an incredible figure.

Since I had broken off with my Norwegian girl friend I had been so busy working I hadn't thought I would ever settle down with anybody again for a while. I was introduced to Helaine a few moments later and I felt that perhaps I would after all. In addition to being so strikingly beautiful, she had a very strange kind of spiritual, mysterious quality that made her different from any girl I had known before. By this time I had arrived at the point in my life when I finally realized every girl was different from the one before but not all were as interesting. I knew that whether or not I was ready to get married and have a family, at least the woman that I was involved with romantically should be a friend and companion as well as a lover. I refused to enter into the war between men and women. I just wanted to be a human being.

Helaine was an actress who had been in several movies and plays but was now in a sort of slump period. That was fine with me, because it meant she would have more free time, hopefully to spend with me. I invited her to my concert and she said she'd be happy to come. She also told me she would bring her mother along.

I spotted her during the concert and wished I were sitting next to her. After the concert I spoke to her backstage.

"How did you like it?"

"It was beautiful," she said.

"How did your mother like it?"

"Well," she said, whispering into my ear, "she turned around to me after the sacred service was completed and said, 'Isn't this a dressy audience?' That's really what she said, I mean that's really what she's like."

"Well," I said, "I'm glad she didn't come to my first concert. Look, tell her to come on down to the Socialist Hall on University Place and Tenth Street and join everybody for some great after-concert sandwiches and beer." Helaine blanched a little. "I know it's not too fancy, but I'm wasted financially. The concert wiped me out. The hall is only charging me fifteen dollars. You'll have a ball. So will your mother. There are all nice people coming."

"No," she said, "but call me tomorrow, I'd really like to see you."

The reception at the Socialist Hall was wild. Everyone was dressed up in tuxedos and tails. Stockbroker Geoffrey Gates financed the kegs of beer and sandwiches from Katz's. The Socialists had all their signs up on the wall saying "Solidarity on May Day," while a man sat outside selling works by Mao Tse-tung, Karl Marx and Hegel. Some people thought the book salesman was part of the party and began laughing. The poor guy didn't sell many copies and he finally quit trying and joined us capitalists in eating sandwiches, drinking beer, flirting with girls and writing down their telephone numbers. I didn't care much about any girls' phone numbers. All I could think about was Helaine.

I saw Helaine the next night and our romance really started flourishing. I felt that at last I'd found my woman. I never had that feeling with any one before physically and spiritually. It was a feeling of love and compassion that I had thought perhaps had died in me forever. We stayed together for a year and it was a rebirth for me as a human being. I saw as time went by that being able to really love and care for someone was just as important as music. In fact it made my music better.

In March I went to Cleveland to stay at Myron Bloom's house. His wife, Nannin, and son, Billy, greeted me and we had a great time for the few days I was in Cleveland. I kept thinking about Helaine and I called her every day I was there.

Myron played my piece brilliantly with Michael Grabanier playing cello. He only had four days' notice because the other cellist found it too difficult and got frightened at the last minute. Mike lived only a few miles from Oberlin. It had been thirteen years since I had been in Cleveland last, but just as I didn't ever visit high school again when I was in Vermont, I decided not to visit Oberlin either. Even though I was free of my antipathy toward most institutions I was still leery of them. My life was getting better each year, not worse. I had no old-grad nostalgia.

I flew back to New York and completed the music for "The American Bell." The director was someone who had worked on *Son et Lumiére* all over Europe. He had a great success in France with the sound and light shows and he was a thorough technician, combining music, sound and lighting cues electronically.

The only problem was he could hardly speak any English. I babbled away in French and found out he had worked as a night-club comic in Paris and knew many of the people that I had known at the Rose Rouge and other parts of Paris night life. He really didn't understand English too well, but he had such great verve that he let nothing bother him. Whenever I asked him about certain problems I saw, he would laugh, *"Ça, c'est rien, alors."* I admired his assurance. As a result, he was not sure as to where and what he wanted in terms of the music, so I just wrote it completely on my own and hoped that it would be able to fit into the production.

The day of the recording came. Part of the Philadelphia Orchestra came by bus. I was petrified. These men had been heroes of mine since I was six years old. I had seen them at the Academy of Music children's concerts, with Stowkowski conducting. Many of the same musicians were still there, including some of the outstanding French hornists. Now I was having a chance to conduct these men in my own music. I studied the scores till I knew every note and rest by heart. I had spent four or five straight hours practicing conducting this relatively simple music. Helaine thought I was losing my mind.

"What are you doing, honey?" she would inquire in her soft, melodious voice as I hacked away at the air, conducting the imaginary orchestra, practicing all the entrances and gesturing for the musicians to bring out the voices I heard in my mind.

"I know it seems far out, but you'll understand when you come to the recording. You have to practice conducting just like you would acting."

As soon as I introduced myself to the orchestra, I got those wonderful vibrations from everybody. I heard one of the string players at the back whisper over to his stand mate, "The kid's all right. He's not a monster. Hard to believe, isn't it?"

We rehearsed for about five minutes and most of the musicians were smiling. I wasn't even thinking about being scared. We were really having a good time. When we got to the overture, the strings played their part so beautifully I almost fell off the podium. The sound was fantastic. I felt as if I were holding on to the back of an enormous space missile about to be shot off to Venus. It was like hugging a woman you were in love with who was five hundred feet tall and all soul. Conducting a great orchestra when they are playing your own music can give you enough energy and inspiration for the rest of your life. It is probably the ultimate experience in music. As the musicians saw that I was really interested in having the music sound good instead of trying to impress them as a conductor, they relaxed even more, made some corrections in the parts, made a few suggestions on how to bow and phrase certain passages and we got done an hour ahead of schedule.

During the recording, I placed a pair of crash cymbals next to the podium. Just before one tremendous climax in the piece I stooped down, picked up the cymbals, and leaped in the air, smashing them over my head. I then resumed conducting, but the musicians almost fell off their chairs, laughing.

"Well," I said, "I finally got to be a soloist with the Philadelphia Orchestra."

Some of the musicians told me they might have a system of choosing guest conductors, like European orchestras did. They asked me if I would guest conduct.

"No, not yet," I said. "I'm just beginning."

"That's all right. You do better than most of the other egomaniacs we work for," said a violinist.

"You keep it up," said a cellist. "Your beat is clear and you're not a faker. We get so tired of phoneys and hackers who can't conduct. It's embarrassing for us to always have to make these guys look good. The great ones—Toscanini, Mitropoulos, Munch, Monteux, Szell, Cantelli—we haven't got too many, most of them are dead. Bernstein's the best American conductor we've got. He knows his business. Now's the chance for young conductors."

As the musicians were leaving I talked to Mason Jones. In addition to being solo horn, he was a fine composer in his own right. I talked to hornist Ward Fearn. I had seen him as a boy. David Madison, the concertmaster for the recording, made some more suggestions, showing me some principles about orchestral bowing and phrasing that were practical. Violinist Norman Black told me that he liked my music and would like to play a piece of mine with his Philadelphia String Orchestra. I also spoke to John de Lancie, the solo oboeist who told me that he might perform my "Shakespearean Concerto" eventually in a concert series with the Amerita Orchestra, a small group composed of members of the Philadelphia Orchestra. I was in seventh heaven.

Maurice had come to help me make sure that the piece was recorded properly. He stayed to help the engineers, check on my conducting and give me criticism. After the last few members of the orchestra had left, we walked together down the street to go home to the Village.

"Isn't it amazing, Maurice?" I said, "you are with the New York Philharmonic and I conducted some of my music with the Philadelphia Orchestra. I never thought anything like that would happen to either of us during our lifetime."

"It's something," said Maurice, "but *some*one's got to do it. Just don't forget to keep on writing music. As long as you do that, nothing else really matters. You're making progress all the time."

"I was scared, Maurice," I told him. "I was terrified at first. The idea of the Philadelphia Orchestra. But it was *fun*."

"You don't ever have to be scared, Davy," Maurice told me. "You did fine. You just acted like yourself and didn't come on. As long as you're for real and know the music, musicians will always play for you, you know that."

Toward the end of April I went to Hollywood with Helaine to work on *The Manchurian Candidate*. It was very different from *The Young Savages*. I thought that it showed a growth in John Frankenheimer as a director. He not only used his great visual gift for individual scenes, but there was also a sense of continuity in the film as a whole. He also got marvelous performances from all the actors.

I had a chance to use contra-bass clarinets, hecklephones, three

piccolos, bass flutes, a harpsichord and many other instruments I had
not used much before. Because I knew I wasn't going to stay in Hollywood, and because I felt my own music was going to find its way
someday, I didn't have too bad a time. But most of my happiness was
because Helaine was with me. When I saw people I had met the first
time I was there, they got a strange look in their eyes.

"You're back," they would say, looking hungrily, "you're going
to stay?"

"No," I said, "I'm finishing this and I'm going back to New York."

"Why don't you stay?" they would say, almost imploring me. Then
they would ask me about New York, desperately, as if it were Mecca.
I saw that most of the people there, even the talented and successful
ones, seemed to feel guilty somehow that they were there and yet
were afraid to come back or to leave. I didn't feel it was a crime to
be there. I just felt that it was not the place for me. I did my work
and tried not to pay any attention to anything except Helaine and
my musician friends.

Stanley Plummer was the concertmaster again and this time no one
gave him any trouble. Fred Dutton and Lou Blackburn from the
Seventh Army Symphony were there. Harold Land played with the
jazz group and Dick Leith was the trombonist. I hadn't seen Dick
since I left for the army.

"You've come quite a way since Washington, Dave," said Dick.

"Man, we're still alive and that's what's most important," I said.

"You know it," said Dick. "Remember when Bird came down to
your basement that night? That was ten years ago. Can you believe
it?"

"No," I said, "doesn't seem that long ago now that you mention it.
How many years would you say it was in subjective time?"

"Not more than three hundred and fifty," said Dick.

Paul Horn and Jack Nimitz, who had played with Buddy Rowell's
Latin band with me in Washington, also played in the recording. It
was wild for all of us to be working again. It was just like the jam
sessions we had in my Washington basement apartment. I realized
that we were still pretty much the same as we had been before. We
still lived for music.

I wrote a lot of jazz for the movie which was never used, partially
just to have all the guys get together to have a session. It was always
there in case it was necessary. The producer of this movie was Howard Koch, a real gentleman, and it was a much different experience

from the first time I was in Hollywood. He and the people connected with the film tried to make it easy for me to do a good job rather than to impress me with the strength of their position. As a result, the music for *The Manchurian Candidate* came out better than any film score that I had ever done. I was proud of the music and again was given many offers to stay in Hollywood. I knew that I couldn't. Helaine decided to stay for a while, but I knew I had to leave. *The Merchant of Venice* was almost ready to open the Shakespeare Festival in Central Park and I hadn't seen a rehearsal or written the music yet.

I took a jet plane back, got off, went right to Ratner's, had a bowl of borscht and almost kissed the ground on Second Avenue. I was really happy to be back in New York. I finished the music for *The Merchant of Venice* in four days. George C. Scott had come back to the Shakespeare Festival to play Shylock. He was better than ever.

I became a shareholder in a large Fire Island house with a mob of other fellow Villagers. I had the room downstairs in the basement and my old piano that I had had at Robin's Rest was moved down in a truck. Although the pipes in my room leaked a little bit, it was good enough to work in and I began writing "Dirge and Variations" during that summer.

Many musicians I knew came out and visited because during the weekdays it was almost empty. When I wasn't working on the "Dirge and Variations," we used to play chamber music and have great jam sessions. The composer and percussionist, Michael Colgrass, came out to visit quite often. By laying a towel over a series of saucepans, he was able to devise a whole percussion unit that sounded like Ceylonese drums. Percy Heath of the Modern Jazz Quartet and his brother, the drummer Albert "Tutti" Heath, also rented a house in Ocean Ridge. Percy had a viola da gamba that he played instead of bass and we had sessions most of the summer.

Seymour came out and brought his kayak. On one stormy day, there were Coast Guard cutters, helicopters and airplanes looking for him. He had kayaked out by himself to go bluefishing in the ocean on a day when there was strong wind blowing offshore. We told him not to go, but he insisted. After he disappeared over the horizon, Spike called up the Coast Guard. I was trying to figure out what to tell his parents when suddenly he showed up in a beach buggy driven by policemen. He had kayaked all the way back against the storm and landed four miles down the beach in the Pines.

He seemed calm and undisturbed. "What's everyone worrying about?" he said, looking up at the airplanes and helicopters that were still circling about.

"How are you feeling?" I asked.

"All right. What's the panic, for Christ sakes?"

"Well, thank God you're O.K.," I said.

"Naturally I'm O.K.," said Seymour. "Whaddya think, I'm suicidal? I don't wanna drown. It was *great* out there. Man," and he rolled his eyes back in his head. "It was byooo-tiful. Ya know the only trouble? I had a bluefish, at least a ten-pounder, and the bastard got away. It was *this close* to the boat."

That night we had a jam session. We were so angry at Seymour for frightening us, we dragged him out of bed and made him play with us. After that he had decided that he had better stop kayaking so much and begin practicing the violin more. Ten days later he went in for an audition and got the job as assistant concertmaster at the Metropolitan Opera. That's how talented he was at music. I continued working on "Dirge and Variations" all summer and even though Helaine would visit me occasionally, she didn't like my relatively cramped living conditions and couldn't understand how I could work in such an atmosphere. "I just turn off my mind when I have to," I told her. "You should have seen the places I used to live in a few years ago. This is paradise in comparison."

I kept thinking of David and Michael playing the Kodály at Marlboro. Remembering their performance as well as just knowing both of them was a great help to me in writing "Dirge and Variations." I mailed them a variation at a time as I copied the score. As work progressed, I felt the entire piece was a statement of how I felt of the idea of a dirge in relation to death. It was not so much that death was tragic to me anymore. Since Mitropoulos had gone, I felt differently. I felt it was a poetic conclusion to the fullness of life itself. I found that the older I was getting, the clearer my music was becoming.

I went into town for the first run-through of "Dirge and Variations." Hearing the Marlboro Trio rehearse it for the first time, I saw that there were not many changes necessary. I had really planned and worked the piece out carefully. I felt I was making progress as a composer.

"We like it," David Soyer told me. "We're going to play it in Philadelphia, October 28, at Town Hall December 18 and at the Library of Congress the following January and on tour."

This was the first time a piece of mine was to be played for more than one performance. I decided I had better get to work on some of my larger pieces now. I began gathering notes and ideas for my opera, *Twelfth Night*, which I had spoken about with Joe Papp so many times before.

As the summer drew to a close I drove back from the island one night with Jim Biderman and Jo Baldwin. Jim had a small moving company in the Village and we drove back with all of us in the cab of his truck. With his good-natured dog slobbering all over our old clothes, we felt like the happiest farmers in the world.

"Let's cut over and look at the Lincoln Center," said Jim, "they're having some big opening there tonight." We went uptown after going through the Midtown Tunnel and went by Lincoln Center. It was opening night at Philharmonic Hall. I looked out of the window of the truck, past the pricked-up ears of Jim's dog. I saw thousands of elegant people, the women in their opening-night furs, the men in white ties and tails, just coming out for intermission. It was quite a sight.

"That's some place, isn't it?" said Jim. "Look at all those fancy people."

"Ugh," said Jo, "I don't like scenes like that. I'd rather hear music like you play it in your jam sessions."

"Well, the music that they play in halls like these has the same spirit," I told Jo. "It's just done in a little more elegant surroundings. And it's *quiet* in there."

We parked outside of Philharmonic Hall and stared for a while. Finally a cop came over and told us we'd better get moving. He flashed his light inside the truck and I guess we didn't look like we were part of the opening-night entourage.

"Well," said Jim, "let's go down to Minetta Lane and have a little taste." We zoomed off down to the Village.

A few days before the Cuban missile crisis, the regular pianist left the Marlboro Trio and Ruth Laredo filled in. The world premier of "Dirge and Variations" took place at the Commercial Museum in Philadelphia, Sunday, October 28, 1962. The next performance took place in Town Hall, December 18 and in spite of the fact that there

was a newspaper strike, the hall was packed to hear the Marlboro
Trio perform. They played my piece beautifully. Ruth's husband,
Jaime Laredo, asked me to write an unaccompanied violin sonata for
him and as I began work on it, Joe Papp and I spent the next few
days going over the libretto for *Twelfth Night*. Before the end of the
year, I began work on the first act. I called Joe up and sang him the
opening bars when Orsino sings, "If Music Be the Food of Love
Play On."

"Beautiful, Amram," said Joe, "a beautiful beginning. Now you've
got to finish it."

Again as New Year's Eve approached, I felt pretty satisfied. I was
still just barely making a living, but I didn't care. That was all I
needed. Helaine and I thought about getting married and decided as
1962 ended that we couldn't, even though we loved each other and
always would. She wanted the life of an actress and she couldn't adjust to my way of life and I couldn't get with hers. I felt at least that
I was able to love another person deeply. We spent our last night
together New Year's Eve. When everyone else was singing "Auld
Lang Syne" and shouting and making noise, I had my own music going in my head again. All I could hear was Sir Toby Belch, Sir Andrew Aguecheek, Feste, Viola, Orsino and all the other characters in
Twelfth Night.

As the new year began, I went down to Washington, where "Dirge
and Variations" was being performed by the Marlboro Trio at the
Library of Congress. I had been to the concerts at the library as a
kid, but I never thought any of my music would be performed there.
I walked into the auditorium with Paul Kline, a tenor saxophonist
whom I had played with before I'd gone into the army, bassoonist
Kenny Pasmanick, who had a night off from the National Symphony,
and Fred Wilkerson, who had O.K.'d my music for the production at
Howard University and given me that scrumptious fried chicken dinner for my first commission twelve years before.

It felt good being back again in Washington, particularly with my
music being performed by a fine and dedicated group like the Marlboro Trio. By this time they really had the piece mastered. They had
found things in it that I didn't even realize were there. Certain tiny
changes and inflections they made actually improved the music. These
were little nuances involving changes of tempo and dynamics. It

showed me again the wonderful way music can evolve when the composer and the performing artists are collaborators.

"It's funny," I said to Paul and Kenny as we walked into the Library of Congress. "I feel scared coming here to have my music played. I associate this place so much with the Budapest String Quartet playing Beethoven."

"That's cool, Dave," said Paul. "You paid your dues."

"I'm still paying them," I told him, "but a different kind and not quite as steep as they were before."

"As long as you're writing down your own story in music, you'll always be paying dues."

"I know that," I said. "But so did every other composer that was any good."

The Marlboro Trio played beautifully that night. As soon as they began my piece I could tell it was going to be their best performance yet. The audience was so attuned to fine chamber music that their presence and acute listening made the music more alive. Harold Spivacke, who was in charge of the concerts, always tried to program contemporary music that he thought was worthwhile. This was one of the few auditoriums in America where you really felt that chamber music belonged and at the same time that you belonged there with it. It made you feel at home.

I worked on the opera day and night when I got back to New York. Joe hoped we might be able to do it in the summer of 1964 if he could raise the money for it. I would compose all day. Then around seven at night I would go off to the YMCA and run around the track. I got to the point where I could make sixty laps, which was the equivalent of three miles. Then I would go through a whole series of exercises, come back home, eat some kind of mysterious health dinner and begin orchestrating. After I orchestrated a few hours I would go out and start sitting in with my horn. I felt I wanted to get back to playing jazz whenever I could. It was important to me as part of my life whether or not it ever made me a dime.

Later that spring I bumped into Elia Kazan.

"Hey, Gadge," I yelled out.

"David," he said to me in his excited, energetic way. "Isn't that something. I was just going to call you."

"Well, here I am," I said.

"Listen," he said, "Bob Whitehead and I are in charge of the new

Lincoln Center Repertory Theatre and would like you to be music
director. You can write music for the plays and have a guaranteed
salary of some sort. It will be just like old times. It's going to be a
wonderful theater without the pressures of Broadway. We have the
best actors. The first play we're doing is *After the Fall*. It's a new
play Arthur Miller is just finishing and we need some music for it.
Can you come meet him in a few weeks?"

"Sure," I said. I went a few weeks later and met Arthur Miller.
He and his wife, Inge, were sitting in Bob Whitehead's office. As
soon as I shook his hand and looked at his eyes and heard him talk
for a few seconds, I could see he had absolutely no Broadway about
him. He was all artist and a real guy. Even though I had more respect for him than any other living playwright, I still felt relaxed in
his presence. I was told that rehearsals would begin in the fall and
that the theater would open that winter.

Arthur Miller turned out to be a great music fan. He had been a
boy crooner when he had lived in Brooklyn and he loved chamber
music, symphonic music, all kinds of classical music and jazz too. I
told him that I had seen him in 1958 when he attended Ettore Rella's
play *Sign of Winter*. I had also seen him at the Actors Studio in 1960
when my band had played there for a party. I explained to him that
I never introduced myself because, not knowing him, I didn't want
to bug him.

"It's too bad more people aren't that way," he said, laughing. "You
know, I had a boy run down the street after me and say, 'Mr. Miller,
Mr. Miller.' I said, 'Yes,' and he said, 'I just want to tell you how
glad I am to meet you at last. I've always enjoyed your music.' You
see, they know they've seen me and identify me with something, but
they're not sure what. I've also met people who tell me their father
had been in college with me and it turns out that while they went
to the same college, they went there ten years after I had graduated.
Still they're convinced they know me. It's funny. The worst one of
all is when a woman drove out to my farm and told me that God
had sent her. She wanted me to come and meet her rabbi. I told her
in as nice a way as possible that she'd better leave."

It really made me feel good to meet him. He was someone whose
work I always admired and who was just as real as what he wrote.

I continued on my opera and when the summer came, I wrote the
music for *Antony and Cleopatra* and *Winter's Tale*. I went back to

Fire Island, but instead of renting the same large blue house with a mob of other people, I found a tiny house in Davis Park right on the bay, and while it was not exactly a showplace, it was ideal for me. It was stuck off in the weeds and because of the strong aroma of marsh gas that came from the bay during the middle of the summer, most people stayed on the ocean side. It was really quiet and I knew I could get even more work done. Also, there would be no pipes dripping on me as there had been the summer before while I was composing. I moved my old piano once more, from the blue house into the tiny bungalow, and continued where I had left off with my opera.

One day after I had finished composing, I received a call from Harold Aks, the conductor at the Interracial Chorale. He wanted me to write a cantata for chorus, orchestra and soloists for the following spring concert at Town Hall. I told him that because of my work with the Lincoln Center Theatre and my opera possibly being done in the summer of sixty-four that it would be better to plan for the spring of sixty-five. He asked me if I had any ideas for a cantata. I remembered Mental File Cabinet ZZ-H2257 in the upper left-hand corner of my brain. That's where I had filed the idea for a large choral work those days in Paris nine and a half years earlier after I had my wisdom teeth taken out.

"I always had the idea of setting the writings of a group of American authors to music," I told him. "What I would like to do would be to have a piece that portrayed the four seasons in America. Each season could be in a different part of the country. We could have spring in the East, summer in the West, fall in the North and winter in the South with possibly a prelude and an epilogue."

"That sounds like a marvelous idea," said Harold. "Did you just think of it?"

"No," I told him, "I've had the idea for years."

"Where will you find the text?"

"There are certain authors' works I'd like to read to see if I could find the text."

"Well, plan on it then," he said, "for the spring of sixty-five."

For the rest of the summer I lugged volumes of books back and forth to the island. I read through a total of fifty-four books and found the text. The prologue was from *Another Country* by James Baldwin, describing the New York landscape as the protagonist landed in a plane. Then for spring in the East I used a section from John Dos

Passos' *Manhattan Transfer* describing a scene by the ferry. For summer in the West I chose a section from *The Lonesome Traveler* by Jack Kerouac, describing the mountains as the author sat in a shack at sunset. For fall in the North I took a selection from *Travels with Charley* by John Steinbeck, a description of the Wisconsin dells at Thanksgiving. For winter in the South I edited a portion from *The Web and the Rock* by Thomas Wolfe which described the snow falling in the South. For the epilogue I chose some lines from Walt Whitman's *Leaves of Grass* which summed up the entire work.

The interesting thing was that when I finally edited the sections down to three pages in length, it looked as if they had been written for the cantata. The different styles contrasted well, but they had an over-all similarity that made the work easy to unify musically. I knew I couldn't begin work on it full-time, but I made some preliminary sketches and thought about it when I wasn't working on *Twelfth Night*.

Toward the end of the summer I met Paddy Chayefsky. He was interested in having me write music for his drama, *The Passion of Joseph D*, a fascinating play about the Russian Revolution. He came down in a beach taxi from the other end of the island on a steaming hot day and we talked all afternoon. I had seen some of his other plays and admired his energy, spirit, humor and dramatic talent. *The Passion of Joseph D* was due to open in January, so I figured I could work on it after I finished the music for *After the Fall*. Since I had been working on my opera now for eight months and was planning a cantata, I really felt in the mood to write choral music anyway. Because Paddy was directing his play as well, I knew it would be fun and stimulating to work on it with him.

As I worked away on my different projects and began attending rehearsals of *After the Fall,* I made one of the most important decisions in my life. I had retained the rights to all my concert music and most of the theater music I had written over the past few years. My original music publisher had never published any of my concert work. He had broken his promise. I had been a sucker to trust him, so we finally "terminated our agreement."

I had such a large pile of music by now that all of the other publishers I spoke to were afraid. "You have too much," I was told. It seemed unbelievable that this was a liability. Apparently the ideal composer would be someone who wrote one piece every other year.

Through Oliver Daniels at BMI, a composer's rights organization, of which I was a member, I went to see Walter Hinrichsen of the C. F. Peters Corporation. They were the original publishers of Mozart and Beethoven and I had collected their editions ever since I was a child. I knew they wouldn't start whining and begging me to write hack music for high school marching bands. They were interested in *music*. I liked Mr. Hinrichsen immediately. He was a real gentleman of the old school. After all of the shifty, sleazy, untrustworthy characters I had met in music publishing, I had almost accepted the fact that music publishers were all petty thieves of one sort or another. To my pleasure, Mr. Hinrichsen and everyone that worked at C. F. Peters were dedicated, intelligent, hard-working people. They all had beautiful manners, seemed to know everything about music from Monteverdi through the most avant-garde works of the day. For the first time in my life, I was in a music publisher's office without feeling sick.

I knew from talking to Oliver Daniels and other composers that if I did not put my music with a serious music publisher at this point, it would never have a chance to be played often in America, much less around the world. There was no guarantee that it would be played even if it was published, but if it wasn't published by a reputable firm like C. F. Peters, it would be next to impossible. I spoke to Mr. Hinrichsen one more time and on October 30 I signed for ten years. Mr. Hinrichsen took me to a fabulous dinner afterwards. It was the most opulent meal I had ever eaten in my life. A few days later, he showed me a green cover of a new C. F. Peters edition with my name on it, just to give me an idea of how my music would look when it came out. It was the first visual realization of the dream I had had when I was six years old.

That fall I began playing again at the Five Spot, which had moved from the Bowery to St. Marks Place. It was the first time I'd worked there since 1957. Six and a half years had passed and it was great to be back again. George Barrow and Arthur Phipps were there and we were even able to work out some of the music that we did for *After the Fall*. At first I felt a little rusty. It had been quite a while since I'd worked in a New York club. After the first few weeks I got with it again and began to feel relaxed.

I loved being back at the Five Spot but I was happy I didn't have to work there six nights a week. Between my work on the play, writing my opera and going to the gym, I felt that I was leading a pretty good life. I was sorry that George, Arthur and I couldn't play more concerts, because we had such a great telepathic rapport after having played together for eight years. I figured eventually that day would come too.

Before *After the Fall* opened I was invited to speak at a conference of psychiatrists and psychologists. I gave a talk that was followed by a discussion with other artists and doctors about the creative process. Lorraine Hansberry, Robert Motherwell, and Pearl Primus also appeared among the participating artists. That night I ran into Ornette Coleman. After speaking and listening to psychiatrists all day, it was nice to hear him. He sounded beautiful. He told me that he was getting into composing more and more. He felt that it helped his playing and that his playing helped his composing.

I was looking forward to hearing what he wrote for groups other than his own quartet. His sincerity, warmth and originality were still like a flame and the new things that he had been doing were no longer laughed at by anybody who knew much about music. There was a whole new vocabulary that was enriching all of jazz. Ornette had been a major force in bringing it about. Even though times were getting hard again for jazz, there had been hard times before. I spoke to Dave Lambert about this a few days later at Joe's Luncheonette on West 4th Street.

Dave said, "Well, man, they say jazz is dying. Well, they've been saying jazz is dying for the last sixty years."

Roswell Rudd, Archie Shepp, Charles Lloyd, Pharoah Sanders (nicknamed Little Rock), Wayne Shorter, Paul Bley and a lot of other gifted musicians used to come by the Five Spot. I began hearing them play other places, at lofts and on the records some of them were making. Wonderful things were happening in jazz even if the music was benefiting from it more than the musicians.

Rehearsals for *The Passion of Joseph D* began at the same time that *After the Fall* was having its final rehearsals. I would dash off from the Lincoln Center Theatre to the *Joseph D* rehearsal hall. The entire score for the play was choral music. The actors and some professional singers sang *a cappella* throughout the play. I conducted the rehearsals. The score for *After the Fall* was largely music performed by our jazz quartet with the exception of a string quartet that played in a few sections. The plays were totally different but both equally interesting.

At first Miller and Kazan were not sure where the music should be used and even if there should be any at all. We would get together and discuss where I thought the music should be. They were afraid almost any music would be inappropriate and would get in the way. But they never discounted the idea that it might work and encouraged me to try. After two months I had recorded about fourteen pieces, but we had still made no decisions about any music. There was a group of teachers from out of town whom we invited as a kind of dummy audience. I had the stage manager set the tape up and without the actors even knowing what the music was going to sound like, we ran it with the play. Miraculously, the music fitted in so well that it was decided to use all of it and add some more as well.

On November 22, 1963, I was at Arnold Arnstein's having a part of my opera copied. He was on the phone, instructing his small army of copyists about details for the five different scores he was able to remember in his head. Suddenly he turned white and hung up the phone.

"The President has just been shot in Texas," he said. We all got up and walked out in the hall to try to find a radio. Everyone was in a daze. Anybody in music or in the arts knew that a President like Kennedy came along once a century. Perhaps it had all been too good to be true. I couldn't say anthing so I just left. By the time I got to the street I saw people crying. I got in the subway and went back to the Village. I saw the look on people's faces in the subway. They all knew as I did that the terrible sickness of America—the repressed violence and hate that were commercialized in so many forms of entertainment, in presentation of news and in people's actions toward one another from the time they were children—had taken its toll.

I had promised Joe Papp to go to Baltimore that day and see the production of a Handel opera at the Peabody Institute which he had directed. I called up Joe's wife to tell him that I didn't want to go, but he had already left. I knew how terrible he must feel. I decided I would go down and stop in Washington to see my family, because I knew it would affect them as much as if a relative of ours had died. I went down, borrowed my family's sedan and drove to Baltimore to find Joe. I was in kind of a daze and I kept listening to the radio reports of the assassination.

"Thank God it wasn't a Jew that killed the President," my mother said just before I left. I thought about this all the time I was driving to Baltimore. Someone who was a third-generation American still had this ancient fear and yet I understood it and know somehow that she was right. There was no doubt in my mind on that terrible night that sickness, violence, prejudice, and hate were the assassins and that we were all guilty in some small way. In music all the people that I'd admired had spent their lives trying to live together on a higher spiritual level. Obviously we all had a long way to go.

Joe was completely shaken.

"I don't know what to do," he said. "I can't call off the performance. What the hell does it all mean? I guess all we can do is go on. I feel like they killed part of me."

I stayed with my family the next day in Washington and watched the proceedings on television. I wanted to go to some of the ceremonies in Washington, but when I saw Jack Ruby shoot Oswald for the fourth re-run within two hours, I was too sickened and ashamed to do anything.

I began to see Arthur Miller even when we weren't working. He was one of the few people I had met in the theater that I felt in tune with. When I would visit him and Inga and their little daughter, Becky, in the Chelsea Hotel, I felt just like I was at home. It made me feel wonderful to know that there were still artists in America who were so dedicated and pure in spirit. We used to go down to Chinatown quite often and wander around and have long talks. He told me about his childhood; when he went to school, college and worked in the Brooklyn Navy Yard, how he had rented a place out in Long Island with no heat; how after *All My Sons* had been a hit, he had turned down several fortunes from Hollywood in order to continue his own work, even though he had very little money and a family.

"When you see those guys who gave up their own dream to do hack work, I can't feel sorry for them. They all grow too rich and fat and lazy. I see the anxiety on their faces and when they start to tell me how awful it is that they've sold out, I can't sympathize with them. It serves them right. Don't ever stop what you're doing. Your own work is the most important thing. It's lucky you didn't get trapped. Don't ever change."

As 1963 ended, I felt that whatever happened I could never be trapped. I had gotten a great deal of *Twelfth Night* written. The first act was almost complete and I had orchestrated almost half the act as well. I was nearly flat broke again, but I knew that even if I had to go out and work at day jobs, my music was going to be published and eventually would be performed. I was working with the kind of artists that I wanted to work with and I was getting in such good condition from my road work in the gym that I could always go back to being a gym teacher.

Just before New Year's Eve, I took Malcolm down to the YMCA. He had not been exactly on a health kick. As fate would have it, he was living with Emma. Her sarcasm and cynicism took on new dimensions with him in her clutches.

"She's really killing me," said Malcolm, "but I can't seem to get away. She has such a wonderful mind that I really enjoy being with her in spite of her craziness."

"Is she writing anything?" I asked him.

"No," said Malcolm. "She is so worried about making the scene and hustling and being with the right people that she has no time left for anything else."

We went to the McBurney Y and Malcolm was gasping after a few laps around the track. To keep himself going he began droning out the names of all the guys we knew over the years who were dead from junk or alcohol. It was quite an impressive list. We went down to the weight room, and as I was lifting dumbbells and doing calisthenics, Malcolm stopped in fascination, watching a Neanderthal-type psychopath who was body-pressing three hundred pounds, flexing his muscles, looking in the mirror and laughing hysterically at Malcolm's thin frame.

"What's that guy's story?" questioned Malcolm. I looked over to catch his bloodshot eyes leering at Malcolm before he bared his fangs and let out a torrent of muscular laughter.

"Well, Malcolm, like they say, man, clean living pays off."

12

After the Fall was about to open. I had written an eerie piece of music based on the theme that had been used for the tragic figure of Maggie. I had tried to make this music represent the emptiness of her aspirations as well as her inability to deal with the real world. In this final statement, a violin held a high harmonic, while other instruments played. Kazan and Miller had not heard it, but because they trusted me at this point they said we should try it during a preview.

I waited until the very end of the play and finally said to Arthur Miller, "Now. Here it comes. Right—now. Listen."

Nothing happened. Maybe it's late, I thought. It still didn't play. The stage manager might have forgotten, I thought to myself. The play ended and after the silence and the final music, people clapped. I went running back to Bob Downing, the stage manager.

"Bob," I said, "you forgot to play that music. What happened?"

"I was just about to," he said, "then the sound man told me that the tape was defective."

"What do you mean?" I said. "It sounded beautiful."

"No," he said, "we listened to it to make sure. There was a tone signal on the tape."

"That wasn't a tone signal. That was part of the music. That's an instrument. A violin playing a high-E harmonic."

"Oh," he said. He played it back. "That doesn't sound like music to me," he said.

Knowing Bob's fondness for more melodic music, I explained to him what I was trying to do and told him to listen to the piano part as well as the high, piercing note. The next night the piece was used, and I had completed my work. Now I could really enjoy the play. I began attending all the rehearsals of *The Passion of Joseph D.* I had written all the music, setting Paddy Chayefsky's short verse poems, stanzas, quatrains and lyrics. There were great, resounding choral numbers, including a huge hallelujah chorus, with an ironic text as well as a lot of music that suggested the religious fervor that the Russian people equated with their revolution. The music and words attempted to portray how so many of the Russian people substituted Lenin for the Tsar as a religious figure.

Paddy's play was brilliant and wild. He directed it himself and if a scene didn't seem to work, he would rush up to his office and come back three hours later with thirty pages of brand-new script as interesting as the script before. Luther Adler, Peter Falk, Milt Kamen and Alvin Epstein were outstanding in their roles. We changed the entire production almost every night. It was the first time Paddy had directed. Staging *The Passion of Joseph D* would have been an almost insurmountable job for anyone. Still it was an unusual and inspired show. The only problem was that most people expected it to be a great, serious tome. Large parts of it were wild parody, almost like cabaret theater. It was really very Brechtian, and like the finest works of Brecht, this ironic kind of writing didn't seem suitable for Broadway. Perhaps if Paddy Chayefsky had an Eric Bentley to "interpret" him, the way Brecht had, the critics would have been kinder. As it was, everyone came expecting to see *Alexander Nevsky* à la 1917 and the play closed rather quickly.

Opening night of *After the Fall* was the best performance yet. Jason Robards, Jr., outdid himself. He was so relaxed, confident and sure of the part that it was as if he were in his living room. His acting and Barbara Lodin's heartbreaking performance as Maggie filled the theater with great bursts of energy. I was proud to be a part of it.

Fortunately *The New York Times* gave it an ultra-rave review. Howard Taubman saw the many levels of the play and realized what the words of the play kept saying over and over again—that we are all responsible and all equally guilty in our treatment of one another. He realized that it was a modern morality play—not an exposé of Marilyn Monroe. Other critics, however, and some show-biz folk apparently could not see past the grease paint. Walter Kerr, author of such dramatic works as the book for the musical *Goldilocks*, thought Arthur Miller didn't really seem to have it. His review was written in his brilliant, acerbic style. I couldn't believe it. I asked Arthur Miller how this was possible.

"This has happened before," he told me. "You know, the funny thing is that often the same critic will come back a year later when the play is still running and review it again and give it an excellent review. Not only that, but they seem to think that they even liked it the first time."

Somehow the entire dramatic structure of *Twelfth Night* seemed so operatic that when Joe Papp and I worked on the libretto we constantly hummed the melody of "The Wind and the Rain" whenever we got stuck. The music we had done for the production of the play helped us to cut Shakespeare's play so that it could be adapted into an opera no more than two and a half hours in length. Because opera generally takes five times longer to do when the libretto is sung than when it is spoken, we were forced to cut *Twelfth Night* a great deal. We finally cut it down to about thirty minutes when spoken. This was murderously difficult work because Joe knew the full uncut version of the play inside out, having directed it several times. I, too, had a great attachment to the play in its entirety. I must have seen the production that we did in the park at least twenty times. The problem had been how to forget about the work we had done on the play and make it something else entirely. While every word we used was Shakespeare's, Joe insisted that the operatic version must be something entirely different from anything we had conceived of when dealing with *Twelfth Night* as a play.

We held a fund-raising reading of the opera at the house of Doctor Sydney Danis and his wife, Herta. They had helped out with the Shakespeare Festival since its humble beginnings on the Lower East Side. Most of the people we had invited from the music and opera world didn't show up. Perhaps they were too busy; perhaps I wasn't well enough known at that time or perhaps the affair wasn't chic enough. For whatever reason, no one showed up but two secretaries from an opera festival in Ohio and the head of a cultural center that was to be built in the Middle West. We went through the first act of the opera anyway. As soon as we began I could feel the excitement in that small room. I had never heard it myself except in my mind. It was really almost like a jam session, with a kind of natural and spontaneous atmosphere. Although it took an hour, the time seemed to go by very rapidly.

At the end I looked at Joe and for the first time since I had known him, he was speechless. He lit a cigar and said, "Don't worry, boychickel, we're going to get this on someday. It's beautiful and much more different than I thought the play could ever be. That's why it's an opera. We'll have to do some changing and I'll have to change my whole idea of staging after listening to the music, but someday we're going to do it. Until we have the money, there's no point in doing it if we can't do it right."

The man from the cultural center in the Midwest told me that if we ever had a production in the East, he would guarantee that it would be put on for two weeks out there.

I went back to work, orchestrating the first act and writing the second act. It had been marvelous to hear the first act sung in a runthrough. A few days later Joe told me it would be impossible to do it in the summer of 1964. It was springtime, so the good weather and the excitement I was finding orchestrating the first act of the opera saved me from really being disappointed. I had been working for nearly a year and a half.

"Perhaps we can do it next summer in 1965," said Joe. "We'll have another reading maybe this coming November and invite a lot of people again. Perhaps they'll want to subsidize it so we can do it. I'm sorry, but we are having enough trouble trying to raise money for the dramatic productions at the new theatre. You know I want to see it done."

"It's O.K., Joe," I said, "as long as I get it written, that's the most important thing."

A little less than two weeks after this disappointment, I was called by Wiley Hance of ABC television. He was in charge of the Directions Series. He and Milton Krents of the Jewish Theological Seminary wanted to commission an opera based on a play by Reginald Rose called *The Final Ingredient*. I went to see a kinescope of the play. It was very moving. I knew I would have to do it. It was a story of a group of prisoners in a concentration camp who tried to break out in order to get an egg from the nest of a nearby tree. This egg was the final ingredient they would need for the illicit Passover service they were going to hold inside the camp.

I was told I could choose the librettist. I thought of Arnold Weinstein. He was a fine poet, a fine librettist, knew a great deal about music and had encouraged me in my composing since I had met him

in 1955, when he lived not too far from me on the Lower East Side.
It was also promised that the full ABC orchestra would be available.
I felt extremely confident. I realized that the work I had done on
Twelfth Night had gotten my mind sufficiently attuned to operatic
writing, so I was ready to undertake another project.

At the same time I worked on "A Year in Our Land," my cantata
based on the works of American authors, and began receiving proofs
of my pieces that were being published. Seeing my music engraved
gave me a new feeling of responsibility toward composing. I saw that
in the near future, my pieces would be available. I realized that I'd
better keep working as hard as possible now that I was getting a
chance to have my music live.

The summer at Davis Park was a very productive one. I shared
the house with Leonard Gross, the young kid I had met at Brooklyn
College when I played there with Jack Kerouac in 1957. Lenny
was the one who asked Jack if his mother got nervous when he was
making his great trips. After he had completed college graduate work,
he had become the editor of the magazine *Sexology*. Because he
looked like a junior Harpo Marx or Marcel Marceau and seemed to
be only fifteen or sixteen years old, no one could believe that this
curly-haired, kind, leprechaunish-looking, twinkle-eyed boy was a
full-fledged editor of a sex magazine. He had the most cheerful disposition of anybody in the history of Long Island. People loved him.
Fans of *Sexology,* mostly young girls, would come by to visit us in
flocks. They could always meet a composer, but it was very rare to
meet a full-fledged sexologist. When I wasn't writing music I would
take time off and Lenny and I would take some young lovely creatures
kayaking in the ocean or to jam sessions. Lenny was an ideal host as
well as a crusading editor-sexologist. He was also a great avant-garde
gourmet and we made some health dinners for his fans that would
have killed anyone with less intestinal fortitude.

Lenny knew a lot of the same people in the Village that I did. We
often had old friends who stayed over for a night and sometimes
weeks. We both joined the Davis Park Fire Department. Lenny was
also a great sports lover. We would shove the eight- and nine-year-
old children out of the way so that we could spear blowfish off the
dock to get our supper. We both survived that summer on fish that
we caught from the dock or from our kayak. Otherwise we always
had food that friends would bring out. They might have appeared to
be freeloaders but like all good Greenwich Villagers, they always

brought along big shopping bags full of goodies whenever they came to visit.

The only guests that overstayed were Jorge and Francess. They were old pals of mine from Christopher Street. Jorge was from Brazil and was a fine photographer. He was doubling at the moment as a cabdriver and bartender. Francess was a social worker–schoolteacher.

I ran into Jorge that summer in the Corner Bistro.

"Man, you lookin' *good!*" he said.

"Well, clean living, Jorge. You know."

"When I gonna come wid Francess an' see you an' Lenny?"

"Anytime, Jorge."

"Beautiful, baby."

Jorge and Francess arrived that weekend. He had two Peruvian girls with him.

"I brung Estella for you, Dave. She crazy about music an' she a *groovy* chick, baby. She don' bug you or nothin'. An' she cook her ass off. *Hasta la pussy!*"

I always liked Jorge's joie de vivre and I didn't want to seem like a grim, gray, soured yanqui.

"Man, there's not too much room," I said.

Lenny and I both had about nine dates that night. It was bad enough as it was.

"It's O.K. O.K.! Estella sleep wid you, her aunt sleep wid Lenny. Dey don' bother nobody!"

Lenny and I prided ourselves on being good hosts. The aunt was no chicken, but she looked good and when she saw Lenny, her eyes lit up.

"It will be a great way to improve our Spanish," said Lenny.

A week later, they were all still there. Lenny and I were trying to drop a hint about maybe it was time to leave, when Jorge came back with forty blowfish.

"Hey, Dave! Lenny!" he shouted joyously. "I got some other frien' comin' out. You gonna really dig dese cats. One of dem, Salvatore, is a big cat in de government. He know all de big musician. Jobim, Gilberto—he friendly wid all dem cats. He fix you guys up when you come an' visit Francess and me in Brazil."

A few minutes later, seven people showed up with bags. The house groaned under their weight as they came in, chatting in Portuguese.

"Dave, you gotta meet Salvatore," said Jorge, introducing me to the fattest man I had ever seen in my life. I noticed his eyes. They were pinned. He was as high as he was fat.

"*Mucho gusto,*" I said in Spanish. I didn't know any Portuguese.

"U-n-n-ngh-h! Eg-g-gh-ank!" he grunted in reply.

The only thing I figured this guy could be in the Brazilian government was the wrestling commissioner.

He lurched over to a young girl in a bikini, one of our charming young neighbors.

"Ag-g-h," he intoned, wrapping his fat arms around her lissome young frame.

"Oooh," she squeaked, "you freshie." She tittered and slid out from the bulging fat.

"Onnnnk!" snorted Salvatore, and collapsed in an almost perfect swan dive on the couch.

He immediately passed out and began snoring so loudly that Lenny's puppy, KoKo, began to whine in fear. We finally got everybody outside. Salvatore snored all day. The two times he got up, he went to the bathroom, then to the icebox, where he swayed back and forth, grunting as he stuffed himself with anything he could reach. He then took a few drinks, tried to grab any girl in sight and passed out again, nearly drowning out the ocean with his snores.

The next morning we were about to tell Jorge it was the end of a lovely visit, when he came up looking guilty.

"Don' be mad at me, fellas."

"Jesus," said Lenny softly. "He's asked someone else out."

"Don' be mad, Dave an' Lenny. I really sorry. We gotta go back. It's a drag man, we gotta get to de city. Salvatore say he don' like it here. It's not enuff to do. Listen, you guys visit me in Brazil, I turn you cats on to some fine herbs and groovy chicks."

I liked Estella, but her aunt wanted to leave. Lenny had been sneaking out late at nights for rendezvous with women more in his age bracket and Estella's aunt was insulted.

We all said good-bye.

"It was beautiful, Dave," said Jorge. "We try an' come back soon, don't worry. *Hasta la pussy!*"

After that, Lenny and I told our friends that we had a full house all the time.

"The aunt was a great cook, but she never taught me any Spanish," said Lenny.

"Well, at least they kept any uninvited guests from barging in," I said.

Toward the end of the summer it was finally decided that the television opera would definitely go through. Arnold Weinstein and his friend Barbara Harris, the actress, came out to visit. I had known Barbara since she had come to New York and we had even been together on a program on WBAI, the listeners' sponsored radio in New York. It was a parody of the Democratic convention. We all had different parts, which we made up on the spot. There was one that Barbara and I did together where she was a lady reporter from the South and I played Mrs. Johnson. It was pretty far out and we did it only one time through—fifteen minutes of spontaneous insanity. Arnold was also a great improviser and their first two or three days on the Island that summer we just sat around laughing. I had been working every day nonstop since our Brazilian visitors had left six weeks before. The three days' relaxation really did my heart good.

Finally Arnold and I began work on the opera. Barbara would cook for us while Arnold and I sat on the back porch and gradually designed the shape of the opera. We realized that this play was a brilliant achievement as it stood, but for an opera we would have to rewrite almost every line. We simplified the original story considerably, and I added sections myself including the part where the women prisoners sing "By the Rivers of Babylon."

I also wanted to make the Nazis stand out. I went into the city and spoke to Igor at the Art Foods Delicatessen. He and his wife had both been in concentration camps and he told me he wanted to see that I got the right attitudes and feelings about the captors and prisoners. It was probably a good thing that I had the three days' laughter before beginning work on the opera. In spite of the triumphant ending, it was really torturous writing. I imagined as I worked on it that I was actually in the concentration camp.

We worked almost around the clock and at the end of two weeks had a complete outline of the libretto. Arnold had to teach at Hollins College and we decided that I would make the final changes. Arnold trusted me to keep the integrity of his libretto and I felt deep inside that Wiley Hance and the people involved in the production of the opera were truly interested in presenting a work of the highest caliber. I tried to write the opera as an opera—not a TV show. Arnold and I wanted something that could be done on the stage as well, something that was a real opera. Now that I had the chance to write a piece of serious music that millions of people could hear, I certainly wasn't going to compromise.

As we packed at the end of the summer I told Lenny, "Man, I've got some great news. You won't have to wait until next summer to visit with me outside the city. I just found out from Arthur Tieger, the painter who lives up in Nanuet, that he found a house for me. I can start renting this place in New City in November. I'll be able to write my opera there. It's only thirty-eight miles from New York." When we got back to the city I drove Lenny out to the house. It was kind of old and ramshackled, but it was really country. The house was across from a huge field and next to an old barn, right by South Mountain Road, one of the last semirural sections this close to New York. Because no one wanted to live in place like this all winter, I was able to rent the house for almost nothing.

The day after that I drove out of the city. Malcolm came along and helped me paint the old house and fix it up. Malcolm was still living with Emma. She was giving him such a hard time and he was happy to get away. We spent three days fixing up the house and I found an old beat-up piano that I thought would be sufficient for working. Richie Budelis, a fine sculptor, who worked part-time for Jerry McGruddy, a distinguished figure of the Village as well as the dean of the movers, came along and helped moved the old piano out.

"This is a great place, Dave," said Richie. "You'll get a lot of work done here."

After they all left and Malcolm fell asleep, I heard the sound of crickets and the soft neighing of a horse in the distance. I realized that it had been a long time since I had spent the fall in the country. My old farm-boy instincts returned. I opened the window just to get some of that beautiful fresh air. The moths that came in didn't even bother me. Sitting in this old ramshackle country house made me feel like a millionaire and I began writing furiously. I found that just as in Fire Island, the calm, fresh air and the whole special kind of feeling that an isolated area has, was an enormous help in getting that inner tranquillity that enabled me to work like a fiend. I remembered how Thelonius Monk had told me how he had written some of his best music when there were ten or fifteen people in the room practicing or just sitting around. Fortunately his music was now finally recognized and he no longer needed to work under these conditions. Neither did I.

The next day Joe Papp called me and told me that on November 19 there was going to be another reading of the opera *Twelfth Night*. He asked me to get a group of singers together in order to have as fine a performance as possible.

"I hope we can raise the money this time," he told me. "I certainly want to see *Twelfth Night* get done."

Joe decided that this time we would invite patrons of the arts, opera lovers and people from the society world. We had the kind help of a really fine lady who had joined the Shakespeare Festival. Judy Peabody and her husband, Sam, are among the handful of people in American society who are as decent and fine as all of us secretly wish our leading citizens would be. When we met at their house, Judy had that way of making all the singers, the pianist, the page turner and myself feel at home immediately. She was not a professional art patron or artsy-craftsy leader, unlike so many people I had bumped into recently. She was for real.

So many people involved in the arts seemed to feel that in exchange for the money they give, they must get a piece of the artist in return. As a result most of these scenes involved a lot of groveling and maneuvering to see who, in fact, was going to become the victim. I wanted to be treated like a man, not a cripple. I wasn't out there in that phony arty social scene. Fortunately Judy and her husband weren't either. They genuinely liked art and music and seemed to understand artists. Because they showed us respect, as soon as we entered their home they had our respect immediately.

"I can't believe it," said one singer. "She lives in this beautiful place and she's doing this for us and she's actually such a nice person." All of us felt the same way. We rehearsed and Judy and her husband would occasionally listen. They became so involved with the rehearsals that all of us had to reassure them.

"Don't worry about it," I said. "Even if we don't raise the money this time, it will get put on someday. It's just great that people will get to hear it."

Engraved invitations were sent out. White satin chairs were put in the music room; a fantastic feast was prepared with champagne by candle light. The entire house was open to make everyone feel at home. You can't imagine what it's like to be welcome in a home like this when you have spent years of your life in a crammed hole-in-the-wall type of apartment like most of us did. The only time we usually had any space is when we were performing in an auditorium. Going to Judy's house to rehearse was like a vacation for all of us. We were looking forward to the arrival of the cream of the cultural world, though we weren't exactly sure who was showing up.

The great moment finally arrived and a small mob descended upon the Peabodys' house. As I was sitting upstairs studying the score for the last time, I could smell the cigarette fumes beginning to pour underneath the door in the room and I could hear the high, whinnying laughter of the women and even caught some of the perfume smells, all of which rose above the sea of New York big-time cocktail-party rumbling and mumbling.

Finally Joe Papp came upstairs and said, "Get downstairs, David. They're tired of seeing me all year long. Go down there and charm them." I noticed that as Joe was lighting his cigar he looked nervous.

"Give me some skin, Gunga Din," I said, knocking the match out of his hand after he blew it out and trying to sound encouraging. "We're going to get the opera put on somehow someday, so don't worry about it, Pops." Joe enjoyed this vintage 1943 hip-talk and he looked a little more cheerful. I walked downstairs and entered the room jammed full of people. I tried to move through the undulating morass of expensive-looking suits and glittering gowns to get one cup of punch before I had to begin conducting. I could see a beautiful glass bowl with a great glittering crystal serving spoon and some gigantic strawberries. Somehow I imagined that if I could sink my teeth into one of those strawberries before I began, everything would go great. I made an attempt to say hello to everyone although I wasn't sure who anybody was. They were giving me that nervous nod, not being sure who I was either but not wishing to snub me for fear I might be someone important.

I saw Arthur Miller in a corner. He was standing by himself, looking over the mob from his great height as if he were Abe Lincoln surveying the stock-market floor.

"Arthur, how are you doing?" I said, really glad to see him.

"Listen, kid," he told me in that beautiful Brooklyn-accented voice that always rang true no matter where he was or what he was doing. "Inge couldn't come tonight because she had to stay with the baby. I just wanted to hear the opera and then I'm going to leave. This isn't exactly my kind of scene."

"It's not mine either, Arthur, they're just trying to raise some money."

"Well, I hope you make it, kid," he said to me. I went across the room toward the music room, managed to get a glass of punch and saw Judy and Sam. I could see that look of apprehension in their eyes.

"Don't worry," I said, "everything will be cool."

I went into the room and the musicians and the singers were all sitting in their satin chairs facing the huge rows of white satin chairs on the other side that were for the audience. The pianist Larry Smith and the singers and I began joking and talking to one another. I suddenly realized the madness of the whole situation. All of us including myself were completely confident and looking forward to what we were doing. We knew that what we were doing was good or none of us would have been there to volunteer our time or to stick our necks out. We were all able to make a living at music. What we would get financially or even professionally from having an operatic production of *Twelfth Night* in Central Park free to the public, outdoors as some kind of wonderful summertime event, was not anything that would be of world-shattering significance. We just all thought it would be a wonderful idea. On the other hand, all the people in the room we saw had that worried, apprehensive look on their faces, torn between the social obligation of coming, wondering who else had come, whether or not they were going to like the opera, and worried that they might have to give some money or time to it if they did.

They all came into the room and sat down. Joe got up and made a brief speech, describing how we had known each other since he first met me on the Lower East Side in 1956. He said how wonderful it would be to have an opera like this as a part of our summer production as free Shakespeare for the public.

Then I made a brief speech thanking Joe. I noticed the conductor of a visiting German opera company in the first row. When he saw that I had a baton in my hand, he gave me a hate ray that looked like two headlights coming over the horizon from way, way far away. I watched the impresario's eyebrows knitting. Then his forehead grew into a scowl. The whole top of his head seemed to be turning into a knot of muscle tension. Wilhelm Reich could have given a two-hour lecture on the tension and anxiety in the small area between the bridge of this man's nose and top of his forehead. Just before I turned to conduct I gave him a wink.

As I began the first act, and Alan Baker sang Orsino's "If Music Be the Food of Love Play On," I could feel a kind of cold draught coming over my shoulder. I suddenly realized that most of the people probably had thought that at most they would only have to hear one singer, preferably one who would go into an Old Broadway shout-honker-extravaganza lasting perhaps two minutes, followed by some more speech making and a lot more partying. These people realized that they were stuck and had to hear some music. Most of them were not only bored, they were infuriated.

By the time we had gotten through the first scene of the first act, it felt like sheets of ice were pouring over all of us. I smiled at the singers. During one piano solo, which accompanied Sir Toby Belch and Andrew Aguecheek dancing the Galliard, one of the singers leaned over and whispered into my ear, "Jesus Christ, this is worse than opening night at the Met."

We continued the opera and it went beautifully. As the more intimate and delicate sections were being sung, especially the parts that had a very soft accompaniment, I could hear heavy breathing, punctuated with an occasional muffled snore. I also heard the writhing of people in their seats, that kind of *squish-squish* sound of expensive clothes twitching with boredom and nervous energy. I could sense that the people had expected, with the word *opera*, to have some great pop-art figure appear in an outrageous beaded gown and gigantic plumed hat, looking like a transvestite tackle with the New York Giants to honk through some familiar Puccini arias. I remembered when a friend who had performed in the Met sneaked me into the orchestra pit for a part of opening night. I walked out during intermission and saw all the men in their top hats getting stoned and obviously intending to spend the rest of the night drinking upstairs while their seats went to waste. Then I went outside and saw people still standing in line waiting for standing room in the very top of the theater. Perhaps opera had to be presented a different way in America.

When the first act of the opera drew to a close there was a groan of relief before the applause. Joe got up and made another speech, saying that before everyone left they should see him if they wished to contribute money to the Shakespeare Festival for this special project. People hit the punch bowl and the food table and in two minutes it was exactly as it was before the opera had begun: the great roar of small talk filled the entire house. Cigar and cigarette smoke and perfume aromas floated about. It was as if this interminable interruption during the social gathering had never really occurred.

A few people came up to me. One was a good-natured hustler whom

I recognized immediately. He had worked as a busboy with me in Nantucket in the summer of 1951. He since had married an American heiress who had divorced a count but kept all her money in the process. She now lavished it all on him.

"God, that was neat," she said nasally. "Niki and I are going to Europe for three years and we do so hope that we shall hear your music there. I'm very close friends with many people in the international music community and I hope we shall be of help to your simply extraordinary musical gift. Are you planning on singing it in English or will you translate it into Italian when you present your opera in the park?" She was absolutely serious. I figured maybe she had never heard an opera in English.

"I thought it was magnificent, David," he said. "It was somehow like Wagner. Still neither myself nor my wife are much for ultramodern music, you know." Seeing as this was perhaps the simplest and least modern piece I was ever to write in my life—in fact parts of it seem as if it could have been written two hundred years ago—I realized that perhaps they were among the beautiful dreamers during its performance. Some other people made some comments, but many people from the musical world, including the conductor of the German opera company, simply shuffled over to the other side of the room whenever I got close to them.

I saw Arthur Miller and he told me in a few sentences what he liked about it, the parts he would like to hear again and how he thought different pacing and tempo in the music might help to hold the opera together dramatically. Because we had worked on *After the Fall* together, we had a great understanding and did not have to waste words talking about nothing.

One man from the Metropolitan Opera, John Gutman, told me that he liked it and that he would help in any way he could in the future. He and conductor Paul Calloway were the most encouraging of anyone.

Gradually people left. Sam and Judy came over, really beaming. I could see from that how much they had enjoyed it and that the whole experience was worthwhile and I suddenly felt very happy that they had had a good time. The singers also seemed very happy.

A baritone came over to me and said, "Don't worry, man, in a few years all these people will be begging you to do things for them."

"I don't care about that, I just want to see this opera get put on," I said, "so that the people in the park can come and see it." The singers and the pianist Larry Smith, the young conductor who had helped during rehearsals and I sat around joking and talking about the opera and music in general. Finally there was no one left but the musicians, the Peabodys and Joe Papp and his wife. Joe looked philosophical. Anyone else in his place might have dived out of a window, but Joe really had a philosophical look on his face. He had been through so many years of constant frustration and perpetual chaos in order to get the Shakespeare Festival launched that nothing could bother him.

"Well, boychick, it looks like we'll have to wait a little longer to have our opera put on. I liked it more this time than the first time and the important thing is that you have it written. We'll have to do another one. I wish the hell I had money of my own. I would put the damn thing on myself. I don't care that I wrote the libretto and really it doesn't mean anything to me anymore that we worked on it together. I just think it's a nice piece of work and that our audience in the park should see it." Then he began to pace back and forth and smoke his cigar furiously. I knew he was a little bugged after all. "Damn it," he said, "there was over a hunder million dollars in this room and we couldn't even raise fifty dollars to help toward getting the parts for the second act copied. Don't let this discourage you, Dave, I have this situation every day, three hundred and sixty-five days a year with the festival. You know because you were there. For the first few years we had to go out after the play and try to raise money from the audience directly. We couldn't get one big-money person or sponsor to come in with a nickel until it got some prestige, and I suspect the same thing's going to happen to you. As you build more of a name in music you'll suddenly find people with a lot of money will begin to think you're a genius."

The next day I went to the YMCA, did my road work and thought to myself, Well, at least I've got most of the opera done and that's something no one can take away from me. The fact that I'd worked eighteen months on some of the best music I'd written in my life only to have it received by snores didn't discourage me. I knew I had nearly completed an opera. And now I had to complete my next one—fast!

I had so much of the feeling of *The Final Ingredient* inside me that I wasn't even worried about finishing it on time. It was an incredible effort, but because I was in such great physical and mental condition, I soared into it with a sense of dedication and joy. I was really turned on to the opera. I was high on life and high on music. I remembered how the heating system had broken down a few years before when I had been out around Woodstock. I kept checking so that this wouldn't happen again in New City. When it really got cold that winter I would go out to the water pump and keep it going by throwing old pieces of insulated cloth on top of it. I would wrap old blankets around the pump and check the heater in the bottom of the pit to make sure it wouldn't break down and let the pipes break.

I worked on the average of fourteen hours a day. I found that there were a few central themes I was able to draw upon, over and over again. By combining them with other themes, it seemed to give the work a cohesive structure dramatically as well as musically. This simplest of compositional devices helped to tie the whole opera together. Even though *The Final Ingredient* was being done on television, Arnold and I decided to make it a real one-act opera. It would then be up to the director, Bob De Laney, to use his considerable skills to make it suitable for television. I had seen a televised production of *Fidelio* which was extremely moving. I knew our opera would be done as well. Television was nothing but a medium. The music, the dramatic story, the singers and the general shape and structure of the work were the message.

We tried to make Aaron, the central character, into a modern Jew, in conflict with his father because of a past grievance. He was also in conflict with his identification as a Jew. He doubted his heritage. Still, at the end of the opera, he gave his life to make the Passover service possible. We were not going to make the Nazis in the play into supermonsters, but we didn't want to make the Jewish prisoners into supermen either. We attempted to make all the characters as human and vulnerable as possible. Otherwise it would be on a religious comic-book level.

Igor Sudarsky helped us write authentic dialogue. He had been in a concentration camp so he knew. I had decided that every time a guard spoke in the opera it would be in German with the exception of the one officer. He had a great sardonic aria but first announced that he was going to speak in the language of the prisoners so that they would understand him better. The rest of the guards brayed in the most horrible German. It made them sound more evil and dehumanized. It was very effective. Igor told me the commands that they used to give to the Jews. We had them usually singing in a southern

German dialect, since a lot of the SS men and noncommissioned offi-cers came from there.

The Nazi officer who sung in English had one great scene where he begged the prisoners to understand him. "Try to understand us, we're doing this for your own good, we're trying to help you. If only you Jews would learn to keep your place." This was followed by a hideous waltzlike section with the ironic text, "We Germans are the friendliest people in the world," answered by the soldiers' repeating it in a monotone similar to the melody of "Ach Du Lieber Augustin." During this scene, I had the "Horst Wessel" song, "Wenn die Soldaten durch die Stadt marschieren," an old marching song and "In München steht ein Hofbräuhaus," all playing at the same time in a gigantic contrapuntal put-down of Germanic beer-hall sentimentality.

The officer was one of the best roles in the opera. In fact, some of the most powerful and frightening music was written for the Nazis. By 1965 there had been a spate of books and articles, implying that the Jews were equally guilty and that in spite of the holocaust, the Nazis really were not such bad guys after all. Some journalists even felt poor Adolph Eichmann was getting a raw deal. Arnold and I knew that we Jews had committed plenty of crimes and sins in our history. But, as one of the characters in the opera sang, "We never built a cage for men."

No one wanted to be reminded of this, exactly twenty years after the worst crime and mass murder in history. Arnold and I felt an obligation.

Beyond that, the opera was a true portrayal of prison, brutality, the relationship between the victim and the executioner and most important, the ultimate triumph of the spirit over degradation and oppression. As a result, a great deal of music had a kind of quiet affirmation, although it was always tinged with a great melancholy and sadness.

The role of Aaron's father, a man misunderstood by his son, was more traditional. In dramatic terms he was a man who was some-what puzzled and beaten by life, even before he was in a concentra-tion camp. The other characters were so understated that we left it to their music and their actions to explain what they were like. They were really only sketches. They were people who were reduced by their bondage to shadows. Arnold and I both felt that the entire opera would be more powerful if these other characters were true prisoners.

By the time I completed the third scene of the opera, I had the entire score clearly worked out in my mind. It was simply a matter of actually being able to put down all the notes on paper. Because I was able to order wood for twenty dollars a cord, my heating problems were solved and I spent almost four straight months writing music, sleeping and keeping the fire burning. As I got farther and farther along, instead of getting more tired I seemed to get more energy and by the time the opera was completed I felt better than I ever had in my life.

During the entire time I worked on *The Final Ingredient* no one asked to hear a note. I had only met once with a rabbi from the Jewish Theological Seminary. We went to lunch at Ratner's, where he checked all the pronunciations of parts of the prayers in Hebrew and asked me to change one line of the libretto, which I did after getting Arnold's permission.

Wiley Hance, the producer, finally asked if he could hear something, as he had no idea what any of it sounded like. I went with a friend of mine, Richard Frisch, a highly gifted bass with perfect pitch, who could sing soprano, mezzo soprano, alto, tenor or baritone parts. With Larry Smith playing the piano and me conducting while playing some percussion, French horn and flute, we tried to play through the opera with Richard singing all the parts and all of us singing when there were sections for trios, quartets or chorus. We went to the Variety Arts recording studio, where I'd recorded Shakespeare in the Park music for so many years, and made a demonstration record of the first four scenes.

It was pretty strange sounding. Still, the director, Bob De Laney, said it helped him to get the feeling of what it was about. He began preparing his shots way in advance. Through an unusual stroke of good luck, he had played cello for years, so with the help of the record and a vocal score, he began planning the shots around the music. Wiley decided that in order to give him more freedom visually, we would record the music first, then have the singers pantomime against the recording of their own singing so that the camera work could be more fluid. Otherwise, they explained to me, we might have a perfect musical take of a scene and have the camera miss a shot. Or have a perfect take visually, only to have somebody miss a note. Although I had never worked this way, it seemed to make sense.

A week later we began casting for the opera, which was to be taped in six weeks' time. We had had to wait this long because of network problems. ABC was not sure that they could afford the great expense of an orchestra. If they could, there was a problem of how large an orchestra. Also, there was a question of whether a professional chorus could be used, how many solo singers could be used, and a thousand other crises that seemed to pop up every day. Wiley handled them with super-Zen calm from his small office.

I knew many singers in addition to the ones who had appeared during our two readings of *Twelfth Night*. Also, Wiley knew a lot of fine singers too. Our only problem was finding people who could work on such short notice. We had to find a complete cast who could attend all the rehearsals, the taping, and the video taping who were not previously committed for some or all of the time. This began a series of phone calls not only in New York but all over the country. Many of the finest singers were on trains, buses and jet planes en route to engagements or on the way home. I had never known until this time how complicated were the travel schedules of accomplished opera singers.

The auditions for the opera began at last. It was much harder to find the right singers for *The Final Ingredient* than it had been for *Twelfth Night*, because this opera was set in 1945 rather than in Shakespeare's time and because it was a tragedy with melodramatic overtones. It required a whole different kind of singing and acting. *The Final Ingredient* required almost a method actor's approach to opera. It was a question of finding singers flexible enough to work, to portray the quality of people who were actually inmates in a concentration camp, even though they were singing.

The father was played by Joseph Sopher, who had just the right quality of gentleness, kindness and a sense of despair. His ability to create a man of overwhelming simplicity made this role much more touching than I had originally imagined it. My friend Ezio Flagello miraculously had just enough time off to make a final rehearsal or two and a taping because of a cancellation of another performance out of town. He played Walter, a man of resignation and a philosophic detachment and bitterness. He had the most powerful aria of the whole opera. I begged Wiley Hance to take my word that Ezio was probably the finest bass in America for this role. Wiley trusted me, and Ezio was hired through his manager, even though he was in Pittsburgh when he agreed to do it.

Richard Frisch, who had sung all twelve roles on the demonstration record, played a small part brilliantly and also helped out with the chorus. John Fiorito agreed to play the part of the Nazi officer. He was a man of great charm, good humor and kindness. John didn't have a mean bone in his body. Yet when he acted he could create a monstrous sadist. Alan Baker, another fine baritone, who had sung at the audition for *Twelfth Night*, played a role that required as much acting ability as it did musical ability. He had both in abundance. Malcolm Smith, one of the busiest bass baritones in America and one of the finest, played a leading role. He was not able to attend the first rehearsal because he was barnstorming the Far West with various opera companies and in concerts. All of us were familiar with his marvelous work and knew he could learn any role in two days.

The only role we had trouble casting was Aaron, the son. John Reardon had agreed to do it, but at the last minute our date had to be changed because of a change in studio time. John was already committed to something else, so we were about to start auditioning all over again when William Covington came in to audition. He sang an aria from *Il Trovatore* and was so outstanding that I told Wiley this was the person we were looking for. His musicianship was of the highest caliber and his acting seemed so natural that I was sure he could bring a great reality to the role. He had sung with the Lake George Opera Company and was just twenty-two years old. Many people's stock response to a young unknown is "Get some more experience and come back," but I always hoped that I would never let this attitude stop me from being able to see what was happening. I had been given chances and come through. I thought William Covington would too. Wiley Hance and Bob De Laney agreed. They were more interested in ability than big names. We hired William that night. There were three solo roles for women, performing with an *a cappella* chorus. Saramae Endich, a brilliant soprano and favorite among musicians for years, Marija Kova, a fine actress as well as singer, and Elaine Bonazzi, a highly gifted mezzo, completed the cast. The chorus of men and women was selected by Tom Pyle.

On a cloudy day in March we all got together for the first run-through. Some of the principal singers couldn't make it, so Richard Frisch agreed to fill in and sing all their parts. Joseph Sopher had a cold, so he sang his part in a whisper so that he wouldn't strain his voice.

It sounded pretty far-out. Wiley Hance and Bob De Laney looked puzzled at times; so did Milton Krents from the Jewish Theological

Seminary. Still, they all trusted me and seemed to feel that when it was all put together, it would be worth the effort.

We began rehearsals the next day. For the next ten days I ran from one rehearsal hall to the other, checking in with the chorus, the soloists, with groups of soloists and with people who played in scenes with one another. The schedule had somehow been figured out in a crazy patchwork-quilt correlation of timetables so that we could rehearse as much as possible. I conducted all the rehearsals from the orchestral score and in that way memorized most of the piece.

I got together with John Fiorito for his important scene as the Nazi officer during an inspection of the prison camp. He asked me my feelings about the part. I tried to sing it myself. He told me that my interpretation of what I had written was too much of a caricature of a Nazi. He said that if the role was to be meaningful and realistic, he would have to play it completely differently. He decided to do it in a less grotesque fashion. The role lost its cartoon flavor and became truly blood-curdling. He sang exactly what I had written. He followed the stage directions and indications that Arnold and I had worked on. But by interpreting the role entirely in his own way, he actually created something of his own that was far more brilliant than anything either Arnold or I had ever imagined.

I found as I worked with the singers that if I concentrated on general musical ideas and let the performers discover their parts themselves, they could make it on their own. The only arguments I had were with tempos. Because of network time, the opera could not last more than fifty-eight and a half minutes. I was responsible to see that it was the right length. I didn't mind slowing down or speeding up in any way that the singers wanted to, as long as the general sections timed out correctly. Otherwise the opera would have to be cut.

Bob De Laney had pretty much the same kind of attitude I had. His staging was simple, direct and forwarded the inherent drama of the story. Rather than trying to impose any superpsychological neo-Freudian acting ideas on the singers, he tried to make the opera come to life by letting it happen. He planned his shots in perfect coordination with the music. They served the simple dramatic framework of the libretto. He left everything else to the performers.

After we had the last rehearsal with the piano, I went home, studied the score all afternoon for the final time so that I could have it memorized for the orchestra rehearsal, then fell asleep for twelve hours. I woke up at seven o'clock the next morning and put on my long moth-eaten fur coat, which was made around the turn of the century in Michigan and I had bought for twenty dollars. It was falling apart but had been an indispensable part of my wardrobe, keeping me warm out in the country while I was writing.

At nine o'clock the studios were open and I went in and introduced myself to the engineers. They were two wonderful guys named Jim and Jack. We went over the placement and set up the microphones. They informed me that we were not able to have a fifteen-inch-per-second tape machine.

"What!" I said, almost falling out of my ratty furs. "Why not? You know only a fifteen-inch machine can get any real fidelity."

"Because ABC only uses seven-and-a-half-inch-per-second equipment," they told me. "The brass felt that if we used a fifteen-inch-per-second machine, it would be wasting tape and set a bad precedent for future productions. We figured between us the cost of recording with fifteen inch as opposed to seven and a half. It would be twenty dollars' difference."

"Perhaps ABC could change their minds," I said hopefully.

"Nope," said Jim, the engineer. "These guys never change their minds about anything. Once they decide they won't budge."

I had forty minutes left before the orchestra was due to arrive for their only rehearsal. I had to act in a hurry. I called up an executive and told him of the problem.

"I'm sorry," he said, "this is a network policy. Seven and a half is good enough for Lawrence Welk, it's good enough for you."

Fortunately by this time, I had learned that shouting and screaming, while it might be great as therapy, doesn't usually accomplish much unless the person you're shouting at enjoys it. I decided that my wits would be my best weapon, so I thanked him and hung up. I called the Variety Arts studio and told them my problem.

"Well, happy times sure are coming back, Dave," said Ferdy, the genial Cuban engineer whom I had known for so many years. "We try and help you all we can. You know we nevair let you down yet, Dave. How can we sneak a machine in?"

"Listen, man," I said, "I have to start the rehearsal in half an hour. If you can get over here between twelve and one and put the fifteen-inch machine in, it's O.K. with the two ABC engineers. They want to do a good job too, but no one will give us a fifteen-inch machine."

"O.K.," he said, "we'll bring it outside in the truck and wrap it up so it look like we're bringing in sandwiches or ice cream. Do that soun' all right?"

"That's great," I said, "just signal me about five after twelve and instead of going to lunch, I'll help you to sneak the machine into the control room."

I ran back and told Jim and Jack that the plot had been hatched and that we would have a fifteen-inch tape machine ferreted in by about twelve five. That would give us a chance to install it before the actual recording began at one that afternoon.

The ABC musicians started arriving for the rehearsal before the recording. I saw many old friends in the orchestra, including French hornist Jim Buffington, Tony Miranda, Warren Smith and other musicians I had known from all over. They didn't know it was going to be my opera they were going to record. They were as happy as I was that something like this was commissied by ABC. So little good music was being done on television that their jobs were gradually dwindling. The ABC Symphony had the finest musicians in New York on staff. They wanted to play music, but there was nothing to play except rock and roll shows. They also admired the Tsar Nicholas lines of my ratty fur coat.

We had exactly two hours to rehearse fifty-eight and a half minutes of music. The singers came so that they could listen to the orchestra for the first time and hum along to themselves. I was still the only one up to this point who had any idea what it would sound like. While it seemed natural to me, many of the singers were extremely surprised when they heard the piano accompaniment replaced with the orchestra. They didn't realize what an important part the orchestra played in the opera. By the time the two hours were up, we had run through the opera once and repeated a few tricky sections. We also corrected errors in the parts. Then everyone went to lunch for an hour.

I ran to the side exit and waited. At 12:05 Ferdy and another engineer from the Variety Arts studio came in, looking like two sandwichmen bringing in a tray of food. We carried the tape recorder, which was on a wheeled cart, into the control room. No one seemed to notice us. This was partly because I put my fur coat over the machine. While Ferdy and his friend were wheeling it past the guards, I picked up Jim Buffington's horn and began to play some jazz to attract their attention. The TV crime of the century had been completed.

We had managed to sneak in the machine. Now we had to try to wire it up. It was a stereophonic machine, but we could only get it to play on one track. That was really sufficient, since television does not broadcast in stereo anyway. But because the wiring was completely different from the setup for the seven-and-a-half-inch machine, we had to readjust all of the wires and cables leading to the microphones.

After lunch, when Wiley and Bob De Laney arrived with several other people, I could see that the control room was going to be the panic scene of the year. Ferdy and his friend stayed on and whispered last-minute instructions to Jim and Jack on how to operate the machine.

At one o'clock sharp we began recording. In order to save time and money, we had to record all the music out of sequence, beginning with the sections that used the most singers and musicians and ending with those sections that used the least. The first portions of the opera we recorded were with the chorus and orchestra and because of the enormous sound were the most difficult to record.

When we finally performed the triumphal ending about the third time, I realized we had a perfect take. "O.K.," I shouted, spinning around on the podium and smiling with joy toward the sound booth. "Let's hear that, man. That was fantastic!" Inside the sound booth I saw nothing but concerned faces and the shaking of heads. "Are you kidding? That was great!" I shouted. "What's wrong?"

"I'm sorry, Dave," said Jack, coming out. "The machine wasn't recording." A gigantic groan came up from the orchestra, chorus and soloists. We began recording again and after several more tries got even a better version than we had before and this time they had all the wires straight.

We kept on at a furious pace and were often able to record an entire scene in the first or second take. Although the singers wanted to slow down the tempos I kept them at the same speed we had rehearsed. This was to make sure that the different sections would time out. I didn't even use a stopwatch or a metronome during the recording, since tempos were memorized in my mind. But without looking at a clock, no scene came out more than two seconds either over or under the length it was supposed to be. The first day we got done with our recording ahead of time and I went home feeling great.

The next day I woke up early again but could hardly move my arm. I had been so carried away the first day that I had just about thrown my arm out of its socket. I did a whole series of calisthenics to loosen up the right side of my body.

Jim and Jack were at the studio early. "We got some kind of damn static on the tape during the women's chorus," they informed me, "but I think we'll be able to get it out. Today we have the sound set up right. You'll be able to hear the difference."

Everything went even better than the day before. During Ezio Flagello's aria, he began to change the tempo in every measure. It was gorgeous. What he did was so musical that without even knowing what would happen next, I was able to follow him and keep the orchestra together at the same time. Ezio's performance had a quality of rubato, an almost-floating feeling that would have taken weeks to rehearse if we had planned it that way. It was one of those really natural and spontaneous moments in music and we managed to record it. I felt it was the best performance of anything I had ever written. Regardless of how the rest of the opera seemed when it was all put together, I knew that Ezio's one moment alone would make it worthwhile.

We actually ended up two hours ahead of schedule. Everyone was exhausted, but I felt great. I was able to move my arm again. I stayed with Jim and Jack for six hours splicing the entire tape, timing it, trying to equalize and balance everything and take the static out of the women's chorus. Then we all went out and celebrated.

Two days later we came back for video taping. The members of the cast were filmed while hearing the playback of the recording of what they had done previously. Then the original sound and video tape would be mixed.

The set looked awfully small. We had originally planned to use Camp Kilmer, where I had been stationed in the army on the way to Germany. I remembered Camp Kilmer as being very much like a concentration camp in many respects. At the last moment, however, we were forced to adapt the set that was generally used for an interview program conducted by Les Crane.

John Dapper made a symbolic design to represent the concentration camp. By the use of different camera shots, Bob De Laney was able to actually make it appear as if this small area were a high series of barracks. The actors got in costume and for the first time I could see as well as hear the opera. The music was played back over loudspeakers and the actors rehearsed while the cameramen went through their series of shots. Everything would be recorded on video tape while the sound was mixed simultaneously. Because the music and singing had already been recorded, the actors had to be able to synchronize their lips with what they had sung two days previously. It was remarkable how well they did it.

The whole opera seemed to work even better in its completed form than it had in my imagination. I had often found in the theater that in the final stages overproduction killed what seemed to be powerful. Grossness and plain bad taste usually leveled everything off. In this case, the production was so simple that it made our opera look real. After two grueling days, the singers had completed their work. We now had to wait for the video tape to be spliced and the final sound to be mixed. Finally, a week later, we went to a viewing room and saw the whole thing.

It was hard to be objective at this point because I was so close to it. In spite of myself, I was conducting and cueing every single bar. Still I saw that if nothing else, the opera held together and that it was what I had dreamed of when I first began *Twelfth Night* several years before. With *The Final Ingredient* I had completed a real opera.

The day of its actual showing, I invited about thirty friends over to my Sixth Avenue apartment. We planned to watch the opera and have a big Passover dinner afterwards. We began to watch the opera with my three rented TV sets. I saw how great television can be as a medium for something serious. It was wonderful to be able to sit at home and watch the opera with my friends. Even though so many subtleties of the sound were lost in the transmission, the intimacy of having the music and drama unfold right in your own living room made television's acoustical shortcomings seem negligible.

It was clear that television wasn't the monstrous medium I had always thought it to be. It was just that there was so much garbage that was presented, many people envisioned the television set as being responsible for what came out of it.

When the opera was over, people were quiet and many of them were crying. We had a traditional Pesach dinner and then the party began. It lasted nine hours during which time I got phone calls from all over the country.

The reviews came and most of them were so encouraging that Wiley Hance told me he would do it on future Passovers. That meant it would get additional performances, something almost unheard of for a new opera on television. ABC had the courage to present a controversial new work and sponsor it themselves. Because of their vision and the dedication of everyone involved in the production, *The Final Ingredient* was no longer an experiment. Like Menotti's *Amahl and the Night Visitors*, it was to become an annual event.

I went down to Igor's to get a sandwich for lunch and we discussed the opera at length.

"Vell, kid," he said to me, "your concentration camp was a lot cleaner than mine, but I think that you got it. Even some of the critics had to finally agree that you did something good."

May 13, "A Year in Our Land" was premiered at Town Hall. My cantata was the first piece on the program and Schubert's C Major Mass the second. Even though the Interracial Chorale was an amateur group, they could really sing, and Harold Aks got a professional sound from them. They had really gotten into the music and the performance was gorgeous. Lynn Blair, Elaine Bonazzi, Seth McCoy and Herbert Beattie were the soloists.

For once I hadn't chosen the orchestra. I didn't have time. I had been so busy the last eight months. To my surprise, Spike was playing the oboe and Henry Nowak was playing trumpet. They had both been with the Seventh Army Symphony and we were really surprised to see one another.

"That's pretty weird there," said Spike, "with all the work that we did with the Shakespeare Festival and all the time we've hung out, it's really strange just to get hired, not even knowing what the job's going to be, and end up playing your music."

"Yeah," said Henry Nowak, "this piece is O.K., Dave. It's really got a lot of soul to it. Don't you know it's unfashionable to write music like that? What are you trying to do, beat Barry Goldwater?"

"No," I said, "I'm trying to make the music sound like me."

"Groovy," said Hank, "stay that way."

Town Hall was packed for the performance. When the chorus got to the fourth movement, "Winter in the South," and arrived at the section after the tolling bells where some of the most moving music of the whole cantata was written, the piece really took off. I could feel it happen and knew at that point if only for those few moments the piece had done what I wanted it to do. Even the soloists in the chorus and Harold got carried away and when they came to the epilogue it was really roaring. I saw that if I could write music that would inspire the performers, it would have an inspiring effect on anyone that heard it. I felt that I had written a piece that served the authors' texts. More than that, it was my thank you to the USA, a musician's tribute to the America that I dreamed of and felt in my heart and mind and soul. I didn't even know if an America like the one described by these six authors could ever exist anymore except in our imaginations and spirits.

I thought more about the piece during intermission. These authors had described the real America. They had written of the poetry that lies in the dream that brought people here from the ghettos of the world. They had voiced the old forgotten love that lay in the hearts of the people who had fought and suffered to get here. And I felt a great sadness when I thought of how all this had been forgotten and ignored. I hoped the cantata might remind all of us who we were.

During the Schubert mass, I decided to go down to the basement before the onslaught of people came backstage. I could never remember having felt so tired. Now the cantata was suddenly over, the panic was off. I hadn't had one real day of rest in an awfully long time. I stretched out chairs underneath the stage and passed out in exhaustion while the Schubert mass was being sung upstairs.

The singers came down after the concert. I guessed they were surprised to find me lying there. One of them poked me and I woke up to see a sea of faces in an oval above me. I felt as if I had been in a car accident with a crowd of onlookers staring down at me. After a second or two I realized what was happening.

"O.K.," I grunted, getting up, "time to go backstage and meet the music lovers of America." I bounded upstairs. People came pouring through.

"Yeah, Davey, byuddiful, byuddiful. Hasta la culture boom, chico, where's the party man?" This was Carlos Anduze, my old buddy from Venezuela. He had played drums at countless sessions at loft parties when he first came to New York. He had about seven delectible teenyboppers with him. I didn't feel tired anymore. Their sunny faces brightened up Town Hall. Dave Lambert, Gil Evans and my favorite composer of theater music, Teiji Ito, came backstage. Suddenly I realized what a lucky man I was. Instead of having to go to some ghoulish stuffy reception, I could go out with my friends and have a ball. "I guess we'll go down to the Socialist Hall," I said. I had rented it out again for fifteen dollars. Lenny Gross was there with Kathy, his sweet young thing. He had been with me all through the summer when I was writing "A Year in Our Land."

"Well, Mr. Amram," he said, "you got it written after all. *Sexology* magazine will nominate you for Clean Liver of the month."

"Come on, man," I said to him, "let's go down to the Socialist Hall and have a sumptuous after-the-concert beer and Katz' Delicatessen soirée."

My parents had come up to hear the work and when I saw my mother in the Socialist Hall she said, "Oh my God, have you become a Socialist after all these years? I think it's a little late for that, don't you?"

"Well, they're nice people, Mom," I told her, "and they rented the hall out cheap."

They were nice people and all the Socialists that worked there really dug my music and my musician friends. They weren't like most people in political groups I know—either lonely-hearts-club types or power-driven, ambitious-looking philistine types. They all seemed kind to one another and they were great hosts.

"I want to congratulate you, Dave," said Wallingford Pickles, the psychedelic airlines pilot, who was also a big-time smuggler and importer of hashish. No one knew his real name, but his pseudonym was unforgettable. I had always figured that he should give a concert himself. An Evening With Wallingford Pickles. If he ever got high and spoke for two and a half hours at Carnegie Hall, it would put all the lecturers in America out of business. He was a matchless raconteur of world-wide low-life scenes. He knew the inner dynamics of every kind of petty hustle, con game and illegal hype that existed. He also had the scientific flair of a Renaissance man. He had invented countless ingenious ways of smuggling all kinds of objects from plane to pad. His Baedeker Guide concentrated solely on drugs, prostitutes, petty crimes and the assorted smorgasbord of international characters he had encountered during his smuggling career.

Still he had a great sense of honor, was always extremely kind and generous to all his friends in the Village, many of whom were destitute. Wallingford never cheated anyone and was really a wonderful guy. I always felt he was just like many other businessmen except that I could trust him much more. The only difference was if anybody could prove what his business was, he would be forced to serve quite a bit of time in the can.

"Out of sight, Jim," he said to me. He came up to the conductor. "I just want to say, Mr. Aks, that I thought your interpretation of Mr. Amram's selection was stupendous. It was outstanding all the way. A real credit to the art of conducting." Wallingford then put his pipe in his mouth and walked away. Harold was surprised and delighted to receive such a compliment from a stranger.

"Who is that guy?" he asked me.

"Oh, he's a friend of mine," I said, "a music lover." And it was true. Although it was the first concert Wallingford had ever been to, he was a music lover. At least during the first half. Lenny had told me that he had seen Wallingford during intermission, puffing away. He got pretty zonked-out after my piece was performed. He returned to his seat just in time to fall asleep during the second half. Because he sat in the very first row in order not to miss anything, he lay with his head on the stage during the entire Schubert mass.

Wallingford was elegantly attired in a beautiful herringbone tweed jacket with leather patches, casually luxuriant knit wool pants with tiny cuffs, and expensive hand-made Moroccan alligator tassel shoes. As he walked around the room, I noticed he would occasionally pass around his meerschaum pipe.

I was completely turned on from the music. I felt relaxed and relieved that the concert was over and that it had gone so well. I also felt a calmness and a sense of brotherhood with everyone in the room. I saw more and more that composing was not a question of building up your ego but of sharing a dream with others.

A group of us went over to my apartment late that night. Carlos and Wallingford and Seymour Krim all entertained us with the tall tales of their travels in Manhattan and throughout the world. I just sat with my girl friend, listening. Jay Cameron was there and we talked about the old days in Paris and I saw how lucky I'd been. I might not have much money, but my hope of working totally in music and keeping some kind of freedom so that I could be an artist was slowly being realized.

My next project, "Let Us Remember," was based on the "Yizkor," a prayer of remembrance. It was commissioned by the Union of American Hebrew Congregations. I met with Langston Hughes, who was to write the text, and with a rabbi. I considered myself very fortunate to be chosen to write this work.

At one point, the rabbi leaned over confidentially to Langston and said, "Of course you have to understand this particular Jewish feeling that we're after."

Langston replied very casually, "I understand, Rabbi, and I think I know the kind of feeling because it's something that's part of me. You see, my grandfather was Jewish." This really blew the rabbi's mind and after this he left us alone to work on the cantata by ourselves.

Because Langston was such a consummate lyric artist and had written so much for voice, he was familiar with the problems that composers have. He presented me with many beautiful poems and allowed me to use whichever parts of them I wished, in order to have the basis for a workable text. While this was a secular text, it had strong roots in the old feelings and ideas of the ancient prayers. In one section there was the constant repetition of the line "Let not the oppressed become oppressors." This section was a brief poetic narrative of tyranny in Jewish and world history and it was one of the most effective parts of the cantata. It was really designed as a concert work and was part of the whole program of modern Jewish music that was to be presented at the San Francisco opera house in November, 1965.

I went up to see Langston at his apartment in Harlem to go over the poems. I hadn't been up in Harlem much since I had played with Oscar Pettiford's band last. We used to rehearse up there and occasionally we would have jobs playing for dances. It brought back a flood of memories as I was driving up, thinking of all the nights I had played there, all of the sessions I had been to and all the musicians and other people I had met who had come from there. I had visited George Barrow a lot when he had lived up there, but when I drove through his old neighborhood, I didn't recognize many faces.

I always thought of Harlem in terms of music and the people that I knew. Now I saw it as an anachronism in these times of plenty. Lyndon Johnson had promised that we were going to have the Great Society, but Harlem didn't look like it was part of it. There was Great activity in the streets, a Great sense of life, energy and style. That was terrific. What I saw that I hadn't noticed before was the Great filth and the Great number of people standing around and a Great variety of angry and desperate looks on people's faces.

Maybe it was just that I was getting older and straighter and saw more of what was really happening. Maybe Harlem had really changed. At any rate, I saw that to even have a Harlem in 1965 was insanity. I didn't feel guilty or ashamed, I just felt sad and angry.

Langston and I spent most of the afternoon talking about his poems. I talked about Harlem with him too, how I'd noticed that it seemed different to me.

"I'm sure you're seeing a little clearer," he told me, "but it has changed. All those hundreds of years of bitterness and frustrations are beginning to overflow. We've been promised so much for so long and now there's so much to be had, a lot of the young people figure if they don't get it they're going to go out and *take* it. I'm a different generation. You see, I love Harlem. I've lived all over the world and I still find it's one of the most beautiful places I know. But the younger people don't feel this way. History is finally catching up with America. Still, I hate to see the anger in the young faces all the time—it's even hard for me to write my Simple stories anymore. There's so much bitterness and anger that they don't seem to be as funny as they used to."

Langston and I then resumed discussion of our piece. As I drove through Harlem on the way out to Fire Island, I could see how ridiculous the whole situation in America was. Here were people crowded in a way that was inexcusable. It was a medieval ghetto in 1965. With all the money we were making in America, and all the money we were spending in Viet Nam, it seemed that there would be a much better way to change the ghettos—other than the obvious way of burning them down. This was something that was being talked about a lot. Not just by speakers on 125th Street. You heard it downtown too. Malcolm X's death had changed things. Yet the way our government seemed to be going, it looked like the only instant slum clearance was going to be arson.

It's horrible, I thought to myself. People have to resort to violence. Still, this was the way business was done in America. Labor unions made great strides in the 1930s as a result of violence. The Indians were put down by violence. Many of our folk heroes like Billy the Kid, Jesse James and Buffalo Bill were violent types. So maybe this was just part of history. I sure hope not, I thought to myself. There must be a better way. I figured if a race war started I'd probably be playing in a band with both black and white musicians and get shot by both sides.

It was also clear to me that race was a dodge for what it was really all about. Money. I had never heard of people who were well-to-do starting a riot. I realized what a gift of God it was to be a musician and to be able to work and to communicate with people on a higher level. This was why I was here, but I couldn't kid myself. The poor people all over America didn't need spiritual elevation as much as they needed the chance to get some money. And right now.

As I got to the bridge at 125th Street, I realized that my life in the jazz world and the places it had taken me had nothing to do with white or black but with music and fellow souls communicating with one another. I didn't give a damn what kind of insanity was taking place in America. No one was going to brainwash me at this point of the game. I had just about learned how to be a human being and I wasn't going to take any steps backward for anyone. I had made my two years in the army. No one was ever going to tell me to go out, get a gun and prepare me to shoot my brothers again.

Instead of having an undeclared war in Asia, we could have a declared war against stupidity, ignorance, hate and fear. That's what most people really wanted, if they looked deep into their souls. That was the reason why most of us had come over here in the first place.

I arrived in San Francisco in November. The performance was November 15, two days before my thirty-fifth birthday. I went to rehearsals and the piece went beautifully. In between I went out and saw North Beach, an area I hadn't seen since I visited Holly and worked as a carpenter's helper in the summer of 1948. Now I was back for the first time since then, about to have a piece performed at the War Memorial Auditorium. It seemed incredible that I was back this way.

North Beach had changed unbelievably since 1948. It was all cement and topless dancers. I visited Herb Gold, whom I hadn't seen since he left New York a few years ago. I also went out and saw Gary Goodrow, and Freddie Redd, who was playing in Haight Ashbury. It was just before the mass media descended upon Haight to make it official Hippieland. It was still a beautiful place. In between rehearsals I had a great time hanging out there. Allen Ginsberg was visiting town and I went down to the Seaman's Institute to a beautiful poetry reading that he and many of the students had. I could see that things in San Francisco were really cooking. Allen had grown to become a leader for a whole new generation.

The entire concert at the War Memorial Auditorium was a very moving experience. The only ironic part was that I wasn't able to get a seat, so I gave Herb and his beautiful girl friend two chairs behind the TV cameramen and I stood off on the side of a box seat and listened. My piece was at the end of the program and I was proud of it. It was a very tightly structured work, with more dense sound and intensity than anything I'd ever written before. It utilized four soloists, a full symphony orchestra, a huge chorus and an extra thirty-voice chorus that sang the one *a cappella* movement near the end.

It got a rousing reception and Paul Kresh, who had planned the whole concert and commissioned "Let Us Remember," came back afterwards bursting with joy.

"You see," he shouted backstage, "the piece really did what it was supposed to. They loved it!"

I didn't care about that so much. People often clap for any composition with a loud ending. I was just happy that it seemed to be a real piece of music. That's all that I really cared about now. Some people involved in the concert were afraid that my piece was too long and wanted me to cut it. I had refused and told them that if they felt that this was necessary, I could understand it but I would rather not have it performed. This was not music for a play or a film where the music had to fit a visual situation. Here the music was the whole situation and I had not wasted any notes in writing it. It turned out that it wasn't too long after all.

I went out to the Haight Ashbury section that night to see Freddie. He was playing with a group and I noticed that the tenor-saxophone player had not shown up. Philly Joe Jones, whom I had played with so many times at sessions at Ken Karpe's, was on drums. There was also a terrific bass player whose name I never did find out. Freddie gave me a signal with his head to come up and play. I ran up, took out my horn and we played a whole set without ever saying a word. Neither of us said what the tunes were going to be or anything. We had that New York telepathy.

A rather dignified professorial type was eyeing us as we played. Afterwards he came over to me as I was packing up my horn.

"Didn't you write that piece that was played tonight at the opera house?"

"Yes," I said. I didn't feel like being interviewed.

"Most interesting. And you play jazz as well?"

"Right."

"You and the pianist Freddie Redd seemed to play without even discussing the pieces you were going to play. Have you often re-hearsed together?"

"No."

"It's extraordinary how musical people don't seem to be verbally oriented. I suppose that's really the essence of the hip mystique. Wouldn't you say so?"

"Maybe."

"There's a great deal of that kind of almost angelic, innocent, trust-ing subconscious communicating going on among the new young community out here. They don't feel the need to talk talk talk. They in*tuit*. Isn't that encouraging to someone like yourself, who is involved in another level of communication?"

"Sure."

"I'm so happy to hear you say that. I imagine you must know a lot of . . . *under*ground types in your work. Tell me, I know its hard to answer a question about yourself. Are you a hippie?"

"No. I'm too old to be a hippie and too young to be a Guru. Good-bye."

Freddie and I left and enjoyed the silence of the quiet streets.

Stanley Plummer had organized a whole concert in Los Angeles of my chamber works plus some Shakespeare songs. The concert went beautifully. A lot of the musicians who had worked with me in Los Angeles came to a party afterwards and they were surprised to see me there as a composer of concert music rather than film music.

"It's beautiful," said the flutist Arthur Gleghorn. "You escaped."

"You're doing your own thing," said Dick Leith. "You're not let-ting them make you into a sandwich or a chocolate bar or any other kind of product. You're going to fool these son of a bitches and be a composer yet. The next seventy years will be the toughest. Can you stay with it and not sell out without wigging?"

"I hope so, man," I said. "I'm sure trying."

The next day I got on the plane and went back to New York, to attend the concert at Carnegie Hall, where Seymour Wakschal was performing my violin sonata in a concert he was giving.

He had taken a whole year off from the Metropolitan Opera in order to give this recital. It was on the evening of December 1. I sat in a box with Lenny Gross and his fiancée and a girl painter I knew who was working part-time as a cigarette girl at the Copacabana. Also with us were Shmuel Ashkenasi, the great Israeli violinist, Arthur Miller and an old friend of Seymour's from Brooklyn. He was from Brownsville and I had snuck him in the back door after he had threatened to get in a fight with the box-office man.

Seymour played more beautifully than I had ever heard him and the whole concert was a real treat for everyone. All of Seymour's friends including me were proud.

13

I WENT on a drive in upstate New York with Dan Cowan and found an old house off in the woods that no one seemed to want. The mortgage payments would be less than the rent I was paying in the city.

"Take it," said Dan. "The best bargain I've ever seen in my life."

"It would take the last cent I have," I told him.

"You're a fool if you don't," he said. "You'll never find a place like this again. It's ideal and you can really fix it up."

Even though it seemed like insanity, something told me that I had to do it. I knew if I didn't I would spend the money anyway and except for my instruments, my music and a few pieces of furniture and my three suits and a kayak, I owned nothing. I had spent it all on my music, given the rest away or wasted it. I had always thought I never would own anything unless I could pay for something outright. This place was so great I couldn't resist.

Barna thought I was crazy. "We have no work for the first time since I've known you," she said.

"It's O.K., Barna," I told her, "I'm big and strong. I can get work playing the horn again or even go out and get a day job if necessary. And they're always looking for gym teachers with a second language."

I had more of my music performed in 1965 than ever before. I felt that with the house I was getting, I would have a place to work for the rest of my life. It was in an undeveloped area way up a hill. I saw that as long as I could make the payments, which were infinitesimal, I would have a perfect hideout.

"What will you do about going out to the beach this summer?" said Dan.

"Well, if I don't get any work I'll rent out my shares and I'll stay up here. I'm happy to have the time off just to write music."

That winter I moved up to the country. Dave Lambert didn't have any musical work either. He was doing carpentry jobs in the neighborhood. We had hung out a lot since his trio had broken up, playing at different bars in the Village. Usually it was for fun. Sometimes we'd get paid. We didn't care; we had such a good time together whenever we played. He was a great woodsman, had been a tree surgeon, was a master carpenter and cabinetmaker and a real outdoorsman. Whenever our girl friends felt like talking to each other, Dave and I would go and work out in the woods a few hours each day, cutting logs, sawing them up with a two-man saw, and splitting them up for firewood. I composed every day too, but for the first time in a long time I didn't have a series of killing deadlines.

My money had run out and the bills were coming in. There were quite a few performances of my music and some conductors wrote me and told me that they were performing my pieces the following year. I knew at this point I wouldn't have enough money to go to out-of-town performances. I didn't care. This was the bed I had been making for so many years and I was happy to lie in it. I'd been writing the kind of music that I wanted to and getting it published and performed. I told Barna that if I didn't get any commissions, I would get a day job the following fall. A friend of mine who owned a bar told me that I could work there and I would be able to make more money in a week than I could doing any other kind of work.

In May I received a letter from the head of an excellent conservatory of music asking me if I would be their composition instructor for a year. The regular instructor was taking a sabbatical. My publisher had sent him some of my music. Without knowing me he had liked my music sufficiently to ask whether or not I would come and teach. I was very flattered. He was an excellent composer and it was a first-rate music school. Also, it would mean that I would be able to get by for the year and continue making small payments on my place in the country.

I was tempted to take the job. Some of the finest composers I knew were teaching school. Still, the more I thought about it, the less I wanted to do it. I enjoyed lecturing about music, and I had been to a few colleges, speaking just for a day. I found that as an outsider, simply coming in as myself, I could tell the students about the best of all possible worlds that I knew about. I knew that as a full-time

instructor I would have to do something else. I respected and understood the needs for institutions and instructors, but I felt that I would
rather wait until a much later point in my life before I taught for any
length of time. I felt that everything I could say to music students
could be boiled down to an hour or two then they could ask questions
just as Mitropoulos had done when he spoke to young people. The
only way you could teach people how to compose was to encourage
them, to kindle the spark that lay in their hearts so that they could
find their own way just as I had done and as I was doing. I knew that
at this point in my life there was certainly no formula and no way.
There was only devotion, love, hard work and patience.

I decided I'd rather take the job as a bartender. I had no offers to
work on plays or films that I thought were first-rate. People were becoming interested in my concert music at last and I had worked too
hard and too long to sell myself down the river. I could have done
that years earlier.

"I don't blame you, man," said Dave Lambert. "Whenever things
get slow, I go back to do my carpentry. I could have been arranging
music for all kinds of trashy vocal music years ago. The only thing
is that every time I'd look at the professional smilers in commercial
music, I felt sick to the stomach. Once you have tasted the truth, you
can't ever live a lie."

"Amen," I told Davey.

I brought a book on mixing drinks and begin to study. I knew I
couldn't use any of the avant-garde recipes I had discovered as a
cook if I was working with real drinkers. I practiced a little each day.
I had worked in bars as a musician and I figured that this wouldn't
be too much different. Of course I wouldn't make any musical strides
on the job, but I didn't give that a second thought. Society wasn't
persecuting me as an artist. I had made my own choice and was
happy to live with it.

I had just received some scores back from a foundation that had
been rejecting me annually for quite a few years. I had never gotten
a grant, but still I felt obligated to go through the process of filling
out all the forms and sending out music and records. A lot of very
talented people I knew never got grants either, but some of them did.
I figured it was like surf casting. If you kept throwing the line out
enough times, the mathematical odds were that you would eventually
end up with a fish.

Before going back up to the country, I got a letter from the Rockefeller Foundation. The letter stated that they had given grants to five different orchestras and were writing to many composers to see if they wanted to be candidates for composer-in-residence at one of the five. Since I had a pile of scores, records and a résumé that had just been returned, it was simply a question of rewrapping all the material. I sent my package off and continued studying the bartending book.

I figured probably I would be subsidizing myself for the following year. I also figured that I would make more money as a bartender than I could teaching. With the one or two days off, I could go out to the country and fix up my place. Dave and I went over to his house. Flutist Jeremy Steig visited us and we played for most of the night. Jeremy was one of the brilliant young new musicians who could play classical music and jazz and was interested in incorporating all of this with rock and roll. The kind of music he was playing was something entirely new. He was also thinking of getting an electrical attachment for his flute and had a whole idea of incorporating all his experiences in music with an electric group.

I had noticed more and more how this kind of music seemed to have real value. Since the advent of the Beatles, pop music was no longer in the clutches of Tin Pan Alley cats, the old cigar-smoking, payola-driven petty crooks who had cheated so many musicians and songwriters throughout the decades of American music. It was becoming more and more the music of young people. They managed their business affairs, had their own groups and their own record companies and their own publishing companies. As a result, not having so many middlemen who knew nothing about music and often hated it, the standard seemed to be getting higher every week. Artists like Tim Hardin, Richie Havens and Arethea Franklin were breaking through to large audiences.

Jeremy and Dave had an idea that they were working on that was different from anything I'd ever heard. I listened to other groups that were coming along and thought that possibly this kind of music would bring back a new renaissance in jazz and help all of us. Most important, it was already turning on a whole generation of people to music in a natural and healthy way.

I got a letter from the Rockefeller Foundation informing me that Leonard Bernstein was interested in having me as the New York Philharmonic's first composer-in-residence. I couldn't believe it. I stared at the letter a few times, put it back in the envelope, took it

out again, sat down and began thinking about all the times I had
seen the Philharmonic playing and had heard them perform on radio.
I remembered seeing Mitropoulos conduct them once in Washington.
One of my dreams when I had been studying horn so many years
before was the possibility that someday I might be able to play with
them. Now it seemed that I was going to be a member of the Philharmonic, not as a player but as their first composer-in-residence.

I took my book on mixing drinks and threw it in the wastebasket.
I wasn't much of a drinker myself and I figured that I wouldn't need
it now. Malcolm was working as the daytime bartender at the Fifty-
Five Bar and I ran over and told him. "Please, don't tell anybody,"
I said to Malcolm, "it's not official."

"That's wonderful," said Malcolm. "How does it feel being a child
prodigy at last?"

"I'm all set," I told him. "I can always get a Little Lord Faunt-
leroy suit made out of blue velvet with a lace collar, a Yo-Yo and
be a boy wonder."

"That's really something," said Malcolm. "Maybe clean living does
pay off after all. I suggest you have a real drink though and forget
about your usual ginger ale. I'll pay for it, don't worry."

"Thanks, man," I said. Malcolm mixed me a Bloody Mary. It
looked and smelled delicious. I gulped it down and ran home. I called
up Barna, but I asked her to sit down before I told her.

A few days later when I received another letter, it seemed definite
and I called up Mr. Hinrichsen of C. F. Peters, my music publisher.

"That's marvelous," he told me, "it's a golden opportunity. For a
young man like yourself who has never been involved in musical politics, it will be an unforgettable experience. Just be sure to get a haircut, wear a suit and tie and keep your ears and your eyes open. You'll
never have an experience like this in your life again."

"I know, Mr. Hinrichsen," I told him, "I'm grateful." It made me
feel great for his sake too because he had published so much of my
music. Now there would be a much better chance that people would
play it. I went out to the country and really drove carefully. I didn't
feel like getting into any accidents now.

I still didn't have any money, since the grant wasn't to start till the
following fall. But I didn't care. I felt like a billionaire inside. "That's
really a groove," said Dave as we were chopping wood one afternoon. "I can hardly wait till they play something of yours. Won't that
be a gas to sit down and listen to them play your music?"

"It's almost impossible to think about it, Dave," I told him. "I never thought that would happen while I was still alive."

That summer I played a concert of my music in Tompkins Square Park with the quartet that George, Arthur Phipps, Al Harewood and I had started. In the first half of the concert Seymour played my violin sonata; some of my Shakespeare songs were done by Lynn Blair and Richard Frisch, and Midhat played "The Wind and the Rain" for viola and piano. For the second half, our jazz group played. Tompkins Square Park was only a block from where we had begun our quartet ten summers before.

I saw the faces in the audience as we played. Many people I knew during the two years I lived on East Eighth Street were there. They were smiling. Our group felt their warmth and it made us play better. We could feel our music getting to them, and the sensation made everybody in the park closer until it seemed we were all one family, and the music was our heartbeat. That was all any musician could hope for, but I knew it was not enough anymore. The people in my old neighborhood and the residents of all the other slums and ghettos of America needed more than good sounds. They had more than enough soul. They needed a chance to join the rest of the United States.

You didn't need a Ph.D. in sociology to realize that if two men were sitting at a table and one had a mountain of food and the other was hungry, that the hungry man could only wait so long to be invited to join his dinner partner in sharing what was there to eat. It was like that afternoon in 1965 when I drove through Harlem. When I looked to my right from the band shell in Tompkins Square Park and saw my old block, I forgot about the strides I had made in music. I remembered the terror of hearing rats at night, the collapsing ceilings and the summertime stench of uncollected garbage. I could feel the dizziness in my stomach and the anger when I sat on the roof and was *really* hungry. But I also knew, even in my most desperate moments, that I could have always given up and moved back home. My old neighbors on the Lower East Side couldn't. This *was* their home.

I couldn't let my sudden good fortunes make me blind. My accomplishments would mean very little in a society that ignored its own citizens. I knew that unless all of us woke up now and changed these conditions, America was in trouble.

What Mitropoulos, Lobo, Oscar Pettiford and so many others had

told me over and over again was true. The best I could do was keep
trying to improve myself as an artist and as a man. Then, perhaps, my
music could be of some value to others. But I also understood that I
could never be free until every one of us in America was free. My
ancestors escaped from Europe and came to America. The ghettos of
Europe, from which so many of us had come, led to concentration
camps. Now we had ghettos here. Beautiful people were living out the
precious days of their lives in filth and fear. Now was the time for the
American Dream to become a reality—and fast! I knew we could do
better, and I prayed that night that we would.

At the end of the concert, Dave Lambert, who was in the audience,
came up and sang with us. The people loved him. We kept playing
until the Parks Department told us we had to stop. That was the last
time that Dave and I ever played together.

Toward the very end of September, the news was announced that
I was chosen as the first composer-in-residence with the New York
Philharmonic. The telephone began ringing the next day. In addition
to people congratulating me, all kinds of people started calling me
up and asking me if I had written music for every conceivable kind of
instrument. I began getting letters from people who had my music to
tell me they were going to perform it. It was less than two months before my thirty-sixth birthday and I was being discovered as a composer of concert music.

I attended my first rehearsal of the New York Philharmonic. Carlos
Moseley, the manager, took me downstairs and I spoke to Leonard
Bernstein briefly.

"It's a fine opportunity and I'm sure it will be rewarding to you,"
he told me. "You'll have a chance to hear a lot of great music and
study scores for some interesting pieces. I hope you are as enthusiastic
by the end of the season as you are now. It's a lot of music, you know,
and we work awfully hard here."

"It's something I never even dreamed would happen," I told him.
"I'll keep out of the way and just look and listen. This will be my
super music education."

I met the three assistant conductors, Sylvia Caduff, Juan Pablo
Izquierdo and Alain Lombard. They were brilliant musicians, accomplished conductors and very friendly. They all spoke many languages
and by the end of the first day, I was speaking French and German
again and fumbling through Italian. I saw even that first day that

hearing the Philharmonic rehearsing and being able to study the scores was more inspiring and more fun than anything I had ever done. I didn't feel like somebody hanging around the rehearsal, trying to get discovered. I was there like a part of the family and it made me feel so good that I had to control myself just to sit down and listen while I read the scores. Watching Leonard Bernstein rehearsing that first day was a whole lesson in conducting and in preparation. I saw how certain musical passages, tempo changes and balance presented difficulties I had forgotten about because of so many years of not playing with a symphony orchestra. Being on the outside in front of the orchestra, I could really hear what was happening. And the Philharmonic reading through a piece sounded better than most orchestras when they give a concert.

Carlos Moseley and his assistant, William Weissel, were friendly, as was all the staff of the orchestra. They weren't sure what a composer-in-residence was supposed to do either, since I was the first one, but I was told I could attend all rehearsals, all concerts and recordings and study the scores. I was also given a small room where I could write and copy music. That meant that instead of having to hear the trucks grinding and scraping outside my window on Sixth Avenue, I could work late at night in a quiet studio right in Lincoln Center. It seemed too good to be true. After the rehearsal, I went up to see Gene Becker, the violist whom I had played with in the Seventh Army Symphony.

"Private Amram," he said to me, "you look so neat and clean I wouldn't have recognized you." I had on my new suit with a black vest.

"You're looking at Mr. Super Conservative himself," I said.

"I hope you're not going to become a stuffed shirt," said Gene.

"No, man, I'll never do that," I said, "but you'll never see me looking sloppy whenever I go above Fourteenth Street from now on."

"Do you think they'll play any of your pieces this year?" he asked me.

"I don't know," I said. "They had already made up the programs in advance before they decided to have a composer-in-residence, but perhaps they will. I know Bernstein must like my music because he chose me."

"When can you come up and have some borscht?" Gene asked. "Ray's been asking when you'll come over."

Ray was Gene's wife and she made the best borscht on the East Coast.

"Soon," I said. "Right now I'm too excited."

It was really like a dream. I attended the opening night performance of the Philharmonic. The great Russian basso Ghiaurov sang sections of *Boris Godounov* and when *Capriccio Espagnole* was played, David Nadien's flawless solos showed he was a born concertmaster. It was his first year with the orchestra. The harp player, Myor Rosen, got together with me and told me that he would help me out with any problems that I might have in writing for the harp. He gave me a manual that he had written on techniques for composing for the harp. Julius Baker was playing solo flute with the orchestra. He had always encouraged me with my flute music since he'd heard the piece I'd written for John Perras back in 1959. I knew many other musicians in the orchestra too and liked to get to rehearsals early just to talk to them. James Chambers and Joe Singer were old heroes of mine since my childhood. I told James Chambers of how I remembered him playing the great horn solo in the last movement of Brahms' First Symphony when I saw Mitropoulos conduct it at the Philadelphia Dell series over twenty years before.

"He was unique," said Chambers. "There was never anyone like him."

A lot of the other musicians I spoke to all said the same thing about Mitropoulos. They all felt that in a certain way he was still here. His spirituality had left a mark on every musician that ever knew him.

About four o'clock in the morning of October 3, Dave Lambert's girl friend Nanya called me up. "I don't know how to tell you this," she said, "but Dave's been killed. A truck ran into him while he was helping someone change a tire."

It seemed impossible that he would be killed this way. He was driving back from a wedding in order to tape the jazz show that he did for WBAI.

I went to the Philharmonic rehearsal that day, but I was in a daze. I didn't know what was happening. A group of his friends got together and we all decided to have a benefit for him at the Village Gate on October 23.

It was a beautiful event, a "happy memorial tribute to Dave Lambert." Because it was hard to find people to come early, George and I came and played at three thirty in the afternoon. Then when Zoot Sims came to play, my girlfriend and I jumped on the train for

Philadelphia to hear my "Autobiography for Strings" performed at the Academy of Music that night. This was where I'd first heard a symphony orchestra when Stowkowski conducted the Philadelphia Orchestra in a children's concert. Now, thirty years later, I was hearing my music performed there for the first time.

It was really an experience, but I couldn't help thinking about Dave's death. I went to the reception for a few minutes, then excused myself. I didn't want to explain. I just told everyone I had to get back.

I got back and at two thirty in the morning went to the Village Gate. The benefit was still going on. I played again, with Jeremy Steig, Buddy Tate, Jimmy Witherspoon, Warren Bernhardt and a drummer I didn't know. They'd all known Dave from different places. I felt a little better. I knew he would not want people to sit around and feel bad. His whole life was so full of good cheer and joy and happiness that he didn't believe in being blue for one second. He could always get that out in his music. I remembered when he and I had gone to the Five Spot a few months before to hear Abby Lincoln and Max Roach play, he and Max gave each other a big hug when they met.

"I'll tell you," said Dave, "everytime we see each other, we hug like that. We're both so glad just to see that we're still alive. He was my first drummer way, way, way back. So many of the cats that we knew are gone. It's really groovy just to know that we're still here."

It didn't seem that Dave had really gone. So many people knew and liked him and would smile and laugh when they reminisced about him. It seemed that maybe he had just traveled to a different place.

Each week the new programs at the Philharmonic renewed my faith in the symphony orchestra as a form of communication unparalleled in music. There wasn't a moment, from the first rehearsal until the final concert, that wasn't exciting. I saw that Leonard Bernstein's ebullience was something he carried with him all the time. He seemed to be born with that fire. I saw him at work as a brother musician, not a celebrity. And that's how he saw himself.

He was able to analyze a piece of music with incredible accuracy and speed. In a few sentences he could describe the whole structure of a piece. He saw at a glance its principle dramatic moments, how it related to the composer's other work, its importance to the history of music, and how the music was related to the time when it was written.

Bernstein was so busy that I would talk to him only from time to time. I respected him enough not to intrude on his few moments of privacy. Occasionally he would speak to the assistant conductors and I would always listen. He was not only a born musician but a born teacher.

He told me how much he missed not being able to compose full-time. I understood how frustrating that could be to anybody. I had no idea then that he was planning to leave the Philharmonic as its full-time music director, but it was an understandable decision. I admired him for doing it. No other human being could possibly keep up his schedule, do all the things he did with such a high level of excellence, and still spend the amount of time necessary to compose music. In addition to having such a brilliant and an all-inclusive musical mind, and being interested in all kinds of music from pre-Bach through Bartók, jazz, and the latest rock and roll music, Bernstein was also interested and informed in politics, art, literature—just about everything.

He had a chance to look at some more of my music and gave me many helpful suggestions, criticisms and, most of all, encouragement. He told me that he hoped the Philharmonic could schedule a work of mine sometime during the year, even though the programs were set before I had been chosen as composer-in-residence. I told him that I was happy just to be there. Each day I had a chance to learn something new. I found as I studied the scores of the masters that when I looked at them now at the age of thirty-six instead of as a teen-ager, I could see them in a completely new light. Having composed a great deal of music myself, I could look at these scores and hear them in a completely fresh way.

I considered myself to be a student of music since the age of six. I knew I would always be. Now I was a more advanced student. The Philharmonic was my graduate school. I understood better what went into making the enormous variety of works that were performed during the Philharmonic season. I was able to see the mind and hear the souls of the more than one hundred composers whose works were being performed. I enjoyed speaking to the three assistant conductors, whom I sat with every day at rehearsals. They would talk about music in a way that was far more objective than any composer. The nature of their work forced them to think of music in another sense. They had to be practical. Their ideas of the function of a composition and of the placement of a particular work on a program opened up a whole new vista for me.

I also had the chance to talk to William Steinberg, Charles Munch and Lorin Maazel, who were guest conductors during the season. I was able to see the masterful work of Abraham Kaplan as he prepared singers for the many programs that included large choruses. I also met a great many other composers I had never known before and had a chance to hear them discuss different pieces. Each day I found that my interest and understanding were increasing.

In the beginning of December I went back to Washington, D.C. Howard Mitchell wanted to perform some of my works with the National Symphony. I went down for rehearsals and saw all my old friends whom I had played with back in 1951. It was a great reunion. When I wasn't at the rehearsals of the two of my works that were being performed, I was being interviewed by the newspapers, radio and television. I didn't even get a chance to visit anybody. In the middle of it all, I had to fly back to New York for a television program called "Bach and Roll," a combination of Bach and pop music on one show.

On this program I had the first chance in my life to state publicly how I felt that music was one entity and that all music affected every other kind of music. I also said that I felt that this new popular music was making people respond naturally to sound. By being able to have their own young heroes and by being able to play and dance naturally, a whole new generation of people would eventually become attuned to all kinds of music, including the treasures that lay in jazz, the works of the masters and hopefully even my fellow contemporary composers. I felt this would happen to them because this is what had happened to me. I also mentioned how Mitropoulos had thought of all music being a mountain and every kind of music being a stone in that mountain without which the mountain could not exist.

I went back to Washington and straight to Constitution Hall. It was here that I had sat as a student and later as a part-time member of the orchestra. Now they were playing my music, "Autobiography for Strings" and "King Lear Variations." The pieces went over beautifully and were the best received of anything of mine that had ever been performed.

I came back to New York and continued to attend rehearsals at the Philharmonic. After the Thursday-night concerts, I would drive to upstate New York and work nonstop until the following rehearsals on Monday morning. A small record company released two LPs of my concert music at that time. My "Shakespearean Concerto," violin sonata, "Dirge and Variations" and piano sonata were the first works that have ever been available for the public to hear. I was working on my horn concerto and had to get a secretary to help me mail out music or answer letters from all over the country, Canada and Europe.

As 1966 came to an end, I felt that I was really getting started. I still played the horn too. I didn't have much time, but after midnight, when everything else was done, I would go down to Casey's Bar on Tenth Street and sit in with Freddie Redd, who was playing there regularly. I felt that my musical life was complete.

On January 16 I was invited by Maurice Peress to Corpus Christi to conduct my "Shakespearean Concerto." Although I had conducted many recordings and rehearsals, this was my concert debut as a conductor. I got a set of tails for the occasion. Maurice had built a first-rate orchestra and they played beautifully. I found that I didn't have to tell jokes or act far-out anymore. I had learned a lot about conducting and rehearsal techniques from my time with the Philharmonic. The performance went beautifully and because I had memorized the music, I was able to enjoy myself and just let it happen.

A month later I made my public New York conducting debut at Carnegie Hall, where my sacred service "Shir L'Erev Shabbat" was programmed. The chorus was made up of the leading professional choral singers in New York. The tenor soloist, Seth McCoy, was also magnificent. Before the concert, I didn't even feel nervous. I knew since I had such wonderful performers that it would be almost impossible for this work not to sound good. Assuming that Carnegie Hall didn't catch on fire, that I didn't fall off the podium or that there was not a subway crash close by the Hall, there was no way to stop the music from speaking for itself.

I noticed that the singers were looking at me.

"You sure look different tonight," said Tom Pyle.

I was wearing my custom-made tails and a new pair of pumps, elegant attire in comparison to the Levis, plaid shirt and hunting jacket I had worn during rehearsals.

"I didn't want to overdress until the concert," I told him.

The singers thought that because it was my New York public conducting debut, I might get panicked and start bombing out—an expression musicians use to describe confused conductors. One real one hundred per cent faker was known as the Mad Bomber, Jr. He was the kind of conductor who during a concert would invariably go into a catatonic state and appear to be conducting a different piece from the one that was being performed. When any conductor panics, he usually conducts everything much too fast and his nervousness is contagious. I told everyone not to worry. I was a peace lover and against any kind of bombs. Because it was a concert of modern religious music, we had to wait backstage for an interminable time. My sacred service was scheduled to end the program. I even danced with one of the beautiful ladies of the chorus backstage during a jazz mass.

The concert stretched on for such a long time that before I even got to conduct my piece, Carlos Moseley, the manager of the Philharmonic who had come to see me conduct, was forced to go home and return to guests he had left there. He had waited until 11 P.M., but my piece was still yet to come.

Finally it was time. I stood offstage waiting for the announcement by a priest who spoke before each piece was performed. As he gave a long pronunciamento about how the Kaddish, part of my sacred service, was in Aramaic, the same language that was spoken by Jesus, my mind suddenly flashed back to the days when I boxed in the army and to the boxers I had watched at Madison Square Garden as they stood during the playing of the "Star-Spangled Banner." First they had to wait for the announcements made in the ring as other famous boxers arrived. Then they had to wait while the referee gave them instructions that they knew about from the time they first started boxing as amateurs. I felt that conducting at Carnegie Hall for the first time was like a boxer who has his first main event at Madison Square Garden. I was keyed up. I had studied the score inside out and could conduct it entirely from memory. Because of the fabulous acoustics in Carnegie Hall and the wonderful chorus and soloists, I was sure it was going to be fun.

Still, I felt the strain a little bit. I had worked out a strategy for the entire performance of the piece, which lasted thirty-five minutes. I could hardly wait to begin. When my name was announced, the final ironic touch was that the manager of the concert slapped me on the rump the same way that seconds do when a boxer enters the ring for the first round. When I walked onstage and stood on the podium, I felt great. I didn't have that nervous feeling that I had had years ago when I played in a symphony orchestra or played as a French-horn soloist. I realized that because I was in charge, there was no one to create those uptight vibrations.

The piece began. I noticed that the singers had their heads pretty much buried in the music. They were afraid I would miscue them. Because I knew the music by heart, I closed the score after the prelude and looked in the eyes of every one of the singers. After about five minutes everyone's head started to come out of the music. All of them were waiting for me to panic, to make a mistake or to be confused. When they saw what a good time I was having, the whole performance began to change and by the time the piece was halfway through, it was so exciting that I could feel the vibrations coming from behind me in the audience. It was like playing jazz when I didn't know which was the instrument, which was me, which were the musicians playing with me and where the audience was. It all became one thing, just the way catharsis is described by Aristotle. I was not conscious of the motions that I was making. I felt that together all of us could do anything.

The main reason was that I had marvelous performers and I knew the music. This is what Mitropoulos had always told me. With fine performers, 95 per cent of the work is done already. Then it is up to the conductor to try to get the other 5 per cent accomplished.

Leonard Bernstein told me one day at rehearsal that he had found a place in a program for my music on March 23, 24 and 27. Sylvia Caduff conducted my "King Lear Variations." The performance was broadcast and heard all over the country. I sat there hypnotized. The Philharmonic played so beautifully that I heard all kinds of things in the piece I had forgotten about.

On April 23, my opera *The Final Ingredient* was performed again on television and the next day I left for Montreal. I had completed the music for the film *We Are Young* for Expo '67. It was shown in the Canadian Pacific Railroad Pavilion. *To Be Alive* was made by Francis Thompson and Alexander Hammid and was done with six screens, six projectors, and three-track stereo sound. It was the first film score I had worked on in five and a half years and it was really fun. Thompson and Hammid were not Hollywood hacks, far from it. They were pioneers in documentary film making. They knew how to take a camera apart and put it together, how to develop film, set up shots, direct actors, edit and do everything themselves. They were real artists and it was a pleasure to work with them.

Montreal was beautiful, but my schedule at this point was so busy that the day that Expo opened, I had to leave to get back to the Philharmonic. I would have loved to stay and see the rest of the exhibitions, but I wasn't sorry. I felt thankful that I had so much to come back to.

I worked away on my horn concerto. During the season, I had a chance to see Salvatore Martirano again. Lorin Maazel conducted a work of his, "Contrasto." It was a brilliant and moving piece. Maazel gave it an exquisite performance, conducting from memory. Salvatore and I talked about the days when we had been the only small group of jazz players along with Ed London and a few others at Oberlin back in 1948. What was then bebop was now absorbed into our musical culture. What we had done that was so different and daring then, was something that was accepted and understood by a whole new generation of musicians. It had become part of the standard jazz vocabulary, and found its way into many other kinds of music. It had inspired some composers like us to write music for the concert hall. Salvatore's piece was beautifully written and just as when he played the piano, it sounded just like him. I could still hear the jazz.

After the regular season at the Philharmonic was over, I went back to Davis Park to complete my horn concerto. I only attended occasional rehearsals and concerts during the summer. I was glad just to concentrate on composing.

That fall, Erick Friedman played my violin sonata at Philharmonic Hall and decided to take it on tour all over Europe. It would be heard in Rome, London and Paris. So many other people were playing my music in so many places that I couldn't attend the performances anymore. It didn't really matter. Other people could hear these pieces now. My job was to write new ones.

In November I received a phone call from David Lloyd. He had decided that the Lake George Opera Company was going to perform the world premiere of my opera *Twelfth Night* for five performances the following summer. Paul Calloway was to be the conductor. I opened up the drawer where *Twelfth Night* had been lying for the last four years. The paper was getting a little yellow. As I looked over the score, I began seeing and hearing Viola, Feste, Sir Toby Belch and Sir Andrew Aguecheek. I had a little more work to do on it. The years that I had put into it before now vanished in my mind forever. The music was still there and that's what counted.

I was invited to a special anniversary concert by the New York Philharmonic on December 7, 1967. All day before the Philharmonic concert, I kept remembering December 7 of 1941. We were on the farm in Feasterville. It was a nice Sunday afternoon. I was working with my father, piling mud and sod on the bank of the pond that we had excavated the summer before. I would drive a tractor while he stood behind with a large scoop, digging out the dirt. I had had a green mallard duck who had been laying eggs and lived in the pond. The duck was no longer there on that December 7 because a few weeks before, my uncle had shot it. He had always promised that he would buy me another one, but of course he never did, being so embarrassed for having shot the proverbial sitting duck. While I was thinking about my lost duck, my mother came running down and told us the news that Pearl Harbor had been bombed and we were at war.

But to the music world, this December 7 was not a commemoration of Pearl Harbor. It was the commemoration of the first concert of the New York Philharmonic, given December 7 of 1842. This was the Philharmonic's one hundred and twenty-fifth anniversary. The program announced that for this celebration, the orchestra had invited "a number of distinguished soloists and conductors and composers who had played a part in the Philharmonic's history, as well as former members and managers of the orchestra." The exact same program that had been played in 1824 was being repeated that night. I could hardly believe that I had been asked. All the musicians, composers, and conductors I had known and admired all my life were listed on the program. I got out my tails and had them cleaned and pressed. I picked up my Land Rover jeep, got my girl and bowled up to Philharmonic Hall. It was one of the few times in my life I had gotten started way ahead of time.

. This was an evening that I didn't want to miss. Philharmonic Hall was packed. Because so many of the audience were musicians, everyone was saying hello, kissing one another and having a good time in general.

We finally got to our seats. We sat down, looked at the orchestra on stage, warming up. It was the first time I had seen the members of the orchestra since the previous August, when my tenure as composer-in-residence with the Philharmonic had ended. Most of the musicians lived uptown. The only other Villager in the orchestra was Sanford Allen. I saw him quite often, because his children went to school at P.S. 41, around the corner from me. I missed seeing everybody but had waited until now to return. I never wanted to be one of those people that appear to be hangers-on.

After a year of sitting through rehearsals, sharing a score with the assistant conductors, there I was in the audience. It felt great. The lights finally dimmed and you could already feel the excitement.

The program opened with Beethoven's Fifth Symphony. As Leonard Bernstein came to the podium, I noticed that he looked different. He seemed a little more rested and a little more at peace. As he bowed to the audience, I could see in his eyes that this event meant as much or more to him than it did to everybody else. The performance of the Fifth was the best I had ever heard him do. The orchestra sounded magnificent, as always. You could see that Bernstein felt he and all of us were part of the continuity of Beethoven's music. We were hearing it played as it had been when it began the Philharmonic's first season. Now it was a hundred and twenty-five years later. Bernstein conducted with insight, spiritual vitality and the experienced authority that still seemed to be growing in him. Even though he was approaching his fiftieth birthday, he still had the energy and enthusiasm of a kid.

As I watched him, I noticed his extraordinary use of the baton. A few critics who had liked his natural kinesthetic response to music had grown tired of his style in recent years. After building him up, they proceeded to tear him down, criticizing him as someone who danced or acted his way through the music. Of course none of these people knew enough about music or conducting, even from the most rudimentary technical point of view, to watch his baton. Specifically, the very end of his baton. If they had, they would have noticed that he had developed a way of conducting that was all his own. He had achieved total clarity of motion. Unlike most conductors, he was actually leading, instead of following. He was able to put himself into the music and make the music his. You had to be a musician to know this. Like ballet or boxing, you had to know what to look for.

The next work was "Ozean, du Ungeheuer" from *Oberon* by Weber. Eileen Farrell was the soloist. She had always been a musician's musician, a singer with such good taste, ability and understanding of every kind of music that she should have been recognized twenty-five years before she was. She had none of the pretentions of a prima donna. She was happily married to a policeman and didn't feel it was necessary to be anything but herself. She always had so much music in her that she made the music world come to her. She came out on stage and took her bows. You could see that wonderful, strong, intelligent face waiting to make the music. She wanted to sing!

Her first note nearly knocked Philharmonic Hall down. It was like a sporting event when a crucial play is executed so brilliantly and perfectly that you know immediately who the winner is going to be. She was saying, "You see, that's how we begin, now perhaps you will join me in the music." As she sang, I could feel her voice and music through my entire body. That's what it's really all about, I said to myself, you can't do better than this. The only other time I had heard a singer do this in recent years was when I heard Birgit Nilsson sing with the Philharmonic a few years earlier. I remember seeing Billie Holiday and Abbey Lincoln. Their singing did this to me, but they were singing in clubs, where I was so relaxed it was possible to get with them immediately. On such an event as the Philharmonic's anniversary, it seemed that the occasion would be bigger than the music. The beautiful part about it was that when Eileen Farrell sang, the music was the star for the evening. This is the way that the Philharmonic Society would have wanted it to be when they began in 1842 and I'm sure it's the way the Philharmonic wanted it to be in 1967.

After the Weber, the extra chairs were moved out and the first movement of the Hummel Piano Quintet in D Minor, Opus 74, was performed. It was a piece that many musicians knew about but almost never played. It certainly was not something you generally heard on symphony programs. Leonard Bernstein played the piano, David Nadien, the violin, William Lincer, the viola, Lorne Munroe, the cello, and Robert Brennand, double bass.

The performance was sensational. Everyone played their parts beautifully and Lorne Munroe showed the audience of distinguished musical artists that he was as fine a cellist as any in the world.

During intermission I wanted to just go out and think about the music. I sneaked out of the side door with my girl and went into the back. I saw Maurice Peress and his wife. "Davey, isn't that fantastic?" said Maurice. "Can you believe that we're really here?"

"No, man," I said, "we're lucky." David Bar-Illan came over and we began talking about the music and soon we were all laughing. This was a night for musicians. You could feel the warmth and happiness as hundreds of musicians greeted one another. It was like a gigantic family meeting. I felt the same vibrations as when I played jazz: all beautiful and free. On my way back to my seat, I saw Rudolph Serkin and his wife. I stopped with my girl and we said hello. He had the same warmth and wonderful smile and twinkle in his eye as when I first met him at Marlboro and his wife, Irene, sat by his side. I wanted to find the words to tell them how much I loved them. I couldn't, but I think they knew anyway. Gunther Schuller was sitting right in front of them with his wife, Margie. We talked, and my mind raced back to the time I had met Gunther at the Jazz Keller in Germany and how he helped me to return to America. His unique talent was now recognized all over the world. There wasn't time to say hello to everybody, so we did it with our smiles.

When I got back to my seat I talked to Leon Kirchner, whom I had met at Marlboro. We talked about the time we had had a great jam session up there when I was playing with other percussionists and ended up playing a solo on a wastebasket. Leon had enjoyed it as much as if he were a jazzman himself. I remembered his daughter singing at Marlboro with her long red hair down her back, playing her guitar under a tree. I spoke with Aaron Copland, whose "Outdoor Overture" was the first contemporary piece I had ever studied. I talked also to David Diamond, another composer whose music and dedication I had always admired since I was a kid. He had sent me the score of his Eighth Symphony after I had heard the Philharmonic play it in 1961. I also sent him some of my music and he had written me some helpful criticisms.

"Isn't this a beautiful concert?" he said. "It's wonderful to know these composers still mean so much. That's really the most encouraging thing for all of us, to know that there are standards in music and music of real value and integrity can last."

Everybody was talking to everybody. This didn't seem like the Establishment. It was the biggest and best birthday party I had ever attended.

The second half of the concert finally began. The overture to *Oberon*, a duet from *Armida* by Rossini with Reri Grist and Nicolai Gedda singing was followed by an aria from *Fidelio* and an aria from *The Abduction from the Seraglio* by Mozart. The final piece on this unusual program was the Overture Number 1 in D Minor, Opus 38, by Kalliwode.

Bernstein made a speech, saying that the real star of the evening was the orchestra. He gave the downbeat and walked offstage. The orchestra played the overture by themselves, without a conductor. At first it seemed strange seeing the musicians playing without someone on the podium. Then I saw in my mind the figure of Mitropoulos. His spirit seemed to fill the hall. It was as if he had actually returned.

As the orchestra played, I thought to myself, Well, the Maestro has done it. He's come back again.

I closed my eyes. I could see him as he had conducted that first time in Philadelphia, over twenty yeare before. I could hear his voice say to me as he had said before, "It's all in the music, there's nothing to conducting. It's the music that means everything. If you love it and you are true to it, it will come out true and pure. You cannot fool a hundred and ten men for one second. They *know*. You must not only know, you must give yourself and be a servant to music. You must never love yourself more than you love music. The joy is in the giving. We come and go, but the music is always there forever. We can have the pleasure of joining in it while we are here."

The orchestra completed the overture. The concert was over. As the audience stood to applaud the men of the Philharmonic, I thought of the last time I had seen Mitropoulos and walked him back to his hotel. I remembered as I had so many times what he said about working in music.

"Aren't we lucky? Aren't we lucky to have music?"

Yes, I thought to myself, we are.

At the reception, I kept hearing the music again in my mind. I left after a while. I had come that night for the music and I wanted to leave while it was still with me. I thought about the compositions I was working on as I drove back downtown to the Village. I knew I had to work that night before I went to sleep. I couldn't be idle. Without music, my life would have no meaning. I owed everything to music. I went home and worked until dawn. I was tired, but couldn't sleep. Time was precious and there wasn't any left to waste.

Epilogue

WHEN I heard the great news that my autobiography *Vibrations* was to be reissued in paperback by Thunder's Mouth Press, thirty-two years after its initial publication in 1968, I didn't have time to celebrate. I had to finish re-orchestrating my score for *The Manchurian Candidate*, written in 1962, for a first concert performance. I also had to finish liner notes for a reissue of my *Triple Concerto for Woodwinds, Brass, Jazz Quintet and Orchestra*. I was also completing *Starry Night for Clarinet and Strings* and the last movement of a flute concerto, *Giants of the Night*, for James Galway. I stayed up until 3:30 A.M. and finally crashed out. At 5:30 A.M. I got up, took a shower, fed the animals on our farm, got the kids off to school, and drove to Stewart Newburgh Airport to catch a 9 A.M. flight.

I stored my instrument box in the overhead compartment and slid my Mexican straw shopping bag full of scores and papers under the seat in front of me. I unpacked it on the empty seat in front of me once the plane took off. I'm exhausted now, but I'm too excited to sleep.

So much is happening in my life, and I have to stay on top of everything. I begin restudying the scores I am going to rehearse and conduct for a pair of symphony concerts in Colorado in four days.

By the time we have flown over Illinois, I have them prepared to conduct. It's all music I have memorized in the past. I take out my score for my latest symphony *Kokopelli*, completed in 1997, which is already being published, and has been recorded. I put in the final corrections in the proofs and look at the title page.

"The world premiere of *Kokopelli,* conducted by the composer at the gracious invitation of his dear friend, Kenneth Schermerhorn, January 17, 1997."

I see his name in print in my score and realize the world will see his name in print in *Vibrations,* along with the names of so many others whose enduring friendships have lasted over a lifetime.

I can't believe it is 47 years ago that Kenneth Schermerhorn and I first met in the Seventh Army Symphony as young soldiers in the U.S. Army, all of which I described in my book.

As the plane flies West, I think of all the other people I wrote about in *Vibrations,* and how our lives intertwined. We were part of a world that even then seemed to be changing as rapidly as the plane's flight carrying me to Colorado is now. We were all so different from one another, and yet we formed friendships that have lasted to this day. What held us all together then, and still holds us together today, was a reckless enthusiasm for life, a sense of adventure, and most important, the positive influence of people older than ourselves. We were the children of the Great Depression. They were the adults of the Great Depression who survived and overcame insurmountable obstacles, but could still smile. We had real life heroes and heroines.

Artists, poets, painters, athletes, sculptors, short order cooks, actors, street philosophers, visionary comedians, farmers, waitresses, garage mechanics, and everyday working people were our mentors. Somehow they always found the time to share a kind word, an encouraging story, or a yea-saying nod of approval to all of us who dreamed of pursuing goals that were outside mainstream America.

None of us considered ourselves to be outsiders. We were following a natural calling *inside* of ourselves, walking on a path guided by our hearts' calling. All of us could identify with the main character of Dickens' *Great Expectations* in the memorable scene where the disenfranchised old man is standing on a dimly lit and snowy street in London, looking through a window, longing to be inside at the table of a magnificent banquet to which he knew he would never receive an invitation. We all could relate to his desire to be *inside*, to be able to share the warmth, approval and camaraderie of a world that excluded him.

But unlike the world that excluded Dickens' tragic character, we had a group of elders who, in spite of being considered outsiders themselves, *welcomed* us to their table, and shared what they had. Anyone with a pure heart, a dream, and a sense of respect was welcome. Many of these people I wrote about in *Vibrations,* to document the generosity and wisdom they shared with our generation.

As the plane flies over Texas and I watch the American landscape rolling slowly below me from the comfort of my window seat on the plane, I remember the endless bus rides, marathon day-night-day shared car journeys, and hitchhiking adventures that all of us experienced as young musicians, and all the people who encouraged us to keep on keeping on. I never dreamed that so many of the people I met as part of this makeshift community of assorted dreamers from every walk of life and from so many disciplines and skills would eventually become acknowledged for sharing their gifts with the world. Most of them are now invited to the banquet table, and they always welcome someone else to sit by their side.

Aloft with my lofty thoughts, I notice passengers on the plane with laptop computers, checking their e-mail, organizing their Web sites, working in their own cyberspatial cocoons with feverish intensity, oblivious to the smiling hostess who graciously serves nitrate-filled greenish-colored stale meat sandwiches wrapped in a plastic bag to the few who wish to eat emergency rations.

I don't imagine there are too many hitchhikers on the plane. Time moves on. We have entered a new millennium. The twenty-first century is here. Plans are on the drawing board to subdivide outer space. Millions of people communicate by computer technology to one another around the world. Anyone can publish their own desktop book, manufacture their own CD recording, or make their own film.

Yet, as we approach the airport in Colorado, I feel more at home and connected to the world at large than I have in decades. I still can't work my computer, but I have hopes for the future.

In my global travels I find this hope for the future in the faces of young people I meet who tell me of their desire to feel connected to one another on a one-to-one level. They tell me that the manufactured role models they are bombarded with send them messages of narcissism and greed that they find repugnant. They express their longing for a community of their own that could be like the spontaneous, informal, ever-changing, joyous community of survival created each day by those of us brought up in the era of post-World War II euphoria. Young people often tell me, "I wish I had been born earlier," to which I respond, "You were born at exactly the right time. Remember Charlie Parker's motto, *"Now's* the Time!"

Over the past ten years, many young people ask me to sign xeroxed passages from *Vibrations* or old remaindered copies found in flea markets or taken from libraries.

"After we read your book and saw your concert, we thought we could just come up and talk to you, like you were a regular person," I was told recently.

"We're all regular people," I answered. "All the people I came up with set an example to us of being *in*-clusive, not *ex*-clusive." I remembered many similar conversations as the pilot of the plane tells us we are about to land.

"Fasten your seat belts and turn off all electronic devices," he intones over the intercom. There is a loud series of slaps, as laptop computer lids close. Now all the passengers must either join me in daydreams or write their thoughts down by hand, as I am doing. There *is* life after computers.

When I wrote *Vibrations* in 1967, I couldn't even type. I did it by hand. My brilliant editor, Alan Rinzler, guided me through mountains of material, always positive and constructive in his criticism. His watchword was, "Always remember this motto, David: give the poor reader a break. Your book will be fine." The final corrections were made by bestselling author and journalist, Larry Merchant, now known by millions as a boxing commentator for HBO. His advice, like his friendship, was, and remains, invaluable.

"Just remember to do the same thing in writing a book that you do when you write a symphony. Just be you. Be honest. Be clear."

I completed *Vibrations* on January 1st, 1968. I have lived several lives since *Vibrations* was completed. These adventures of the past thirty-two years will be recounted in a new book I'm writing. I am fortunate that Paul Maher Jr. is writing a book about my major compositions and all the life experiences that led me to write them. Certainly, *Vibrations* shows the reader that the first 37 years of my life were far from perfect. Still, all the experiences I recounted in this first book could never be duplicated. I am overjoyed to have it reissued, with a foreword by Douglas Brinkley, who is currently writing the authorized biography of Jack Kerouac. This edition of *Vibrations* includes a selected discography of my music and an index of the names of the people I wrote about. Some are now celebrated, some forgotten, but all of them were part of my early journeys and adventures, down the highway of life. *Vibrations* is a thank-you letter to all the men and women who shared these experiences.

Shortly after I had handed Alan Rinzler the final manuscript, I was told by a friend who worked for the publisher that the head of the sales department was worried that what I had written about in my book did not relate in any way to the burgeoning pop culture of 1968. My friend suggested I consult with a brilliant young writer, who could help guide me towards rewriting the book to make it more commercial.

"He has written reviews for his college paper about rock and roll. He's very with it," I was told by the head of the sales department, when I went to his office to inquire about this mystery man. "He's *extremely* hip. He knows all about the ins and outs of flower power, and what the trends are, *before* they become trendy. He can help you with your wardrobe for when you make personal appearances, to give you a more *groovy* image. Today, it's not enough to *write* a book. You need a *look!*"

I saw him grimacing at me, like an angry owl through his horn rimmed glasses, as he checked out my janitorial garb. I was wearing my old stained floppy gray turtle neck sweater that I wore when I played Mezz McGillicuddy, the deranged French hornist in Jack Kerouac, Alfred Leslie, and Robert Frank's underground 1959 film, *Pull My Daisy*. I got the sweater in 1953 in the Army, and always kept it for special occasions.

I told him a rambling history of the places the sweater and I had been over the last fifteen years. "This is my lucky literary sweater. The hole in this sleeve was burned there by mistake when Terry Southern lurched into me with his cigarette in 1955 during a jam session I was playing with Lionel Hampton in Paris."

"That's what I mean," said the head of the sales department, in a clipped quasi-Edwardian-tinged executive-ese nasal tone.

"You're *dated*, David. You're dropping names that no longer mean anything. You've got to learn the lingo of Psychedelia! This young man we are recommending can help your case. He's *very* bright. He's a personal friend of the Monkees' manager. He's very *with* it, tuned into the dynamics of today's youth market's vast purchasing power!"

"Sounds like a fabulous cat. I'm sure I'll learn something new," I said. "And I can never resist a good meal."

As I went home on the subway, I wondered what the brilliant young advisor would be like. I was curious to see where he was coming from. I met the young trouble-shooting youth culture expert two days later. He looked like a razor-thin version of Groucho Marx. He was wearing bell bottom pants, a Nehru jacket with Tantric beads, topped with a gigantic hairdo that sprouted like a thick mass of porcupine quills from his head. He squinted at me through his magenta-tinted granny glasses, with a far-away terminally stoned-out look that seemed focused on an extraterrestrial traveling in outer space.

"As you may know, David, I've been recently hired as the company freak, to be a sales liaison to today's youth market. I drop acid at least three times a week. I'm in tune with the new Revolutionary consciousness of the Age of Aquarius. Let's be brutally frank, David. The people you wrote about in your book may be important to you. They no longer are to anyone else. They are has-beens and nobodies. No one cares about jazz and symphonic music anymore. The theater and painting and poetry are obsolete. You can no longer *epater la bourgoisie* with old art forms. Life is now expressed by *flashes of the moment*! TV commercials are the only true art form. The media is the message. Your book will never make it. There's no real sex described in detail. You're living in the past. This is the *Sixties,* man!"

"Thank you for your advice," I said. "I respect your knowledge of merchandising. But I think young people today need to hear about something they have not heard about. That's why I wrote the book. I told the truth. I'm keeping it exactly the way I wrote it. No one else has lived my life. I tried to honor those who have made it possible for me to do what I have done. No one does it alone."

"Yes, but . . . I don't know how to say this, David, without hurting your feelings, but the people you mention in your book are . . . not only passe, but totally *irrelevant*!"

"Time will tell," I said. We finished our meal in silence.

That night I called Jack Kerouac and told him of my conversation. He roared with laughter.

"Send me the book, Davey, and I'll critique it for you. We've both shared each other's endless monologues and stories. Everyone has a story to tell. If you've written it the way you talk, it will have its own sound, just like your music. They say my work is no longer relevant. Some of my books are being remaindered, others are already out of print. I can't even get *Visions of Cody* published. The critics are ignoring my work as if I never existed. But we're not irrelevant, Davey. We're here for the duration. Turn your back and the other cheek to the Philistines. Stick to your guns."

I mailed Jack the manuscript and he sent me a quote for the publisher to use for the dust jacket. He called the following week to congratulate me. We talked for about an hour, laughing about our spontaneous barnstorming tours through New York City parties, bars, coffee houses and park benches, after our first-ever-jazz-poetry readings given in 1957. Then I played the French horn and piano into the phone as he read the parts of *On the Road* we used to do together, and then we improvised words and music.

"The ghosts of Eric Satie and Beaudelaire have now completed their monthly *soiree* of words and music over the phone. *Beaux sejours,* Davey. *Soit tranquil.* Stick to your guns. Remember Ruskin in his tortured night shirt, saying 'An artist must burn with a hard and gem-like flame.' Or was it Slim Gaillard or Harry the Hipster, or Fats Navarro or Lord Buckley? *Qui sait? Je m'en fou.* But don't ever give up. We'll be relevant when all these shysters and Philistines have had their day. Charlie Parker, Bartok, Proust, Thomas Wolfe and Walt Whitman . . . they're yet to be truly appreciated. They're yet to be discovered. Some day when we're old men, we'll lie in our hammocks with tooth picks and rejoice in all the work we've done, and smile like Buddha and pray for all our friends yet to be discovered."

In the past thirty-two years since *Vibrations* was published, Jack and many of us have been discovered or rediscovered. I was, and still am, one of the lucky ones of our generation. I was blessed with health and energy, and in 1979 I finally got married, had three incredible children, and gave up my remaining bad habits so that I could bring them up and try to be as good an example to them as my father had been to me.

I'm still writing music non-stop, which is now being recorded and performed all over the world. I guest-conduct orchestras in all kinds of new programs and often am asked to conduct my own symphonies and operas. I utilize my skills as an improviser of music and words in concerts with my quartet, playing all the musics I have been touched by on all the instruments and styles I am at home with, through years of collaborating with musicians in thirty-five countries. Often, I use these elements of music in my compositions for orchestra, to bring something new to the symphonic arena, and honor those who shared their music with me. I'm writing a new book about these adventures.

Still, wherever I am in the world, I can hear that distant sound of the silver train "The Crusader" in my memory as it makes its late night rackety journey from Philadelphia to New York, speeding mysteriously through the night, a few miles from my father's long-gone farm in Feasterville, Pennsylvania, where I lay in bed in the lonely waking hours of the 1930s, dreaming of being on that train some day and traveling around the world, making music.

Now, as the twenty-first century is here, my dream has come true. I am on that journey, bringing music and all I have learned from music to young people all over the world, sharing my blessings and keeping alive the memories of the people I honored in *Vibrations,* my early book of life. I hope this book can inspire others to dare to dream, to work hard, to never give up, to see the joy beyond the struggle, and be buoyed in spirit by Duke Ellington's motto for music and life: "It don't mean a thing if it ain't got that swing." And what Dimitri Mitropolous told me as a young boy: "Always love the music more than you love yourself."

All of these thoughts about my whole life go through my mind as the plane finally lands. I pack up my scores, papers, and instruments, ready to embark on a new adventure. Enough of the past. This is 2000. I'll phone my wife and kids, then I'll go to my motel room to write more music and finish this epilogue for *Vibrations.* I'll have a new home for a few days, filling the motel room with fresh fruit, vegetables, pictures of my family, and music. I'll see old friends and make new ones. As long as I'm inhaling and exhaling, I'll be making music. And I'll go anywhere to do it.

"Life is the Road," Jack Kerouac told me one night on Macdougal Street in Greenwich Village, before *On the Road* was published.

When we played in Havana, Cuba, in 1977, Dizzy Gillespie was asked when he planned to stop traveling and retire.

"Never happen," he said. "I'll do this forever. That's why God put me here. To play this music."

In the fall of 1999, I was invited by Willie Nelson to play the Farm Aid concert with him for the fifth time. I told Willie what a pleasure it was to perform with him and his great band.

"I'm a lucky man, David. Doing what I love to do. And able to do it."

I go to the baggage claim area and I'm met by an old friend who greets me with a sunny Western smile.

"Everyone told me you'd be here again. Give me a Kerrville, Texas hug, Maestro Dave. They've been playing your symphonies and operas and jazz on the radio. You're a senior citizen overnight success story! And both of your concerts are sold out. My baby that you used to sing to is in high school now. All her friends are coming to the concert. They're all reading *On the Road* and listening to Charlie Parker and Thelonious Monk and Charles Mingus records. They have an old hardback copy of *Vibrations,* probably stolen from the Denver library. They read all about you guys. Could you sign it? I wish we could buy a copy."

"You can pretty soon," I said. "It's coming out in paperback this fall."

Almost thirty-three years to the day that *Vibrations* was completed and sent to the copy editor, I realized it was finally taking a curtain call.

I want to thank Sterling Lord, Douglas Brinkley, and Neil Ortenberg for bringing *Vibrations* back to life. I thank my wife Lora Lee and our three children, Alana, Adira, and Adam for giving me a life beyond music.

And I want to thank all the people I wrote about in *Vibrations,* who still mean so much to me every day of my life.

David Amram
August 1, 2000

David Amram's Selected Discography

Orchestral Chamber and Operatic Works

David Amram: An American Original
  The Manhattan Chamber Orchestra
  Richard Auldon Clark, Conductor
  American Dance Suite
  Theme and Variations on "Red River Valley" for Flute and Strings
    Julius Baker, Flute
  Travels for Trumpet and Orchestra
    Chris Gekker, Trumpet
  Three Songs for America for Bass Voice, Woodwind Quintet, and String Quintet
    James Courtney, Bass
  Newport Classics, NPD 85546 (Recorded 1993)

David Amram: Three Concertos
  The Manhattan Chamber Orchestra
  Richard Auldon Clark, Conductor
  Concerto for Violin and Orchestra
    Charles Castleman, Violin
  Honor Song for Sitting Bull for Cello and Orchestra
    Nathaniel Rosen, Cello

Concerto for Bassoon and Orchestra
Kenneth Pasmanick, Bassoon
Newport Classics NPD 85601 (Recorded 1995)

The Final Ingredient
An Opera of the Holocaust in One Act
Libretto by Arnold Weinstein
Conducted by David Amram
Premier Recordings PRCD 1056—(Recorded 1996 from 1965 television premiere)
Distributed by Empire Music

Triple Concerto for Woodwind, Brass, Jazz Quintets and Orchestra
Pepper Adams, Jerry Dodgion and David Amram, soloists
Elegy for Violin and Orchestra
Howard Weiss, Violin
Rochester Philharmonic Orchestra conducted by David Zinman
Flying Fish FF 751 (Recorded 1973)
Distributed by Rounder Records

Kokopelli: A Symphony in Three Movements
The Nashville Symphony conducted by Kenneth Schermerhorn
Magnatone Records MGT 119-2 (Recorded 1998)

Ode to Lord Buckley for Saxophone and Orchestra
Harvey Pittel, Saxophone
Louisville Orchestra conducted by Akira Endo (Recorded 1982)

Songs of the Soul: A Symphony in Three Movements
The Rundfunk Sinfonie Berlin Orchestra conducted by Christopher Wilkins
Milken Archive of American Jewish Music Recordings (Recorded 1999)
To be released 2002

Excerpts from The Final Ingredient: An Opera of the Holocaust
The University of Michigan Opera Theater conducted by Ken Kiesler
Milken Archive of American Jewish Music Recordings (Recorded 2001)
To be relased 2002

Selections from Sacred Service (Shir l'Erev Shabat) *for Tenor, Mixed Chorus, and Orchestra*
Milken Archive of American Jewish Music Recordings (Recorded 2001)
To be released 2002

Three Songs for Marlboro for French Horn and Cello
   Phillip Meyers, French Horn
   CAL #513 (New York Legends) (Recorded 1997)

Conversations for Flute, Violin, Viola, Cello and Piano
   Atlanta Chamber Players
   ACAD 20038 (Recorded 1995)

Autobiography for Strings, Shakespearean Concerto for Oboe, Two Horns and Strings and King Lear Variations for Winds, Brass and Percussion
   New York Chamber Orchestra conducted by David Amram
   RCA Red Seal LP VCS 7089 (2) (Recorded 1971)
   To be reissued on CD

The Complete Score for The Manchurian Candidate
   Conducted by David Amram
   Premier Recordings PRCD 1059 (Recorded 1962)
   Distributed by Empire Music

The Complete Score for Elia Kazan's The Arrangement
   Conducted by David Amram
   Warner Brothers LP WS 1824 (Recorded 1969)
   To be reissued as a CD

The Complete Score for The Young Savages
   Conducted by David Amram, and a Jazz Quartet led by Amram featuring
      Harold Land
   Columbia Records LP WS 1824 (Recorded 1960)
   To be reissued as a CD

Jazz, Latin and World Music Recordings

Jack Kerouac and David Amram: Pull My Daisy and other Jazz Classics
   With David Amram Quartet featuring Paquito de Rivera, Saxophone, Vic
      Juris, Guitar,
   Victor Venegas, Bass, and Akira Tana, Drums
   Premier Recordings PRCD 1046 (Recorded 1988 and 1989)
   Distributed by Empire Music

Havana New York: The Historic U.S.-Cuban Musical Exchange of 1977
   Arturo Sandoval, Trumpet
   Paquito de Rivera, Alto Saxophone

Los Papines Congas
Pepper Adams, Baritone Saxophone
Eddie Gomez, Bass
Thad Jones, Trumpet
Candido, Congas
David Amram, Piano, French Horn, Wooden Flutes, Spanish Guitar and
    Percussion
Flying Fish Records CD FF 70057 (Recorded 1977)
Distributed by Rounder Records

David Amram and Friends: A Home/Around the World
Pepper Adams, Odetta, Candido, Ramblin' Jack Elliott, Floyd Red Crow
    Westerman,
George Mrgdichian, Patty Smyth, Victor Venegas, Steve Berrios,
    Mohammed El Akkad, Jerry Dodgion and Nicky Marrero
Flying Fish FFCD 094 (Recorded 1978)
Distributed by Rounder Records

David Amram: No More Walls
Pepper Adams, Jerry Dodgion, Candido, Ramblin' Jack Elliott
George Mrgdichian and Ali Hafid
Flying Fish CD FF 752 (Recorded 1971)
Distributed by Rounder Records

David Amram and Friends: Latin-Jazz Celebration
Machito, Paquito de Rivera, Candido, Pepper Adams, Jerry Dodgion,
    Duduca Fonseca, George Barrow, and Victor Venegas
Electra Musician LP 60195-1 (Recorded 1982)
To be reissued on CD

Jazz Studio 6: Amram/Barrow Quartet
Decca Records (Recorded 1957)
To be reissued on CD

David Amram Quartet in Paris with Bobby Jaspar
Swingtime Records (Recorded 1955 in Paris)
To be reissued on CD

Amram as a Conductor and Sideman/Soloist, for other jazz artists

Betty Carter: Whatever happened to Love
Betty Carter Trio with Strings
Conducted by David Amram (Recorded 1982)
Reissued on CD

Hannibal Marvin Peterson: Children of the Fire
The Sunrise Orchestra conducted by David Amram
(Recorded 1974)

Charles Mingus Quintet Live at the Café Bohemia with Max Roach
David Amram, French Horn
Debut Box Set (recorded 1955)
Distributed by Fantasy Records

Kenny Dorham: But Beautiful
"Cannonball" Adderley, Alto Saxophone, Cedar Walton, Piano, Paul
    Chambers, Bass,
Jimmy Cobbs, Drums, Cecil Payne, Baritone Saxophone, David Amram,
    French Horn
Milestone LP M-47036 (Recorded in 1959)
Reissued on CD

Monk on Monk
T.S. Monk, Wynton Marsalis, Herbie Hancock, David Amram, French
    Horn, and others
N2KE 10017 (Recorded July 1997)

Four French Horns
Julius Watkins and David Amram, soloists, with Matt Matthews, Accordion
    and his ensemble, Milt Hinton, Bass, Osie Johnson, Drums, and others
Electra Records (Recorded 1957)
Reissued on CD

Teddy Charles
Julius Watkins and David Amram, French Horns, Hampton Hawes, Piano,
    Curtis Fuller, Trombone, Teddy Charles, Vibraphone
Prestige Records (Recorded 1957)
Reissued on CD

Mary Lou Williams: Mary Lou's Mass (Music for Peace)
Mary Lou Williams, Piano, David Amram, French Horn, Pakistani Flute, and others
Mary 102 Records (Recorded 1970)

Oscar Pettiford's Big Band, Vols. 1 and 2
Julius Watkins, David Amram, French Horn soloists, with Art Farmer, Trumpet, Tommy Flanagan, Piano, Sahib Shahab and Gigi Gryce, Saxophones, Jimmy Cleveland, Trombone, and others
Paramount Records (Recorded 1957)
Reissued on CD

Lionel Hampton in Paris: Crazy Hamp
Lionel Hampton, Vibraphone, Nat Adderley, Trumpet, David Amram, French Horn, and others
Emarcy Recordings (Recorded 1955 in Paris)
Reissued on CD

Willie Nelson and Family: It Could Have Been Tonight (Volume 2)
Willie Nelson and his band, live on 2000 tour
David Amram, Pennywhistles, Percussion, and French Horn
CD WN-1002 (Two CD set recorded live at Irving Plaza, New York, April 9, 2000)

Amram Singing His Song Stories

Southern Stories
Vassar Clements, Fiddle, Mickey Raphael, Harmonica, Reggie Young, Guitar, Michael Rhodes, Bass, Fred Bogert, Acoustic Guitar
Chrome Records CR 4202 (Recorded 1998)

Three Jammin' Gents
Vassar Clements, Fiddle, John McEuen, Banjo and Vocals, and David Amram, Pennywhistles, Piano, Clay Drums, Dumbek, Shanai, Vocals and improvised scat

Subway Night
Ten different Amram songs, each accompanied by their own orchestra
RCA LSP-4820 (Recorded 1972)

Spoken Word Collaborations

Jack Kerouac: Visions of Cody
Narrated by Graham Parker, all music composed and performed by David
Amram on 12 instruments
Penguin Audio Books (Recorded 1996)

Jack Kerouac Reads On the Road
Music composed and performed by David Amram and friends
Ryko Disc RCD 10474 (Recorded 1998)

Selected Musical Videos

Origins of Symphonic Instruments
Amram narrating and conducting members of the Corpus Christi
Orchestra, and demonstrating folk instrumental roots of modern
symphonic orchestral instruments
Educational Video Network Film #768-V (Recorded 1990)
Available via e-mail: edvidnet.com

Pull my Daisy (Documentary Film)
Directed by Alfred Leslie, photographed by Robert Frank, spontaneously
narrated by Jack Kerouac, title song and score composed by Amram, who
appears in film as Mezz McGillicudy, the deranged French Horn player.
The cast includes artists Larry Rivers, Dody Muller, Alice Neal, and Mary
Frank, poets Gregory Corso and Allen Ginsberg, and actress Delphine
Seyrig (Filmed in 1959)
Now available on VHS)

Celebrating a Jazz Master: Thelonius Sphere Monk
Amram performing in a quintet with Dizzy Gillespie, Roy Haynes, Percy
Heath, Walter Davis Jr. in concert with Wynton Marsalis, Herbie Hancock,
Gerry Mulligan, Billy Taylor and others, hosted by Bill Cosby
Laser Disc SM-068-3289 or VHS (Recorded live Constitution Hall,
Washington, D.C., 1986)

CBS Sunday
Rev. Andrew Young, Host, Bill Evans and Sadik Hakim, Pianos, and David
Amram, Piano and French Horn with Nat Hentoff, Moderator
Available for viewing at the Museum of Broadcasting, New York City
(Recorded Live Network Broadcast 1959)

The World of David Amram (Documentary Film)
David Amram Quartet, members of the Houston Symphony, Soloists, and
Chorus performing excerpts from his cantata A Year in Our Land,
conducted by Amram, and performance of Amram's Three Songs for
America for Bass-Baritone, Woodwind and String Quartets and Erik
Friedman, performing Amram's Violin Sonata at Avery Fisher Hall
NET (PBS) Network Broadcast (Recorded 1969)

Sound Stage: David Amram and Friends (Documentary Film)
Members of the Chicago Symphony conducted by Amram, Dizzy Gillespie,
Trumpet, Vocals and Jews Harp, Jerry Dodgion and Pepper Adams,
Saxophone, Steve Goodman, Vocals and Guitar, Jethro Burns, Mandolin,
Nicky Marrero, Ray Mantilla, Johnny Rodriguez Jr., Percussion, Al
Harewood, Drums, Bonnie Koloc, Vocals, Brian Torff, Bass, and others
PBS Network Broadcast (Recorded 1977)

Amram Jam (Documentary Film)
Clark Terry, Trumpet, Al Grey, Trombone, Paquito D'Rivera, Saxophone,
Victor Venegas, Bass, Johnny Almendra, Congas, Jimmy Madison, Drums,
Joanne Shenendoah, Vocals, Keir Dullea, Reader, Manhattan Chamber
Orchestra conducted by Richard Auldon Clark with flutist Julius Baker
performing Amram's Theme and Variations on Red River Valley, members
of the Amram family and others
Winner of the Best Documentary Film Award, NYU Film Festival, 1995

Dizzy Gillespie's 70th Birthday at Wolftrap (Documentary Film)
Amram playing French Horn, Pennywhistles and Percussion in program
with Wynton Marsalis, Jimmy Owens, Freddie Hubbard, John Faddis,
Trumpets, Sonny Rollins, Benny Carter and James Moody, Saxophones,
Mongo Santa Maria, Candido, Airto, and Nicky Marrero, Percussion,
Charlie Persip, Drums, Rufus Ried, Bass, J.J. Johnson, Slide Hampton,
Steve Turre, Trombones, Lalo Shiffren, Piano, Walter Davis Jr., Piano,
Dave Valentin, Flute, Carmen McCrae, Vocals, and others
PBS Great Performances Series Network Broadcast 1987

Amram at 70 (Documentary Film)
Live performance of 70th birthday concert at the Paramount Center for the
Arts, with Odetta and Joanne Shenendoah, Vocals, Charles Castleman, and
Heidi Upton, performing Amram's Violin Concerto, David Kellett and
Ann McKenna performing excerpts from Amram's opera Twelfth Night
with Libretto by Joseph Papp, Amram's Middle Eastern Trio, and Jazz

Quartet, actors Keir Dullea and Maya Dillon reading, T.S. Monk, Drums,
Victor Venegas, Bass, and others
To be released in 2002 as part of Chris Felver's documentary

For other Amram recordings, videos, and listings of over 100 compositions published by C.F. Peters Corporation, see Amram's web site,
www.DavidAmram.com

Index